Human Resource Management

TWELFTH EDITION

Human Resource Management

TWELFTH EDITION

ROBERT L. MATHIS
University of Nebraska at Omaha

•

JOHN H. JACKSON
University of Wyoming

THOMSON
™
SOUTH-WESTERN

Australia · Brazil · Canada · Mexico · Singapore · Spain · United Kingdom · United States

THOMSON
SOUTH-WESTERN

Human Resource Management, Twelfth Edition
Robert L. Mathis, John H. Jackson

VP/Editorial Director:
Jack W. Calhoun

Editor-in-Chief:
Melissa S. Acuña

Senior Acquisitions Editor:
Joseph A. Sabatino

Senior Developmental Editor:
Susanna C. Smart

Editorial Assistant:
Ruth Belanger

Senior Marketing Manager:
Kimberly Kanakes

Senior Marketing Communications Manager:
Jim Overly

Content Project Manager:
Patrick Cosgrove

Manager, Editorial Media:
John Barans

Technology Project Manager:
Kristen Meere

Senior Manufacturing Coordinator:
Doug Wilke

Production House:
Graphic World Inc.

Printer:
RR Donnelley, Inc.
Willard, OH

Art Director:
Stacy Shirley

Cover and Internal Designer:
Joe DeVine, Red Hangar Design

Cover Images:
© Digital Stock

For permission to use material
from this text or product,
submit a request online at
http://www.thomsonrights
.com.

For more information about
our products, contact us at:

Thomson Learning Academic
Resource Center
1-800-423-0563
Thomson Higher Education
5191 Natorp Boulevard
Mason, OH 45040
USA

TO

Jo Ann Mathis,
who manages me

R. D. and M. M. Jackson,
who were successful managers of people for many years

Contents in Brief

Contents

S E C T I O N   2

STAFFING THE ORGANIZATION 97

SECTION 3

DEVELOPING HUMAN RESOURCES 257

SECTION 4
COMPENSATING HUMAN RESOURCES 357

SECTION 5

MANAGING EMPLOYEE RELATIONS 453

Preface

Organizations today face challenges in management of human resources. To provide a current understanding of developments in the field of human resource (HR) management, the authors are pleased to provide the twelfth edition of Mathis and Jackson's *Human Resource Management*. The authors of this book are gratified that this book has become the leader both in the academic market for HR texts and in the market for HR professionals.

For academics, the book is a standard in HR classes and is also used to provide HR knowledge as part of other professional degree programs. For HR professionals, the book is extensively used to provide HR knowledge in the pursuit of HR professional education and certifications, specifically the PHR and SPHR from the Human Resource Certification Institute (HRCI). See Appendix A for the most recent test specifications from HRCI.

In preparing this edition of the book, we extensively reviewed the academic and practitioner literature published since the last revision. We have incorporated a large number of new topics and references so that readers can be certain that they are getting the most up-to-date HR content possible. Further, we asked academics and practitioners, both those who use this book and those who do not, to provide input on the previous edition and what coverage should be added, deleted, or changed. We have always been receptive to input from our reviewers and have made extensive use of their observations and ideas.

THE TWELFTH EDITION

The twelfth edition has evolved to reflect the changing nature of HR management today in organizations globally. In addition to the new research content, this edition has other useful additions that are worth noting. Two major forces are affecting all aspects of HR management:

- *Changing workforce composition:* The aging and retirement of many workers, the increasing diversity of the workplace (both racial/ethnic and other factors), and the growth of work-life issues are crucial issues. Throughout the chapters these issues are discussed as part of the context for many different HR topics.
- *Globalization:* The global economy is impacting both large and small organizations in the United States. Outsourcing, international competition, employees who are located and moved throughout the world, and different cultural considerations all affect HR management. Rather than having a separate chapter on global HR management, the coverage of global issues has been integrated throughout the various chapters. This is a reflection of the integration of global competition into almost all HR issues and practices. In the chapters, global material is indicated with a small global

icon:

Several significant features in this edition should be noted. The following are some of the key ones.

Strategic HR Management

It is becoming more crucial for HR management to understand organizational strategy and to contribute directly to it. In most chapters, the topical connection to strategy is discussed. For example, the strategic natures of recruiting (Chapter 7), training (Chapter 9), talent management (Chapter 10), compensation (Chapter 12), and benefits (Chapter 14) are all examples of the inclusion of strategic HR throughout the book.

Attracting, Retaining, and Managing Talent

Having the right people with the right capabilities—and being able to retain them—are crucial current HR concerns in many organizations and are emphasized in separate chapters. The importance of these activities is also emphasized in coverage throughout the text. Additionally, specific chapters contain related content on recruiting and selection, training and development, talent management, and succession planning. These topics emphasize HR's role in ensuring that organizations have sufficient and productive workforces, both currently and in the future.

HR, Technology, and the Internet

The use of technology, the Internet, Web-based resources, and blogs is affecting HR management. Throughout the chapters of this edition is a feature titled "HR Online" that highlights how technology is being used in HR. Also, many chapters cover e-HR topics in the specific content areas.

The Internet has become a valuable tool for HR professionals and affects a number of HR activities. To provide immediate links for readers to access, about 100 "Internet Resource" features have been placed throughout the text. This feature identifies Websites that contain useful sources of HR information about the topics being discussed and contains specific Web address links. Also, a number of references from Web addresses are cited in the chapter notes as appropriate.

HR Metrics

The value of HR management activities increasingly has to be justified to executives in organizations by using financial and other data. By using analytic measures of cost-benefit profit per employee, new hire success, and the like, HR efforts can be justified and the value HR management contributes to the company's goals can be documented.

The twelfth edition includes sections in most chapters called "HR Metrics" that identify how different HR management activities can be measured.

A special metrics icon is also used to identify this content.

ORGANIZATION OF THE TWELFTH EDITION

The twelfth edition reflects both the continuity and changes occurring in HR management. The following overview highlights some of the significant content throughout the book.

HR's Strategic Contribution to Organizational Effectiveness

This book stresses how HR professionals and the activities they direct contribute to the strategic business success of organizations. The first chapter looks at human capital, HR as a core competency, and typical HR activities. The competencies for HR careers are also discussed. Chapter 2 addresses the strategic factors affecting HR, such as planning, productivity, and metrics, to evaluate the effectiveness of HR management.

Individual Performance and Employee Retention

Organizations need individuals who perform well and remain as employees. Chapter 3 contains extensive content on job satisfaction, loyalty, commitment, and employee retention. No other general HR text provides comparable in-depth coverage of retention.

Equal Employment and Diversity Management

Chapters 4 and 5 cover equal employment opportunity (EEO). Chapter 4 addresses the various laws, regulations, and court decisions that determine the legal framework of EEO. Because the issues of diversity and equal employment are so closely linked, Chapter 5 looks at various aspects of implementing equal employment, such as affirmative action, sexual harassment, age discrimination, and other issues. This chapter concludes with a discussion of diversity and the importance of managing diversity as a critical part of HR management.

Staffing the Organization

Chapter 6 describes workflow, scheduling, and other job design issues that have an impact on organizations and the people working in them. The chapter then provides coverage of job analysis and various approaches to job analysis.

Chapter 7 focuses on recruiting in various labor markets. It discusses the difficulties of recruiting employees with special skills—and new methods to attract those individuals. The chapter contains significant content on Internet recruiting and the evaluation of recruiting efforts. An expansion of the coverage on selection in Chapter 8 encompasses the selection strategy choices that management must make. The discussion of testing and interviewing approaches and techniques reflects current research and practices in HR management.

Training, Development, and Talent Management

As mentioned earlier, talent management is a growing concern of many employers. Major content additions in this area have been made to emphasize the nature and importance of talent management. Chapter 9 discusses the strategic role training plays in organizations and how training must be linked to business strategies and organizational competitiveness. Specific content on adult learning and new training design and means of delivery is provided. As the text addresses the growing use of *e-learning*, it discusses both the contributions and problems associated with Web-based training. Chapter 10 on talent management and development looks at the methods organizations use to expand the capabilities of their human resources. The chapter contains significantly expanded content on the nature of talent management and succession planning.

Performance Management

Chapter 11 emphasizes performance management and the role of the performance appraisal process in enhancing the performance of human resources in organizations. The chapter expands the material on identifying and measuring employee performance, including additional information on the numerous approaches used.

Total Rewards and Human Resources

Total rewards include compensation, variable pay, and benefits. Employers are facing great pressure to control those expenditures while also being competitive to attract and retain employees. Chapter 12 discusses the strategic nature of total rewards and then looks at compensation. The well-regarded cov-

erage of base compensation, pay for performance, and variable pay programs has been revised and updated in Chapters 12 and 13, including coverage of variable pay metrics in Chapter 13.

Chapter 14 highlights the growing concerns over the cost of benefits that are facing HR professionals and their organizations. Specific expanded content discusses health-care costs and issues, including evolving solutions such as consumer-driven health-care programs.

Risk Management and Employee Relations

One of the growing issues in HR management is risk management, which incorporates health, safety, and security. The coverage in Chapter 15 identifies the nature of risk management, current health and safety issues, OSHA compliance requirements, health promotion, prevention of workplace violence, and the importance of workplace security. New content identifies the need for HR to develop disaster and recovery plans for such situations as natural disasters, terrorist threats, or avian flu outbreaks.

The various issues associated with employee rights and discipline—such as employment-at-will, privacy rights, and substance abuse—have been highlighted in Chapter 16. The chapter also looks at such emerging issues as electronic monitoring, privacy, e-mail, and other employee rights issues affected by technology.

Union/Management Relations

The changing role of unions in the U.S. economy and the reasons for the decline in the percentage of workers in unions are discussed in Chapter 17. In addition to covering the basic laws and regulations governing union/management relations in the United States, the chapter concludes with coverage of collective bargaining and grievance management as key components of union/management relations.

CHAPTER FEATURES

Each chapter begins with specific learning objectives. Next, the "HR Headline" feature contains a concise example of a contemporary HR problem, situation, or practice to illustrate topics covered. Throughout the text, most chapters also include an "HR Best Practices" feature that highlights effective

HR management in real-world companies. Additionally, all chapters contain "HR On-the-Job," a feature that presents suggestions on how to handle specific HR issues or situations. The "Internet Research" feature provides links to additional materials beyond the text content. To highlight how information technology affects HR management, most chapters contain an "HR Online" feature. In some chapters, "HR Perspectives" features address other specific HR issues, ethical concerns, or interesting approaches.

Each chapter concludes with a point-by-point summary, and the review and discussion questions provide critical thinking queries. At the end of every chapter, a case presents a real-life HR problem or situation using real organizations as examples. Further, a Supplemental Case is available on the text Website that briefly describes typical HR problems faced in organizations. Finally, reference notes cite sources used in the chapter, with particular attention given to the inclusion of the most current references and research. Over 80% of the references are new or updated from the previous edition.

SUPPLEMENTS

Instructor's Manual with Video Guide

The instructor's manual, revised by Dr. Fraya Wagner-Marsh, Eastern Michigan University, represents one of the most exciting and useful instructor's aids available. Comprehensive teaching materials are provided for each chapter—including overviews, outlines, instructor's notes, suggested answers to end-of-chapter Review and Application Questions, suggested questions for the "HR Headline," "HR Online," "HR Best Practices," and "HR On-the-Job" features, suggested answers to the end-of-chapter case questions, and suggested questions and comments on the supplemental case for each chapter. In addition, a video guide section describes the video segments that are available on the Instructor's Resource CD to help integrate chapter content through current, interesting examples.

Test Bank

The twelfth edition test bank is significantly revised and upgraded from previous editions. The test bank contains more than 1,800 test questions prepared by Janelle Dozier. Multiple-choice, true/false, and essay questions are provided for every chapter.

Answers are cross-referenced to pages within the text so that it is easy to pinpoint where relevant material is found. Questions are identified by type—definition, application, and analytical—and also include AACSB tags for general (NATIONAL) and topic-specific (LOCAL) designations.

ExamView

ExamView contains all of the questions in the printed test bank. This program is easy-to-use test creation software that is compatible with Microsoft Windows. Instructors can add or edit questions, instructions, and answers. Questions may be selected by previewing them on screen, selecting them randomly, or selecting them by number. Instructors can also create quizzes on-line whether over the Internet, a local area network, or a wide area network.

PowerPoint Slide Presentation

Instructor's PowerPoint slides, prepared by Charlie Cook of the University of West Alabama, are available on both the Instructor's Resource CD and on the password-protected Instructor's Resources Website. Approximately 400 slides are included.

Instructor's Resource CD

The Instructor's Resource CD includes the instructor's manual, test bank, ExamView, the HR Handbook, and PowerPoint presentation slides.

ThomsonNOW

This powerful and fully integrated on-line teaching and learning system provides you with flexibility and control, saves valuable time, and improves outcomes. Your students benefit by having choices in the way they learn through our unique personalized learning path. All this is made possible by ThomsonNOW.

■ Homework, assignable and automatically graded
■ Integrated e-book
■ Personalized learning paths
■ Interactive course assignments
■ Assessment options, including AACSB learning standards achievement reporting
■ Test delivery
■ Course management tools, including Grade Book
■ WebCT and Blackboard integration

Speak with your Thomson South-Western sales representative about integrating ThomsonNOW into your courses. Visit *http://www.thomsonedu.com/ thomsonnow* today to learn more!

Video

A completely new video collection features companies with innovative HR practices, many of which have been recognized for their excellence in HR practices. Both small and large companies are featured in the videos, and all video content is closely tied to concepts within the text. These include interviews with Xerox, Burton Snowboards, MacLean Law, Zappos, and many others. The videos are available on DVD for the instructor and on-line in ThomsonNOW for the students.

Student Resource Guide

Designed from a student's perspective by Tonya Vogel, a certified HR professional, this useful study guide provides aids that students can use to maximize results in the classroom and on exams and, ultimately, in the practice of HR. Chapter objectives and chapter outlines aid students in reviewing for exams. Study questions include matching, true/ false, idea completion, multiple-choice, and essay questions. Answer keys are provided for immediate feedback to reinforce learning.

Product Support Website

Please visit our product support Website, *http:// www.thomsonedu.com/management/mathis*, which offers additional instructional and learning tools to complement our text.

WebTutor™ for Blackboard® or WebCT®

This dynamic learning and instructional resource harnesses the power of the Internet to deliver innovative learning aids that actively engage students. Multimedia resources include animated tutorials, quizzes with immediate feedback, on-line exercises to reinforce principles learned, and on-line discussion to encourage continuing communication between students and instructors.

ACKNOWLEDGMENTS

The success of each edition of *Human Resource Management* can largely be attributed to our reviewers, who have generously offered both suggestions

for improvements and new ideas for the text. The twelfth edition reviewers whom we would like to sincerely thank include:

Bob Meier	*Robert Morris College*
Cathy Dubois	*Kent State University*
David Nye	*Athens University*
Fraya Wagner-Marsh	*Eastern Michigan University*
K. J. Tullis	*University of Central Oklahoma*
Larry Siefert	*Webster University*
Romilia Singh	*University of Wisconsin, Milwaukee*
Ryan D. Zimmerman	*Texas A&M*
Stan Malos	*San Jose State University*
Thomas Kanick	*Southern New Hampshire University*
Yezdi Godiwalla	*University of Wisconsin, Whitewater*

Finally, some leading HR professionals provided ideas and assistance. Appreciation is specifically expressed to Sean Valentine, Nicholas Dayan, Jennifer Graber, Beverly Clampett, Michael Sabbag, Gary Berg, Frank Giancola, and Sandra Washa.

Those involved in changing messy scrawls into printed ideas deserve special recognition. At the top of that list is Jo Ann Mathis, whose guidance and diligence have made this book better than before. Others who assisted with many critical details include Carolyn Foster and our copyeditor, Lorretta Palagi of Quantum Publishing Services, Inc.

The authors thank Joe Sabatino, Executive Editor, and Susan Smart, Senior Developmental Editor, for their guidance and involvement. We also appreciate the support of our Content Project Manager, Patrick Cosgrove, whose efforts contributed significantly to making the final product appealing. Thanks go also to our Technology Project Manager, Kristen Meere, and to our Senior Marketing Manager, Kimberly Kanakes.

The authors feel confident that this edition will continue as the standard for the HR field. We believe it offers a relevant and current look at HR management, and we are optimistic that those who use the book will agree.

Robert L. Mathis, SPHR   John H. Jackson
Omaha, Nebraska   Laramie, Wyoming

ABOUT THE AUTHORS

Dr. Robert L. Mathis

Dr. Robert L. Mathis is Professor Emeritus of Management at the University of Nebraska at Omaha (UNO). Born and raised in Texas, he received a B.B.A. and M.B.A. from Texas Tech University and a Ph.D. in Management and Organization from the University of Colorado. At UNO he has received the University's "Excellence in Teaching" award.

Dr. Mathis has co-authored several books and has published numerous articles covering a variety of topics over the last 25 years. Dr. Mathis also has held national offices in the Society for Human Resource Management (SHRM) and served as President of the Human Resource Certification Institute (HRCI). He also is certified as a Senior Professional in Human Resources (SPHR) by HRCI.

He has had extensive consulting experiences with organizations of all sizes and in a variety of areas. Firms assisted have been in the telecommunications, telemarketing, financial, manufacturing, retail, health-care, and utility industries. He has extensive specialized consulting experience in establishing or revising compensation plans for small- and medium-sized firms. Internationally, Dr. Mathis has consulting and training experience with organizations in Australia, Lithuania, Romania, Moldova, and Taiwan.

Dr. John H. Jackson

Dr. John H. Jackson is Professor of Management at the University of Wyoming. Born in Alaska, he received his B.B.A. and M.B.A. from Texas Tech University. He then worked in the telecommunications industry in human resources management for several years. After leaving that industry, he completed doctoral studies at the University of Colorado and received his Ph.D. in Management and Organization.

During his academic career, Dr. Jackson has authored six other college texts and over 50 articles and papers, including those appearing in *Academy of Management Review, Journal of Management, Human Resources Management,* and *Human Resources Planning.* He has consulted widely with a variety of organizations on HR and management development matters. During the past several years, Dr. Jackson has served as an expert witness in a number of HR-related cases.

At the University of Wyoming, he has served three terms as Department Head in the Department of Management and Marketing. Dr. Jackson has received the top teaching award at the University of Wyoming and was one of the first to work with two-way interactive television for MBA students in the state. He has served on the boards of directors of the Wyoming Business Council and the Wyoming Workforce Development Council. In addition to teaching, Dr. Jackson is president of Silverwood Ranches, Inc.

Human Resource Management

TWELFTH EDITION

Nature of Human Resource Management

CHAPTER

1

Changing Nature of Human Resource Management

After you have read this chapter, you should be able to:

- Define human capital and explain its importance.

- Identify the seven categories of HR activities.

- Describe how the major roles of HR management are being transformed.

- Discuss four challenges facing HR today.

- Identify the purposes and uses of HR technology.

- Discuss why ethical issues affect HR management.

- Explain the key competencies needed by HR professionals and why certification is important.

(HR) Headline

Why HR Is Not Always Respected

Many people in organizations do not like how their human resource (HR) departments operate. Some argue that HR is at best a necessary evil—at worst a bureaucratic force that routinely enforces unnecessary detailed rules, resists creativity, and impedes needed changes. Common criticisms include: Why are performance appraisals so useless? Why is HR always involved in cutting payroll and benefits expenditures at the command of the chief financial officers, which leads to higher employee turnover rates?

HR management is necessary of course, especially due to the huge number of government regulations enacted over the past decades. Legal requirements are complex in nature and HR must be cautious. This role of protecting corporate assets against the never-ending lawsuits often puts HR in the role of being the "bad cop." But many managers wonder why HR insists on treating everyone equally, which often leads to protecting poor performers rather than aiding retention of high performers.

Ideally, HR should be finding the best hires, nurturing the stars, and enhancing a productive work environment. Instead, too often HR departments concern themselves with the administrivia of personnel policies and practices—which companies are increasingly outsourcing to contractors who can do them more cheaply and more efficiently. Frequently, HR managers are seen as more concerned about *activities* than *results*. They tell how many people were hired, the number of performance appraisals completed, and

3

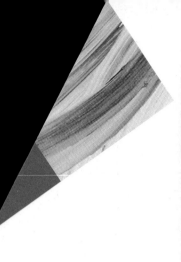

whether employees are satisfied with their orientation sessions. But too seldom does HR link those details to employee, managerial, and business performance measurement and metrics.

Despite many of these criticisms, there is evidence that HR *can be* respected if done well. Hunter Douglas, Yahoo!, Cardinal Health, Procter & Gamble, Pitney Bowes, Goldman Sachs, General Electric, and others truly bring HR into the realm of business strategy. HR can and should be a special part of any organization, which means viewing the people and their talents as an opportunity for creating greater organizational competitive advantages. But in many companies, that opportunity is seen by managers and employees as wasted, and that is why HR is not highly respected. Clearly, HR needs to change even more to overcome its current image.[1]

Human Resource (HR) management Designing management systems to ensure that human talent is used effectively and efficiently to accomplish organizational goals.

As a field, human resource management is undergoing significant transformation. **Human resource (HR) management** is designing management systems to ensure that human talent is used effectively and efficiently to accomplish organizational goals. Whether employees are in a big company with 10,000 positions or a small non-profit agency with 10 positions, employees must be recruited, selected, trained, and managed effectively. They also must be adequately and competitively compensated, and many will be given a range of benefits. Additionally, appropriate and legal HR systems are needed to comply with numerous legal requirements. In an environment in which the workforce keeps changing, laws and the needs of employers change too. Therefore, HR management activities continue to change and evolve.

However, as the HR Headline suggests, managing people in an organization is about more than simply administering a pay program, designing training, or avoiding lawsuits.[2] If human resources are to be an important part of successfully competing in the marketplace, a different level of thinking about HR management is necessary. Productive, creative people working in a flexible, effective organization that provides rewarding work with an earned reputation as an excellent employer should be the goal. However, too often HR managers and professionals primarily concentrate on HR *activities* such as job analysis or safety training—and those things certainly *do* need to be done. But today, a traditional activities approach to HR is necessary but insufficient. Part of the newer thinking is to treat people as part of the capital assets of the firm.

HUMAN CAPITAL IN ORGANIZATIONS

In all organizations there are many resources that affect organizational performance. Organizations must manage four types of assets:

- *Physical:* Buildings, land, furniture, computers, vehicles, equipment, etc.
- *Financial:* Cash, financial resources, stocks, financial securities, etc.
- *Intangible:* Specialized research capabilities, patents, information systems, designs, operating processes, etc.
- *Human:* Individuals with talents, capabilities, experience, professional expertise, relationships, etc.

All these assets are crucial in varying degrees in different organizations. But the human assets are the "glue" that holds all the other assets together and guides their use to achieve results.[3] Certainly, the cashiers, supervisors, and other employees at Wendy's or Lowe's or the doctors, nurses, receptionists, technical professionals, and other employees at a hospital allow all the other assets of their organization to be used to provide customer or patient services. Effective use of the firm's human capital may explain as much as 43% of the difference in higher market value between one company and another.[4]

Human Capital and HR

Human capital The collective value of the capabilities, knowledge, skills, life experiences, and motivation of an organizational workforce.

Human capital is not solely the people in organizations—it is what those people bring and contribute to organizational success. Human capital is the collective value of the capabilities, knowledge, skills, life experiences, and motivation of an organizational workforce.

Sometimes it is called *intellectual capital* to reflect the thinking, knowledge, creativity, and decision making that people in organizations contribute. For example, firms with high intellectual capital may have technical and research employees who create new biomedical devices, formulate pharmaceuticals that can be patented, and develop new software for specialized uses. All these organizational contributions illustrate the potential value of human capital.

Measuring the Value of Human Capital A fundamental question is whether better human capital management strategies create higher market values for companies, or whether financially successful companies have more resources to allocate to human capital initiatives. Research by Watson Wyatt on 750 large U.S., Canadian, and European firms concludes that superior human capital practices are a leading indicator of increased shareholder value rather than the reverse. Hiring the right people, supporting their creative thinking and productivity, and levering it all with the right technology seems to build superior business performance and shareholder value.[5]

In the United States, firms spend nearly twice as much as European firms on employee salary and benefits. Yet a ratio of pretax profit divided by compensation and benefit costs (Dollars of profit ÷ Dollars paid to employees) shows a "Human Capital Return on Investment" of 1.52 in the United States versus 1.14 for Europe. The interpretation of this difference is as follows: For $1,000 spent on employees in the U.S. a company returns $1,520. The same $1,000 in Europe generates $1,140. U.S. firms tend to be more flexible with their human capital investments and more likely to use pay-for-performance systems, which explains part of the difference.[6]

The value of human capital in organizations can be seen in various ways. One is sheer costs. In some industries, such as the hospitality industry, employee-related expenditures exceed 60% of total operating costs. With that recognition comes an increasing need to measure how the value of human capital is changing.[7] One study by Mercer, a global consulting firm, found that most chief financial officers (CFOs) see human capital as a key factor in creating value for shareholders. However, only 16% of the CFOs have calculated the return on human capital investments.[8] Also, less than half of them assess the value of human capital and its impact on business performance.[9] The measurement of human capital is discussed more in Chapter 2.

Human Resources as a Core Competency

The development and implementation of specific organizational strategies must be based on the areas of strength in an organization. Referred to as *core competencies,* those strengths are the foundation for creating a competitive advantage for an organization. A core competency is a unique capability that creates high value and differentiates an organization from its competition.

Certainly, many organizations have stated that their human resources differentiate them from their competitors and are a key determinant of competitive advantages. Studies also have documented that HR practices help create competitive advantages. Organizations as widely diverse as FedEx, Nordstrom, and Dell Computer have focused on human resources as having special strategic value for the organization.[10]

In small companies the same can be true. For example, small community banks have added numerous small- and medium-sized commercial loan customers because those banks emphasize that their customers can deal with the same employees directly every time they need help, rather than having to call an automated service center in another state, which occurs with some larger nationwide banks. This focus of community banks is on developing and retaining human resources to give competitive advantage with commercial and retail customers and using people as a core competency.

Core competency A unique capability that creates high value and differentiates an organization from its competition.

HR ACTIVITIES

One aspect of getting the greatest contributions from human capital in an organization requires that a fit be made with how people are treated and the long-term effect on the company's bottom line. The way that happens is through HR activities that are based on research, best practices, and continuing enhancement of HR efforts.

HR management can be thought of as seven interlinked activities taking place within organizations, as depicted in Figure 1-1. Additionally, external forces—legal, economic, technological, global, environmental, cultural/geographic, political, and social—significantly affect HR activities and how they are designed, managed, and changed. The HR activities are:

- **Strategic HR Management:** As part of maintaining organizational competitiveness, *HR effectiveness* can be increased through the use of *HR measurement* and *HR technology.* Through *HR planning,* managers anticipate the future supply of and demand for employees. An additional strategic HR concern is the *retention* of employees. All these topics are discussed in Chapters 2 and 3.
- **Equal Employment Opportunity:** *Compliance* with equal employment opportunity (EEO) laws and regulations affects all other HR activities. The *diversity* of a workforce creates additional challenges. For instance, a company must have sufficient diversity to meet *affirmative action* requirements. The nature of EEO and diversity management is discussed in Chapters 4 and 5.
- **Staffing:** The aim of staffing is to provide a sufficient supply of qualified individuals to fill jobs in an organization. *Job analysis* lays the foundation for staffing by identifying what people do in their jobs. These analyses are used when *recruiting* applicants for job openings. The *selection* process is concerned with choosing qualified individuals to fill those jobs. Staffing activities are discussed in Chapters 6, 7, and 8.

FIGURE 1-1   HR Management Activities

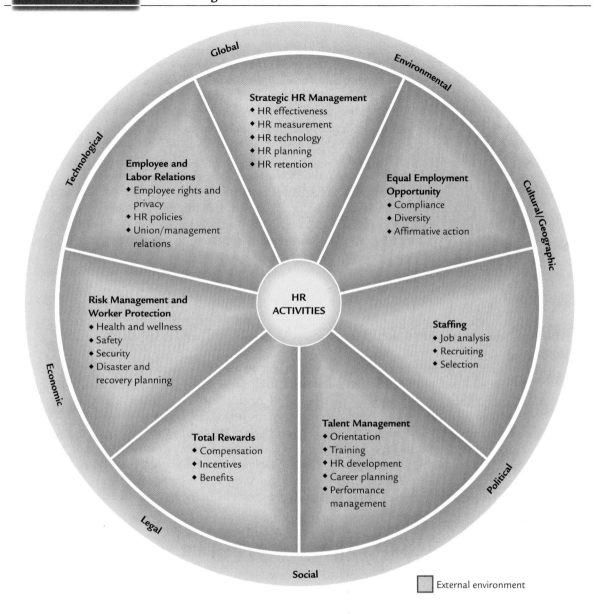

- **Talent Management and Development:** Beginning with the *orientation* of new employees, talent management and development includes different types of *training*. Also, *HR development* of employees and managers is necessary to prepare for future challenges. *Career planning* identifies paths and activities for individual employees as they move within the organization. Assessing how well employees perform their jobs is the focus of *performance management*. Activities associated with talent management are examined in Chapters 9, 10, and 11.
- **Total Rewards:** *Compensation* in the form of *pay, incentives,* and *benefits* rewards people for performing organizational work. To be competitive, employers develop and refine their basic *compensation* systems and may

use *variable pay programs* such as gainsharing and productivity rewards. The rapid increase in the cost of benefits, especially for health-care benefits, will continue to be a major issue for most employers. Compensation, variable pay, and benefits activities are discussed in Chapters 12, 13, and 14.

■ **Risk Management and Worker Protection:** Employers need to address an increasing number of workplace risks to ensure worker protection. For decades employers have had to meet legal requirements and be more responsive to concerns for workplace *health* and *safety*. Also, workplace *security* has grown in importance along with *disaster and recovery planning*. Health, safety, and security activities are examined in Chapter 15.

■ **Employee and Labor Relations:** The relationship between managers and their employees must be handled effectively. *Employee rights* and *privacy* issues must be addressed. It is important to develop, communicate, and update *HR policies and procedures* so that managers and employees alike know what is expected. In some organizations, *union/management relations* must be addressed as well. Activities associated with employee rights and labor/management relations are discussed in Chapters 16 and 17.

MANAGING HUMAN RESOURCES IN ORGANIZATIONS

In a real sense, *every* manager in an organization is an HR manager. Sales managers, head nurses, drafting supervisors, college deans, and accounting supervisors all engage in HR management, and their effectiveness depends in part on the success of organizational HR systems. However, it is unrealistic to expect a nursing supervisor or an engineering manager to know about the nuances of equal employment regulations or how to design and administer a compensation and benefits system. For that reason, many organizations have people in an HR department who specialize in these activities. The HR On-the-Job illustrates the HR manager's job with a week of typical activities.

Smaller Organizations and HR Management

In the United States and worldwide, the number of small businesses continues to grow. According to data from the U.S. Small Business Administration (SBA), small businesses employ more than 50% of all private-sector employees and generate 60% to 80% of all net new jobs each year.[11]

In surveys over several years by the SBA, the issues identified as the greatest concerns in small organizations are consistently: (1) shortages of qualified workers, (2) increasing costs of benefits, (3) rising taxes, and (4) compliance with government regulations. Notice that three of the top four concerns have an HR focus, especially when governmental compliance with wage/hour, safety, equal employment, and other regulations are considered.

As a result, for many smaller organizations HR issues are often significant. But not every organization is able to maintain an HR department. In a company with an owner and only three employees, the owner usually takes care of HR issues. As an organization grows, often a clerical employee is added to

HR ON-THE-JOB

What Do HR Managers Do?

Management of human resources requires a wide range of effects. Here are some of the activities that an HR manager in a 700-employee firm dealt with during one week:

- Met with the CEO and CFO to plan compensation budgets for the following year.
- Discussed with an outside lawyer a racial discrimination complaint by a former employee who had been terminated because of performance problems.
- Negotiated with the provider of health-care insurance benefits to bring a projected 22% increase in premiums down to a 14% increase.
- Reviewed an employee performance appraisal with a supervisor and discussed how to communicate both positive feedback and problem areas.
- Advised an executive on the process for terminating a sales manager whose sales performance and efforts were significantly below the goals set.

- Addressed a manager's report of an employee's accessing pornographic Websites on his company computer.
- Resolved an individual employee complaint about "offensive" comments and insults being made by a co-worker.
- Chaired an employee recognition luncheon.
- Discussed succession plan for the Customer Operations Division, consisting of 400 employees.
- Discussed with the other members of the Executive Leadership Team (the CEO, the CFO, and division heads) an employee staffing plan for the following year and ways to reduce employee turnover.

Many other topics were part of this HR manager's job that week. However, this list illustrates one fact: "There are a wide range of issues that are part of the regular work in HR management."

handle payroll, benefits, and required HR recordkeeping. If new employees are hired, supervisors and managers usually do the recruiting, selecting, and training. These HR activities reduce the time that supervisors and managers have to focus on operations, sales and marketing, accounting, and other business areas. At 80 to 100 employees, an organization typically needs to designate a person to specialize in HR management. Other HR jobs are added as the company gets larger and as HR technology increasingly becomes available for small- and medium-sized organizations.[12]

HR Cooperation with Operating Managers

Cooperation between operating managers, such as those in sales and manufacturing, and HR staff is necessary for HR efforts to succeed. In many cases, the HR professionals and staff members design processes and systems that the operating managers must help implement. The exact division of labor between HR and other departments varies from organization to organization.

Throughout this book, figures labeled "Typical Division of HR Responsibilities" illustrate how HR responsibilities in various areas are typically divided in organizations having specialized HR departments. The first such example, Figure 1-2, shows how the responsibilities for a familiar activity—training—might be divided between the HR department and operating managers in an organization.

FIGURE 1-2	Typical Division of HR Responsibilities: Training

HR Unit	Managers
• Prepares skill-training materials • Coordinates training efforts • Conducts or arranges for off-the-job training • Coordinates career plans and employee development efforts • Provides input and expertise for organizational development	• Provide technical information • Monitor training needs • Conduct and monitor continuing on-the-job training • Continually discuss employees' growth and future potential • Participate in organizational change

HR MANAGEMENT ROLES

Several roles can be fulfilled by HR management. The nature and extent of these roles depend on both what upper management wants HR management to do and what competencies the HR staff have demonstrated. Three roles are typically identified for HR:

■ *Administrative:* Focusing on HR clerical administration and recordkeeping
■ *Operational and employee advocate:* Managing most HR activities in keeping with the strategy that has been identified by management and serving as employee "champion"
■ *Strategic:* Helping to define the strategy relative to human capital and its contributing to organizational results

The administrative role traditionally has been the dominant role for HR. However, as Figure 1-3 indicates, a significant transformation in HR is occurring. The HR pyramid is being turned upside down so that significantly less HR time and fewer HR staff are used for clerical administration. Notice in Figure 1-3 that the percentage of emphasis on the operational and employee advocate role is remaining constant. The greatest challenge is for HR to devote more emphasis to strategic HR management. A study by Towers-Perrin, a large consulting firm, found that HR is being pressured to change because of four critical business issues identified by senior HR managers: cost-reduction pressures, business restructuring, broadscale downsizing/layoffs, and globalization of business.[13] A look at each of the roles of HR and how they are being transformed follows.

Administrative Role of HR

The administrative role of HR management has been heavily oriented to processing and recordkeeping. This role has given HR management in some organizations the reputation of being staffed by paper shufflers who primarily tell managers and employees what cannot be done. If limited to the administrative

FIGURE 1-3   Changing Roles of HR Management

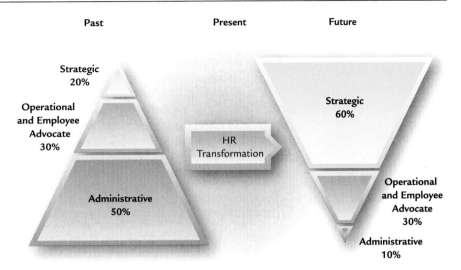

Note: Example percentages are based on various surveys.

role, HR staff are seen primarily as clerical and lower-level administrative aides to the organization. Two major shifts driving the transformation of the administrative role are greater use of technology and outsourcing.

Technology Transforming HR To improve the administrative efficiency of HR and responsiveness of HR to employees and managers, more HR functions are becoming available electronically or are being done on the Internet. Web-based technology is reducing the amount of HR administrative time and staff needed. Technology is being used in all HR activities, from employment application and employee benefits enrollment to e-learning using Internet-based resources. Later in this chapter there is more discussion on the nature, types, and uses of HR technology.

Outsourcing of HR Increasingly, many HR administrative functions are being outsourced to vendors. Outsourcing of HR administrative activities has grown dramatically with the value of outsourcing contracts tripling recently, and there are projections of large increases occurring over the next several years.[14] The HR areas most commonly outsourced are employee assistance (counseling), retirement planning, benefits administration, payroll services, and outplacement services.[15]

The primary reasons why HR functions are outsourced is to save money on HR staffing, to take advantage of specialized vendor expertise and technology, and to be able to focus on more strategic HR activities. These activities are being outsourced to firms both in the United States and worldwide. For example, a major firm offering administrative services for retirement benefits is using a customer service center on a Caribbean island to answer questions from employees of a number of large U.S. firms. Estimates have been that outsourcing arrangements such as that save employers 30% or more on labor costs.

However, there have been some problems with outsourcing HR activities as well. The 30% cost savings does not always materialize because the process has been more complex than initially imagined.[16] For example, Marathon Oil in Houston outsourced its recruiting process, then demand grew rapidly for petroleum engineers, geologists, and other skilled positions. The outsourcing firm fell behind in meeting the company's needs. After examining its options, Marathon returned the recruiting function to internal control.[17]

There is apparently general satisfaction with outsourcing benefits, payroll, and information systems administration. But the "judgment services" or the more strategic parts of HR, such as compensation, recruiting, and performance management, are more likely to be less successfully outsourced.[18] However, the idea that even those HR functions should *not* be outsourced, is not held by everyone; for instance, DuPont outsources performance management and employee development.[19] Such contracting for HR services is an evolving practice that promises to change the administrative HR functions for many employers.[20]

Operational and Employee Advocate Role for HR

HR often has been viewed as the "employee advocate" in organizations. As the voice for employee concerns, HR professionals traditionally have been seen as "company morale officers" who do not understand the business realities of the organizations and do not contribute measurably to the strategic success of the business.

HR professionals spend considerable time on HR "crisis management" dealing with employee problems that are both work and non-work related. Employee advocacy helps ensure fair and equitable treatment for employees regardless of personal background or circumstances. Sometimes the HR advocate role may create conflict with operating managers. However, without the advocate role, employers would face even more lawsuits and regulatory complaints than they do now.

The operational role requires HR professionals to cooperate with operating managers, to identify and implement needed programs and policies in the organization. Operational activities are tactical in nature. Compliance with equal employment opportunity and other laws is ensured, employment applications are processed, current openings are filled through interviews, supervisors are trained, safety problems are resolved, and wage and benefit questions are answered. These efforts require matching HR activities with the strategies of the organization. However, HR often does not help formulate strategies for the organization as a whole; instead it merely carries them out through HR activities.

Strategic Role for HR

Differences between the operational and strategic roles exist in a number of HR areas. As shown in Figure 1-4, the strategic HR role requires that HR professionals be proactive in addressing business realities and focusing on future business needs, such as workforce planning, compensation strategies, and the performance of HR.

Many executives, managers, and HR professionals increasingly see the need for HR management to become a greater strategic contributor to the "business" success of organizations. Even not-for-profit organizations, such as governmental and social service entities, must manage their human resources in a "business-oriented" manner. In fact, it has been suggested that the HR function should be managed as its own

FIGURE 1-4   Operational to Strategic Transformation of HR

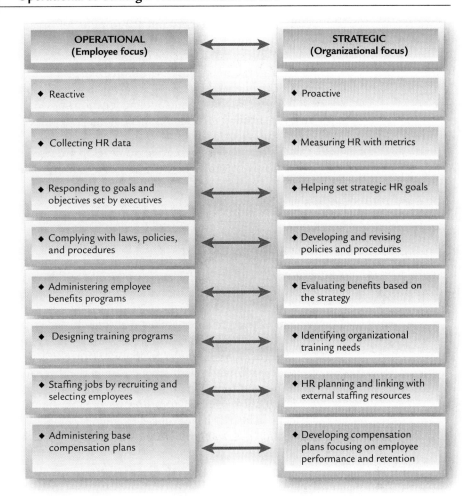

"business." HR should be responsible for knowing what the true cost of human capital is for that employer. For example, it may cost two times key employees' annual salaries to replace them if they leave. Turnover is something HR can help control, and if it is successful in saving the company money with good retention management strategies, those are contributions to the bottom line.[21]

"Contributing at the Table" The role of HR as a *strategic business partner* is often described as "having a seat at the table," and contributing to the strategic directions and success of the organization. That phrase means HR is involved in *devising* strategy in addition to *implementing* strategy.[22] For instance, at Target, a large retailer, HR is accountable for workforce planning, staffing, and employee retention, all of which affect customer service in Target stores.[23]

At a much smaller firm, Wegman's Food Markets in New York, HR is focusing on controlling benefit costs by educating employees about increasing their use of generic drugs, which has cut the firm's prescription drug costs while preserving benefits for employees.[24] However, even though this role of HR is recognized, many organizations still need to make significant progress toward fulfilling it. Some examples of areas where strategic contributions should be made by HR are as follows:

- Evaluating mergers and acquisitions for organizational "compatibility," structural changes, and staffing needs
- Conducting workforce planning to anticipate the retirement of employees at all levels and identify workforce expansion in organizational strategic plans
- Leading site selection efforts for new facilities or transferring operations to international outsourcing locations based on workforce needs
- Instituting HR management systems to reduce administrative time and staff
- Working with executives to develop a revised sales compensation and incentives plan as new products/services are rolled out to customers

CURRENT HR MANAGEMENT CHALLENGES

As the way HR is managed in organizations changes, some challenges are affecting all employers. Responding effectively requires a competent HR presence to deal with them.[25] The environment faced by organizations and their managers is also changing. A force affecting the management of human resources is the *globalization of business,* as evidenced by international outsourcing and global competitive pressures. Other challenges include significant changes in *economic forces* and the rapid growth in *technology* that have changed how people work. *Changing demographics* in the workforce are significantly affecting management, particularly with the increase in the diversity of employees and the aging of the workforce in many countries. All of these factors and others are combining to put more *cost pressures* on organizations. Consequently, employers in many industries have reduced the number of jobs and employees as part of *organizational restructuring.* A look at some of these challenges for HR follows.

Globalization of Business

The internationalization of business has proceeded at a rapid pace. Many U.S. firms, both large and small, receive a substantial portion of their profits and sales from other countries. Firms such as Coca-Cola, Exxon, Mobil, Microsoft, Ford, and General Electric derive half or more of total sales and profits outside the United States. The reverse is also true. For example, Toyota, based in Japan, is growing its market share and its number of jobs in the United States, and North American sales provide 70% of its profits worldwide.[26] Also, Toyota, Honda, Nissan, and other Japanese automobile manufacturers, electronics firms, and suppliers have expanded their operations in the United States.

The globalization of business has shifted from trade and investment to the integration of global operations, management, and strategic alliances, which has significantly affected the management of human resources. Attracting global talent has created political issues. For instance, U.S. employers are having a difficult time hiring enough engineers and educated tech workers, but Congress is restricting the quota for high-skilled workers to be admitted from other countries in light of the large amount of illegal immigration that is occurring.[27]

The HR profession is changing under the force of globalization.[28] Ethical issues and difficult adjustments for countries are

Internet Research

Human Resource Management in the News
HRM in the News is South-Western's service to provide summaries of the latest human resource management news stories. For news stories on the globalization of human resources, link to their site at:
http://thomsonedu.com/management/mathis.

HR PERSPECTIVE

Globalization Affecting German Companies

Globalization is affecting HR management in many industries in countries throughout the world, not just in the United States. One illustration is seen in Germany, where worldwide free-market capitalism has created challenges for German employers traditionally known for providing high wages but being part of a rigid labor market. German firms have avoided as long as possible the impact of global competition that requires costs to be kept under control or sales will be lost to producers who can make the same product and charge less. Consider Grohe Water Technology AG, a medium-sized German firm that makes upscale faucets and showers.

After World War II, Germany built an economy designed to harness the power of capitalism while smoothing out its harsher effects. Most people worked for family-owned businesses like Grohe that provided generous pay, training, and time-off benefits. However,

in the 1970s the high payroll taxes needed to fund the generous welfare and pension benefits caused companies to defer job creation, which meant that German unemployment rates continued to rise. Also, many competitors of Grohe had already shifted production operations to lower wage areas. For instance, the average worker in Germany costs €51,000 per year, while workers in Portugal cost only one-third as much and those in Thailand one-tenth as much. Thus, Grohe is likely to be less successful if it doesn't cut costs.

The unions representing most Grohe workers contend that the firm is doing fine, but that viewpoint may be unrealistic given what is occurring in the global economy. The employees do not want to reduce their pay levels, benefits, or the number of jobs. Yet the "invisible hand" of competition will continue to affect Grohe and other German companies unless they can raise productivity and cut costs.[30]

occurring in many areas.[29] As the HR Perspective shows, firms in countries such as Germany are facing major HR pressures.

Moving jobs to countries with lower labor rates, such as China, Thailand, or India, is another indication of the globalization of HR. Employers in many developed countries are offshoring jobs, usually to cut costs.[31] Offshoring of jobs affects not only the number of jobs in both countries involved, but the occupations and skills needed as well.[32] The final effect is complex, but the following distinctions in terminology can be made[33]:

- **Offshoring:** U.S. businesses contracting out activities to unaffiliated companies or their affiliates in another country
- **In-shoring:** Foreign businesses shifting activities to the United States
- **Outsourcing:** Businesses contracting out activities to unaffiliated companies either at home or abroad

Whenever international outsourcing occurs, HR management should be involved to ensure the appropriate consideration of various laws, cultural factors, and other issues.[34]

Global Security and Terrorism Another global challenge for international employers is the threat of terrorism. Following the terrorist attacks of September 11, 2001, firms around the world had to develop terror response and security plans. International firms in many industries have dramatically increased security for both operations and employees. Terrorist threats and incidents have significantly affected airlines, travel companies, construction firms, and even retailers such as McDonald's. HR management must respond to such concerns as part of transnational operations and risk management efforts.

Off-shoring U.S. businesses contracting out activities to unaffiliated companies or their affiliates in another country.

In-shoring Foreign businesses shifting activities to the United States.

Outsourcing Businesses contracting out activities to unaffiliated companies either at home or abroad.

Economic and Technological Changes

Several changes are discussed next.

Occupational Shifts A major change is the shift of jobs from manufacturing and agriculture to service and telecommunications. In general, the U.S. economy has become predominantly a service economy, and that shift is expected to continue. More than 80% of U.S. jobs are in service industries, and most new jobs created by 2014 will also be in services.[35] Projections of growth in some jobs and decline in others illustrate the shifts occurring in the U.S. economy. Figure 1-5 lists occupations that are expected to experience the greatest growth in percentage and numbers for the period ending in 2014. Most of the fastest-growing occupations percentage-wise are related to health care. The anticipated increase in the growth in health-care jobs is primarily due to the demands of an aging population. In contrast, many of the fastest-growing jobs in terms of numbers are in lower-skilled service fields.

Workforce Availability and Quality Concerns Many parts of the United States face significant workforce shortages that exist due to an inadequate supply of workers with the skills needed to perform the jobs being added. It is not that there are too few people—only that there are too few with many of the skills being demanded. For instance, a study of U.S. manufacturing firms revealed that about 80% of them have been experiencing a moderate to serious shortage of qualified specialized workers. The primary reasons were shifting demographics, the negative image of the manufacturing industry, and inadequately educated U.S. workers.[36]

Even though many Americans are graduating from high school (84% over age 25 have high school diplomas) and from college (almost 26% over age 25 now have college degrees), employers are concerned about the preparation and specific skills of new graduates. Comparisons of international test results show that students in the United States perform slightly above average in math and science, but *well below* students in some other directly competitive nations. Also, graduates with degrees in computers, engineering, and the health sciences

FIGURE 1-5   Fastest Growing Jobs to 2014

Percentage Increase in Jobs		Increase in Job Numbers	
Medical assistants	59%	Retail sales workers	736,000
Network analysts	57%	Registered nurses	703,000
Social service assistants	49%	Post-secondary teachers	524,000
Physician's assistants	49%	Customer service representatives	471,000
Home health aides	48%	Janitors	440,000
Medical records technicians	47%	Waiters/servers	376,000

Source: U.S. Bureau of Labor Statistics, www.bls.gov.

Internet Research

**Workforce Information
Council**

The Workforce Information
Council provides a wide variety of information
on labor market trends and conditions, including
job outlook and wages and skill requirements
of jobs. Visit their site at: http://thomsonedu
.com/management/mathis.

remain in short supply relative to the demand for them. That is another reason why international outsourcing has grown. Unless major improvements are made to U.S. educational systems, U.S. employers will be unable to find enough qualified workers for the growing number of skilled jobs of all types.

Growth in Contingent Workforce *Contingent workers* (temporary workers, independent contractors, leased employees, and part-timers) represent more than 20% of the U.S. workforce. Many employers operate with a core group of regular employees who have critical skills, and then expand and shrink the workforce through the use of contingent workers.

The use of contingent workers has grown for many reasons. A significant one is that many contingent workers are paid less and/or receive fewer benefits than regular employees. Omitting contingent workers from health-care benefits saves some firms 20% to 40% in labor costs. Another reason for the increased use of contingent workers is that doing so may reduce legal liability for employers. As more and more employment-related lawsuits are filed, some employers have become more wary about adding regular full-time employees. By using contract workers, employers reduce the number of legal issues they face regarding selection, discrimination, benefits, discipline, and termination.

Technological Shifts and the Internet Globalization and economic shifts have been accelerated by technological changes, with the Internet being a primary driver. The explosive growth in information technology and in the use of the Internet has driven changes in jobs and organizations of all sizes. For employees and managers, technology means always being "available." Cell phones, wireless networks for laptop computers, and personal digital organizers allow many workers to be always "on call." Technology is also enabling more people to work from home and at night and during weekends. This technology is resulting in more weekly hours worked and more stress on balancing work and personal lives. Further, organizations have to deal with the management of "virtual employees," who may not be working on-site, and of employees and vendors in other countries.

Workforce Demographics and Diversity

The U.S. workforce has been changing dramatically. It is more diverse racially and ethnically, more women are in it than ever before, and the average age of its members is now considerably older. As a result of these demographic shifts, HR management in organizations has had to adapt to a more varied labor force both externally and internally.

Racial/Ethnic Diversity Racial and ethnic minorities account for a growing percentage of the overall labor force, with the percentage of Hispanics equal to or greater than the percentage of African Americans. Immigrants will continue to expand that growth. An increasing number of individuals characterize themselves as *multi-racial*, suggesting that the American "melting pot" is blurring racial and ethnic identities.

Racial/ethnic diversity has created greater cultural diversity as well because of its accompanying differences in traditions, languages, religious practices, etc. For example, global events have increased employers' attention to individuals who are Muslim, and more awareness and accommodation for Islamic religious beliefs and practices have become a common concern.

Women in the Workforce Women constitute about 47% of the U.S. work-force.[37] Many women workers are single, separated, divorced, or widowed, and therefore are "primary" income earners. Many women who are married have spouses who are also employed. A growing number of U.S. households include "domestic partners," who are committed to each other though not married and who may be of the same or the opposite sex.

For many workers in the United States, balancing the demands of family and work is a significant challenge. Although that balancing has always been a concern, the increased number of working women and dual-career couples has resulted in greater tensions for many workers, both male and female. Employers have had to respond to work/family concerns in order to retain employees. Responses have included greater use of flexible hours, job sharing, the establishment of child-care referral services or on-site child-care facilities, and more flexible leave programs.[38] Figure 1-6 shows changes in family friendly benefits during the past few years.

Aging Workforce In many economically developed countries, the population is aging, resulting in a significantly aging workforce. In the United States, during the next decade a significant number of experienced employees will

FIGURE 1-6   Family-Friendly Benefit Offerings

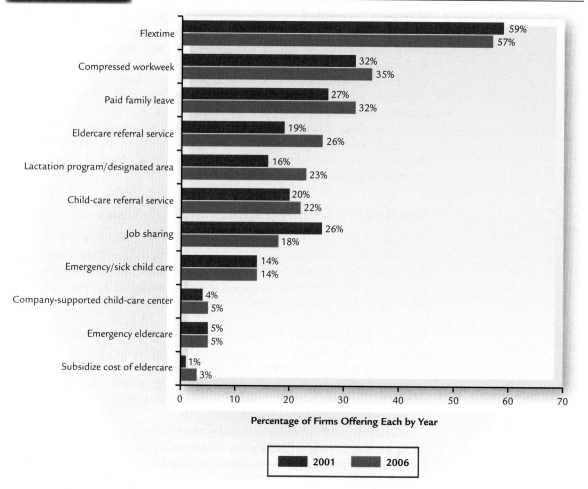

Percentage of Firms Offering Each by Year

■ 2001   ■ 2006

Source: Adapted from *Benefits Survey Report* (Alexandria, VA: Society for Human Resource Management, 2006).

be retiring, changing to part-time, or otherwise shifting their employment. Replacing the experience and talents of longer-service workers is a growing challenge facing employers in all industries.

Overall, the growing diversity and aging of the workforce are creating more tensions and a greater likelihood of individuals filing employment discrimination complaints against employers. Therefore, employers are having to devote more time and effort to ensuring that non-discriminatory policies and practices are followed. Training on diversity issues and the effective management of diversity issues in organizations are getting more attention.

Organizational Cost Pressures and Restructuring

An overriding theme facing managers and organizations is to operate in a "cost-less" mode, which means continually looking for ways to reduce costs of all types—financial, operations, equipment, and labor. Pressures from global competitors have forced many U.S. firms to close facilities, use international outsourcing, adapt their management practices, increase productivity, and decrease labor costs in order to become more competitive. The growth of information technology, particularly that linked to the Internet, has influenced the number, location, and required capabilities of employees.

A familiar example is Wal-Mart, the giant retailer, whose corporate strategy is providing the lowest prices to customers. As a result, Wal-Mart has driven its vendors and suppliers to reduce their costs. One result has been for suppliers to manufacture their goods overseas in order to use cheaper labor rates. Another consequence has been for many suppliers to cut jobs and close factories that were not as cost efficient and productive as foreign competitors. So while Wal-Mart has grown and Wal-Mart's customers have gotten lower prices, many suppliers and other retailers have had to follow the "cost-less" strategy.[39]

As part of organizational changes, many organizations have "rightsized" by: (1) eliminating layers of managers, (2) closing facilities, (3) merging with other organizations, and (4) outplacing workers. To improve productivity, quality, and service while also reducing costs, they are redesigning jobs and affecting people. The human cost associated with downsizing has resulted in increased workloads and a "survivor's mentality" for those employees who remain. Additionally, downsizing often led to loss of employee and customer loyalty, unmet cost savings, and, ultimately, increased turnover of the remaining employees.

These organizational shifts have caused some organizations to reduce the number of employees, while at the same time scrambling to attract and retain employees with different capabilities than were previously needed. To respond to organizational cost pressures and restructurings, as well as the other HR challenges it faces, the use of information technology of all types is transforming HR management.

Internet Research

International Association for Human Resource Management

The International Association for Human Resource Information Management (IHRIM) is the world's leading clearinghouse for the HRMS industry for information management, systems issues, trends, and technology. Visit their site at: http://thomsonedu.com/management/mathis.

HR TECHNOLOGY

Human resource management system (HRMS) An integrated system providing information used by HR management in decision making.

Greater use of technology has led to organizational use of a **human resource management system (HRMS)**, which is an integrated system providing information used by HR management in decision making. This terminology emphasizes that making HR decisions, not just building databases, is the primary reason for compiling data in an information system.

Purposes of an HRMS

An HRMS serves two major purposes in organizations. One relates to administrative and operational efficiency, the other to effectiveness. The first purpose is to improve the efficiency with which data on employees and HR activities are compiled. If automated, many HR activities can be performed more efficiently and quickly and with less paperwork. One survey of about 200 companies found a 60% decline in HR administrative work when employees were given self-service access to HR information and forms through Web-based systems.[40]

A major advantage of implementing an HRMS is that as users access information and input changes, the system will guide them through all the steps of the transaction. An increasing number of firms have HR technology systems that allow employees to access Web-based 401(k) information, and employees and managers are able to make changes to their own data without the assistance of an HR professional.[41]

The second purpose of an HRMS is more strategic and is related to HR planning. Having accessible data enables HR planning and managerial decision making to be based to a greater degree on information rather than relying on managerial perceptions and intuition.[42]

A different use of technology in HR is a "wiki," which is best known for its use in Wikipedia, a collaborative encyclopedia that anyone can add content to at any time. The Wikipedia is used as a place to get current information on topics that are explained by a wide variety of people. Wikis can be part of HR collaboration efforts and information exchange, as discussed in the HR On-Line.

HR ONLINE

Wikis and Collaborative HR

The growth of the Internet has resulted in creation of a large number of wikis. A *wiki* is a Web page with no formal oversight and no managing editor. Each contributor adds input to the product and revises what is collectively known about the subject. One might suspect such a process would only produce graffiti, but wikis can work well in organizations because well-intentioned users can provide a wide range of insights and useful information.

For employers, wikis and other technology have led to creation of collaborative networks to foster the exchange of ideas and information among a wide range of individuals both inside and outside a firm. Wikis are one example of *collaborative HR*. This process of collaboration can lead to HR professionals from several different organizations jointly working to address shared business problems and interacting

regularly with individuals from a number of different firms in various industries. These firms can be part of industry or professional associations, so that limited competitive conflicts potentially arise.

The HR individuals in such collaborative efforts can participate in exchanging details and research such as that related to employee turnover issues or training plans. This sharing of information and programs allows each firm to benefit from the expertise of other firms, without having the time and expense of developing some of their own HR practices. Such collaborative HR practices are well suited to the use of wikis, which use software to harness the group's collaborative energy. Thus, collaborator networks provide a technological way to share a wide range of useful information about HR management. [43]

Other Uses of HR Technology

HR technology has many uses in an organization. The most basic is the automation of payroll and benefits activities. Another common use of technology is tracking EEO/affirmative action activities. Beyond those basic applications, the use of Web-based information systems has allowed the HR unit in organizations to become more administratively efficient and to deal with more strategic and longer-term HR planning issues. Web-based systems include these:

- *Bulletin boards:* Information on personnel policies, job postings, and training materials can be accessed by employees globally.
- *Data access:* Linked to databases, an extranet or an intranet allows employees to access benefits information such as sick leave usage or 401(k) balances. This access frees up time for HR staff members who previously spent considerable time answering routine employee inquiries.
- *Employee self-service:* Many HR technology activities enable employees to access and update their own personnel records, change or enroll in employee benefits plans, and respond to employment opportunities in other locations. Obviously, maintaining security is critical when the employee self-service option is available.
- *Extended linkage:* Integrating an HRMS allows the databases of vendors of HR services and an employer to be linked so that data can be exchanged electronically. Also, employees can communicate directly from throughout the world to submit and retrieve their own personnel details, take on-line training courses, and provide complete career planning data.

The greater use of HRMS technologies is affecting how HR activities are performed in many ways. To illustrate, Coca-Cola provides a Web-based employee self-service program to its worldwide staff in more than 200 countries. Employees can go on-line to access and change their personal data, enroll in or change benefits programs, and prepare for performance reviews. The employee self-service system is available in various languages and reflects country and cultural differences.[44] Additional examples of how various HR activities are being transformed by technology will be presented throughout the chapters of this text.

ETHICS AND HR MANAGEMENT

Closely linked with the strategic role of HR is the way HR management professionals influence the organizational ethics practiced by executives, managers, and employees. On the strategic level, organizations with high ethical standards are more likely to meet long-term strategic objectives and profit goals. Organizations that are seen as operating with integrity are viewed more positively by individuals in the community and industry, as well as by consumers and employees.[45] That positive view often translates into bottom-line financial results and the ability to attract and retain human resources.

The need for great attention to ethics has grown in the past few years, as evidenced by the corporate scandals in the United States at Enron, WorldCom, Tyco, numerous financial and investment firms, and other organizations. Ethical problems at Parmalat (an Italian-based food company), Credit Lyonnais (a French financial firm), and other companies illustrate that ethical lapses are not problems just in the United States.

Ethics and Global Differences

Differences in legal, political, and cultural values and practices in different countries often raise ethical issues for global employers. Those employers also must comply with their home-country laws. The United States and some Western European countries have laws regarding the conduct of firms based domestically. For example, the Foreign Corrupt Practices Act (FCPA) prohibits U.S. firms from engaging in bribery and other practices in foreign countries that would be illegal in the United States. However, competing firms from certain other countries are not bound by similar restrictions, which may create competitive disadvantages for U.S. and European firms.

The impact of those laws often requires global managers to draw some fine ethical distinctions between bribery and gift-giving, particularly given differences in business practices in various Asian and Eastern European countries. Two examples illustrate typical ethical dilemmas:

- Many global firms have found that establishing or expanding operations in some Asian, African, and Latin American countries is much easier if the global firm arranges for the children of key government officials to be admitted to and receive scholarships from colleges and universities in the United States or Great Britain. Without this "sponsorship," the global firms often face endless delays in obtaining the necessary government agency approvals for its operations.
- In some Eastern European and Asian countries, obtaining a new telephone line in less than three months requires making a cash payment, referred to as an "expediting charge," to the local manager of the telephone office. All parties to the deal know that the manager personally will retain the cash, but a telephone is essential for doing business internationally.

These and other situations reflect how different legal, political, and cultural factors in other countries can lead to ethical conflicts for global managers. Some global firms have established guidelines and policies to reduce the payments of bribes, but even those efforts do not provide detailed guidance on handling the situations that can arise.

Ethical Behavior and Organizational Culture

Organizational culture The shared values and beliefs in an organization.

Numerous writers on business ethics consistently stress that the primary determinant of ethical behavior is organizational culture, which is the shared values and beliefs in an organization. Basically, organizational culture is "how things are done here." Every organization has a culture, and that culture influences how executives, managers, and employees act in making organizational decisions. For example, the more common it is for employees to lie about why they missed work in order to use sick leave, the more likely it is that new employees adopt that behavior. Or, if meeting objectives and financial targets is stressed, then it should not be a surprise when executives and managers fudge numbers or falsify cost records. The financial scandals in many firms in recent years illustrate the consequences of an "anything goes" organizational culture. However, a positive ethical culture exists in many organizations, as the HR Best Practices describes. Organizational culture is discussed in more detail in the next chapter.

HR plays a key role in ensuring ethical behavior in organizations. The number of incidents of employees reporting ethical misconduct has grown in the past decade, primarily because of such corporate scandals as the Enron

How UPS Delivers Ethics and Corporate Integrity

With all the reports of corporate scandals in the past several years, one company whose name has not appeared in them is UPS, a transportation and logistics firm. The "Big Brown" company, as UPS is also called, sees ethics as a primary part of achieving competitive advantage with customers, as well as an aid in attracting and retaining employees at all levels. HR executives and key staff members are ensuring that UPS has ethical practices in place throughout the firm's worldwide operations.

UPS has taken a number of actions to, as it says, "lead with integrity." A detailed code-of-conduct manual is given to and reviewed with all employees. The manual includes specific examples of ethical situations that employees may face and how to respond to them. The manual itself is updated regularly, and

the code of conduct is reinforced annually through training sessions and communications.

Additionally, UPS contracts with an external firm to provide a hotline for receiving confidential calls on ethical problems. The vendor notes the information and sends it to a special compliance department at UPS where investigations and follow-up are handled. Regular summaries of the hotline reports are presented to department managers and senior executives. Annually, managers complete a "conduct code" report that asks specific questions about ethical problems that have arisen during the year. In summary, an emphasis on ensuring corporate integrity and ethical behavior permeates UPS, and HR plays both strategic and operational roles in delivering on ethics at UPS.[46]

scandal and others. When the following four elements of ethics programs exist, ethical behavior is likely to occur:

- A written code of ethics and standards of conduct
- Training on ethical behavior for all executives, managers, and employees
- Means for employees to obtain advice on ethical situations they face, often provided by HR
- Systems for confidential reporting of ethical misconduct or questionable behavior

HR's Role in Organizational Ethics

Organizations that are seen as ethical in the way they operate have longer-term success. Because people in organizations are making ethical decisions on a daily basis, HR management plays a key role as the "keeper and voice" of organizational ethics. All managers, including HR managers, must deal with ethical issues and be sensitive to how they interplay with HR activities. To help HR professionals deal with ethical issues, the Society for Human Resource Management has developed a code of ethics for its members. There are a number of different views about the importance of HR in ensuring that ethical practices, justice, and fairness are present throughout HR practices. Figure 1-7 identifies some of the most frequent areas of ethical misconduct involving HR activities.

Ethical issues pose fundamental questions about fairness, justice, truthfulness, and social responsibility.[47] Ethics deals with what "ought" to be done. Just complying with the laws does not guarantee ethical behavior. Laws and regulations cannot cover every situation executives, managers, and employees

FIGURE 1-7	Examples of Ethical Misconduct in HR Activities

Types of Misconduct	Examples of Employee, Supervisor, and Managerial Behavior
Compensation	· Misrepresenting hours and time worked · Falsifying expense reports · Personal bias in performance appraisals and pay increases · Inappropriate overtime classifications
Employee Relations	· Employees lying to supervisors · Executives/managers providing false information to public, customers, and vendors · Personal gains/gifts from vendors · Misusing/stealing organizational assets and supplies · Intentionally violating safety/health regulations
Staffing and Equal Employment	· Favoritism in hiring and promotion · Sexual harassment · Sex, race, and age discrimination in hiring, discipline, and termination

will face. Instead of relying on laws, people must be guided by values and personal behavior "codes," including the following two questions:

■ Does the behavior or result meet all applicable *laws, regulations, and government codes*?
■ Does the behavior or result meet both *organizational standards* and *professional standards* of ethical behavior?

Yet, having all these elements may not prevent individual managers or executives from engaging in or failing to report unethical behavior.[48] Even HR staff members may be reluctant to report ethics concerns, primarily because of fears that doing so may affect their current and future employment. Specific ethical issues that have created difficulty in the HR area include the following:

■ How much information on a problem employee should be given to or withheld from another potential employer?
■ Should an employment manager check credit agency or law enforcement records on applicants without informing them?
■ What obligations are owed a long-term employee who has become an ineffective performer because of changes in the job skills required?
■ What impact should an employee's off-the-job lifestyle have on promotion decisions if on-the-job work performance has been satisfactory?
■ Should employees who smoke be forced to stop smoking on the job when new no-smoking restrictions are implemented by the employer? Also, should an employer be allowed to reject a job applicant solely on the basis of off-the-job smoking?
■ Should an otherwise qualified applicant be refused employment because the applicant's dependent child has major health problems that would significantly raise the employer's insurance costs?
■ How should co-workers' "right to know" be balanced with individual privacy rights when a worker discloses he or she has AIDS, hepatitis C, or other serious communicable diseases?

HR Ethics and Sarbanes-Oxley The Sarbanes-Oxley Act (SOX) was passed by Congress to make certain that publicly traded companies followed accounting controls that would reduce the likelihood of illegal and unethical behaviors. A number of HR facets must be managed in line with SOX. The biggest issues are linked to executive compensation and benefits. But SOX Sections 406 and 806 require companies to establish ethics codes, develop employee complaint systems, and have anti-retaliation policies for employees who act as whistle blowers to identify wrongful actions. HR has been involved in routing people through the massive compliance verification effort that has occurred. Further, the whole verification process has caused employers to check time and attendance and payroll. In the past, time and attendance often were not checked very carefully.[49]

A broad study of ethics is philosophical, complex, and beyond the scope of this book. The intent here is to highlight ethical aspects of HR management. Various ethical issues in HR management are highlighted throughout the text as appropriate.

HR MANAGEMENT COMPETENCIES AND CAREERS

As HR management becomes more complex, greater demands are placed on individuals who make HR their career specialty. Even readers of this book who do not become HR managers and professionals will find it useful to know about the competencies required for effective HR management.

HR Competencies

Internet Research

Society for Human Resource Management
The Society for Human Resource Management is the largest association devoted to Human Resource Management. Some of the most essential and comprehensive resources available for Human Resource professionals are contained within the SHRM Website at:
http://thomsonedu.com/management/mathis.

The transformation of HR toward being more strategic has implications for the competencies needed by HR professionals. To identify those competencies, the University of Michigan (UM) and the Society for Human Resource Management (SHRM) recently conducted a cooperative study. The results of the study have been summarized to identify five basic sets of HR competencies.[50] One useful product of the UM/SHRM study is the development of an HR competency self-assessment, which individual HR professionals can complete.[51] The five areas of HR competencies are described briefly as follows:

■ *Strategic contribution:* The key competency that HR needs to fulfill its strategic role is the ability to be a strategic contributor to organizational success. That means that HR must focus on the long-term implications of HR issues.

■ *Business knowledge:* HR professionals must have business knowledge of the organization and its strategies if they are to contribute strategically. They must understand the financial, technological, and other facets of the industry and the organization.

■ *HR delivery:* The HR activities must be delivered effectively and efficiently in ways that meet the needs of both the organization and its employees.

■ *HR technology:* Technology, particularly information systems and Web-based resources, have become a significant part of HR management today. HR professionals must develop the abilities needed to work effectively with various dimensions of an HRMS.

■ *Personal credibility:* HR professionals must have credibility personally and professionally. That means they must develop effective internal relationships with individual executives, employees, managers, and supervisors. Also, HR professionals must establish personal and professional credibility in various external relationships.

HR Management as a Career Field

HR generalist A person who has responsibility for performing a variety of HR activities.

HR specialist A person who has in-depth knowledge and expertise in a limited area of HR.

There are a variety of jobs within the HR career field, ranging from executive to clerical. As an employer grows large enough to need someone to focus primarily on HR activities, the role of the HR generalist emerges—that is, a person who has responsibility for performing a variety of HR activities. Further growth leads to the addition of HR specialists, or individuals who have in-depth knowledge and expertise in limited areas of HR. Figure 1-8 shows the most common areas of HR specialists, with benefits being the most prevalent.

FIGURE 1-8   HR Specialists

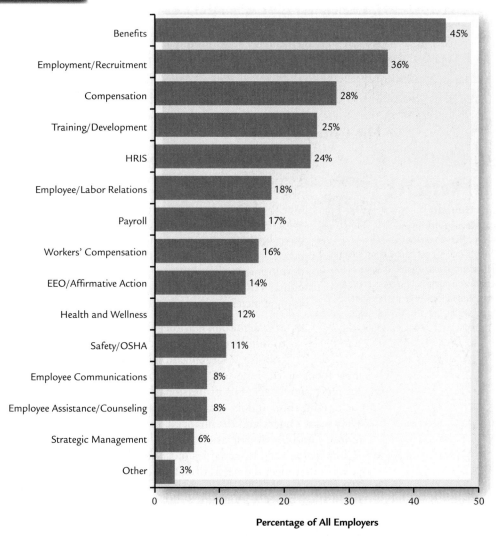

Percentage of All Employers

Source: *HR Department Benchmarks and Analysis 2007* (Washington, DC: Bureau of National Affairs, 2007), 131. To purchase this publication and find out more about BNA HR solutions, visit http://hrcenter.bna.com or call 800-372-1033. Used with permission.

HR jobs can be found in both corporate headquarters and field/subsidiary operations. A compensation analyst or HR director might be found at a corporate headquarters. An employment manager for an auto parts manufacturing plant and a European HR manager for a global food company are examples of field and subsidiary HR professionals. The two types of jobs have different career appeals and challenges.[52]

HR Professionalism and Certification

The idea that "liking to work with people" is the major qualification necessary for success in HR is one of the greatest myths about the field. Depending on the job, HR professionals may need considerable knowledge about employment regulations, finance, tax law, statistics, and information systems. In most cases, they also need extensive knowledge about specific HR activities.

Professional Involvement and Development The broad range of issues faced by HR professionals has made involvement in professional associations and organizations important. For HR generalists, the largest organization is the Society for Human Resource Management (SHRM). Public-sector HR professionals tend to be concentrated in the International Personnel Management Association (IPMA). Other major specialized HR organizations include the International Association for Human Resource Information Management, (IHRIM), the WorldatWork Association, and the American Society for Training and Development (ASTD).

One of the characteristics of a professional field is having a means to certify the knowledge and competence of members of the profession. The CPA for accountants and the CLU for life insurance underwriters are examples. The most well-known certification programs for HR generalists are administered by the Human Resource Certification Institute (HRCI), which is affiliated with SHRM.

Internet Research

Human Resource Certification Institute
For information on the HRCI certification process, link to their Website at:
http://thomsonedu.com/management/mathis.

PHR/SPHR Certification The most widely known HR certifications are the Professional in Human Resources (PHR) and the Senior Professional in Human Resources (SPHR), both sponsored by HRCI. More than 50,000 HR professionals are certified as PHR or SPHR. Annually, thousands of individuals take the certification exams. HRCI also sponsors a Global Professional in Human Resources (GPHR) certification. Eligibility requirements for PHR, SPHR, and GPHR certification are shown in Figure 1-9. Appendix A

FIGURE 1-9   HR Certification

The Human Resource Certification Institute offers three types of professional certifications for HR generalists.

PHR Certification	SPHR or GPHR Certification
· Complete at least 2 years of exempt-level (professional) HR experiencce (recommended: 2–4 years). · Pass the PHR certification exam. · Students may take and pass exam, and receive certification after 2 years of experience.	· Complete at least 2 years of exempt-level (professional) HR experience (recommended: 6–8 years). · Pass the SPHR or GPHR exam.

Details on these certifications are available from the Human Resources Certification Institute, *www.hrci.org.*

identifies test specifications and knowledge areas covered by the PHR and SPHR. Additionally, those who want to succeed in the field must update their knowledge continually. One way of staying current on HR is to tap information available in current HR literature, as listed in Appendix B.

GPHR Certification HRCI has established a certification for global HR professionals. The addition of global certification recognizes the growth in HR responsibilities in organizations throughout the world. The subject areas for the global certification are as follows:

- Strategic international HR management
- Organizational effectiveness and employee development
- Global staffing
- International assignment management
- Global compensation and benefits
- International employee relations and regulations

Other HR Certifications Increasingly, employers hiring or promoting HR professionals are requesting certification as a "plus." HR professionals feel that HR certification gives them more credibility with corporate peers and senior managers. Additional certification programs for HR specialists and generalists are sponsored by various organizations. For specialists, some well-known programs include the following:

- Certified Compensation Professional (CCP), sponsored by the Worldat-Work Association
- Certified Employee Benefits Specialist (CEBS), sponsored by the International Foundation of Employee Benefits Plans
- Certified Benefits Professional (CBP), sponsored by the WorldatWork Association
- Certified Performance Technologist (CPT), co-sponsored by the American Society for Training & Development and the International Society for Performance Improvement
- Certified Safety Professional (CSP), sponsored by the Board of Certified Safety Professionals
- Occupational Health and Safety Technologist (OHST), given by the American Board of Industrial Hygiene and the Board of Certified Safety Professionals
- Certified Professional Outsourcing, provided by New York University and the Human Resource Outsourcing Association

Certifying knowledge is a trend in numerous professions, and HR has many certifications. Given that many people may enter HR jobs with limited formal HR training, certification helps both individuals and their employers to make HR management a better performing part of organizations.

SUMMARY

- HR management ensures that human talent is used effectively and efficiently to accomplish organizational goals.
- There are four types of assets in organizations: physical, financial, intangible, and human.
- Human assets should be seen as human capital, which is the collective value of the capabilities, knowledge, skills, life experiences, and motivation of an organizational workforce.
- HR management activities can be grouped as follows: strategic HR management; equal employment opportunity; staffing; talent management; compensation and benefits; health, safety, and security; and employee and labor relations.
- All organizations need HR management, but larger ones are more likely to have a specialized HR function.
- HR management must fulfill three roles: (1) administrative, (2) operational and employee advocate, and (3) strategic.
- HR roles are being transformed by technology, outsourcing, and the need for HR to become a more strategic contributor.

- Four major HR challenges faced by managers and organizations now and in the future are the globalization of business, economic and technological changes, workforce demographics and diversity, and organizational cost pressures and restructuring.
- HR technology in the form of human resource management systems (HRMSs) helps improve administrative efficiencies and expand information for strategic HR planning.
- Ethical behavior is crucial in HR management, and HR professionals regularly face a number of HR ethical issues.
- The five areas of competencies needed by HR professionals are strategic contribution, business knowledge, HR delivery, HR technology, and personal credibility.
- Current knowledge about HR management is required for professionals in the HR career field, and professional certification has grown in importance for HR generalists and specialists.

REVIEW AND APPLICATION QUESTIONS

1. Why is it important for HR management to transform from being primarily administrative and operational to becoming a more strategic contributor?
2. Describe how economic and workforce changes are affecting organizations in which you have worked, and give specific examples of how these changes should be addressed.
3. Assume you are an HR director with a staff of seven people. A departmental objective is for all staff members to become professionally certified

within a year. Using Internet resources of associations listed in Appendix B, develop a table that identifies six to eight certifications that could be obtained by your staff members, and show the following details for each certification:
- Name of sponsoring organization
- Names and types of certification
- Addresses for relevant Websites containing more information
- Experience and education requirements
- Nature of certification process

CASE

HR Contributes at SYSCO

Many people in the United States are not familiar with SYSCO, but they see its results because SYSCO is the largest food services and distribution company with almost $24 billion in annual sales. SYSCO supplies food products to customers in restaurants, hotels, supermarkets, hospitals, and other companies. In a firm the size of SYSCO with more than 40,000 employees, HR management is making significant contributions to organizational success. As an indication of this success, SYSCO received the Optimas award for general HR Excellence from *Workforce Magazine*.

Beginning several years ago, the need to revitalize HR activities was recognized by both executives and senior HR staff members. At the time, the SYSCO operating regions had administered many of their own HR practices. To bring change to HR corporate-wide, while preserving the entrepreneurial independence of the regions, a "market-driven" HR approach was developed. In this approach, corporate HR identified ways it could assist regional operations, and then developed programs and services that met regional needs. However, unlike in many other corporations where corporate HR programs would be "mandated" to operating units, SYSCO took a different approach. Key to market-driven HR is that managers in the regional operations must be convinced to "buy" the corporate HR services. For example, if a supervisory training program is developed by corporate HR, regional managers decide if they want to use the program for supervisory training in their regions.

Another part of creating HR as market driven was the establishment by corporate HR of a Virtual Resource Center (VRC) to provide services to managers and employees. A key aspect of the VRC is use of HR technology to gather extensive data on HR activities and provide that data to operating managers. One source of data is workplace climate surveys of employees.

Using the survey data, HR developed initiatives to increase safety, which reduced workers' compensation claims by 30%, resulting in savings of $10 million per year.

Another problem that SYSCO had was high turnover rates of night shift warehouse workers. Recruiting these workers has been a constant challenge for SYSCO and other distribution firms. By implementing a variety of programs and services, based on employee and managerial input from surveys, the retention rate for these warehouse employees has been increased by 20%, resulting in savings of $15 million per year. These savings are due to reduced time and money spent recruiting, selecting, and training new employees. Also, employees with more experience are more productive and more knowledgeable about SYSCO operations and products.

Another area where HR has contributed is with truck and delivery drivers. Data gathered through the VRC has been used to revise base pay and incentive programs, increase driver retention rates, and improve driver safety records. Additionally, customer satisfaction rates increased and delivery expenses declined.

All of these changes illustrate that HR efforts at SYSCO have been paying off for the company, managers, and employees. But as the value of HR efforts is recognized by more managers, HR's role at SYSCO is likely to continue growing and changing.[53]

Questions

1. How does the market-driven approach illustrate that HR has strategic, operational, and administrative roles at SYSCO?

2. Discuss what types of HR changes could have affected reductions in workers' compensation expenses, employee turnover, and increases in customer satisfaction.

SUPPLEMENTAL CASE

Phillips Furniture

This case describes a small company that has grown large enough to need a full-time HR person. You have been selected to be the HR manager, and you have to decide what HR activities are needed and the role HR is to play. (For the case, go to http://thomsonedu.com/management/mathis.)

NOTES

1. Based on Keith Hammonds, "Why We Hate HR," *Fast Company,* August 2005, 40.
2. Mark Roehling and Patrick Wright, "Organizationally Sensible vs. Legal-Centric Approaches to Employment Decisions," *Human Resources Management,* 45 (2006), 605–627.
3. Vaughan Limbrick and Tom Baldwin, "Out with the Old HR, In with the New," *Workindex.com,* July 20, 2005, *www.workindex.com.*
4. Patrick J. Kiger, "Research Backs Up HR's Impact on Value," *Workforce Management,* June 26, 2006, 40.
5. "Watson Wyatt Human Capital Index: Human Capital as a Lead Indicator of Shareholder Value," *Watson Wyatt Worldwide Research Report,* 2005, *www.watsonwyatt.com/research.*
6. Jon Burton and Scott Pollak, "The ROI of Human Capital: The U.S. and Europe," *Workspan,* November 2006, 24–26.
7. Alan P. Brache, "Managing Human Capabilities," *Journal of Organizational Excellence,* (2003), 61.
8. *Human Capital Management: The CFO's Perspective* (New York: Mercer Human Resource Consulting, 2003).
9. Ann Pomeroy, "People Are Our Greatest Asset," *HR Magazine,* (April 2005), 20.
10. Christopher J. Collins and Kevin D. Clark, "Strategic Human Resource Practices, Top Management Team Social Networks, and Firm Performance," *Academy of Management Journal,* 46 (2003), 740–751.
11. *Small Business by the Numbers* and other reports from the U.S. Small Business Administration, *www.sba.gov.*
12. Jennifer Schramm, "HR from the Top," *HR Magazine,* (May 2005), 144.
13. *Tough Times, Tougher HR* (New York: Towers-Perrin, 2003).
14. Pamela Babcock, "A Crowded Space," *HR Magazine,* (March 2006), 68–73.
15. Kathy Gorchiek, "Record Growth Seen in Outsourcing HR Functions," *HR News,* April 20, 2005, 1–2.
16. "A Watershed Year Predicted for HR Outsourcing," *HR Magazine,* (February 2006), 16–20; and Debra White, "Managing the Handoff," *Human Resource Executive,* March 2, 2005, 18–47.
17. Carol Patton, "Grabbing the Reins," *Human Resource Executive,* November 2005, 81–83.
18. David Rhodes and Cary Sparrow, "Taking the Next Step," *Human Resource Executive Online,* November 17, 2006, 1–3, *www.hreonline.com.*
19. Paul Harris, "Outsourcing Spreads Its Wings," *Benefitsnews.com,* April 15, 2006, 1–4, *www.benefitnews.com.*
20. Stephan R. Barley and Gideon Kunda, "Contracting: A New Form of Professional Practice," *Academy of Management Perspective,* (February 2006), 45–66.
21. Lydell C. Bridgeford, "Paint It Black," *Employee Benefit News,* September 15, 2006, 18–21.
22. Theresa M. Welbourne, "Human Resource Management: At the Table or Under It?," *Workforce Management Online,* August 2006, 1–5, *www.workforce.com.*
23. Barbara Parus, "HR: From Paper Pusher to Strategic Partner," *Workspan,* November 2003, 26–29.
24. Theresa Minton-Eversole, "HR Must Forge Partnerships . . . ," *HR News,* October 10, 2003, *www.shrm.org/hrnews.*
25. Peter Cappelli, "The Future for Human Resources," *Human Resource Executive Online,* November 17, 2006, 1–3, *www.hreonline.com.*
26. Alex Taylor III, "The Americanization of Toyota," *Fortune,* December 8, 2003, 17.
27. Devesh Kapur and John McHale, "Are We Losing the Global Race for Talent?," *The Wall Street Journal,* November 21, 2005, A17.
28. Emily Lawson et al., "A Dearth of HR Talent," *The McKinsey Quarterly,* 2 (2005), 1–5; and Peter Cappelli, "Visions of HR," *Human Resource Executive Online,* July 24, 2006, 1–2, *www.hreonline.com.*
29. Janet L. Morrison, "The Global HR Professional—Establishing an Ethically Effective Global Framework," *SHRM Whitepaper,* November 2005, 2–6.
30. Marcus Walker, "Unwanted Arrivals," *The Wall Street Journal,* June 30, 2005, A1.
31. Bill Leonard, "Cutting Costs Top Reason for Off-Shoring," April 2006, 2, *www.shrm.org/global.*
32. Jennifer Schramm, "Offshoring," *SHRM Research: Workplace Visions,* 2004, 1–8.
33. Ann E. Harrison and Margret E. McMillan, "Dispelling Some Myths About Offshoring," *Academy of Management Perspectives,* November 2006, 6–22.
34. Andy Meisler, "Think Globally, Act Rationally," *Workforce Management,* January 2004, 40–45.
35. U.S. Bureau of Labor Statistics, 2006, *www.bls.gov.*
36. *Keeping America Competitive: How a Talent Shortage Threatens U.S. Manufacturing* (Washington, DC: National Association of Manufacturers, 2003).
37. U.S. Census Bureau, *Current Population Survey,* 2006, *www.census.gov.*
38. Jennifer Schramm, *Workplace Visions: Exploring the Future of Work,* (Alexandria, VA: SHRM Research Department, 2006), 1–8.

39. Charles Fishman, "The Wal-Mart You Don't Know," *Fast Company,* December 2003, 68.

40. *HR on the Web: The Investment Is Paying Off* (New York: Towers-Perrin, 2003).

41. Paige Mazzoni, "Technology's Increasing Role in Workforce Management," *Workspan,* August 2006, 52–55.

42. Bill Roberts, "New HR Systems on the Horizon," *HR Magazine,* May 2006, 103–111.

43. Philip Evans, "The Wiki Factor," *Bized,* January/February 2006, 28–32; and Desda Moss, "New Tools of the Trade," *HR Magazine Anniversary Issue,* 2005, 40.

44. Kristen B. Frasch, "Coca-Cola Talent Leader Shares Story of a Self-Service 'Soft Sell,'" *Workindex.com,* October 13, 2003, *www.workindex.com.*

45. Mike Cherenson, "Rethinking Reputation," *Workforce Management,* November 20, 2006, 23–26.

46. Adapted from Richard Stolz, "What HR Will Stand For," *Human Resource Executive,* January 2003, 20–28.

47. Kathryn Tyler, "Do the Right Thing," *HR Magazine,* February 2005, 99–102.

48. *National Business Ethics Survey Executive Summary 2005, ethics@ethics.org.*

49. Robert J. Grossman, "Are You Clear?" *HR Magazine,* October 2005, 54–59; and "Heightened Security," *Human Resource Executive,* April 2005, 26–28; and Diya Gullapall, "Living with Sarbanes-Oxley," *The Wall Street Journal,* October 17, 2005, Section R.

50. The summary of the five competencies is based on Wayne Brockbank and Dave Ulrich, *Competencies for the New HR Guidebook* (Alexandria, VA: Society for Human Resource Management, 2003).

51. For details, see *The HR Competency Self-Assessment,* available at *www.shrm.org/competencies.*

52. C. J. Collins and K. G. Smith, "Knowledge Exchange and Combination: The Role of Human Resources Practices in the Performance of High-Technology Firms," *Academy of Management Journal,* 49, (2006), 544–560.

53. Based on Patrick J. Kiger, "HR Proves Its Value," *Workforce,* March 2002, 28–33.

CHAPTER

2

Strategic HR Management and Planning

After you have read this chapter, you should be able to:

- Explain strategic HR management and how it is linked to organizational strategies.

- Discuss two possible contributors to competitive advantage and how HR contributes to each.

- Describe how legal, political, cultural, and economic factors affect global HR management.

- Define HR planning and outline the HR planning process.

- Describe the means for assessing the external and internal environments of HR management.

- Discuss several ways of managing a surplus and a shortage of human resources.

- Identify why HR metrics must consider both strategic and operational HR measures.

HR Headline

Strategy Mistakes and HR Consequences at Automakers

In the mid-1980s, due to competition from Japanese automakers, General Motors (GM), Ford, and Chrysler each entered into an agreement with the United Automobile, Aerospace and Agricultural Implement Workers of America (UAW) union that has become very expensive. Instead of reducing total workforce costs, these firms "stored" laid-off workers in "job banks" in case sales increased.

GM originated the idea and Ford and Chrysler followed suit. The original job bank idea was intended to help train or find jobs for UAW employees who would otherwise be permanently laid off. But it has morphed into a nightmare for the automakers. Laid-off employees in the job bank program continue to receive full pay and benefits even when they are no longer needed. They must perform some company-approved activity—doing volunteer work, going back to school, or merely sitting in a room killing time. In a recent year, about 7,500 GM workers were in the job bank; each person costs GM $100,000 to $130,000 in wages and benefits *not to produce cars*. The Chrysler unit had 2,500 employees in the bank, and Ford had 1,100.

Unfortunately, this approach in a very competitive industry simply did not work. Subsequently, these automakers have negotiated plant closings, bought out existing employees, and spent huge amounts to adjust their workforce costs to align with current and future strategic needs.[1]

Strategy The strategy an organization follows is its proposition for how to compete successfully and thereby survive and grow.

The strategy an organization follows is its proposition for how to compete successfully and thereby survive and grow. There are several different approaches to strategy formation. For example, an organization might have a formal written strategy encompassing a five-year period with objectives and goals for each unit. Alternatively, the strategy may be identified less formally by the CEO and changed by that person's decisions alone.[2]

Strategic approaches that companies might choose vary from acquiring new or even unrelated businesses to revising products, or maybe involve developing new products or approaches internally. Other approaches might be to maintain a secure position with a single stable product or to emphasize a constant stream of new products. These are all viable strategies for different businesses, but one major point should be made. The strategies chosen will determine the number, nature, and capabilities of people needed in the organization. Further, the people already in the organization may limit the strategies that might be successful.[3]

Regardless of which specific strategies are chosen for promoting an organization, the HR strategy to have the right people in the right place at the right time will be necessary to make the overall strategies work. That is why it is commonly argued that HR should have input into the organization's overall strategy. After all, if a strategy requires individual skills that are currently not available in the company, a certain amount of time is necessary to find and hire people with those skills. Strategic HR management entails not only input into organizational strategic planning, but also a series of "blueprints" as to how HR will help achieve the needed performance from people in the operations critical to meeting key organizational goals.[4]

To contribute more effectively, HR must move beyond the administrative and legally mandated tasks that it has traditionally performed. Although those tasks still must be done as well, more HR efforts are needed to add value by improving the performance of the business. Although some businesses are very dependent on human capital for a competitive advantage, others are less so. But to be able to identify the value of the human capital, there must be sufficient measurements (metrics) about the HR side of the business as part of strategic HR management.[5]

NATURE OF STRATEGY AND HR MANAGEMENT

Strategic HR management Use of employees to gain or keep a competitive advantage.

Strategic HR management refers to the use of employees to gain or keep a competitive advantage. Figure 2-1 shows the factors that affect strategic HR management. Because business strategies affect HR plans and policies, consideration of human resource issues should be part of the strategy formulation process. It may be important to identify competitive advantage opportunities that fit the existing employees or to assess strategic alternatives given the current capabilities of organizational human resources. HR managers should be scanning the environment to pinpoint what workforce skills are and are not available. HR professionals also should be able to estimate lead times for adjusting to labor shortages or surpluses. In summary, HR should be involved in implementing strategies that affect and are influenced by people.

FIGURE 2-1	Strategic HR Management Process

Strategic Success with HR Practices

Although the logic of having HR involved with strategic planning seems clear enough, the implementation is apparently not as widespread as expected. A BNA study summarized HR's strategic performance notes[6]:

- Top management usually does not assess HR on its strategic contributions.
- Only about one-quarter of firms monitor effectiveness/productivity statistics—measures clearly tied to business strategic performance.
- Around one-half of organizations do not have an HR strategy.
- Forty percent of firms report weak or no links between HR and overall strategic planning.

HR Best Practices A wide array of data from both academics and consulting firms shows that HR practices really do make a significant difference to business outcomes.[7] For instance, companies that follow HR best practices have more than 50% higher market value than those who do not.[8] Some recognized HR best practices include[9]:

- Employment security
- Selective recruiting
- High wages/incentives
- Information sharing/participation
- Training/cross-training
- Promotion from within
- Measurement

The use of these HR best practices are identified in chapters throughout this book. The examples will illustrate that HR strategies that help foster these practices pay off for both employers and employees.

FIGURE 2-2	Common Areas for HR Strategies

PLANNING	PERFORMANCE ENHANCEMENTS
• Organizational restructuring • Job redesign • Critical staffing levels • Workforce additions/reductions • Succession planning	• Training and development • Productivity/performance management • Compensation/benefits review • Retention increase • Technology systems

Operationalizing HR Strategy

Specific HR strategies depend on the strategies and plans of an organization. However, Figure 2-2 highlights some common areas in need of HR strategies. But how specifically can HR professionals provide the perspective and expertise to be a successful part of the strategic planning process?[10] They can:

- *Understand the business.* Knowing the financials and the key drivers of business success are important to understanding the need for certain strategies.
- *Focus on the key business goals.* Programs that have the greatest relevance to business objectives should get priority.
- *Know what to measure.* Metrics are a vital part of assessing success, which means picking those measures that directly relate to the business goals.
- *Prepare for the future.* Strategic thinking requires preparing for the future, not focusing on the past—except as a predictor of the future.

Using Human Resources as a Core Competency

Human resources are a core competency in many organizations, as mentioned in Chapter 1. As such, they create value and create organizational results that are better than those of competitors.

Some ways in which human resources might become a core competency are through attracting and retaining employees with unique professional and technical capabilities, investing in training and development of those employees, and compensating them in ways that retain and keep them competitive with their counterparts in other organizations.[11]

Figure 2-3 shows some possible areas where human resources may become part of a core competency. People can be an organizational core competency when they have special skills or are innovative in ways that competitors cannot easily imitate. In addition, high productivity or outstanding quality or service can be an area in which people might provide a core competency for a firm.

Organizational Culture and HR

The ability of an organization to use its human capital as a core competency depends at least in part on the organizational culture that is operating. As mentioned in Chapter 1, organizational culture consists of the shared values and beliefs that give members of an organization meaning and provide them

FIGURE 2-3   Possible HR Areas for Core Competencies

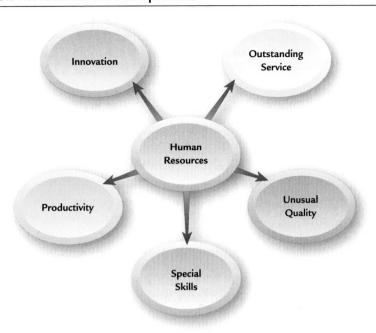

with rules for behavior. These values are inherent in the ways organizations and their members view themselves, define opportunities, and plan strategies. Much as personality shapes an individual, organizational culture shapes its members' responses and defines what an organization can or is willing to do.

The culture of an organization is seen in the norms of expected behaviors, values, philosophies, rituals, and symbols used by its employees. Culture evolves over a period of time. Only if an organization has a history in which people have shared experiences for years does a culture stabilize. A relatively new firm, such as a business existing for less than 2 years, probably has not developed a stabilized culture.

Culture is important because it tells people how to behave (or not to behave). It is relatively constant and enduring over time. Newcomers learn the culture from the senior employees; hence, the rules of behavior are perpetuated. These rules may or may not be beneficial, so that the culture can either facilitate or limit performance.

Managers must consider the culture of the organization because otherwise excellent strategies can be negated by a culture that is incompatible with the strategies. In one culture, external events in an industry might be seen as threatening, whereas another culture might view risks and changes as challenges requiring immediate responses. The latter type of culture can be a source of competitive advantage, especially if it is unique and hard to duplicate.

Organizational culture should be seen as the "climate" of the organization that employees, managers, customers, and others experience. This culture affects service and quality, organizational productivity, and financial results. Critically, it is the culture of the organization, as viewed by the people in it, that affects the attraction and retention of competent employees. Alignment of the organizational culture and HR strategy help effect such aspects as merger success, productivity, and whether human capital can indeed be a core competency.

HR AS ORGANIZATIONAL CONTRIBUTOR

Because HR management plays a significant strategic role in organizations where there are identifiable core competencies that relate to people, organizational effectiveness is enhanced. Strategic HR management plays a significant role in the following strategies:

- Organizational productivity
- Customer service and quality
- Financial contributions

Organizational Productivity

Productivity Measure of the quantity and quality of work done, considering the cost of the resources used.

Productivity can be a competitive advantage because when the costs to produce goods and services are lowered by effective processes, lower prices can be charged. Better productivity does not necessarily mean more output; perhaps fewer people (or less money or time) are used to produce the same amount. In its most basic sense, productivity is a measure of the quantity and quality of work done, considering the cost of the resources used. A useful way to measure the productivity of a workforce is to determine the total cost of people required for each unit of output. For example, a retailer may measure productivity as a ratio of employee payroll and benefits to sales, or a bank may compare the number and dollar amount of loans made to the number of loan officers employed. This example provides a metric of productivity per loan officer.

Unit labor cost Computed by dividing the average cost of workers by their average levels of output.

A useful way of measuring the productivity of human resources is to consider unit labor cost, which is computed by dividing the average cost of workers by their average levels of output. Using unit labor costs, one can see that paying relatively high wages still can result in a firm being economically competitive if high productivity levels are achieved. Low unit labor costs can be a basis for a strategy focusing on human resources. Productivity and unit labor costs can be evaluated at the global, country, organizational, departmental, or individual level.

Improving Organizational Productivity Productivity at the organizational level ultimately affects profitability and competitiveness in a for-profit organization and total costs in a not-for-profit organization. Perhaps of all the resources used for productivity in organizations, the most closely scrutinized is human resources. Many strategic HR management efforts are designed to enhance organizational productivity, as Figure 2-4 indicates.

- *Organizational restructuring* involves eliminating layers of management and changing reporting relationships, as well as cutting staff through downsizing, layoffs, and early retirement buyout programs
- *Re-designing work* often involves having fewer employees who work longer hours and perform multiple job tasks. It may also involve replacing workers with capital equipment or making them more efficient by use of technology or new processes.
- *Aligning HR activities* means making HR efforts consistent with organizational efforts to improve productivity. This alignment includes ensuring that staffing, training and development, performance management, compensation, and other HR activities are not working against productivity.
- *Outsourcing analyses* involve HR in conducting cost-benefit analyses to justify outsourcing. Additional factors may include negotiating with outsourcing vendors, ensuring that contractors domestically and internationally are operating legally and appropriately, and linking organizational employees to the outsourcing firm's employees.

FIGURE 2-4	Approaches to Improving Organizational Productivity

Restructuring the Organization
- Revising organizational structure
- Reducing staff
- Aiding in mergers and acquisitions

Re-Designing Work
- Changing workloads and combining jobs
- Re-shaping jobs due to technology changes

Goals
- Increase organizational productivity
- Reduce unit labor costs

Aligning HR Activities
- Attracting and retaining employees
- Training, developing, and evaluating employees
- Compensating employees and other HR activities

Outsourcing
- Using domestic vendors/contractors instead of employees
- Outsourcing operations internationally

Customer Service and Quality Linked to HR Strategies

In addition to productivity, customer service and quality significantly affect organizational effectiveness. Having managers and employees focus on customers contributes significantly to achieving organizational goals and maintaining a competitive advantage. In most organizations, service quality is greatly influenced by the individual employees who interact with customers. For instance, organizations with high employee turnover rates have seen slow sales growth.[12] It seems customers consider continuity of customer service representatives as important in making sales decisions.

Unfortunately, overall customer satisfaction with sales quality has declined in the United States and other countries.[13] One example illustrates the importance of service excellence. Within the first six months after being hired, a new CEO at Home Depot directed that labor costs and staffing in the company stores be reduced. As a result, over several years a significant number of customers complained about not being able to find employees to help them, having to wait a long time to check out, and encountering shortages of merchandise on shelves. At the same time, Lowe's, a major competitor, expanded staff and advertised its "customer service" emphasis. The result was that Lowe's sales and profitability grew significantly, while Home Depot's "cost-cutting" approach created customer problems and significantly affected the performance of the firm. After several years, the Home Depot CEO resigned and since then, Home Depot has been taking steps to repair its customer service image.

Quality Delivering high-quality services and/or products can significantly influence organizational effectiveness. Whether producing automobiles, as General Motors and Toyota do, or providing cellular phone service, as Verizon and Cingular Wireless do, a firm must consider how well its products and services meet customer needs. Therefore, many organizations have emphasized efforts to enhance quality. The thrust of all these programs is to get tasks done correctly and efficiently so that quality services are delivered the first time, every time. The problems with quality that some U.S. auto manufacturers have had, compared with other firms such as Toyota and Honda, illustrate the important effect of quality on sales, revenue, costs, and ultimately organizational effectiveness. Attempts to improve quality have worked better for some organizations than for others.

HR Effectiveness and Financial Performance

Effectiveness The extent to which goals have been met.

Efficiency The degree to which operations are done in an economical manner.

Effectiveness for organizations is defined as the extent to which goals have been met. Efficiency is the degree to which operations are done in an economical manner. Efficiency can also be thought of as a short-term measure that compares inputs and costs directly against outputs and benefits. During the past several years, HR management has given significant attention to working more effectively with financial executives to make certain that HR is a financial contributor to organizational effectiveness.[14] The return on investment (ROI) of all resources and expenditures in organizations can be calculated, including the ROI of human expenditures.

There are many different ways of measuring the financial contributions of HR and many difficulties associated with doing so.[15] For example, if a firm invests $20,000 for a supervisory training program, what does it gain in lower worker compensation costs, lower legal costs, higher employee productivity, and lower employee turnover? Or if it introduces new HR management system software that costs $800,000, what will it save in reduced staffing, lowered response times, and other factors? Questions such as these illustrate that HR must be able to provide financial justification for its activities.[16] Later in this chapter, the discussion of HR metrics will highlight some specific HR measurement approaches.

GLOBAL COMPETITIVENESS AND STRATEGIC HR

The globalization of business has meant that more organizations are operating in multiple countries or have foreign operational links to international suppliers, vendors, and outsourced contributors. Rapid growth of international outsourcing also indicates the linkage between global competitiveness and HR management.[17]

Types of Global Organizations

A growing number of organizations that traditionally operated in only one country have recognized the need to develop more global operations. As they broaden their operations worldwide, organizations may pass through three stages.

Importing and exporting Buying and selling goods and services with organizations in other countries.

Importing and Exporting The first phase of international interaction consists of importing and exporting. Here, an organization begins buying and selling goods and services with organizations in other countries. Generally, HR activities are not affected except for travel policies for those going abroad.

Multi-National Enterprises As firms develop and expand, they identify opportunities to begin operating in other countries. A multi-national enterprise (MNE) is an organization that has operating units located in foreign countries. As the MNE expands, it hires workers from the countries in which it has operations. Because laws and regulations in those countries usually differ from those in the home country, the HR professionals in the parent organization must become knowledgeable about each country in which the MNE operates and must know how to adapt staffing, training, compensation, health and safety, and labor relations.

Multi-national enterprise (MNE) Organization that has operating units located in foreign countries.

Global Organization An MNE can be thought of as an international firm in that it operates in various countries, but each foreign business unit is operated separately. In contrast, a global organization has corporate units in a number of countries integrated to operate as one organization worldwide. All managers and employees in global organizations need a global "mindset." HR management in truly global organizations moves people, especially key managers and professionals, throughout the world. Individuals who speak several languages fluently are highly valued, and they will move among divisions and countries as they assume more responsibilities and experience career growth.

Global organization Firm that has corporate units in a number of countries integrated to operate as one organization worldwide.

Internet Research

Organization for Economic Cooperation and Development (OECD)
The OECD is an organization of 30 member countries that work to influence economic and social policies. Visit the Website at: http://thomsonedu.com/management/mathis.

Having a global HR mindset means looking at HR issues from a global perspective, using ideas and resources throughout the world, and ensuring openness to other cultures and ideas. This global mindset requires consideration of a number of factors, including legal, political, cultural, and economic forces that significantly affect the competitiveness of organizations and global HR management.[18]

Global Legal and Political Factors

Firms in the United States, Europe, and elsewhere are accustomed to relatively stable political and legal systems. However, many nations function under turbulent and varied legal and political systems. Therefore, HR-related laws vary in character and stability. Compliance with laws on wages, benefits, union relations, worker privacy, workplace safety, and others illustrate the importance of HR management when operating transnationally. As a result, it is crucial for HR professionals to conduct a comprehensive review of the political environment and employment laws before beginning operations in a country.[19] The role and nature of labor unions also should be a part of that review.

Global Cultural Factors

Culture Societal forces affecting the values, beliefs, and actions of a distinct group of people.

Cultural forces represent another important concern affecting international HR management. Culture is composed of societal forces affecting the values, beliefs, and actions of a distinct group of people. Cultural differences certainly exist between nations, and significant cultural differences also exist within countries. One has only to look at the conflicts caused by religion or ethnicity in Africa, the Middle East, and other parts of the world to see the importance of culture in international organizations. Convincing individuals from different religious, ethnic, or tribal backgrounds to work together in a global firm may be difficult in some parts of the world.

One widely used way to classify and compare cultures was developed by Geert Hofstede, a Dutch scholar and researcher. Hofstede conducted research on more than 100,000 IBM employees in 53 countries, and he defined five dimensions useful in identifying and comparing cultures[20]:

- Inequality in power
- Individualism/group orientation
- Masculinity/femininity
- Uncertainty avoidance
- Long-term/short-term orientation

Differences in many other facets of culture could be discussed. But it is enough to note that international HR managers and professionals must recognize that cultural dimensions differ from country to country and even within countries. Therefore, the HR activities appropriate in one culture or country may have to be altered to fit appropriately into another culture.

Global Economic Factors

Economic factors are linked to political, legal, and cultural issues, and different countries have different economic systems. In many developed countries, especially in Europe, employment restrictions and wage levels are high. The differences between labor costs in the United States compared with those in Germany and Norway are significant. Figure 2-5 shows the differences in manufacturing unit labor costs in various countries. As a result of these differences, many U.S. and European firms are moving jobs to lower-wage countries such as China and Thailand.

Critics of globalization cite the extremely low wage rates paid by the international firms and the substandard working conditions that exist in some underdeveloped countries. Examples include Cambodians making $40 a month sewing garments for U.S. retailers, and workers in many Chinese toy manufacturing firms earning $1 a day. Various advocacy groups have accused Nike, Adidas, Levi Strauss, Liz Claiborne, and other global firms of being

---

FIGURE 2-5   **Hourly Compensation Costs for Manufacturing Production Workers**

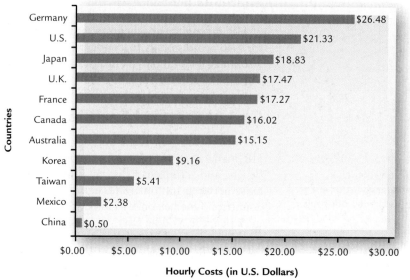

Source: U.S. Bureau of Statistics, *www.bls.gov.*

"sweatshop employers." Those and some other employers have made efforts to ensure that foreign factories adhere to more appropriate HR standards.

Global employers counter that even though the wage rates in some countries are low, their employees often receive the highest wages and experience the best working conditions that exist in the local countries. Also, many employees in the host countries now have jobs, which allows them to improve their living standards.[21]

HUMAN RESOURCE PLANNING

Human resource planning
Process of analyzing and identifying the need for and availability of human resources so that the organization can meet its objectives.

Human resource planning is the process of analyzing and identifying the need for and availability of human resources so that the organization can meet its objectives. The focus of HR planning is to ensure the organization has the *right number of human resources,* with the *right capabilities,* at the *right times,* and in the *right places.* In HR planning, an organization must consider the availability of and allocation of people to jobs over long periods of time, not just for the next month or even the next year.

This level of planning requires knowledge of expansions or reductions in operations and any technological changes that may affect the organization. To illustrate, Walgreens, the large retail drugstore chain, has had an aggressive expansion plan. Each new Walgreens store must be staffed with pharmacists, managers, and customer service employees. For this firm, one of the biggest pressures is ensuring that enough pharmacists are available—a challenge that has resulted from a continuing shortage of graduates in pharmacy as well as from Walgreens retail service setting, which requires pharmacists to work different hours and face different demands than those in hospitals and clinics. Therefore, HR planning at Walgreens has had to identify how and where to find enough pharmacists to fill openings caused by turnover and retirement, as well as to staff all the new stores. This example also illustrates that HR planning must identify the knowledge, skills, abilities, experience, and other characteristics affecting the capabilities of employees for current and future jobs.

Internet Research

Human Resource Planning Society
This Website contains a Knowledge Resource Center for building a strategic HR function. Link to their site at:
http://thomsonedu.com/management/mathis

Additionally, as part of the analyses, HR plans can be made for shifting employees within the organization, laying off employees or otherwise cutting back the number of employees, retraining present employees, or increasing the number of employees in certain areas. Factors to consider include the current employees' knowledge, skills, and abilities in the organization and the expected vacancies resulting from retirements, promotions, transfers, and discharges. In summary, doing HR planning right requires significant time and effort by HR professionals working with executives and managers.

HR Planning Responsibilities

In most organizations that do HR planning, the top HR executive and subordinate staff specialists have most of the responsibilities for this planning. However, as Figure 2-6 indicates, other managers must provide information for the HR specialists to analyze. In turn, those other managers need to receive data from the HR unit. Because top managers are responsible for overall strategic planning, they usually ask the HR unit to project the human resources needed to implement overall organizational goals.

FIGURE 2-6   Typical Division of HR Responsibilities: HR Planning

HR Unit	Managers
• Participates in strategic planning process for entire organization • Identifies HR strategies • Designs data systems for HR planning • Compiles and analyzes data from managers on staffing needs • Implements HR plan as approved by top management	• Identify supply-and-demand needs for each division/department • Review/discuss HR planning information with HR specialists • Integrate HR plan with departmental plans • Monitor HR plan to identify changes needed • Review employee succession plans associated with HR plan

Small Businesses and HR Planning

The need for HR planning in larger organizations is vital. If some formal adjustments to changes are not made, people or even entire divisions might be working at cross-purposes with the rest of the company. In a smaller business, even though the owner/manager knows on a daily basis what is happening and what should be done, planning is still important. Perhaps the most difficult area for HR planning in small businesses is family matters and succession.[22]

Particular difficulties arise when a growing business is passed from one generation to another, resulting in a mix of family and non-family employees. Key to a successful transition is having a clear HR plan. In small businesses, such a plan includes incorporating key non-family members in HR planning efforts because non-family members often have important capabilities and expertise that family members do not possess. Planning for the attraction and retention of these "outsiders" may be vital to the future success of smaller organizations. Small businesses, depending on how small they are, may use the HR planning process discussed next, but in very small organizations, the process is much more intuitive and is often done entirely by the top executives, who often are family members.

HR Planning Process

The steps in the HR planning process are shown in Figure 2-7. Notice that the HR planning process begins with considering the organizational objectives and strategies. Then HR needs and supply sources must be analyzed both externally and internally and forecasts must be developed. Key to assessing internal human resources is having solid information accessible through a human resource management system.

Once the assessments are complete, forecasts must be developed to identify the relationship between supply and demand for human resources. Management then formulates HR strategies and plans to address imbalances, both short-term and long-term.

Specific strategies may be developed to fill vacancies or deal with surplus employees. For example, a strategy might be to fill 50% of expected vacancies

FIGURE 2-7	HR Planning Process

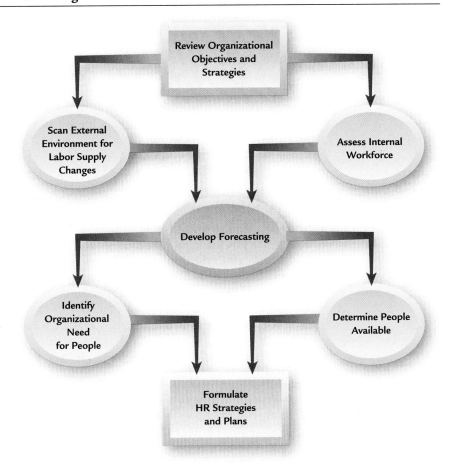

by training good lower level employees and promoting them into anticipated needed openings—a promotion from within strategy.

Finally, specific HR plans are developed to provide more specific direction for the management of HR activities. The most telling evidence of successful HR planning is a consistent alignment of the availabilities and capabilities of human resources with the needs of the organization over a period of time.

SCANNING THE EXTERNAL ENVIRONMENT

Environmental scanning
Process of studying the environment of the organization to pinpoint opportunities and threats.

At the heart of strategic planning is environmental scanning, a process of studying the environment of the organization to pinpoint opportunities and threats. The external environment affects HR planning in particular because each organization must draw from the same labor market that supplies all other organizations, including competitors. Indeed, one measure of organizational effectiveness is the ability of an organization to compete for a sufficient supply of human resources with the appropriate capabilities. All elements of the external environment—government influences, economic conditions, geographic and competition issues, and workforce changes—must be part of the scanning process.

Government Influences

An expanding and often bewildering array of government regulations affects the labor supply and therefore HR planning. As a result, HR planning must be done by individuals who understand the legal requirements of various government regulations.

In the United States and other countries, tax legislation at local, state, and federal levels also affects HR planning. Pension provisions and Social Security legislation may change retirement patterns and funding options. Elimination or expansion of tax benefits for job-training expenses might alter some job-training activities associated with workforce expansions. In summary, an organization must consider a wide variety of government policies, regulations, and laws during the HR planning process.[23]

Economic Conditions

The general business cycle of economic recessions and economic booms also affects HR planning.[24] Factors such as interest rates, inflation, and economic growth affect the availability of workers and should figure into organizational and HR plans and objectives. There is a considerable difference between finding qualified applicants in a 3% unemployment market and in a 7% unemployment market. As the unemployment rate rises, the number of qualified people looking for work increases, making it easier to fill jobs.

Geographic and Competition Concerns

In making HR plans, employers must consider a number of geographic and competition concerns. The *net migration* into a particular region is important. For example, in the past decade, the populations of U.S. cities in the South, Southwest, and West have grown rapidly and provided a source of labor. However, many areas in the Northeast and Midwest have experienced declining populations.

Direct competitors are another important external force in HR planning. Failure to consider the competitive labor market and to offer pay scales and benefits competitive with those of organizations in the same general industry and geographic location may cost a company dearly in the long run.

Finally, the impact of *international competition* must be considered as part of environmental scanning. Global competition for labor intensifies as global competitors shift jobs and workers around the world, as illustrated by the outsourcing of jobs from the United States to countries with cheaper labor.

Workforce Composition

Changes in the composition of the workforce, combined with the use of different work patterns, have created workplaces and organizations that are notably different from those of a decade ago. Many organizations face major concerns about having sufficient workers with the necessary capabilities. When scanning the workforce, it is important to consider a number of variables, including these:

- Aging of the workforce
- Growing diversity of workers
- Women workers and work/life balancing concerns
- Availability of "contingent workers"
- Outsourcing possibilities

Mattel Assesses Its Management

Mattel had been successful with Barbie, Hot Wheels, and Elmo dolls, but it was losing at its own game: Mattel had followed a growth-by-acquisition strategy that failed. Stock prices were significantly down and a new CEO was hired. Because the toy maker had 25,000 employees in 36 countries and sold products in 150 different countries, obviously the turnaround strategy had to be global.

Mattel was willing to dump its unprofitable businesses, but found a major need to develop the management team that remained. This was a key strategy to the human resources turnaround that was deemed necessary to change the company's future. Of course, motivating the managers to help with the turnaround was difficult after the shakeup. Mattel launched a set of leadership programs throughout the global company. The programs were held in corporate offices and on an e-learning network. Global business growth was a topic, as were the most critical strategic issues facing the company. The result was that global management was more closely aligned with corporate strategies and goals. This in turn resulted in innovative products and reduced costs.

But the company went further. It initiated its first performance-management, succession management, and career opportunities systems. In five years the company increased in value by about $5 billion. This illustrates how leaders view their companies and how human resources can contribute significantly to changing corporate culture.[25]

When considering these factors, it is important to analyze how they affect the current and future availability of workers with specific capabilities and experience. For instance, in a number of industries, the median age of engineers is over 50 years, and the supply of engineering graduates is not sufficient to replace such employees as they retire.

ASSESSING THE INTERNAL WORKFORCE

Analyzing the jobs that will need to be done and the skills of people who are currently available in the organization to do them is the next part of HR planning. The needs of the organization must be compared against the labor supply available inside the organization. A good example is found in the HR Best Practices feature.

Jobs and Skills Audit

The starting point for evaluating internal strengths and weaknesses is an audit of the jobs being done in the organization. A comprehensive analysis of all current jobs provides a basis for forecasting what jobs will need to be done in the future. Much of the data to answer the questions in the audit should be available from existing staffing and organizational databases. The following questions are addressed during the internal assessment:

- What jobs exist now?
- How many individuals are performing each job?
- What are the reporting relationships of jobs?
- How essential is each job?
- What jobs will be needed to implement future organizational strategies?
- What are the characteristics of anticipated jobs?

Organizational Capabilities Inventory

As HR planners gain an understanding of the current and future jobs that will be necessary to carry out organizational plans, they can conduct a detailed audit of current employees and their capabilities. The basic source of data on employees is the HR records in the organization. Different HR information databases can be used to identify the knowledge, skills, and abilities (KSAs) of employees. Planners can use KSA inventories to determine future needs for recruiting, selection, and HR development. The information in those inventories can also provide a basis for determining what additional capabilities will be needed in the future workforce. For example, IBM offers a consulting service that allows clients to profile their workforces based on skills and competencies, identify areas where they are most at risk of losing talent, and determine a strategy to deal with problems.[26]

Using a Skills Database

An inventory of organizational skills and capabilities may consider a number of elements. The following ones are important:

- Individual employee demographics (age, length of service in the organization, time in present job)
- Individual career progression (jobs held, time in each job, promotions or other job changes, pay rates)
- Individual performance data (work accomplishment, growth in skills)

All the details on an individual employee's skills that go into a databank may affect the employee's career. Therefore, the data and their use must meet the same standards of job relatedness and non-discrimination as when the employee was initially hired. Furthermore, security measures must ensure that sensitive information is available only to those who have a specific use for it.

Managers and HR staff members can gather data on individual employees and aggregate details into a profile of the current organizational workforce. This profile may reveal many of the current strengths and deficiencies of the organization. If some specialized expertise, such as advanced computer skills, is absent, the organization may find it difficult to take advantage of new technological developments. Or if a large group of experienced employees are all in the same age bracket, their eventual retirements about the same time might lead to future "gaps" in the organization. For example, see the accompanying HR On-the-Job box.

FORECASTING HR SUPPLY AND DEMAND

Forecasting Using information from the past and the present to identify expected future conditions.

The information gathered from scanning the external environment and assessing internal strengths and weaknesses is used to predict HR supply and demand in light of organizational objectives and strategies. Forecasting uses information from the past and the present to identify expected future conditions. Projections for the future are, of course, subject to error. Fortunately, experienced people usually are able to forecast with enough accuracy to benefit long-range organizational planning.

Forecasting Methods and Periods

Forecasting methods may be either judgmental or mathematical. Methods for forecasting human resources range from a manager's best guess to a rigorous and complex computer simulation. Despite the availability of sophisticated

HR ON-THE-JOB

Discovering What Works with a "Skills Database"

When Dell needed a sales executive in China, managers looked in a database that the company kept internally to track employees' skills and experience and they found a male candidate. He had Asia-Pacific region experience and high marks in setting business goals and leading others—both requirements for the job. He got the job.

Skills databases are an increasingly popular tool employers use to track employee talent. The concept is simple: Put employees' skills and technical expertise, prior jobs, training, coaching aptitude, certifications, geographical experience, languages, career aspirations, etc., in a database. The finished product can be queried to fill jobs or analyzed to identify strengths and weaknesses of a division or the whole company. It is a great concept—but difficult to operationalize as it turns out.

Some systems rely on managers to enter and update employee information in the database. Managers may fail to do so or may withhold information fearing they might lose their most skilled employees to someone else in the company. Other approaches call for employees to enter their skills and proficiency levels and for managers to review the reports. But overworked managers can rubber-stamp gross overstatements of skills and the result is poor data. At a financial services company, executives tried to track proficiency on a few "core" skills such as "leadership" or "project management," but the skills were poorly defined and employees used their own judgments. Consequently, the data were not helpful.

Such failures are not always the case. For example, a health systems company instituted a skills database that tracked what training courses employees had completed. It has been successful, so now the company plans to add a more sophisticated database that includes information on skills "gaps" in the workforce as baby boomers retire. Such software would identify people whose credentials suggest they might be ready for management. But it is much harder to gauge the necessary "soft skills," such as whether they can manage others.[27]

---

mathematical models and techniques, forecasting is still a combination of quantitative methods and subjective judgment. The facts must be evaluated and weighed by knowledgeable individuals, such as managers or planners, who use the mathematical models as tools and make judgments to arrive at decisions.

HR forecasting should be done over three planning periods: short range, intermediate range, and long range. The most commonly used planning period of six months to one year focuses on *short-range* forecasts for the immediate HR needs of an organization. Intermediate- and long-range forecasting are much more difficult processes. *Intermediate-range* plans usually project one to three years into the future, and *long-range* plans extend beyond three years.

Forecasting the Demand for Human Resources

The demand for employees can be calculated for an entire organization and/or for individual units in the organization. For example, a forecast might indicate that a firm needs 125 new employees next year, or that it needs 25 new people in sales and customer service, 45 in production, 20 in accounting and information systems, 2 in HR, and 33 in the warehouse. The unit breakdown obviously allows HR planners to better pinpoint the specific skills needed than the aggregate method does.

Demand for human resources can be forecast by considering specific openings that are likely to occur. The openings (or demands) are created when new jobs are being created or current jobs are being reduced. Additionally, forecasts must consider when employees leave positions because of promotions, transfers, turnovers, and terminations.

An analysis is used to develop decision rules (or "fill rates") for each job or level. For example, a decision rule for a financial institution might state that 50% of branch supervisor openings will be filled through promotions from customer service tellers, 25% through promotions from personal bankers, and 25% from new hires. Forecasters must be aware of chain effects throughout the organization, because as people are promoted from within, their previous positions become available. Continuing our example, forecasts for the need for customer service tellers and personal bankers would also have to be developed. The overall purpose of the forecast is to identify the needs for human resources by number and type for the forecasting period.

Forecasting the Supply of Human Resources

Once human resources needs have been forecast, then availability of human resources must be identified. Forecasting the availability considers both *external* and *internal* supplies. Although the internal supply may be somewhat easier to calculate, it is important to calculate the external supply as accurately as possible.

External Supply The external supply of potential employees available to the organization needs to be identified. Extensive use of government estimates of labor force populations, trends in the industry, and many more complex and interrelated factors must be considered. Such information is often available from state or regional economic development offices, including these items:

- Net migration into and out of the area
- Individuals entering and leaving the workforce
- Individuals graduating from schools and colleges
- Changing workforce composition and patterns
- Economic forecasts for the next few years
- Technological developments and shifts
- Actions of competing employers
- Government regulations and pressures
- Circumstances affecting persons entering and leaving the workforce

Internal Supply Figure 2-8 shows in general terms how the internal supply can be calculated for a specific employer. Estimating internal supply considers the number of external hires and the employees who move from their current jobs into others through promotions, lateral moves, and terminations. It also considers that the internal supply is influenced by training and development programs, transfer and promotion policies, and retirement policies, among other factors. In forecasting the internal supply, data from the replacement charts and succession planning efforts are used to project potential personnel changes, identify possible backup candidates, and keep track of attrition (resignations, retirements, etc.) for each department in an organization.

Succession Planning

Succession planning
Process of identifying a long-term plan for the orderly replacement of key employees.

One important outcome of HR planning is succession planning, which is a process of identifying a long-term plan for the orderly replacement of key employees. In larger organizations, such as the U.S. federal government, the aging of the workforce has significant implications for HR planning and succession planning. For instance, U.S. government agencies as varied as the National Park Service, Army Corps of Engineers, Department of Veterans Affairs, and

| FIGURE 2-8 | Estimating Internal Labor Supply for a Given Unit |

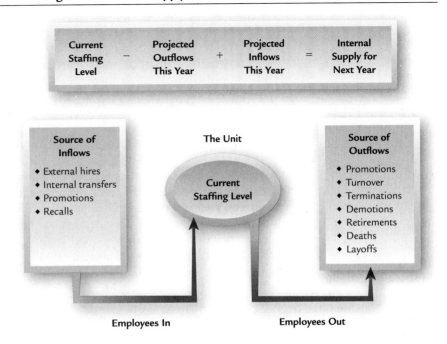

Department of Agriculture are just some of the ones facing significant possible losses of experienced workers. Veterans Affairs is already facing competitive challenges in recruiting nurses due to the high demand in health care generally. Other agencies are concerned about finding a significant number of specialized and experienced engineers, technical workers, and scientists.

One common flaw in succession planning is that too often it is limited to key executives. It may be just as critical to replace several experienced mechanical engineers or specialized nurses as to plan for replacing the CEO. Succession planning is discussed in detail in Chapter 10.

WORKFORCE REALIGNMENT

With all the data collected and forecasts done, an organizational plan can be developed. Such a plan can be extremely sophisticated or rather rudimentary. Regardless of the degree of complexity, the ultimate purpose of the plan is to enable managers in the organization to match the available supply of labor with the demand that is expected given the strategies of the organization. If the necessary skill levels do not exist in the present workforce, the organization can train employees in the new skills or undertake outside recruiting. If the plan reveals that the firm employs too many people for its needs, a human resource surplus exists; if too few, an HR shortage.

Managing a Human Resources Surplus

HR planning is of little value if no subsequent action is taken. The action taken depends on the likelihood of a human resources surplus or shortage. A surplus of workers can be managed within an HR plan in a variety of ways. Regardless of the means, the actions are difficult because workforce reductions often are ultimately necessary.

Workforce Reductions and the WARN Act In this era of mergers, acquisitions, and downsizing, many workers have been laid off or had their jobs eliminated due to the closing of selected offices, plants, and operations. To provide employees with sufficient notice of such losses, a federal law was passed, the Worker Adjustment and Retraining Notification (WARN) Act. This law requires employers to give a 60-day notice before implementing a layoff or facility closing that involves more than 50 people. However, part-time employees working fewer than 20 hours per week do not count toward the 50 employees. Also, seasonal employees do not have to receive WARN notification. The WARN Act imposes stiff fines on employers who do not follow the required process and give proper notice.[28]

Workforce Downsizing It has been given many names, including *downsizing, rightsizing,* and *reduction in force (RIF),* but it almost always means cutting employees. Focusing on trimming underperforming units or employees as part of a plan that is based on sound organizational strategies may make sense. After a decade of many examples and studies, it is clear that downsizing has worked for some firms. However, it usually does not generate additional revenue, and it only generates lower costs in the short term.[29] When companies cannibalize the human resources needed to change, restructure, or innovate, disruption follows for some time. Also, downsizing can hurt productivity by leaving "surviving" employees overburdened and demoralized.

A common myth is that those who are still around after downsizing are so glad to have a job that they pose no problems to the organization. However, some observers draw an analogy between those who survive downsizing and those who survive wartime battles. Bitterness, anger, disbelief, and shock all are common reactions. For those who survive workforce cuts, the culture and image of the firm as a "lifetime" employer often are gone forever.

The need for downsizing has inspired various innovative ways of removing people from the payroll, sometimes on a massive scale. Several different methods can be used when downsizing must occur: attrition, early retirement buyouts, and layoffs are the most common.

Attrition and Hiring Freezes *Attrition* occurs when individuals quit, die, or retire and are not replaced. By use of attrition, no one is cut out of a job, but those who remain must handle the same workload with fewer people. Unless turnover is high, attrition will eliminate only a relatively small number of employees in the short run, but it can be a viable alternative over a longer period of time. Therefore, employers may combine attrition with a freeze on hiring. Employees usually understand this approach better than they do other downsizing methods.

Voluntary Separation Programs Organizations can downsize while also reducing legal liabilities if employees volunteer to leave. Often firms entice employees to volunteer by offering them additional severance and benefit payments.

Early retirement buyouts are widely used to encourage more senior workers to leave organizations early. As an incentive, employers make additional payments to employees so that they will not be penalized as much economically until their pensions and Social Security benefits take effect. These buyouts are widely viewed as ways to accomplish workforce reductions without resorting to layoffs and individual firings. Some plans offer eligible employees expanded health coverage and pension benefits to entice them to take early retirement.[30]

Volunteer separation programs appeal to employers because they can reduce payroll costs significantly over time. Although the organization faces some up-front costs, it does not incur as many continuing payroll costs. Using such programs is also viewed as a more humane way to reduce staff than terminating long-service, loyal employees. In addition, as long as buyouts are truly voluntary, the organization offering them is less exposed to age discrimination suits. One drawback is that some employees the company would like to see stay might take advantage of a buyout. Also, employers must comply with WARN and other laws.

Layoffs Layoffs occur when employees are put on unpaid leaves of absence. If business improves for the employer, then employees can be called back to work. Layoffs may be an appropriate downsizing strategy during a temporary economic downturn in an industry. Nevertheless, careful planning of layoffs is essential. Care must be taken to ensure that age and other types of EEO discrimination do not occur.

Companies have no legal obligation to provide a financial cushion to laid-off employees; however, many do. When firms do provide severance pay, the most common formula is one week of pay for every year of employment. Larger companies tend to be more generous. Loss of medical benefits is a major problem for laid-off employees. However, under the federal Consolidated Omnibus Budget Reconciliation Act (COBRA), displaced workers can retain their group medical coverage for up to 18 months for themselves, and for up to 36 months for their dependents, if they pay the premiums themselves.

Outplacement Services

Outplacement occurs when a group of services are provided to give displaced employees support and assistance. It is most often used with those who have been involuntarily removed because of performance problems or job elimination. Outplacement services typically include personal career counseling, résumé preparation services, interviewing workshops, and referral assistance. Such services are generally provided by outside firms that specialize in outplacement assistance and whose fees usually are paid by the employer. It is important that outplacement be viewed as part of strategic HR planning. Figure 2-9 shows that it is only one of five factors that should be considered to make downsizing more effective.

Managing a Shortage of Employees

Managing a shortage of employees seems simple enough—simply hire more people. Among the occupations that currently are experiencing shortages are nurses, miners, truck drivers, and welders.[31] However, there are consequences to hiring full-time employees in terms of costs, benefits, and other factors. Other options are available that should be considered *before* recruiting and hiring to fill a shortage:

- Use overtime.
- Add contingent workers.
- Bring back recent retirees.
- Outsource work.
- Reduce turnover.

Where possible, the use of contingent workers or recent retirees is a possibility, although challenges may be associated with options.[32] If that is not possible, two longer-term possibilities are outsourcing some of the work or trying to reduce turnover, which will reduce the shortage as well.[33]

| **FIGURE 2-9** | **Making Downsizing More Effective** |

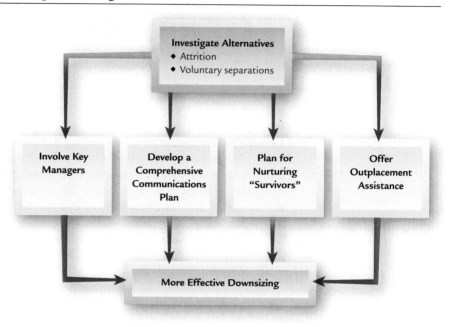

HR PLANNING IN MERGERS AND ACQUISITIONS

HR management can contribute to the success of mergers and acquisitions (M&As). Experience with the failures shows clearly that for M&As to succeed, organizations have to ensure that different organizational cultures mesh. *Cultural compatibility* is the extent to which such factors as decision-making styles, levels of teamwork, information-sharing philosophies, the formality of the two organizations, etc., are similar.

To address organizational culture concerns, HR professionals should be involved before, during, and after M&As.[34] Significant time must be spent identifying the cultural differences, how they are to be addressed, and ways to integrate managers and employees from both entities.

The failures of M&As often are attributed to the incompatibility of the different organizational cultures involved. What changes will be made to the organization structure, how employee benefits will be meshed, what jobs and locations will get more or less staff, and many other issues must be decided and communicated. The longer such issues are left unanswered, the greater employee anxiety will be, and the more rumors will proliferate. For instance, when Daimler and Chrysler merged, it was portrayed as a very smart deal for both—"a combination of equals" whose markets barely overlapped. The strategic fit was thought to be perfect. Yet within two years the combined company was worth less than Daimler alone before the merger, and a hostile relationship between entrepreneurial U.S. management and conservative German management was evident.[35] Continuing efforts with such conflicts affected the firm's ongoing performance, resulting in its split apart.

Internet Research

Mercer Human Resource Consulting
The on-line Knowledge Center contains articles on human resource planning in mergers and acquisitions. Link to their Website at: http://thomsonedu.com/management/mathis.

Revising the Structure

A common result of most M&As is an excess of employees once the firms have been combined due to redundant departments, plants, and people. Because much of the rationale for combinations is strategic and financial, eliminating employees with overlapping responsibilities is a primary concern. A crucial part of an M&A is being sure that employee downsizing is handled legally and effectively. Also critical is the impact of job elimination on the remaining employees. Often, employee morale declines in the short term, and some firms see longer-term declines in employee morale after downsizing. Additionally, resignations and employee turnover may increase substantially in the year following downsizing if the HR issues are mismanaged.

Key Factors in Cultural Fit Key factors in assessing the culture fit between two firms include the following[36]:

- *Degree of internal integration.* Strong integration is indicative of cooperative relationships and common objectives. Weak integration is conducive to strong subcultures and conflicts.
- *Autonomy.* This is the extent to which individuals have freedom to make decisions about their jobs. Weak autonomy leads to poor M&A performance.
- *Adaptability.* An ability to adapt, develop, and survive is helpful. Adaptability between the two entities should be similar.
- *Employees' trust.* Higher levels of trust may bode well for a successful merger.
- *Diversity.* The more diverse the organization, the more likely it will be able to cope with even more diversity after the merger.

General Electric and CISCO have made M&A into a core competency. With a clear strategic vision and logic to how smaller companies will fit with their companies, these two successfully merge with others regularly. They pay a great deal of attention to "due diligence" in the HR area. One important way in which value is lost in a merger is through the loss of key staff—researchers, managers, salespeople. The value of the merger may be lost if much of that value walks out the door. General Electric's formula for acquisition success is simple but useful: $E = Q \times A$. Effectiveness of the acquisition (E) depends on the quality of the financial/strategic analysis (Q) times the acceptance (A) of the acquisition decision by the people involved.[37]

Merging HR Activities Another key role played by HR in mergers and acquisitions is melding together the HR activities in each organization. Compensation, benefits, performance appraisal systems, and employee relations policies all require significant attention by HR staff in both organizations. Who will head HR and which employees will and will not have jobs in the new HR function must be addressed. Compatibility of databases and information systems must be considered. Ultimately, how HR contributes to various aspects of mergers and acquisitions likely affects the overall effectiveness of the newly combined organizations.[38]

MEASURING EFFECTIVENESS USING HR METRICS

A long-standing myth perpetuates the notion that one cannot really measure what the HR function does. That myth has hurt HR departments in some cases, because it suggests that any value added by HR efforts is somehow "mystical." That notion is, of course, untrue; HR—like marketing, operations, or finance—must be evaluated by considering the results of its actions and the value it adds to the organization.

Other departments, managers, and employees are the main "customers" for HR services. If those services are lacking, too expensive, or of poor quality, then HR loses some credibility in the organization. Unfortunately, the perceptions of managers and employees in many organizations are mixed because HR has not always measured and documented its contributions or communicated those results to executives, managers, and employees. It is through the development and use of metrics that HR can better demonstrate its value and track its performance.[39]

Developing and Using HR Metrics

HR metrics Specific measures tied to HR performance indicators.

HR metrics are specific measures tied to HR performance indicators. A metric can be developed using costs, quantity, quality, timeliness, and other designated goals. One pioneer in developing HR measurements, Jac Fitz-Enz, has identified a wide range of HR metrics. In fact, most HR activities can be measured and benchmarked.[40] Some examples are shown in Figure 2-10.

Whether determining the cost of turnover, the average time needed to fill job openings, scores on employee satisfaction surveys, or the ratio of payroll expenditures to revenues, metrics provide specific data to track HR performance. Characteristics for developing HR metrics include the following:

- Accurate data can be collected.
- Measures are linked to strategic and operational objectives.
- Calculations can be clearly understood.
- Measures provide information expected by executives.
- Results can be compared both externally and internally.
- Measurement data drive HR management efforts.

Internet Research

HR Metrics
For an on-line database of HR metrics information, link to the HR Metrics Website at: http://thomsonedu.com/management/mathis.

Data to evaluate performance can come from several sources. Some of those sources are already available in most organizations, but some data may have to be collected from existing HR records or HR research. For example, HR data can identify units with high turnover or an usual number of disciplinary problems. Or HR records on training can be compared with subsequent employee performance to determine if additional training expenditures are justified. Much of what has typically been measured by HR has focused on internal HR expenditures and effectiveness. A broader strategic perspective in measuring HR effectiveness is needed.[41]

Measures of Strategic HR Effectiveness

For HR to fulfill its role as a strategic business partner, HR metrics that reflect organizational strategies and actions must be used. Some of the more prevalent measures compare *full-time equivalents* (FTEs) with organizational measures. An FTE is a measure equal to one person working full-time for a year. For instance, two employees, each working half-time, would count as one FTE.

| **FIGURE 2-10** | **Examples of Strategic and Operational HR Metrics** |

Strategic	Operational
· Revenue generated per FTE · Net income before taxes per FTE · Ratio of managers to non-managers · Labor costs as percentage of total operating costs · ROI of human capital expenditures · HR department expenses as percentage of total expenses · Payroll/benefits costs as percentage of revenues	· Annual turnover rate · Benefits costs as percentage of payroll · Training expenditures per FTE · Average time to fill openings · Workers' compensation costs per FTE · Number of applicants per opening · Absenteeism by employee level/department

When analyzing revenue and income per FTE, what is obtained are not answers but better questions for analyzing HR in an organization. The two figures represent employer productivity. Revenue minus expenses equals income.[42] Figure 2-11 shows a comparison across industries of the two metrics.

Return on investment (ROI) Calculation showing the value of expenditures for HR activities.

Return on Investment A widely used financial measure that can be applied to measure the contribution and cost of HR activities is return on investment (ROI), which is a calculation showing the value of expenditures for HR activities. It can also be used to show how long it will take for the activities to pay for themselves. The following formula can be used to calculate the potential ROI for a new HR activity:

$$ROI = \frac{C}{A + B}$$

where:

A = Operating costs for a new or enhanced system for the time period
B = One-time cost of acquisition and implementation
C = Value of gains from productivity improvements for the time period

ROI is stressed because it is used in most other parts of organizations. It also is the "language" used by CFOs, CEOs, and Boards of Directors. To conduct ROI analyses, firms complete three stages:

■ Identify all potential/actual costs.
■ Determine the potential/actual benefits.
■ Calculate the ROI.

Economic value added (EVA) Net operating profit of a firm after the cost of capital is deducted.

Economic Value Added Another measure used is economic value added (EVA), which is the net operating profit of a firm after the cost of capital is deducted. Cost of capital is the minimum rate of return demanded by shareholders. When a company is making more than the cost of capital, it is creating wealth for shareholders. An EVA approach requires that all policies, procedures, measures, and methods use cost of capital as a benchmark against which their return is judged. Human resource decisions can be subjected to the same analyses.

HR and the Balanced Scorecard One effective approach to the measurement of the strategic performance of organizations, including their HR departments,

FIGURE 2-11 Revenue and Income per Full Time Employment (FTE)

	Median Revenue per FTE	Median Income per FTE
All industries	$142,857	$10,131
Educational services	$76,896	$263
Finance	$162,712	$41,361
Government	$134,691	$0
Health-care services	$103,166	$5,000
High-tech	$211,111	$16,250
Insurance	$159,150	$46,667
Manufacturing (durable goods)	$190,213	$16,463
Manufacturing (non-durable goods)	$222,222	$33,810
Retail/wholesale trade	$214,706	$41,528
Services (non-profit)	$90,563	$1,867
Services (profit)	$113,374	$18,866
Transportation & warehousing	$192,593	*
Utilities	$374,932	$53,702
Government agency	$99,622	$725
Non-profit organization	$107,031	$2,818
Privately owned for-profit organization	$148,148	$18,602
Publicly owned for-profit organization	$210,673	$38,751
Commercial sector	$163,848	$19,065
Defense sector	$171,004	$20,507
Government (non-defense) sector	$92,165	$155

*Data not reliable.
Source: Human Capital Benchmarking Study (Alexandria, VA: SHRM, 2006).

is the *balanced scorecard.* Use of the balanced scorecard stresses measuring the strategic performance of organizations on four perspectives:

■ Financial
■ Internal business processes
■ Customer
■ Learning and growth

Organizational measures in each of these areas are calculated to determine if the organization is progressing toward its strategic objectives. For example, some firms have noticed that when survey results show a decline in employee satisfaction, several months later there is a decline in customer loyalty and repeat customer sales. Or expenditures in employee leadership development training can be linked to lower employee turnover and reduced time to hire managers from outside the organization.

Several years ago Verizon began using 17 questions to evaluate HR activities as part of a "balanced scorecard" process. Questions look at factors such as talent availability, turnover reduction and retention plans, HR service delivery, and the firm's return on investment on its people expenditures. These evaluation efforts continue to give Verizon a better understanding of the cost-benefit payoffs of its HR efforts and how well these efforts contribute to attainment of Verizon's strategic and operational goals.

Using the balanced scorecard requires spending considerable time and effort to identify the appropriate HR measures in each of the four areas and how they tie to strategic organizational success. Various companies as diverse as Verizon, EDS, and Union Pacific, as well as small firms, are using the balanced scorecard to ensure better alignment of HR measurement efforts and strategic goals.[43] However, regardless of the time and effort spent trying to develop and use objective measures in the balanced scorecard, subjectivity in what is selected and how the measures are interpreted can still occur. In this book, HR metrics sections will be highlighted throughout the discussion of the various HR activities, using the special HR metrics icon that appears at the beginning of this section.

HR Measurement and Benchmarking

Benchmarking Comparing specific measures of performance against data on those measures in other organizations.

One approach to assessing HR effectiveness is benchmarking, which compares specific measures of performance against data on those measures in other organizations. HR professionals interested in benchmarking compare their measurement data with those from outside sources, including individual companies, industry sources, and professional associations.

Some diagnostic measures can be used to check the effectiveness of the HR function.[44] For benchmarking overall HR costs, one useful source is data gathered each year by the Society for Human Resource Management and BNA, Inc. This survey shows that HR expenditures by workforce size vary significantly. As might be expected, the total number of staff needed to serve 1,000 employees is not significantly different from the number needed to serve 2,500 employees. But the cost per employee of having an HR department is greater in organizations with fewer than 250 employees.

Using benchmarking, HR effectiveness is best determined by comparing ratios and measures from year to year. But it is crucial that the benchmarking look at the strategic contributions HR makes to the organization, not just the operating efficiency measures.[45]

HR Audit

HR audit Formal research effort that evaluates the current state of HR management in an organization.

One general means for assessing HR is through an HR audit, which is similar to a financial audit. An HR audit is a formal research effort that evaluates the current state of HR management in an organization. This audit attempts to evaluate how well HR activities in each of the HR areas (staffing, compensation, health and safety, etc.) have been performed, so that management can identify areas for improvement. An HR audit often helps smaller organizations without a formal HR professional identify issues associated with legal compliance, administrative processes and recordkeeping, employee retention, etc.

Regardless of the time and effort placed on HR measurement and HR metrics, the most important consideration is that HR effectiveness and efficiency must be measured regularly for HR staff and other managers to know how HR is contributing to organizational success.

Internet Research

HR Audit, Inc.

HR Audit, Inc., provides functional and strategic audits. Visit their Website at: http://thomsonedu.com/management/mathis.

SUMMARY

- Organizational strategy focuses on how to successfully compete and how HR should be involved in strategy decisions both at the organizational level and in making HR strategies.
- Organizational effectiveness and strategic HR management must focus on organizational culture, as well as productivity, customer service and quality, and financial contributions.
- Organizations doing business internationally may evolve from organizations engaged in importing and exporting, to multi-national enterprises, to global organizations.
- Legal, political, cultural, and economic factors influence global HR management.
- One scheme for classifying national cultures considers inequality in power, individualism, masculinity/femininity, uncertainty avoidance, and long-term orientation.
- HR planning involves analyzing and identifying the need for and availability of human resources so that the organization can meet its objectives.
- The HR unit has major responsibilities in HR planning, but managers must provide supportive information and input.
- When developing HR plans, it is important for managers to scan the external environment to identify the effects of government influences, economic conditions, geographic and compe-

tition concerns, and workforce composition changes.
- Assessing internal strengths and weaknesses as a part of HR planning requires auditing and inventorying current jobs and employee capabilities.
- The supply and demand for human resources can be forecast with a variety of methods and for differing periods of time.
- Management of HR surpluses may require downsizing through use of attrition and hiring freezes, early retirement buyouts, layoffs, and outplacement assistance.
- Managing a workforce shortage should be multi-faceted, not just solved with hiring.
- HR plays a crucial role in mergers and acquisitions, particularly in dealing with organizational culture issues.
- HR effectiveness must be measured using HR metrics that consider both strategic and operational effectiveness.
- The ROI of human capital, economic value added (EVA), and the balanced scorecard are common means for HR measurement.
- Benchmarking allows an organization to compare its practices against "best practices" in different organizations, and HR audits can be used to get a comprehensive overview on HR activities.

REVIEW AND APPLICATION QUESTIONS

1. Discuss how cultural factors, both globally and inside organizations, must be addressed as part of strategic HR management.
2. What steps can HR professionals take to overcome the view that what HR accomplishes is not measurable?

3. As a newly hired HR manager for a medical clinic with 20 physicians and 100 employees, you want to identify and develop some HR metrics. Using the various metrics discussed at *www.saratogainstitute.com* and other Web sources, identify five specific metrics and discuss why those measures could be useful.

CASE

Xerox Focuses on HR

Xerox is a widely known firm worldwide, but it has been through numerous crises in the past decade. In fact, at one point several years ago, there were questions about Xerox surviving as a firm. But no longer. Under the leadership of Anne Mulcahy as CEO, Xerox has rebounded. Numerous strategic business and financial decisions had to be made, including reducing the workforce by 30,000. But Mulcahy also stressed that HR had to become a more strategic contributor.

One of the actions taken was to consolidate a number of HR functions from different business units into a corporate HR Service Center. This center performs many administrative transactions, and has added Internet-based systems to make HR services more accessible to managers and employees.

To track employees' views on the company and HR, employee surveys on the company intranet have been used for several years. Areas at which lower scores were recorded have been addressed by HR staff and other managers. The survey results have led to another primary focus at Xerox: employee retention. With all of

the reductions and organizational restructurings, keeping the remaining employees, especially high-potential ones, has been a continuing emphasis. Xerox has invested significant time and resources into training and development of its employees, an important retention factor. Greater use of e-learning, technology, and leadership development have paid off in reducing turnover and convincing employees that career opportunities exist at Xerox. Continuing competitive pressures are presenting new challenges for Xerox and its HR staff. The strategic importance of HR has been demonstrated in the past, and looks to be a part of the firm's future.[46]

Questions

1. Discuss the challenges faced by HR management when significant staff cutbacks occur and how they should be addressed.
2. Use of technology, employee retention, and HR development have been at the core of HR becoming more strategic at Xerox. Why have those areas been so key?

SUPPLEMENTAL CASE

Where Do You Find the Bodies?

This case identifies problems associated with HR planning and recruiting in a tight labor market. (For the case, go to http://thomsonedu.com/management/mathis.)

NOTES

1. Jeffrey McCracken, "Detroit's Symbol of Dysfunction: Paying Employees Not to Work," *The Wall Street Journal*, March 1, 2006, A1; and Adam Aston and David Welch, "A Wrench for Parts Suppliers," *Business Week*, March 14, 2005, 46.
2. "Improving Strategic Planning: A McKinsey Survey," *The McKinsey Quarterly*, September 2006, 1–10.
3. Evan H. Offstein et al., "A Strategic Human Resource Perspective of Firm Competitive Behavior," *Human Resource Management Review*, 15 (2005), 305–318.
4. James D. Werbel and Samuel M. DeMarie, "Aligning Strategic Human Resource Management and Person–Environment Fit," *Human Resource Management Review*, 15 (2005), 247–262.
5. Edward E. Lawler III, "From Human Resources Management to Organizational Effectiveness," in Mike Losey, Sue Meisinger, and Dave Ulrich, eds., *The Future of Human Resource Management* (Alexandria, VA: SHRM/John Wiley, 2005), 144–146.
6. "Strategic HR Planning—Targeting the Business Goals that Organizations Value Most," *BNA Workforce Strategies*, June 2005, 1–48.
7. "Research Backs Up HR's Impact on Value," *Workforce Management*, June 26, 2006, 40.

8. Dave Ulrich and David Creelman, "In Touch with Intangibles," *Workforce Management*, May 8, 2006, 39–42.

9. Jeffrey Pfeffer, "Producing Sustainable Competitive Advantage Through the Effective Management of People," *Academy of Management Executive*, November 2005, 95–109.

10. Kathy Gurchiek, "Ten Steps for HR to Earn That Seat at the Table," *HR News*, April 11, 2006, *www.shrm.org/hrnews;* and "Strategic Workforce Strategies," 11–13.

11. David E. Bowen and Cheri Ostroff, "Understanding HRM—Firm Performance Linkages: The Role of the 'Strength of the HRM System,'" *Academy of Management Review*, 29 (2004), 203–221.

12. Rosemary Batt, "Managing Customer Services: Human Resource Practices, Quit Rates, and Sales Growth," *Academy of Management Journal*, 45 (2003), 587–597.

13. Regular updates on customer satisfaction generally and by industry are available at *www.theacsi.org.*

14. Karen M. Krol, "Repurposing Metrics for HR," *HR Magazine*, July 2006, 64–69.

15. Saba Colakoglu et al., "Measuring HRM Effectiveness: Considering Multiple Stakeholders in a Global Context," *Human Resource Management Review*, 16 (2006), 209–218.

16. John Dooney, "Measuring Human Capital: Getting Started," *Briefly Stated ROI, www.shrm.org.*

17. Lars W. Mitlacher, "The Organization of HRM in Temporary Work Agencies," *Human Resource Management Review*, 16 (2006), 67–81.

18. Wendy M. Becker and Vanessa M. Freeman, "Going from Global Trends to Corporate Strategy," *The McKinsey Quarterly*, 3, 2006, 1–7.

19. Richard F. Stolz, "World Leaders," *Human Resource Executive Online*, December 1, 2006, 1–5. *www.hreonline.com.*

20. Geert Hofstede, *Culture's Consequences: Comparing Values, Behaviors, Institutions, and Organizations Across Cultures*, 2nd ed. (Thousand Oaks, CA: Sage, 2001); and John W. Bing, "Hofstede's Consequences: The Impact of His Work on Consulting and Business Practices," *Academy of Management Executive*, February 2004, 80–87.

21. "Free Trade on Trial," *The Economist*, January 3, 2004, 13–16.

22. K. S. Lee, G. H. Lim, and W. S. Lim, "Family Business Succession: Appropriation Risk and Choice of Successor," *Academy of Management Review*, 28 (2003), 657–666.

23. C. Geissler et al., "The Cane Mutiny: Managing a Grazing Workforce," *Harvard Business Review*, October 2005, 1–9.

24. Michael Mandel, "Why the Economy Is a Lot Stronger Than You Think," *Business Week*, February 13, 2006, 63–70.

25. Based on Leslie G. Klaff, "Many People, One Matter," *Workforce Management*, March 2004, 42–44.

26. Mark McGraw, "Bye-Bye Boomers," *Human Resource Executive*, March 22, 2006, 34–37.

27. Based on Erin White, "Skills Tracking Lets Firms Measure Bench Strength," *The Wall Street Journal*, February 13, 2006, B3.

28. Joshua L. Ditelberg, "A Practical Guide to Workforce Reductions," *SHRM Legal Report*, March/April 2002.

29. Wayne F. Cascio, "Strategies for Responsible Restructuring," *Academy of Management Executive*, November 2005, 39–50.

30. "More Workers Choosing to Retire Early," *Omaha World-Herald*, January 12, 2004, 2D.

31. Kris Maher, "Coal Companies Are Slowed by Severe Shortage of Workers," *The Wall Street Journal*, May 5, 2005, A1; and Julie Schmit, "Nursing Shortage Drums Up Demands for Happy Nomads," *USA Today*, June 9, 2005, 3B.

32. Bas Koene and Marten van Riemsdijk, "Managing Temporary Workers: Work Identity, Diversity and Operational HR Choices," *Human Resource Management Journal*, 15 (2005), 76–92.

33. Leslie A. Weatherly, "HR Outsourcing: Reaping Strategic Value for your Organization," *SHRM Research Quarterly*, 2005, 1–11.

34. Moira Donoghue, "Is Human Resources Ready?" *Workspan*, May 2006, 62–65.

35. Susan Cartwright and Simon McCarthy, "Developing a Framework for Cultural Due Diligence in Mergers and Acquisitions," in G. K. Stahl and M. E. Mendenhall, eds., *Mergers and Acquisitions* (Stanford, CA: Stanford Business Books, 2005), 252–263.

36. Ibid., 206–263.

37. Paul Evans and Vladimir Pucik, "People and Cultural Aspects of Mergers and Acquisitions," in G. K. Stahl and M. E. Mendenhall, eds., *Mergers and Acquisitions* (Stanford, CA: Stanford Business Books, 2005), 413–416.

38. Leah Carlson, "Smooth Transition," *Employee Benefits News*, June 1, 2005, 12; and Ann Pomeroy, "A Fitting Role," *HR Magazine*, June 2005, 54–60.

39. Robert Grossman, "Measuring the Value of HR," *HR Magazine*, December 2006, 44–49.

40. *HR Department Benchmarks and Analysis 2007* (Washington, DC: BNA 2007), iii.

41. L. L. Bryan and M. Zanini, "Strategy in the Era of Global Giants," *The McKinsey Quarterly*, No. 4 2005, 1–11.

42. Karen M. Kroll, "Repurposing Metrics for HR," *HR Magazine*, July 2006, 65–74.

43. Nancy R. Lockwood, "The Balanced Scorecard: An Overview," *SHRM Research*, June 2006, 1–9.

44. F. E. Reichheld and P. Rogers, "Motivating Through Metrics," *Harvard Business Review*, September 2005, 20–24.

45. C. Cornell, "The Metric System," *Human Resource Executive*, June 2, 2005, 52–54.

46. Adapted from Ed Santalone, "Processing a Turnaround," *Human Resource Executive*, June 28, 2004, 16–23.

CHAPTER

3

Organization/Individual Relations and Retention

After you have read this chapter, you should be able to:

- Identify the changing nature of the psychological contract.
- Discuss how motivation is linked to individual performance.
- List the five major drivers of retention and activities related to them.
- Describe different kinds of absenteeism and turnover.
- Explain two ways to measure absenteeism and turnover.
- Outline the steps in managing retention.

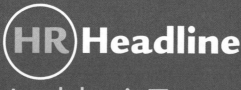

(HR) Headline

Applebee's Turnover Recipe

Applebee's International of Overland Park, Kansas, is a large "casual dining" chain with more than 1,600 restaurants, 25% of which are company owned and 75% franchised. Applebee's has been adding about 100 restaurant locations a year. However, like many businesses in a low-wage environment, Applebee's has been plagued by high turnover among the more than 29,000 company employees. Among restaurant managers the industry averages around 50% turnover per year. But Applebee's has reduced its turnover rate to about 14% annually, and keeps 80% of hourly workers in the desired categories. How they got these results illustrates the importance of HR retention efforts.

The key to their success has been a system based on the working knowledge that the loss of a top 20% performing and experienced hourly employee costs $2,500, the loss of a middle 60% employee costs $1,000, but the loss of a bottom 20% employee *makes* the company $500. Of course, to focus retention on good performers the company needs a good way of tracking performance. Their "people metrics" approach is based on hiring hourly employees based on their competencies, rating managers in the three groups, and rewarding managers who are able to keep high performers. The decisions are based on a software program that reports specific data on turnover, sales, and profits, as well as details on customer satisfaction ratings and performance reviews.

Managers have retention targets set: keep 80% of the top 20% group, 70% of the middle 60% segment, and none of the bottom 20%. The company does not require that the bottom 20% be fired as some companies do, but the low performers must be informed of their status and the need to improve their performance results.

As a result of the corporate program, franchisees have begun asking about the "people metrics" approach and have suggested that it become mandatory for all sites. Thus, Applebee's focus on turnover and retention has been a key part of its strategic growth.[1]

Recent studies raise the specter of an expanding economy restrained by a shrinking labor pool—a scenario that will drive up the cost of getting and maintaining a workforce.[2] When good, experienced employees leave, valuable knowledge leaves too. Given the difficulty and expense of replacing good employees who leave, an important strategy is to keep them as long as possible.

Relationships between individuals and their employing organizations can vary widely. Both parties may view the employer/employee relationship as satisfactory. Or one may see it as satisfactory and one may not. Or both may be looking for a way to end the relationship. *Job satisfaction* and *commitment* often help determine whether an employee will want to stay or leave. The *individual's performance* is a major part of whether the employer wants the employee to stay. Understanding the relationship between individuals and organizations is more than just academically interesting. It is the basis for employee retention.

Competent employees who are satisfied with their employers, who know what is expected, and who have minimal absenteeism and reduced turnover potential are assets to the organization. But just as individuals in an organization can be a competitive advantage, they can also be a liability. When few employees know how to do their jobs, when people are constantly leaving, and when the employees who do remain work ineffectively, human resources are a *problem* that puts the organization at a competitive *disadvantage*. Individual performance, motivation, and employee retention are key for organizations to maximize the effectiveness of human resources.

INDIVIDUAL/ORGANIZATIONAL RELATIONSHIPS

The long-term economic health of most organizations depends on the efforts of employees with both the appropriate capabilities and the motivation to do their jobs well. Organizations that are successful over time can usually demonstrate that relationships with their employees *do* matter. Key considerations in these relationships include the psychological contract, job satisfaction, and loyalty.

The Psychological Contract

Psychological contract
The unwritten expectations employees and employers have about the nature of their work relationships.

One concept that has been useful in discussing employees' relationships with organizations is that of a psychological contract, which refers to the unwritten expectations employees and employers have about the nature of their work relationships. Because the psychological contract is individual and subjective, it focuses on expectations about "fairness" that may not be defined very clearly by either party.

Expectations about both tangible items (such as wages, benefits, employee productivity, and attendance) and intangible items (such as loyalty, fair treatment, and job security) are encompassed by unwritten psychological contracts between employers and employees. Many employers attempt to detail their expectations through employee handbooks and policy manuals, but those materials are only part of the total "contractual" relationship.

The Changing Psychological Contract At one time, employees expected to exchange their efforts and capabilities for a secure job that offered rising pay, good benefits, and career progression within the organization. But as organizations have downsized and cut workers who have given long and loyal service, a growing number of employees question whether they should or should not be loyal to their employers. Closely related to the psychological contract is the concept of *psychological ownership*.[3] When individuals feel that they have some control and perceived rights in the organization, they are more likely to be committed to the organization.

Rather than just paying employees to follow orders and put in time, increasingly, employers are expecting them to utilize their knowledge, skills, and abilities to accomplish results. A psychological contract that can help achieve those ends recognizes the following components:

Employers Provide:
- Competitive compensation and benefits
- Flexibility to balance work and home life
- Career development opportunities

Employees Contribute:
- Continuous skill improvement and increased productivity
- Reasonable time with the organization
- Extra effort when needed

Recent research suggests that psychological contracts can be strengthened and employee commitment enhanced when the organization is involved in a cause the employee values highly. Conversely, psychological contracts can be violated not only in reaction to personal mistreatment but from a perception that the organization has abandoned an important principle or cause. The unethical and illegal behavior of upper management at Enron and WorldCom in the early 2000s is a good example of psychological contract violation. When a psychological contract is violated, employees may feel anger, distrust, reduced loyalty and commitment, and increased willingness to leave.[4]

Generational Differences

Much has been written about the differing expectations of individuals in different generations.[5] Many of these observations are anecdotal and give only generalizations about individuals in the various age groups. Some common generational labels are:

- Matures (born before 1945)
- Baby boomers (born 1945–1965)
- Generation Xers (born 1966–1980)
- Generation Yers (born 1981–1990)

Rather than identifying the characteristics cited for each of these groups, it is most important here to emphasize that people's expectations about psychological contracts differ between generations, as well as within generations. For employers, the differing expectations present challenges. For instance, many baby boomers and matures are concerned about security and experience. However, younger generation Yers are often seen as the "why" generation, who expect to be rewarded quickly, are very adaptable, and tend to ask more questions about why managers and organizations make the decisions they do. Consider the dynamics of a mature manager directing generation X and Y individuals, or generation X managers supervising older, more experienced baby boomers.[6] Generational differences are likely to continue to create challenges and conflicts in organizations because of the different expectations inherent in different generations.[7]

JOB SATISFACTION, LOYALTY, AND COMMITMENT

Employees *do* behave as if there is a psychological contract, and hope their employers will honor the "agreement." Many employees want security and stability, interesting work, a supervisor they respect, and competitive pay and benefits. If these elements are not provided, employees may feel a diminished need to contribute.[8] When organizations merge, lay off large numbers of employees, outsource work, and use large numbers of temporary and part-time workers, employees experience job security concerns and in turn see fewer reasons to give their loyalty to those employers.

Job satisfaction A positive emotional state resulting from evaluating one's job experiences.

In its most basic sense, job satisfaction is a positive emotional state resulting from evaluating one's job experiences. Job *dis*satisfaction occurs when one's expectations are not met. For example, if an employee expects clean and safe working conditions, then the employee is likely to be dissatisfied if the workplace is dirty and dangerous.

Dimensions of job satisfaction frequently mentioned include work, pay, promotion opportunities, supervision, and co-workers. Job satisfaction appears to have declined somewhat in recent years, and elements of the employee/employer relationship have been cited. More demanding work, fewer traditional hierarchical relationships with management, shorter relationships, and less confidence in long-term rewards are frequently cited reasons.[9]

Loyalty and Organizational Commitment

Even though job satisfaction itself is important, perhaps the "bottom line" is how job satisfaction influences organizational commitment, which then affects employee turnover. As Figure 3-1 depicts, the interaction of the individual and the job determines levels of job satisfaction and organizational commitment.

"Loyal" employees are more than just satisfied with their jobs; they are pleased with the relationships with their employers. Additionally, employers find that in tight labor markets, turnover of key people occurs more frequently when employee loyalty is low, which in turn emphasizes the importance of a loyal and committed workforce.[10]

Organizational commitment The degree to which employees believe in and accept organizational goals and desire to remain with the organization.

Organizational commitment is the degree to which employees believe in and accept organizational goals and desire to remain with the organization. A related idea is *employee engagement,* which is the extent to which an employee is willing and able to contribute. Various research studies have revealed that people who are relatively satisfied with their jobs are somewhat more committed to the organization.[11]

FIGURE 3-1   Factors Affecting Job Satisfaction and Organizational Commitment

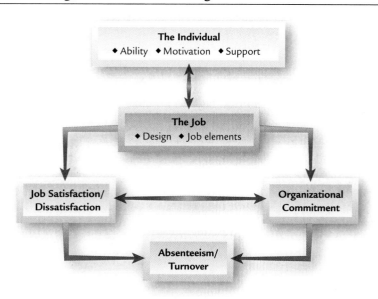

A logical extension of organizational commitment focuses more specifically on *continuance commitment* factors, which suggests that decisions to remain with or leave an organization ultimately are reflected in employee absenteeism and turnover statistics. Individuals who are not as satisfied with their jobs or who are not as committed to the organization are more likely to withdraw from the organization. The relationships among satisfaction, commitment, and absenteeism and turnover have been affirmed across cultures, full- and part-time workers, genders, and occupations.

INDIVIDUAL EMPLOYEE PERFORMANCE

The relationship between the individual employee and the organization helps clarify why people might leave a job, as does satisfaction, loyalty, and commitment. But for an employer to *want* to keep an employee, that employee must be performing well.

The HR unit in an organization exists in part to analyze and address the performance of individual employees. Exactly how that should be done depends on what upper management expects. Like any management function, HR management activities should be developed, evaluated, and changed as necessary so that they can contribute to the competitive performance of the individuals at work and therefore of the organization.

Individual Performance Factors

The three major factors that affect how a given individual performs are illustrated in Figure 3-2. They are: (1) individual ability to do the work, (2) effort expended, and (3) organizational support. The relationship of those factors is widely acknowledged in management literature as follows:

$$\text{Performance } (P) = \text{Ability } (A) \times \text{Effort } (E) \times \text{Support } (S)$$

FIGURE 3-2	Components of Individual Performance

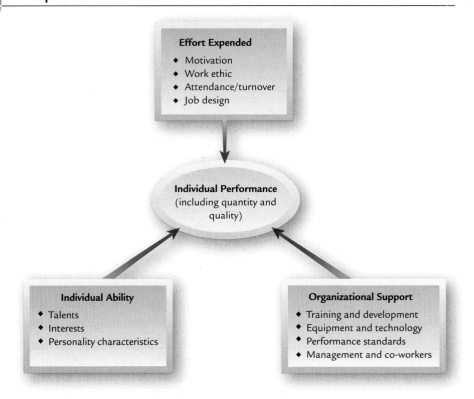

Individual performance is enhanced to the degree that all three components are present with an individual employee, and diminished if any of these factors is reduced or absent. For instance, assume that several production workers have the abilities to do their jobs and work hard, but the organization provides outmoded equipment or the management style of supervisors causes negative reactions by the workers. Or assume that a customer service representative in a call center has the necessary abilities and the employer provides excellent support, but the individual hates "being tied to a telephone cord" all day and is frequently absent because of that dislike, even though the job pays well. In both cases, individual performance is likely to be lower than it would be if all three components were present. Individual motivation, one of the variables that affects effort, is often missing from the performance equation.

Individual Motivation

Motivation The desire within a person causing that person to act.

Motivation is the desire within a person causing that person to act. People usually act for one reason: to reach a goal. Thus, motivation is a goal-directed drive, and it seldom occurs in a void.[12] The words *need, want, desire,* and *drive* are all similar to *motive,* from which the word *motivation* is derived. Understanding motivation is important because performance, reaction to compensation, turnover, and other HR concerns are affected by and influence motivation.

Approaches to understanding motivation vary because different theorists have developed their own views and models.[13] Each approach has contributed to the understanding of human motivation, and details on different approaches can be found in various organizational behavior textbooks.

Management Implications for Motivating Individual Performance

Motivation is complex and individualized, and managerial strategies and tactics must be broad based to address the motivation concerns of individuals. For instance, managers must determine whether inadequate individual behavior is due to employee deficiencies, inconsistent reward policies, or low desire for the rewards offered. Additionally, managers may try training to improve employee performance or look at the methods by which they appraise and reward performance.

Many organizations spend considerable money to "motivate" their employees, using a wide range of tactics. For example, firms hire motivational speakers to inspire employees, with some of those "motivational coaches" commanding fees of as much as $50,000 a speech. Other employers give T-shirts, mugs, books, and videos to employees as motivators. Such efforts, not including sales motivation rewards, are estimated to cost in the billions of dollars a year. However, the effectiveness of those expenditures has been questioned, particularly given the short-term nature of many of the programs and rewards. See the HR Perspective for an example of motivation that works.

The relationship between individuals and their employers clearly affects retention of employees. That is the topic for the remainder of the chapter.

HR PERSPECTIVE

Nucor Steel Motivates Employees

Three Nucor Corporation electricians who were out of town got a call from colleagues at the plant telling them that the electrical grid had failed. For a company that uses electric-arc furnaces to make steel from scrap, it was the worst possible news. All three dropped what they were doing and drove or flew to the plant. They camped out in the electrical substation with other staff and worked 20-hour shifts to get the plant running again in three days instead of the expected week.

No supervisor had ordered them to come back and there was no extra money in the next paycheck. But, at Nucor *money* is indeed where the rubber meets the road. At another company an experienced steelworker earns $21/hour. At Nucor it is $10/hour. But the average Nucor steelworker took home $79,000 last year plus a $2,000 bonus for record earnings plus $18,000 in profit sharing. Managers have their own pay at risk for results as well. Nucor profit sharing is the key—when the company performs well, managers and employees do well financially. If it does poorly, individuals receive less compensation.

Newly acquired plants have a hard time getting used to this high-stakes teamwork. For example, Nucor acquired a rolling mill. Prior to the takeover, if there was a problem that backed up work, people would sit, have a cup of coffee, and wait for "them" to fix it. But at Nucor it is not "you guys"; it is "all us guys," and if there is a holdup everyone works on it because it costs everyone money. During the first six months after the takeover, Nucor paid the acquired employees at their old pay rate, but showed them what they would have made under Nucor's formula. Employees saw their pay climb from $53,000 before the takeover to $92,000 two years later.

The payoff for Nucor was in the second year of operation of the acquired facility, with fewer employees and no new capital investments, the plant saw a 14% increase in total shipments. It is not just pay but cooperation, ideas, and competition, resulting from the motivation of the people in the mills, that makes Nucor perform well.[14]

RETENTION OF HUMAN RESOURCES

Retention of human resources must be viewed as a strategic business issue. Until a few years ago, the opposite of retention, turnover, was a routine HR matter requiring records and reports, but top management did not get involved. However, what was once a bothersome detail has become a substantial money issue for many employers. There are now fewer qualified and productive people in the workforce, and the high performers are even more in demand. Thus, companies are being forced to study why employees leave and why they stay. While experts can (and do) make some observations, each organization must determine the causes for its own specific retention situation.

Some employers have placed such a high priority on employee retention that they have designated retention officers. Often an individual in the HR area is assigned to specifically focus on retention to ensure that it receives high priority.

Internet Research

Employee Retention
For a six-part e-mail series, "Designing and Implementing a Successful Employee Retention Strategy," visit this Website at: http://thomsonedu.com/management/mathis.

Myths About Retention

Keeping good employees is a challenge that all organizations share and that becomes even more difficult as labor markets tighten. Unfortunately, some myths have arisen about what it takes to retain employees. Consultants have identified some of the most prevalent of these myths:

1. *Money is the main reason people leave.* Money certainly is a powerful recruiting tool, and if people feel they are being paid inadequately, they are clearly more likely to leave. But if they are paid a competitive wage or salary, other parts of the job are more important.
2. *Hiring has nothing to do with retention.* This is not true. Recruiting and selecting the people who fit the jobs and who are less likely to leave in the first place, and then orienting them to the company, can greatly increase retention. Select for retention!
3. *If you train people, you are only training them for another employer.* Developing skills in employees may indeed make them more marketable, but it also tends to improve retention. When an employer provides employees with training and development assistance, job satisfaction may increase and employees are more likely to stay.
4. *Do not be concerned about retention during a merger.* That is exactly the time to worry about retention. Although some people's jobs may have to be cut after a merger, the employees the company would like to keep may have the most opportunity to leave voluntarily. During a merger, all employees are concerned about job security, and if they do not feel a part of the new organization early on, many will leave.
5. *If solid performers want to leave, the company cannot hold them.* Employees are best viewed as free agents. They can indeed leave when they want. The key to keeping solidly performing employees is to create an environment in which they want to stay and grow.

Why People Stay or Leave

Conventional wisdom says that employees leave if they are dissatisfied, and that money will make them stay. That greatly oversimplifies the issue.[15] People often leave jobs for reasons that have nothing to do with the jobs themselves.

FIGURE 3-3	Drivers of Retention

Mergers, unsolicited job offers, family responsibilities, a spouse's relocation, a poor performance appraisal, and administrative changes are all "shocks" that can bring on serious thoughts of leaving, even when people are not dissatisfied with their jobs. Further, people sometimes stay with jobs for non-work reasons. Some factors that limit individuals' willingness to leave the jobs are *links* between themselves and others; compatibility or *fit* with the job/organization/community; and potential *sacrifice*, or what they would have to give up if they left the job.

Those characteristics of the "stay or go" decision are personal and not entirely within the control of an employer. However, there are factors related to those individual decisions that an employer can control.[16] Figure 3-3 shows those factors, and also indicates that they are "drivers" of retention, or forces that an employer can manage to improve retention.

DRIVERS OF RETENTION

If employees choose to leave an organization for family reasons—because a spouse is transferring, to raise children, etc.—there may be a limited number of actions the employer can take to keep them on the job. However, there are significant actions that an employer *can* do to retain employees in most other circumstances.

Characteristics of the Employer

A number of organizational characteristics influence individuals in their decisions to stay with or leave their employers. Organizations experience less turnover when they have positive and distinctive cultures, effective management, and recognizable job security.

Organizational culture The shared values and beliefs of a workforce.

Culture and Values Organizational culture is a pattern of shared values and beliefs of a workforce. Those items provide organizational members with meaning and rules for behavior. In one study, employees gave employers a B+ on average, with 44% calling their employers' cultures "excellent" or "very good."[17]

One corporation well known for its culture and values is Southwest Airlines. The firm focuses considerable HR efforts on instilling its values of customer service and employee involvement. Those efforts have yielded greater performance, retention of employees, and a reputation as an "employer of choice" in the airline industry. Even after the terrorist attacks of September 11, 2001, Southwest was the only airline that did not cut staff and significantly reduce its flights. The initiator of Southwest's culture, founding CEO Herb Kelleher, has repeatedly stated that showing respect for people is central to that culture.

The "100 Best Companies to Work For" have somewhat different cultures and values, yet their commitment to treating their employees well is a constant in good times and bad. Those firms are also performing better financially as the positive culture is reflected in better results.[18] Additionally, executives who have tried to build a "truth-telling" culture have found that frank feedback can be both good and bad, but they have succeeded in increasing retention and revenues.[19]

Management and Retention Other organizational components that affect employee retention are related to the management of the organization. Some organizations see external events as threatening, whereas others see changes as challenges requiring responses. The latter approach can be a source of competitive advantage, especially if an organization is in a growing, dynamic industry. The attitudes and approaches of management are the key.

Another factor affecting how employees view their organizations is the visionary quality of organizational leadership.[20] Often, leaders demonstrate their vision by having an identified strategic plan that guides how the firm responds to changes. If a firm is not effectively managed, then employees may be turned off by the ineffective responses and inefficiencies they deal with in their jobs.[21] Organizations that have clearly established goals and hold managers and employees accountable for accomplishing results are viewed as better places to work, especially by individuals wishing to progress both financially and career-wise. Further, effective management provides the resources necessary for employees to perform their jobs well.

Job Security Many individuals have seen a decline in job security during the past decade. All the downsizings, layoffs, mergers and acquisitions, and organizational restructurings have affected employee loyalty and retention. Also, as co-workers experience layoffs and job reductions, the anxiety levels of the remaining employees rise. Consequently, employees start thinking about leaving before they too get cut.[22] On the other hand, organizations in which job continuity and security are high tend to have higher retention rates. Younger employees experience more concern about job security than do older workers.

But job security is not solely about one's personal security. A major issue in retention is the extent to which high-caliber top performers are retained by the company. Other employees view high turnover in this group and the company as a negative in the retention equation.

Job Design/Work

Some jobs are considered "good" and others are thought to be "bad," but not all people agree on which are which. People vary considerably in their preferences for particular job features. As a result, some people like some kinds of work and others like different kinds of work. That is fortunate, because it means there are people willing to do most jobs.

Job/Person Match Matching people with jobs they like and fit can be a challenge. Figure 3-4 shows some characteristics of people and jobs that might need to be matched.

If people do not fit their jobs well, they are more likely to look for other employment, so retention is affected by the *selection process*. A number of organizations have found that high turnover rates in the first few months of employment are often linked to inadequate selection screening efforts.

Once individuals have been placed in jobs, other job/work factors affect retention. Because individuals spend significant time on the job, they expect to have modern equipment, technology, and *good working conditions*, given the nature of the work. Physical and environmental factors such as space, lighting, temperature, noise, and layout affect retention of employees.

Additionally, workers want a *safe work environment*, in which risks of accidents and injuries have been addressed. That is especially true for employees in such industries as manufacturing, agriculture, utilities, and transportation, which have higher safety risks than do many service industries and office environments.

FIGURE 3-4   Some Characteristics of People and Jobs

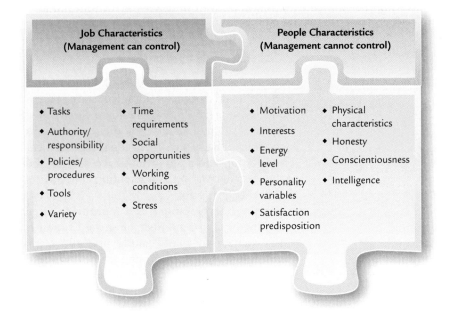

Time Flexibility Flexibility in work schedules has grown in importance.[23] Workload pressures have increased because of downsizing. On average, employees work 41.2 hours a week at their main jobs, but would prefer to work 34.5 hours a week. That discrepancy leads to employees working more than they want to and feeling overworked. Further, with more Americans living longer, the need for elder care is increasing. Dual-income couples in the "sandwich generation," caring for children *and* aged parents, may find flexible scheduling options very desirable.[24]

Internet Research

Work Options

For employee flexible work schedule proposal templates, link to the Work Options Website at: http://thomsonedu.com/management/mathis.

Various work scheduling alternatives (discussed in more detail in Chapter 6) can be used to improve time flexibility. Options include compressed scheduling, flexplace or telecommuting, flextime, part-time work, job sharing, and phased retirement.[25]

Many approaches to time flexibility are informal. However, informal schedule arrangements can cause communication problems among people who do not see each other and hostility among some employees. Formal policies indicating who is eligible for schedule flexibility and how problems will be handled also are needed to provide guidance to managers and employees, as well as to ensure that more consistency and fairness result.

Work Flexibility Balancing the demands of work with the responsibilities of life, including family and personal responsibilities, is a challenge; some may say it is an impossibility.[26] Work/life balancing programs commonly used include:

- Different work arrangements
- Leave for children's school functions
- Compressed workweek
- Job sharing
- On-site child/adult care

- Telecommuting
- Employee assistance plans
- On-site health services
- Wellness programs
- Fitness facility

The purpose of all these offerings is to convey that employers recognize the challenges employees face when balancing work/life demands. The value of work/life programs has been documented by a number of employers. One large manufacturer worked to reduce absenteeism and increase employee commitment to the firm. A revised time-off program and more flexible work arrangements have reduced absenteeism and unscheduled time off and increased employee satisfaction with the company.[27]

Career Opportunities

Surveys of workers in all types of jobs consistently indicate that organizational efforts to aid career development can significantly affect employee retention.[28] Such surveys have found that *opportunities for personal growth* lead the list of reasons why individuals took their current jobs and why they stay there. That component is even more essential for technical professionals and those under age 35, for whom opportunities to develop skills and obtain promotions rank above compensation as a retention concern.

Training/Development and Mentoring Organizations address training and development in a number of ways. Tuition aid programs, typically offered as a benefit by many employers, allow employees to pursue additional educational and training opportunities. These programs often contribute to higher employee retention rates. However, just offering such programs is not sufficient. Employers must also identify ways to use employees' new knowledge and capabilities inside the organization. Otherwise, employees are likely to feel that their increased "value" is not being recognized. Overall, training and development efforts are designed to meet many individuals' expectations that their employers are committed to keeping employees' knowledge, skills, and abilities current.[29]

Orientation is a type of training offered to new employees to help them adapt to their new jobs and employers. Increasing employee integration with the job through orientation during the first 90 days gets people proficient and makes them feel part of the company "team." Orientation that is well administered may increase employee retention rates.

Mentoring can increase retention because it provides both career opportunities and development. Mentoring can be formal or informal. As the number of contacts grows through mentors or others, it turns into a career networking system, either inside the organization or outside, or perhaps both.

Career Planning/Advancement Organizations also increase employee retention through formal career planning efforts. Employees discuss with their managers career opportunities within the organization and career development activities that will help the employees grow. Career development and planning efforts may include formal mentoring programs. Also, companies can reduce attrition by showing employees that they are serious about promoting from within. In very large companies, it is not always easy to know who might be qualified for an open job. HR On-Line describes an effective solution.

Promotions reward individuals with status, security, and the opportunity for further development. They reward the organization by contributing to retention, therefore reducing the costs of training, recruiting, and turnover. Individuals consider their own and others' promotion experiences in weighing opportunities, and eventually in deciding whether to stay or leave. As would be expected, when people have been promoted, they are less likely to leave the organization.

HR ONLINE

Opportunities for Promotion

By taking an electronic look within companies for candidates to promote, firms may not only save money, but also enhance the prospects for retention of current employees. Numerous employers are using HR technology systems to identify entrance employee capabilities. For instance, Hyatt Hotels now fills 70% of management positions from within the company. It has been able to do so by using its internal talent pool to better advantage. Another firm, Fireman's Fund Insurance, has implemented an electronic system for internal recruiting. The advantage of this Web-based system is seen in statistics that show that in one year 38% of the positions at Fireman's Fund were filled internally, compared with 5% in the previous year.

By logging on to the company intranet, an employee can create a personal profile including career objectives, education, skills, and salary expectations. When a job opens up, the program automatically looks in the company database for matches. Then appropriate candidates are notified by e-mail, and they can choose to go through the regular hiring process. Employees can register their profiles easily and quickly. Previously, the task took employees 15–30 minutes to complete. It was so cumbersome that only 2,000 of the 7,000 employees submitted information to be considered for transfers or promotions.[30] Thus the changes have helped with employee retention.

Rewards

The tangible rewards that people receive for working come in the form of pay, incentives, and benefits. Numerous surveys and experiences of HR professionals reveal that one key to retention is having *competitive compensation practices*. Many managers believe that money is the prime retention factor. Often, employees cite better pay or higher compensation as a reason for leaving one employer for another. However, the reality is a bit more complex.[31]

Competitive Pay and Benefits Pay and benefits *must be competitive*, which means they must be close to what other employers are providing and what individuals believe to be consistent with their capabilities, experience, and performance. If compensation is not close, often defined as within 10% of the "market" rate, then turnover is likely to be higher. This is especially true for individuals making less than $25,000 to $30,000 annually. If those lower-paid workers can get $1 per hour more or add employer-paid family benefits elsewhere, they are more likely to move.

On the other hand, for more highly paid individuals, especially those earning $80,000 and more, retention is less affected by how close compensation is to the market rate. Other considerations are more likely to enter into their decisions to stay or leave. In fact, money may be why some people leave a job, but other factors may be why many stay. Offering health insurance, 401(k) retirement, tuition assistance, and other benefits commonly provided by competing employers often is vital to retention.

A number of employers have used a wide range of special benefits and perks to attract and retain employees. Some of the more exotic benefits offered are dry cleaning pickup and dropoff, car maintenance services in company parking lots, coffee and latte kiosks, and ATM machines in break rooms. By offering special benefits and perks, employers hope to be seen more favorably by employees, which may increase retention rates.

Performance and Compensation Many individuals expect their rewards to be differentiated from those of others based on performance. That means, for instance, that if an employee receives about the same pay increase and overall pay as others who produce less, are absent more and work fewer hours, then that person may feel that the situation is "unfair." This perception may prompt the individual to look for another job where compensation recognizes performance differences.

Generally, individuals are more satisfied with the actual levels of their pay than with the processes used to determine pay. That is why the performance management systems and performance appraisal processes in organizations must be designed so they are linked to compensation increases. To strengthen links between organizational and individual performance, a growing number of private-sector firms are using variable pay and incentives programs. These programs offer cash bonuses or lump-sum payments to reward extra performance.

Recognition Employee recognition as a form of reward can be either tangible or intangible. Tangible recognition comes in many forms, such as "employee of the month" plaques and perfect-attendance certificates. Intangible and psychological recognition includes feedback from managers and supervisors that acknowledges extra effort and performance, even if monetary rewards are not given.[32]

One franchise firm uses both tangible and intangible recognition as part of its employee retention efforts. Employees who receive recognition cards from customers or co-workers can exchange them for movie tickets and other rewards. Also, managers have been trained to make special efforts to recognize employee performance and service. However, recognition programs *do not work* when used as substitutes for pay, when viewed as "negative recognition" by those who are not recognized, or when the recognition is insincere.

Employee Relationships

A final set of factors found to affect retention is based on the relationships that employees have in organizations. Such areas as the reasonableness of HR policies, the fairness of disciplinary actions, and the means used to decide work assignments and opportunities all affect employee retention. If individuals feel that policies are unreasonably restrictive or are applied inconsistently, then they may be more likely to look at jobs offered by other employers.

The increasing demographic diversity of U.S. workplaces makes *fair* and *non-discriminatory treatment* of employees, regardless of gender, age, and other characteristics, particularly important. The organizational commitment and job satisfaction of ethnically diverse individuals are affected by perceived discriminatory treatment. A number of firms have recognized that proactive management of diversity issues results in greater retention of individuals of all backgrounds.

Other relationships that affect employee retention are *supervisory/ management support* and *co-worker relations*. A supervisor or manager builds positive relationships and aids retention by being fair and non-discriminatory, allowing work flexibility and work/family balancing, giving feedback that recognizes employee efforts and performance, and supporting career planning and development.[33]

Many individuals build close relationships with co-workers. Such friendships do not appear on employee records, but research suggests that they can be an important signal that a workplace is positive.[34]

EMPLOYEE ABSENTEEISM

Absenteeism is any failure to report for work as scheduled or to stay at work when scheduled. The cause does not matter when counting someone absent. Absenteeism is expensive, costing an estimated $645 per employee each year.[35] Being absent from work may seem like a small matter to an employee. But if a manager needs 12 people in a unit to get the work done, and 4 of the 12 are absent most of the time, the work of the unit will decrease some or additional workers will have to be hired to provide results.

Internet Research

CCH Incorporated
CCH Incorporated conducts an Annual Unscheduled Absence Survey. For information on the rate and financial impact of employee absenteeism, visit their Website at: http://thomsonedu.com/management/ mathis.

Though some absences are justified, many are of the "three-day weekend" or "mental health days" variety. Many employees feel that such absences are acceptable. Such incidental absences account for as much as 80% of all absences and 33% of lost workdays.[36] For a company with 16,000 employees who cost the employer an average of $50,000 a year each (in compensation, benefits, etc.), incidental absences will incur about $16 million annually in direct costs. One study suggested that companies spend 15% of their payrolls on absenteeism each year.[37]

Types of Absenteeism

Employees can be absent from work for several reasons. Clearly, some absenteeism is inevitable because illness, death in the family, and other personal reasons. Such absences are unavoidable and understandable. Many employers have sick leave policies that allow employees a certain number of paid days each year for those types of *involuntary* absences.

However, much absenteeism is avoidable, or *voluntary*. Often, a relatively small number of individuals are responsible for a disproportionate share of the total absenteeism in an organization.[38] One problem is that a number of employees see no real concern about being absent or late to work because they feel that they are "entitled" to some absenteeism. Figure 3-5 shows the most common reasons for unscheduled absences.

Controlling Absenteeism

Voluntary absenteeism is better controlled if managers understand its causes clearly. Once they do, they can use a variety of approaches to reduce it. Organizational policies on absenteeism should be stated clearly in an employee handbook and stressed by supervisors and managers. Approaches to control absenteeism fall into several categories:

- *Disciplinary approach:* Many employers use a disciplinary approach. People who are absent the first time receive an oral warning, and subsequent absences bring written warnings, suspension, and finally dismissal.
- *Positive reinforcement:* Positive reinforcement includes such methods as giving employees cash, recognition, time off, or other rewards for meeting attendance standards. Offering rewards for consistent attendance, giving bonuses for missing fewer than a certain number of days, and "buying back" unused sick leave are all positive methods of reducing absenteeism.

FIGURE 3-5   Reasons for Unscheduled Absences

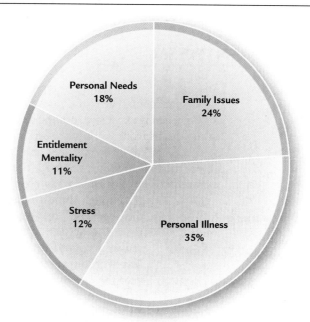

Source: Based on data from "2006 CCH Unscheduled Absence Survey," CCH, Inc., October 26, 2006, www.cch .com/press/news/2006. All Rights Reserved. Reprinted with permission.

FIGURE 3-6   Employee Absenteeism Control Actions

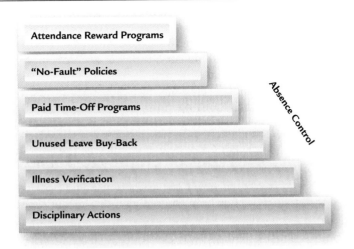

- *Combination approach:* A combination approach ideally rewards desired behaviors and punishes undesired behaviors. This "carrot and stick" approach uses policies and discipline to punish offenders and various programs and rewards to recognize employees with outstanding attendance. One firm that has used attendance incentives effectively is Continental Airlines. As part of its "Go Forward" program, employees with perfect attendance receive incentives of travel and other rewards.
- *"No fault" policy:* With a "no fault" policy, the reasons for absences do not matter, and the employees must manage their own attendance unless they abuse that freedom. Once absenteeism exceeds normal limits, then disciplinary action up to and including termination of employment can occur. The advantages of the "no fault" approach are that all employees can be covered by it, and supervisors and HR staff do not have to judge whether absences count as excused or unexcused.
- *Paid-time-off (PTO) programs:* Some employers have paid-time-off programs, in which vacation time, holidays, and sick leave for each employee are combined into a PTO account. Employees use days from their accounts at their discretion for illness, personal time, or vacation. If employees run out of days in their accounts, they are not paid for any additional days missed. PTO programs generally have reduced absenteeism, particularly one-day absences, but they often increase overall time away from work because employees use all of "their" time off by taking unused days as vacation days.

The disciplinary approach is the most widely used means for controlling absenteeism, with most employers using policies and punitive practices. Figure 3-6 shows that the other actions that employers use to control employee absenteeism are important also.

EMPLOYEE TURNOVER

Some people contend that turnover and absenteeism are different reactions to the same problems. That may be true—both can be classified as organizational withdrawal. Absenteeism is temporary withdrawal and turnover is permanent

Turnover The process in which employees leave an organization and have to be replaced.

withdrawal. Like absenteeism, turnover is related to job satisfaction and organizational commitment. Turnover occurs when employees leave an organization and have to be replaced.

Many organizations have found that turnover is a costly problem. In many service industries, the turnover rates and costs are frequently very high. In the retail industry, turnover averages more than 100% a year for part-time workers and around 75% a year for full-time workers. For instance, the nation's supermarkets, fast-food restaurants, and other service-industry firms spend billions on turnover. For higher-level executives and professionals, turnover costs can run as much as two times the departing employees' annual salaries.

Types of Employee Turnover

Turnover is classified in a number of ways. Each of the following classifications can be used, and the various types are not mutually exclusive:

■ **Involuntary Turnover**
Employees are terminated for poor performance or work rule violations

■ **Voluntary Turnover**
Employees leave by choice

Involuntary turnover is triggered by organizational policies, work rules, and performance standards that are not met by employees. Voluntary turnover can be caused by many factors, including career opportunities, pay, supervision, geography, and personal/family reasons. Voluntary turnover also appears to increase with the size of the organization, most likely because larger firms are less personal, are permeated by an "organizational bureaucracy," and have more employees who are inclined to move.

■ **Functional Turnover**
Lower-performing or disruptive employees leave

■ **Dysfunctional Turnover**
Key individuals and high performers leave at critical times

Not all turnover is negative for organizations; on the contrary, some workforce losses are desirable, especially if those who leave are lower-performing, less reliable individuals, or disruptive co-workers. Unfortunately for organizations, dysfunctional turnover does occur. That happens when key individuals leave, often at crucial work times.[39] For example, a software project leader left in the middle of a system upgrade in order to take a promotion at another firm in the city. His departure caused the system upgrade timeline to slip by two months due to the difficulty of replacing that project leader.

■ **Uncontrollable Turnover**
Employees leave for reasons outside the control of the employer

■ **Controllable Turnover**
Employees leave for reasons that could be influenced by the employer

Employees quit for many reasons that cannot be controlled by the organization. These reasons include: (1) the employee moves out of the geographic area, (2) the employee decides to stay home with young children or elder relatives, (3) the employee's spouse is transferred, and (4) the employee is a student worker who graduates from college. Even though some turnover is inevitable, many employers today recognize that reducing turnover is crucial. Therefore, they must address turnover that is controllable. Organizations are better able to retain employees if they deal with the concerns of employees that are leading to this type of turnover.

It appears that the amount of money an organization invests in its employees is one of those concerns because it increases the costs of turnover. With respect to turnover and expense, firms that have invested significantly in employees have had lower turnover rates and their profits are affected positively. Tactics for adapting to ongoing turnover include simplifying jobs, outsourcing, and cross training.

Turnover and "Churn"

Churn Hiring new workers while laying off others.

Hiring new workers while laying off others is the definition of **churn**. This practice raises a paradox in which employers complain about not being able to find skilled workers while they are laying people off.[40] For example, Hewlett-Packard laid off 30% of its workforce worldwide over four years, but did not change the total number of employees significantly because it hired other individuals at the same time. For nearly 60 years HP avoided layoffs—the financial hardships were spread around and workers retrained when times got tough. But HP's intentional churn today represents a major change in its culture. The company felt it had too many workers in information technology, HR, and finance and too few in sales. Expensive members of the workforce in the United States and western Europe were laid off and work was sent to less expensive workers in Asia, eastern Europe, and Latin America.[41]

HR METRICS: MEASURING ABSENTEEISM AND TURNOVER

A major step in reducing the expense of absenteeism and turnover is to decide how the organization is going to record those events and what calculations are necessary to maintain and benchmark their rates. A number of considerations are required.

Measuring Absenteeism

Controlling or reducing absenteeism must begin with continuous monitoring of the absenteeism statistics in work units. Such monitoring helps managers pinpoint employees who are frequently absent and departments that have excessive absenteeism. Various methods of measuring or computing absenteeism exist. One formula suggested by the U.S. Department of Labor is as follows:

$$\frac{\text{Number of person-days lost through job absence during period}}{(\text{Average number of employees}) \times (\text{Number of workdays})} \times 100$$

(This rate also can be based on number of hours instead of number of days.)

One source of extremely detailed information on absenteeism and turnover calculation has been prepared by Wayne Cascio. He suggests calculating the employee hours lost each month (or some other period) and the cost of those hours (including benefits), then calculating the cost of supervisory time lost to the management of absenteeism problems. The combination of the two costs is the cost of absenteeism for that period.[42] Sometimes it takes a six- or seven-figure cost number to get the attention of management to address absenteeism levels. Calculations of the costs of absenteeism should usually include these variables:

- Lost wages
- Benefits
- Overtime for replacements

- Fees for temporary employees, if incurred
- Supervisor's time
- Substandard production
- Overstaffing necessary to cover anticipated absences

Additional information can be gained by separating absenteeism data into long- and short-term categories. Different problems are caused by employees who are absent for one day 10 times during a year, and employees who are absent one time for 10 days. Other useful measures of absenteeism might include:

- *Incidence rate:* The number of absences per 100 employees each day
- *Inactivity rate:* The percentage of time lost to absenteeism
- *Severity rate:* The average time lost per absent employee during a specified period of time (a month or a year)

Measuring Turnover

The U.S. Department of Labor estimates that the cost of replacing a lower-level employee is one-third of the new hire's annual salary. Using only $8 an hour for an example, that equals $5,440 for each departing employee. Professional and managerial replacement rates are higher—perhaps as much as 2 or 2.5 times the new hire's annual salary.[43]

The turnover rate for an organization can be computed in different ways. The following formula from the U.S. Department of Labor is widely used; in it, *separations* means departures from the organization.

$$\frac{\text{Number of employee separations during the month}}{\text{Total number of employees at midmonth}} \times 100$$

Common turnover rates range from almost 0% to more than 100% a year and vary among industries. Often a part of HR management systems, turnover data can be gathered and analyzed in a number of different ways, including the following categories:

- Job and job level
- Department, unit, and location
- Reason for leaving
- Length of service
- Demographic characteristics
- Education and training
- Knowledge, skills, and abilities
- Performance ratings/levels

Two examples illustrate why detailed analyses of turnover are important. One manufacturing organization had a company-wide turnover rate that was not severe, but 80% of the turnover occurred within one department. That imbalance indicated that some action was needed to resolve problems in that unit. A health-care institution found that its greatest turnover in registered nurses occurred 24–36 months after hire, so the firm instituted a two-year employee recognition program and expanded the career development and training activities for employees with at least two years' service. For these example employers, the targeted turnover rates declined as a result of the actions taken in response to the turnover analyses that were done.

Determining Turnover Costs Determining turnover costs can be relatively simple or very complex, depending on the nature of the efforts and data used. Figure 3-7 shows a simplified costing model. In this model, if a job pays $20,000 (A) and benefits cost 40% (B), then the total annual cost for one

| **FIGURE 3-7** | Simplified Turnover Costing Model |

Job Title: _____

A. Typical annual pay for this job   _____
B. Percentage of pay for benefits multiplied by annual pay   _____
C. Total employee annual cost (add A + B)   _____
D. Number of employees who voluntarily quit the job in the past   _____
   12 months
E. Number of months it takes for 1 employee to become fully productive _____
F. Per person turnover cost (multiply [E ÷ 12] × C × 50%*)   _____
G. Annual turnover cost for this job (multiply F × D)   _____

*Assumes 50% productivity throughout the learning period (E).

Internet Research

Talent Keepers

This organization offers Web-based employee retention solutions. Link to their Website at: http://thomsonedu.com/management/mathis.

employee is $28,000. Assuming that 20 employees quit in the previous year (D) and that it takes three months for 1 employee to be fully productive (E), the calculation in (F) results in a per person turnover cost of $3,500. Overall, the annual turnover costs would be $70,000 for the 20 individuals who left. In spite of its conservative and simple nature, this model makes the point that turnover is costly. For instance, if the job is that of a teller in a large bank where more than 150 people leave in a year, the conservative model produces turnover costs of more than $500,000 a year. More detailed and sophisticated turnover costing models consider a number of factors. Some of the most common areas considered include the following:

- *Separation costs:* Includes HR staff and supervisor time and salaries to prevent separations, exit interview time, unemployment expenses, legal fees for separations challenged, accrued vacation, continued benefits, etc.
- *Replacement costs:* Includes recruiting and advertising expenses, search fees, HR interviewer and staff time and salaries, employee referral fees, relocation and moving costs, supervisor and managerial time and salaries, employment testing costs, reference checking fees, pre-employment medical expenses, etc.
- *Training costs:* Includes paid orientation time, training staff time and salaries, costs of training materials, supervisors' and managers' time and salaries, co-worker "coaching" time and salaries, etc.
- *Hidden costs:* Includes costs not obvious but that affect lost productivity, decreased customer service, other unexpected employee turnover, missed project deadlines, etc.

MANAGING RETENTION

The foregoing section summarized the results of many studies and HR practices to identify factors that can cause retention difficulties. Retention is critical because turnover (and absenteeism) can cause poor performance in otherwise productive units.[44] Now our focus turns toward what a manager can do about retention issues. Figure 3-8 shows the keys to managing retention.

FIGURE 3-8   **Managing Retention**

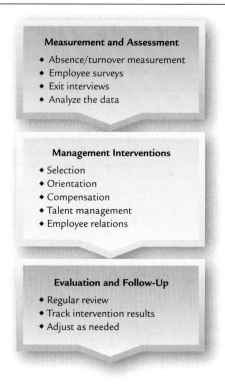

Measurement and Assessment
- Absence/turnover measurement
- Employee surveys
- Exit interviews
- Analyze the data

Management Interventions
- Selection
- Orientation
- Compensation
- Talent management
- Employee relations

Evaluation and Follow-Up
- Regular review
- Track intervention results
- Adjust as needed

Global Retention

The same core elements that help retention in the United States are important across the globe according to a Mercer study.[45] A look at India's $3 billion call center industry helps illustrate the problem. Many of India's call center jobs are monotonous, and as the need for English-speaking call center employees has grown dramatically, turnover rates have risen too. Turnover rates in some Indian firms have jumped to 35% to 45% annually. That is much lower than rates for similar jobs in the United States, but it is "the single biggest issue" in the industry, according to the CEO of one of the Indian call center firms. Companies see their costs go up as they have to invest in ongoing training and recruiting. Also, productivity dips until new people learn their jobs, and customer satisfaction has declined with some Indian call centers.

Companies are taking several actions to retain employees—agreeing not to poach workers from other firms, recruiting from rural areas in India, giving more attention to increasing workers' job satisfaction—much as American call centers have. But turnover is forcing the Indian companies to overstaff in anticipation of more turnover as they are tapping ever deeper into the pool of English speakers. Turnover, or attrition, as it is often referred to, has become an industry issue there just as it has in the United States, the country that popularized call centers.[46]

High turnover is also seen among U.S. expatriates.[47] Also, repatriating those who have been overseas only to return to less than an ideal situation later in the United States is another source of international retention difficulties.[48]

Retention Measurement and Assessment

To ensure that appropriate actions are taken to enhance retention, management decisions require data and analyses rather than subjective impressions, anecdotes of selected individual situations, or panic reactions to the loss of key people.[49] Having several *absence and turnover measurements* to analyze is important. Two other sources of information might be useful before analysis is done: employee surveys and exit interviews.[50]

Exit interview An interview in which individuals are asked to give their reasons for leaving the organization.

Exit Interviews One widely used type of interview is the exit interview, in which individuals are asked to give their reasons for leaving the organization. In one survey of employers, 87% of them claimed to conduct exit interviews, and more than half used the information gathered to make changes to aid retention. A wide range of issues can be examined in exit interviews, as described in the HR On-the-Job feature.[51]

Employee Surveys Employee surveys can be used to diagnose specific problem areas, identify employee needs or preferences, and reveal areas in which HR activities are well received or are viewed negatively. For example, questionnaires may be sent to employees to collect ideas for revising a performance appraisal system or to determine how satisfied employees are with their benefits programs. Regardless of the topic of a survey, obtaining employee input provides managers and HR professionals with data on the "retention climate" in an organization.

HR ON-THE-JOB

Conducting Exit Interviews

Departing employees may be reluctant to divulge their real reasons for leaving. A skilled HR interviewer may be able to gain useful information that departing employees may not wish to share with managers and supervisors.

The following suggestions may be useful when conducting exit interviews:

■ Decide who will conduct the exit interviews and when the discussions will occur. Often, they are done on the last day of a departing individual's employment.

■ Develop a checklist or a set of standard questions so that the information can be summarized. Typical areas covered include reasons for leaving, supervision, pay, training, best- and least-liked aspects of the job, and organization to which the employee is moving.

■ Emphasize that the information provided by departing employees will be treated confidentially and used to make improvements.

■ Regularly summarize the data by reasons for leaving, department, length of service, etc., to provide information for improving company retention efforts.

■ Contact departed employees a month or so after they leave. The "real reasons" for departure may be voiced at that time.

■ Recognize that former employees may be more willing to provide information on questionnaires mailed to their homes or in telephone conversations conducted some time after they have left the organization.

Attitude survey A survey that focuses on employees' feelings and beliefs about their jobs and the organization.

One specific type of survey used by many organizations is an attitude survey, which focuses on employees' feelings and beliefs about their jobs and the organization. By obtaining data on how employees view their jobs, their supervisors, their co-workers, and organizational policies and practices, these surveys can be starting points for reducing turnover and increasing the length of time that employees are retained. Some employers conduct attitude surveys regularly (such as every year) while others do so intermittently. As the use of the Internet has spread, more organizations have begun conducting attitude surveys electronically.[52]

Attitude surveys are developed by consulting firms, academicians, and others. They can also be custom designed to address specific issues and concerns in an organization. Regardless of their type, only surveys that are valid and reliable can measure attitudes accurately. Often a "research" survey developed in-house is poorly structured, asks questions in a confusing manner, or leads employees to respond in ways that will give "favorable" results.

By asking employees to respond candidly to an attitude survey, management is building up employees' expectations that action will be taken on the concerns identified. Therefore, a crucial part of conducting an attitude survey is providing feedback to those who participated in it. It is especially important that even negative survey results be communicated, to avoid fostering the appearance of hiding the results or placing blame.

Retention Management Interventions

The analysis of data mined from turnover and absenteeism records, surveys of employees, and exit interviews is an attempt to get at the cause of retention problems. Analysis should recognize that turnover and absenteeism are symptoms of other factors that may be causing problems.[53] When the causes are treated, the symptoms will go away. Some of the first areas to consider when analyzing data for retention include the work, pay/benefits, supervision, and management systems.

There are numerous actions management might take to deal with retention issues. The choice of a particular action depends on the analysis of the turnover and retention problems in a particular organization and should be custom tailored for that organization. Figure 3-9 shows possible actions.

Retention Evaluation and Follow-Up

Once appropriate management actions have been implemented, it is important that they be evaluated and that appropriate follow-up be conducted and adjustments made. *Regular review of turnover data* can identify when turnover increases or decreases among different employee groups classified by length of service, education, department, and gender, etc.

Tracking of intervention results and *adjustment of intervention efforts* also should be part of evaluation efforts. Some firms may use pilot programs to see how changes affect turnover before extending them to the entire organization. For instance, to test the effect of flextime scheduling on employee turnover, a firm might try flexible scheduling in one department. If the turnover rate in that department drops in comparison with the turnover rates in other departments still working set schedules, then the experimental project may indicate that flexible scheduling can reduce turnover. Next, the firm might extend the use of flexible scheduling to other departments.

FIGURE 3-9   **Possible Retention Interventions**

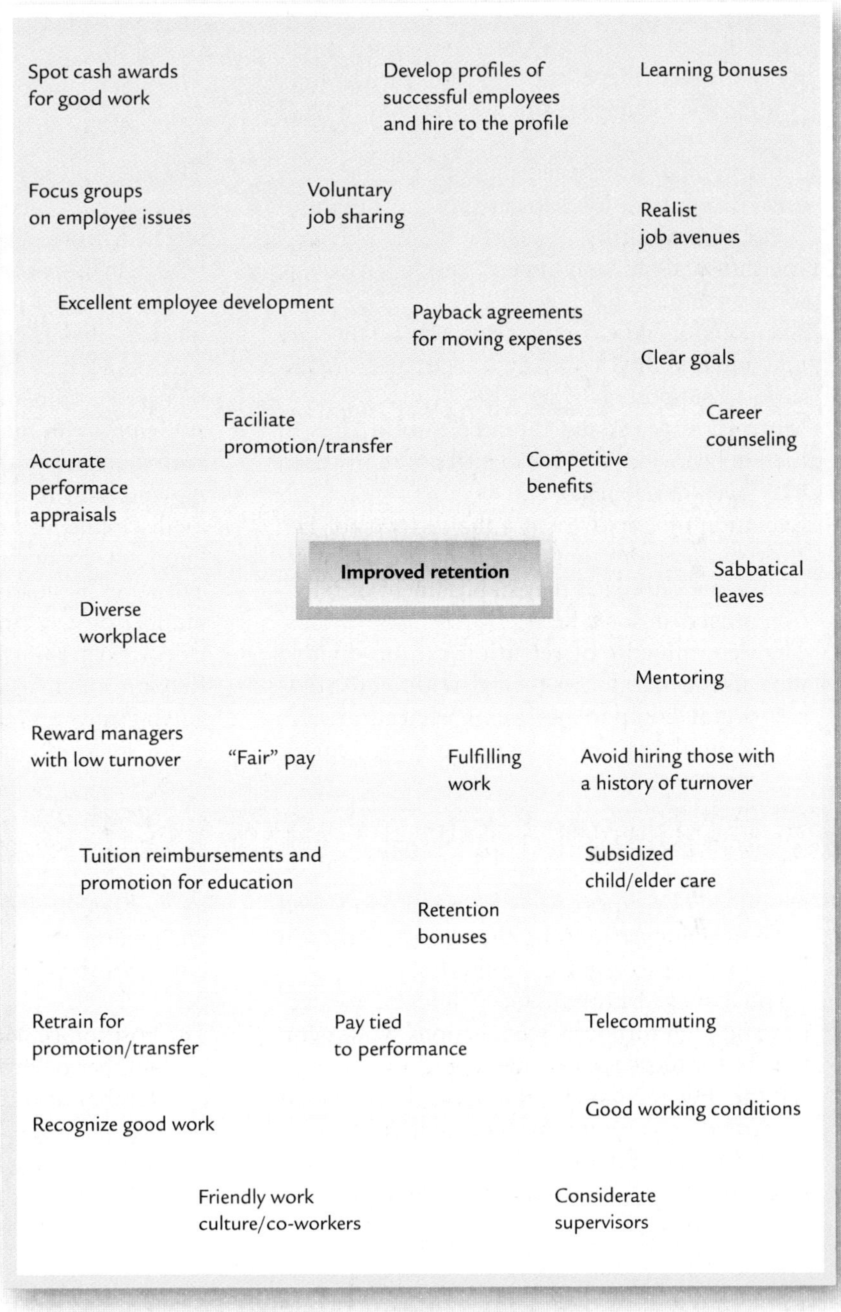

Spot cash awards
for good work

Develop profiles of
successful employees
and hire to the profile

Learning bonuses

Focus groups
on employee issues

Voluntary
job sharing

Realist
job avenues

Excellent employee development

Payback agreements
for moving expenses

Clear goals

Faciliate
promotion/transfer

Accurate
performace
appraisals

Competitive
benefits

Career
counseling

Improved retention

Sabbatical
leaves

Diverse
workplace

Mentoring

Reward managers
with low turnover

"Fair" pay

Fulfilling
work

Avoid hiring those with
a history of turnover

Tuition reimbursements and
promotion for education

Subsidized
child/elder care

Retention
bonuses

Retrain for
promotion/transfer

Pay tied
to performance

Telecommuting

Recognize good work

Good working conditions

Friendly work
culture/co-workers

Considerate
supervisors

SUMMARY

- Psychological contracts are unwritten expectations that employees and employers have about the nature of their work relationships. Those contracts are changing along with employee loyalty to their employers.
- The interaction between individuals and their jobs affects both job satisfaction and organizational commitment.
- Job satisfaction, commitment, and loyalty relate to turnover and absenteeism.
- The components of individual performance are individual ability, effort expended, and organizational support.
- Motivation deals with the needs and desires of human behavior. Various theories of motivation have been developed.
- Retention of employees is a major focus of HR efforts in organizations, as seen by the use of retention measures and the establishment of retention officers in some firms.
- The determinants of retention can be divided into five general categories, with key organizational components being characteristics of the employer, job design and work, career opportunities, rewards, and employee relationships.
- The culture and values of the employer, management performance, and job security are employer characteristics that affect retention.
- The jobs and work done by employees affect retention, particularly if individuals are properly selected, work schedules are flexible, and work/life balancing programs are offered.
- Organizational career opportunities are frequently cited as crucial to employee retention.
- To enhance employee retention, rewards must be relatively competitive and tied to performance, and employees must have effective relationships with managers and co-workers.
- Absenteeism is expensive. It can be controlled by discipline, positive reinforcement, or use of a "no fault" policy and paid-time-off programs.
- Turnover is costly and can be classified in a number of ways, but it should be measured and its costs determined.
- Retention management should be a process involving measurement and assessment, interventions, and evaluation and follow-up.

REVIEW AND APPLICATION QUESTIONS

1. Describe your expectations for a job. How well is your employer meeting the expectations you bring to the psychological contract?
2. If you managed a restaurant with high absenteeism and high turnover, what actions would you take to get those issues under control?
3. As the HR manager, you have been asked to provide the senior management team with turnover costs for the following high-turnover position. Using *www.talentkeepers.com* and *www.keepemployees.com*, calculate turnover and analyze the variables involved. Also identify any other data that might be relevant.

The position is: **Machine Operator**
 Number of employees: 250
 Number of turnovers: 85
 Average wage: $11.50/hour
 Cost of benefits: 35% of payroll

CASE

Alegent Health

Alegent Health, based in Omaha, Nebraska, is a non-profit health-care system composed of seven hospitals with about 2,000 beds and more than 200 clinic and outpatient locations, 1,200 physicians, and more than 7,500 other employees who work throughout the organization. Several years ago, Alegent recognized that HR issues needed "acute care treatment." Turnover rates of 24%, coupled with more than 500 unfilled positions, were costing the firm more than $15 million annually.

Four years later, the turnover rates had declined to 12% and open positions had dropped to fewer than 100. Because of their improvements, Alegent's HR practices, and especially its retention successes, won several local and national awards. Alegent was named one of the "Best Places to Work in Omaha." The award was based on surveys of employees that asked about credibility, respect and fairness, pride, and camaraderie. Alegent also received a *Workforce Management* Optimas Award in the financial impact category for its success at recruiting and retaining key staff. Winning these awards indicates that Alegent is clearly being effective with its HR activities.

Specifically regarding retention efforts, Alegent created an Employee Retention Task Force whose focus was to decrease turnover and increase employee satisfaction. The task force identified several strategies to be used.

One program illustrates how Alegent approached retention of nurses. The Nursing Residence Program has caught national attention. Each resident (or new nurse) is paired with an experienced nurse or "preceptor" based on interests, personality, and so on. Also, a mentor outside the nursing department adds support and encouragement to individuals. Nursing staff meet monthly for training. In addition, they can visit various other departments (pediatrics, cardiology, etc.) in which they may have career interests. Nurses interested in management can shadow the department director to see how the department is managed. Returning nurses who have been out of the field five or more years are enrolled, retrained, and paired with recently finished residents.

Alegent Health is the exception to the turnover levels in nursing. Compared with the U.S. health-care industry rate of 20%, Alegent's turnover rate of 7.6% is exceptionally low. Another key to aiding nursing recruitment and retention is an extensive training and development program. Many different short courses and classes are provided to Alegent employees at no cost. As part of this program, Alegent pays up to $20,000 for employees selected for a career advancement program to obtain nursing degrees.[54]

Questions

1. Discuss how Alegent's practices match with the recommended retention practices covered in the chapter.

2. Why was Alegent's broad-based approach to nursing retention important?

SUPPLEMENTAL CASE

The Clothing Store

This case describes one firm's approach to improving employee retention. (For the case, go to http://thomsonedu.com/management/mathis.)

NOTES

1. Based on Frank Jossi, "Turning Turnover Around," *Human Resources Executive*, October 16, 2004, 28; and Aaron Dalton, "Applebee's Turnover Recipe," *Workforce Management*, May 2005, 1–5.
2. Susan Meisinger, "Workforce Retention: A Growing Concern," *HR Magazine*, April 2006, 12.
3. Denise Rousseau and Zipi Shperling, "Piece of the Action: Owners and the Changing Employment Relationship," *Academy of Management Review*, 28 (2003), 553–570.
4. Lisa Scherer, et al., "Breach and Fulfillment of the Psychological Contract: A Comparison of Traditional and Expanded Views," *Personnel Psychology*, 56 (2003), 895–934.
5. Julia Chang, "Age Defying," *Sales and Marketing Management*, August 2005, 1.
6. "Exploding Generation X Myths," *Journal of Accountancy*, August 2005, 38–40.
7. Charlotte Huff, "Consider Employee Age When Choosing Awards," *Workforce Management*, September 11, 2006, 28.
8. Thomas A. Wright, "To Be or Not to Be Happy: The Role of Employee Well-Being," *Academy of Management Perspective*, 20 (2006), 118–120.
9. Dean B. McFarlin, "Hard Day's Work: A Boon for Performance But a Bane for Satisfaction?" *Academy of Management Perspectives*, November 2006, 115–116.
10. Steve Bates, "Workers' Loyalty to Employers Rising, Survey Finds," *HR News*, November 22, 2005, 1–3.
11. P. A. Siegel et al., "The Moderating Influence of Procedural Fairness on the Relationship Between Work–Life Conflict and Organizational Commitment," *Journal of Applied Psychology*, 90 (2005), 13–24.
12. Gary Latham and C. T. Ernst, "Keys to Motivating Tomorrow's Workforce," *Human Resource Management Review*, June 2006, 181–198.
13. Piers Steel and Cornelius König, "Integrating Theories of Motivation," *Academy of Management Review*, 31 (2006), 889–913.
14. Based on Nanette Byrnes, "The Art of Motivation," *Business Week*, May 1, 2006, 57–62.
15. Jon Hanabides, "Reducing Staff Turnover in Communications Centers," *Emergency Number Professional Magazine*, May 2005, 84–87.
16. Nanette Byrnes, "Star Search," *Business Week*, October 10, 2005, 69–78.
17. Robert Morgan, "Does Your Organization Make the Grade?" *Workspan*, February 2004, 19–20.
18. Ingrid Smithley Fulmer et al., "Are the 100 Best Better?" *Personnel Psychology*, 56 (2003), 965–993.
19. Carol Hymorwitz, "Executives Who Build Truth-Telling Cultures Learn Fast What Works," *The Wall Street Journal*, June 12, 2006, B1.
20. Eric Krell, "Do They Trust You?" *HR Magazine*, June 2006, 58–65.
21. Richard Florida and Jim Goodnight, "Managing for Creativity," *Harvard Business Review*, July/August 2005, 124–131.
22. David Welch, "Getting Out of Dodge," *Business Week*, April 17, 2006, 80–82.
23. Sue Shellenbarger, "Companies Retool Time-Off Policies," *The Wall Street Journal*, January 3, 2006, D1.
24. Patrick J. Kiger, "Throw Out the Rules of Work," *Workforce Management*, September 25, 2006, 16–23.
25. "Live a Little," *Fortune* (Europe), January 23, 2006, 69.
26. Jeffrey H. Greenhaus and G. N. Powell, "When Work and Family Are Allies: A Theory of Work–Family Enrichment," *Academy of Management Review*, 31 (2006), 72–92.
27. F. D. Blau et al., *The Economics of Women, Men, and Work* (Upper Saddle River, NJ: Pearson, 2006), 348–369.
28. "Professional Development Opportunities Key to Retaining Talented Employees," *www.shrm.org/press*.
29. Todd Henneman, "Peer Coaching Helps WFS Financial Curb Turnover," *Workforce Management*, February 2005, 1–6.
30. Based on Cindy Waxes, "Inside Jobs," *Human Resource Executive*, March 2, 2003, 36–37; and "Hyatt Hotels Reduces Turnover with Taleo," *Human Resource Executive*, June 2, 2006, 50.
31. "Study: Link Between Employee Turnover and Retirement Plan Participation Rates," *Newsline*, May 8, 2006, 1.
32. Stephen Miller, "More Than Money Needed to Motivate and Retain Employees," *SHRM Forum*, June 2005, 1.
33. Adrian Gostick, "People Don't Leave Companies, They Leave Managers," *Human Capital*, May/June 2005, 24.
34. Erin White, "Praise from Peers Goes a Long Way," *The Wall Street Journal*, December 19, 2005, B3.
35. "2006 CCH Unscheduled Absence Survey," *CCH Inc.*, October 26, 2006, 1, *www.cch.com/press/news*.
36. Sharon Kaleta and Edward Anderson, "Here Today, Gone Tomorrow," *National Underwriter*, November 3, 2003, 28.
37. Sarah Fister Gale, "The Insider," *Workforce Management*, September 2003, 72.
38. Gordon Steele, "Understanding Absence Management," *Workspan*, August 2006, 57–60.
39. Jeffrey McCracken and Joan Lublin, "Managers See Leaving Ford as a Better Idea," *The Wall Street Journal*, August 28, 2006, B1.
40. David Wessel, "Factory-Worker Shortage Amid Layoffs Isn't Paradoxical, After All," *The Wall Street Journal*, December 1, 2005, A2.
41. Nicole C. Wong, "HP Turns to Churn for Survival," *The Denver Post*, December 25, 2006, 1.
42. Wayne Cascio, *Costing Human Resources*, 4th ed. (Cincinnati: South-Western College Publishing, 2003), 62–70.
43. Ibid., 24–25.
44. K. Michele Kacmar et al., "Sure Everyone Can Be Replaced . . . But at What Cost? Turnover as a Predictor of Unit-Level Performance," *Academy of Management Journal*, 49 (2006), 133–144.
45. "Employee Engagement Depends on HR Effectiveness," *Benefits.com*, May 2006, 1, *www.benefits.com*.
46. John Larkin, "India's Talent Pool Drying Up," *The Wall Street Journal*, January 4, 2006, A9.
47. Riki Takevchi et al., "A Model of Expatriate Withdrawal Related Outcomes," *Human Resource Management Review*, 15 (2005), 119–138.

48. Kathryn Tyler, "Retaining Repatri-
ates," *HR Magazine,* March 2006,
1–4.
49. Leigh Branham, "Why Employee
Retention Fails," *Optimize,* February
2005, 1–2.
50. "America's Fast-Growth Companies Spend Half Their Budget on
Workforce But Few Spend on Employee Retention," *World at Work,*
September 12, 2006, 1–2, *www
.worldatwork.com.*

51. Eilene Zimmerman, "Use of Exit
Interviews Grows, Gets More Sophisticated," *Workforce Management Online,* September 2005, 1–6,
www.workforce.com.
52. K. D. Scott et al., "Employee Opinion Surveys in the Internet Age,"
Worldatwork Journal, Fourth Quarter 2005, 32–42; and Gail Dutton,
"What They're Really Saying,"
Human Resource Executive, June
16, 2006, 48–51.

53. M. R. Barrick and R. D. Zimmerman, "Reducing Voluntary, Avoidable Turnover through Selection,"
Journal of Applied Psychology, 90,
2005, 159–166.
54. Based on Eilene Zimmerman,
"Strong Medicine," *Workforce Management,* March 2004, 40–42.

Staffing the Organization

CHAPTER

4

Legal Framework of Equal Employment

After you have read this chapter, you should be able to:

- Explain four basic EEO concepts.

- Describe key provisions in Title VII of the Civil Rights Acts of 1964 and 1991.

- Indicate important requirements of four other key EEO-related laws.

- Discuss the two general approaches for complying with the 1978 Uniform Guidelines on Employee Selection Procedures.

- Identify typical EEO enforcement and compliance requirements.

HR Headline

Paying for Employment Discrimination

For decades many employers have had to pay significant amounts to resolve EEO charges and lawsuits. But illegal employment discrimination continues to be expensive for employers, whether based on race, sex, age, disability, religion, or other factors. Some recent claims settled include the following[1]:

- Target Corporation paid $95,000 to an employee with multiple sclerosis for refusing to transfer her to a vacant position because of her disability.
- The Stillwater (Minnesota) School District paid $1.12 million to settle age-bias claims for reducing early retirement incentives based on age.
- Verizon Communications settled a pregnancy bias case by paying $48.9 million for denying female employees leaves of absence for pregnancy and newborn care.
- Wal-Mart spent $315,000 to settle race and sexual harassment claims by five women at a Florida store.
- Red Robin restaurant chain paid $150,000 to settle a religious discrimination suit filed by a food server fired for not concealing religious-faith tattoos.

These examples illustrate that employers must constantly be aware of and address worker discrimination issues. As part of HR management, equal employment likely will be a major concern as more employees are added who are covered under various EEO laws and regulations.

Internet Research

Equal Employment Opportunity Commission

For information on the Equal Employment Opportunity Commission's purpose, employment discrimination facts, enforcement statistics, and details on technical assistance programs, link to their site at: http://thomsonedu .com/management/mathis.

Inequality in the treatment of people with different backgrounds has been a concern for years. Some countries have "castes" where individuals in some groups are treated better or worse based on race, ethnicity, religion, or other factors. In the United States, slavery was a major concern until amendments to the U.S. Constitution gave all citizens rights to due process (Fifth Amendment), freedom from slavery (Thirteenth Amendment), and equal protection under the law (Fourteenth Amendment). Despite these protections, discrimination in employment has a long history. Women and men working in similar jobs sometimes have been paid differently; African Americans and Latinos/Hispanics simply have not been considered for some jobs even if they are qualified, or they have been treated differently or terminated unfairly.

The civil rights movement of the late 1950s and 1960s influenced public attitudes toward members of racial minorities and women. That influence ultimately resulted in four decades of legislation designed to level the playing field in employment. Beginning in 1963 with the Equal Pay Act and then the Civil Rights Act of 1964, numerous Title VII provisions, Executive Orders, regulations, and interpretations by courts and administrative agencies continue to affect every part of HR management.

Equal employment opportunity (EEO) The concept that all individuals should have equal treatment in all employment-related actions.

The focus of all these legal items is equal employment opportunity (EEO), the concept that all individuals should have equal treatment in all employment-related actions. Initial concerns primarily addressed discrimination based on race, gender, and religion. But the idea spread to include age, pregnancy, and individuals with disabilities.

The fact that many companies have had to make significant payments for violating EEO laws makes the point that employers *must* be familiar with these laws and ensure that their practices are not illegally discriminatory. For employers operating worldwide, similar laws exist in other countries. This chapter focuses on EEO concepts and the major legal structures that support them. The next chapter will focus on managing for EEO compliance and diversity in the workforce.

NATURE OF EQUAL EMPLOYMENT OPPORTUNITY (EEO)

At the core of equal employment is the concept of discrimination. Objectively, the word *discrimination* simply means "recognizing differences among items or people." For example, employers must discriminate (choose) among applicants for a job on the basis of job requirements and candidates' qualifications. But when discrimination is based on race, gender, or some other factors, it is illegal and employers face problems.

Protected class Individuals within a group identified for protection under equal employment laws and regulations.

Various laws have been passed to protect individuals who share designated characteristics, such as race, age, gender, or disabilities. Those having the designated characteristics are referred to as a protected class, which is composed of individuals who fall within a group identified for protection under equal employment laws and regulations. The following bases for protection have been identified by various federal, state, and/or local laws:

- Race, ethnic origin, color (including multi-race/ethnic backgrounds)
- Sex/gender (including pregnant women and also men in certain situations)
- Age (individuals over age 40)
- Individuals with disabilities (physical or mental)
- Military experience (military status employees and Vietnam-era veterans)

FIGURE 4-1   Illegal Employment Discrimination

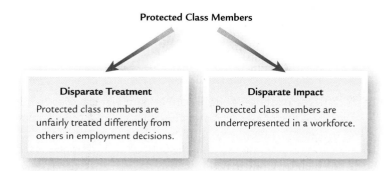

Discrimination in equal employment has been a growing concern as the U.S. workforce becomes more diverse. As Figure 4-1 indicates, there are two types of illegal employment discrimination: disparate treatment and disparate impact.

- Religion (special beliefs and practices)
- Marital status (some states)
- Sexual orientation (some states and cities)

Disparate Treatment

Disparate treatment
Occurs when members of a protected class are treated differently from others.

The first main type of illegal discrimination occurs with employment-related situations in which either: (1) different standards are used to judge different individuals, or (2) the same standard is used, but it is not related to the individuals' jobs. Disparate treatment occurs when members of a protected class are treated differently from others. For example, if female applicants must take a special skills test not given to male applicants, then disparate treatment may be occurring. If disparate treatment has occurred, the courts generally have indicated that intentional discrimination exists.

It would seem that the motives or intentions of the employer might enter into the determination of whether discrimination has occurred—but they do not. The outcome of the employer's actions, not the intent, is considered by the regulatory agencies or courts when deciding whether or not illegal discrimination has occurred. The HR Perspective highlights some emerging disparate treatment factors that employers must consider.

Often disparate treatment cases are based on both direct and circumstantial evidence that an employer's actions were intentionally discriminatory. A manufacturing firm in Cleveland, Ohio, paid almost $1 million to settle an EEO lawsuit involving 20 people, charging that S&Z Tool & Die Company refused to hire African Americans and women except in clerical jobs.[5]

Disparate Impact

Disparate Impact
Occurs when members of a protected class are substantially underrepresented as a result of employment decisions that work to their disadvantage.

The second type of employment discrimination that has been legally supported focuses on the proportion of protected-class members in the workforce of employers. Disparate impact occurs when members of a protected class are substantially underrepresented as a result of employment decisions that work to their disadvantage. The landmark case that established the importance of disparate impact as a legal foundation of EEO law is *Griggs v. Duke*

Hidden or Implicit Bias and Employment Discrimination

A number of different ideas have been researched and used to identify causes of employment discrimination. One of the views is that hidden or implicit bias occurs whereby whites and males, naturally and unconsciously but inevitably, will treat women and racial minorities differently, even if they do not mean to do so.

According to this view, often the males and whites who have significant flexibility in making employment decisions revert to stereotypes. Companies that have faced illegal discrimination charges or have settled complaints based on this concept include FedEx, Wal-Mart, Cargill, and Johnson & Johnson. For example, the large investment firm Morgan Stanley spent over $40 million to settle a sex discrimination case that claimed hidden biases led to illegal employment actions.[2]

Various research has focused on identifying this type of hidden bias because it may lead to illegal employment discrimination.[3] The extent to which these concepts will be accepted by the legal system, regulatory agencies, and courts is uncertain.

To address these concepts and perceptions, employers should develop objective-based systems, establish and enforce non-discrimination policies, and train managers and employees to use job-related factors when making employment decisions.[4]

Power (1971).[6] The decision of the U.S. Supreme Court established two major points:

1. It is not enough to show a lack of discriminatory intent if the employment tool results in a disparate impact that discriminates against one group more than another or continues a past pattern of discrimination.
2. The employer has the burden of proving that an employment requirement is directly job related as a "business necessity." Consequently, the intelligence test and high school diploma requirements of Duke Power were ruled not to be related to the job.

This and a number of other decisions make it clear that employers must be able to document through statistical analyses that disparate treatment and disparate impact have not occurred.[7] How to perform these analyses is discussed later in this chapter.

Equal Employment Opportunity Concepts

Several basic EEO concepts have been applied as a result of court decisions, laws, and regulatory actions. The four key areas discussed next (Figure 4-2) have evolved to clarify how disparate treatment and disparate impact have been interpreted and enforced.

Business necessity Practice necessary for safe and efficient organizational operations.

Business Necessity and Job Relatedness A business necessity is a practice necessary for safe and efficient organizational operations. Business necessity has been the subject of numerous court decisions. Educational requirements often are based on business necessity. However, an employer who requires a minimum level of education, such as a high school diploma, must be able to defend the requirement as essential to the performance of the job. For instance, equating a degree or diploma with the possession of math or reading abilities is considered questionable.

FIGURE 4-2   **EEO Concepts**

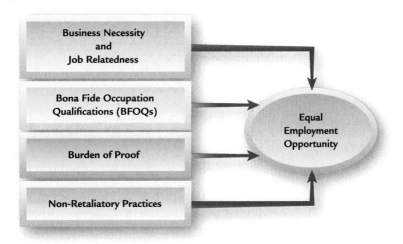

Closely related, employers are expected to use job-related employment practices. The *Washington v. Davis* case involved the hiring of police officers in Washington, D.C. The issue was a reading comprehension and aptitude test given to all applicants for police office positions. The test contained actual material that the applicants would have to learn during a training program. The city could show a relationship between success in the training program and success as a police officer, although a much higher percentage of women and blacks than white men failed this aptitude test.

The Supreme Court ruled that the City of Washington, D.C., did not discriminate unfairly because the test was definitely job related. If a test is clearly related to the job and tasks performed, it is *not illegal* simply because a greater percentage of minorities or women do not pass it. The crucial outcome is that the test must be specifically job related and cannot be judged solely on its disparate impact.[8]

Bona Fide Occupational Qualification (BFOQ) Title VII of the 1964 Civil Rights Act states that employers may discriminate on the basis of sex, religion, or national origin if the characteristic can be justified as a "bona fide occupational qualification reasonably necessary to the normal operation of the particular business or enterprise." Thus, a bona fide occupational qualification (BFOQ) is a characteristic providing a legitimate reason why an employer can exclude persons on otherwise illegal bases of consideration.

What constitutes a BFOQ has been subject to different interpretations in various courts across the United States. Legal uses of BFOQs have been found for hiring Asians to wait on customers in a Chinese restaurant or Catholics to serve in certain religious-based positions in Catholic churches. One case found that under certain circumstances, it is not illegal for a religious institution to discriminate against an employee for "objectionable religious speech." A clerk had been warned three times not to attempt "saving souls" on the premises of a Catholic non-profit clinic. He was fired and he filed a lawsuit. The court held that religious organizations have the right to "define themselves and their religious message" and may fire workers for violating that right.[9] However, other cases involving religious colleges that have terminated transexual employees or homosexuals have been filed and are still under court review in some states.

Bona fide occupational qualification (BFOQ) Characteristic providing a legitimate reason why an employer can exclude persons on otherwise illegal bases of consideration.

Burden of Proof Another legal issue that arises when discrimination is alleged
is the determination of who has the burden of proof, which is what individuals
who file suit against employers must prove in order to establish that illegal
discrimination has occurred. The *McDonnell-Douglas v. Green* case decided
by the U.S. Supreme Court identified how to determine burden of proof.
The case involved the rejection of a qualified African American individual
for employment.[10] The court ruled that a *prima facie* (preliminary) case of
discrimination existed by showing: (1) the person (Green) was a member of a
protected group, (2) the person applied for and was qualified for a job but was
rejected, and (3) the employer (McDonnell-Douglas) continued to seek other
applicants after the rejection occurred. Decisions in numerous other cases have
been built on that case. For example, the U.S. Supreme Court in *Reeves v.
Sanderson Plumbing Products* ruled that circumstantial evidence can shift the
burden of proof to the employer.[11]

Based on the evolution of court decisions, current laws and regulations
state that the plaintiff charging discrimination:

- must be a *protected-class member* and
- must prove that *disparate impact* or *disparate treatment* existed.

Once a court rules that a *prima facie* case has been made, the burden of proof
shifts to the employer. In another case, *Desert Palace v. Costa,*[12] the U.S. Supreme Court emphasized that the plaintiff only has to present enough evidence, both direct and circumstantial, that would be reasonable to show that
protected-class status was a motivating factor for an employment action.[13]
The employer then must show that the bases for making employment-related
decisions were specifically job related and consistent with considerations of
business necessity.

Non-Retaliatory Practices Employers are prohibited by EEO laws from
retaliating against individuals who file discrimination charges. Retaliation
occurs when employers take punitive actions against individuals who exercise
their legal rights. For example, a construction company was ruled to have
engaged in retaliation when an employee who filed a discrimination complaint
had work hours reduced, resulting in a loss of pay, and no other employees'
work hours were reduced.[14]

The importance of employers avoiding retaliation was clarified further in a
U.S. Supreme Court case, *Burlington Northern & Santa Fe Railway v. White.*
The plaintiff employee, Sheila White, was sole female forklift operator at a
Tennessee facility. She filed a sex discrimination charge because she alleged her
supervisor repeatedly made disparaging remarks about women working in her
department. After filing a complaint inside the company, the supervisor was
suspended for 10 days and further disciplined. But White was removed from
forklift duties and assigned to perform only laborer work.

The decision indicated that retaliation claims are valid if workers demonstrate they were victims of reprisals, such as being moved to different work
shifts or jobs, excluded from training, or harassed outside of work.[15] To avoid
retaliation the following actions are recommended for employers[16]:

- Train supervisors on what retaliation is and what is and is not appropriate.
- Conduct a thorough internal investigation and document the results.
- Take appropriate action when any retaliation occurs.
- Review any HR or job-related changes when taking actions involving
  individuals who have filed EEO complaints.

Progressing Toward Equal Employment Opportunity

Equal employment
Employment that is not affected by illegal discrimination.

Blind to differences
Differences among people should be ignored and everyone should be treated equally.

Affirmative action
Employers are urged to hire groups of people based on their race, age, gender, or national origin to make up for historical discrimination.

After 40-plus years equal employment continues to be a significant focus of HR management. One study identified discrimination, harassment, and retaliation lawsuits as the legal actions of most concern to HR professionals.[17] But the number of EEO complaints and lawsuits remains significant, indicating that continuing progress is needed to reduce employment discrimination.

Not everyone agrees on the best way to achieve equal employment opportunity. There seems to be little disagreement that the goal is equal employment, or employment that is not affected by illegal discrimination. However, the way to achieve that goal is open to debate. One way is to use the "blind to differences" approach, which argues that differences among people should be ignored and everyone should be treated equally.[18] The second common approach is affirmative action, through which employers are urged to employ people based on their race, age, gender, or national origin. The idea is to make up for historical discrimination by giving groups who have been affected enhanced opportunities for employment. Affirmative action, covered in more detail in Chapter 5, is an outgrowth of a number of major laws and regulations.

MAJOR EQUAL EMPLOYMENT LAWS

Even if an organization has little regard for the principles of equal employment opportunity, it must follow federal, state, and local EEO laws and some affirmative action regulations to avoid costly penalties. Numerous federal, state, and local laws address equal employment opportunity concerns, as shown in Figure 4-3. An overview of the major laws, regulations, and concepts follows.

Civil Rights Act of 1964, Title VII

Although the first civil rights act was passed in 1866, it was not until passage of the Civil Rights Act of 1964 that the keystone of anti-discrimination employment legislation was put into place. The Equal Employment Opportunity Commission (EEOC) was established to enforce the provisions of Title VII, the portion of the act that deals with employment.

Title VII of the Civil Rights Act states that it is illegal for an employer to:

1. *fail or refuse to hire or discharge any individual, or otherwise discriminate against any individual with respect to his compensation, terms, conditions, or privileges of employment because of such individual's race, color, religion, sex, or national origin, or*
2. *to limit, segregate, or classify his employees or applicants for employment in any way that would deprive or tend to deprive any individual of employment opportunities or otherwise adversely affect his status as an employee because of such individual's race, color, religion, sex, or national origin.*

Title VII Coverage Title VII, as amended by the Equal Employment Opportunity Act of 1972, covers most employers in the United States. Any organization meeting one of the criteria in the following list is subject to

FIGURE 4-3	Major Federal Equal Employment Opportunity Laws and Regulations

Act	Year	Key Provisions
Broad-Based Discrimination		
Title VII, Civil Rights Act of 1964	1964	Prohibits discrimination in employment on basis of race, color, religion, sex, or national origin
Executive Orders 11246 and 11375	1965 1967	Require federal contractors and subcontractors to eliminate employment discrimination and prior discrimination through affirmative action
Executive Order 11478	1969	Prohibits discrimination in the U.S. Postal Service and in the various government agencies on the basis of race, color, religion, sex, national origin, handicap, or age
Vietnam Era Veterans' Readjustment Assistance Act	1974	Prohibits discriminations against Vietnam-era veterans by federal contractors and the U.S. government and requires affirmative action
Civil Rights Act of 1991	1991	Overturns several past Supreme Court decisions and changes damage claims provisions
Congressional Accountability Act	1995	Extends EEO and Civil Rights Act provisions to U.S. congressional staff
Race / National Origin Discrimination		
Immigration Reform and Control Act	1986 1990 1996	Establishes penalties for employers who knowingly hire illegal aliens; prohibits employment discrimination on the basis of national origin or citizenship
Gender / Sex Discrimination		
Equal Pay Act	1963	Requires equal pay for men and women performing substantially the same work
Pregnancy Discrimination Act	1978	Prohibits discrimination against women affected by pregnancy, childbirth, or related medical conditions; requires that they be treated as all other employees for employment-related purposes, including benefits
Age Discrimination		
Age Discrimination in Employment Act (as amended in 1978 and 1986)	1967	Prohibits discrimination against persons over age 40 and restricts mandatory retirement requirements, except where age is a bona fide occupational qualification
Older Workers Benefit Protection Act of 1990	1990	Prohibits age-based discrimination in early retirement and other benefits plans
Disability Discrimination		
Vocational Rehabilitation Act and Rehabilitation Act of 1974	1973 1974	Prohibit employers with federal contracts over $2,500 from discriminating against individuals with disabilities
Americans with Disabilities Act	1990	Requires employer accommodations for individuals with disabilities

rules and regulations that specific government agencies have established to administer the act:

- All private employers of 15 or more persons who are employed 20 or more weeks a year
- All educational institutions, public and private
- State and local governments
- Public and private employment agencies
- Labor unions with 15 or more members
- Joint labor/management committees for apprenticeships and training

Title VII has been the basis for several extensions of EEO law. For example, in 1980, the EEOC interpreted the law to include sexual harassment. Further, a number of concepts identified in Title VII are the foundation for court decisions, regulations, and other laws discussed later in the chapter.

Executive Orders 11246, 11375, and 11478

Changing laws during the last 30 years have forced employers to address additional areas of potential discrimination. Several acts and regulations apply specifically to government contractors. These acts and regulations specify a minimum number of employees and size of government contracts. The requirements primarily come from federal Executive Orders 11246, 11375, and 11478. Many states have similar requirements for firms with state government contracts.

Numerous executive orders require that employers holding federal government contracts not discriminate on the basis of race, color, religion, national origin, or sex. An *Executive Order* is issued by the president of the United States to provide direction to government departments on a specific area. The Office of Federal Contract Compliance Programs (OFCCP) in the U.S. Department of Labor has responsibility for enforcing nondiscrimination in government contracts.

Civil Rights Act of 1991

The Civil Rights Act of 1991 requires employers to show that an employment practice is *job related for the position* and is consistent with *business necessity*. The act clarifies that the plaintiffs bringing the discrimination charges must identify the particular employer practice being challenged and must show only that protected-class status played *some role*. For employers, this requirement means that an individual's race, color, religion, sex, or national origin *must play no role* in their employment practices. It allows people who have been targets of intentional discrimination based on sex, religion, or disability to receive both compensatory and punitive damages. One key provision of the 1991 act relates to how U.S. laws on EEO are applied globally. The HR Perspective highlights some of the issues.

Sex/Gender Discrimination Laws and Regulations

A number of laws and regulations address discrimination based on sex or gender. Historically, women experienced employment discrimination in a variety of ways. The inclusion of sex as a basis for protected-class status in Title VII of the 1964 Civil Rights Act has led to various areas of protection for women.

HR PERSPECTIVE

Global Employees and EEO

Many U.S. firms operating internationally have had to adapt their employment practices to reflect the cultures and customs of the countries in which they operate. The Civil Rights Act of 1991 extended coverage of EEO laws and regulations to U.S. citizens working internationally for U.S.-controlled companies. However, the act states that if laws in a foreign country require actions in conflict with U.S. EEO laws, the foreign laws will apply. If no laws exist, only customs or cultural considerations, then the U.S. EEO laws will apply.

One specific area of global EEO concerns is related to the growing number of women expatriates. Estimates are that over half of all multinational corporations will be increasing the number of women internationally. Consequently, these firms must ensure that

they do not engage in illegal employment discrimination with these female employees, as well as others in protected classes.[19] For example, due to cultural roles of women in certain foreign countries, some women expatriates may not be considered for sales, marketing, or other managerial jobs. Such actions would violate U.S. EEO regulations.

In a related area, some foreign firms, have "reserved" top-level positions for those from the home country. A U.S. Circuit court decision ruled that because of a treaty between Japan and the United States, Japanese subsidiaries can give preference to Japanese over U.S. citizens.[20] However, it should be noted that most of the other EEO regulations and laws apply to foreign-owned firms.

Pregnancy Discrimination The Pregnancy Discrimination Act (PDA) of 1978 requires that any employer with 15 or more employees treat maternity leave the same as other personal or medical leaves. Closely related to the PDA is the Family and Medical Leave Act (FMLA) of 1993, which requires that individuals be given up to 12 weeks of family leave without pay and also requires that those taking family leave be allowed to return to jobs (see Chapter 14 for details). The FMLA applies to both men and women.

Courts have generally ruled that the PDA requires employers to treat pregnant employees the same as non-pregnant employees with similar abilities or inabilities. Therefore, in one case, an employer was ruled to have acted properly when terminating a pregnant employee for excessive absenteeism due to pregnancy-related illnesses, because the employee was not treated differently from other employees with absenteeism problems.[21]

Two other areas somewhat related to pregnancy and motherhood have also been subjects of legal and regulatory action. The EEOC has ruled that denial of health insurance coverage for prescription contraceptives under employer-provided health plans violates the PDA. Also, a number of states have passed laws that guarantee breast-feeding rights at work for new mothers.

Equal Pay and Pay Equity The Equal Pay Act of 1963 requires employers to pay similar wage rates for similar work without regard to gender. A *common core of tasks* must be similar, but tasks performed only intermittently or infrequently do not make jobs different enough to justify significantly different wages. Differences in pay may be allowed because of:

1. Differences in seniority
2. Differences in performance
3. Differences in quality and/or quantity of production
4. Factors other than sex, such as skill, effort, and working conditions

For example, a university was found to have violated the Equal Pay Act by paying a female professor a starting salary lower than salaries paid to male professors with similar responsibilities. In fact, the court found that the woman professor taught larger classes and had more total students than some of the male faculty members.[22]

Ledbetter v. Goodyear Tire and Rubber Co. was a significant U.S. Supreme Court decision on pay discrimination.[23] Ledbetter, a female manager with Goodyear in Alabama, claimed that she was subjected to pay discrimination because she received lower pay during her career back to 1979, even though she did not file suit until 1998.[24] The decision examined this view and stated that the rights of workers to sue for previous years of paid discrimination is limited.

Pay equity is the idea that pay for jobs requiring comparable levels of knowledge, skill, and ability should be similar, even if actual duties differ significantly. This theory has also been called *comparable worth* in earlier cases. Some state laws have mandated pay equity for public-sector employees. However, U.S. federal courts generally have ruled that the existence of pay differences between different jobs held by women and men is not sufficient to prove that illegal discrimination has occurred.

A major reason for the development of the pay equity idea is the continuing gap between the earnings of women and men. For instance, in 1980, the average annual pay of full-time female workers was 60% of that of full-time male workers. By 2006, the reported rate of about 77% showed some progress. More in-depth data and research studies have shown that when differences between the education, experience, and time at work of men and women are considered, women earn about 90% of what comparable male workers earn.[25]

Pay equity Idea that pay for jobs requiring comparable levels of knowledge, skill, and ability should be similar, even if actual duties differ significantly.

Sexual Harassment The Equal Employment Opportunity Commission has issued guidelines designed to curtail sexual harassment. Sexual harassment refers to actions that are sexually directed, are unwanted, and subject the worker to adverse employment conditions or create a hostile work environment. Sexual harassment can occur between a boss and a subordinate, among co-workers, and when non-employees have business contacts with employees.

Sexual harassment Actions that are sexually directed, are unwanted, and subject the worker to adverse employment conditions or create a hostile work environment.

According to EEOC statistics, more than 80% of the sexual harassment charges filed involve harassment of women by men. However, some sexual harassment cases have been filed by men against women managers and supervisors, and for same-sex harassment. An in-depth discussion of prevention and investigation of sexual harassment complaints appears in Chapter 5.

Americans with Disabilities Act (ADA)

The passage of the Americans with Disabilities Act (ADA) in 1990 expanded the scope and impact of laws and regulations on discrimination against individuals with disabilities. The ADA affects employment matters as well as public accessibility for individuals with disabilities and other areas. Organizations with 15 or more employees are covered by the provisions of the ADA, which are enforced by the EEOC, and the act applies to private employers, employment agencies, and labor unions. State government employees are not covered by the ADA, which means that they cannot sue in federal courts for redress and damages. However, they may still bring suits under state laws in state courts.

Internet Research

Americans with Disabilities Act

To access the U.S. Department of Justice's home page on the Americans with Disabilities Act (ADA), link to their site at:

http://thomsonedu.com/management/mathis.

| FIGURE 4-4 | Most Frequent ADA Disabilities Cited |

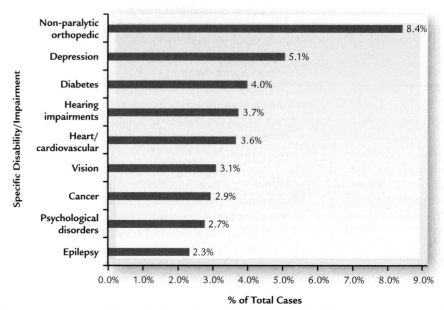

Source: Based on data from U.S. Equal Employment Opportunity Commission, 1992–2005; see www.eeoc.gov for details.

Disabled person Someone who has a physical or mental impairment that substantially limits life activities, who has a record of such an impairment, or who is regarded as having such an impairment.

Who Is Disabled? As defined by the ADA, a disabled person is someone who has a physical or mental impairment that substantially limits that person in some major life activities, who has a record of such an impairment, or who is regarded as having such an impairment. Notice in Figure 4-4 the most frequent disabilities identified in ADA charges. In spite of the EEOC guidelines, some confusion still remains as to who is disabled. Court decisions have found individuals who have high blood pressure, epilepsy, allergies, obesity, color blindness, and hearing impairments to be disabled. However, various court decisions have narrowed the definition of who is disabled.[26]

The Supreme Court has said that the means used to mitigate an individual's physical or mental impairments, such as corrective eyeglasses or controlling medications, must be considered when determining if someone is disabled as defined by the ADA. For example, in a case involving United Parcel Service, the court ruled that an employee who had high blood pressure but was on blood pressure medications was not disabled under the ADA.[27] But it should be noted that a U.S. Supreme Court case found that an employee who had been fired for drug addiction was not entitled to be rehired because his addiction was not a disability. The ADA does not protect current users of illegal drugs and substances, but it does protect those who are recovering addicts.

Mental Disabilities A growing area of concern under the ADA is individuals with mental disabilities. A mental illness is often more difficult to diagnose than a physical disability. Employers must be careful when considering "emotional" or "mental health" factors such as depression in employment-related decisions. They must not stereotype individuals with mental impairments or disabilities but must instead base their evaluations on sound medical information.[28]

Life-Threatening Illnesses In recent years, the types of disabilities covered by various local, state, and federal acts prohibiting discrimination have been expanded. One of the most feared contagious diseases is acquired immunodeficiency syndrome (AIDS). A U.S. Supreme Court decision ruled that individuals infected with human immunodeficiency virus (HIV), not just those with AIDS, have a disability covered by the ADA.[29]

Genetic Bias Regulations Somewhat related to medical disabilities is the emerging area of workplace genetic bias. As medical research has revealed the human genome, medical tests have been developed that can identify an individual's genetic markers for various diseases. Whether these tests should be used and how they are used raise ethical issues.

Employers that use genetic screening tests do so for two primary reasons. Some employers use genetic testing to make workers aware of genetic problems that may exist so that medical treatments can begin. Others use genetic testing to terminate employees who may make extensive use of health insurance benefits and thus raise the benefits costs and utilization rates of the employer. A major railroad company, Burlington Northern Santa Fe, had to publicly apologize to employees for secretly testing to determine if they were genetically predisposed to carpal tunnel syndrome. Several other statutes may potentially provide protection against genetic discrimination.[30]

ADA and Job Requirements The ADA contains a number of specific requirements that deal with employment of individuals with disabilities. Discrimination is prohibited against individuals with disabilities who can perform the essential job functions—the fundamental job duties—of the employment positions that those individuals hold or desire. These functions do not include marginal functions of the position.

For a qualified person with a disability, an employer must make a reasonable accommodation, which is a modification to a job or work environment that gives that individual an equal employment opportunity to perform. EEOC guidelines encourage employers and individuals to work together to determine what are appropriate reasonable accommodations, rather than employers alone making those judgments.

Some cases have considered individuals who have primary care responsibilities for individuals with disabilities to be protected under the ADA. For example, an employee who must take an older relative to kidney dialysis weekly has been seen in some cases as being eligible for reasonable accommodation of work schedules.

Reasonable accommodation is restricted to actions that do not place an undue hardship on an employer. An undue hardship is a significant difficulty or expense imposed on an employer in making an accommodation for individuals with disabilities. The ADA offers only general guidelines in determining when an accommodation becomes unreasonable and places undue hardship on an employer.

ADA Restrictions and Medical Information The ADA contains restrictions on obtaining and retaining medically related information on applicants and employees. Restrictions include prohibiting employers from rejecting individuals because of a disability and from asking job applicants any question about current or past medical history until a conditional job offer is made. Also, the ADA prohibits the use of pre-employment medical exams, except for drug tests, until a job has been conditionally offered. Use of personality tests as employment screening means have been ruled in some court cases to violate the ADA because such tests may eliminate individuals with perceived psychological impairments.[31]

Essential job functions Fundamental job duties.

Reasonable accommodation A modification to a job or work environment that gives a qualified individual an equal employment opportunity to perform.

Undue hardship Significant difficulty or expense imposed on an employer in making an accommodation for individuals with disabilities.

HR BEST PRACTICES

Recruiting and Retaining Older Workers

The health-care industry is facing a growing shortage of workers. Because of this shortage, many hospitals are focusing on recruiting and retaining older workers.

Baptist Health South Florida received a *Workforce Optimas Award* for its efforts with older workers. With 25% of its 10,000 employees over age 50, Baptist sees keeping older employees as crucial for its HR staffing. Baptist changed its pension plan to allow part-time workers to receive retirement benefits but continue working. That way older Baptist employees can work fewer hours, but add retirement benefits in order to maintain their overall income level. A "Bridgement of Service" program also helps Baptist because it allows workers who quit and return to work within five years to renew their seniority and benefits status.

The advantages of creating a positive environment for older workers is evident at Baptist. Workers over age 50 are the most satisfied individuals, according to employee surveys, and the turnover rate for these employees is very low. Other employers in health-care and different industries facing the same workforce challenges may need to expand efforts for attracting and keeping older workers, while also ensuring that age discrimination against older workers does not occur.[33]

An additional requirement of the ADA is that all medical information be maintained in files separated from the general personnel files. The medical files must have identified security procedures, and limited access procedures must be identified.

Age Discrimination in Employment Act (ADEA)

The Age Discrimination in Employment Act (ADEA) of 1967, amended in 1978 and 1986, prohibits discrimination in terms, conditions, or privileges of employment against all individuals age 40 years or older working for employers having 20 or more workers. However, the U.S. Supreme Court has ruled that state employees may not sue state government employers in federal courts because the ADEA is a federal law. The impact of the ADEA is increasing as the U.S. workforce has been aging. Consequently, the number of age discrimination cases has been increasing, according to EEOC reports. However, as the HR Best Practices describes, some employers are viewing older workers as key resources.

A number of countries have passed age discrimination laws. For example, age discrimination regulations in Great Britain focus on preventing age discrimination in recruitment, promotion, training, and retirement-related actions.[32]

Internet Research

Administration on Aging
Information on aging and age discrimination from government agencies, associations, and organizations is available by linking to the Administration on Aging's site at: http://thomsonedu.com/management/mathis.

Disparate Impact and ADEA A U.S. Supreme Court ruling in the *Smith v. Jackson* case stated that employees could use disparate impact as a basis for suing. In this case, the city of Jackson, Mississippi, gave higher percentage pay raises to police officers with five years or less service in order to attract and retain younger employees. Older officers claimed that they were being discriminated against because of age. However, the court also ruled that employers are not liable if the disparate impact was due to non-age factors such as seniority and jobs.[34] Thus the phrase, "reasonable factors other than age" (RFOA), has become a part of ADEA legal terminology.[35]

This ruling and others indicate that the act does not apply if age is a job-related occupational qualification. Age discrimination does not apply when an individual is disciplined or discharged for good cause, such as poor job performance. But targeting older workers for replacement is illegal.

However, employers that focus on recruiting or providing "preferential treatment" of older workers do not violate the ADEA. The Supreme Court ruled that, although older workers can sue if they are not treated the same as younger workers, the reverse is *not* true. Two hundred General Dynamics employees had sued because they were too young to get benefits offered to co-workers age 50 and over. The workers (who were all in their 40s) argued for reverse discrimination and lost their case.[36]

Older Workers Benefit Protection Act (OWBPA) This law is an amendment to the ADEA and is aimed at protecting employees when they sign liability waivers for age discrimination in exchange for severance packages. To comply with the act, employees must be given complete accurate information on the available benefits. For example, an early retirement package that includes a waiver stating the employee will not sue for age discrimination if he or she takes the money for early retirement must[37]:

- Include a written, clearly understood agreement.
- Offer value beyond what the employee will receive without the package.
- Advise the employee to consult an attorney.
- Allow the employee at least 21 days to consider the offer.
- Allow the employee 7 days to revoke the agreement after signing it.

The impact of the OWBPA is becoming more evident. Industries such as manufacturing and others offer early retirement buy-outs to cut their workforces. For instance, Ford and General Motors have offered large buyouts of which thousands of workers have taken advantage.

OTHER EMPLOYMENT DISCRIMINATION LAWS AND REGULATIONS

Several types of employment circumstances have resulted in passage of a variety of anti-discrimination and other laws and regulations. Some of the key ones deal with immigration, religion, military service, and other issues.

Immigration Reform and Control Acts (IRCA)

The United States has always had a significant number of immigrants who come to work in this country. The increasing number of immigrants who have entered illegally has led to extensive political, social, and employment-related debates. The existence of more foreign-born workers means that employers must comply with the provisions of the Immigration Reform and Control Acts (IRCA). Employers are required to obtain and inspect I-9 forms, and verify documents such as birth certificates, passports, visas, and work permits. They can be fined if they knowingly hire illegal aliens.

Visas and Documentation Requirements Various revisions to the IRCA changed some of the restrictions on the entry of immigrants to work in U.S. organizations, particularly organizations with high-technology and other "scarce skill" areas. More immigrants with specific skills have been allowed legal entry, and categories for entry visas were revised.

Visas are granted by U.S. consular officers (there are more than 200 such officers throughout the world). Many different types of visas exist. Among those most commonly encountered by employers are the B1 for business visitors, H-1B for professional or specialized workers, and L-1 for intracompany transfers.

Usually an employer must sponsor the workers. Companies are not supposed to hire employees to displace U.S. workers, and they must file documents with the Labor Department and pay prevailing U.S. wages to the visa holders. Despite these regulations, a number of unions and other entities view such programs as being used to circumvent the limits put on hiring foreign workers to displace U.S. workers. Given the volatile nature of this area, changes in federal, state, and local laws are likely to continue to be discussed, implemented, and reviewed in court decisions.

Religious Discrimination

Title VII of the Civil Rights Act identifies discrimination on the basis of religion as illegal. The increasing religious diversity in the workforce has put greater emphasis on religious considerations in work places. However, religious schools and institutions can use religion as a bona fide occupational qualification for employment practices on a limited scale. Also, the employers must make *reasonable accommodation* efforts regarding an employee's religious beliefs.

A major guide in this area was established by the U.S. Supreme Court in *TWA v. Hardison*. In this case, the Supreme Court ruled that an employer is required to make reasonable accommodation for an employee's religious beliefs. Because TWA had done so, the ruling denied the plaintiff's discrimination charges.[38]

Since the September 11, 2001, terrorist attacks, increased discrimination complaints have been filed by Muslims because of treatment or insults made by co-workers and managers. In a recent case, Alamo Rent-A-Car refused to allow a female Muslim customer service representative to wear a religious head scarf when assisting customers. Despite her offer to wear a head scarf with an Alamo logo, that offer was refused and she was terminated. A court decision ruled that Alamo had not made reasonable accommodation for the employee.[39]

Cases also have addressed the issues of beards, mustaches, and hair length and style. African American men, who are more likely than white men to suffer from a skin disease that is worsened by shaving, have filed suits challenging policies prohibiting beards or long sideburns. Generally, courts have ruled for employers in such cases, except where certain religious standards expect men to have beards and facial hair.

An EEOC religious discrimination complaint was filed by a Rastafarian male who was denied a job at UPS as a driver helper because of his beard. UPS disputed his claims and cited company guidelines that prohibit beards and goatees for employees who have public contact. The final decision is in court at present.[40]

Military Status and USERRA

The employment rights of military veterans and reservists have been addressed in several laws. The two most important laws are the Vietnam Era Veterans Readjustment Assistance Act of 1974 and the Uniformed Services Employment and Reemployment Rights Act (USERRA) of 1994. Under the latter, employees

FIGURE 4-5   Uniformed Services Employment and Reemployment Rights Act (USERRA) Provisions

Common Issues
- Leaves of absence
- Return to employment rights
- Prompt re-employment on return
- Protection from discharge/retaliation
- Health insurance continuation
- Continued seniority rights

Internet Research

Uniformed Services Employment and Reemployment Rights Act
To access the U.S. Department of Labor's home page on the Uniformed Services Employment and Reemployment Rights Act (USERRA), link to their site at: http://thomsonedu.com/management/mathis.

are required to notify their employers of military service obligations. Employers must give employees serving in the military leaves of absence protections under the USERRA, as Figure 4-5 highlights.

With the increasing use of reserves and National Guard troops abroad, the provisions of USERRA have had more impact on employers. This act does not require employers to pay employees while they are on military leave, but many firms provide some compensation, often a differential. Many requirements regarding benefits, disabilities, and re-employment are covered in the act as well.[41]

Other Discrimination Issues

A number of other employment issues must be addressed by employers when considering discriminatory concerns. Some common ones are highlighted next.

Sexual Orientation Recent battles in a number of states and communities illustrate the depth of emotions that accompany discussions of "gay rights." Some states and cities have passed laws prohibiting discrimination based on sexual orientation or lifestyle. Even the issue of benefits coverage for "domestic partners," whether heterosexual or homosexual, has been the subject of state and city legislation. No federal laws of a similar nature have been passed. Whether gays and lesbians have any special rights under the equal protection amendment to the U.S. Constitution has not been decided by the U.S. Supreme Court.

A related issue is dealing with transgender individuals who have had sex-change surgery. Court cases and the EEOC have ruled that sex discrimination under Title VII applies to a person's gender at birth. Thus, it does not apply to the new gender of those who have had gender-altering operations. Transvestites and individuals with sexual behavior disorders are specifically excluded from being considered as disabled under the Americans with Disabilities Act of 1990. However, eight states and several cities have laws prohibiting bias against transgender persons.

Appearance and Weight Discrimination Several EEO cases have been filed concerning the physical appearance of employees. Court decisions consistently have allowed employers to set dress codes as long as they are applied uniformly. For example, establishing a dress code for women but not for men has been ruled discriminatory. Also, employers should be cautious when enforcing dress standards for women employees who are members of certain religions that prescribe appropriate and inappropriate dress and appearance standards. Some individuals have brought cases of employment discrimination based on height or weight. The crucial factor that employers must consider is that any weight or height requirements must be related to the job, such as when excess weight would hamper an individual's job performance.[42]

Seniority and Discrimination Conflicts between EEO regulations and organizational practices giving preference to employees on the basis of seniority represent another area of regulation. Employers, especially those with union contracts, frequently make layoff, promotion, and internal transfer decisions by giving employees with longer service first consideration. However, the use of seniority often results in disparate impact on protected-class members, who may be the workers most recently hired. The result of this system is that protected-class members who have obtained jobs through an affirmative action program are at a disadvantage because of their low levels of seniority. They may find themselves "last hired, first fired" or "last hired, last promoted." In most cases, the courts have held that a valid seniority system does not violate rights based on protected-class status. However, in a few cases, gender, racial, disability, or age considerations have been given precedence over seniority.

Conviction and Arrest Records Court decisions have consistently ruled that using records of arrests, rather than records of convictions, has a disparate impact on some racial and ethnic minority groups protected by Title VII. An arrest, unlike a conviction, does not show guilt. Statistics indicate that in some geographic areas, the arrest rates are higher for members of some minority groups than for others, creating possible disparate impact.

Generally, courts have held that conviction records may be used in determining employability if the offense is job related. For example, a bank could use an applicant's conviction for embezzlement as a valid basis for rejection. Some courts have held that only job-related convictions occurring within the most recent five to seven years may be considered. Consequently, employers inquiring about convictions often add a phrase such as "indication of a conviction will not be an absolute bar to employment."

Pre-Employment Inquiries

Given all of the previous protected-class groups, many EEO complaints arise because of inappropriate pre-employment inquiries. Questions asked of applicants may be viewed as discriminatory or biased against protected-class applicants.

Figure 4-6 identifies pre-employment inquiries that may or may not be discriminatory. The pre-employment inquiries labeled "may be discriminatory" have been so designated because of findings in a variety of court cases. Those labeled "may not be discriminatory" are legal, but only if they reflect a business necessity or are job related. Once an employer tells an applicant he or she is hired (the "point of hire"), inquiries that were prohibited earlier may be made. After hiring, medical examination forms, group insurance cards, and other enrollment cards containing inquiries related directly or indirectly to sex, age, or other bases may be requested.

FIGURE 4-6	Guidelines to Lawful and Unlawful Pre-Employment Inquiries

Subject of Inquiry	It May Not Be Discriminatory to Inquire About. . .	It May Be Discriminatory to Inquire About. . .
1. Name	a. Whether applicant has ever worked under a different name	a. The original name of applicant whose name has been legally changed b. The ethnic association of applicant's name
2. Age	a. If applicant is over the age of 18 b. If applicant is under the age of 18 or 21 if that information is job related (e.g., for selling liquor in a retail store)	a. Date of birth b. Date of high school graduation
3. Residence	a. Applicant's place of residence b. Alternative contact information	a. Previous addresses b. Birthplace of applicant or applicant's parents c. Length lived at current and previous addresses
4. Race or Color		a. Applicant's race or color of applicant's skin
5. National Origin and Ancestry		a. Applicant's lineage, ancestry, national origin, parentage, or nationality b. Nationality of applicant's parents or spouse
6. Sex and Family Composition		a. Sex of applicant b. Marital status of applicant c. Dependents of applicants or child-care arrangements d. Whom to contact in case of emergency
7. Creed or Religion		a. Applicant's religious affiliation b. Applicant's church, parish, mosque, or synagogue c. Holidays observed by applicant
8. Citizenship	a. Whether the applicant is a U.S. citizen or has a current permit/visa to work in U.S.	a. Whether applicant is a citizen of a country other than the U.S. b. Date of citizenship
9. Language	a. Language applicant speaks and/or writes fluently, if job related	a. Applicant's native tongue b. Language used at home

(Continued on next page.)

FIGURE 4-6   Guidelines to Lawful and Unlawful Pre-Employment Inquiries

Subject of Inquiry	It May Not Be Discriminatory to Inquire About. . .	It May Be Discriminatory to Inquire About. . .
10. References	a. Names of persons willing to provide professional and/or character references for applicant b. Previous work contacts	a. Name of applicant's religious leader b. Political affiliation and contacts
11. Relatives	a. Names of relatives already employed by the employer	a. Name and/or address of any relative of applicant b. Whom to contact in case of emergency
12. Organizations	a. Applicant's membership in any professional, service, or trade organization	a. All clubs or social organizations to which applicant belongs
13. Arrest Record and Convictions	a. Convictions, if related to job performance (disclaimer should accompany)	a. Number and kinds of arrests b. Convictions, unless related to job requirements and performance
14. Photographs		a. Photographs with application, with résumé, or before hiring
15. Height and Weight		a. Any inquiry into height and weight of applicant, except where a BFOQ exists
16. Physical Limitations	a. Whether applicant has the ability to perform job-related functions with or without accommodation	a. The nature or severity of an illness or physical condition b. Whether applicant has ever filed a workers' compensation claim c. Any recent or past operations, treatments, or surgeries and dates
17. Education	a. Training applicant has received, if related to the job b. Highest level of education applicant has attained, if validated that having certain educational background (e.g., high school diploma or college degree) is needed to perform the specific job	a. Date of high school graduation
18. Military	a. Branch of the military applicant served in and ranks attained b. Type of education or training received in military	a. Military discharge details b. Military service records
19. Financial Status		a. Applicant's debts or assets b. Garnishments

UNIFORM GUIDELINES ON EMPLOYEE SELECTION PROCEDURES

Internet Research

Office of Personnel Management
This office provides advice and assistance to federal agencies regarding non-discriminatory practices. Visit their site at:
http://thomsonedu.com/management/mathis.

The 1978 Uniform Guidelines on Employee Selection Procedures are used by the U.S. EEOC, the U.S. Department of Labor's OFCCP, the U.S. Department of Justice, and the U.S. Office of Personnel Management. These guidelines attempt to explain how an employer should deal with hiring, retention, promotion, transfer, demotion, dismissal, and referral. Under the uniform guidelines, if sued, employers can choose one of two routes to prove they are not illegally discriminating against employees: no disparate impact and job-related validity.

"No Disparate Impact" Approach

Generally, the most important issue regarding discrimination in organizations is the *effect* of employment policies and procedures, regardless of the *intent* of the employer. *Disparate impact* occurs when protected-class members are substantially underrepresented in employment decisions. Under the guidelines, disparate impact is determined with the 4/5ths rule. If the selection rate for a protected group is less than 80% (4/5ths) of the selection rate for the majority group or less than 80% of the majority group's representation in the relevant labor market, discrimination exists. Thus, the guidelines have attempted to define discrimination in statistical terms. The use of the statistical means has been researched and some methodological issues have been identified.[43] However, the guidelines have continued to be used because disparate impact is checked by employers both internally and externally.

4/5ths rule Discrimination exists if the selection rate for a protected group is less than 80% (4/5ths) of the selection rate for the majority group or less than 80% of the majority group's representation in the relevant labor market.

Internal Metrics for Disparate Impact Internal disparate impact compares the results of employer actions received by protected-class members with those received by non-protected–class members inside the organization. HR activities that can be checked most frequently for internal disparate impact include the following:

- Selection of candidates for interviews from those recruited
- Pass rates for various selection tests
- Performance appraisal ratings as they affect pay increases
- Promotions, demotions, and terminations
- Identification of individuals for layoffs

Figure 4-7 calculates the internal disparate impact for men and women who were interviewed for jobs at a firm. In this case, the figure indicates that the selection process does have a disparate impact internally. The practical meaning of these calculations is that statistically, women have less chance of being selected for jobs than men do. Thus, illegal discrimination may exist unless the firm can demonstrate that its selection activities are specifically job related.

External Metrics for Disparate Impact Employers can check for disparate impact externally by comparing the percentage of protected-class members in their workforces with the percentage of protected-class members in the relevant labor markets. The relevant labor markets consist of the areas where the firm recruits workers, not just where those employed live. External comparisons can also consider the percentage of protected-class members who are recruited and who apply for jobs to ensure that the employer has drawn a "representative sample" from the relevant labor markets. Although employers are not required

FIGURE 4-7   **Internal Disparate Impact Example**

Female applicants: 25% were selected for jobs
Male applicants: 45% were selected for jobs

<u>Disparate Impact Determination (4/5 = 80%)</u>

♦ Male selection rate of 45% × (80%) = 36%
♦ Female selection rate = 25%

Disparate impact exists because the female selection rate is less than 4/5 of the male selection rate.

to maintain exact proportionate equality, they must be "close." Courts have applied statistical analyses to determine if any disparities that exist are too high.

Figure 4-8 illustrates external disparate impact using impact analyses for a sample metropolitan area, Valleyville. Assume that a firm in that area, Acme Company, has 500 employees, including 50 African Americans and 75 Hispanics. To determine if the company has external disparate impact, it is possible to make the following comparisons:

Protected Class	% of Total Employees at Acme Company	4/5ths of Group in the Population (from Figure 4-8)	Disparate Impact?
African American	10% (50/500)	13.6%	Yes (10% <13.6%)
Latino/Hispanic	15% (75/500)	14.4%	No (15% >14.4%)

At Acme, external disparate impact exists for African Americans because the company employs fewer of them than the 4/5 threshold of 13.6%. How-

FIGURE 4-8   **Racial Distribution in Valleyville (Example)**

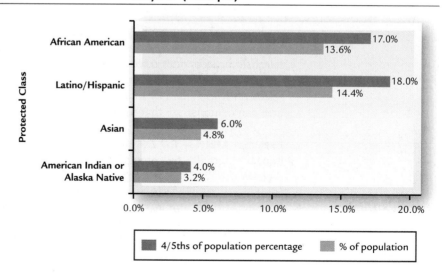

ever, because Acme has more Latino/Hispanic employees than the 4/5 threshold of 14.4%, there is no disparate impact for this group.

Statistical comparisons for determining disparate impact may use more complex methods.[44] HR professionals need to know how to do such calculations because external disparate impact must be computed and reported in affirmative action plans that government contractors submit to regulatory agencies.

Job-Related Validation Approach

Under the job-related validation approach, virtually every factor used to make employment-related decisions is considered an employment "test." Such activities as recruiting, selection, promotion, termination, discipline, and performance appraisal all must be shown to be job related. Hence, two basic concepts affect many of the common means used to make HR decisions. Validity and reliability are discussed further in Chapter 8.

Employment "test" Any employment factor used as the basis for making an employment-related decision.

Validity and Reliability The first concept is validity, which is simply the extent to which a test actually measures what it says it measures. The concept relates to inferences made from tests. For instance, it may be valid to assume that performance on a mechanical knowledge test may predict performance of a machinist in a manufacturing plant. However, it is probably not valid to assume that the same test scores indicate general intelligence or promotability for a manufacturing sales representative. For instance, for a general intelligence test to be valid, it must actually measure intelligence, not just a person's vocabulary.

Validity Extent to which a test actually measures what it says it measures.

Therefore, an employment test that is valid must measure the person's ability to perform the job for which she or he is being hired. For example, R. R. Donnelly & Sons of Lancaster, Pennsylvania, reached agreement with the OFCCP to pay $610,000 to protected-class applicants for unintentionally discriminating against them. The OFCCP found that Donnelly limited minority hires by requiring a high school diploma or its equivalent for certain jobs without being able to show that a high school education made a valid difference between good and poor employee performance. In this case, the diploma was considered a "test."[45]

Ideally, employment-related tests will be both valid and reliable. Reliability refers to the consistency with which a test measures an item. For a test to be reliable, an individual's score should be about the same every time the individual takes the test (allowing for the effects of practice). Unless a test measures a factor consistently (reliably), it is of little value in predicting job performance.

Reliability Consistency with which a test measures an item.

Validity and Equal Employment

If a charge of discrimination is brought against an employer on the basis of disparate impact, a *prima facie* case must be established. The employer then must be able to demonstrate that its employment procedures are valid and job related. A key element in establishing job relatedness is conducting a *job analysis* to identify the *knowledge, skills, and abilities (KSAs)* and other characteristics needed to perform a job satisfactorily. In one sense, then, current requirements have done management a favor by forcing employers to use job-related employment procedures.

There are two categories of validity in which employment tests attempt to predict how well an individual will perform on the job. In measuring

Criterion-related validity Validity measured by a procedure that uses a test as the predictor of how well an individual will perform on the job.

Content validity Validity measured by a logical, non-statistical method to identify the KSAs and other characteristics necessary to perform a job.

criterion-related validity, a test is the *predictor,* and the measures for job performance are the *criterion variables.* Job analysis determines as exactly as possible what KSAs and behaviors are needed for each task in the job. Two types of criterion-related validity are *predictive validity* and *concurrent validity,* both of which are discussed in more detail in Chapter 8 on selection means such as interviews and tests.

Content validity is validity measured by a logical, non-statistical method to identify the KSAs and other characteristics necessary to perform a job. Then managers, supervisors, and HR specialists must identify the most important KSAs needed for the job. Finally, a "test" is devised to determine if individuals have the necessary KSAs. The test may be an interview question about previous supervisory experience, or an ability test in which someone types a letter using a word-processing software program, or a knowledge test about consumer credit regulations.

A test has content validity if it reflects an actual sample of the work done on the job in question. For example, an arithmetic test for a retail cashier might contain problems about determining amounts for refunds, purchases, and merchandise exchanges. Content validity is especially useful if the workforce is not large enough to allow other, more statistical approaches.

Many practitioners and specialists see content validity as a commonsense standard for validating staffing and other employment dimensions, and as more realistic than other means. Research and court decisions have shown that content validity is consistent with the Uniform Guidelines also.[46] Consequently, content validity approaches are growing in use.

EEO ENFORCEMENT

Enforcement of EEO laws and regulations in the United States must be seen as a work in progress that is inconsistent and confusing at times. The court system is left to resolve the disputes and interpret the laws. Often the lower courts have issued conflicting rulings and interpretations. The ultimate interpretation often has rested on decisions by the U.S. Supreme Court, although those rulings also have been interpreted differently.

EEO Enforcement Agencies

Government agencies at several levels can investigate illegal discriminatory practices. At the federal level, the two most prominent agencies are the Equal Employment Opportunity Commission and the Office of Federal Contract Compliance Programs.

Equal Employment Opportunity Commission (EEOC) The EEOC has enforcement authority for charges brought under a number of federal laws. Further, the EEOC issues policy guidances on many topics influencing EEO. Although the policy statements are not "law," they are "persuasive authority" in most cases.

Internet Research

Office of Federal Contract Compliance Programs
To access the Department of Labor's Office of Federal Contract Compliance Programs (OFCCP) site within the Employment Standards Administration, link to:
http://thomsonedu.com/management/mathis.

Office of Federal Contract Compliance Programs (OFCCP) While the EEOC is an independent agency, the OFCCP is part of the U.S. Department of Labor and ensures that federal contractors and subcontractors use non-discriminatory practices. A major thrust of OFCCP efforts is to require that covered employers take affirmative action to counter prior discriminatory practices.

State and Local Agencies In addition to federal laws and orders, many states and municipalities have passed their own laws prohibiting discrimination on a variety of bases, and state and local enforcement bodies have been established. Compared with federal laws, state and local laws sometimes provide greater remedies, require different actions, or prohibit discrimination in more areas.

EEO Compliance

Employers must comply with a variety of EEO regulations and guidelines. To do so, it is crucial that all employers have a written EEO policy statement. They should widely communicate this policy by posting it on bulletin boards, printing it in employee handbooks, reproducing it in organizational newsletters, and reinforcing it in training programs. The contents of the policy should clearly state the organizational commitment to equal employment and incorporate a listing of the appropriate protected classes.

Additionally, employers with 15 or more employees may be required to keep certain records that can be requested by the Equal Employment Opportunity Commission, the Office of Federal Contract Compliance Programs, or numerous other state and local enforcement agencies. Under various laws, employers are also required to post an "officially approved notice" in a prominent place for employees. This notice states that the employer is an equal opportunity employer and does not discriminate.

EEO Records Retention All employment records must be maintained as required by the EEOC. Such records include application forms and documents concerning hiring, promotion, demotion, transfer, layoff, termination, rates of pay or other terms of compensation, and selection for training and apprenticeship. Even application forms or test papers completed by unsuccessful applicants may be requested. The length of time documents must be kept varies, but generally *three years is recommended as a minimum*. Complete records are necessary to enable an employer to respond should a charge of discrimination be made.

EEOC Reporting Forms Many private-sector employers must file a basic report annually with the EEOC. Slightly different reports must be filed biennially by state/local governments, local unions, and school districts. The following private-sector employers must file the EEO-1 report annually:

- All employers with 100 or more employees, except state and local governments
- Subsidiaries of other companies if the total number of all combined employees equals 100 or more
- Federal contractors with at least 50 employees and contracts of $50,000 or more
- Financial institutions with at least 50 employees, in which government funds are held or saving bonds are issued

In 2007, changes were made in the EEO-1 data collected.[47] Details on employees must be reported by gender, race/ethnic group, and job levels. The most significant change was adding the phrase "two or more races," in order to reflect the multi-diverse nature of a growing number of employees.[48]

Applicant-Flow Data Under EEO laws and regulations, employers may be required to show that they do not discriminate in the recruiting and selection of members of protected classes. Because employers are not allowed to collect such data on application blanks and other pre-employment records, the EEOC allows them to do so with a separate *applicant-flow form* that is not used in the selection process. The applicant-flow form is filled out voluntarily by the applicant, and the data must be maintained separately from other selection-related materials. With many applications being made via the Internet, employers must collect this data electronically to comply with regulations on who is an applicant. Analyses of the data collected in applicant-flow forms may help show whether an employer has underutilized a protected class because of an inadequate flow of applicants from that class, in spite of special efforts to recruit them. Also, these data are reported as part of affirmative action plans that are filed with the OFCCP.

EEOC Compliance Investigation Process

When a discrimination complaint is received by an employer, it must be processed whether it is made internally by a disgruntled employee or by an outside agency. Figure 4-9 shows the steps required in an employer's response to an EEO complaint.

Notice that the employer should have a formal complaint process in place and should be sure that no retaliatory action occurs. Internal investigations can be conducted by HR staff, but they often utilize outside legal counsel to provide expert guidance in dealing with agency investigations. Internal investigations should occur also when employees make complaints without filing them with outside agencies. Once the employer's investigation is completed, then the decision must be made within to negotiate and settle the complaint or oppose the complaint.

EEOC Complaint Process To handle a growing number of complaints, the EEOC and other agencies have instituted a system that puts complaints into three categories: *priority, needing further investigation,* and *immediate dismissal.* If the EEOC decides to pursue a complaint, it uses the process outlined here, and an employer must determine how to handle it.[49]

In a typical situation, an EEO complaint goes through several stages before the compliance process is completed. First the charges are filed by an individual, a group of individuals, or a representative. A charge must be filed within 180 days of the alleged discriminatory action. Then the EEOC staff reviews the specifics of the charges to determine if it has *jurisdiction,* which means that the agency is authorized to investigate that type of charge.[50] If the EEOC has jurisdiction, it must serve a notice of the charge on the employer within 10 days of the filing; then the employer is asked to respond. Following the charge notification, the major effort of the EEOC turns to investigating the complaint.

During the investigation, the EEOC may interview the complainants, other employees, company managers, and supervisors. Also, it can request additional records and documents from the employer. If sufficient cause is found to support charges that the alleged discrimination occurred, the next stage involves mediation efforts by the agency and the employer. Mediation is a dispute resolution process in which a third party helps negotiators reach a settlement. The EEOC has found that use of mediation has reduced its backlog of EEO complaints and has resulted in faster resolution of complaints.

Mediation Dispute resolution process in which a third party helps negotiators reach a settlement.

| FIGURE 4-9 | Stages in the Employer's Response to an EEO Complaint |

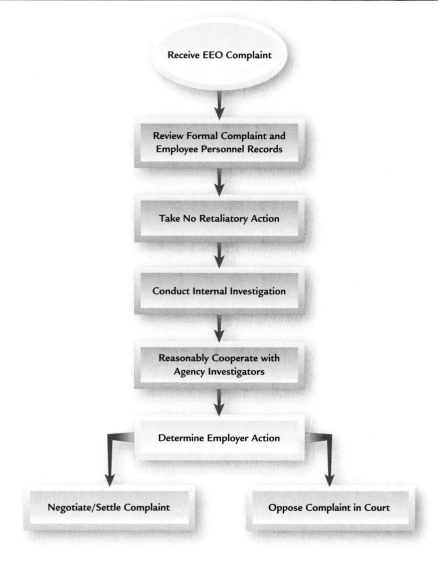

If the employer agrees that discrimination has occurred and accepts the proposed settlement, then the employer posts a notice of relief within the company and takes the agreed-on actions. If the employer objects to the charge and rejects conciliation, the EEOC can file suit or issue a *right-to-sue letter* to the complainant. The letter notifies the complainant that he or she has 90 days to file a personal suit in federal court.

In the court litigation stage, a legal trial takes place in the appropriate state or federal court. At that point, both sides retain lawyers and rely on the court to render a decision. The Civil Rights Act of 1991 provides for jury trials in most EEO cases. If either party disagrees with the court ruling, either can file appeals with a higher court. The U.S. Supreme Court becomes the ultimate adjudication body.

SUMMARY

- Equal employment is an attempt to level the field of opportunity for all people at work.
- Disparate treatment occurs when members of a protected class are treated differently from others, regardless of discriminatory intent.
- Disparate impact occurs when employment decisions work to the disadvantage of members of protected classes, regardless of discriminatory intent.
- Employers may be able to defend their management practices using business necessity, job relatedness, and bona fide occupational qualifications (BFOQ).
- Employers have the burden of proof once a *prima facie* case of discrimination has been shown, and they should take care to avoid retaliation against individuals who exercise their rights.
- Title VII of the 1964 Civil Rights Act was the first significant equal employment law. The Civil Rights Act of 1991 both altered and expanded on the 1964 provisions.
- Several laws on sex/gender discrimination have addressed issues regarding pregnancy discrimination, unequal pay for similar jobs, and sexual harassment.
- The Americans with Disabilities Act (ADA) requires that most employers identify the essential functions of jobs and that they make reasonable accommodation for individuals with disabilities unless doing so results in undue hardship.
- Age discrimination against persons older than age 40 is illegal, according to the Age Discrimination in Employment Act.

- The Immigration Reform and Control Acts identify employment regulations affecting workers from other countries.
- A number of other concerns have been addressed by laws, including discrimination based on religion, military status, and other factors.
- The 1978 Uniform Guidelines on Employee Selection Procedures are used by enforcement agencies to examine recruiting, hiring, promotion, and many other employment practices. Two alternative compliance approaches are no disparate impact and job-related validation.
- Job-related validation requires that tests measure what they are supposed to measure (validity) in a consistent manner (reliability).
- Disparate impact can be determined through the use of the 4/5ths rule.
- One primary type of validity is content validity, which uses a sample of the actual work to be performed.
- The Equal Employment Opportunity Commission (EEOC) and the Office of Federal Contract Compliance Programs (OFCCP) are the major federal enforcement agencies in the area of equal employment.
- Implementation of equal employment opportunity requires appropriate recordkeeping, completing the annual report (EEO-1), keeping applicant-flow data, and investigating EEO complaints.

REVIEW AND APPLICATION QUESTIONS

1. If your employer asked you to review the decision *not to hire* an African American applicant for a job, what would you need to consider?
2. Explain why the broadening diversity of the U.S. workforce is making EEO issues more important and give several examples.
3. Use the text and the U.S. Department of Justice Website (www.usdoj.gov/crt/ada/) to identify what is reasonable accommodation and how it is determined.

CASE

Mitsubishi Believes in EEO—NOW

Several years ago the Mitsubishi auto plant in Normal, Illinois, had a negative reputation. A lawsuit told the story: it alleged that sexual graffiti was written on the fenders of cars being assembled before they passed female production workers, pornographic photos hung on the walls, male workers taunted women, and women who complained were not promoted or perhaps were even fired.

Ultimately, Mitsubishi paid $34 million to settle a sexual harassment lawsuit brought on behalf of 500 workers at the plant. Further, Mitsubishi agreed to pay a multi-million-dollar settlement to African American and Hispanic employees who had claimed racial discrimination during the same time period as the sexual harassment claims. The plant's image was so bad that people were embarrassed to wear the company colors outside of work.

Productivity was bad as well, and the company headquarters in Japan considered closing the American plant. Rich Gilligan, a former Ford manager, was hired to run the plant and began to change the humiliating and illegal ways its women and racial minority employees were treated.

Over time the plant has moved toward being a solid workplace of equal employment oppor-

tunity. Gilligan set up a department to investigate all employee complaints and to train employees in avoiding illegal discrimination issues. During monitoring for three years, there were 140 discrimination and harassment complaints. Fifty-two of those cases violated the zero-tolerance policy and resulted in 8 dismissals, 14 suspensions, and 30 additional disciplinary actions. These actions reinforced the efforts to move the Mitsubishi plant culture toward equal employment.[51]

The Mitsubishi case illustrates that there are consequences for violating EEO laws. Employers who choose not to deal with violations of EEO laws have paid hundreds of millions of dollars in fines to state and federal governments and in back wages and damages to employees.

Questions

1. Discuss why making changes such as Mitsubishi did is important both legally and for improving HR management with the employees and managers.

2. Describe how disparate treatment and disparate impact were factors affecting this case.

SUPPLEMENTAL CASE

Keep on Trucking

This case illustrates the problems that can be associated with the use of employment tests that have not been validated. (For the case, go to http://thomsonedu.com/management/mathis.

NOTES

1. To review these and other examples, go to *www.eeoc.gov/press/index .html.*
2. Michael Orey, "White Men Can't Help It," *Business Week,* May 15, 2006, 54–57.
3. J. C. Ziegret and P. J. Hanges, "Employment Discrimination: The Role of Implicit Attitudes, Motivation, and a Climate for Racial Bias," *Journal of Applied Psychology* 90 (2005), 553–562; and A. P. Brief et al., "Just Doing Business: Modern Racism and Obedience to Authority as Explanations for Employment Discrimination," *Organizational Behavior and Human Decision Processes,* 81 (2000), 72–97.
4. Pamela Babcock, "Detecting Hidden Bias," *HR Magazine,* February 2006, 50–55.
5. Mike Tobin, "S&Z Settles 2003 Bias Case," *The Cleveland Plain Dealer,* August 26, 2006, C1.
6. *Griggs v. Duke Power Co.,* 401 U.S. 424 (1971).
7. Jon D. Bible, "Right Without a Remedy? Supreme Court Allows Disparate Impact Claims under the ADEA," *Labor Law Journal* 56 (2005), 161–172.
8. *Washington, Mayor of Washington D.C. v. Davis,* 74 U.S. 1492 (1976).
9. "State Court Backs Catholic Employer in Religious-Bias Case," *Omaha World-Herald,* May 17, 2002, 8A.
10. *McDonnell-Douglas v. Green,* 411 U.S. 972 (1973).
11. *Reeves v. Sanderson Plumbing Products, Inc.,* 530 U.S. 99–536 (June 12, 2000).
12. *Desert Palace v. Costa,* 539 U.S. 90 (2003).
13. David A. Drachsler, "Proof of Disparate Treatment Under Federal Civil Rights Laws, *Labor Law Journal* 56 (2005), 229–238.
14. *O'Neal v. Ferguson Construction Co.,* 10th Cir., No. 99-2037 (January 24, 2001).
15. *Burlington Northern & Santa Fe Railway v. White,* 126 U.S. 2405 (2006).
16. Jathan Janove, "Retaliation Nation," *HR Magazine,* October 2006, 63–67.
17. Linda A. Jones, "HR Fears Discrimination Lawsuits Most," *Human Resource Executive,* May 16, 2005, 44.
18. William J. Collins, "The Labor Market Impact of State-Level Anti-Discrimination Laws, 1940–1960," *Industrial and Labor Relations Review,* 56 (2003), 1–35.
19. J. J. Smith, "Most Firms' Policies Do Not Reflect Needs of Growing Number of Female Expats," *Global HR News,* October 26, 2006, *www.shrm .org/globalnews.*
20. *Fortino v. Quasar Co.,* 950 F. 2d. 389 (7th Cir. 1991).
21. *Arimindo v. Padlocker, Inc.,* 11th Cir., No. 99-4144 (April 20, 2000).
22. *EEOC v. Eastern Michigan University,* E. D. Mich., No. 98-71806 (September 3, 1999).
23. *Ledbetter v. Goodyear Tire and Rubber Co.* Need copy. Need copy. Need copy. Need copy.
24. Allen Smith, "Pay Bias Figures Prominently in New Supreme Court Form," *HR News,* September 26, 2006, *www.shrm.org/hrnews.*
25. Anne M. Alexander et al., "A Study of the Disparity in Wages and Benefits Between Men and Women in Wyoming," 2003, www.wyoming-business.org/women.
26. John W. Sheffield, "Navigating Current Trends Under the ADA," *Employee Relations Law Journal,* Summer 2005, 3–21.
27. *Murphy v. United Parcel Service,* 527 U.S. 516 (1999).
28. *Quiles-Quiles v. Henderson,* 1st Cir., U.S. No 05-5191 (February 21, 2006).
29. *Bragdon v. Abbott,* U.S. No. 97-156 (June 25, 1998).
30. "Genetic Information," *www.shrm .org/government.*
31. *Karrake v. Rent-A-Center,* 7th Cir., No. 04-2881 (June 14, 2005).
32. "Hire the Aged," *The Economist,* September 30, 2006, 66.
33. Based on Joe Mullich, "New Ideas Draw Older Workers," *Workforce Management,* March 2004, 44–46.
34. *Smith v. City of Jackson Mississippi,* 125 U.S. 1536 (2005).
35. Margaret Clark, "ADEA: Prevention, Not Panic," *HR Magazine,* September 2005, 58–62.
36. *General Dynamics Land Systems, Inc. v. Cline,* 540 U.S. 581 (2004).
37. For specifics, see "Older Workers Benefit Protection Act," *Ceridian Abstracts,* July 20, 2005, *www .hrcompliance.ceridian.com.*
38. *TransWorld Airlines v. Hardison,* 432 U.S. 63 (1977).
39. For discussion, see Christopher Cornell, "EEOC Wins a Round in Alamo Head Scarf Case," *Human Resource Executive,* September 1, 2006, 12.
40. Kathy Gurchiek, "EEOC Claims Bias Against Bearded Candidate," *HR News,* April 4, 2006, *www.shrm .org/hrnews.*
41. James B. Thelen, "Workplace Rights for Service Members: The USERRA Regulations Deconstructed," *HR Legal Report,* March/April, 2006, 1–8.
42. Mark V. Roehling, "Weight Discrimination in the American Workplace," *Journal of Business Ethics,* 40 (2002), 177–189.
43. P. L. Roth, P. Bobko, and F. S. Switzer III, "Modeling the Behavior of the 4/5th Rule for Determining Adverse Impact: Reasons for Caution," *Journal of Applied Psychology,* 91 (2006), 507–522.
44. Kenneth M. York, "Disparate Results in Adverse Impact Tests: The 4/5th Rule and the Chi Square Test," *Public Personnel Management,* 31 (2002) 253–262.
45. Jennifer L. Gatewood, "Company Pays for Unintentional Bias," *Human Resource Executive,* October 20, 2002, 14.
46. M. A. Buster, P. L. Roth, and P. Bobko, "A Process for Content Validation of Education and Experienced-Based Minimum Qualifications: An Approach Resulting in Federal Court Approval," *Personnel Psychology,* 58 (2005), 771–799.
47. Rita Zeidner, "Planning for EEO-1 Changes," *HR Magazine,* May 2006, 61–64.
48. For details, see *www.eeoc.gov/eeo1.*
49. Donald R. Livingston, *EEOC Litigation and Charge Resolution* (Washington, DC: Bureau of National Affairs, Inc., 2005).
50. David Bojorquez and Brian H. Kleiner, "How to Validate Conclusions Regarding Discrimination Based on EEOC Criteria," *Equal Opportunities International,* July/August, 2005, 59–69.
51. Based on David Kiley, "Workplace Woes Almost Eclipse Mitsubishi Plant," *USA Today,* October 21, 2002, 1B.

CHAPTER

5

Managing Equal Employment and Diversity

After you have read this chapter, you should be able to:

- Discuss racial/ethnic discrimination concerns involved with harassment and language issues.

- Describe how women are affected by pay, job assignment, and career issues in organizations.

- Define the two types of sexual harassment and how employers should respond to sexual harassment complaints.

- Identify two means that organizations are using to deal with the aging of their workforces.

- Discuss how reasonable accommodation is made when managing individuals with disabilities and differing religious beliefs.

- Evaluate several arguments supporting and opposing affirmative action.

- Explain diversity management and discuss why diversity training is important.

HR Headline

Facing the Workforce of the Future

The composition of the U.S. population has changed significantly during the past decade, and more shifts are expected during the next 20 years. Industries and employers are having to adapt to these changes. Some examples include the following[1]:

- Many construction firms are growing and need more workers. To fill these jobs, many Latinos/Hispanics are employed in the construction industry. Consequently, those employers have adapted their HR practices. For instance, communications, particularly those related to safety practices, have had to be presented in English, Spanish, and other languages to ensure better workplace efficiency.
- During the past decade the Harley-Davidson motorcycle firm identified the need to expand sales to ethnic minorities and female customers. One aspect of this effort has been to increase by 20% the number of minority and female managers and workers. Doing so has given the firm greater involvement in various motorcycle clubs, community groups, and rider safety programs.
- To counter an expected shortage of 111,000 drivers by 2014, long-haul trucking companies are focusing on recruiting and training women, who currently make up only 5% of drivers.

These examples indicate why equal employment and diversity management are becoming more important. Changes in HR practices are crucial to effective management of the workforce of the future.

| **FIGURE 5-1** | **Equal Employment and Diversity Management** |

The philosophy and legal requirements of equal employment opportunity (EEO) were discussed in Chapter 4. Understanding what the laws say is important, but knowing about managing human resources for EEO requires significant efforts. EEO is the foundation for HR management in dealing with a varied workforce and legal compliance. Two approaches that are at the forefront of these efforts are: (1) non-discriminatory practices and (2) affirmative action.

Although both of these approaches are controversial at times, they are widely used to ensure that workforce diversity management occurs. Such a broad focus is crucial given the changing composition of the workforce in the United States and other countries. To manage diversity, organizations develop initiatives and take actions that use the capabilities of all people. Figure 5-1 depicts three major components of workforce diversity management.

This chapter considers the EEO areas covered in Chapter 4 with a different emphasis, focusing on the special issues in managing each. The second part of this chapter examines affirmative action, and the final section discusses diversity in the workforce and HR approaches and responses to that diversity.

RACE, NATIONAL ORIGIN, AND CITIZENSHIP ISSUES

The original purpose of the Civil Rights Act of 1964 was to address race and national origin discrimination. This concern continues to be important today, and employers must be aware of potential HR issues that are based on race, national origin, and citizenship in order to take appropriate actions. The attention is especially important given the shifting racial/ethnic mix of the U.S. population.

Racial/Ethnic Discrimination

Employment discrimination can occur in numerous ways, from refusal to hire someone because of their race/ethnicity to treatment of those protected class employees. FedEx Freight East, a trucking company, settled a discrimination lawsuit by 20 African American employees who were denied job assignments and promotions because of racial bias. In addition to paying $500,000, the firm must report to the EEOC on promotions from part-time to full-time for dock worker jobs.[2] This case illustrates that firms must continually monitor actions through all departments to assure that racial/ethnic bias does not occur.

The significant increase in workers with different ethnic backgrounds makes preventing racial/ethnic discrimination even more important. To illustrate the scope of these issues, under federal law discriminating against people because of skin color is just as illegal as discriminating because of race. For example, one might be guilty of color discrimination but not racial discrimination if someone hired light-skinned African Americans over dark-skinned people. Many color bias situations go unreported because people simply do not understand that such a distinction is covered by law on racial and ethnic discrimination.

In a recent year, about 35% of the charges filed with the EEOC were on racial complaints, and about 10% were on national origin complaints. Racial discrimination still represents the highest percentage of discrimination complaints, as Figure 5-2 shows.

Racial/Ethnic Harassment The area of racial/ethnic harassment is such a concern that the EEOC has issued guidelines on it. It is recommended that employers adopt policies against harassment of any type, including ethnic jokes, vulgar epithets, racial slurs, and physical actions. The consequences of not enforcing these policies are seen in a case involving a Las Vegas cabinet maker that subjected Latinos to physical and verbal abuse. Hispanic males at the firm were subjected to derogatory jokes, verbal abuse, physical harm, and other humiliating experiences. Settling the case cost the firm $600,000.[3]

Contrast this case with the advantage of taking quick remedial action. In *Hollins v. Delta Airlines*, an employee filed a lawsuit against Delta Airlines because co-workers told racist jokes and hung nooses in his workplace. Delta was able to show that each time any employee, including the plaintiff, reported

FIGURE 5-2   Recent Year Charge Statistics from EEOC

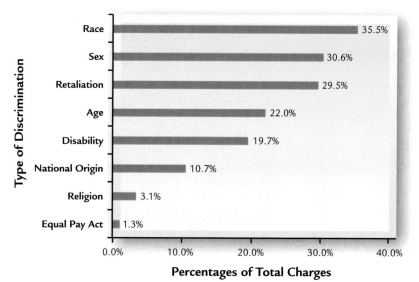

Note: Because individuals often file charges claiming multiple types of discrimination, the total percentages may exceed 100%. Total charges = 75,428.

Source: U.S. Equal Employment Opportunity Commission, 2006, *www.eeoc.gov/stats/charges.html.*

an incident, management quickly conducted an investigation and took corrective and disciplinary actions against the offending employees. Following the management actions, further incidents did not occur, so the court ruled for Delta Airlines in this case.[4]

Language Issues and EEO

As the diversity of the workforce increases, more employees have language skills beyond English. Interestingly, some employers have attempted to restrict the use of foreign languages, while other employers have recognized that bilingual employees have valuable skills. Regardless of the HR policies and practices used, the reality is that language issues must be dealt with as part of managing a racially and ethnically diverse workforce.

English-Only Requirements A number of employers have policies requiring that employees speak only English at work. These employers contend that the policies are necessary for valid business purposes. For instance, a manufacturer requires that employees working with dangerous chemicals use English to communicate hazardous situations to other workers and to read chemical labels.

The EEOC has issued guidelines clearly stating that employers may require workers to speak only English at certain times or in certain situations, but the business necessity of the requirements must be justified.[5] Teaching, customer service, and telemarketing are examples of positions that may require English skills and voice clarity. However, because language characteristics are closely related to national origin, employers must make sure that the business reasons justify any impingement on workers' rights.

Bilingual Employees A growing number of employers have found it beneficial to have bilingual employees so that foreign-language customers can contact someone who speaks their language. Some employers do not pay bilingual employees extra, believing that paying for the jobs being done is more appropriate than paying for language skills that are used infrequently on those jobs. Other employers pay "language premiums" if employees must speak to customers in another language. For instance, one employer pays workers in some locations a bonus if they are required to use a foreign language a majority of the time with customers. Bilingual employees are especially needed among police officers, airline flight personnel, hospital interpreters, international sales reps, and travel guides.

To help employees learn languages, employers are using various means. For example, fast food firms such as Wendy's and Jack in the Box are widely using "Sed de Saber." This interactive system trains Spanish speakers in English by providing a record and playback device. Usage has benefited the companies by reducing turnover and improving customer service. Employees have benefited from expanding English skills in both work- and non–work-related situations.[6]

Requirements for Immigrants and Foreign-Born Workers

Much of the growth in various racial and ethnic groups is due to immigrants from other countries who are here as temporary workers, visitors, students, illegals, etc. For many types of jobs, particularly the lower-skilled jobs in such

HR PERSPECTIVE

Employers and Illegal Immigrants

Illegal immigrants are estimated to comprise about 5% of the total U.S. labor force. In certain industries, such as construction and agriculture, they comprise more than 20% of the workers. The greatest growth is in the number of Latino/Hispanic illegals who come across the southern border of the United States. The United States has a population of 300 million. About 40 million are Hispanics, and an estimated 30% of those are thought to be immigrants; many are legal, but a sizable number are illegal.

A widespread political debate has been occurring for several years on how to control illegal immigration. Some advocate establishing processes for those here illegally to take steps to become legal residents. Other critics suggest limiting the influx of immigrants. A key part of these political and social debates is that employers may be required to expand the means used to check individual immigration status. Also, more effort

may be made to penalize employers more heavily for hiring illegal immigrants

Conflicting laws can present some real problems for an employer in deciding who is legal and who is not. For example, the government fined Wal-Mart $60,000 for requiring too much information (more verification than was required by law) to prove prospective hires were citizens. Later, in a series of raids, federal agents rounded up 250 illegal immigrants in 21 states from contractors who were cleaning stores for Wal-Mart. But anti-discrimination sections of the immigrant code had severely limited Wal-Mart's ability to investigate an individual's legal status.[7]

Ultimately, the federal, state, and local laws being discussed and revised will determine how employers must handle this issue. It is likely these discussions will continue to be contentious.[8]

---

areas as hospitality and agricultural businesses, workers with limited educational skills are coming from Mexico, Sudan, the Balkan countries, and Latin American and Asian countries. The HR Perspective discusses the significant issue of illegal immigrants.

Employers are required to comply with provisions of the Immigration Reform and Control Acts, as mentioned in Chapter 4. Foreign-born workers are required to have visas and other documents. It is crucial that employers verify the legal work status of all individuals.

SEX/GENDER ISSUES

The influx of women into the workforce has major social, economic, and organizational consequences. The percentage of women in the total U.S. civilian workforce has increased dramatically since 1950, to almost 50% today.

Sex Discrimination

Internet Research

Catalyst Organization
For information from a non-profit research and advisory organization dedicated to advancing women in business, link to their Website at: http://thomsonedu.com/management/mathis.

The growth in the number of women in the workforce has led to more sex/gender issues related to jobs and careers. A significant issue is related to biology (women bear children) and to tradition (women have a primary role in raising children). A major result of the increasing share of women in the workforce is that more women with children are working. According to the U.S. Bureau of Labor Statistics, about three-fourths of women aged 25–54 are in the workforce. Further, about half of all women currently working are single, separated, divorced, widowed, or otherwise single heads of households. Consequently, they are "primary" income earners, not co-income providers, and must balance family and work responsibilities.

The increasing number of working mothers with children has led employers to take steps to establish compatible policies. Due to the Pregnancy Discrimination Act discussed in Chapter 4, employers must not discriminate against pregnant women when making selection, promotion, training, or other employment-related decisions. Another law, the Family and Medical Leave Act (FMLA), also affects the management of pregnant workers and new parents. This act applies to both female and male employees who are new parents, through either adoption or natural birth. Many employers have policies allowing new mothers to leave their work sites during business hours in order to nurse or use breast pumps.

Pay Inequity On average, women annually receive about 77% of men's earnings, and that percentage has increased over time, as Figure 5-3 indicates. That discrepancy depends to a large extent on differences between jobs, industries, and time spent at work. One study found that when race/ethnicity is considered, the gap widens. However, there is probably a discrimination component to the problem as well.[9] To guard against pay inequities that are considered illegal under the Equal Pay Act, employers should follow these guidelines[10]:

- Include benefits and other items that are part of remuneration to calculate total compensation for the most accurate overall picture.
- Make sure people know how the pay practices work.
- Base pay on the value of jobs and performance.
- Benchmark against local and national markets so that pay structures are competitive.
- Conduct frequent audits to ensure there are no gender-based inequities and that pay is fair internally.

Nepotism Practice of allowing relatives to work for the same employer.

Nepotism Many employers have policies that restrict or prohibit nepotism, the practice of allowing relatives to work for the same employer. Other firms require only that relatives not work directly for or with each other or not be placed in positions where collusion or conflict could occur. The policies

FIGURE 5-3   Female Annual Earnings as Percentage of Male Earnings

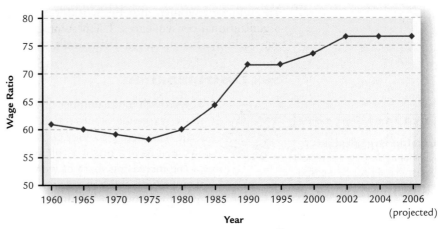

Source: U.S. Department of Labor, Bureau of Labor Statistics, 2006, *www.bls.gov.*

most frequently cover spouses, brothers, sisters, mothers, fathers, sons, and daughters. Generally, employer anti-nepotism policies have been upheld by courts, in spite of the concern that they tend to discriminate against women more than men (because women tend to be denied employment or to leave employers more often as a result of marriage to other employees).[11]

Nontraditional Jobs An increasing number of women in the workforce are moving into jobs traditionally held by men. The U.S. Department of Labor defines nontraditional occupations for women as those in which women constitute 25% or less of the total number employed. Even though the nature of the work and working conditions may contribute some to this pattern, many of these jobs pay well, and as more women enter these occupations, women's earnings will rise.

The right to re-assign women from hazardous jobs to ones that may be lower paying because of health-related concerns is another gender-related issue encountered by employers. Fears about higher health insurance costs and possible lawsuits involving such problems as birth defects caused by damage sustained during pregnancy have led some employers to institute reproductive and fetal protection policies. However, the U.S. Supreme Court has ruled that such policies are illegal. Also, having different job conditions for men and women is usually held to be discriminatory. Figure 5-4 shows some of the occupations in which women constitute high percentages and low percentages of those employed.

Glass ceiling
Discriminatory practices that have prevented women and other protected-class members from advancing to executive-level jobs.

Glass Ceiling For years, women's groups have alleged that women in workplaces encounter a glass ceiling, which refers to discriminatory practices that have prevented women and other protected-class members from advancing to executive-level jobs. Women in the United States are making some progress in getting senior-level, managerial, or professional jobs. Nevertheless, women hold only 12% of the highest-ranking executive management jobs in Fortune 500 companies. By comparison, women hold much lower percentages of the same kinds of jobs in France, Germany, Brazil, and many other countries.[12]

"Glass Walls" and "Glass Elevator" A related problem is that women have tended to advance to senior management in a limited number of support or

FIGURE 5-4   Women as Percentage of Total Employees by Selected Industries

Higher Percentages		Lower Percentages	
Child day care	95.5%	Taxi/limousine services	10.5%
Home health care	91.3%	Coal mining	10.2%
Hospitals	79.2%	Construction	9.7%
Elementary and secondary schools	75.0%	Automotive repair	9.4%
Veterinary services	73.2%	Landscaping services	9.2%
Travel/reservation services	71.7%	Logging	8.9%
Pharmacies and drug stores	63.9%	Rail transportation	8.4%

Source: U.S. Bureau of Labor Statistics, "Employed Persons by Detailed Industry and Sex," 2006, www.bls.gov.

staff areas, such as HR and corporate communications. Because executive jobs in these "supporting" areas tend to pay less than jobs in sales, marketing, operations, or finance, the overall impact is to reduce women's career progression and income. Limits that keep women from progressing only in certain fields have been referred to as "glass walls" or "glass elevators." These limitations are seen as tied to organizational, cultural, and leadership issues.[13]

"Breaking the Glass" A number of employers have recognized that "breaking the glass," whether ceilings, walls, or elevators, is good business for both women and racial minorities. Some of the most common means used to "break the glass" are as follows:

■ Establish formal mentoring programs for women and members of racial/ethnic minorities.
■ Provide opportunities for career rotation into operations, marketing, and sales for individuals who have shown talent in accounting, HR, and other areas.
■ Increase the memberships of top management and boards of directors to include women and individuals of color.
■ Establish clear goals for retention and progression of protected-class individuals and hold managers accountable for achieving these goals.
■ Allow for alternative work arrangements for employees, particularly those balancing work/family responsibilities.

Individuals with Differing Sexual Orientations

As if demographic diversity did not place enough pressure on managers and organizations, individuals in the workforce today have widely varying lifestyles that can have work-related consequences. Legislative efforts have been made to protect individuals with differing lifestyles or sexual orientations from employment discrimination, though at present only a few cities and states have passed such laws.[14]

One visible issue that some employers have had to address is that of individuals who have had or are undergoing sex-change surgery and therapy. As mentioned in Chapter 4, federal court cases and the EEOC have ruled that sex discrimination under Title VII applies to a person's gender at birth. Thus, it does not apply to the new gender of those who have had gender-altering operations. Sexual orientation or sex-change issues that arise at work include the reactions of co-workers and managers and ensuring that such individuals are evaluated fairly and not discriminated against in work assignments, raises, training, or promotions.

SEXUAL HARASSMENT AND WORKPLACE RELATIONSHIPS

As more women have entered the workforce, more men and women work in teams and on projects. Consequently, more employers are facing issues involving the close personal relationships that develop at work.

Consensual Relationships and Romance at Work

When work-based friendships lead to romance and off-the-job sexual relationships, managers and employers face a dilemma: Should they "monitor" these relationships to protect the firm from potential legal complaints, thereby "meddling" in employees' private, off-the-job lives? Or do they simply ignore these relationships and the potential problems they present? These concerns are significant, given a survey that found that about 40% of workers have dated co-workers.[15]

A survey by SHRM found that most executives and HR professionals (as well as employees) agree that workplace romances are risky because they have great potential for causing conflict. Seventy percent agreed that romance must not take place between a supervisor and a subordinate.[16] Some employers have addressed the issue of workplace romances by establishing policies dealing with them.[17]

Different actions may occur if a relationship is clearly consensual than if it is forced by a supervisor–subordinate relationship. One consideration is illustrated by a California court ruling that stated that consensual workplace romances can create hostile work environments for others in organizations.[18]

Nature of Sexual Harassment

Sexual harassment is a significant concern in many organizations and can occur in a variety of workplace relationships. As shown in Figure 5-5, individuals in many different roles can be sexual harassers. For example, third parties who are not employees also have been found to be harassers. Both customer service representatives and food servers have won sexual harassment complaints because their employers refused to protect them from regular sexual harassment by aggressive customers.

Most frequently, sexual harassment occurs when a male in a supervisory or managerial position harasses women within his "power structure." However, women managers have been found guilty of sexually harassing male employees. Also, same-sex harassment has occurred. Court decisions have held that a person's sexual orientation neither provides nor precludes a claim of sexual harassment under Title VII. It is enough that the harasser engaged in pervasive and unwelcome conduct of a sexual nature.

FIGURE 5-5   **Potential Sexual Harassers**

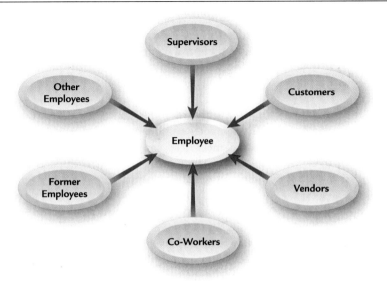

Cyber and Electronic Sexual Harassment

Electronic information technology is creating new problems for HR managers because sexual harassment is increasingly occurring in "cyberspace" via e-mails and Internet access systems. Cyber sexual harassment may occur when an employee forwards an e-mail joke with sexual content. Or, it may take the form of accessing pornographic Websites at work and then sharing content with other employees. Cyber stalking, in which a person continually e-mails an employee requesting dates and sending personal messages, is growing as instant messaging and cybertext equipment expands.

Many employers have policies addressing the inappropriate use of e-mail, company computer systems, and electronic technology usage. Serious situations have led to employee terminations, as evidenced by

Dow Chemical who disciplined more than 200 employees and fired 50 of them for having e-mailed pornographic images and other inappropriate materials using the company information system.[20]

It is crucial to train all employees on sexual harassment and electronic usage policies. Additionally, many employers have equipped their computer systems with scanners that screen for inappropriate words and images. Offending employees receive warnings and/or disciplinary actions associated with "flagged" items. Also, employees subjected to severe sexual harassment may receive counseling assistance. As with all sexual harassment situations, HR professionals should document the incidents, their investigative efforts, and the actions taken to prevent further cyber sexual harassment.[21]

Quid pro quo Sexual harassment in which employment outcomes are linked to the individual granting sexual favors.

Hostile environment Sexual harassment in which an individual's work performance or psychological well-being is unreasonably affected by intimidating or offensive working conditions.

Types of Sexual Harassment Two basic types of sexual harassment have been defined by EEOC regulations and a large number of court cases. The two types are different in nature and defined as follows:

1. **Quid pro quo** is harassment in which employment outcomes are linked to the individual granting sexual favors.
2. **Hostile environment** harassment exists when an individual's work performance or psychological well-being is unreasonably affected by intimidating or offensive working conditions.

In quid pro quo harassment, an employee may be promised a promotion, a special raise, or a desirable work assignment, but only if the employee grants some sexual favors to the supervisor. The second type, hostile environment harassment, is much more prevalent, partially because the standards and consequences are more varied.

A number of court cases have emphasized that commenting on appearance or attire, telling jokes that are suggestive or sexual in nature, allowing revealing photos and posters to be on display, or making continual requests to get together after work can lead to the creation of a hostile work environment. Research has also found that rude and discourteous behavior often is linked to sexual harassment.[19] As computer and Internet technology has spread, the number of electronic sexual harassment cases has grown, as the HR On-Line discussion describes.

Regardless of the type, it is apparent that sexual harassment has significant consequences on the organization, other employees, and especially those harassed. Follow-up interviews and research with victims of sexual harassment reveal that the harassment has both job-related and psychological effects. Also, harassment even has a ripple effect on others who fear being harassed or view their employer more negatively if prompt remedial actions do not occur. Thus, how employers respond to sexual harassment complaints is crucial for both legal reasons and employee morale.

Employer Responses to Sexual Harassment It is crucial that employers respond proactively to prevent sexual and other types of harassment. If the workplace culture fosters harassment, and if policies and practices do not inhibit harassment, an employer is wise to re-evaluate and solve the problem before lawsuits follow.

Only if the employer can produce evidence of taking reasonable care to prohibit sexual harassment does the employer have the possibility of avoiding liability through an affirmative defense. Critical components of ensuring reasonable care include the following:

- Establish a sexual harassment policy.
- Communicate the policy regularly.
- Train employees and managers on avoiding sexual harassment.
- Investigate and take action when complaints are voiced.

As Figure 5-6 indicates, if an employee suffered any tangible employment action (such as being denied raises, being terminated, or being refused access to training) because of sexual harassment, then the employer is liable. Even if the employee suffered no tangible employment action, if the employer has not produced an affirmative defense, then employer liability still exists.

FIGURE 5-6   Sexual Harassment Liability Determination

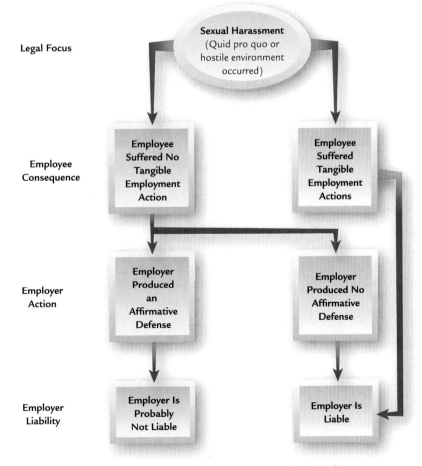

Source: Virginia Collins, PhD, SPHR, and Robert L. Mathis, PhD, SPHR, Omaha, Nebraska.

AGE ISSUES AND EEO

The populations of most developed countries—including Australia, Japan, most European countries, and the United States—are aging. These changes mean that as older workers with a lifetime of experiences and skills retire, HR faces significant challenges in replacing them with workers having the capabilities and work ethic that characterize many mature workers. Employment discrimination against individuals age 40 and older is prohibited by the Age Discrimination in Employment Act (ADEA), as mentioned in Chapter 4. Therefore, employers must be aware of a number of HR issues associated with managing older workers.

One issue that has led to age discrimination charges is labeling older workers as "overqualified" for jobs or promotions. In a number of cases, courts have ruled that the term *overqualified* may have been used as a code word for workers being too old, thus causing them not to be considered for employment. Also, selection and promotion practices must be "age neutral." Older workers face substantial barriers to entry in a number of occupations, especially those requiring significant amounts of training or ones where new technology has been recently developed.

Age Discrimination and Workforce Reductions

In the past decade, many employers have used early retirement programs and organizational downsizing to reduce their employment costs. The Older Workers Benefit Protection Act (OWBPA) was passed to ensure that equal treatment for older workers occurs in early retirement or severance situations. Illegal age discrimination sometimes occurs when an individual over the age of 40 is forced into retirement or is denied employment or promotion on the basis of age. If disparate impact or treatment for those over age 40 exists, age discrimination occurs. In some cases involving older employees, age-related comments such as "That's just old Fred" or "We need younger blood" in conversations were used as evidence of age discrimination.

Attracting, Retaining, and Managing Older Workers

To counter significant staffing difficulties, some employers are recruiting older people to return to the workforce through the use of part-time and other scheduling options. During the past decade, the number of older workers holding part-time jobs has increased. It is likely that the number of older workers interested in working part-time will continue to grow.

Phased retirement
Approach in which employees gradually reduce their workloads and pay levels.

A strategy used by employers to retain the talents of older workers is phased retirement, whereby employees gradually reduce their workloads and pay levels. This option is growing in use as a way to allow older workers with significant knowledge and experience to have more personal flexibility, while the organizations retain them for their valuable capabilities. Some firms also re-hire their retirees as part-time workers, independent contractors, or consultants. Some provisions in the Pension Protection Act of 2006 allow pension distributions for employees who are reducing their work hours.[22]

INDIVIDUALS WITH DISABILITIES IN THE WORKFORCE

Employers looking for workers with the knowledge, skills, and abilities to perform jobs often have neglected a significant source: individuals with physical or mental disabilities. Based on a U.S. government survey, individuals with disabilities or work-limiting problems have an employment rate of 20.8% compared with non-disabled workers' employment rate of 78%.[23] One concern is that discrimination against individuals is often based on misperceptions about the controllability and stability of different disabilities.[24]

Making Reasonable Accommodations

At the heart of employing individuals with disabilities is for employers to make reasonable accommodations in several areas. Common means of reasonable accommodation are shown in Figure 5-7. First, architectural barriers should not prohibit disabled individuals' access to work areas or restrooms. Second, appropriate work tasks must be assigned. Satisfying this requirement may mean modifying jobs, work area layouts, or work schedules or providing special equipment.

Key to making reasonable accommodations is identifying the essential job functions and then determining which accommodations are reasonable so that the individual can perform the core job duties. Fortunately for employers, most accommodations made are relatively inexpensive.[25] Employers who show a positive interest in making accommodations are more likely to encourage individuals with disabilities to believe that they will receive appropriate considerations for employment opportunities.

Recruiting and Selecting Individuals with Disabilities

Numerous employers have specifically targeted the recruitment and selection of individuals with disabilities. However, as the HR On-the-Job on the next page indicates, questions asked in the employment process should be job related.

The means used to screen individuals for positions also should be reviewed. One common means is the use of physical abilities tests, which can be challenged as discriminatory. The physical tests must be specifically job related, not general in nature. Thus, having all applicants lift 50-pound weights, even

---

FIGURE 5-7   **Common Means of Reasonable Accommodation**

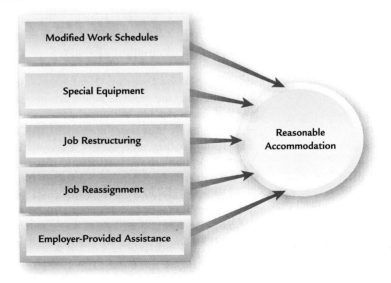

HR ON-THE-JOB

ADA and the Employment Questions

The Americans with Disabilities Act prohibits asking job applicants questions about past or current health history until a conditional job offer is made. The offer often is based on passing a physical exam or a medical background check. Any physical or medical requirements must be related to the specific job for which the applicant is being considered. Two HR areas that are affected are employment applications and interviews. In these areas a general question such as the following is often used:

Can you perform the essential functions of the job for which you are applying with or without accommodation?

Several examples of specific questions concerning disabilities that should and should not be asked in employment interviews are shown below in the chart. As is evident, the questions that should be asked are specifically related to the job and address essential job functions.

DO NOT ASK	✔ DO ASK
■ Do you have any physical or mental disabilities? ■ Why are you using crutches, and how did you become injured? ■ How many times were you absent due to illness in the past two years? ■ Have you been treated for any of the following medical conditions? ■ Have you ever filed for or collected workers' compensation?	■ How would you perform the essential tasks of the job for which you have applied? ■ If hired, which tasks outlined in the job description that you reviewed would be more enjoyable and which ones most difficult? ■ Describe your attendance record on your last job. ■ Describe any problems you would have reaching the top of a six-foot filing cabinet. ■ What did your prior job duties consist of, and which ones were the most challenging?

though only some warehouse workers will have to lift that much, could be illegal. Also, rather than lifting barbells, the employer should use actual 50-pound boxes for specific jobs, rather than artificial weights.

Managing Individuals with Disabilities

Employers increasingly are facing more employees who have or may develop disabilities. It is important that employers handle various types of employee disability situations appropriately.

Employees Who Develop Disabilities For many employers, the impact of the ADA has been the greatest when handling employees who develop disabilities, not just when dealing with applicants who have disabilities. As the workforce ages, it is likely that more employees will develop disabilities. For instance, a warehouse worker who suffers a serious leg injury while motorcycling away from work may request reasonable accommodation.

Employers must develop responses for handling accommodation requests from individuals who have been satisfactory employees without disabilities, but who now must be considered for accommodations if they are to be able to continue working. Handled inappropriately, these individuals are likely to file either ADA complaints with the EEOC or private lawsuits.

Employees sometimes can be shifted to other jobs where their disabilities do not affect them as much. For instance, the warehouse firm might be able to move the injured repair worker to a purchasing inventory job inside so that climbing and lifting are unnecessary. But the problem for employers is what to do with the next worker who develops problems if an alternative job is not available. Even if the accommodations are just for one employee, the reactions of co-workers must be considered.

Individuals with Mental Disabilities More ADA complaints are being filed by individuals who have or claim to have mental disabilities. The cases that have been filed have ranged from individuals with a medical history of paranoid schizophrenia or clinical depression to individuals who claim that job stress has affected their marriage or sex life. Regardless of the type of employees' claims, it is important that employers respond properly by obtaining medical verifications for claims of mental illnesses and considering accommodation requests for mental disabilities in the same manner as accommodation requests for physical disabilities.[26]

Individuals with Life-Threatening Illnesses The U.S. Supreme Court has determined that individuals with life-threatening illnesses are covered by the ADA. Individuals with leukemia, cancer, or AIDS are all considered as having disabilities, and employers must respond to them appropriately or face charges of discrimination. Numerous individuals with life-threatening illnesses may intend to continue working, particularly if their illness is forecast to be multi-year in nature.[27]

Unfortunately, employers and employees often react with fear about working with someone who has AIDS or a life-threatening illness. Educating other employees may be more appropriate than terminating the person who is ill. A medical leave of absence (without pay, if that is the general policy) can be used to assist the afflicted employee during medical treatments. Also, employees who indicate that they will not work with an afflicted employee should be told that their refusal to work is not protected by law, and that they could be subject to disciplinary action up to and including discharge.

RELIGION AND SPIRITUALITY IN THE WORKPLACE

Title VII of the Civil Rights Act of 1964 prohibits discrimination at work on the basis of religion; also, employers are prohibited from discriminating against employees for their religious beliefs and practices. Since the terrorist attacks on September 11, 2001, such considerations have become even more important in protecting Muslim individuals and others from discrimination and harassment. Concerns exist about continuing discriminatory beliefs that may lead to inappropriate workplace actions. More than 2,000 complaints were filed by Muslim-Americans over five years, and numerous firms have had to settle lawsuits. For example, Bechtel Corporation paid $90,000 to settle a hostile work environment complaint by an Iraqi employee in New Jersey who received disparaging comments and was excluded from meetings.[28]

Managing Religious Diversity in the Workplace

Employers increasingly are having to balance the rights of employees with differing religious beliefs.[29] One way to do that is to make reasonable accommodation for employees' religious beliefs when assigning and scheduling

FIGURE 5-8   Religion and Spirituality in Workplaces

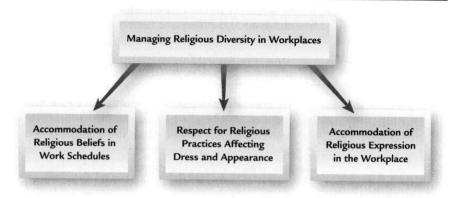

work, because many religions have differing days of worship and holidays. For example, some firms have established "holiday swapping pools," whereby Christian employees can work during Passover or Ramadan or Chinese New Year, and employees from other religions work Christmas. Other firms allow employees a set number of days off for holidays, without specifying the holidays in company personnel policies. Figure 5-8 indicates common areas for accommodating religious diversity.

One potential area for conflict between employer policies and employee religious practices is dress and appearance. Some religions have standards about appropriate attire for women. Also, some religions expect men to have beards and facial hair, which may violate company appearance policies.

Another issue concerns religious expression. In the last several years, employees in several cases have sued employers for prohibiting them from expressing their religious beliefs at work. In other cases, employers have had to take action because of the complaints by workers that employees were aggressively "pushing" their religious views at work, thus creating a "hostile environment." Executives and owners of some firms have strong evangelical Christian beliefs that are carried over into their companies. Some display crosses, have Bible study groups for employees before work, sponsor Christian prayer groups, and support other efforts.[30] But such actions can lead to non-Christians feeling discriminated against, thus creating a "hostile environment." Other areas that may need to be considered when dealing with religion at work are food, on-site religion-based groups, office decorations, and religious practices at work.

AFFIRMATIVE ACTION

Affirmative action
Employers are urged to hire groups of people based on their race, age, gender, or national origin to make up for historical discrimination.

Through affirmative action employers are urged to hire groups of people based on their race, age, gender, or national origin to make up for historical discrimination. Affirmative action was mentioned previously in Chapter 4 as a requirement for federal government contractors to document the inclusion of women and racial minorities in the workforce. As part of those government regulations, covered employers must submit plans describing their attempts to narrow the gaps between the composition of their workforces and the composition of labor markets where they obtain employees. But affirmative action has been the subject of numerous court cases and an ongoing political and social debate both in the United States and globally.

Affirmative Action and the U.S. Courts

Generally, the courts have upheld the legality of affirmative action, but recently they have limited it somewhat. One major case involved a University of Michigan policy of allotting every minority applicant 20 out of the 150 points necessary to guarantee admission. The U.S. Supreme Court held that the system violated the Fourteenth Amendment's "equal protection" clause. However, in another case, the Supreme Court upheld affirmative action, ruling that the University of Michigan law school was justified in trying to ensure that a "critical mass" of minority students was admitted, even if that meant denying admission to white students with better grades or higher test scores.[31] These court decisions provided both guidance and confusion, so additional cases are likely to be appealed to various courts. Thus, it is important for HR professionals to monitor both court decisions and political efforts, given the continuing controversies and debate over the fairness of affirmative action.

Internet Research

The Affirmative Action and Diversity Project
For differing opinions surrounding the issues of affirmative action and its cultural and economic aspects, visit the Affirmative Action and Diversity Project site at:
http://thomsonedu.com/management/mathis.

Debate on Affirmative Action

Employers use affirmative action *goals,* *targets,* and *timetables* to specify how many of which types of individuals they hope to have in their workforces in the future. By specifying these goals, employers say they are trying to "appropriately include protected group members" or "ensure a balanced and representative workforce." These claims and others like them are commonly used to describe affirmative action, which leads to specific debate points.

Supporters offer many reasons why affirmative action is important, while opponents argue firmly against it. Individuals can examine the points of both sides in the debate and compare them with their personal views of affirmative action. The authors of this text believe that whether one supports or opposes affirmative action, it is important to understand why its supporters believe that it is needed and why its opponents believe it should be discontinued. The reasons given most frequently by both sides are highlighted next.

Debate: Why Affirmative Action Is Needed Without affirmative action, proponents argue that many in the United States will be permanently economically disadvantaged. Proponents argue for programs to enable women, minorities, and members of other protected groups to be competitive with males and whites. Otherwise, they will never "catch up" and have appropriate opportunities. Specific points made by advocates include the following:

- Affirmative action is needed to overcome past injustices or eliminate the effects of those injustices.
- Affirmative action creates more equality for all persons, even if temporary injustice to some individuals may result.
- Raising the employment level of protected-class members will benefit U.S. society in the long run.
- Properly used, affirmative action does not discriminate against males or whites.
- Goals indicate progress is needed, not quotas.

Debate: Why Affirmative Action Is No Longer Needed Opponents of affirmative action believe that it establishes two groups: (1) women, racial minorities, and others in protected classes, and (2) everyone else. For any job, a person will clearly fall into one group or the other. Critics of affirmative action say that regardless of the language used, subsequent actions lead to the use of *preferential selection* for protected-class members over equally qualified white males and others not covered by the EEO regulations. The result is reverse discrimination, which occurs when a person is denied an opportunity because of preferences given to protected-class individuals who may be less qualified. Other points made by opponents include the following:

Reverse discrimination
When a person is denied an opportunity because of preferences given to protected-class individuals who may be less qualified.

- Affirmative action penalizes individuals (males and whites) even though they have not been guilty of practicing discrimination.
- Creating preferences of certain groups results in discrimination against others.
- Affirmative action results in greater polarization and separatism along gender and racial lines.
- Affirmative action stigmatizes those it is designed to help.
- Goals become quotas by forcing employers to "play by the numbers."

Affirmative Action Debate Review The debate over affirmative action is likely to continue. Surveys of Americans' beliefs on affirmative action show that 63% feel that affirmative action has been good for minorities. However, only 42% say affirmative action is still necessary to achieve diversity at work.[32]

Various research studies on affirmative action have been done to identify how it is perceived by different groups. A number of the studies have been done using surveys of students or other study groups.[33] One study found that a hiring decision was seen as fairer when no justification was provided than when the reason for the hiring choice was affirmative action. Also, men had stronger views this way than women.[34]

Other research on affirmative action suggests that increases in diversity recruiting efforts by employers results in raising employer willingness to hire minority applicants, increasing the numbers of minority applicants and employees, and increasing tendencies to provide training and formally evaluate employees. Overall, the research found that affirmative action generally does not lead to lower credentials of workers.[35]

What studies, surveys, and employer experiences all indicate is that affirmative action is a controversial subject, and it will continue to be so. Despite this, employers must comply with the regulations, which are discussed next.

Affirmative Action Compliance Requirements

Affirmative action focuses on hiring, training, and promoting protected-class members who are *underrepresented* in an organization in relation to their availability in the labor markets from which recruiting occurs. Sometimes, employers have instituted affirmative action voluntarily, but many times, employers have been required to do so because they are government contractors. They develop detailed reports to submit to governmental agencies.

Affirmative action plan (AAP) Formal document that an employer compiles annually for submission to enforcement agencies.

Affirmative Action Plans (AAPs) Federal, state, and local regulations require many government contractors to compile affirmative action plans to report on the composition of their workforces. An affirmative action plan (AAP) is a formal document that an employer compiles annually for submission to enforcement agencies. Generally, contractors with at least 50 employees and $50,000 in government contracts annually must submit these plans. Courts have noted that any employer *may* have a *voluntary* AAP, although employers *must* have such a plan if they are government contractors. Some courts have ordered employers that are not government contractors to submit required AAPs because of past discriminatory practices and violations of laws.

The contents of an AAP and the policies flowing from it must be available for review by managers and supervisors within the organization. Plans vary in length; some are long and require extensive staff time to prepare. Figure 5-9 depicts the phases in the development of an AAP.

Availability analysis
Identifies the number of protected-class members available to work in the appropriate labor markets for given jobs.

Affirmative Action Plan Measures The second phase is a crucial but time-consuming one in which two types of analyses and comparisons are done. The availability analysis identifies the number of protected-class members available to work in the appropriate labor markets for given jobs. This analysis can be developed with data from a state labor department, the U.S.

FIGURE 5-9   Components of an Affirmative Action Plan (AAP)

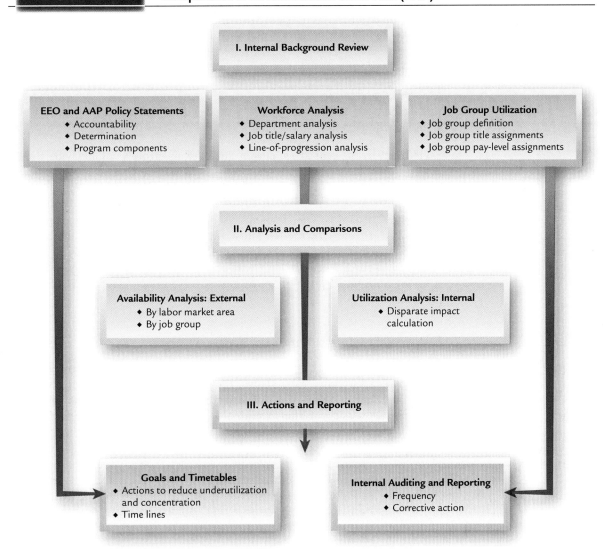

Utilization analysis
Identifies the number of protected-class members employed in the organization and the types of jobs they hold.

Census Bureau, and other sources. The utilization analysis identifies the number of protected-class members employed in the organization and the types of jobs they hold.

Once all the data have been analyzed and compared, then *underutilization* statistics must be calculated by comparing the workforce analyses with the utilization analysis. It is useful to think of this stage as a comparison of whether the internal workforce is a "representative sampling" of the available external labor force from which employees are hired.

Using the underutilization data, *goals and timetables* for reducing underutilization of protected-class individuals must then be identified. Actions that will be taken to recruit, hire, promote, and train more protected-class individuals are described. The AAP must be updated and reviewed each year to reflect changes in the utilization and availability of protected-class members. If the AAP is audited by the Office of Federal Contract Compliance Programs (OFCCP), the employer must be prepared to provide additional details and documentation.

MANAGING DIVERSITY

As the foregoing discussions have shown, the U.S. workforce has become quite diverse. The tangible indictors of diversity that employers must consider are as follows:

- Age
- Marital and family status
- Disabilities
- Race/ethnicity

- Religion
- Gender
- Sexual orientation

Further, by the year 2025, current racial/ethnic groups will likely be almost 40% of the U.S. population. The Census Bureau says non-Hispanic whites represent 69% of the population currently, and will be about 60% in 2025. The African American population will grow some, but not nearly as much as Latinos/Hispanics. The Hispanic population will increase dramatically, to about 20% to 25% of the overall population and will exceed the number of African Americans. The Asian population will triple.[36] Many organizations have already begun to deal with the diversity challenge. According to a study by SHRM, 75% of organizations surveyed have diversity policies and practices.[37]

Diversity Management Approaches

Different organizations approach the management of diversity from several perspectives. As Figure 5-10 shows, the continuum can run from resistance to creation of an inclusive diversity culture. The increasing diversity of the available workforce, combined with growing shortages of workers in many occupations and industries, has resulted in more employers recognizing that diversity must be managed. Organizational experiences and research have indicated that establishing broad responsibility for diversity leads to more effective diversity training, networking, mentoring, and other efforts.[38]

Internet Research

Diversity Central
Diversity Central is a business center for diversity articles, tools, and resources. Link to their site at: http://thomsonedu.com/management/mathis.

FIGURE 5-10	**Various Approaches to Diversity and Their Results**

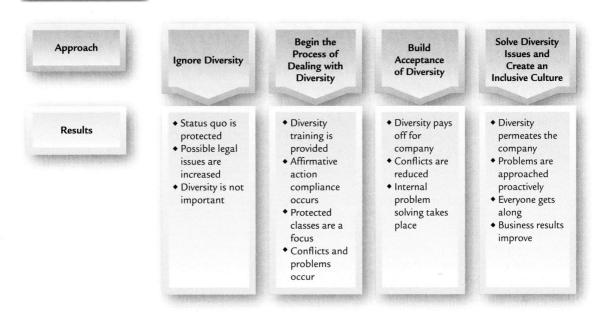

Approach	**Ignore Diversity**	**Begin the Process of Dealing with Diversity**	**Build Acceptance of Diversity**	**Solve Diversity Issues and Create an Inclusive Culture**
Results	• Status quo is protected • Possible legal issues are increased • Diversity is not important	• Diversity training is provided • Affirmative action compliance occurs • Protected classes are a focus • Conflicts and problems occur	• Diversity pays off for company • Conflicts are reduced • Internal problem solving takes place	• Diversity permeates the company • Problems are approached proactively • Everyone gets along • Business results improve

Diversity: The Business Case

Diversity can be justified on the basis of social justice, but does it make business sense? The "business case" for diversity is based on the following points:

- Diversity allows new talent and new ideas from employees of different backgrounds, which may enhance organizational performance.
- Diversity helps recruiting and retention because protected-class individuals often prefer to work in organizations with co-workers having various demographics.
- Diversity allows for an increase of market share because customers can be attracted to purchase products and services with varied demographic marketing activities.
- Diversity leads to lower costs because there may be fewer discrimination lawsuits.

Whether or not the money spent by employers is producing results has been researched. A five-year study of several companies examined how diversity affects performance. It found that managing diversity leads to more effective performance on gender issues, but that racial and ethnic diversity may, in fact, have a negative impact on business performance unless specific controls are in place. If not managed properly, diversity can produce miscommunication, conflict, higher turnover, and lower performance.[39] Additionally, diversity was found to have enhanced performance when diversity *was* treated as a source of innovation and learning. A final result showed that customers did not care whether they were served by people of the same gender or race.[40] Another study found that firms with diverse workforces do not have higher turnover rates than less diverse firms.[41]

HR BEST PRACTICES

Diversity Management Pays Off for PepsiCo

Many employers have recognized that diversity management is important. But a number of leading firms have seen ways in which diversity contributes to organizational success and growth. One example is seen at PepsiCo, a large food and beverage company.

As part of a broad program, PepsiCo has developed and implemented a Diversity and Inclusion Council so that diversity considerations are part of all strategic efforts. Also, PepsiCo has regular diversity celebrations, newsletters, and other events. The value of such a program is illustrated by the Latino Employee Network in its Frito-Lay division. Individuals in that group were asked to use their applicable knowledge to provide input on the taste and packaging of

Doritos Guacamole Tortilla Chips. Based on those ideas and others, once that produce was released, it generated sales of more than $100 million in its first year on the market.

Key to PepsiCo's effective diversity efforts is that they begin at the top level of management, with the CEO and executive staff. All executives are responsible for ensuring that diversity management occurs with all types of employees. That commitment then establishes that diversity is crucial. It also means that throughout the company, inclusion of diversity issues continues to contribute to PepsiCo's success with employees, managers, and customers.[43]

These studies illustrate that the impact of diverse workforces is still being identified. It does appear that if diversity is to contribute to business success, organizations need to learn how to maximize its benefits and minimize its problems.[42] The HR Best Practices illustrates one example.

Diversity Management Programs and Activities

A wide variety of programs and activities have been used in organizations as part of diversity management efforts. Almost half of companies in one survey have a written policy on employee diversity, a significant increase over a 12-year span.[44] That is an essential beginning, but there are a number of common components of diversity management efforts, as Figure 5-11 illustrates. For diversity to succeed, the most crucial component is seeing it as a commitment throughout the organization, beginning with top management. Diversity results must be measured, and management accountability for achieving these results must be emphasized and rewarded. Once management accountability for diversity results has been established, then it is important that policies and activities provide organizational justice and fairness in work treatment for employees.[45] A number of different activities can be implemented as part of a diversity management program, including diversity training.

DIVERSITY TRAINING

Traditional diversity training has a number of different goals. One prevalent goal is to minimize discrimination and harassment lawsuits. Other goals focus on improving acceptance and understanding of people with different backgrounds, experiences, capabilities, and lifestyles.

FIGURE 5-11   Common Diversity Management Components

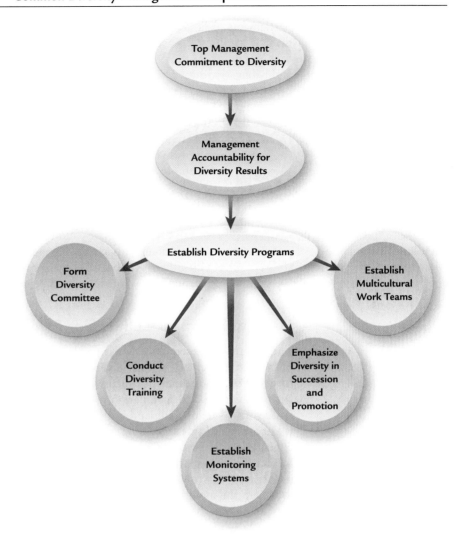

Components of Traditional Diversity Training

Approaches to diversity training vary, but often include at least three components. *Legal awareness* is the first and most common component. Here, the
training focuses on the legal implications of discrimination. A limited approach
to diversity training stops with these legal "do's and don'ts."

By introducing *cultural awareness*, employers hope to build greater understanding of the differences among people. Cultural awareness training helps
all participants to see and accept the differences in people with widely varying
cultural backgrounds.

The third component of diversity training—*sensitivity training*—is more
difficult. The aim here is to "sensitize" people to the differences among
them and how their words and behaviors are seen by others. Some diversity training includes exercises containing examples of harassment and other
behaviors.

Effects of Diversity Training

The effects of diversity training are viewed as mixed by both organizations and participants. A limited number of studies have been done on the effectiveness of diversity training.[46] There is some concern that the programs may be interesting or entertaining, but may not produce longer-term changes in people's attitudes and behaviors toward others with characteristics different from their own.

Some argue that traditional diversity training more often than not has failed, pointing out that it does not reduce discrimination and harassment complaints. Rather than reducing conflict, in a number of situations diversity training has heightened hostility and conflicts.[47] In some firms, it has produced divisive effects, and has not taught the behaviors needed for employees to work well together in a diverse workplace.

This last point, focusing on behaviors, seems to hold the most promise for making diversity training more effective. For instance, dealing with cultural diversity as part of training efforts for sales representatives and managers has produced positive results. Teaching appropriate behaviors and skills in relationships with others is more likely to produce satisfactory results than focusing just on attitudes and beliefs among diverse employees.

Internet Research

American Institute for Managing Diversity
To learn about the nation's leading non-profit think tank dedicated to promoting and furthering the field of diversity management, link to their site at: http://thomsonedu.com/management/mathis.

Backlash Against Diversity Efforts

The negative consequences of diversity training may manifest themselves broadly in a backlash against diversity efforts. This backlash takes two main forms. First, and somewhat surprisingly, the individuals in protected groups, such as women and members of racial minorities, sometimes see the diversity efforts as inadequate and nothing but "corporate public relations." Thus, it appears that by establishing diversity programs, employers are raising the expectation levels of protected-group individuals but the programs are not meeting the expectations. This failure can result in further disillusionment and more negativity toward the organization by those who would initially appear to benefit the most from such programs.

On the other side, a number of individuals who are not in protected groups, primarily white males, believe that the emphasis on diversity sets them up as scapegoats for the societal problems created by increasing diversity. Sometimes white males show hostility and anger at diversity efforts. Those programs are widely perceived as benefiting only women and minorities and taking away opportunities for men and non-minorities. This resentment and hostility is usually directed at affirmative action programs that employers have instituted.

The backlash against diversity efforts is not limited to white males. For example, diversity training that includes lesbian, gay, and bisexual content has created resistance from employees with certain religious beliefs.[48] Those employees have felt discriminated against because of their beliefs, and some have been reprimanded for bringing Bibles to read in the training classes. It appears that problems such as this one stem from what employees see as attempts to change what they believe. Trainers emphasize that the key to avoiding backlash in diversity efforts is to stress that people can believe whatever they wish, but at work their values are less important than their *behaviors*. Dealing with diversity is not about what people can and cannot *say*, it is about being *respectful* to others.

Managing diversity training, and indeed diversity itself, must be well thought out and implemented. Diversity is a reality for employers today, and effective diversity management is crucial to HR management.

SUMMARY

- Discrimination on the basis of race and national origin is illegal, and racial harassment and language issues are two important concerns.
- As more women have entered the workforce, sex/gender issues in equal employment have included discrimination in both pay inequity and discrimination in jobs and careers.
- Sexual harassment can occur in two forms, quid pro quo and hostile environment, and employers should develop policies on sexual harassment.
- It is vital that employers train all employees on what constitutes sexual harassment, promptly investigate complaints, and take action when sexual harassment is found to have occurred.
- Aging of the U.S. workforce has led to more concerns about age discrimination, especially in the form of forced retirement and termination.
- Employers are recognizing the value of attracting and retaining older workers through greater use of part-time work and phased retirement programs.

- Individuals with disabilities represent a significant number of current and potential employees.
- Employers are making reasonable accommodations for individuals with disabilities, including those with mental or life-threatening illnesses.
- Reasonable accommodation also is a strategy that can be used to deal with the religious diversity of employees.
- Affirmative action has been intensely litigated, and the debate continues today.
- Diversity management focuses on organizational efforts to ensure that all people are valued regardless of their differences.
- The "business case" for diversity is built on its ability to allow new talent and ideas, aid in employee attraction and retention, allow for an increase in market share, and lead to lower costs.
- Diversity training has had limited success, possibly because it too often has focused on beliefs rather than behaviors.

REVIEW AND APPLICATION QUESTIONS

1. From your own experience or that of someone you know, give examples of the two types of sexual harassment.
2. Explain why you agree or disagree with affirmative action and how it will be affected by the growing workforce diversity.
3. You need to convince upper management of the usefulness of a company-wide diversity program. How will you define diversity and what arguments can be made for doing so? Use the Website *www.diversityinc.com* and other sources to gather the necessary information.

Diversity and Discrimination in the Restaurant Industry

The experiences of different restaurant industry firms illustrate how employment issues can affect organizations. Several examples are described next.

McDonald's Corporation has placed significant emphasis on ensuring that all employees are treated appropriately. The firm has a large number of racial/ethnic minority managers and employees. So that all individuals involved in hiring handle the employment processes legally and effectively, McDonald's does the same training for everyone. This training is done for managers at stores, regional offices, and corporate headquarters. Also, at the firm's "Hamburger University," additional seminars on diversity are conducted as part of its broad training curriculum.

A different focus is occurring at Starbucks Corporation. As it expands its number of stores and adds more employees, a specific effort is being made to recruit individuals with disabilities. To aid customers and employees with disabilities, Starbucks has been redesigning service counters and facilities to make them more usable for those with disabilities. Special recruiting efforts have resulted in the growth of employees with cerebral palsy, hearing deficiencies, and those with physical limitations.

Contrast these efforts with lawsuits filed against other restaurants for illegal discrimination. Cracker Barrel restaurants in Illinois had to pay $2 million to settle EEOC charges for race and sexual harassment against 51 employees. African American employees were insulted through racially specific wording, and women were subjected to offensive sexual comments and conduct. Note that Cracker Barrel has more than 500 stores in 40 states, but these charges only applied to three restaurants.

Denny's Restaurants have also been sued for disability bias against workers nationwide. The EEOC lawsuit charged that Denny's did not make reasonable accommodation for employees with different disabilities. That lawsuit is still under review and being challenged by Denny's. Note that a decade ago Denny's was subjected to racial bias legal claims. As a result, Denny's responded by aggressively hiring minorities and proactively addressing diversity problems, which led it to receive a national award as a minority friendly firm.

These varied examples in just one industry illustrate how employment discrimination and diversity continue to be HR challenges for employers. This is especially true given the widely varying workforces, numerous different managers, and many different locations.[49]

Questions

1. Discuss why the various diversity efforts of McDonald's and Starbucks are good business practices.
2. Describe what HR efforts are needed by employers such as Cracker Barrel and Denny's to reduce discrimination charges and complaints when they occur in individual locations.

Discrimination?

This case illustrates issues involved in a disciplinary action when a protected-class individual is involved. (For the case, go to http://thomsonedu.com/management/mathis.)

NOTES

1. Based on Carol Hymowitz, "The New Diversity," *The Wall Street Journal*, November 14, 2005, R1; Stacie Hamel, "Women at the Wheel," *Omaha World Herald*, November 12, 2006, D1; and Roger O. Crockett, "Why Are Latinos Leading Blacks in the Job Market?" *Business Week*, March 15, 2004, 70.

2. "EEOC Settles Suit for Qualified Black Workers Denied Promotions at Trucking Company," *EEOC News Release*, October 25, 2005.

3. "EEOC Suit Said Cabinet Maker Subjected Class of Latinos to Physical and Verbal Abuse," *EEOC News Release*, July 22, 2005.

4. *Hollins v. Delta Airlines*, 10th Cir., No. 99-4072 (January 29, 2001).

5. "English-Only Rules," *HR Compliance Abstracts*, March 28, 2007, www.hrcompliance.ceridian.com.

6. Miriam Jordan, "Employers Provide Language Aid," *The Wall Street Journal*, November 8, 2005, B13.

7. Catherine Yang, "The Economic Case for Legalizing Illegals," *Business Week*, May 8, 2006, 43; and Ann Zimmerman, "Labor Pains," *The Wall Street Journal*, December 19, 2003, A1, A8.

8. Susan Ladika, "Trouble on the Hiring Front," *HR Magazine*, October 2006, 56–61.

9. For detailed studies, see Francine D. Dlau and Lawrence M. Kahn, "The Gender Pay Gap: Have Women Gone As Far As They Can?" *Academy of Management Perspectives*, 21 (2007), 7–23; and "Women's Economic Status in the States: Wide Disparities by Race, Ethnicity, and Region" (Washington, DC: Institute for Women's Policy Research, 2004).

10. "Diffusing the Equity Issue: How BC-BS Instituted a Gender-Balanced Pay Plan," *Pay for Performance Report*, July 2003, 1–2.

11. Tracey Levy, "Hiring and Promotion Policies," June 16, 2006, www.hreonline.com.

12. "Glass Ceiling Not Cracked for Executives," *T&D*, June 2006, 19.

13. Barbara Reinhold, "Smashing Glass Ceilings: Why Women Still Find It Tough to Advance to the Executive Suite," *Journal of Organizational Excellence*, 24 (2005), 43–56.

14. Matthew Heller, "More Employers Broadening Nondiscrimination Policies to Include Transgender Workers," *Workforce Management*, June 26, 2006, 62–63.

15. "Nearly 40% of Workers Have Had Workplace Romance," *Newsline*, January 31, 2007, www.spherion.com.

16. "HR Managers/Executives Worry About Workplace Romance," *Human Resource Department Management Report*, April 2002, 1; and "Workplace Romance," *SHRM Research*, April 2002, 3, 6.

17. Janet Lever, Gail Zellman, and Stephen J. Hirschfeld, "Office Romance," *Across the Board*, March/April 2006, 32–41.

18. Jonathan A. Segal, "Dangerous Liaisons," *HR Magazine*, December 2005, 104–108.

19. Sandy Lim and Lilia Cortina, "Interpersonal Mistreatment in the Workplace: The Interface and Impact of General Incivility and Sexual Harassment," *Journal of Applied Psychology*, 90 (2005), 483–496.

20. Karyn-Siobhan Robinson, "Cyber-Sex Permeates the Workplace," *HR News*, April 2001, 10.

21. Michelle Conlin, "Harassers in High Places," *Business Week*, November 13, 2006, 44; Michael W. Johnson, "California Requires Sexual Harassment Training," *SHRM Legal Report*, January/February, 2005, 1–4; and "Harassment and Discrimination Through Electronic Communications," *Ceridian Abstracts*, www.hrcompliance.ceridian.com.

22. Joanne Sammer, "Pension Law Eases Way for Phased Retirement Plans," *SHRM OnLine*, Summer 2006, www.shrm.org/rewards.

23. Mark Schoeff, Jr., "Advocates Seek Greater Voice for Disabled," *Workforce Management*, October 23, 2006, 8.

24. Chan Fong et al., "Drivers of Workplace Discrimination Against People with Disabilities: The Utility of Attribution Theory," *Work*, 25 (2005), 77.

25. Kelley M. Butler, "10 Million Ways to Fill the Talent Gap," *Employee Benefit News*, March 2007, 22; and Allen Smith, "ADA Accommodation Is Not One-Stop Shopping," *HR Magazine*, May 2006, 34.

26. "ADA Protections for Employees with Mental Illness," *Best Practices in HR*, October 6, 2006, 1.

27. James D. Westaby, Andrea Versony, and Robert C. Hausmann, "Intentions to Work During Terminal Illness: An Exploratory Study of Antecedent Conditions," *Journal of Applied Psychology*, 90 (2005), 1297–1305.

28. Bruce Shutan, "Battling the 9/11 Backlash," *Human Resource Executive*, June 16, 2006, 73–76.

29. J. D. Prenkart and J. M. Magid, "A Hobson's Choice for Religious Accommodation," *American Business Law Journal*, 43 (2006), 967.

30. Phred Dvorak, "Managing by the (Good) Book," *The Wall Street Journal*, October 19, 2006, B1.

31. M. Lee Pelton, "After the Supreme Court Michigan Cases," *The Presidency*, Fall 2003, 18–27.

32. Stephen J. Hirschfeld, "Americans Believe Affirmative Action in Hiring Has Been Good," *Press Releases Polls/Surveys*, www.employmentlaw-alliance.com.

33. For example, see R. Cropanzano, J. E. Slaughter, and P. D. Bachiochi, "Organizational Justice and Black Applicants' Reactions to Affirmative Action," *Journal of Applied Psychology*, 90 (2005), 1168–1184.

34. Amy McMillan-Capehart and Orlando Richard, "Organizational Justice and Perceived Fairness of Hiring Decisions Related to Race and Gender: Affirmative Action Reactions," *Equal Opportunities International*, 24 (2005), 44–58.

35. Harry Holzer and David Neumark, "What Does Affirmative Action Do?" *Industrial and Labor Relations Review*, 53 (2000), 240–271.

36. For details and statistics, go to www.census.gov.

37. *Workplace Diversity Practices and Changes to the EEO-1 Process Survey Report* (Alexandria, VA: Society for Human Resource Management, 2006).

38. Alexandra Kalev, Erin Kelly, and Frank Dobbin, "Best Practices or Best Guesses: Assessing the Efficacy of Corporate Affirmative Action and Diversity Policies," *American Sociological Review*, 71 (2006), 589–618.

39. Thomas Kochan et al., "The Effects of Diversity on Business Performance: Report of the Diversity Research Network," *Human Resource Management*, 42 (2003), 3–21.

40. Mary Kwak, "The Paradoxical Effects of Diversity," *MIT Sloan Management Review,* 44 (2003), 7.

41. Jonathan Leonard and David Levine, "The Effect of Diversity on Turnover: A Large Case Study," *Industrial & Labor Relations Review,* 59 (2006), 547.

42. Rebecca R. Hastings, "SHRM Research Report Shows Diversity Making Progress," *HR News,* October 17, 2006, *www.shrm.org/hrnews.*

43. Robert Rodriguez, "Diversity Finds Its Place," *HR Magazine,* August 2006, 56–61.

44. M. R. Carrell, E. E. Mann, and T. H. Sigler, "Defining Workforce Diversity Programs and Practices in Organizations: A Longitudinal Study," *Labor Law Journal,* Spring 2006, 5–12.

45. Q. M. Roberson and C. K. Stevens, "Making Sense of Diversity in the Workplace. . . .," *Journal of Applied Psychology,* 91 (2006), 379–391.

46. Elizabeth L. Paluck, "Diversity Training and Intergroup Contact: A Call to Action Research," *Journal of Social Issues,* 62 (2006), 577–595.

47. C. W. Von Bergen et al., "Unintended Negative Effects of Diversity Management," *Public Personnel Management,* 31 (2002), 1–12.

48. David M. Kaplan, "Can Diversity Training Discriminate? Backlash to Lesbian, Gay, and Bisexual Diversity Initiatives," *Employee Responsibilities and Rights Journal,* 18 (2006), 61.

49. Julie C. Ramirez, "A Different Bias," *Human Resource Executive,* May 15, 2006, 37–39; Michael Corkery, "A Special Effort," *The Wall Street Journal,* November 14, 2005, R8; *EEOC v. Cracker Barrel Old Country Store, Inc., and CBOCX West, Inc.,* N.D. Illinois, No. 04-C5273 (March 2006); "Denney's Sued for Disability Bias Against Class of Workers Nationwide," *Ceridian Abstracts, www.hrcompliance.ceridian.com;* and Bill Leonard, "EEOC Sues Denny's over Disability Practices," *HR News,* October 2, 2006, *www.shrm.org/hrnews.*

CHAPTER

6

Jobs and Job Analysis

After you have read this chapter, you should be able to:

- Discuss workflow analysis and business process re-engineering as approaches to organizational work.

- Define job design and identify five design characteristics for jobs.

- Explain how work schedules and telework can change jobs and work.

- Describe job analysis and the stages and methods used in the process.

- Identify both behavioral and legal aspects of job analysis.

- List the components of job descriptions.

HR Headline

Global Jobs Have Demanding Differences

Virtually every job has its good and bad points. When Travis Damon was stationed in Hong Kong—a good point—he had to leave his amateur basketball team's playoff game at half time for a conference call with the U.S. headquarters. For his colleagues in America, it was after breakfast and the morning coffee, but for Travis it was 9:30 on a Friday night and personal time—a bad point. It was the last straw in the frequently 24-hour Asian workday for American expatriates, so Travis transferred back to the United States, but he found that living in America did not solve his problem. He still reported to a work team based in Asia, so he ended up staying up late for business once again. A year later he moved back to Hong Kong.

Sometimes bad timing cannot be helped—especially when tri-continental conferences are necessary. Odd hours are part of the job for U.S. East Coast–centric businesses that tie expatriates to their cell phones. Some expatriates are searching for solutions to the "timing" problems.

Kelly Allen, a Hong Kong–based IT manager, has her colleagues in the United States condense all of their communications to one weekly call on Tuesdays from 8:45 to 10 P.M. Hong Kong time. They call that meeting the "Flight Club," and it is a good solution.[1]

These two examples illustrate just some of the job challenges facing individuals working globally. In designing jobs or identifying accurate job descriptions, significant requirements should be recognized and made apparent to potential expatriates and their domestic counterparts.

Work and jobs in organizations throughout the world are changing dramatically. Globalization and technology are primary drivers of this change. Consider the number of jobs that have been shifted from the United States and Europe to China, India, Romania, Mexico, the Philippines, and other lower-wage countries.

These drivers of change and other elements such as IT, demographics, and worker shortages are providing employers with multiple opportunities to change how work is done and the number of jobs necessary to carry out the work of the organization. Changing work and jobs requires an understanding of the options for building different jobs and clear knowledge of what employees do now in their jobs.

NATURE OF JOBS AND WORK

Work Effort directed toward accomplishing results.

Job Grouping of tasks, duties, and responsibilities that constitutes the total work assignment for an employee.

One way to visualize an organization is as an entity that takes inputs from the surrounding environment and then, through some kind of "work," turns those inputs into goods or services. Work is effort directed toward accomplishing results. The work may be done by humans, machines, or both. But the total amount of work to be done in an organization must be divided into jobs so that it can be coordinated in some logical way. A job is a grouping of tasks, duties, and responsibilities that constitutes the total work assignment for an employee. These tasks, duties, and responsibilities may change over time, and therefore the job may change. Ideally, when all the jobs in an organization are added together, they should equal the amount of work that the organization needs to have done—no more, no less. The degree to which this ideal is or is not met drives differences in organizational productivity.

Jobs increase in number, evolve and change in duties, and are combined or eliminated as the needs of the organization change. If this does *not* happen, the organization is failing to adapt to the changes in its environment and may be becoming outmoded or non-competitive.[2] Several different approaches are used to deal with the common issues surrounding jobs in any organization. The discussion in this chapter will follow the topics in Figure 6-1.

For Southwest Airlines, organizational values and strategies are tied to having involved employees working in an enjoyable culture that delivers dependable service at low fares. Thus, Southwest employees have a high degree of flexibility in how they perform the work, even to the point that customer service agents may help clean planes or unload luggage if the workload demands it. Other airlines, such as American and United, have higher fares, more service amenities, and employees with more narrowly defined jobs. The way work is done and how jobs are designed and performed vary significantly under these two approaches, and the differences impact the number of jobs and people needed.

For HR, how work flows through the organization and how to make that work more efficient is important. Changing the way jobs are done through re-design, perhaps by using teams or flexible scheduling, may make people more satisfied with their jobs. Formally reviewing jobs and workflow analysis to identify what is expected to be accomplished is part of a framework for training, pay, performance, and other aspects of HR management.

WORKFLOW ANALYSIS

Workflow analysis Study of the way work (outputs, activities, and inputs) moves through an organization.

Workflow analysis is the study of the way work moves through an organization. Usually, it begins with an examination of the quantity and quality of the desired and actual *outputs* (goods and services). Then, the *activities* (tasks and jobs) that lead to the outputs are evaluated to see if they are achieving

FIGURE 6-1   Approaches to Dealing with Jobs

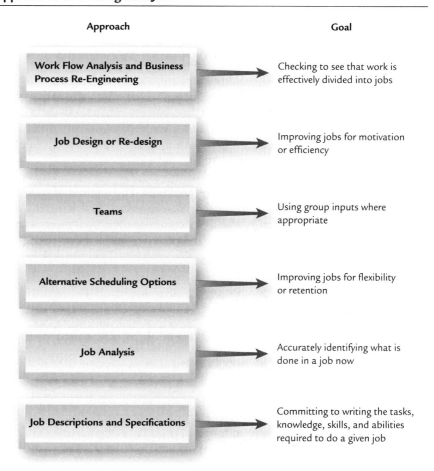

Approach	Goal
Work Flow Analysis and Business Process Re-Engineering	Checking to see that work is effectively divided into jobs
Job Design or Re-design	Improving jobs for motivation or efficiency
Teams	Using group inputs where appropriate
Alternative Scheduling Options	Improving jobs for flexibility or retention
Job Analysis	Accurately identifying what is done in a job now
Job Descriptions and Specifications	Committing to writing the tasks, knowledge, skills, and abilities required to do a given job

the desired outputs. Finally, the *inputs* (people, material, information, data, equipment, etc.) must be assessed to determine if they make the outputs and activities more efficient and better.

At one electric utility company, if a customer called with a service outage problem, a customer service representative typically took the information and put it into a database. Then, in the operations department, a dispatcher accessed the database to schedule a line technician to repair the problem. Then, someone else called to tell the customer when the repair would be done. The line technician also received instructions from a supervisor, who got information on workload and locations from the dispatcher.

A workflow analysis of this process showed that there were too many steps involving too many different jobs. So the utility implemented a new customer service system and combined the dispatching function with customer service. The re-design permitted the customer service representatives to access workload information and schedule the line technicians as part of the initial customer phone call, except in unusual situations. The re-design required redefining the tasks, duties, and responsibilities of several jobs. Implementing the new jobs required training the customer service representatives in dispatching, as well as moving dispatchers into the customer service department and training them in all facets of customer service. The result was a more responsive workflow for customers, more efficient scheduling of line technicians, and broader jobs for customer service representatives. Ultimately, through retirements and employee attrition, the firm has reduced the number of customer service employees by 20% because the work could be done with fewer individuals.

Technology and Workflow

The utility company example illustrates how technology must be viewed as part of workflow analysis. With the rapid growth of the Internet and Web-based information systems, changes in the workflow are occurring in many organizations. For instance, having employees access and change their personal benefits information themselves has reduced HR administrative work by 60%, according to one survey.[3]

Another example of why workflow analysis may be helpful involves administrative secretarial jobs. The number of secretaries has declined sharply during the last decade as technology has changed. Also, the demand has dropped as more managers compose their own memos and reports on e-mail. Voice mail has reduced the need for someone to take messages, and copying and filing are done in many organizations through electronic systems in office service centers, not by individual secretaries. On the other hand, current office support functions require greater responsibility and entail more coordination and authority than in the past.[4] The job title today is more likely to be "administrative coordinator" or "administrative assistant" to reflect these changes, and organizations are doing workflow analysis to make adjustments.

Business Process Re-Engineering

Business process re-engineering (BPR)
Measures for improving such activities as product development, customer service, and service delivery.

After workflow analysis provides an understanding of how work is being done, re-engineering generates the needed changes in the operations. The purpose of business process re-engineering (BPR) is to improve such activities as product development, customer service, and service delivery. BPR consists of three phases:

1. *Re-think:* Examine how the current organization of work and jobs affects customer satisfaction and service.
2. *Re-design:* Analyze how jobs are put together, the workflow, and how results are achieved; then re-design the process as necessary.
3. *Re-tool:* Look at new technologies (equipment, computers, software, etc.) as opportunities to improve productivity, service quality, and customer satisfaction.

In the past, HR has been excluded from BPR in organizations because the focus of BPR has been on the operations areas. However, because of the desire to improve HR efficiency and effectiveness, BPR is increasingly being applied to HR management. Global banks such as Barclays, Deutsche, and Standard Chartered have engaged in re-engineering and restructuring of their HR departments.[5] Key to the successful re-engineering of HR or other organizational areas is providing effective and continuous communication, doing detailed planning, and training managers on the BPR processes. Without these efforts, the success rates of BPR are low, around 30%.[6]

Process analysis/management techniques such as workflow analysis and re-engineering may work best when applied to routine rather than more creative areas of work.[7] Their success depends on several factors important in managing change.

Internet Research

ProSci Learning Center
The ProSci Learning Center is a good source for on-line reference material for business process re-engineering. Visit their Website at: http://thomsonedu.com/management/mathis.

JOB DESIGN/RE-DESIGN

Job design Organizing tasks, duties, responsibilities, and other elements into a productive unit of work.

Job design refers to organizing tasks, duties, responsibilities, and other elements into a productive unit of work. It addresses the content of jobs and the effect of jobs on employees. Identifying the components of a given job is an integral part of job design.[8] Currently, job design is receiving greater attention for three major reasons:

■ Job design can influence *performance* in certain jobs, especially those where employee motivation can make a substantial difference. Lower costs resulting from reduced turnover and absenteeism also are related to the effective design of jobs.

■ Job design can affect *job satisfaction*. Because people are more satisfied with certain job configurations than with others, identifying what makes a "good" job becomes critical.

■ Job design can affect both *physical* and *mental health*. Problems such as hearing loss, backache, and leg pain sometimes can be traced directly to job design, as can stress, high blood pressure, and heart disease.

Person/job fit Matching characteristics of people with characteristics of jobs.

Not everyone would enjoy being an HR manager, an engineer, a nurse, or a drill-press operator. But various people like and do well at each of these jobs. The person/job fit is a simple but important concept of matching characteristics of people with characteristics of jobs. If a person does not fit a job, theoretically either the person can be changed or replaced or the job can be altered. For instance, an employer can try to make the "round" person fit the "square" job, but it is hard to successfully reshape people. By re-designing jobs, the person/job fit may be improved more easily. Improving the person/job fit may affect individual responses to jobs because a job may be motivating to one person but not to someone else. Also, depending on how jobs are designed, they may provide more or less opportunity for employees to satisfy their job-related needs. For example, bank tellers talk to people all day; an individual who would rather not talk to others all day may be better in a job that does not require so much interaction because that part of the bank teller job probably cannot be changed.

Figure 6-2 shows a variety of elements in a job that can be changed to make it a different job. Consider how the "levers" shown in the figure would be different for a bank teller's job and a timber cutter's job. Some of the elements in each job would appeal to some people but not to others. Some aspects in each job could be changed but many others could not. For example, the job content and working conditions are quite different. The final configuration of all these elements is the design for a particular job. Re-design involves changing some of the elements.[9]

Classic Approaches to Job Design

One approach for designing or re-designing jobs is to simplify the job tasks and responsibilities. Job simplification may be appropriate for jobs that are to be staffed with entry-level employees. However, making jobs too simple may result in boring jobs that appeal to few people, causing high turnover. Several different approaches have been used as part of job design.

Job enlargement Broadening the scope of a job by expanding the number of different tasks to be performed.

Job Enlargement and Job Enrichment Attempts to alleviate some of the problems encountered in excessive job simplification fall under the general headings of job enlargement and job enrichment. Job enlargement involves

FIGURE 6-2   Possible "Levers" for Job Design

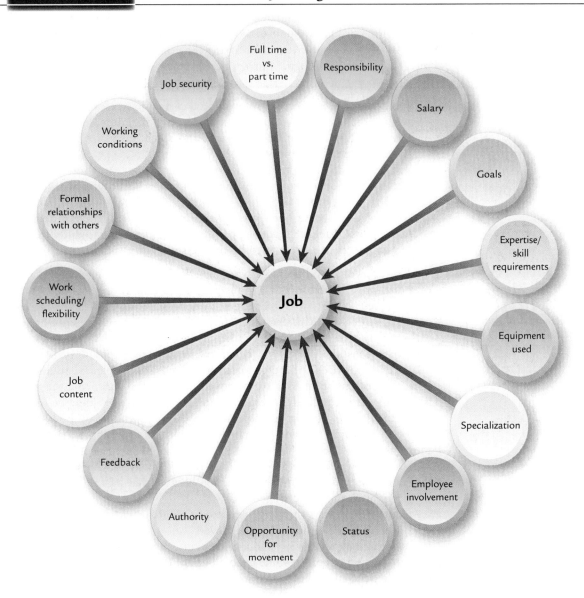

Job enrichment Increasing the depth of a job by adding responsibility for planning, organizing, controlling, or evaluating the job.

broadening the scope of a job by expanding the number of different tasks to be performed. Job enrichment is increasing the depth of a job by adding responsibility for planning, organizing, controlling, or evaluating the job. A manager might enrich a job by promoting variety, requiring more skill and responsibility, providing more autonomy, and adding opportunities for personal growth. Giving an employee more responsibility for planning and controlling the tasks to be done also enriches a job. However, simply adding more similar tasks does not enrich a job. Some examples of job enrichment are:

- Giving the employee an entire job rather than just a piece of the work
- Providing the employee more freedom and authority to perform the job as necessary
- Increasing the employee's accountability for work by reducing external control

■ Expanding assignments so that the employee can learn to do new tasks and develop new areas of expertise

■ Directing feedback reports to the employee rather than only to management

Job Rotation One technique that can break the monotony of an otherwise simple, routine job is job rotation, which is the process of shifting a person from job to job. Some argue that job rotation does little in the long run—that although rotating a person from one boring job to another may help somewhat initially, the jobs are still perceived as boring. The advantage of job rotation is that it develops an employee's capabilities for doing several different jobs.

Job rotation Process of shifting a person from job to job.

Characteristics of Jobs

A model developed by Hackman and Oldham focuses on five important design characteristics of jobs. Figure 6-3 shows that *skill variety, task identity,* and *task significance* affect the meaningfulness of work; *autonomy* stimulates responsibility; and *feedback* provides knowledge of results. Each aspect can make a job better for the jobholder to the degree that each is present.

Skill Variety The extent to which the work requires several different activities for successful completion indicates its skill variety. For example, lower skill variety exists when an assembly-line worker performs the same two tasks repetitively. The more skills involved, the more meaningful the work becomes. Skill variety is not to be confused with *multi-tasking,* which is doing several tasks at the same time with computers, telephones, personal organizers, and other gadgets. The price of multi-tasking may be never getting away from the job—not a "better" outcome for everyone.

Skill variety Extent to which the work requires several different activities for successful completion.

Task identity Extent to which the job includes a "whole" identifiable unit of work that is carried out from start to finish and that results in a visible outcome.

Task Identity The extent to which the job includes a "whole" identifiable unit of work that is carried out from start to finish and that results in a visible outcome is its task identity. For example, in the utility company mentioned

FIGURE 6-3   **Job Characteristics Model**

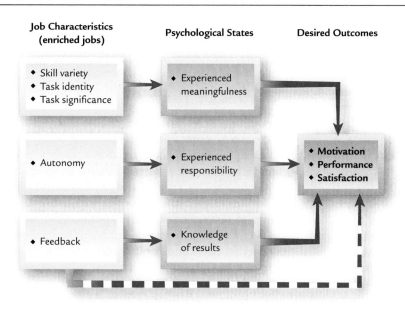

previously, now when a customer calls with a problem, one employee, called a Customer Care Advocate, handles problems from maintenance to repair. As a result, more than 40% of customer problems are resolved by one person while the customer is still on the line. Previously, fewer than 1% of customer problems were resolved immediately because the customer service representative had to complete paperwork and forward it to operations, which then followed a number of separate steps using different people to resolve problems. In the current system, the Customer Care Advocate generally follows the problem from start to finish, solving the whole problem, not just a part of it, which makes the job more meaningful to the employees involved.

Task Significance The impact the job has on other people indicates its task significance. A job is more meaningful if it is important to other people for some reason. For instance, soldiers may experience more fulfillment when defending their country from a real threat than when merely training to stay ready in case a threat arises.

Autonomy The extent of individual freedom and discretion in the work and its scheduling indicates autonomy. More autonomy leads to a greater feeling of personal responsibility for the work.

Feedback The amount of information employees receive about how well or how poorly they have performed is feedback. The advantage of feedback is that it helps employees to understand the effectiveness of their performance and contributes to their overall knowledge about the work. At one firm, feedback reports from customers who contact the company with problems are given directly to the employees, who then handle the customers' complaints, instead of being given only to the department manager.

USING TEAMS IN JOBS

Typically, a job is thought of as something done by one person. However, where appropriate, jobs may be designed for teams. In an attempt to make jobs more meaningful and to take advantage of the increased productivity and commitment that can follow such a change, more organizations are assigning jobs to teams of employees instead of individuals. Some firms have gone as far as dropping such terms as *workers* and *employees*, replacing them with *teammates, crew members, associates,* and other titles that emphasize teamwork.

Types of Teams

Organizations use several types of teams that function outside the scope of members' normal jobs and meet from time to time. One is the special-purpose team, which is formed to address specific problems, improve work processes, and enhance the overall quality of products and services. Often, special-purpose teams are a mixture of employees, supervisors, and managers.

The self-directed team is composed of individuals who are assigned a cluster of tasks, duties, and responsibilities to be accomplished. Unlike special-purpose teams, self-directed work teams become the regular entities that use internal decision-making processes. Use of self-directed work teams must be planned well and fit the culture of the organization.[10]

Task significance Impact the job has on other people.

Autonomy Extent of individual freedom and discretion in the work and its scheduling.

Feedback Amount of information employees receive about how well or how poorly they have performed.

Special-purpose team Organizational team formed to address specific problems, improve work processes, and enhance the overall quality of products and services.

Self-directed team Organizational team composed of individuals who are assigned a cluster of tasks, duties, and responsibilities to be accomplished.

The role of supervisors and managers changes with use of teams.[11] An interesting challenge for self-directed work teams involves the emergence or development of team leaders. The role of the team leader differs from the traditional role played by supervisors or managers. Rather than giving orders, the team leader becomes a facilitator to assist the team, to mediate and resolve conflicts among team members, and to interact with other teams and managers in other parts of the organization. Team members may need to share or rotate leadership for different phases of projects in which special expertise may be beneficial.

With more firms operating globally, the use of global teams has increased significantly. Many times, members of global teams seldom or never meet in person. Instead, they "meet" electronically using Web-based systems.

The virtual team is composed of individuals who are separated geographically but linked by communications technology. The success of virtual work teams depends on a number of factors, some of which are depicted in Figure 6-4.[12]

Virtual team
Organizational team composed of individuals who are separated geographically but linked by communications technology.

Advantages and Disadvantages of Team Jobs

Doing work with teams has been a popular form of job re-design for the last decade. Improved productivity, increased employee involvement, more widespread employee learning, and greater employee ownership of problems are among the potential benefits.[13] For example, the United Auto Workers (UAW) and Chrysler have used work teams effectively in a number of facilities, though this cooperative effort has not been successful in all locations.

One study on the use of self-directed work teams found that productivity increased, especially when both individual and team compensation were used.[14] However, how to measure the performance of teams poses a problem. Compensating individual team members so that they see themselves as a team rather than just a group of individuals is a related issue not adequately addressed in many team situations.

Teams are more likely to be successful if they are allowed to function with sufficient authority to make decisions about their activities and operations. As a transition to work teams occurs, significant efforts are necessary to define the areas of work, scope of authority, and goals of the teams. Additionally, teams must recognize and address dissent and conflict. Contrary to what some

FIGURE 6-4   **Factors Affecting Virtual Team Success**

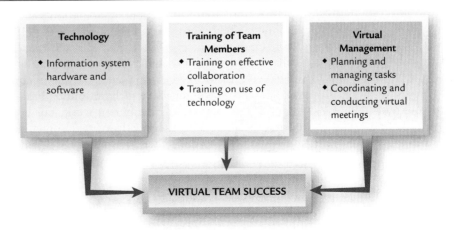

might believe, suppressing dissent and conflict to preserve harmony ultimately becomes destructive to the effective operation of a team.

As seen in the example of the UAW and Chrysler, not every use of teams as a part of job design has been successful. In some cases, employers find that teams work better with "group-oriented" employees than with more individualistically focused workers. Further, much work is not really suited to a team environment, and many companies have used teamwork without much thought. Too often, *teamwork* can be a buzzword or "feel-good" device that may actually get in the way of effective decision making.

JOBS WITH ALTERNATIVE SCHEDULING/LOCATIONS

A job consists of the tasks an employee does, the relationships required on the job, the tools the employee works with, and many other elements. Considerations that can be used to affect job design for both employers and employees are the time during which work is scheduled and the location of employees when working.

The main causes of job-related stress appear to be time pressures, fears of losing a job, deadlines, and fragmented work. The increasing use of technology means that many employees are "always on call" and can "burn out" on work. How employees view the demands of work have been identified in a study that found the following[15]:

- More than half of U.S. workers (52%) say they would be willing to trade a day off a week for a day's less pay a week.
- Over 80% wish they had more time to spend with family, and this view is shared among adults with and without children.
- About 60% feel pressure to work too many hours.

To respond to stress and other concerns, employers are using work schedule alternatives and telework.

Work Schedules

The work schedules associated with different jobs vary. Some jobs must be performed during "normal" daily work hours and workdays, and some jobs require employees to work nights, weekends, and extended hours.

Global Work Schedule Differences The number of work hours in a week varies from country to country. For a look at how Spain has tried to build more flexibility into work scheduling, see the HR Perspective discussion. The European Union (EU) has issued the Working Time Directive, which states that employees in EU countries should work a maximum of 48 hours a week. However, EU workers can opt out of the maximum, and over one-third of British workers have such opt-outs.[16] France has a law limiting working hours to 35 hours a week, but because various exceptions are made, the weekly average sometimes is lower than 35. Workers in the United States average significantly more work hours than do workers in many other developed countries.

Work Schedule Alternatives The traditional work schedule in the United States, in which employees work 8 hours a day, 5 days a week, at the employer's place of operation, is in

HR PERSPECTIVE

Work Schedules and Job Security

The differences in job security and work schedules for both employers and employees can be traced in part to differences in the duration of the job. Europe has had high unemployment for years because workers often cannot be fired or removed if the economy takes a downturn. For instance, in an effort to alleviate this situation, Spain has expanded use of "short-term employment contracts" that can be eliminated with little cost when they no longer need certain employees. Workers in such jobs now account for almost one-third of Spain's labor force.

Spanish workers on short-term employment often subsist on salaries barely above the national minimum of $725 per month and get no severance payments when they move on to the next job. For example, an interpreter in such a job teaches French to Spanish students from October to June. She teaches 17 hours of classes a week, some running as late as 10 P.M., for about $900 per month. She gets no pay over the summer and no paid vacation.

Compare that with another Spaniard with the job security of the "long-term contract." This person, a tax collector, averages about $3,600 per month with an inflation-indexed raise each year. He gets 24 days of paid vacation per year, can leave for up to 15 years, and will be hired back if he returns to his job. When he retires his pension will be 70% of his last salary.

The two jobs are very different in both their impact on employees and their costs to employers. Between the two extremes in job design, Europe continues to struggle with the optimal amount of work schedules and job security in job design.[17]

transition. Throughout many organizations, many different work scheduling arrangements are being used, including the 4-day, 40-hour week; the 4-day, 32-hour week; the 3-day week; shift work and the compressed workweek; flexible scheduling; and job sharing.

Shift Work and the Compressed Workweek *Shift work* is a commonly used work schedule design. Many organizations need 24-hour coverage and therefore schedule three 8-hour shifts each day. Many employers provide some form of additional pay, called a *shift differential,* for working the evening or night shift. Shift work has been found to increase the number of workplace accidents, with employees who work the "graveyard" shift (11 p.m. to 7 a.m.) having 20% more accidents and five times as many work-related mistakes.[18] Also, shift work has long been known to cause difficulties for many employees with families. Twelve-hour shifts, which some employees choose, often involve significant life changes. Nevertheless, many employers must have 24-hour, 7-day coverage, so shift work is likely to continue to be an HR concern.[19]

Compressed workweek
Schedule in which a full week's work is accomplished in fewer than five 8-hour days.

One type of shift work is the compressed workweek, in which a full week's work is accomplished in fewer than five 8-hour days. Compression simply alters the number of hours an employee works each day, usually resulting in more work hours each day and fewer workdays each week. The use of the compressed workweek illustrates how greater flexibility in work schedules is occurring.

Flextime Scheduling arrangement in which employees work a set number of hours a day but vary starting and ending times.

Flexible Scheduling Flexible work schedules allow organizations to make better use of workers by matching work demands to work hours. One type of flexible scheduling is flextime, in which employees work a set number of hours a day but vary starting and ending times. In another variation, employees work 30 minutes longer Monday through Thursday, take short lunch breaks, and leave work at 1 P.M. or 2 P.M. on Friday. Some firms allow employees to work reduced schedules and receive proportionally reduced wages/salaries. Certain levels of hours are worked weekly or monthly.[20]

Flexible scheduling allows management to relax some of the traditional "time clock" control of employees, while still covering workloads. In the United States, numerous full-time workers vary their work hours from those in the traditional model.[21] Also, many employees have increasing control over their work schedules to balance work/life concerns, which may affect organizational productivity.[22] The HR Best Practices highlights the value of Best Buy's more flexible scheduling program.

Job Sharing   Another alternative used to add flexibility and more work/life balancing is job sharing, in which two employees perform the work of one full-time job. For instance, a hospital allows two radiological technicians to fill one job, whereby each individual works every other week. Such arrangements are beneficial for employees who may not want to or be able to work full-time because of family, school, or other reasons. Job sharing also can be effective because each person can substitute for the other when illness, vacation, or other circumstances occur. The keys to successful job sharing are that both "job sharers" must work effectively together and each must be competent in meeting the job requirements.

Job sharing Scheduling arrangement in which two employees perform the work of one full-time job.

Telework

The developments in information and communications technology mean that employees can work anywhere and anytime. As a result, a growing number of employers are allowing employees to work from widely varied locations, as

HR BEST PRACTICES

Best Buy Workplace Change

Best Buy, a large national retailer with over 4,000 employees, has made major changes in its workplace schedules. Rather than emphasizing fixed hours, Best Buy is increasing use of more flexible work hours in its corporate headquarters and stores. Based on the success of an experimental program with 300 employees in some departments, the changes have evolved into a more broadly used program labeled ROWE—Results Only Work Environment.

At the heart of ROWE is the philosophy of focusing on employees getting their work done, not just meeting clock hours. To implement ROWE, managers and employees have had to identify performance result expectations and measures for all jobs. One of the greatest advantages of the ROWE program is the ability of employees to achieve a better work/life balance in their lives. From mothers of school-age children to

single males involved in hobbies and sports, employees can adjust schedules to meet their personal and professional needs.

The HR payoff of ROWE has been significant. According to metrics, voluntary employee turnover has declined in some divisions by as much as 75% to 90% over three years. Average worker productivity in the same period increased 35%.

The ROWE program now is being expanded to include retail store managers and workers. Doing so may require some modifications to ensure that sufficient salespersons are available to serve customers. But with Best Buy retail stores previously experiencing turnover of 60% plus, the hope is that adapting ROWE will help increase employee retention and also make Best Buy a more attractive workplace for recruiting new employees.[23]

FIGURE 6-5   Growth of Telecommuting

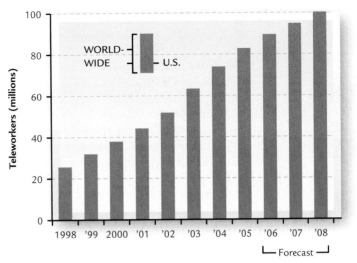

Dialing In
Employees telecommuting more than eight hours per month.

*Estimated.
Source: Gartner Dataquest.

Figure 6-5 indicates. Some employees work partly at home and partly at an office while others share office space with other "office nomads." Many teleworkers are self-employed individuals who have their own businesses or work as independent contractors or contingent workers.[24]

Some employees *telecommute,* which means they work via electronic computing and telecommunications equipment. Many U.S. employers have employees who telecommute one or more days a week and who may work from home, a client's facility, an airport conference room, a work suite in a hotel resort, a business-class seat on an international airline flight, or even a vacation condominium. Telecommuting allows employees to work from home when bad weather or family illness prevents them from coming to office facilities.

Employer Issues with Telework A number of HR management issues and employee concerns must be addressed with teleworkers. Because managers have less direct supervision of teleworkers, there is more self-scheduling by employees. Thus, employees have to be evaluated more on producing results and less on "putting in time."[25]

Employers usually are concerned about maintaining appropriate control over employees when they work from home or away from the office. Further, employers must attend to legal compliance requirements at both federal and state levels. Some of the legal issues include wage and hour laws, health and safety laws, workers' compensation, property insurance, and general liability.

HR must develop policies regarding teleworkers and must train supervisors and managers on how to "lead" employees who may not be physically present much of the time.[26] An effective way to handle the issues that can impact the success of a telework relationship is to begin with a carefully worded policy that considers the following questions:

- How will employers monitor the work of teleworkers?
- How will the use of company equipment and systems be monitored?
- How will expenses for home offices be handled?
- How will employee time records be tracked?
- Is work time being managed properly?

Telework and Employee Concerns Other issues affect employees and their relationships with co-workers and managers. One aspect is overwork when having to balance home and work requirements. Maintaining employee motivation when individuals are not physically present at company facilities can also be challenging and may increase employee stress.[27]

Another concern comes from evidence that telecommuting employees may not advance as quickly as office-based executives because of an "out-of-sight, out-of-mind" framework on the part of some managers.[28] This is a special concern for global employees, whose working hours may not be consistent with U.S. working times.[29] For instance, the 15-hour time zone difference between the United States and some Asian countries may make it difficult for global employees to participate in conference calls.

NATURE OF JOB ANALYSIS

Job design attempts to develop jobs that fit effectively into the flow of the organizational work that needs to be done. The more narrow focus of job analysis centers on using a formal system to gather data about what people do in their jobs. These data are used to generate job descriptions and job specifications.

Job analysis Systematic way of gathering and analyzing information about the content, context, and human requirements of jobs.

The most basic building block of HR management, job analysis, is a systematic way of gathering and analyzing information about the content, context, and human requirements of jobs. Using job analysis to document HR activities is important because the legal defensibility of an employer's recruiting and selection procedures, performance appraisal system, employee disciplinary actions, and pay practices rests in part on the foundation of job analysis.

Various methods and sources of data can be used to conduct job analyses. The real value of job analysis begins as the information is compiled into job descriptions and job specifications for use in virtually all HR activities. To justify HR actions as job related for EEO matters, accurate details on job requirements are needed. To be effective, HR planning, recruiting, and selection all must be based on job requirements and the capabilities of individuals.[30] Additionally, compensation, training, and employee performance appraisals all should be based on the specific needs of the job. Job analysis also is useful in identifying job factors and duties that may contribute to workplace health and safety issues. For instance, one study used job analysis to identify physical demands causing work-related injuries, and the steps to be taken to reduce those injuries.[31] Finally, job analysis plays a key role in employee/labor relations issues.

Job analysis involves collecting information on the characteristics of a job that differentiate it from other jobs. The information generated by job analysis may be useful in redesigning jobs, but its primary purpose is to capture a clear understanding of what is done on a job and what capabilities are needed to do it as designed. There are two approaches to job analysis; one focuses on tasks performed in the job, the other on competencies needed for job performance. An overview of job analysis is depicted in Figure 6-6.

FIGURE 6-6	Job Analysis in Perspective

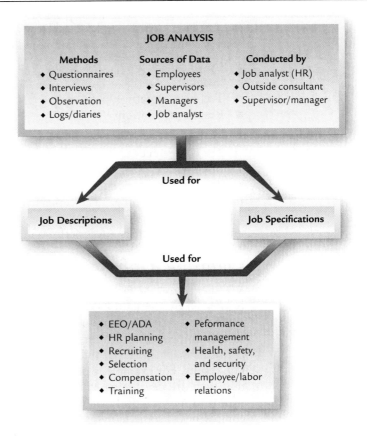

JOB ANALYSIS

Methods	Sources of Data	Conducted by
◆ Questionnaires	◆ Employees	◆ Job analyst (HR)
◆ Interviews	◆ Supervisors	◆ Outside consultant
◆ Observation	◆ Managers	◆ Supervisor/manager
◆ Logs/diaries	◆ Job analyst	

Used for

Job Descriptions   **Job Specifications**

Used for

◆ EEO/ADA	◆ Peformance management
◆ HR planning	
◆ Recruiting	◆ Health, safety, and security
◆ Selection	
◆ Compensation	◆ Employee/labor relations
◆ Training	

Task-Based Job Analysis

Task Distinct, identifiable work activity composed of motion.

Task-based job analysis is the most common form and focuses on the tasks, duties, and responsibilities performed in a job. A **task** is a distinct, identifiable work activity composed of motions, whereas a **duty** is a larger work segment composed of several tasks that are performed by an individual. Because both tasks and duties describe activities, it is not always easy or necessary to distinguish between the two. For example, if one of the employment supervisor's duties is to interview applicants, one task associated with that duty would be asking questions. Responsibilities are obligations to perform certain tasks and duties.

Duty Work segment composed of several tasks that are performed by an individual.

Responsibilities Obligations to perform certain tasks and duties.

Competency-Based Job Analysis

Competencies Individual capabilities that can be linked to enhanced performance by individuals or teams.

Unlike the traditional approach to analyzing jobs, which identifies the tasks, duties, knowledge, and skills associated with a job, the competency approach considers how the knowledge and skills are used. Competencies are individual capabilities that can be linked to enhanced performance by individuals or teams.

Some organizations use some facets of competency analysis in various HR activities.[32] Organizations cite three primary reasons for using a competency approach: (1) to communicate valued behaviors within the organization; (2) to raise competency levels throughout the organization; and (3) to emphasize people's capabilities for enhancing the competitive advantage of the organization.

The concept of competencies varies widely from organization to organization.[33] *Technical competencies* often refer to specific knowledge and skills employees have. For example, skills for using specialized software to design Web pages or for operating highly complex machinery and equipment may be cited as competencies. Some of the following have been identified as *behavioral competencies:*

- Customer focus
- Team orientation
- Technical expertise
- Results orientation
- Communication effectiveness

- Leadership
- Conflict resolution
- Innovation
- Adaptability
- Decisiveness

The competency approach also attempts to identify the hidden factors that are often critical to superior performance. For instance, many supervisors talk about employees' attitudes, but they have difficulty identifying exactly what they mean by "attitude." The competency approach uses a variety of methodologies to help supervisors articulate examples of what they mean by attitude and how those factors affect performance.

Choosing a Job Analysis Approach

Whether to use the task-based or competency-based approach to job analysis is affected by the nature of jobs and how work is changing. In some high-technology industries, employees work in cross-functional project teams and shift from project to project. Organizations in these industries focus less on performing specific tasks and duties and more on competencies needed to attain results. For example, a project team of eight employees in different countries who are developing software that will allow various credit cards to be used with ATMs worldwide will work on many different tasks and use various competencies, some individually and some with other team members. When that project is finished, those employees will move to other projects, possibly with different team members. Such shifts may happen several times a year. Therefore, the basis for recruiting, selecting, and compensating these individuals is their competencies and capabilities, not just the tasks they perform.

However, in many industries, traditional jobs will continue to exist. Traditional task-based job analysis can provide a defensible basis for such activities as compensation, selection, and training, all of which may be the subject of legal action by employees if they believe they are being wronged in some way. The traditional job analysis approach has been used successfully to substantiate employment decisions. Currently, there is little legal precedent regarding competency analysis, which leaves it open to legal challenge as not being documented as well as the traditional approach. For that reason, task-based job analysis is more widely used, and it is the primary focus of the rest of this chapter.

Job Analysis Responsibilities

Job analysis requires a high degree of coordination and cooperation between the HR unit and operating managers. Figure 6-7 shows a typical division of responsibilities in organizations with an HR unit. The assignment of responsibility for job analysis depends on who can best perform various aspects of the process. In large companies, the HR unit supervises the process to maintain its integrity and writes the job descriptions and specifications for uniformity. The managers review the efforts of the HR unit to ensure accuracy and completeness. They also may request new job analyses when jobs change significantly. In small organizations, managers may perform all job analysis responsibilities.

FIGURE 6-7   Typical Division of HR Responsibilities: Job Analysis

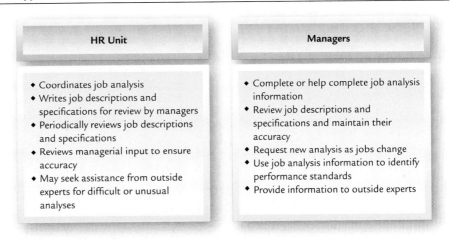

HR Unit

- Coordinates job analysis
- Writes job descriptions and specifications for review by managers
- Periodically reviews job descriptions and specifications
- Reviews managerial input to ensure accuracy
- May seek assistance from outside experts for difficult or unusual analyses

Managers

- Complete or help complete job analysis information
- Review job descriptions and specifications and maintain their accuracy
- Request new analysis as jobs change
- Use job analysis information to identify performance standards
- Provide information to outside experts

Stages in the Job Analysis Process

The process of job analysis must be conducted in a logical manner, following appropriate management and professional psychometric practices. Therefore, analysts usually follow a multi-stage process, regardless of the specific job analysis methods used.[34] The stages for a typical job analysis, as outlined in Figure 6-8 (on the next page), may vary somewhat with the number of jobs included.

Planning the Job Analysis A crucial aspect of the job analysis process is the planning done before gathering data from managers and employees. Probably the most important consideration is to identify the objectives of the job analysis, from just updating job descriptions to revising the compensation programs in the organization. Whatever the purpose identified, it is vital to obtain the support of top management.

Preparing for and Introducing the Job Analysis Preparation for job analysis begins with identification of the jobs under review. For example, are the jobs to be analyzed hourly jobs, clerical jobs, all jobs in one division, or all jobs in the entire organization? Reviewing existing job descriptions, organization charts, previous job analysis information, and other industry-related resources is part of the planning. This phase identifies those who will be involved in conducting the job analysis and the methods to be used. A crucial step is communicating and explaining the process to managers, affected employees, and other concerned people.

Conducting the Job Analysis If questionnaires are used, it is often helpful to have employees return them to supervisors or managers for review before giving them back to those conducting the job analysis. Questionnaires should be accompanied by a letter explaining the process and instructions for completing and returning them. Once data from job analyses are compiled, the information should be sorted by job, organizational unit, and job family.

FIGURE 6-8   Stages in the Job Analysis Process

I. **Planning the Job Analysis**
A. Identify objectives of job analysis
B. Obtain top management support

II. **Preparing For and Introducing Job Analysis**
A. Identify jobs and methodology
B. Review existing job documentation
C. Communicate process to managers/employees

III. **Conducting the Job Analysis**
A. Gather job analysis data
B. Review and compile data

IV. **Developing Job Descriptions and Job Specifications**
A. Draft job descriptions and specifications
B. Review drafts with managers and employees
C. Finalize job descriptions and recommendations

V. **Maintaining and Updating Job Descriptions and Job Specifications**
A. Update job descriptions and specifications as organization changes
B. Periodically review all jobs

Developing Job Descriptions and Job Specifications At the fourth stage, the job analysts draft job descriptions and job specifications. Generally, organizations find that having managers and employees write job descriptions is not recommended for several reasons. First, it reduces consistency in format and details, both of which are important given the legal consequences of job descriptions. Second, managers and employees vary in their writing skills. Also, they may write the job descriptions and job specifications to reflect what they do and what their personal qualifications are, not what the job requires. However, completed drafts should be reviewed with managers and supervisors.

Maintaining and Updating Job Descriptions and Job Specifications Once job descriptions and specifications have been completed and reviewed by all appropriate individuals, a system must be developed for keeping them current. One effective way to ensure that appropriate reviews occur is to use job descriptions and job specifications in other HR activities. For example, each time a vacancy occurs, the job description and specifications should be reviewed and revised as necessary *before* recruiting and selection efforts begin. Similarly, in some organizations, managers and employees review their job descriptions during each performance appraisal interview.

JOB ANALYSIS METHODS

Job analysis information about what people are doing in their jobs can be gathered in a variety of ways. One consideration is who should conduct the job analysis. Most frequently, a member of the HR staff coordinates this effort. Depending on which of the methods discussed next is used, others who often participate are managers, supervisors, and employees doing the jobs. For more complex analyses, industrial engineers may conduct time-and-motion studies.

Another consideration is the method to be used. Whatever method is chosen, it should be content based and should not reflect rater bias.[35] Common methods are observation, interviewing, questionnaires, and computerized systems. The use of a combination of these approaches depends on the situation and the organization. Each of these methods is discussed next.

Internet Research

Job-Analysis.NETwork
Find resources for conducting a job analysis, including different types of methods, legal issues, questionnaires and job descriptions, by visiting this Website at:
http://thomsonedu.com/management/mathis.

Observation

With the observation method, a manager, job analyst, or industrial engineer observes the individual performing the job and takes notes to describe the tasks and duties performed. Use of the observation method is limited because many jobs do not have complete and easily observed job duties or complete job cycles. Thus, observation may be more useful for repetitive jobs and in conjunction with other methods.

Work Sampling One type of observation, work sampling, does not require attention to each detailed action throughout an entire work cycle. This method allows a manager to determine the content and pace of a typical workday through statistical sampling of certain actions rather than through continuous observation and timing of all actions. Work sampling is particularly useful for routine and repetitive jobs.

Employee Diary/Log Another method requires employees to "observe" their own performances by keeping a diary/log of their job duties, noting how frequently those duties are performed and the time required for each one. Although this approach sometimes generates useful information, it may be burdensome for employees to compile an accurate log. Also, employees sometimes perceive this approach as creating needless documentation that detracts from the performance of their work.

Interviewing

The interview method of gathering information requires a manager or an HR specialist to visit each job site and talk with the employees performing each job. A standardized interview form is used most often to record the information. Frequently, both the employee and the employee's supervisor must be interviewed to obtain a complete understanding of the job.

Sometimes, group or panel interviews are used. A team of *subject matter experts* (SMEs) who have varying insights about a group of jobs is assembled to provide job analysis information. This option may be particularly useful for highly technical jobs and others for which a range of individuals can provide input.

The interview method can be quite time consuming, especially if the interviewer talks with two or three employees doing each job. Professional and managerial jobs are often more complicated to analyze and usually require longer interviews. For these reasons, combining the interview method with one of the other methods is suggested.

Questionnaires

The questionnaire is a widely used method of gathering data on jobs. A survey instrument is developed and given to employees and managers to complete. The typical job questionnaire often covers the areas shown in Figure 6-9.

The questionnaire method offers a major advantage in that information on a large number of jobs can be collected inexpensively in a relatively short period of time. However, the questionnaire method assumes that employees can accurately analyze and communicate information about their jobs. Employees may vary in their perceptions of the jobs, and even in their literacy. Using interviewing and observation in combination with the questionnaire method allows analysts to clarify and verify the information gathered in questionnaires.

Position Analysis Questionnaire (PAQ) The Position Analysis Questionnaire is a specialized instrument that incorporates checklists. Each job is analyzed on 27 dimensions composed of 187 "elements." The PAQ has a number of divisions, each containing numerous job elements. The divisions include:

- *Information input:* Where and how does the worker get information to do the job?
- *Mental process:* What levels of reasoning are necessary on the job?
- *Work output:* What physical activities are performed on the job?
- *Relationships with others:* What relationships are required while performing the job?
- *Job context:* What working conditions and social contexts are involved in the job?
- *Other:* What else is relevant to the job?

FIGURE 6-9   Typical Areas Covered in a Job Analysis Questionnaire

Duties and Percentage of Time Spent on Each	Contact with Other People
· Regular duties · Special duties performed less frequently	· Internal contacts · External contacts
Supervision	**Physical Dimensions**
· Supervision given to others · Supervision received from others	· Physical demands · Working conditions
Decisions Made	**Jobholder Characteristics**
· Records and reports prepared · Materials and equipment used · Financial/budget responsibilities	· Knowledge · Skills · Abilities · Training needed

The PAQ focuses on "worker-oriented" elements that describe behaviors necessary to do the job rather than on "job-oriented" elements that describe the technical aspects of the work. Although its complexity may deter many potential users, the PAQ is easily quantified and can be used to conduct validity studies on selection tests. It also may contribute to internal pay fairness because it considers the varying demands of different jobs.

Managerial Job Analysis Questionnaire Because managerial jobs differ in character from jobs with clearly observable routines and procedures, some specialized methods have evolved for their analysis. One well-known and widely used method is the Management Position Description Questionnaire (MPDQ). Composed of more than 200 statements, the MPDQ examines a variety of managerial dimensions, including decision making and supervising.

Computerized Systems

With the expansion of information technology, computerized job analysis systems have been developed. These systems have several common characteristics, including the way they are administered. First, analysts compose task statements that relate to all jobs. Then, those statements are listed in questionnaires, which are distributed to employees. Next, employees respond on computer-scannable documents, which are fed into computer-based services capable of scoring, recording, analyzing, and reporting thousands of pieces of information about any job.

An important feature of computerized job analysis is the specificity of data that can be gathered. All this specific data is compiled into a job analysis database. As a result, a computerized job analysis system can often reduce the time and effort involved in writing job descriptions. These systems often store banks of job duty statements that relate to each of the task and scope statements of the questionnaires. Interestingly, a study found little variation in the results of job analysis data obtained by paper questionnaires and by computerized methods.[36] Thus, use of computerized methods will likely grow.

Job Analysis and the U.S. Department of Labor

A variety of resources related to job analysis are available from the U.S. Department of Labor (DOL). The resources have been developed and used over many years by various entities within the DOL, primarily the Employment and Training Administration.

Functional Job Analysis (FJA) This method is a comprehensive approach to job analysis. FJA considers: (1) the goals of the organization, (2) what workers do to achieve those goals in their jobs, (3) the level and orientation of what workers do, (4) performance standards, and (5) training content. A functional definition of what is done in a job can be generated by examining the three components of *data, people,* and *things.* The levels of these components traditionally have been used to identify and compare important elements of jobs in the *Dictionary of Occupational Titles* and through O*Net.

O*Net On-Line The DOL has made a major commitment to provide usable information on skills, abilities, knowledge, work activities, and interests associated with a wide range of jobs and occupations. O*Net is a database

Using O*Net

O*Net is a database of worker attributes and job characteristics that can be used to describe jobs and the skills workers will need to perform. It can be accessed at *www.onetcenter.org/rd/index.html*.

O*Net can be used in different ways—for example, to see what skills will be needed in the future for the fastest-growing jobs. One state did this exercise to identify what skills the state workforce would need in the future. A different employer can use the same approach for its jobs. The skills might vary some from state to state, but the skills most in demand for the future are:

- Active listening
- Speaking
- Reading comprehension
- Problem identification
- Math
- Information organization
- Product inspection
- Writing

These skills are, for the most part, fundamental skills, illustrating the need for strong basic education in the workforce. They also suggest recruiting strategies that can be followed by employers.[37]

Internet Research

O*Net On-Line
For a wide array of occupational information, visit this Website at:
http://thomsonedu.com/management/mathis.

compiled by the U.S. Department of Labor to provide basic occupational data to anyone who is interested. Information in O*Net covers more than 950 occupations based on the Standard Occupational Classification (SOC) developed by the government.

O*Net also provides extensive links to additional resources on workplace issues. It is a valuable and time-saving resource for job analysis and for writing good descriptions and specifications. To see an example of O*Net use, see the HR On-Line feature.

Combination Methods

As just identified, there are a number of different ways to obtain and analyze information about a job. Therefore, in dealing with issues that may end up in court, HR specialists and others doing job analysis must carefully document all steps taken. Each method has strengths and weaknesses, and a combination of methods generally may be more appropriate than one method alone. Regardless of the methods used, in its most fundamental form, job analysis provides the information necessary to develop job descriptions and job specifications.

BEHAVIORAL ASPECTS OF JOB ANALYSIS

Job analysis involves determining what the "core" job is. A detailed examination of jobs, although necessary, sometimes can be a demanding and disruptive experience for both managers and employees, in part because job analysis can identify the difference between what currently is being performed in a job and what *should* be done. This can be of concern because employees may fear that as a result of the analysis of their job, the job will be downgraded and they will be paid less.

This is a major issue people always seem to have about job analysis, but it is not the only concern. Consequently, a number of behavioral factors can affect job analysis, some of which are discussed next.

"Inflation" of Jobs and Job Titles

Employees and managers have some tendency to inflate the importance and significance of their jobs. Because job analysis information is used for compensation purposes, both managers and employees hope that "puffing up" jobs will result in higher pay levels and greater "status" for résumés and more possible promotion opportunities.

Titles of jobs often get inflated too.[38] Some firms give fancy titles in place of pay raises, and others do it to keep well-paid employees from leaving for "status" reasons. Some industries, such as banking and entertainment, are well known for their title inflation. For instance, banking and financial institutions use officer designations to enhance status. In one small Midwestern bank, an employee who had three years' experience as a teller was "promoted" with no pay increase to Second Vice President and Senior Customer Service Coordinator. She basically became the lead teller when her supervisor was out of the bank, and now could sign a few customer account forms, but her duties remained basically the same.

Offbeat titles are very common in the "creative" areas of advertising and marketing. But what *is* a "group idea management director," "chief transformation officer," or a "marketing evangelist"? What does the director of the "Department of Human Nature" really do?[39]

Employee and Managerial Anxieties

Both managers and employees have concerns about job analysis. Through the information developed in a job analysis, the job description is ideally supposed to identify what is done in a job. However, it is difficult to capture all facets of a job, particularly for jobs in which employees perform a variety of duties and operate with a high degree of independence.

Managerial Straitjacket One primary concern of managers and supervisors is that the job analysis and job descriptions will unrealistically limit managerial flexibility. Because workloads and demands change rapidly, managers and supervisors want to be able to move duties to other employees, cross-train employees, and have more dynamic, flexible means available to accomplish work. If job descriptions are written restrictively, some employees may use an omission to limit managerial flexibility. The resulting attitude, "It's not in my job description," puts a straitjacket on a manager. In some organizations with unionized workforces, very restrictive job descriptions exist. Because of such difficulties, the final statement in many job descriptions is a *miscellaneous clause,* which consists of a phrase similar to "Performs other duties as needed upon request by immediate supervisor." This statement covers unusual situations that may occur in an employee's job. However, duties covered by this phrase cannot be considered essential functions under the Americans with Disabilities Act.

Employee Fears One fear that employees may have concerns the purpose of a detailed investigation of their job. Perhaps they feel that such a detailed look means someone thinks they have done something wrong. The attitude behind such a fear might be "As long as no one knows precisely what I am supposed to be doing, I am safe."

Often the content of a job may reflect the desires and skills of the incumbent employee. For example, in one firm, an employee promoted to customer service supervisor continued to spend considerable time answering customer calls, rather than supervising employees taking the calls. As part of job analysis discussions, the customer service manager and the supervisor discussed the need for the supervisor to train his employees on handling special customer requests and to delegate more routine duties to the customer service representatives.

Also, some employees may fear that an analysis of their jobs will put a straitjacket on them, limiting their creativity and flexibility by formalizing their duties. However, analyzing a job does not necessarily limit job scope or depth. In fact, having well-written, well-communicated job descriptions can assist employees by clarifying their roles and the expectations within those roles. One effective way to handle anxieties is to involve the employees in the revision process.

Current Incumbent Emphasis

As illustrated by the example of the customer service supervisor, a job analysis and the resulting job description and job specifications should not describe just what the person currently doing the job does and what his or her qualifications are. The incumbent may have unique capabilities and the ability to expand the scope of the job to assume more responsibilities. The company would have difficulty finding someone exactly like that individual if he or she left. Consequently, it is useful to focus on *core* duties and *necessary* knowledge, skills, and abilities by determining what the jobs would be if the incumbents quit or were no longer available to do the jobs.

LEGAL ASPECTS OF JOB ANALYSIS

The previous chapters on equal employment laws, regulations, and court cases emphasized that legal compliance must focus on the jobs that individuals perform. The 1978 Uniform Guidelines on Employee Selection Procedures make it clear that HR requirements must be tied to specific job-related factors if the employers are to defend their actions as a business necessity.

Job Analysis and the Americans with Disabilities Act (ADA)

HR managers and their organizations must identify job activities and then document the steps taken to identify job responsibilities. One result of the ADA is increased emphasis by employers on conducting job analyses, as well as developing and maintaining current and accurate job descriptions and job specifications.

The ADA requires that organizations identify the *essential job functions*, which are the fundamental duties of a job. These do not include the marginal functions of the positions. Marginal job functions are duties that are part of a job but are incidental or ancillary to the purpose and nature of the job. Figure 6-10 shows three major considerations used in determining essential functions and marginal functions. Job analysts, HR staff members, and operating managers must evaluate and make decisions when information on the three considerations is not clear.

Job analysis also can identify the physical demands of jobs. An understanding of the skills and capabilities used on a job is critical. For example, a

Marginal job functions
Duties that are part of a job but are incidental or ancillary to the purpose and nature of the job.

| FIGURE 6-10 | Determining Essential and Marginal Job Functions |

Considerations	Essential Functions	Marginal Functions
Percentage of time spent on task	Significant percentage of time, often 20% or more, is spent on task.	Generally less than 10% of time is spent on task.
Frequency of task	Task is performed regularly: daily, weekly, or monthly.	Task is performed infrequently or when substituting in part of another job.
Importance of task	Task affects other parts of job and other jobs.	Task is unrelated to job, and there are few consequences if not performed.

customer service representative must be able to hear well enough to take customer orders. However, hearing may be less essential for a heavy equipment operator in a quarry.

An important part of job analysis is obtaining information about what duties are being performed and what percentage of time is devoted to each duty. As the ADA suggests, the percentage of time spent on a duty generally indicates its relative importance. Also, if duties are regularly performed daily, weekly, and/or monthly, they are more likely to be seen as essential. In contrast, a task performed only infrequently or when helping another worker on a totally unrelated job more likely falls in the marginal category.

Another consideration is the ease or difficulty of assigning a duty to be performed by someone else, or in a different job. For instance, assume an assembler of electronic components places the completed parts in a bin next to the work area. At the end of each day, the bin of completed parts must be carried to another room for use in the final assembly of a product. Carrying the bin to the other room probably would be defined as a marginal task because assigning someone else to carry it would not likely create major workflow problems with other jobs and workers.

Job Analysis and Wage/Hour Regulations

Typically, job analysis identifies the percentage of time spent on each duty in a job. This information helps determine whether someone should be classified as exempt or non-exempt under the wage/hour laws.

As will be noted in Chapter 12, the federal Fair Labor Standards Act (FLSA) and most state wage/hour laws indicate that the percentage of time employees spend on manual, routine, or clerical duties affects whether they must be paid overtime for hours worked in excess of 40 hours a week. To be exempt from overtime, the employees must perform their *primary duties* as executive, administrative, professional, or outside sales employees. *Primary* has been interpreted to mean occurring at least 50% of the time.

Other legal-compliance efforts, such as those involving workplace safety and health, can also be aided through the data provided by job analysis. In summary, it is extremely difficult for an employer to have a legal staffing system without performing job analysis. Truly, job analysis is the most basic HR activity and the foundation for most other HR activities.

JOB DESCRIPTIONS AND JOB SPECIFICATIONS

The output from analysis of a job is used to develop a job description and its job specifications. Together, these two documents summarize job analysis information in a readable format and provide the basis for defensible job-related actions. They also identify individual jobs for employees by providing documentation from management.[40]

In most cases, the job description and job specifications are combined into one document that contains several sections. A job description identifies the tasks, duties, and responsibilities of a job. It describes what is done, why it is done, where it is done, and, briefly, how it is done.

Job description
Identification of the tasks, duties, and responsibilities of a job.

Job Specifications

Job specifications
The knowledge, skills, and abilities (KSAs) an individual needs to perform a job satisfactorily.

While the job description describes activities to be done, the job specifications list the knowledge, skills, and abilities (KSAs) an individual needs to perform a job satisfactorily. KSAs include education, experience, work skill requirements, personal abilities, and mental and physical requirements. It is important to note that accurate job specifications identify what KSAs a person needs to do the job, not necessarily the current employee's qualifications.

Performance Standards

Performance standards
Indicators of what the job accomplishes and how performance is measured in key areas of the job description.

Performance standards flow directly from a job description and indicate what the job accomplishes and how performance is measured in key areas of the job description. The reason for establishing performance standards linked to job descriptions and job responsibilities is clear. If employees know what is expected and how performance is to be measured, they have a much better chance of performing satisfactorily. To illustrate, for a customer service job duty stating "Reviews and records trouble complaints from customer and dispatches appropriate reports," the following could be set as performance standards:

- Completes all information on the trouble-reporting system accurately, with less than five errors annually.
- Dispatches trouble ticket information to voice mail with 100% accuracy.
- Tests line if needed or as requested by technician for telephone troubles.

Unfortunately, performance standards are often not developed as supplemental items from job descriptions. Even if performance standards have been identified and matched to job descriptions, they may not be communicated to employees if the job descriptions are not provided to employees but are used only as tools. Such an approach limits the value of job descriptions.

Job Description Components

A typical job description contains several major parts. The HR On-the-Job shows suggestions for writing job descriptions. Overviews of the most common components are presented next.

Identification The first part of the job description is the identification section, in which the job title, department, reporting relationships, location, and date of analysis may be given. Usually, it is advisable to note other information that is useful in tracking jobs and employees through HR systems. Additional items commonly noted in the identification section are job code, pay grade, exempt/

HR ON-THE-JOB

Writing Job Descriptions

Although not the most exciting part of HR manage-ment, developing and maintaining current job de-scriptions is important. Some key suggestions for writ-ing the essential functions and duties of a job follow:

- *Compose specific duty statements that contain most of the following elements:*
  - A precise action verb
  - An object of the verb
  - The expected outcomes
  - The frequency of the duties
  - The tools, equipment, aids, and processes to be used
- *Be logical:* If the job is repetitive, describe the tasks as they occur in the work cycle. For varied jobs, list the major tasks first and follow those with the less frequent and/or less important tasks in order.
- *Use proper detail:* Make sure the description covers all the meaningful duties of the job, but avoid too many details.
- *Use the active voice:* Start each statement with a functional verb in the present tense (third-person

singular)—for instance, "Bends," "Approves," or "Analyzes." Avoid terms like *prepares, handles, main-tains,* and *processes.*

- *Be specific:* For example, instead of saying "Lifts heavy packages," say "Frequently lifts heavy pack-ages weighing up to 50 pounds."
- *Describe, do not prescribe:* Say "Operates electronic imaging machine," not "Must know how to oper-ate electronic image machine." (The latter is a job specification, not a job description.)
- *Be consistent:* Define terms like *may, occasionally,* and *periodically.* For example, say "*May* is used to describe tasks that only some of the employees in a job perform; *occasionally* can describe tasks performed once in a while and not by a particular employee on a job."
- *Prepare a miscellaneous clause:* This clause pro-vides flexibility, and may be phrased as follows: "Performs other related duties as assigned by supervisory personnel."[41]

non-exempt status under the Fair Labor Standards Act (FLSA) and the EEOC classification (from the EEO-1 form).[42]

General Summary The second part, the general summary, is a concise statement of the general responsibilities and components that make the job different from others. One HR specialist has characterized the general summary statement as follows: "In thirty words or less, describe the essence of the job." It is generally recommended that the summary be written after all other sections are completed so that a more complete overview is prepared.

Essential Job Functions and Duties The third part of the typical job description lists the essential functions and duties. It contains clear, precise statements on the major tasks, duties, and responsibilities performed. Writing this section is the most time-consuming aspect of preparing job descriptions.

Job Specifications The next portion of the job description gives the qualifications needed to perform the job satisfactorily. The job specifications typically are stated as: (1) knowledge, skills, and abilities; (2) education and experience; and (3) physical requirements and/or working conditions. The components of the job specifications provide information necessary to determine what accommodations might and might not be possible under the Americans with Disabilities Act.

Figure 6-11 shows a sample job description and also contains job specifications.

FIGURE 6-11   Sample Job Description

Identification Section:
Position Title: Human Resource Manager
Department: Human Resources   EEOC Class: O/M
Reports to: President   FLSA Status: Exempt

General Summary: Directs HR activities of the firm to ensure compliance with laws and policies, and assists President with overall HR planning

Essential Job Functions:
1. Manages compensation and benefits programs for all employees, resolves compensation and benefits questions from employees, and negotiates with benefits carriers (20%)
2. Ensures compliance with both internal policies and applicable state and federal regulations and laws, including EEO, OSHA, and FLSA (20%)
3. Identifies HR planning issues and suggested approaches to President and other senior managers (15%)
4. Assists managers and supervisors to create, plan, and conduct training and various development programs for new and existing employees (15%)
5. Recruits candidates for employment over telephone and in person. Interviews and selects internal and external candidates for open positions (10%)
6. Reviews and updates job descriptions, assisted by department supervisors, and coordinates performance appraisal process to ensure timely reviews are completed for all employees (10%)
7. Administers various HR policies and procedures and helps managers resolve employee performance and policy issues (10%)
8. Performs other duties as needed and directed by President

Knowledge, Skills, and Abilities:
· Knowledge of HR policies, HR practices, and HR-related laws and regulations
· Knowledge of company products and services and policies and procedures
· Knowledge of management principles and practices
· Skill in operating equipment, such as personal computer, software, and IT systems
· Skill in oral and written communication
· Ability to communicate with employees and various business contacts in a professional and courteous manner
· Ability to organize multiple work assignments and establish priorities
· Ability to negotiate with others and resolve conflicts, particularly in sensitive situations
· Ability to pay close attention to detail and to ensure accuracy of reports and data
· Ability to make sound decisions using available information while maintaining confidentiality
· Ability to create a team environment and sustain employee commitment

Education and Experience: Bachelor's degree in HR management or equivalent, plus 3–5 years' experience

Physical Requirements:	Percentage of Work Time Spent on Activity			
	0%–24%	25%–49%	50%–74%	75%–100%
Seeing: Must be able to read computer screen and various reports				X
Hearing: Must be able to hear well enough to communicate with employees and others				X
Standing/walking	X			
Climbing/stooping/kneeling	X			
Lifting/pulling/pushing	X			
Fingering/grasping/feeling: Must be able to write, type, and use phone system				X

Working Conditions: Good working conditions with the absence of disagreeable conditions

Note: The statements herein are intended to describe the general nature and level of work performed by employees, but are not a complete list of responsibilities, duties, and skills required of personnel so classified. Furthermore, they do not establish a contract for employment and are subject to change at the discretion of the employer.

Disclaimer and Approvals The final section on many job descriptions contains approval signatures by appropriate managers and a legal disclaimer. This disclaimer allows employers to change employees' job duties or to request employees to perform duties not listed, so that the job description is not viewed as a contract between the employer and the employee.

SUMMARY

- Work is organized into jobs for people to do. Both workflow analysis and business process re-engineering are approaches used to check how well this has been done.
- Job design involves developing jobs that people like to do. It may include simplification, enlargement, enrichment, or rotation.
- Designing jobs so that they incorporate skill variety, task identity and significance, autonomy, and feedback is important for both employers and employees.
- The use of teams in jobs, especially self-directed work and virtual teams, is growing.
- Greater flexibility in work schedules and the use of telework have affected the design of many jobs.
- Job analysis is a systematic investigation of the content, context, and human requirements of a job.
- Task-based job analysis focuses on the tasks, duties, and responsibilities associated with jobs.

- Competency-based job analysis focuses on basic characteristics that can be linked to enhanced performance, such as technical and behavioral competencies.
- The job analysis process has five stages, beginning with planning and ending with maintaining and updating job descriptions and job specifications.
- A number of methods of job analysis are used, with interviews and questionnaires being the most popular.
- Both the behavioral reactions of employees and managers and legal-compliance issues must be considered as part of job analysis.
- The end products of job analysis are job descriptions, which identify the tasks, duties, and responsibilities of jobs, and job specifications, which list the knowledge, skills, and abilities needed to perform a job satisfactorily.

REVIEW AND APPLICATION QUESTIONS

1. For many individuals, the nature of work and jobs is changing. Describe some reasons for the changes and how they are affecting HR management and organizations.
2. Explain how you would conduct a job analysis in a company that has never had job descriptions.
3. As an HR specialist, you have been asked to develop job descriptions for a *computer support specialist* who assists with LAN/WAN networks. Using O*Net (*http://online.onetcenter.org*), job boards, and other Web-based resources, locate the details needed and prepare a job description using the format shown in Figure 6-11.

CASE

Jobs and Work at R. R. Donnelley

Changes in many industries are occurring in an effort to increase productivity. Re-designing jobs, integrating information technology, and increasing HR training efforts are all critical. One example illustrates what happens when jobs and work are changed.

R. R. Donnelley is a leading U.S. commercial printing firm. One of its primary facilities is in Roanoke, Virginia, where 3.5 million books a month are produced with about 300 employees. To improve productivity and profitability, Donnelley focused on lowering costs, improving workplace safety, and reducing errors. Because making numerous changes was likely to increase employees' concerns, significant time and effort were spent communicating with employees about the need for change, improvement in quality, and higher productivity. Training for all employees on quality and workflow changes was conducted that focused on specialized methods such as Six Sigma and other process improvement means. In addition, greater use was made of digital technology to receive and make printing film and plates, which changed numerous

jobs at the plant and required employees to learn a number of new methods and technologies.

The payoff of these changes is seen in a number of ways. The production time for printing four-color books has been cut by 50% or more. Productivity is up 20% in the past three years. In fact, the increase in productivity has been great enough that Donnelley did not have to set up an additional production line, savings millions of dollars. For Donnelley employees, their fears that the Roanoke plant might close were reduced. They have been trained in new technology, have changed jobs, and work in a highly successful plant.[43]

Questions

1. Discuss why Donnelley had to coordinate HR activities with the changes in jobs and work.

2. Identify examples of how technology has changed jobs where you have worked and which HR activities were handled well and which poorly.

SUPPLEMENTAL CASE

The Reluctant Receptionist

This case illustrates how incomplete job analysis and job descriptions create both managerial and employee problems. (For the case, go to http://thomsonedu.com/management/mathis.)

NOTES

1. Based on Geoffrey A. Fowler, "For Asia Based Staff, the Typical Workday Lasts about 24 Hours," *The Wall Street Journal,* August 22, 2006, B1.
2. Martin J. Conyon, "Executive Compensation and Incentives," *The Academy of Management Perspective,* February 2006, 25–44.
3. "Study: Self-Service Is Finally Delivering," *Human Resource Executive,* January 2004, 52.
4. For details, see the International Association of Administrative Profes-

sionals, *www.iaap-hq.org,* and the International Association of Virtual Office Assistants, *www.iavoa.com.*
5. "Banks Invest in a New Look at HR," *Human Resource Management International Digest,* 11 (2003), 19–23.
6. Martin Smith, "Business Process Design: Correlates of Success and Failure," *Quality Management Journal,* 10 (2003), 38–50.
7. Erin White, "Rethinking the Quality-Improvement Programs," *The Wall Street Journal,* September 19, 2005, B5.

8. "Organizing for Successful Change Management," *The McKinsey Quarterly: The Online Journal of McKinsey and Co.,* July 2006.
9. Stephanie Armour, "Job Opening? Work-at-Home Moms Fill the Bill," *USA Today,* July 20, 2005, 3B; and Ed Frauenheim, "Permatemp Legal Worries Wane," *Workforce Management,* October 10, 2005, 1–4.
10. Robert J. Trent, "Planning to Use Work Teams Effectively," *Team Performance Management,* 9 (2003), 50.

11. Ceasar Douglas and William L. Gardner, "Transition to Self-Directed Work Teams," *Journal of Organizational Behavior,* 25 (2004), 47.

12. Jessica Marquez, "Virtual Workspaces," *Workforce Management,* May 22, 2006, 38; and Carla Joinson, "Managing Virtual Teams," *HR Magazine,* June 2002, 69–73.

13. James O'Toole and Edward E. Lawler III, "A Piece of Work," *Fast Company,* June 2006, 87–89.

14. Larry W. Hunter, John P. Macduffie, and Lorna Doucet, "What Makes Teams Take?—Employee Reactions to Work Teams," *Industrial and Labor Review,* 55 (2002), 448.

15. "Poll Shows Americans Eager to Take Back Their Time," *Newsline,* October 6, 2003, *www.timeday .com.*

16. "Put Down That Tool," *The Economist,* January 10, 2004, 55–56.

17. Based on Keith Johnson and John Carreyrou, "Amid Euro's Gloom, Spain Blossoms with Short-Term Jobs," *The Wall Street Journal,* September 28, 2005, A1.

18. Acacia Aguirre, *Health in Extended Hours Operations: Understanding the Challenges, Implementing Solutions,* 2003, *www.circadian.com.*

19. Sue Shellenbarger, "Companies Retool Time-Off Policies," *The Wall Street Journal,* January 5, 2006, 1.

20. Sue Shellenbarger, "Fairer Flextime: Employers Try New Policies for Alternative Schedules," *The Wall Street Journal,* November 17, 2005, D1.

21. Sonya Goshe et al., "Current Methods and Practices," *Workspan,* August 2006, 25–26.

22. John Kirchhoff, "Understanding Work/Life Balance and Organizational Productivity," *SHRM Research Series,* April 2006, 1–4.

23. Based on Michelle Conlin, "Smashing the Clock," *Business Week,* December 11, 2006, 60–68; and Lynn Gresham, "Best Buy Puts Work-Life Balance on New Axis," *Employee Benefit Advisor,* March 2007, 24–26.

24. International Telework Association and Council, *American Interactive Consumer Survey,* *www.telecommute.org.*

25. Sarah Flannery, "Telecommuting: Issues to Consider . . . ," *Workspan,* April 2007, 58–62.

26. Sue Shellenbarger, "When Working at Home Doesn't Work," *The Wall Street Journal,* August 24, 2006, D1.

27. Christopher Rhoads and Sara Silvers, "Working at Home Gets Easier," *The Wall Street Journal,* December 29, 2005, B4.

28. Michelle Conlin, "The Easiest Commute of All," *Business Week,* December 12, 2005, 78–80.

29. Michael Mandel, "The Real Reasons You Are Working So Hard," *Business Week,* October 3, 2005, 60–73; and Lina Yoon, "More Play, Less Toil Is a Stressful Shift for Some Koreans," *The Wall Street Journal,* August 10, 2006, 1.

30. Theresa Minton-Eversole, "Job Analysis, Behavioral Interviews Key to Hiring Process," *Recruiting and Staffing News,* March 2006, 1.

31. W. M. Keyserling et al., "Using Multiple Information Sources to Identify Opportunities for Ergonomic Interventions in Automotive Parts Distribution: A Case Study," *AIHA Journal,* 64 (2003), 690–702.

32. Donna Rodriguez et al., "Developing Competency Models to Promote Integrated Human Resource Practices," *Human Resource Management,* 41 (2002), 309.

33. Marcel R. Vander Klink and Jo Boon, "Competencies: The Triumph of a Fuzzy Concept," *International Journal of Human Resources Development and Management,* 3 (2003), 125.

34. For a detailed discussion of the job analysis process and methods, see Michael T. Brannick and Edward Levine, *Job Analysis: Methods, Research, and Applications for Human Resource Management in the New Millennium* (Thousand Oaks, CA: Sage Publishing, 2002).

35. Kristen O. Prien, Erich P. Prien, and William Wooten, "Interrater Reliability in Job Analysis," *Public Personnel Management,* 32 (2003), 125–141.

36. Jeanne D. Mackiney et al., "Examining the Measurement Equivalence of Paper and Computerized Job Analysis Scales" (paper presented at the 18th annual conference of the Society for Industrial and Organizational Psychology, 2003).

37. Sylvia D. Jones, "Using O*Net to Identify Skill Needs for the Available, Critical, and Projected Jobs," *Outlook 2010 Revisited,* Wyoming Department of Employment, May 2006, 51–56.

38. Patrick Shannon and Bob Miller, "What's in a Title?" *WorldatWork Journal,* Fourth Quarter 2003, 26–34.

39. "Offbeat Titles Let Clients Know 'We Got It,'" *Omaha World Herald,* September 25, 2006, D1.

40. "Can You Provide Guidance on Writing Job Descriptions?," *HR Comply/Newsletter Abstracts,* July 7, 2004, *www.hrcomply .com/newsletter.*

41. John Sullivan, "Boring Position Descriptions Are Dramatically Decreasing Your Application Rates, Part 1," *Electronic Recruiting Exchange,* July 31, 2006, 1–3.

42. "The ABC's of Job Descriptions," *Workspan,* March 2005, 58.

43. Adapted from Gene Bylinsky, "Elite Factories," *Fortune,* September 1, 2003, 154B–154J.

CHAPTER

7

Recruiting in Labor Markets

After you have read this chapter, you should be able to:

- Identify different ways that labor markets can be identified and approached.

- Discuss advantages and disadvantages of internal and external recruiting.

- Specify three internal sources for recruiting and issues associated with their use.

- List and briefly discuss five external recruiting sources.

- Explain why Internet recruiting has grown and how employers are conducting it.

- Discuss three factors to consider when evaluating recruiting efforts.

HR Headline

Global Recruiting of High-Tech Employees

Stanford University awarded 88 PhDs in electrical engineering in a recent year. Over half of the recipients were foreign born. High-tech employers are particularly dependent on these foreign-born students as employees because too few American students graduate in science, math, technology, and engineering from U.S. universities. When companies run out of U.S.-born workers and cannot hire immigrants, projects get dropped, delayed, or sent offshore.

When U.S. employers try to hire the foreign-born graduates of U.S. colleges and universities, they run into a roadblock because of the limit on available visas for these highly skilled workers. The issue has become tangled with the politics of illegal immigration and low-skilled immigrants. The 65,000 yearly quota of three-year visas for highly skilled workers that are available to employers were snapped up in eight months in a recent year. An employer hoping to hire a Chinese- or Indian-born worker now may have to wait years before the application will get any attention.

U.S. employers argue that educating foreign-born talent in the United States, but then having those individuals go elsewhere to work for global competitors is not logical. This is especially ironic when you consider that firms in competing countries such as Britain are streamlining their immigration systems to recruit and hire these high-talent employees.[1]

The staffing process matches people with jobs through recruiting and selection. This chapter examines recruiting and the next examines selection. Recruiting is the process of generating a pool of qualified applicants for organizational jobs. If the number of available candidates equals the number of people to be hired, no real selection is required—the choice has already been made. The organization must either leave some openings unfilled or take all the candidates.

Recruiting Process of generating a pool of qualified applicants for organizational jobs.

Recruiting is about finding *qualified* applicants, and doing that often requires much more than just running an ad in a newspaper. For example, simply acquiring the human capital necessary to replace normal workforce attrition and provide for growth probably will require an employer to:

- Know the industry to successfully recruit qualified employees
- Identify keys to success in the labor market, including competitors' recruiting efforts
- Cultivate networks and relationships with sources of prospective employees
- Promote the company brand so that the organization is known as a good place to work
- Create recruiting metrics in order to measure the effectiveness of recruiting efforts

Without significant HR attention, recruiting can become just a set of administrative functions: coordinating internal openings, handling the flow of candidate data, dealing with regulatory reporting, and moving candidates through the system. These steps are important, but more important is tying the employer's recruiting strategy to its business strategy.

STRATEGIC RECRUITING

Strategic recruiting becomes more important as labor markets shift and become more competitive. HR planning helps to align HR strategies with organizational goals and plans. It is important that recruiting be viewed as a part of strategic HR planning because recruiting is the mechanism that makes the plans work. For example, Walgreens, the drugstore chain, at times has had to cut back its strategy to expand and open new stores because of a shortage of trained pharmacists. Extensive recruiting and more lead time are now a key part of Walgreens' strategic expansion efforts.

Strategy A general framework that provides guidance for actions.

Strategy is a general framework that provides guidance for actions. If a company is driven by technology, recruiting must determine how to bring in the best technologists. If the strategy of a company is based on marketing, the focus should be on where the company will look to find the best marketing candidates.

Recruiting can be expensive. But an offsetting concept that must be considered is the *cost of unfilled jobs*. For example, consider a company in which three important related jobs are vacant. These three vacancies cost the company $300 for each business day the jobs remain vacant. If the jobs are not filled for four months, the cost is about $26,000 for the failure to recruit for those jobs in a timely fashion.

Certainly, cost is an issue, and some employers are quite concerned about cost per hire, but quality might be the trade-off. For example, if an HR strategy focuses on *quality* as a competitive advantage, a company might choose to hire only from the top 15% of candidates for critical jobs, and from the top

FIGURE 7-1   **Strategic Recruiting Stages**

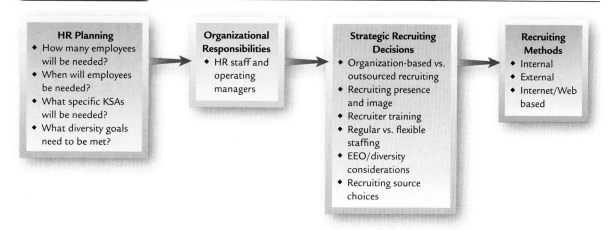

30% of candidates for all other positions. This approach likely would improve workforce quality, but it would cost more per hire.

Strategic recruiting may sometimes need to go beyond just filling empty positions. It can focus on discovering talent *before* it is needed, capitalizing on windfall opportunities when there is an abundance of highly qualified people, or perhaps developing strong Internet recruiting abilities.[2] Generally, such strategic recruiting decisions dictate not only the kinds and numbers of applicants, but also how difficult or successful recruiting efforts may be. Figure 7-1 shows an overview of the strategic recruiting stages.

Even during periods of reduced hiring, the ability to implement long-range plans may mean keeping in contact with outside recruiting sources to maintain visibility, while also maintaining employee recruiting channels inside the organization. These efforts allow management to match people with organizational and human resource plans when they are needed.

Employers face shortages of workers who have the appropriate knowledge, skills, and abilities (KSAs) from time to time.[3] Further, as business cycles fluctuate, demand for labor changes and the number of people looking for work changes. Understanding such labor market adjustments is key for adapting recruiting successfully.

LABOR MARKETS

Labor markets External supply pool from which organizations attract employees.

Because staffing takes place in different labor markets that can vary a great deal, learning some basics about labor markets aids in understanding recruiting.[4] Labor markets are the external supply pool from which employers attract employees. To understand where recruiting takes place, one can think of the sources of employees as a funnel, in which the broad scope of labor markets narrows progressively to the point of selection and job offers (see Figure 7-2). Of course, if the selected candidate rejects the offer, then HR staff members must move back up the funnel to the applicant pool for other candidates, and in extreme cases they re-open the recruiting process.

FIGURE 7-2   Labor Market Components

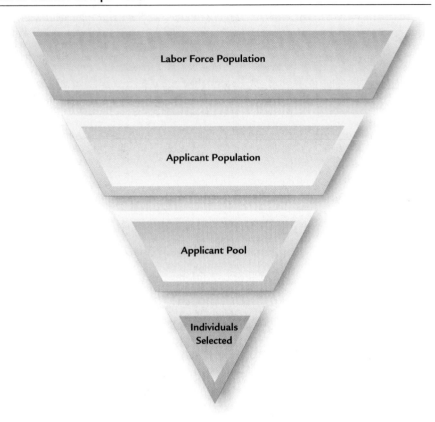

Labor Market Components

Labor force population
All individuals who are available for selection if all possible recruitment strategies are used.

The broadest labor market component and measure is the labor force population, which is made up of all individuals who are available for selection if all possible recruitment strategies are used. This large number of potential applicants may be reached using many different recruiting methods—for example, newspaper ads, job boards, college job fairs, and word of mouth. Each recruiting method will reach different segments of the labor force population.

Applicant population A subset of the labor force population that is available for selection using a particular recruiting approach.

The applicant population is a subset of the labor force population that is available for selection if a particular recruiting approach is used. For example, an organization might limit its recruiting for management trainees to MBA graduates from major universities. This recruiting method results in a different group of applicants from those who might apply if the employer advertises openings for management trainees on a local radio station or posts a listing on an Internet jobs board. At least four recruiting decisions affect reaching the applicant population:

- *Recruiting method:* Advertising medium chosen, including use of employment agencies
- *Recruiting message:* What is said about the job and how it is communicated
- *Applicant qualifications required:* Education level and amount of experience necessary, for example
- *Administrative procedures:* When recruiting is done, applicant follow-up, and use of previous applicant files

In tight labor markets, many employers try to expand the applicant population in a number of ways. One method that employers have used to expand the applicant population is to consider *ex-convicts*. But care is needed in evaluating these individuals and ensuring appropriate placements given their criminal backgrounds. Giving individuals a second chance has paid off in some situations and not in others, for both small and large employers.

Applicant pool All persons who are actually evaluated for selection.

The applicant pool consists of all persons who are actually evaluated for selection. Many factors can affect the size of the applicant pool, including the reputation of the organization and industry as a place to work, the screening efforts of the organization, the job specifications, and the information available. If a suitable candidate can be found, the organization then selects the individual and makes the job offer.

Different Labor Markets and Recruiting

The supply of workers in various labor markets differs substantially and affects staffing. An organization recruits in a number of different labor markets, including geographic, industry and occupational, and educational and technical. The labor markets can be viewed in several ways to provide information that is useful for recruiting. Looking at projections for the labor force by age, participation rates, annual rates of labor force growth, and growth in employment in certain occupations will help alert recruiters to trends in the labor markets.[5]

Geographic Labor Markets One common way to classify labor markets is based on geographic location. Some markets are local, some area or regional, some national, and others international. Local and area labor markets vary significantly in terms of workforce availability and quality. For instance, the state of Iowa found that even if it retained every high school graduate for 10 years, at the end of that time it still would be short of workers for many jobs because of the aging populations in many Iowa counties. This shortage of workers had caused employers in some locations to close operations and relocate to areas with greater numbers of potential workers. Therefore, state agencies and Iowa employers developed an aggressive campaign to "import" workers. Efforts included recruiting native Iowans to return to the state, encouraging foreign immigrants to move to Iowa, and encouraging graduates of Iowa high schools and colleges to remain in the state.

Changes in a geographic labor market may force changes in recruiting efforts. If a new major employer locates in a regional labor market, then other employers may see a decline in their numbers of applicants. For instance, following the opening of large automobile manufacturing plants in South Carolina, Tennessee, Kentucky, and Alabama, some nearby employers, particularly smaller manufacturing firms, had to raise their wages to prevent turnover of existing workers.

Attempting to recruit locally for a job market that is really a nationally competitive market will likely result in disappointing applicant rates. For example, a catalog retailer will likely not be able to recruit a senior merchandising manager from only the small town where the firm is located. Conversely, it may not need to recruit nationally for workers to fill administrative support jobs.

Global Labor Markets U.S. employers tap global labor markets when necessary and export work to overseas labor markets when doing so is advantageous. For example, U.S. hotels are likely to hire housekeeping staff from Croatia, Poland, Jamaica, Sudan, and the Philippines. Manufacturers, meatpackers, and roofing companies regularly use workers from Mexico, Haiti, Honduras, Sudan, Albania, and other countries. But use of illegal immigrants has become a volatile political and social issue.

The migration of U.S. work overseas has been controversial. While many decry the loss of American jobs, some employers respond that they cannot be competitive in a global market if they fail to take advantage of labor savings. Scores of Western firms have farmed out software development and back-office work to India and other countries with lower wages. However, enormous advancements in American productivity mean that it takes fewer employees in America to produce certain items, which results in a cost savings—even at the American employees' higher wage rates. Hence, those types of jobs are not being exported to other countries.[6]

Recruiting employees for global assignments requires approaches and understanding different from those used for typical recruiting efforts in the home country. The recruiting processes must consider differences in culture, laws, and language. For instance, in Eastern Europe, potential recruits like to work for European and U.S. firms, so recruiters emphasize the "Western" image. In Hong Kong, recruiting ads often stress success factors by showing "typical employees" of a firm wearing expensive watches and stylish clothes.

Dealing with foreign labor markets can present challenges. In China, for example, recruiting is regulated and generally requires the approval of local personnel or labor authorities. Article 8 of China's Labor Market Regulations sets out the specific channels that may be used for recruiting. Recruitment agencies, employment fairs, mass media, and the Internet are allowed. Unfortunately, two government bureaucracies, with different rules, have overlapping authority in recruiting, and the result is bureaucratic confusion as to what recruiting can be done.[7] This example illustrates that government regulation very much affects recruiting. The HR Perspective on global labor markets expands the example.

HR PERSPECTIVE

Governmental Issues in Global Labor Markets

Governments and their regulations can make recruiting globally challenging. Consider the following examples:

- In Dubai the labor ministry announced that companies had 18 months to replace all expatriate HR managers with locals. But qualified locals were in *very* short supply.
- In South Africa, affirmative action appears to be at odds with rapid economic growth because of a lack of trained and experienced protected-class members.
- Singapore significantly raised the monthly tax paid by companies who recruit foreign workers, thus making it expensive *not* to hire locals.

- A change in U.S. tax law is causing some Americans stationed overseas by their employers to consider coming home because the cost for them personally of staying abroad has gone up markedly.
- India has a significant shortage of middle managers, but government regulations that reserve education and employment for a percentage of lower-caste citizens make that labor shortage worse.[8]

Effective recruiting can be difficult any time, but when different governments' regulations must be met, it can place even greater demands on HR management. But meeting these demands is crucial for HR and organizational strategic success.

Industry and Occupational Labor Markets Labor markets also can be classified by industry and occupation. The demand for truck drivers, hotel workers, nurses, teachers, and others has been strong, creating tight labor markets in the industries served by those occupations.

Educational and Technical Labor Markets Occupational labor markets are based on the KSAs required for the jobs. These markets include physical therapists, HR managers, engineers, accountants, welders, and bank tellers. One occupational area of extreme volatility in the past several years has been the *information technology* (IT) labor market, which has fluctuated from being extremely tight several years ago, to rather soft after many dot.coms failed and now is becoming more limited as IT jobs are expanding. Another example is that currently welders are in very tight supply, with pay over $50,000/year and sign-on bonuses and good benefits available.[9]

Another way to look at labor markets is by considering educational and technical qualifications to define the people being recruited. Employers may need individuals with specific licenses, certifications, or educational backgrounds. For instance, a shortage of business professors with PhDs is forecasted to affect many colleges and universities in the next few years due to the retirement of many baby boomers from faculty positions. Other examples include shortages of certified auto mechanics, heating and air-conditioning technicians, and network-certified computer specialists.

Unemployment Rate and Labor Markets

When the unemployment rate is high in a given market, many people are looking for jobs. When the unemployment rate is low, there are few applicants. Of course, unemployment rates vary with the business cycle and present very different challenges for recruiting.[10] For instance, in Michigan, due to the closing of automobile plants and layoffs of many workers, the manufacturers in other Michigan industries, and even retailers, are getting a significant number of job applicants.

STRATEGIC RECRUITING DECISIONS

An employer must make a number of recruiting decisions based on these needs identified as part of HR planning. The way these decisions affect the strategy the company has chosen will be a critical part of deciding which is the "right" choice. Important strategic decisions for recruiting are discussed next.

Organization-Based vs. Outsourced Recruiting

An initial and basic decision is whether the recruiting will be done by the employer or outsourced to someone else. This decision need not be an "either–or" decision entirely. In most organizations, HR staff members handle the bulk of recruiting efforts. The distribution of recruiting responsibilities between the HR department and operating managers shown in Figure 7-3 is typical for all but the smallest organizations.

Because recruiting can be a time-consuming process, given all the other responsibilities of HR staff and other managers in organizations, outsourcing it is a way to both decrease the number of HR staff needed and free up time

FIGURE 7-3 Typical Division of HR Responsibilities: Recruiting

HR Unit	Managers
• Forecasts recruiting needs • Prepares copy for recruiting ads and campaigns • Plans and conducts recruiting efforts • Audits and evaluates all recruiting activities	• Anticipate needs for employees to fill vacancies • Determine KSAs needed from applicants • Assist in recruiting efforts with information about job requirements • Review success/failure of recruiting activities

for HR staff members. Recruiting can be outsourced in a number of ways. For example, some large employers outsource such functions as placement of advertisements, initial screening of résumés, and initial phone contacts with potential applicants. Once those activities are done, then the employer's HR staff members take over the rest of the recruiting activities.

A common means of outsourcing is retaining search firms and employment agencies to recruit candidates. About 10% of all firms outsource large parts of recruiting operations, and about 58% plan to increase outsourcing at some point.[11] Outsourcing gives a firm more flexibility because a vendor may be able to fill those positions faster and cheaper than in-house recruiters can.[12]

Professional Employer Organizations and Employee Leasing A specific type of outsourcing uses professional employer organizations (PEOs) and employee leasing. This approach has grown rapidly in recent years. The employee leasing process is simple: An employer signs an agreement with the PEO, after which the existing staff is hired by the leasing firm and leased back to the company. For a fee, a small-business owner or operator turns the staff over to the leasing company, which then writes the paychecks, pays the taxes, prepares and implements HR policies, and keeps all the required records.

Internet Research

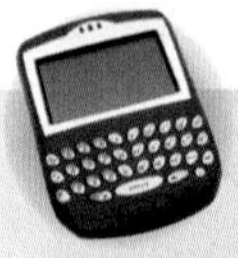

Professional Employer Organizations
For information and a directory of PEOs, link to their site at: http://thomsonedu.com/management/mathis.

PEOs and employment agencies are different entities. An *employment agency* provides a "work-finding" service for job seekers and supplies employers with applicants they may then hire. A PEO has its own workforce, which it supplies by contract to employers with jobs. Small-business owners do not always know how to comply with EEOC, ADA, COBRA, OSHA, and other government requirements, and using a PEO can be an advantage because PEOs handle the HR complexities. However, some legal and tax-related issues must be considered when using a PEO, so employers should consult outside experts before shifting to PEOs for staffing.

One advantage for employees of leasing companies is that they may receive better benefits than they otherwise would get in many small businesses. All this service comes at a cost. Leasing companies often charge employers between 4% and 6% of employees' monthly salaries. Thus, while leasing may save employers money on benefits and HR administration, it may also increase total payroll costs.

Recruiting Presence and Image

Recruiting efforts may be viewed as either continuous or intensive. *Continuous* efforts to recruit offer the advantage of keeping the employer in the recruiting market. For example, with college recruiting, some organizations may find it advantageous to have a recruiter on a given campus each year. Employers that visit a campus only occasionally are less likely to build a following at that school over time.

Intensive recruiting may take the form of a vigorous recruiting campaign aimed at hiring a given number of employees, usually within a short period of time. Such efforts may be the result of failure in the HR planning system to identify needs in advance or to recognize drastic changes in workforce needs due to unexpected workloads.

Employment "Branding" and Image A factor impacting recruiting is portraying a positive image of the employer. The way the "employment brand" of the organization is viewed by both employees and outsiders is crucial to attracting applicants and retaining employees, who also may describe the organization in positive or negative terms to others.

Organizations seen as desirable employers are better able to attract more qualified applicants than are organizations with poor reputations. For example, one firm had good pay and benefits, but its work demands were seen as excessive, and frequent downsizings had resulted in some terminations and transfers. The result was high turnover and a low rate of applicants interested in applying for employment at the company.

Companies spend considerable effort and money establishing brand images for their products. Firms that regularly appear in the "100 Best Companies to Work For" as designated by *Fortune* magazine, such as Southwest Airlines, Cisco Systems, and Edward Jones, have achieved success in establishing a brand image as an employer that helps their recruiting.

Not only can the brand help generate more recruits, but it can also help with applicant self-selection because it affects whether individuals ever consider a firm and submit applications.[13] Thus, recruiting and employer branding should be seen as part of organizational marketing efforts and linked to the overall image and reputation of the organization and its industry.

Training of Recruiters

Another important strategic issue is how much training will be given to recruiters. In addition to being trained on interviewing techniques, communications skills, and knowledge of the jobs being filled, it is crucial that recruiters learn the types of actions that violate EEO regulations and how to be sensitive to diversity issues with applicants. Training in those areas often includes interview do's and don'ts and appropriate language to use with applicants. Racist, sexist, and other inappropriate remarks hurt the image of the employer and may result in legal complaints. For instance, a male college recruiter regularly asked female candidates about their marital status, and if they were single and attractive, he later called applicants and asked them for dates. Only after two students complained to the university placement office did the employer learn of the recruiter's misconduct.

Incidents such as this one reinforce the importance of the need for employers to train and monitor recruiters' behaviors and actions. Some employers send interviewees follow-up surveys asking about the effectiveness of the recruiters and the image the candidates have of the employers as a result of their recruiting contacts.

Regular vs. Flexible Staffing

Another strategic decision affects how much recruiting will be done to fill staffing needs with regular full-time and part-time employees. Decisions as to who should be recruited hinge on whether to seek traditional employees or to use more flexible approaches, which might include temporaries or independent contractors. A number of employers feel that the cost of keeping a regular workforce has become excessive and is growing worse due to increasing government-mandated costs. However, not just the money is at issue. The number of regulations also constrains the employment relationship, making many employers reluctant to hire new employees.

Flexible staffing Use of workers who are not traditional employees.

Flexible staffing uses workers who are not traditional employees. Using flexible staffing arrangements allows an employer to avoid some of the cost of full-time benefits such as vacation pay and pension plans, as well as to recruit in a somewhat different market. These arrangements can use temporary workers or independent contractors.

Temporary Workers Employers who use temporary employees can hire their own temporary staff members or contract with agencies supplying temporary workers on a rate-per-day or rate-per-week basis. Originally developed to provide clerical and office workers to employers, such agencies now provide workers in many other areas. The use of temporary workers may make sense for an organization if its work is subject to seasonal or other fluctuations. Hiring regular employees to meet peak employment needs would require that the employer find some tasks to keep employees busy during less active periods or resort to layoffs.

Some employers hire temporary workers as a way for individuals to move into full-time, regular employment. Better-performing workers may move to regular positions when they become available. This "try before you buy" approach is potentially beneficial to both employers and employees. However, most temporary service firms bill client companies a placement charge if a temporary worker is hired full-time within a certain time period—usually 90 days.

Independent contractors Workers who perform specific services on a contract basis.

Independent Contractors Some firms employ independent contractors, workers who perform specific services on a contract basis. These workers must be independent as determined by regulations used by the U.S. Internal Revenue Service and the U.S. Department of Labor, which is discussed in greater detail in Chapter 12. Independent contractors are used in a number of areas, including building maintenance, security, advertising, and others. One major reason for use of independent contractors is that some employers get significant savings by using independent contractors because benefits do not have to be provided to those individuals.

Recruiting and Diversity Considerations

As Figure 7-4 indicates, a number of factors go into ensuring that recruiting decisions meet diversity considerations. Recruiting as a key employment-related activity is subject to various legal considerations, especially equal employment

| FIGURE 7-4 | Recruiting and Diversity Considerations |

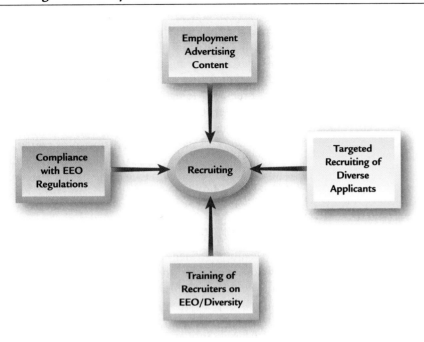

laws and regulations. When a particular protected class is underrepresented in an organization, word-of-mouth referral by existing employees has been considered a violation of Title VII of the Civil Rights Act of 1964, because it continues a past pattern of discrimination.

Employment Advertising The Equal Employment Opportunity Commission (EEOC) guidelines state that no direct or indirect references implying gender or age are permitted. Some examples of impermissible terminology are: "young and enthusiastic," "recent college graduate," "Christian values," and "journeyman lineman."

Additionally, employment advertisements should indicate that the employer has a policy of complying with equal employment regulations. Advertisements should contain a general phrase, such as Equal Opportunity Employer, or more specific designations, such as EEO/M-F/AA/ADA. Employers demonstrate inclusive recruiting by having diverse individuals represented in company materials, in advertisements, and as recruiters. Microsoft, Prudential Insurance, Bristol-Myers Squibb, and other firms have found that making diversity visible in recruiting efforts has helped them recruit more individuals with more varied backgrounds.[14]

Recruiting Nontraditional Workers

The growing difficulty that many employers have had in attracting and retaining workers has led them to recruit workers from what, for some, are nontraditional labor pools. Nontraditional sources may include:

- Older workers
- Stay-at-home moms
- Single parents
- Welfare-to-work workers
- Homeless/substance abuse workers
- Workers with disabilities

Older workers may include retirees who have become bored (or need money), those who have been involuntarily laid off, or career changers wanting to try a new field in mid-career. Single parents may be attracted to a family-friendly employer that offers flexibility because it is frequently difficult to balance job and family life. Stay-at-home moms may consider part-time work that is available during times when the children are at school.[15] Welfare-to-work applicants often need training in basic work skills such as reporting to work on time and doing what they are told—putting a premium on an employer's training program. Employees with disabilities present a variety of challenges depending on the nature of the disability, but if an employer can be flexible, such workers can be a good source of employees.[16] Homeless and substance abusers also come with a variety of problems. Some cities have non-profit groups interested in seeing these people succeed at work that provide support and some training to them.

Recruiting Source Choices: Internal vs. External

Recruiting strategy and policy decisions entail identifying where to recruit, whom to recruit, and how to recruit. One of the first decisions determines the extent to which internal or external sources and methods will be used. Both promoting from within the organization (internal recruitment) and hiring from outside the organization (external recruitment) come with advantages and disadvantages. Figure 7-5 shows some of the major pluses and minuses of each.

FIGURE 7-5   **Advantages and Disadvantages of Internal and External Recruiting Sources**

Recruiting Source	Advantages	Disadvantages
Internal	• The morale of the promotee is usually high. • The firm can better assess a candidate's abilities. • Recruiting costs are lower for some jobs. • The process is a motivator for good performance. • The process causes a succession of promotions. • The firm has to hire only at entry level.	• "Inbreeding" results. • Those not promoted may experience morale problems. • Employees may engage in "political" infighting for promotions. • A management development program is needed.
External	• New "blood" brings new perspectives. • Training new hires is cheaper and faster because of prior external experience. • The new hire has no group of "political supporters" in the organization. • The new hire may bring new industry insights.	• The firm may not select someone who will fit the job or the organization. • The process may cause morale problems for internal candidates not selected. • The new employee may require a longer adjustment or orientation time.

A possible strategy might be to promote from within if a qualified applicant exists and to go external if not.[17] Most employers combine the use of internal and external methods. Organizations that face rapidly changing competitive environments and conditions may need to place a heavier emphasis on external sources in addition to developing internal sources. However, for organizations existing in environments that change slowly, promotion from within may be more suitable. Once the various recruiting policy decisions have been addressed, then the actual recruiting methods can be identified and used. These include internal and external methods and Internet/Web-based approaches.

INTERNAL RECRUITING METHODS

The most common internal recruiting methods include: organizational databases, job postings, promotions and transfers, current-employee referrals, and re-recruiting of former employees and applicants.

Internal Recruiting Processes

Within the organization, tapping into employee databases, job postings, promotions, and transfers provides ways for current employees to move to other jobs. Filling openings internally may add motivation for employees to stay and grow in the organization rather than pursuing career opportunities elsewhere.

Employee Databases The increased use of HR management systems allows HR staff members to maintain background and KSA information on existing employees. As openings arise, HR can access databases by entering job requirements and then get a listing of current employees meeting those requirements. Various types of employment software sort employee data by occupational fields, education, areas of career interests, previous work histories, and other variables. For instance, if a firm has an opening for someone with an MBA and marketing experience, the key words *MBA* and *marketing* can be entered in a search field, and the program displays a list of all current employees with these two items identified in their employee profiles.

The advantage of such databases is that they can be linked to other HR activities. Opportunities for career development and advancement are major reasons why individuals stay or leave their employers. With employee databases, internal opportunities for individuals can be identified. Employee profiles are continually updated to include such items as additional training or education completed, special projects worked on, and career plans and desires noted during performance appraisal and career mentoring discussions.

Job posting System in which the employer provides notices of job openings and employees respond by applying.

Job Posting The major means for recruiting current employees for other jobs within the organization is job posting, a system in which the employer provides notices of job openings and employees respond by applying for specific openings. Without some sort of job posting system, it is difficult for many employees to find out what jobs are open elsewhere in the organization. The organization can notify employees of job vacancies in a number of ways, including posting notices on the company intranet and Internet Website, using employee newsletters, and sending out e-mails to managers and employees. In a unionized organization, job posting and bidding can be quite formal because the procedures are often spelled out in labor agreements. Seniority lists may be used by organizations that make promotions based strictly on seniority.

HR BEST PRACTICES

Recruiting for Internal Promotions and Transfers

Recruiting tools can help identify prospective candidates internally. It has been noted that "if you are not recruiting your own employees, someone else will," and that if employees have no internal opportunities to advance, the best performers will look outside.

Most companies historically have had some kind of job posting system in place for internal jobs; today many companies use proactive efforts to get employees to apply through Web-based systems. For example, the job posting system at Fireman's Fund Insurance works like this: Employees log on to the company intranet and create personal profiles including career objectives, education, skill sets, and salary expectations. They may also attach a résumé. When a job opens, the placement program automatically mines the database for matches. Candidates are notified by e-mail and go through the regular hiring cycle.

At Whirlpool, employees can use a somewhat similar system, making it simpler for them to access job openings. They can go on-line to retrieve a list of jobs that match their backgrounds and to apply for jobs. Further, managers can enter job criteria and instantly receive names of internal and external candidates who fit them. More than half of the people Whirlpool hired in one year were internal candidates. The company estimated that it saved $1 million with the system that year.

These examples illustrate how best practices in automated job posting are paying off for employers. Use of such systems has been growing rapidly, and is expected to continue to do so in the future.[18]

Some organizations use automated systems that combine elements of databases and job postings. The HR Best Practices presents examples of such systems.

Regardless of the means used, the purpose of the job posting system is to provide employees with more opportunities to move within the organization. When establishing and managing a job posting system, answers to a number of potential questions must be addressed:

- What happens if no qualified candidates respond to postings?
- Must employees inform their supervisors that they are applying for another job?
- Are there restrictions on how long an employee must stay in a job before applying for another one?
- How much notice should an employee be required to give before transferring to a new department?
- What types of or levels of jobs will not be posted?

Job posting systems can be ineffective if handled improperly. Jobs generally are posted before any external recruiting is done. The organization must allow a reasonable period of time for present employees to check notices of available jobs before it considers external applicants. When employees' bids are turned down, they should discuss with their supervisors or someone in the HR area the knowledge, skills, and abilities they need in order to improve their opportunities in the future.

Promotions and Transfers Many organizations choose to fill vacancies through promotions or transfers from within whenever possible. Although most often successful, promotions and transfers from within have some drawbacks as well. A person's performance on one job may not be a good predictor of performance on another, because different skills may be required on the new job. For example, not every high-performing worker makes a successful supervisor. In most supervisory jobs, an ability to accomplish the work through others requires skills in influencing and dealing with people, and those skills may not have been a factor in non-supervisory jobs.

As employees transfer or are promoted to other jobs, individuals must be recruited to fill their vacated jobs. Planning on how to fill those openings should occur before the job transfers or promotions, not afterward. It is clear that people in organizations with fewer levels may have less frequent chances for promotion.

Employee-Focused Recruiting

One reliable source of potential recruits is suggestions from current or former employees. Because current and former employees are familiar with the employer, most employees usually do not refer individuals who are likely to be unqualified or to make the employees look bad. Also, follow-up with former employers is likely to be done only with persons who were solid employees previously.

Current-Employee Referrals A reliable source of people to fill vacancies is composed of acquaintances, friends, and family members of employees. The current employees can acquaint potential applicants with the advantages of a job with the company, furnish letters of introduction, and encourage candidates to apply. However, using only word-of-mouth or current-employee referrals can violate equal employment regulations if protected-class individuals are underrepresented in the current organizational workforce. Therefore, some external recruiting might be necessary to avoid legal problems in this area.

Utilizing this source is usually one of the most effective methods of recruiting because many qualified people can be reached at a low cost. In an organization with numerous employees, this approach can develop quite a large pool of potential employees. New workers recruited by current-employee referrals have longer tenure with organizations than do those recruited through other sources and cost less to hire than advertising and hiring externally.

Tight labor markets in many geographic areas and certain occupational fields prompted many employers to establish employee referral incentive programs. Mid-sized and larger employers are much more likely to use employee referral bonuses. Some referral programs provide different amounts for hard-to-fill jobs compared with common openings.

Re-Recruiting of Former Employees and Applicants Former employees and former applicants represent another source for recruitment. Both groups offer a time-saving advantage because something is already known about them. Seeking them out as candidates is known as *re-recruiting* because they were successfully recruited previously. Former employees are considered an internal source in the sense that they have ties to the employer, and may be called "boomerangers" because they left and came back.

Individuals who left for other jobs might be willing to return because the other jobs and employers turned out to be less attractive than initially thought. For example, a consulting firm attracted more than 100 people who had left in the prior two years by contacting them and offering them "loyalty grants." Other firms have established "alumni reunions" to keep in contact with individuals who have left, and also to allow them to re-recruit individuals as appropriate openings arise. Key issues in the decision to re-recruit someone include the reasons why the individual left originally and whether or not the individual's performance and capabilities were good.

Another potential source of applicants is former applicants. Although these are not entirely an internal source, information about them can be found in the organizational files or an applicant database. Re-contacting those who have previously applied for jobs can be a quick and inexpensive way to fill unexpected openings. For instance, one firm that needed two cost accountants immediately contacted qualified previous applicants and was able to hire individuals who were disenchanted with their current jobs at other companies.

Re-recruiting has another meaning as well. The idea is to treat the best current employees as if they were top recruits. For example, if a company is giving signing bonuses to top recruits, perhaps it should give retention bonuses to top existing staff members.

EXTERNAL RECRUITING SOURCES

What makes an external applicant consider a specific employer? What attracts the right kind of applicants? Characteristics of the job and organization, how the recruiting is conducted, and whether the applicant sees a fit are important elements in successfully recruiting external candidates according to recent research.[19] These attractions apply regardless of the source of the applicants. Many external sources are available for recruiting. In some tight labor markets, multiple sources and methods will be used to attract candidates for the variety of jobs available in organizations. Some of the more prominent methods are highlighted next.

College and University Recruiting

College or university students are a significant source for entry-level professional and technical employees. Most universities maintain career placement offices in which employers and applicants can meet. A number of considerations affect an employer's selection of colleges and universities at which to conduct interviews. The major determinants are:

- Current and anticipated job openings
- Reputations of the colleges and universities
- Experiences with placement offices and previous graduates
- Organizational budget constraints
- Market competition for graduates
- Cost of available talent and typical salaries

College recruiting can be expensive; therefore, an organization should determine if the jobs it is trying to fill really require persons with college degrees. A great many jobs do not, yet many employers often insist on filling them with college graduates. The result may be employees who must be paid more and who are likely to leave if the jobs are not sufficiently challenging.

There is a great deal of competition for the top students in many college and university programs, and less competition for students with less impressive records.[20] Attributes that recruiters seem to value most highly in college graduates—poise, oral and written communication skills, personality, and appearance—all are typically mentioned ahead of grade point average (GPA). However, for many employers, a high GPA is a major criterion for considering candidates for jobs during on-campus interviews. Recruiters use GPA decision rules in a variety of ways to initially screen applicants in college recruiting, such as setting minimum GPA requirements to screen large applicant pools, not considering GPA at all, or even screening out students with *high* GPAs.[21]

A number of factors determine success in college recruiting. Some employers actively build continuing relationships with individual faculty members and career staff at designated colleges and universities. Maintaining a presence on campus by providing guest speakers to classes and student groups increases the contacts for an employer. The important point is that employers that show continuing presence and support on a campus are more likely to see expanded college recruiting results.

Many other firms stress internships in college recruiting. Companies using internships believe they achieve better retention through the use of internships and cooperative programs. Well-planned internships can be excellent sources for talented job candidates. For successful internship suggestions, see the HR On-the-Job feature.

School Recruiting

High schools or vocational/technical schools may be valuable sources of new employees for some organizations. Many schools have a centralized guidance or placement office. Promotional brochures that acquaint students with starting jobs and career opportunities can be distributed to counselors, librarians, or others. Participating in career days and giving company tours to school groups are other ways of maintaining good contact with school sources. Cooperative programs in which students work part-time and receive some school credits also may be useful in generating qualified future applicants for full-time positions.

HR ON-THE-JOB

Making Internships Work

An internship has the potential to benefit both the individual student intern and the employer. The student gets an opportunity to see if the employer and its culture fit, and the employer gets the equivalent of a 90-day interview instead of a 30-minute one. But not all internships actually are good situations for either party. Some basic guidelines for the employer can help improve the odds that internships will be rewarding:

■ *Decide what the company needs.* A specific project is more challenging for the student and a better predictor of future employment capabilities for the company than just providing a job.

■ *Require meaningful work.* Challenging assignments are best. Using interns as clerical replacements is usually not the best way to impress them.

■ *Pay well.* Competitive wages help attract talent. In the past, many internships were unpaid, but now most interns are paid.

■ *Treat the intern like a new employee.* Interns need work space, appropriate tools for the job, Internet access, a telephone, training feedback, and someone to provide guidance when needed.

■ *Look at several candidates.* Use a broad internship description to increase the chances of finding a talented person with appropriate capabilities.

Until recently, students not going on to college received little guidance or training on finding jobs after high school. However, the number of "partnerships" with schools through "school-to-work" programs has grown. Companies are entering the classroom not only to recruit, but to tutor students in skills such as the reading and math needed for work. Internships during the summer and work/school programs also are widely used.[22]

Employers recognize that they may need to begin attracting students with capabilities while those students are in high school. For example, GE, IBM, and other corporations fund programs to encourage students with science and math skills to participate in engineering internships during summers. These and other employers specifically target talented members of racial minorities in high schools and provide them with career encouragement, summer internships, and mentoring programs. In addition to fulfilling some social responsibilities and aiding in workforce diversity, the organizations hope to generate employment interest from the students they assist and hope that interest may help fill future openings.

Labor Unions

Labor unions are a good source of certain types of workers. In such industries as electric and construction, unions have traditionally supplied workers to employers. A labor pool is generally available through a union, and workers can be dispatched from it to particular jobs to meet the needs of the employers.

In some instances, the union can control or influence recruiting and staffing needs. An organization with a strong union may have less flexibility than a non-union company in deciding who will be hired and where that person will be placed. Unions can also benefit employers through apprenticeship and cooperative staffing programs, as they do in the building and printing industries.

Employment Agencies and Headhunters

Every state in the United States has its own state-sponsored employment agency. These agencies operate branch offices in many cities throughout the states and do not charge fees to applicants or employers.

Private employment agencies also operate in most cities. For a fee collected from either the employee or the employer, these agencies do some preliminary screening and put the organization in touch with applicants. Private employment agencies differ considerably in the levels of service, costs, policies, and types of applicants they provide. Employers can reduce the range of possible problems from these sources by giving complete descriptions and specifications for jobs to be filled.

Some employment agencies focus their efforts on executive, managerial, and professional positions. These executive search firms are split into two groups: (1) contingency firms that charge a fee only after a candidate has been hired by a client company, and (2) retainer firms that charge a client a set fee whether or not the contracted search is successful. Most of the larger firms work on a retainer basis. The fee charged by executive search firms may be 30% or more of the employee's first-year salary. In most cases, the employer pays the fee, but in some circumstances, the employee does. For placing someone in a high-level executive job, a search firm may receive $300,000 or more, counting travel expenses and the placement fee.[23] The size of the fees and the aggressiveness with which some firms pursue candidates for openings have led to such firms being called *headhunters*. However, search firms are ethically bound not to approach employees of client companies in their search for job candidates for another employer.

Competitive Sources

Other sources for recruiting include professional and trade associations, trade publications, and competitors. Many professional societies and trade associations publish newsletters or magazines and have Websites containing job ads. Such sources may be useful for recruiting the specialized professionals needed in an industry.

Some employers have extended recruiting to customers. Retailers such as Target, Home Depot, and Best Buy have aggressive programs to recruit customers to become employees in stores. Customers at these firms can receive applications blanks, apply on-line using kiosks, or schedule interviews with managers or HR staff members, all while in the stores. Other firms have included employment announcements when sending out customer bills or newsletters.

Media Sources

Media sources such as newspapers, magazines, television, radio, and billboards are widely used.[24] Some firms have used direct mail with purchased lists of individuals in certain fields or industries. Whatever medium is used, it should be tied to the relevant labor market and should provide sufficient information on the company and the job. Figure 7-6 shows the information a good recruiting advertisement should include. Notice that details about the job and the application process, desired candidate qualifications, and an overview of the organization are all important.

FIGURE 7-6   **What to Include in an Effective Recruiting Ad**

Information on the Job and on the Application Process

- Job title and responsibilities
- Location of job
- Starting pay range
- Closing date for application
- Whether or not to submit a résumé and a cover letter
- Whether or not calls are invited
- Where to mail application or résumé

Desired Candidate Qualifications

- Years of experience
- Three to five key characteristics of successful candidates

Information on the Organization

- That it is an EEO employer
- Its primary business

Evaluating Ads HR recruiters should measure the responses they generate in order to evaluate the effectiveness of various media. The easiest way to track responses to ads is to use different contact names, e-mail addresses, or phone number codes in each ad. Then the employer can note which advertisement prompted each applicant response that is received.

Although the total number of responses to each ad should be tracked, judging the success of an ad only by this number is a mistake. For example, it is better to have 10 responses with two qualified applicants than 30 responses with only one qualified applicant. Therefore, after the individuals are hired, follow-up should be done to see which sources produced employees who stayed longer and performed better.

Job Fairs and Special Events

Employers in tight labor markets or needing to fill a large number of jobs quickly have used job fairs and special recruiting events. Job fairs also have been held by economic development entities, employer and HR associations, and other community groups to help bring employers and potential job candidates together. For instance, to fill jobs in one metropolitan area, the local SHRM chapter annually sponsors a job fair at which 75–125 employers can meet applicants. Publicity in the city draws more than 1,000 potential recruits. One cautionary note: Some employers at this and other job fairs may see current employees "shopping" for jobs at other employers.

Another cautionary note: "General" job fairs are likely to attract many people including more unemployed (and unemployable) attendees. Industry or skill-specific events offer more satisfactory candidates. Such job fairs can attract employed candidates who are looking casually but may not put their resumes out on the Internet.

"Virtual" job fairs that have Web-based links have been used by the federal government and others. "Drive-through" job fairs at shopping malls have been used by employers in a number of communities. At one such event, interested persons can drive up to a tent outside the mall and pick up applications from a "menu board" of employers, then park and interview in the tent with recruiters if time allows. Some firms also use other methods as noted next.

Creative Recruiting Methods

In labor markets that are tight and in industries with significant shortages of qualified applicants, employers turn to more creative recruiting methods. Regardless of the methods used, the goal is to generate a pool of qualified applicants so that the jobs in organizations are filled in a timely manner. Some methods may be more effective at recruiting for certain jobs than others. To illustrate, here are some examples:

- Using a plane towing an advertising banner over beach areas
- Advertising jobs on local movie theater screens as pre-show entertainment
- Holding raffles for employees who refer candidates, with cars and trips being used as prizes
- Offering free rock concert tickets to the first 20 applicants hired
- Setting up recruiting tables at bowling alleys, minor-league baseball games, or stock car races
- Recruiting younger technical employees at video game parlors
- Arranging partnerships with downsizing firms to interview those being laid off

- Connecting with outplacement firms to find out about individuals who have lost their jobs
- Offering tuition assistance for those willing to work their way through college
- Sponsoring book fairs to recruit publishing company sales representatives
- Interviewing two hours a week even if the organization does not have any openings—and maintaining good files on those interviewed
- Taking candidates from among those who leave the armed forces (About 275,000 women and men, plus many of their spouses, leave the armed forces each year.)
- Partnering with U.S. military recruiters and guaranteeing enlistees jobs after they complete military service
- Parking motor homes—all set up for interviews, testing, and hiring—in parking lots at malls, with signs saying "Want a job? Apply here."

INTERNET RECRUITING

The Internet has become the primary means for many employers to search for job candidates and for applicants to look for jobs. The explosive growth in general Internet use is a key reason. Internet users tap the Internet to search for jobs almost as frequently as they read classified ads in newspapers. Many of them also post or submit resumes on the Internet.

E-Recruiting Places

Several sites are used for Internet recruiting. The most common ones are Internet job boards, professional/career Websites, and employer Websites.

Internet Job Boards Numerous Internet job boards, such as Monster, Yahoo!, and HotJobs, provide places for employers to post jobs or search for candidates. Job boards provide access to numerous candidates. However, many individuals accessing the sites are "job lookers" who are not serious about changing jobs, but are checking out compensation levels and job availability in their areas of interest. Despite these concerns, HR recruiters find general job boards useful for generating applicant responses. Also, a recruiter for a firm can pretend to be an applicant in order to check out what other employers are looking for in similar job candidates and offering as compensation, in order to maintain recruiting competitiveness.

Professional/Career Websites Many professional associations have employment sections at their Websites. As illustration, for HR jobs see the Society for Human Resource Management site, *www.shrm.org*, or the American Society for Training and Development site, *www.astd.org*. A number of private corporations maintain specialized career or industry Websites to focus on IT, telecommunications, engineering, medicine, or other areas. Use of these more targeted Websites limits somewhat the recruiters' search time and efforts. Also, posting jobs on such Websites is likely to target applicants specifically interested in the job field and may reduce the number of less-qualified applicants who actually apply.

Employer Websites Despite the popularity of job boards and association job sites, many employers have found their own Websites to be more effective and

HR ONLINE

Effective Recruiting Through a Company Website

Effective company recruiting Websites should meet certain criteria. The primary ones are:

- Make the site easy to navigate. The "Careers" button should be on the home page and clearly labeled. Job information should be no more than three clicks away.
- Build a strong image for the company and the job. One company lists open positions and also describes the kind of work people would be doing in those positions, shows pictures of facilities and the people who work there, and describes the company climate and location.
- Make it easy to apply for a job. There should be a résumé builder, or a place to paste an existing résumé. On-line applications should also be provided.
- Use qualifying categories (location, job function, skills, keyword search, etc.) to help candidates find the jobs for which they are eligible. Use of such categories saves time, especially in a big company.

- Use self-assessment checklists to ask candidates about experience and interests and to direct them to the jobs that fit them the best.
- Include items people care about. Describe the company, its products and services, careers, and other unique advantages of working for the company.
- Link the site to a database. Doing this provides recruiters with an additional way to post jobs, search for résumés and applications, and screen applicants. Without this necessary step, it is impossible to manage a busy Website.
- Collect metrics on the site. To see how effective the site is, gather information such as the numbers of visitors, hits from ads, actual hires, and other details.

efficient when recruiting candidates. See HR On-Line for advice on designing an effective careers or employment section for a Website.

Numerous employers have included employment and career information on their sites. Many company Websites have a tab labeled "Employment" or "Careers." This is the place where recruiting (internal and external) is often conducted. On many of these sites, job seekers are encouraged to e-mail résumés or complete on-line applications. According to one survey, about 16% of hires come through a company's Website—a much higher proportion than come from on-line job boards.[24]

A good Website can also help reach "passive" job seekers—those who have a good job and are not really looking to change but might consider a better opportunity if it were presented. These individuals often do not list themselves on job boards, but they might visit a company Website for other reasons and check out the careers or employment section. A well-designed corporate Website can help stimulate interest in some of passive job seekers, as well as other potential candidates.[25]

It is important for the recruiting and employment portions of an employer Website to be seen as part of the marketing efforts of the firm. Therefore, the employment section of an organizational Website must be shaped to market jobs and careers effectively. Also, a company Website should market the employer by outlining information on the organization, its products and services, organizational and industry growth potential, and organizational operations.

Advantages of Internet Recruiting

Employers have found a number of advantages to using Internet recruiting. A primary one is that many employers have saved money using Internet recruiting versus other recruiting methods such as newspaper advertising, employment agencies, and search firms.

Internet Research

Recruiters Network

This Website provides resources and information on the recruiting and Internet recruiting industries. Link to the site at: http://thomsonedu.com/management/mathis.

Internet recruiting also can save considerable time. Applicants can respond quickly to job postings by sending e-mails, rather than using "snail mail." Recruiters can respond to qualified candidates more quickly, and establish times for interviews or request additional candidate information.

An expanded pool of applicants can be generated using Internet recruiting. In fact, a large number of candidates may see any given job listing, although exposure depends on which Internet sources are used. One side benefit of the Internet is that jobs literally are posted globally, so potential applicants in other geographic areas and countries can view job openings posted on the Internet. The Internet also improves the ability to target specific audiences through the use of categories, information, and other variables.

Disadvantages of Internet Recruiting

The positives associated with Internet recruiting come with a number of disadvantages. In getting broader exposure, employers also may get more unqualified applicants. HR recruiters find that Internet recruiting creates additional work for HR staff members. More résumés must be reviewed, more e-mails need to be dealt with, and expensive specialized software may be needed to track the increased number of applicants resulting from many Internet recruiting efforts. A primary concern is that many individuals who access job sites are just browsers who may submit résumés just to see what happens but are not seriously looking for new jobs.

Another issue with Internet recruiting is that some applicants may have limited Internet access, especially individuals from lower socioeconomic groups and from certain racial/ethnic minority groups. A "digital divide" separates those who have Internet access from those who do not—and fewer Hispanic and African American job seekers than whites have Internet access at home or at all. Consequently, employers using Internet recruiting may not be reaching as diverse a recruitment pool as might be desired.

Privacy is another potential disadvantage with Internet recruiting. Sharing information gleaned from people who apply to job boards or even company Websites has become common. But information sharing is being done in ways that might violate discrimination and credit reporting laws.

Internet recruiting is, of course, only one approach to recruiting, but it has been expanding in use. Information about how Internet recruiting methods compare with other, more traditional, approaches is relevant. For example, one study found that the most effective approach to recruiting (combining the numbers of hires with the total cost to hire them) is employee referrals. Referral through social networking Websites is the second most effective approach, followed by use of employer Websites. Additional means evaluated for effectiveness, in descending order, were found to be campus recruiting and specialty job boards. Commercial résumé databases, general job boards, newspapers, and job fairs were found to be among the less cost effective recruiting sources.[25] What this study and the experiences of a broadening number of employers show is that it is important to use both the Internet and traditional approaches in different situations for successful recruiting, depending upon the jobs to be filled.

Blogs and Social Networks

The informal use of the Web can cause some interesting recruiting advantages and disadvantages for both employers and employees. For example, some employers are using blogs to recruit for specialty positions among the participants who read the blog. More employers are looking at on-line journals and social networking sites such as Facebook to discover potentially damaging personal information about high school and college applicants.[26]

Other social networking sites allow job seekers to connect with employees of potential hirers. Jobster Inc. includes posts on what it is like to work for a boss, and job hunters can contact the posters and ask questions. LinkedIn has a job-search engine that lets one see if any contacts *or their contacts* work for employers who have posted job openings. Again, this approach makes it easy to ask current employees for an evaluation of their own employers.[27]

Legal Issues in Internet Recruiting

With Internet recruiting comes new legal concerns. Several of the concerns have ethical and moral implications, as well as legal ones. For example:

- When companies use screening software to avoid looking at each of the thousands of résumés they receive, are rejections really based on the qualifications needed for the job?
- Are protected classes being excluded from the process?
- As a company receives résumés from applicants, it is required to track those applicants and report to the federal government. How can a person's protected-class and other information be collected and analyzed for those reports?
- Who are really applicants? Is someone who sent an e-mail asking if the employer has a job open really an applicant?
- General informality on-line can lead to discussions or information that might be improper if the person does not get the job.

RECRUITING EVALUATION AND METRICS

To determine how effective various recruiting sources and methods have been, it is important to evaluate recruiting efforts. The primary way to find out whether recruiting efforts are cost effective is to conduct formal analyses as part of recruiting evaluation. Although various areas can be measured when trying to analyze recruiting effectiveness; five specific areas that usually *need* to be considered include: quantity of recruits, quality of recruits, time available for filling empty positions, cost per recruit, and satisfaction of parties involved. Metrics that look at the quality of the selection decisions made are also included.

Evaluating Recruiting Quantity and Quality

As one means of evaluating recruiting, organizations can see how their recruiting efforts compare with past patterns and with the recruiting performance of other organizations. Certain measures of recruiting effectiveness are quite useful in indicating whether sufficient numbers of the targeted applicant population group are being attracted. Information about job performance, absenteeism, cost of training, and turnover by recruiting source also helps adjust future recruiting efforts. For example, some companies find that recruiting at certain colleges or universities furnishes stable, high performers, whereas recruiting at other schools provides employees who are more prone to leave the organization. General metrics for evaluating quantity and quality of recruiting include the following variables:

- *Quantity of applicants:* Because the goal of a good recruiting program is to generate a large pool of applicants from which to choose, quantity is a natural place to begin evaluation. The basic measure here considers whether the quantity of recruits is sufficient to fill job vacancies. A related question is: Does recruiting at this source provide enough qualified applicants with an appropriate mix of protected-class individuals?
- *Quality of applicants:* In addition to quantity, a key issue is whether or not the qualifications of the applicant pool are sufficient to fill the job openings. Do the applicants meet job specifications, and do they perform the jobs well after hire? What is the failure rate for new hires for each recruiter? Measures that can be used include items such as performance appraisal scores, months until promotion, output, and sales volume for each hire.

Evaluating the Time Required to Fill Openings

Looking at the length of time it takes to fill openings is a common means of evaluating recruiting efforts. If openings are not filled quickly with qualified candidates, the work and productivity of the organization are likely to suffer. If it takes 75 days to fill empty positions, managers who need those employees will be unhappy. Also, as noted earlier, unfilled positions cost money. Generally, it is useful to calculate the average amount of time it takes from contact to hire for each source of applicants, because some sources may produce recruits faster than others. For example, one firm calculated the following averages:

Source	Average Time from Contact to Hire
Agencies	25 days
Walk-ins	7 days
Internet	12 days

These data reveal that, at least for this firm, the use of agencies takes significantly longer to fill openings than does relying on other means. Therefore, it suggests matching the use of sources to the time available.

Evaluating the Cost of Recruiting

The major calculation used to measure cost is to divide recruiting expenses for the year by the number of hires for the year:

$$\frac{\text{Recruiting expenses}}{\text{Number of recruits hired}}$$

The problem with this approach is accurately identifying what details should be included in the recruiting expenses. Should expenses for testing, background checks, relocations, or signing bonuses be included, or are they more properly excluded?

Once those questions are answered, the costs can be allocated to various sources to determine how much each hire from each source costs. The costs also can be sorted by type of job—costs for hiring managers, secretaries, bookkeepers, and sales personnel will all be different.

Evaluating Recruiting Satisfaction

The satisfaction of two groups is useful in evaluating recruiting. Certainly the views of managers with openings to fill are important, because they are "customers" in a very real sense. But the applicants (those hired and those not hired) also are an important part of the process and can provide useful input.

Managers can respond to questions about the quality of the applicant pool, the recruiter's service, the timeliness of the process, and any problems that they see. Applicants might provide input on how they were treated, their perceptions of the company, and the length of the recruiting process.

General Recruiting Process Metrics

Because recruiting activities are important, the costs and benefits associated with them should be analyzed. A cost-benefit analysis of recruiting efforts may include both direct costs (advertising, recruiters' salaries, travel, agency fees, etc.) and indirect costs (involvement of operating managers, public relations, image, etc.). Cost-benefit information on each recruiting source can be calculated. Comparing the length of time that applicants hired from each source stay in the organization with the cost of hiring from that source also offers a useful perspective.

Yield ratios Comparisons of the number of applicants at one stage of the recruiting process with the number at the next stage.

Yield Ratios One means for evaluating recruiting efforts is yield ratios, which compare the number of applicants at one stage of the recruiting process with the number at another stage. The result is a tool for approximating the necessary size of the initial applicant pool. It is useful to visualize yield ratios as a pyramid in which the employer starts with a broad base of applicants that progressively narrows. As Figure 7-7 depicts, to end up with five hires for the job in question, a sample company must begin with 100 applicants in the pool, as long as yield ratios remain as shown.

A different approach to using yield ratios suggests that over time, organizations can develop ranges for crucial ratios. When a given indicator ratio falls outside that range, it may indicate problems in the recruiting process. As an example, in college recruiting the following ratios might be useful:

$$\frac{\text{College seniors given second interview}}{\text{Total number of seniors interviewed}} = \text{Range of 30\%–50\%}$$

| FIGURE 7-7 | Sample Recruiting Evaluation Pyramid |

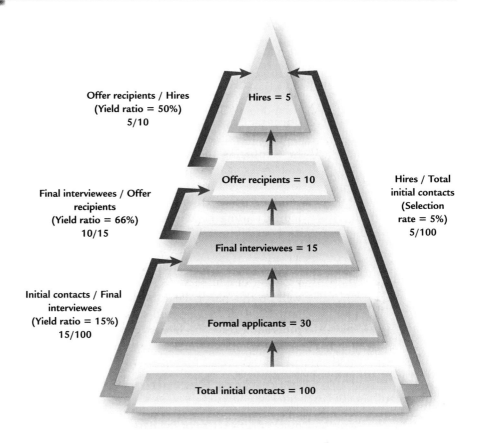

$$\frac{\text{Number who accept offer}}{\text{Number invited to the company to visit}} = \text{Range of } 50\%-70\%$$

$$\frac{\text{Number hired}}{\text{Number offered a job}} = \text{Range of } 70\%-80\%$$

$$\frac{\text{Number finally hired}}{\text{Total number interviewed on campus}} = \text{Range of } 10\%-20\%$$

Selection rate Percentage hired from a given group of candidates.

Selection Rate Another useful calculation is the selection rate, which is the percentage hired from a given group of candidates. It equals the number hired divided by the number of applicants; for example, a rate of 30% indicates that 3 out of 10 applicants were hired. The selection rate is also affected by the validity of the selection process. A relatively unsophisticated selection program might pick 8 out of 10 applicants for the job. Four of those might turn out to be good employees. A more valid selection process might pick 5 out of 10 applicants but all perform well. Selection rate measures not just recruiting but selection issues as well. So do acceptance rate and success base rate.

Acceptance rate Percent of applicants hired divided by total number of applicants offered jobs.

Acceptance Rate Calculating the acceptance rate helps identify how successful the organization is at hiring candidates to employ. The acceptance rate is the percent of applicants hired divided by the total number of applicants offered jobs. After the company goes through all the effort to screen, interview, and make job offers, hopefully, most candidates accept job offers. If they do not, then HR might want to look at reasons why managers and HR staff cannot "close the deal." It is common for HR staff members to track the reasons candidates turn down job offers, which helps explain the rejection rate in order to learn how competitive the employer is compared with other employers and what factors are causing candidates to choose employment elsewhere.

Success Base Rate A longer-term measure of recruiting effectiveness is the success rate of applicants. The *success base rate* can be determined by comparing the number of past applicants who have become successful employees against the number of applicants they competed against for their jobs, using historical data within the organization. Also, the success base rate can be compared with the success rates of other employers in the area or industry using benchmarking data. This rate indicates whether the quality of the employees hired results in employees who perform well and have low turnover. For example, assume that if 10 people were hired at random, one would expect 4 of them to be good employees. Thus, a successful recruiting program should be aimed at attracting the 4 in 10 who are capable of doing well on this particular job. Realistically, no recruiting program will attract only the 4 in 10 who will succeed. However, efforts to make the recruiting program attract the largest proportion of those in the base rate group can make recruiting efforts more effective.

Increasing Recruiting Effectiveness

The efforts to evaluate recruiting should be used to make recruiting activities more effective. Use of the data to target different applicant pools, tap broader labor markets, use different recruiting methods, improve internal handling and interviewing of applicants, and train recruiters and managers can increase recruiting effectiveness. The following technology-aided approaches to recruiting have made recruiting more effective for big employers[28]:

- *Résumé mining*—a software approach to getting the best résumés for a fit from a big database
- *Applicant tracking*—an approach that takes an applicant all the way from a job listing to performance appraisal results
- *Employer career Websites*—a convenient recruiting place on an employer's Website where applicants can see what jobs are available and apply
- *Internal mobility*—a system that tracks prospects in the company and matches them with jobs as they come open

The non-technical issues make a big difference in recruiting too, however:

- Personable recruiters who communicate well with applicants
- Emphasizing positives about the job and employer within a realistic job preview
- Fair and considerate treatment of applicants in the recruiting process
- Enhancing applicants' perceived fit with the organization

When the unemployment rate is low and good employees are difficult to hire, the preceding suggestions can help. These approaches and others are part of effective recruiting, which is crucial for HR management.

SUMMARY

- Recruiting is the process of generating a pool of qualified applicants for organizational jobs through a series of activities.
- Recruiting must be viewed strategically, and discussions should be held about the relevant labor markets in which to recruit.
- A strategic approach to recruiting begins with human resource planning and decisions about organizational recruiting responsibilities.
- The components of labor markets are labor force population, applicant population, and the applicant pool.
- Labor markets can be categorized by geographic area, industry, occupation, qualifications, and other characteristics.
- Employers must make decisions about organization-based versus outsourced recruiting, regular versus flexible staffing, and other strategic aspects of recruiting.
- Efforts should be made to recruit a diverse workforce, including older workers, individuals with disabilities, women, and members of racial/ethnic minorities.
- The decision to use internal or external sources should consider both the advantages and disadvantages of each source.

- The most common methods of internal recruiting include organizational databases, job postings, promotions and transfers, current-employee referrals, and re-recruiting of former employees and applicants.
- The most common external recruiting sources are colleges and universities, schools, labor unions, employment agencies and headhunters, competitive sources, media sources, job fairs and special events, and other creative methods.
- Internet recruiting has grown in use through job boards and various Websites.
- Internet recruiting can save costs and time, but also can generate more unqualified applicants and frequently may not reach certain groups of potential applicants.
- Recruiting efforts should be evaluated to assess how effective they are.
- Recruiting evaluation typically includes evaluating recruiting quantity and quality, tracking the time to fill openings, examining the costs and benefits of various recruiting sources, and recruiting satisfaction.

REVIEW AND APPLICATION QUESTIONS

1. What labor markets should be considered when recruiting to fill an opening for a sales representative for a pharmaceutical manufacturer?
2. Discuss ways a bank could effectively use the Internet to recruit management trainees.
3. Go to *www.recruitusa.com* and other sites to get ideas on evaluating recruiting efforts and then prepare a report for review.

CASE

Enterprise Recruiting

Many customers use Enterprise Rent-A-Car each year, and it is bigger than its competitors Hertz, Avis, and National. In 10 years Enterprise has doubled the number of cars in its fleet and increased its workforce over 30%, to 54,000 employees. What may not be widely known is that Enterprise recruits large numbers of college graduates each year for its management training program and other jobs. About 6,000 college graduates are hired annually so that Enterprise can staff its expanding number of offices. Several innovative recruiting methods have been used in the past few years by Enterprise. On the company's Website the on-line game called "Give Me the Business" has gotten many hits. The game is not directly related to renting cars, but it lets people experience the challenges of a customer service business. The hidden message is its "virtual marketing" of Enterprise and its fun culture.

Another creative approach used was sponsorship of Personal Enterprise show on MTV, in which candidates for a job at Enterprise were viewed during two rounds of behavioral interviews. The candidates were asked questions, and they were "judged" on their answers. But unlike other TV reality shows where only one person wins, three of the four candidates were offered jobs.

The on-line games and the TV show were attention-getters, but the greatest source of Enterprise recruits comes from employee referrals. Enterprise employees who refer candidates who are hired and remain with the firm can receive incentives of $500 to $1,500 each. Often, referrals check out Enterprise or its Website and mention the firm to others, which expands the pool of potential recruits.

Enterprise is somewhat unusual as an employer because it uses both traditional and creative recruiting means. The wide range of activities has helped Enterprise recruit more effectively, which aids its strategic goal of establishing its "employment brand." At the heart of its branding efforts has been a program called *My Personal Enterprise*. This program combines all of Enterprise's recruiting materials and advertisements, its Website, and its other recruiting efforts. The main focus of *My Personal Enterprise* has been to convince college graduates that there are career opportunities in the rental car firm and that jobs in the company can be fun and fulfilling.[29]

Questions

1. How does having multiple recruiting means help Enterprise establish its brand?
2. Go to the Enterprise Website (*www.erac.com/recruit*) and then click on the tab "About Enterprise." Check out the on-line game, career opportunities, and other components. Then evaluate how effective you feel the Website is as an employment branding and recruiting resource.

SUPPLEMENTAL CASE

Northwest State College

This case shows how recruiting policies can work against successful recruiting when a tight labor market exists. (For the case, go to http://thomsonedu.com/management/mathis.)

NOTES

1. Based on June Kronholz, "Businesses Push for High Skilled Foreign Workers," *The Wall Street Journal,* April 6, 2006, B1.
2. Derek Moscato, "Using Technology to Get Employees on Board," *HR Magazine,* April 2005, 1–4.
3. Susan Meisinger, "Looming Talent, Skills Gap Challenge HR," *HR Magazine,* October 2005, 1–2.
4. Grace Lee, "Epidemics, Labour Markets and Unemployment," *International Journal of Human Resource Management,* 16, (2005), 752–771.
5. Alain Belda, "Dealing with the Global Transformation," *Metal Center News,* April 2005, 4–6.
6. Fay Hansen, "Running the Global Recruiting Machine," *Workforce Management* Online, August 2006, 1–5.
7. Dene Yeaman, "New Opportunities Old Shackles," *China Staff,* nd 7, 51–53, no. 02856020; and Cui Rong, "Firms in China Think Globally, Hire Locally," *The Wall Street Journal,* February 27, 2006, B1.
8. Fay Hansen, "Regulating the Recruitment Mix in Global Markets," *Workforce Management Online,* August 2006, 1–5; and Cris Prystay and Tom Herman, "Tax Hike Hits Home for Americans Abroad," *The Wall Street Journal,* July 19, 2006, D1.
9. Ilan Brat, "Where Have All the Welders Gone?" *The Wall Street Journal,* August 15, 2006, B1.
10. Martha Frase-Blunt, "Candidate Glut," *HR Magazine,* August 2003, 1.
11. Rachel King, "The Messy Challenge and Big Payoff of Outsourced Recruiting," *Workforce Management Online,* October 2003, 1.
12. Michelle Martinez, "Recruiting Here and There," *HR Magazine,* September 2002, 96–97.
13. Gene C. George et al., "Building the Brand Through People," *Worldatwork Journal,* First Quarter 2004, 39–45.
14. William H. Burgess III, "Dibs on Diversity Recruiting," *Network Journal,* June 2003, 12–13.
15. Sue Shellenbarger, "Employers Step Up Efforts to Lure Stay at Home Mothers Back to Work," *The Wall Street Journal,* February 9, 2006, D1.
16. Sue Shellenbarger, "Work and Family," *The Wall Street Journal,* October 12, 2006, D1.
17. George Anders, "When Filling Top Jobs, Inside Makes Sense—and When It Doesn't," *The Wall Street Journal,* January 16, 2006, B1.
18. Based on Leslie Klaff, "New Internal Hiring Systems Reduce Cost and Boost Morale," *Workforce Management,* March 2004, 76–79; Cindy Waxer, "Inside Jobs," *Human Resource Executive,* June 10, 2003, 1; D. J. Chhabra, "Turbo Hiring," *Human Resource Executive,* March 2, 2004, 56–59; Patrick J. Kiger, "CISCO's Homegrown Gamble," *Workforce,* March 2003, 28; and "Staffing," *HR Magazine,* November 2005, 135.
19. D. S. Chapman et al., "Applicant Attraction to Organization and Job Choice: A Meta-Analytic Review of the Correlates of Recruiting Outcomes," *Journal of Applied Psychology,* 90 (2005), 928–944.
20. D. J. Brown et al., "Proactive Personality and Successful Job Search: A Field Investigation with College Graduates," *Journal of Applied Psychology,* 91 (2006), 717–727.
21. Arlise P. McKinney et al., "Recruiters' Use of GPA in Initial Screening Decisions," *Personnel Psychology,* 56 (2003), 823–845.
22. Sue Shellenbarger, "In Their Search for Skilled Workers Big Employers Go to Summer Camp," *The Wall Street Journal,* February 27, 2006, D1.
23. Fay Hansen, "Managing the Search Firm," *Workforce Management Online,* May 2006, 1–6.
24. Mo Edjlali, "The 2 Keys to Killer Job Ads," *Electronic Recruiting Exchange,* July 27, 2006, 1–3.
25. Tom Sarner, "Great Expectations," *Human Resource Executive,* August 2006, 1.
26. Derek Kravitz, "In What Has Been Called the 'Newest Phenomenon' in Recruiting, Employers Are Trolling the Web," *Sunday Omaha World Herald,* July 23, 2006, D1; and Bill Leonard, "Blogs Could Become Newest Recruiting Tool," *SHRM Online,* August 2006, 104.
27. Anjali Anthaualey, "Getting the Inside Scoop on a Future Boss," *The Wall Street Journal,* July 13, 2006, D1.
28. Fay Hansen, "Growing into Applicant Tracking Systems," *Workforce Management,* 2003, *www.workforce.com;* Talk by Barry Siegel, Spring 2006, *www.resjobs.com;* and Chapman et al., "Applicant Attraction to Organization and Job Choice," 940.
29. Based on Alison Stein Wellnar, "The Pickup Artists," *Workforce Management Online,* July 2004, *www.workforce.com.*

CHAPTER

8

Selecting Human Resources

After you have read this chapter, you should be able to:

- Discuss how validity and reliability are related to selection.

- Diagram the sequence of a typical selection process.

- Explain the importance of realistic job previews and application screening efforts to the selection process.

- Identify three types of selection tests and legal concerns about their uses.

- Discuss several types of selection interviews and some key considerations in conducting these interviews.

- Explain how legal concerns affect background investigations of applicants and use of medical examinations in the selection process.

- Describe the major issues to be considered when selecting candidates for global assignments.

HR Headline

A Las Vegas Hotel's On-Line Approach to Hiring

Before opening its doors, the multi-billion-dollar Wynn Las Vegas resort had to hire over 9,000 service employees to work in the various functional areas necessary for the efficient operation of a hotel and casino property. Arte Nathan, the organization's seasoned chief human resource officer, was responsible for tackling this extremely challenging task. His primary strategy for getting an adequate pool of applicants involved running a series of advertisements and messages in a regional newspaper; surprisingly, this effort generated over 100,000 applications. After conducting many interviews a day over several weeks, the company was able to hire over 1,000 people and make plans to employ many more individuals in the future.

Although this hiring scenario was challenging for the staff of Wynn Las Vegas, the company's unique on-line approach to hiring eased some of the workload. Nathan developed the hiring system collaboratively with a software developer. The procedure requires applicants to submit and track their application information on-line, greatly improving the efficiency and effectiveness of the staffing function. Other contact methods are offered to individuals who cannot gain access to a computer, as well as to those who are English-language challenged. Applicants are rated based on their answers to a variety of different hospitality-specific and experiential questions, and those individuals who achieve a certain number of points are invited for a formal interview. However, the "human side" of the hiring process is not forgotten in the company. According to Nathan, "Software is just a tool, but something like this requires a great deal of human intervention."[1]

Selection decisions are an important part of successful HR management. Some managers would even state that selection is the *most* important part of running a sound organization. There are many reasons why a company can succeed; however, unless managers can hire the right people for the right jobs, a company might not be able to fully satisfy its mission, vision, and overarching long-term objectives. The University of Texas M.D. Anderson Cancer Center, located in Houston, Texas, is one such successful organization that has effectively utilized its employees through positive selection and staffing processes. Even though the organization operates in a competitive labor market, it has been able to hire and retain personnel by giving employees the opportunity to learn different jobs and to change career tracks.[2]

SELECTION AND PLACEMENT

Selection Process of choosing individuals with qualifications needed to fill jobs in an organization.

Selection is the process of choosing individuals with qualifications needed to fill jobs in an organization. Without these qualified employees, an organization is far less likely to succeed. Perhaps the best perspective on selection and placement comes from two HR beliefs that underscore the importance of effective staffing:

- *"Hire hard, manage easy."* The amount of time and effort spent selecting the right people for jobs may make managing them as employees much less difficult because many problems are eliminated.
- *"Good training will not make up for bad selection."* When the right people with the appropriate capabilities are not selected, employers will have difficulty later adequately training the lesser qualified individuals who were selected.

Placement

Placement Fitting a person to the right job.

The ultimate purpose of selection is placement, or fitting a person to the right job. Placement of human resources should be seen primarily as a matching process that can affect many different employment outcomes. How well an employee is matched to a job can affect the amount and quality of the employee's work, as well as the training and operating costs required to prepare the individual for work life. Finally, employee morale can also be an issue because good fit encourages individuals to be positive about what they accomplish on the job.[3]

Applicant Knowledge, Skills, and Abilities

Selection and placement activities typically focus on applicants' knowledge, skills, and abilities (KSAs), but these activities should also focus on the degree to which job candidates "generally" match the situations experienced both on the job and in the company. For instance, the match between a person and the job and/or company could impact such factors as an individual's attraction to work and intentions to take a job.[4] One study found that different types of fit were related to satisfaction with work, commitment to a company, and quitting intentions.[5] Consequently, managers should definitely consider the work relationship between personal and occupational characteristics.

Person/job fit Matching the KSAs of individuals with the characteristics of jobs.

Person/job fit is an important concept that involves matching the KSAs of individuals with the characteristics of jobs. People already in jobs can help identify the most important KSAs for success as part of job analysis. The fit between the individual and job characteristics is particularly important when dealing with overseas assignments because employees must have the proper personality, skills, and interpersonal abilities to be effective in the international environment.[6]

Person/organization fit The congruence between individuals and organizational factors.

In addition to matching people to jobs, employers are also increasingly concerned about the congruence between people and companies, or person/organization fit. For instance, a recent study of person/organization fit showed that congruence was related to various attitudes about work, suggesting that fit is important when managers make placement decisions.[7] Person/organization fit is also important from a "values" perspective, with many organizations trying to positively link a person's principles to the company's values. Organizations tend to favor job applicants who effectively blend into how business is conducted.[8] Person/organization fit can also influence employees' and customers' beliefs about the organization, making such a fit a key strategic consideration.[9]

Criteria, Predictors, and Job Performance

Regardless of whether an employer uses specific KSAs or a more general approach, effective selection of employees involves using criteria and predictors of job performance. At the heart of an effective selection system must be knowledge of what constitutes appropriate job performance, as well as what employee characteristics are associated with that performance. First, an employer needs to identify the criteria associated with successful employee performance. Using these criteria as a generalized definition, an employer must then determine the KSAs required for individuals to be successful on the job. A selection criterion is a characteristic that a person must possess to successfully perform work. Figure 8-1 shows that ability, motivation, intelligence, conscientiousness, appropriate risk, and permanence might be good selection criteria for many jobs. Factors that might be more specific to managerial jobs include "leading and deciding," "supporting and cooperating," "organizing and executing," and "enterprising and performing."[10]

Selection criterion Characteristic that a person must possess to successfully perform work.

Predictors Measurable or visible indicators of a selection criterion.

To determine whether or not candidates might possess a certain selection criterion (such as ability or motivation), employers try to identify predictors that are measurable or visible indicators of that positive characteristic (or criterion). As Figure 8-1 indicates, three good predictors of "permanence" might be individual interests, salary requirements, and tenure on previous jobs. If a candidate possesses any or all of these predictor criteria, it might therefore be assumed that the person would stay on the job longer than someone without those predictors.

The information gathered about an applicant through predictors should focus on the likelihood that the individual will execute the job competently once hired. Predictors can also take many forms such as application forms, tests, interviews, education requirements, or years of experience, but these factors should be used only if they are found to be valid predictors of specific job performance. Using invalid predictors can result in selecting the "wrong" candidate and rejecting the "right" one, affecting the ability to accomplish operational objectives.

FIGURE 8-1   Job Performance, Selection Criteria, and Predictions

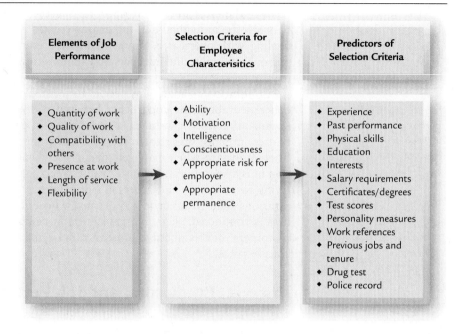

Elements of Job Performance	Selection Criteria for Employee Characterisitics	Predictors of Selection Criteria
• Quantity of work • Quality of work • Compatibility with others • Presence at work • Length of service • Flexibility	• Ability • Motivation • Intelligence • Conscientiousness • Appropriate risk for employer • Appropriate permanence	• Experience • Past performance • Physical skills • Education • Interests • Salary requirements • Certificates/degrees • Test scores • Personality measures • Work references • Previous jobs and tenure • Drug test • Police record

Correlation coefficient
Index number that gives the relationship between a predictor and a criterion variable.

Concurrent validity
Measured when an employer tests current employees and correlates the scores with their performance ratings.

Predictive validity
Measured when test results of applicants are compared with subsequent job performance.

Validity In selection, validity is the correlation between a predictor and job performance. In other words, validity occurs to the extent that the predictor actually predicts what it is supposed to predict. Several different types of validity are used in the selection function. For example, *synthetic validity* involves the degree to which areas of a particular job are associated with assessments of the individual characteristics required to complete these areas.[11] Most validity decisions use a correlation coefficient, an index number that gives the relationship between a predictor variable and a criterion (or dependent) variable. Correlations always range from −1.0 to +1.0 with higher scores suggesting stronger relationships.

Concurrent validity is one method for establishing the validity associated with a criterion variable. Concurrent means "at the same time" and suggests that an employee's performance information is collected at one point in time and then compared statistically. As shown in Figure 8-2, concurrent validity is measured when an employer tests current employees and correlates the scores with their performance ratings on such measures as accident rates, absenteeism records, and supervisory performance appraisals.

A disadvantage of the concurrent validity approach is that employees who have not performed satisfactorily at work are probably no longer with the firm and therefore cannot be tested. Also, extremely good employees may have been promoted or have left the company for better work situations. Any learning on the job might also confound test scores.

Another method for establishing criterion-related validity is considered a "before-the-fact" approach. To measure predictive validity, test results of applicants are compared with their subsequent job performance (see Figure 8-2). Job success is measured by assessing factors such as absenteeism, accidents, errors, and performance appraisal ratings. If the employees who had one year of experience at the time of hire demonstrate better performance than those without such experience, as calculated through statistical comparisons, then

| **FIGURE 8-2** | Concurrent and Predictive Validity |

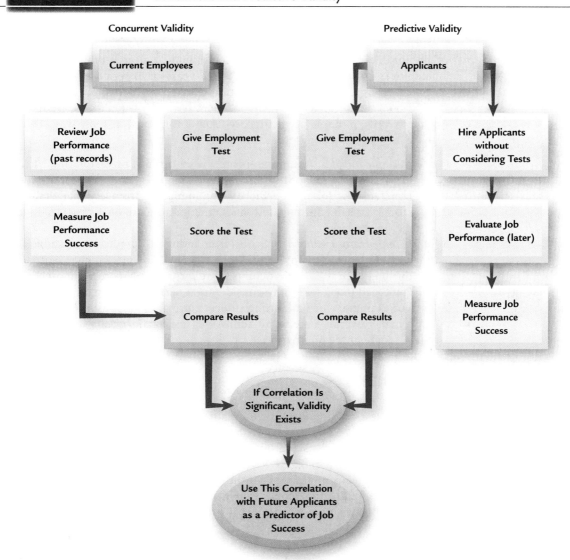

the experience requirement can be considered a valid predictor of job performance. In addition, individual experience may be utilized as an important "selection criteria" when making future staffing decisions.

In the past, the EEOC has favored predictive validity because it includes the full range of performance and test scores. However, establishing predictive validity can be challenging for managers because a large sample of individuals is needed (usually at least 30) and a significant amount of time must transpire (usually one year) to facilitate the analysis. Because of these limitations, other types of validity tests tend to be more popular in organizations.

Reliability Reliability of a predictor is the extent to which it repeatedly produces the same results over time. For example, if a person took a test in December and scored 75, then took the same test again in March and scored 76, the exam is probably a reliable instrument. Consequently, reliability involves the consistency of predictors used in selection procedures.

Combining Predictors

If an employer chooses to use only one predictor such as a pencil-and-paper test to select the individuals to be hired, the decision becomes straightforward. If the test is valid and encompasses a major dimension of a job, and the applicant does well on the test, he or she should be given a job offer. When an employer uses predictors such as "three years of experience," "possesses a college degree," and "acceptable aptitude test score," job applicants are evaluated on all of these requirements to identify the best-qualified candidates. In other words, multiple predictors are usually combined in some way. Two approaches for combining predictors are:

- *Multiple hurdles:* A minimum cutoff is set on each predictor, and each minimum level must be "passed." For example, a candidate for a sales representative job must achieve a minimum education level, a certain score on a sales aptitude test, and a minimum score on a structured interview to be hired.
- *Compensatory approach:* Scores from individual predictors are added and combined into an overall score, thereby allowing a higher score on one predictor to offset, or compensate for, a lower score on another. The combined index takes into consideration performance on all predictors. For example, when admitting students into graduate business programs, a higher overall score on an admissions test might offset a lower undergraduate grade point average.

SELECTION RESPONSIBILITIES

Selection is a key responsibility for all managers and supervisors in a company. However, organizations vary in how they allocate selection responsibilities between HR specialists and operating managers. The typical selection responsibilities are shown in Figure 8-3. The need to meet EEO requirements and the inherent strategic implications of the staffing function have caused many companies to place greater emphasis on hiring procedures and techniques. In many other companies, each department (or its management team) screens and hires

FIGURE 8-3   Typical Division of HR Responsibilities: Selection

HR Unit	Managers
• Provides initial reception for applicants • Conducts initial screening interview • Administers appropriate employment tests • Obtains background and reference information and sets up a physical examination, if used • Refers top candidates to managers for final selection • Evaluates success of selection process	• Requisition employees with specific qualifications to fill jobs • Participate in selection process as appropriate • Interview final candidates • Make final selection decision, subject to advice of HR specialist • Provide follow-up information on the suitability of selected individuals

its own personnel. Many managers, especially those working in smaller firms, prefer to select their own employees because these individuals directly impact their work areas. But the validity and effectiveness of this approach may be questionable.

Other organizations have HR professionals initially screen the job candidates and the managers or supervisors make the final selection decisions from the qualified applicant pool. Generally, the higher the position being filled, the greater the likelihood that the ultimate hiring decisions will be made by operating managers rather than HR professionals.

Selection responsibilities are affected by the existence of a central employment office, which is often housed within a human resources department. In smaller organizations, especially in those with fewer than 100 employees, a full-time employment specialist or group might be impractical. But for larger firms, centralizing activities in an employment office might be appropriate.

The employment function in any organization may be concerned with some or all of the following activities: (1) receiving applications, (2) interviewing the applicants, (3) administering tests to applicants, (4) conducting background investigations, (5) arranging for physical examinations, (6) placing and assigning new employees, (7) coordinating follow-up of these employees, (8) conducting exit interviews with departing employees, and (9) maintaining appropriate records and reports.

The Selection Process

Most organizations take a series of consistent steps to process and select applicants for jobs. Company size, job characteristics, the number of people needed, the use of electronic technology, and other factors cause variations on the basic process. Selection can take place in a day or over a much longer period of time, and certain phases of the process may be omitted or the order changed, depending on the employer. If the applicant is processed in one day, the employer usually checks references after selection. Figure 8-4 (on the next page) shows a typical selection process.

Applicant Job Interest

Individuals wanting employment can indicate interest in a number of ways. Traditionally, individuals have submitted résumés by mail or fax, or applied in person at an employer's location. But with the growth in Internet recruiting, many individuals complete applications on-line or submit résumés electronically.

Regardless of how individuals express interest in employment, the selection process has an important public relations dimension. Discriminatory hiring practices, impolite interviewers, unnecessarily long waits, unreturned telephone inquiries, inappropriate testing procedures, and lack of follow-up responses can produce unfavorable impressions of an employer. Job applicants' perceptions of the organization will be influenced by how they are treated.

Realistic job preview
Process through which a job applicant receives an accurate picture of a job.

Realistic Job Previews Many individuals know little about companies before applying for employment. Consequently, when deciding whether or not to accept a job, they pay particularly close attention to the information received during the selection process, including compensation data, work characteristics, job location, and promotion opportunities. Unfortunately, some employers make the jobs appear better than they really are. Realistic job previews provide

FIGURE 8-4   Selection Process Flowchart

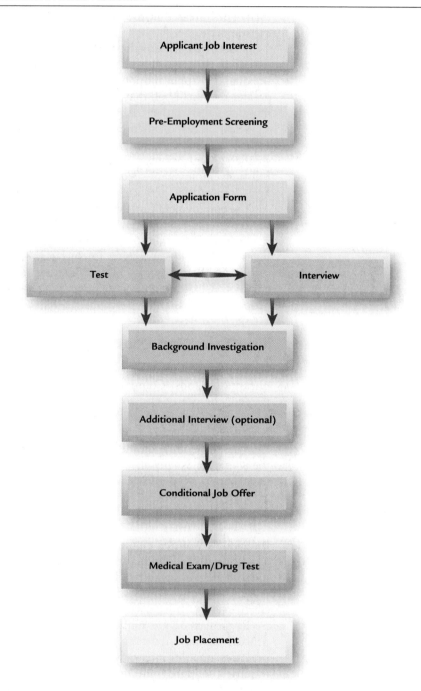

potential employees with an accurate introduction to a job so that they can better evaluate the employment situation. Indeed, a realistic job preview can directly enhance individual training beliefs and clarify a job role.[12] Also, the use of "self-assessment" realistic job previews increases individual confidence and decision making about the acceptance of an expatriate position.[13] The HR Best Practices discusses further the importance of providing job candidates and current employees with useful realistic job previews.

HR BEST PRACTICES

Using Realistic Job Previews to Establish Positive "Recruitment Branding"

Companies need to provide potential employees with a realistic overview of what work life is really like, and this can include the *realistic job preview*. However, a company must think broadly when recruiting new employees—it must consider initially developing or strengthening an already existing "recruiting brand." This brand should establish in the minds of recruits the company's overall purpose for being in business and it should honestly portray the jobs that are performed by individuals already employed in the firm. According to a manager at Edward Jones investment firm, it is inappropriate to distort the characteristics of particular jobs to candidates and employees.

A company should consider several strategies when developing a recruiting brand and conveying it to potential employees via realistic job previews. A project director of a New York recruiting firm suggests that a firm should evaluate its own strengths and develop a list of employment benefits that would make the company attractive to potential employees. These points could include building human capital, good compensation, and ethics and social responsibility. At the same time, a company needs to convey the less attractive aspects of work, such as work schedules or extensive travel. These negative job attributes, however, can be outweighed by the positive factors already covered.[14]

Pre-Employment Screening

Many employers conduct pre-employment screening to determine if applicants meet the minimum qualifications for open jobs. Other employers have every interested individual complete an application first. While these completed application forms become the basis for pre-screening information, collecting, storing, and tracking the forms can create significant work for HR staff members.

Electronic Screening The use of electronic pre-employment screening has grown. Much of this screening utilizes computer software to review the many résumés and application forms received during the recruiting and selection process. Many large companies use different types of software to receive, evaluate, and track the applications of many potential employees. For example, Plantronics Inc., a California-based "communications headsets" developer, and Southern Co., a southern-based energy organization, both adopted application/selection software. This software enables companies to recruit through electronic means, track the application process, and evaluate various staffing issues.[15]

Application Forms

Application forms are universally used and can take on different formats. Properly prepared, the application form serves four purposes:

- It is a record of the applicant's desire to obtain a position.
- It provides the interviewer with a profile of the applicant that can be used during the interview.
- It is a basic employee record for applicants who are hired.
- It can be used for research on the effectiveness of the selection process.

Many employers use only one application form for all jobs, but others need several. For example, a hotel might need one form for management and supervisory staff and another for line employees.

Application Disclaimers and Notices Application forms should contain disclaimers and notices so that appropriate legal protections are clearly stated. These recommended disclosures include:

- *Employment-at-will:* Indicates the right of the employer or the applicant to terminate employment at any time with or without notice or cause (where applicable by state law).
- *Reference contacts:* Requests permission to contact previous employers listed by applicants as references on the application form or résumé.
- *Employment testing:* Notifies applicants of required drug tests, pencil-and-paper tests, physical exams, or electronic or other tests that will be used in the employment decision.
- *Application time limit:* Indicates how long application forms are active (typically six months), and that persons must reapply or reactivate their applications after that period.
- *Information falsification:* Conveys to an applicant that falsification of application information can be grounds for serious reprimand or termination.

Immigration Forms The Immigration Reform and Control Act of 1986, as revised in 1990, requires that within 72 hours of hiring, an employer must determine whether a job applicant is a U.S. citizen, registered alien, or illegal alien. Figure 8-5 shows documents that can be used to verify that new hires are eligible to work in the United States. Applicants who are not eligible to work in this country are not supposed to be hired.

Employers use the Federal I-9 form to identify the status of potential employees. Employers are responsible for ensuring the legitimacy of documents submitted by new employees, such as U.S. passports, birth certificates, original Social Security cards, and driver's licenses. Also, employers who hire employees on special visas must maintain appropriate documentation and records.[16] However, many employers are not performing these immigration status background checks for different reasons, even though they can be performed quickly online and with limited cost the employer.[17] That is why legislation to restrict hiring illegal immigrants has become such a controversial political issue.

EEO Considerations and Application Forms An organization should retain all applications and hiring-related documents and records for *three years*. Guidelines from the EEOC and court decisions require that the data requested on application forms must be job related. Illegal questions frequently found on application forms ask for the following information:

- Marital status
- Height/weight
- Number and ages of dependents
- Information on spouse
- Date of high school graduation
- Contact in case of emergency

Concerns about inappropriate questions stem from their potential disparate impact on some protected groups because of the potential to provide information that should not be used in the hiring decision. A recent study found that a majority of the litigation surrounding application forms involved questions regarding the sex and age of a potential employee, so special consideration

| FIGURE 8-5 | Acceptable Documents for Verifying Eligibility to Work in the United States |

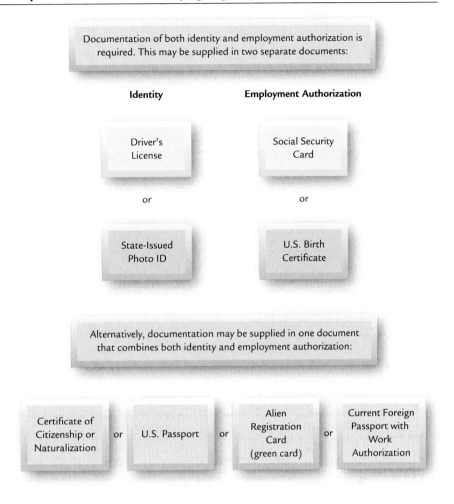

should be dedicated to removing any items that relate to these personal characteristics.[18] Figure 8-6 (on the next page) shows a sample application form containing appropriate questions.

Résumés as Applications Applicants commonly provide background information through résumés. When the situation arises, EEO standards require that an employer treat a résumé as an application form. As such, if an applicant's résumé voluntarily furnishes some information that cannot be legally obtained, the employer should not use that information during the selection process. Some employers require those who submit résumés to complete an application form as well.

Regardless of how the background information is collected, companies should be dutiful about checking the truthfulness of the information presented on résumés and application forms. Various accounts suggest that a noteworthy percentage of applicants knowingly distort their past work experiences, and an experiment involving undergraduate students showed that many individuals were willing to fabricate their qualifications to get a competitive scholarship.[19] For example, former RadioShack CEO David Edmondson resigned after it was determined that he had embellished his educational background.[20]

FIGURE 8-6 **Sample Application Form**

Application for Employment
An Equal Opportunity Employer*

Today's Date _____

PERSONAL INFORMATION Please Print or Type

Name (Last) (First) (Full middle name)	Social Security number
Current address City State Zip code	Phone number ( )
What position are you applying for?	Date available for employment?	E-mail address

Are you willing to relocate? ☐ Yes ☐ No	Are you willing to travel if required? ☐ Yes ☐ No	Any restrictions on hours, weekends, or overtime? If yes, explain.
Have you ever been employed by this Company or any of its subsidiaries before? ☐ Yes ☐ No		Indicate location and dates
Can you, after employment, submit verification of your legal right to work in the United States? ☐ Yes ☐ No	Have you ever been convicted of a felony? ☐ Yes ☐ No	*Convictions will not automatically disqualify job candidates. The seriousness of the crime and the date of conviction will be considered.*

PERFORMANCE OF JOB FUNCTIONS

Are you able to perform all the functions of the job for which you are applying, with or without accommodation?

☐ Yes, without accommodation ☐ Yes, with accommodation ☐ No

If you indicated you can perform all the functions with an accommodation, please explain how you would perform the tasks and with what accommodation.

EDUCATION

School level	School name and address	No. of years attended	Did you graduate?	Course of study
High school				
Vo-tech, business, or trade school				
College				
Graduate school				

PERSONAL DRIVING RECORD

This section is to be completed ONLY if the operation of a motor vehicle will be required in the course of the applicant's employment.

How long have you been a licensed driver?	Driver's license number	Expiration date	Issuing State

List any other state(s) in which you have had a driver's license(s) in the past:

Within the past five years, have you had a vehicle accident? ☐ Yes ☐ No	Been convicted of reckless or drunken driving? ☐ Yes ☐ No If yes, give dates:	Been cited for moving violations? If yes, give dates: ☐ Yes ☐ No
Has your driver's license ever been revoked or suspended? ☐ Yes ☐ No If yes, explain:		Is your driver's license restricted? ☐ Yes ☐ No If yes, explain:

*We are an Equal Opportunity Employer. We do not discriminate on the basis of race, religion, color, gender, age, national origin, or disability.

SELECTION TESTING

Many different kinds of tests can be used to help select qualified employees. Literacy tests, skill-based tests, psychological measurement tests, and honesty tests are often utilized to assess various individual factors that are deemed important for the work to be performed. These useful employment tests allow companies to predict which applicants will be the most successful after being hired.

Because of the increased numbers of résumés and application forms submitted through electronic means, many more organizations are using assessment tools to select individuals for interviews. Capital One, Alex Reed, Inc., and Century Theatres are but a few companies that currently utilize tests that assist in the evaluation of important behavioral and cultural-fit job criteria, and these tests appear to be saving these organizations money and resources.[21]

However, selection tests must be evaluated extensively before being utilized as a recruiting tool. The development of the test items should be linked to a thorough job analysis. Also, initial testing of the items should include an evaluation by knowledge experts, and statistical and validity assessments of the items should be conducted. Furthermore, adequate security of the testing instruments should be coordinated, and the monetary value of these tests to the firm should be determined.[22]

Ability Tests

Cognitive ability tests
Tests that measure an individual's thinking, memory, reasoning, verbal, and mathematical abilities.

Tests that assess an individual's ability to perform in a specific manner are grouped as ability tests. These are sometimes further differentiated into *aptitude tests* and *achievement tests*. Cognitive ability tests measure an individual's thinking, memory, reasoning, verbal, and mathematical abilities. Tests such as these can be used to determine applicants' basic knowledge of terminology and concepts, word fluency, spatial orientation, comprehension and retention span, general and mental ability, and conceptual reasoning. The Wonderlic Personnel Test and the General Aptitude Test Battery (GATB) are two widely used tests of this type. Managers need to ensure that these tests assess cognitive abilities that are job related.

Physical ability tests
Test that measure an individual's abilities such as strength, endurance, and muscular movement.

Physical ability tests measure an individual's abilities such as strength, endurance, and muscular movement. At an electric utility, line workers regularly must lift and carry equipment, climb ladders, and perform other physical tasks; therefore, testing of applicants' mobility, strength, and other physical attributes is job related. Some physical ability tests measure such areas as range of motion, strength and posture, and cardiovascular fitness. As noted later, care should be taken to limit physical ability testing until after a conditional job offer is made, in order to avoid violating the provisions of the Americans with Disabilities Act (ADA).

Psychomotor tests Tests that measure dexterity, hand–eye coordination, arm–hand steadiness, and other factors.

Different skill-based tests can be used, including psychomotor tests, which measure a person's dexterity, hand–eye coordination, arm–hand steadiness, and other factors. Tests such as the MacQuarie Test for Mechanical Ability can measure manual dexterity for assembly-line workers and others using psychomotor skills regularly.

Work sample tests Tests that require an applicant to perform a simulated task that is a specified part of the target job.

Many organizations use situational tests, or work sample tests, which require an applicant to perform a simulated task that is a specified part of the target job. Requiring an applicant for a secretarial job to type a business letter as quickly as possible would be one such test. An "in-basket" test is a work sample test in which a job candidate is asked to respond to memos in a hypothetical in-basket that are typical of the problems experienced in that job. Once again, these tests should assess criteria that are embedded in the job that is to be staffed.

Situational judgment tests Tests that measure a person's judgment in work settings.

Situational judgment tests are designed to measure a person's judgment in work settings. The candidate is given a situation and a list of possible solutions to the problem. The candidate then has to make judgments about how to deal with the situation. Situational judgment tests are a form of job simulation.[23]

Assessment Centers An assessment center is not a place but an assessment composed of a series of evaluative exercises and tests used for selection and development. Evidence suggests that the use of assessment centers that incorporate varied exercises is becoming more popular in companies as a selection tool.[24]

Most often used in the selection process when filling managerial openings, assessment centers consist of multiple exercises and are evaluated by multiple raters. In one assessment center, candidates go through a comprehensive interview, a pencil-and-paper test, individual and group simulations, and work exercises. Individual performance is then evaluated by a panel of trained raters. It is crucial that the tests and exercises in an assessment center reflect the content of the job for which individuals are being screened, and the types of problems faced on that job. Recently, Energis, a technology communications organization, utilized a series of assessment centers to facilitate the hiring of employees who would interact with clients. The company found that these centers enhanced the selection process and provided new employees with a road map for individual development.[25]

Personality Tests

Personality is a unique blend of individual characteristics that can affect how a person interacts with his or her work environment. As such, many organizations utilize various personality tests that assess the degree to which candidates' attributes match specific job criteria. For instance, the Finish Line, a large retail chain specializing in sporting goods, offers job applicants a Web-based test. The test evaluates their personal tendencies, and test scores are used to categorize individuals for the hiring decision. Blockbuster and Sports Authority also use similar tools in their pre-employment personality screening.[26] A California-based technology firm also found that the use of personality tests enhanced the selection decisions made in the company.[27] Many types of personality tests are available, including the Minnesota Multiphasic Personality Inventory (MMPI) and the Myers-Briggs test.

Although many different personality characteristics exist, some experts believe that there is a relatively small number of underlying *major* traits. The most widely accepted approach to studying these underlying personality traits (although not the only one) is the "Big Five" personality framework. The Big Five traits are generally considered to be useful predictors of various types of job performance in different occupations.[28] The factors are shown in Figure 8-7. Several of the Big Five traits are related to various dimensions of burnout[29] and accident involvement in both non-work and work contexts.[30]

"Fakability" and Personality Tests "Faking" is a major concern for employers using personality tests. Many test publishers admit that test profiles can be falsified, and they try to reduce faking by including questions that can

FIGURE 8-7   Big Five Personality Characteristics

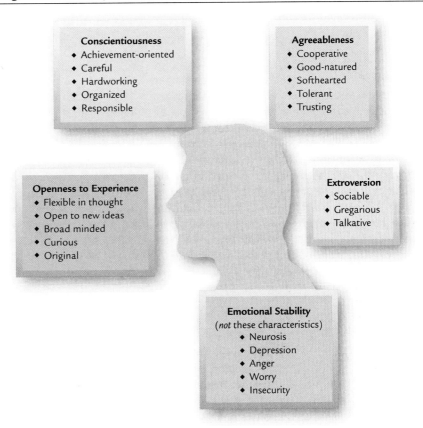

Conscientiousness
- Achievement-oriented
- Careful
- Hardworking
- Organized
- Responsible

Agreeableness
- Cooperative
- Good-natured
- Softhearted
- Tolerant
- Trusting

Openness to Experience
- Flexible in thought
- Open to new ideas
- Broad minded
- Curious
- Original

Extroversion
- Sociable
- Gregarious
- Talkative

Emotional Stability
(*not* these characteristics)
- Neurosis
- Depression
- Anger
- Worry
- Insecurity

be used to compute a social desirability or "lie" score.[31] Researchers also favor the use of "corrections" based on components of the test to account for faking—a preference that also constitutes an argument for professional scoring of personality tests.[32] Another possibility is use of a "fake warning," which instructs applicants that faking can be detected and can result in a negative hiring impression.

Honesty/Integrity Tests

Companies are utilizing different tests to assess the honesty and integrity of applicants and employees. Employers use these tests as a screening mechanism to prevent the hiring of unethical employees, to reduce the frequency of lying and theft on the job, and to communicate to applicants and employees alike that dishonesty will not be tolerated. In other words, honesty/integrity tests may be valid as broad screening devices for organizations if used properly. One survey found that about 28% of employers are using honesty/integrity tests, and 22% use violence potential testing means.[33]

However, these instruments have limitations. For instance, socially desirable responding is a key concern; some questions can be considered overly invasive, insulting, and not job related; sometimes "false positives" are generated (or an honest person is scored as "dishonest"); and test scores might be affected by individual demographic factors such as gender and race.[34] The HR Perspective discusses several recent cases where the use of integrity and personality tests in the workplace has been challenged.

Internet Research

Uniform Guidelines
This Website is a free site on the use of selection procedures and tests to ensure compliance with federal laws. Visit their Website at: http://thomsonedu .com/management/mathis.

Integrity and Personality Tests—Are They Fair?

Many employers are using integrity and personality tests to evaluate the degree to which job candidates or current employees might exhibit questionable behaviors in the workplace. However, some of these tests are being called into question based on various employment laws. For instance, the Seventh U.S. Circuit Court of Appeals recently determined in a class-action lawsuit that the Americans with Disabilities Act was not followed when Rent-A-Center, a furniture-rental organization, made employees who were seeking advancement complete the MMPI personality test. A panel of judges concluded that the instrument's use probably prevented individuals who were mentally challenged from getting promotions in the company.

Shortly after this ruling, Jeannine Cruz sued the Louisiana State Police, claiming that she was discriminated against based on sex because her scores on several employment tests (including the MMPI) were not high enough to warrant promotion into a trooper position. In fact, her performance on the tests indicated that she was a candidate for "sexual misconduct" and "chemical dependency." She claimed in her suit that the tests utilized are not fair to women because men tend to score more positively than do women. According to some experts, similar lawsuits can be expected based on the Rent-A-Center case if companies do not relate the test content to specific job content.[35]

Polygraphs The polygraph, more generally and incorrectly referred to as the "lie detector," is a mechanical device that measures a person's galvanic skin response, heart rate, and breathing rate. The theory behind the polygraph is that if a person answers a question incorrectly, the body's physiological responses will "reveal" the falsification through the polygraph's recording mechanisms.[36] As a result of concerns about polygraph validity, Congress passed the Employee Polygraph Protection Act, which prohibits the use of polygraphs for pre-employment screening purposes by most employers. Federal, state, and local government agencies are exempt from the act. Also exempted are certain private-sector employers such as security companies and pharmaceutical companies. The act does allow employers to continue to use polygraphs as part of internal investigations of thefts or losses. But in those situations, the polygraph test should be taken voluntarily, and the employee should be allowed to end the test at any time.

SELECTION INTERVIEWING

Selection interviewing of job applicants is done both to obtain additional information and to clarify information gathered throughout the selection process. Interviews are commonly conducted at two levels: first, as an initial screening interview to determine if the person has met minimum qualifications, and then later, as an in-depth interview with HR staff members and/or operating managers to determine if the person will fit into the designated work area.

Before the in-depth interview, information from all available sources is pooled so that the interviewers can reconcile conflicting information that may have emerged from tests, application forms, and references. Also, interviewers must obtain as much pertinent information as possible about the applicants given the limited time of the interview itself, and evaluate this information against job standards.

Inter-Rater Reliability and Face Validity

Interviews must be reliable, allowing interviewers, despite their limitations, to pick the same applicant capabilities again and again. High *intra*-rater reliability (within the same interviewer) can be demonstrated, but only moderate-to-low *inter*-rater reliability (across different interviewers) is generally shown. Inter-rater reliability becomes important when each of several interviewers is selecting employees from a pool of applicants, or if the employer uses team or panel interviews with multiple interviewers.

Employers prefer all types of interviews over other selection activities because they have high "face validity" (or it makes sense to them). It is often assumed that if someone interviews well and that the information obtained in the interview is useful, then the individual will be a good hire. However, an unstructured interview does not always provide much validity, causing a growth in the popularity of structured interviews.

Structured Interviews

Structured interview
Interview that uses a set of standardized questions asked of all applicants.

A **structured interview** uses a set of standardized questions asked of all applicants so that comparisons can more easily be made. This type of interview allows an interviewer to prepare job-related questions in advance and then complete a standardized interviewee evaluation form that provides documentation indicating why one applicant was selected over another. The structured interview is useful in the initial screening process because many applicants can be effectively evaluated and compared. However, the structured interview does not have to be rigid. The predetermined questions should be asked in a logical manner but do not have to be read word for word down the list. Also, the applicants should be allowed adequate opportunity to explain their answers, and each interviewer should probe with additional questions until she or he fully understands the responses. Because of this process, the structured interview can be more reliable and valid than other interview approaches. As Figure 8-8 shows, the various types of interviews range from structured to unstructured, and they vary in terms of appropriateness for selection.

The structured format ensures that a given interviewer has similar information on each candidate. It also ensures that when several interviewers ask the same questions of applicants, there is greater consistency in the subsequent

FIGURE 8-8   Types of Selection Interviews

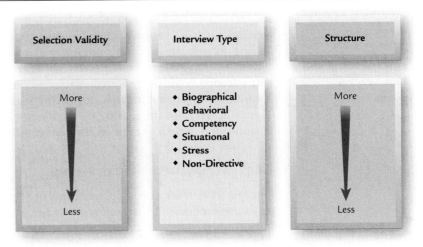

evaluation of those candidates. In fact, the Merit Systems Protection Board recommended that structured interviews be utilized in selection efforts for federal jobs because individual work performance can be better forecasted.[37] However, one study determined that various types of structure in interviews resulted in mixed reactions from interviewers and interviewees.[38] Companies might therefore have to provide additional guidance to enhance interviewers' implementation of this structure. These reasons point to why structured interviews—in any of several forms, including biographical, behavioral, competency, and situational—are important when making selection decisions.

Biographical Interview A *biographical interview* focuses on a chronological assessment of the candidate's past experiences. This type of interview is widely used and is often combined with other collected information. Overall, the process provides a sketch of past experiences.

Behavioral Interview Interviewers often utilize an experiential type of structured interview. In the behavioral interview, applicants are asked to describe how they have performed a certain task or handled a problem in the past, which ideally predicts future actions and shows how applicants are best suited for current jobs. A recent study showed that "past behavior" structured-type interviews are better at identifying achievement at work than are situational interviews, hence demonstrating the efficacy of this interview strategy.[39] In addition, the Studer Group consulting firm, after working with a multitude of health-care firms across the nation, identified the use of behavioral interviews as a positive practice in organizations.[40] However, companies must provide interviewer training to enhance behavioral interviews, and numerous organizations have done that effectively.[41]

Competency Interview The *competency interview* is similar to the behavioral interview except that the questions are designed to provide the interviewer with something to measure the applicant's response against. A *competency profile* for the position is often utilized, which includes a list of competencies necessary to do that particular job.[42] Using competencies as a benchmark to predict job candidate success is useful because interviewers can identify the factors needed in specific jobs.[43] However, these interviews take time and sometimes benefit articulate or impression management-oriented people.

Situational Interview The situational interview contains questions about how applicants might handle specific job situations. Interview questions and possible responses are based on job analysis and checked by job experts to ensure content validity. The interviewer typically codes the suitability of the answer, assigns point values, and adds up the total number of points an interviewee received. The situational interview is a highly recommended approach to candidate selection because of its predictive capabilities, uniformity, and accuracy.[44] A variation of the situational format that is used by companies such as GE and Microsoft is termed the *case study interview,* which requires a job candidate to diagnose and correct organizational challenges during the meeting.[45]

Less-Structured Interviews

Some interviews are done unplanned and are not structured. Often, these interviews are conducted by operating managers or supervisors who have had little interview training. An *unstructured interview* occurs when the interviewer

Behavioral interview
Interview in which applicants give specific examples of how they have performed a certain task or handled a problem in the past.

Situational interview
Structured interview that contains questions about how applicants might handle specific job situations.

improvises by asking questions that are not predetermined. A *semistructured interview* is a guided conversation in which broad questions are asked and new questions arise as a result of the discussion.

Non-directive interview
Interview that uses questions developed from the answers to previous questions.

A non-directive interview uses questions that are developed from answers to previous questions. The interviewer asks general questions designed to prompt applicants to describe themselves. The interviewer then uses applicants' responses to shape the next question. With a non-directive interview, as with any less-structured interview, difficulties include keeping the conversation job related and obtaining comparable data on various applicants. Many non-directive interviews are only partly organized; as a result, a combination of general and specific questions is asked in no set order, and different questions are asked of different applicants for the same job. The comparing and ranking of candidates are more open to subjective judgments and legal challenges, so they are best used sparingly.

Stress Interview

Stress interview Interview designed to create anxiety and put pressure on applicants to see how they respond.

A stress interview is designed to create anxiety and put pressure on applicants to see how they respond. In a stress interview, the interviewer assumes an extremely aggressive and insulting posture. Firms using this approach often justify doing so because employees will encounter high degrees of job stress. The stress interview can be a high-risk approach for an employer because an applicant is probably already anxious, and the stress interview can easily generate a poor image of the interviewer and the employer. Consequently, an applicant that the organization wishes to hire might turn down the job offer.

Who Conducts Interviews?

Job interviews can be conducted by individuals, by several individuals sequentially, or by panels or teams. For some jobs, such as entry-level jobs requiring lesser skills, applicants might be interviewed solely by a human resource professional. For other jobs, employers screen applicants by using multiple interviews, beginning with a human resource professional and followed by the appropriate supervisors and managers. Then, a selection decision is made collectively. Managers need to ensure that multiple interviews are not redundant.

Panel interview Interview in which several interviewers meet with candidate at the same time.

Team interview Interview in which applicants are interviewed by the team members with whom they will work.

Other interview formats are also utilized. In a panel interview, several interviewers meet with the candidate at the same time so that the same responses are heard. Panel interviews may be combined with individual interviews. However, without proper planning, an unstructured interview can result and applicants are frequently uncomfortable with the group interview format. In a team interview, applicants are interviewed by the team members with whom they will work. This approach can improve team success, but training is required to educate team members about the selection process, and consensus over the hiring decision should be established. Note that research indicates group interviews might be less effective than individual interviews.[46]

Effective Interviewing

Many people think that the ability to interview is an innate talent, but this contention is difficult to support. Just being personable and liking to talk is no guarantee that someone will be an effective interviewer. Figure 8-9 lists questions commonly used in selection interviews.

FIGURE 8-9   Questions Commonly Used in Selection Interviews

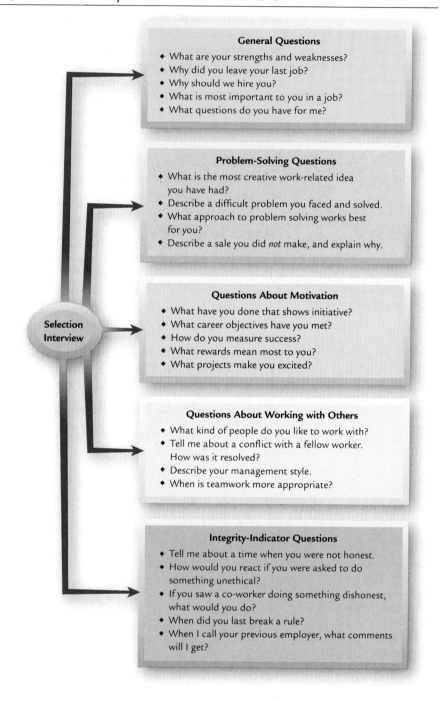

General Questions
- What are your strengths and weaknesses?
- Why did you leave your last job?
- Why should we hire you?
- What is most important to you in a job?
- What questions do you have for me?

Problem-Solving Questions
- What is the most creative work-related idea you have had?
- Describe a difficult problem you faced and solved.
- What approach to problem solving works best for you?
- Describe a sale you did *not* make, and explain why.

Questions About Motivation
- What have you done that shows initiative?
- What career objectives have you met?
- How do you measure success?
- What rewards mean most to you?
- What projects make you excited?

Questions About Working with Others
- What kind of people do you like to work with?
- Tell me about a conflict with a fellow worker. How was it resolved?
- Describe your management style.
- When is teamwork more appropriate?

Integrity-Indicator Questions
- Tell me about a time when you were not honest.
- How would you react if you were asked to do something unethical?
- If you saw a co-worker doing something dishonest, what would you do?
- When did you last break a rule?
- When I call your previous employer, what comments will I get?

Selection Interview

Interviewing skills are developed through training. A number of suggestions for making interviewing more effective are as follows:

- *Plan the interview.* Interviewers should review all information before the interview, and then identify specific areas for questioning. Preparation is critical because many interviewers have not done their research.[47]
- *Control the interview.* This includes knowing in advance what information must be collected, systematically collecting it during the interview,

and stopping when that information has been collected. An interviewer should not monopolize the conversation.

- *Use effective questioning techniques.* Utilize questions that will produce full and complete answers that can be evaluated based on job relatedness.

Questions to Avoid Certain kinds of questions should be avoided in selection interviews that are conducted:

- *Yes/no questions:* Unless verifying specific information, the interviewer should avoid questions that can be answered "yes" or "no." For example, "Did you have good attendance on your last job?" will probably be answered simply "yes."
- *Obvious questions:* An obvious question is one for which the interviewer already has the answer and the applicant knows it.
- *Questions that rarely produce a true answer:* Avoid questions that prompt a less than honest response. An example is "How did you get along with your co-workers?" The likely answer is "Just fine."
- *Leading questions:* A leading question is one to which the answer is obvious from the way that the question is asked. For example, "How do you like working with other people?" suggests the answer "I like it."
- *Illegal questions:* Questions that involve information such as race, age, gender, national origin, marital status, and number of children are illegal. They are just as inappropriate in the interview as on the application form.
- *Questions that are not job related:* All questions should be directly job related.

Listening Responses to Avoid Effective interviewers should avoid listening responses such as nodding, pausing, making casual remarks, echoing, and mirroring. The applicant might try to please the interviewers by examining the feedback provided. However, giving no response to applicants' answers may imply boredom or inattention. Therefore, interviewers should use friendly but neutral comments when acknowledging the answers.

Problems in the Interview

Operating managers and supervisors are more likely than HR personnel to use poor interviewing techniques because they do not interview often or lack training. Several problems include:

- *Snap judgments:* Some interviewers decide whether an applicant is suitable within the first two to four minutes of the interview, and spend the rest of the time looking for evidence to support their judgment.
- *Negative emphasis:* Unfavorable information about an applicant is often emphasized more than favorable information when evaluating suitability.
- *Halo effect:* The *halo effect* occurs when an interviewer allows a positive characteristic, such as agreeableness, to overshadow other evidence. *Devil's horns* is the reverse of the halo effect and occurs when a negative characteristic, such as inappropriate dress, overshadows other traits.
- *Biases and stereotyping:* "Similarity" bias occurs when interviewers favor or select people that they believe to be like themselves based on a variety of personal factors. Interviewers should also avoid any personal

tendencies to stereotype individuals because of demographic characteristics and differences. For instance, age disparities may be a concern as younger executives are interviewing more senior personnel.[48] Additionally, applicants' ethnic names and accents can negatively impact personal evaluations.[49] Also, older workers are sometimes less likely to get interviewed and hired than are younger applicants.[50]

■ *Cultural noise:* Interviewers must learn to recognize and handle cultural noise, which stems from what applicants believe is socially acceptable rather than what is factual.[51]

BACKGROUND INVESTIGATION

Background investigation may take place either before or after the in-depth interview. Although the process requires time and money, it generally proves beneficial when making selection decisions. The value of background investigation is evident when the investigation reveals that applicants have misrepresented their qualifications and backgrounds. Some of the more common types of false information given during the application process are the dates of employment and academic study, past jobs, and academic credentials.[52] Universities also report that inquiries on former students often reveal that "graduates" never graduated or did not even attend the university. The only protection is to get verification on applicants either before or after hire, and to never assume that applicant information is accurate. If hired, an employee can be terminated for falsifying employment information.

Internet Research

Business.Com

This Website provides resources and links to companies that provide employee background checks, criminal history checks, and pre-employment screening. Visit their site at: http://thomsonedu.com/management/mathis.

Sources of Background Information and Reference Checking

Background information can be obtained from a number of sources. Some of these sources are identified in Figure 8-10, which include criteria such as past job records, credit history, testing, and educational and certification records.

Work-related references from previous employers and supervisors provide a valuable snapshot of a candidate's background and characteristics. Telephoning references is common. Managers should consider using a form that facilitates the factual verification of information given by the applicant, such as employment dates, salary history, type of job responsibilities, and attendance record. Other items might include subjective information such as reasons for leaving the previous job and employee interaction style. Written methods of reference checking are also useful. Some organizations send preprinted reference forms to individuals who are giving references for applicants. These forms often contain a release statement signed by the applicant, so that those providing references can see that they have been released from liability on the information they furnish. Specific letters of reference also are requested by some employers or provided by applicants.

Criminal background checks are also common because there has been an increase in claims that companies are staffing irresponsibly.[53] Based on information compiled in a survey of human resource professionals, a majority of large U.S. firms including Ford Motor, General Electric, and General Motors

FIGURE 8-10   Sources of Background Information

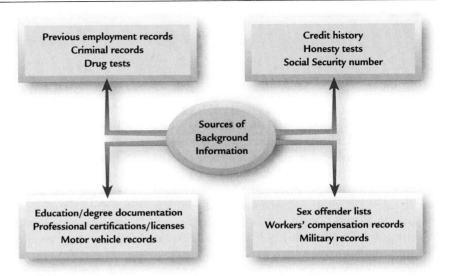

conduct such checks to avoid negligent staffing lawsuits, corporate theft, and terrorism.[54] In fact, many organizations use outside vendors that specialize in conducting background checks because these outside firms can provide such services much more efficiently and effectively.

Despite their use, criminal background checks can negatively affect ex-criminals. Decision makers should be aware that, if used incorrectly, criminal background investigations could contradict federal law indicating that checks should not be an "absolute bar to hiring." Furthermore, background checks have some candidates and employees concerned because the information reported might be inaccurate or outdated.[55] For instance, a woman living in Minneapolis was denied employment by Office Depot because a background report provided by an outside firm contained adverse information. However, after getting the report corrected, she was hired by the company.[56] Consequently, the information provided in criminal record checks should be used judiciously and with caution.

A growing number of companies are using personal Web pages and the Internet to perform more in-depth background checks on employees. The HR On-Line (on the next page) discusses this growing trend in selection.

Legal Constraints on Background Investigations

Various federal and state laws protect the rights of individuals whose backgrounds may be investigated during pre-employment screening. An employer's most important action when conducting a background investigation is to obtain from the applicant a signed release giving the employer permission to conduct the investigation.

Under the Federal Privacy Act of 1974, a government employer must have a signed release from a person before it can give information about that person to someone else. The recommendation is that during an exit interview, an employer should obtain a signed release authorizing the employer to provide reference information on the former employee in the future.

HR ONLINE

Searching the Web for Candidate Information

Managers involved in selection are beginning to browse the Internet for nontraditional sources of employee background information, such as personal Websites, on-line networking groups, and Web search engines. Many believe that these Websites provide a more "in-depth" snapshot of a job candidate's individual characteristics, despite the information that has been submitted to the company through traditional means with the application form or résumé. More specifically, managers are using Google.com to obtain data such as demographics and other highly personal information that cannot be covered in the interview session. On-line network sites such as MySpace and Facebook are also being utilized to obtain personal information,

some of which involves sexual activity, drug use, and other questionable behavior.

Unfortunately, much of this information appears to be difficult to erase or alter, so some candidates and employees just have to live with the "less than flattering" content once it is posted. Also, damaging information can be posted about individuals by anyone on the Internet, further complicating the process of performing fair and legitimate background checks if this information is utilized in job selection. Job candidates (and current employees) must therefore realize the potential for problems when posting personal information on-line and recognize that this information might be used in future hiring decisions.[57]

Risks of Negligent Hiring and Negligent Retention As indicated previously, failing to check references and candidate backgrounds can cost a company greatly. Some organizations have become targets of lawsuits that charge them with negligence in hiring workers who have committed violent acts on the job. Lawyers say that an employer's liability hinges on how well it investigates an applicant's background. Consequently, details provided on the application form should be investigated extensively, and these efforts should be documented.

Negligent hiring Occurs when an employer fails to check an employee's background and the employee injures someone on the job.

Negligent hiring occurs when an employer fails to check an employee's background, and the employee later injures someone on the job. There is a potential negligent hiring problem when: the employer hired an unfit employee, the background check was insufficient, or the employer did not research potential risk factors that would have prevented the positive hire decision.[58] Similarly, negligent retention occurs when an employer becomes aware that an employee may be unfit for employment, but continues to employ the person, and the person injures someone.

Negligent retention Occurs when an employer becomes aware that an employee may be unfit for work, but continues to employ the person, and the person injures someone.

Fair Credit Reporting Act Many employers check applicants' credit histories. The logic is that poor credit histories may signal either correctly or incorrectly a certain level of irresponsibility. Firms that check applicants' credit records must comply with the federal Fair Credit Reporting Act. This act basically requires disclosing that a credit check is being made, obtaining written consent from the person being checked, and furnishing the applicant with a copy of the report. Some state laws also prohibit employers from getting certain credit information. Credit history should be checked on applicants for jobs in which use of, access to, or management of money is an essential job function. Commonly, financial institutions check credit histories on loan officers or tellers, and retailers conduct credit checks on cashiers and managerial staff. But unnecessary credit checks may be illegal, according to some EEOC cases.[59]

Medical Examinations and Inquiries

Medical information on applicants may be used to determine their physical and mental capabilities for performing jobs. Physical standards for jobs should be realistic, justifiable, and linked to job requirements. Even though workers with disabilities can competently perform many jobs, they sometimes may be rejected because of their physical or mental limitations.

ADA and Medical Inquiries The Americans with Disabilities Act (ADA) prohibits the use of pre-employment medical exams, except for drug tests, until a job has been conditionally offered. Also, the ADA prohibits a company from rejecting an individual because of a disability and from asking job applicants any question related to current or past medical history until a conditional job offer has been made. Once a conditional offer of employment has been made, then some organizations ask the applicant to complete a pre-employment health checklist or the employer pays for a physical examination of the applicant. It should be made clear that the applicant who has been offered the job is not "hired" until successful completion of the physical inquiry.

Drug Testing Drug testing may be conducted as part of a medical exam, or it may be done separately. Use of drug testing as part of the selection process has increased in the past few years. If drug tests are used, employers should remember that their accuracy varies according to the type of test used, the item tested, and the quality of the laboratory where the test samples are sent. Because of the potential impact of prescription drugs on test results, applicants should complete a detailed questionnaire on this matter before the testing. If an individual tests positive for drug use, then an independent medical laboratory should administer a second, more detailed analysis. Whether urine, blood, saliva, or hair samples are used, the process of obtaining, labeling, and transferring the samples to the testing lab should be outlined clearly and definite policies and procedures should be established.

MAKING THE JOB OFFER

The final step of the selection process is offering someone employment. Job offers are often extended over the phone, and many are then formalized in letters and sent to applicants. It is important that the offer document be reviewed by legal counsel and that the terms and conditions of employment be clearly identified. Care should be taken to avoid vague, general statements and promises about bonuses, work schedules, or other matters that might change later. These documents also should provide for the individual to sign an acceptance of the offer and return it to the employer, who should place it in the individual's personnel files.

GLOBAL STAFFING ISSUES

Staffing global assignments involves making selection decisions that impact (or take place in) other countries. When staffing global assignments, cost is a major consideration because establishing a business professional in another country can run as high as $1 million for a three-year job assignment. Further, if a business professional quits an international assignment prematurely or wants to transfer home, associated costs can be even grater. "Failure" rates for global assignments can run as high as 40% to 50% in some situations.[60]

Types of Global Employees

Internet Research

World Federation of Personnel Management Associations (WFPMA)

For a report on the *Survey of Global HR Challenges: Yesterday, Today and Tomorrow*, link to the WFPMA Website at: http://thomsonedu .com/management/mathis.

Global organizations can be staffed in a number of different ways, including with expatriates, host-country nationals, and third-country nationals. Each staffing option presents some unique HR management challenges. For instance, when staffing with citizens of different countries, different tax laws and other factors apply. HR professionals need to be knowledgeable about the laws and customs of each country represented in their workforce. Experienced expatriates can provide a pool of talent that can be utilized as the firm expands operations into other countries.[61]

Selection Process for Global Assignments

The selection process for an international assignment should provide a realistic picture of the life, work, and culture to which the employee may be sent. HR managers start by preparing a comprehensive description of the job to be done. This description notes responsibilities that would be unusual in the home nation, including negotiating with public officials; interpreting local work codes; and responding to ethical, moral, and personal issues such as religious prohibitions and personal freedoms.[62] Figure 8-11 shows the most frequently cited key competencies for successful global employees. The five areas are as follows:

■ *Cultural adjustment:* Individuals who accept foreign job assignments need to successfully adjust to cultural differences.

FIGURE 8-11   **Selection Factors for Global Employees**

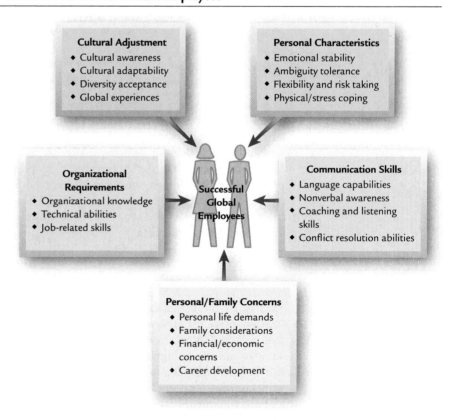

- *Personal characteristics:* The experiences of many global firms demonstrate that the best employees in the home country may not be the best employees in a global assignment, primarily because of personal characteristics of individuals.
- *Organizational requirements:* Many global employers find that knowledge of the organization and how it operates is important.
- *Communication skills:* Expatriate employees should be able to communicate in the host-country language both orally and in writing.
- *Personal/family concerns:* The preferences and attitudes of spouses and other family members can influence the success of expatriate assignments.

A growing issue for U.S. firms that hire individuals to fill jobs in other countries is the need for adequate background checks. Global companies want to ensure that their employees have acceptable work histories and personal characteristics. To satisfy this demand, a number of firms have begun to specialize in pre-employment screening of global employees.[63]

Some countries have varying government-controlled employment processes that require foreign employers to obtain government approval in order to hire local employees. Many countries such as the United States and Australia require foreign workers to obtain work permits or visas.

For U.S.-based firms, the assignment of women and members of racial/ethnic minorities to international posts involves complying with U.S. EEO regulations and laws. Also, most U.S. EEO regulations and laws apply to foreign-owned firms operating in the United States.

LEGAL CONCERNS IN THE SELECTION PROCESS

Selection is subject to a number of legalities, especially many of the EEO regulations and laws discussed previously. Throughout the selection process, application forms, interviews, tests, background investigations, and any other selection activities must be conducted in a non-discriminatory manner. Also, applicants who are not hired should be rejected only for job-related reasons; rejections based on protected-class status are illegal.

Defining Who Is an Applicant

Employers are required to track applicants who apply for jobs at their companies. Such applicant tracking should be comprehensive and consistent. It is increasingly important for employers to carefully define exactly who is an applicant and who is not, because many employers are required to track and report applicant information as part of equal employment and affirmative action plans. It is also important because employers may be negatively affected by individuals who claim to have applied for jobs but really just want to file lawsuits.

One court case determined that basic interest in a particular job type is considered part of the application process. This ruling stands even if "no formal posting of the job opening in question had been made, the employee had not filed any sort of formal application, and the employee did not meet the minimum qualifications for the job." Additionally, the EEOC stated that an individual applicant did not have to meet the minimum requirements of a particular job, suggesting further that any person who is interested in a position should be considered an applicant.[64]

Without a clear definition of who is an applicant, employers might have to count as applicants all individuals who submit unsolicited résumés, respond electronically to Website employment postings, or walk in to apply for jobs. The EEOC and OFCCP have agreed on this definition of "applicant" to be used when an application has been submitted electronically. An applicant is a person who[65]:

■ Has expressed interest through the Internet or electronically and is being considered for a specific position by the employer.
■ Has identified that he or she has the basic position qualifications.
■ Does not remove his or her interest in the position at anytime during the selection process.
■ Has been ranked using "hit features" by employer software or other data techniques that are not linked to assessment qualifications.

Applicant Flow Documentation

Employers must collect applicant data on race, sex, and other demographics to fulfill EEO reporting requirements. Many employers ask applicants to provide EEOC reporting data in a flow form that may be attached to the application form. It is important that employers review this flow form separately and not use it in any other selection efforts to avoid claims of impropriety. Because completing the form is voluntary, employers can demonstrate that they tried to obtain the data.

SUMMARY

- Selection is the process that matches individuals and their qualifications to jobs in an organization.
- Placement of people should consider both person/job fit and person/organization fit.
- Predictors linked to criteria are used to identify the applicants who are most likely to perform jobs successfully.
- The selection process—from applicant interest through pre-employment screening, application, testing, interviewing, and background investigation—must be handled by trained, knowledgeable individuals.
- A growing number of employers are using electronic pre-employment screening.
- Application forms must meet EEO guidelines and must ask only for job-related information.
- Selection tests include ability tests, assessment centers, personality tests, honesty/integrity tests, and other more controversial types of tests.
- Structured interviews, including behavioral and situational ones, are more effective and face fewer

- EEO compliance concerns than do unstructured interviews and non-directive interviews.
- Interviews can be conducted individually, by multiple individuals, or by video technology. Regardless of the method, effective interviewing questioning techniques should be used.
- Background investigation can be conducted in a variety of areas. When either requesting or giving reference information, employers must take care to avoid potential legal concerns such as negligent hiring and negligent retention.
- Global organizations can be staffed by individuals who are expatriates, host-country nationals, or third-country nationals.
- Selection factors for global employees include cultural adjustment, personal characteristics, communication skills, personal/family concerns, and organizational requirements.
- Selection decisions must be based on job-related criteria in order to comply with various legal requirements.
- HR professionals must be careful to properly identify, track, and document applicants.

REVIEW AND APPLICATION QUESTIONS

1. Develop a structured interview for hiring assistant managers at a large retail store.
2. How would you do a complete background investigation on applicants to minimize concerns about negligent hiring?
3. Your Accounting Manager has decided that a behavioral interview to select accountants will solve many hiring problems. What can you tell him? Check *www.job-interview.net* and other sources to gather information.

CASE

Strategic Selection: A Review of Two Companies

Managers are proactively improving the employee selection process with various strategies that will ideally enhance corporate success. Some of these strategies focus on improving the quality of the individuals who apply for work, as well as those individuals who are actually hired into the organization. Other strategies target the selection process itself and seek to improve the various activities involved in proper hiring. The overriding theme of these efforts is that the staffing/selection function is a key component of an organization's strategy because the process ideally provides highly motivated and qualified employees who can ultimately impact the financial and operational well-being of a company.

Hallmark Cards is one company that emphasizes selection. It recently developed a recruiting metric called a "staffing index" that enables management to track the degree to which newly hired employees are performing as expected on the job. A series of evaluations are conducted over time, and scores are compared to obtain a longitudinal perspective on the quality of the hiring decisions.[66]

UnitedHealth Group is another organization that has improved its selection activities with proper strategic planning and execution. The company's Vice President of Recruitment Services decided to modify hiring procedures within the organization by splitting job candidates into two basic groups. The first group of individuals was comprised of high-level professionals who would be recruited by internal staffing specialists, while the second group included various staff and line personnel who would be acquired with outsourcing contacts. This "two-pronged" strategy enabled the company to save money through increased control and efficiency.[67]

These various strategic selection approaches enable companies to improve the manner in which employees are hired and placed within a hierarchy of jobs. Many other strategies could be employed in different employment situations to improve the efficiency and effectiveness of selection. Overall, these efforts should increase the degree of fit between employees and organizations and increase the completion of strategic objectives.

Questions

1. Compare and contrast the two selection strategies used by the organizations discussed in the case.
2. What other strategies might help organizations better utilize and manage selection activities?

SUPPLEMENTAL CASE

Selecting a Programmer

This case shows that using a test after a pool of candidates has already been interviewed can present some difficulties. (For the case, go to http://thomsonedu .com/management/mathis.)

NOTES

1. Based on Jennifer C. Berkshire, "For Massive Hiring Effort, Vegas Resort Wagers on High-Tech, Tried-and-True," *Workforce Management,* March 2005, 65–67.

2. Leslie Stevens-Huffman, "Could Your Best New Hire be a 'Recareering' Boomer?" *Workforce Management,* December 12, 2005, *www.workforce.com.*

3. Lisa Daniel and Carolyn Brandon, "Finding the Right Job Fit," *HR Magazine,* March 2006, 62–67.

4. Sally A. Carless, "Person-Job Fit Versus Person-Organization Fit as Predictors of Organizational Attraction and Job Acceptance Intentions: A Longitudinal Study," *Journal of Occupational & Organizational Psychology,* 78 (2005), 411–429.

5. Amy L. Kristof-Brown, Ryan D. Zimmerman, and Eric C. Johnson, "Consequences of Individuals' Fit at Work: A Meta-Analysis of Person-Job, Person-Organization, Person-Group, and Person-Supervisor Fit," *Personnel Psychology,* 58 (2005), 281–342.

6. Ed Silverman, "The Global Test," *Human Resource Executive,* June 2006, 30.

7. Winfred Arthur, Jr., Suzanne T. Bell, Anton J. Villado, and Dennis Doverspike, "The Use of Person-Organization Fit in Employment Decision Making: An Assessment of Its Criterion-Related Validity," *Journal of Applied Psychology,* 91 (2006), 786–801.

8. Christopher Cornell, "The Value of Values," *Human Resource Executive,* November 2004, 68–72.

9. Eitan Yaniv and Ferenc Farkas, "The Impact of Person-Organization Fit on the Corporate Brand Perception of Employees and of Customers," *Journal of Change Management,* 5 (2005), 447–461.

10. Dave Bartram, "The Great Eight Competencies: A Criterion-Centric Approach to Validation," *Journal of Applied Psychology,* 90 (2005), 1185–1203.

11. Charles A. Scherbaum, "Synthetic Validity: Past, Present, and Future," *Personnel Psychology,* 58 (2005), 481–515.

12. Hiram C. Barksdale, Jr., et al., "The Impact of Realistic Job Previews and Perceptions of Training on Salesforce Performance and Continuance Commitment: A Longitudinal Test," *Journal of Personal Selling and Sales Management,* 23 (2003), 125–138.

13. Paula M. Caligiuri and Jean M. Phillips, "An Application of Self-Assessment Realistic Job Previews to Expatriate Assignments," *International Journal of Human Resource Management,* 14 (2003), 1102–1116.

14. Carolyn Brandon, "Truth in Recruitment Branding," *HR Magazine,* November 2005, 89–96.

15. Drew Robb, "Screening for Speedier Selection," *HR Magazine,* September 2004, 143–148.

16. W. J. Manning and Jorge R. Lopez, "New Concerns About Immigration Procedures Merit Review of I-9 Requirements," Jackson/Lewis, *www.Jacksonlewis.com/legalupdates.*

17. Bruce Finley, "Bosses Bypass Worker-Status Website," *Denver Post,* April 30, 2006, 4A.

18. Bryan R. Kethley and David E. Terpstra, "An Analysis of Litigation Associated with the Use of the Application Form in the Selection Process," *Public Personnel Management,* 34 (2005), 357–376.

19. Joey George and Kent Marett, "The Truth About Lies," *HR Magazine,* May, 2004, 87–91.

20. Gary McWilliams, "RadioShack CEO Agrees to Resign," *The Wall Street Journal,* February 21, 2006, A3.

21. Anne Freedman, "Front-Line Defense," *Human Resource Executive,* December 2005, 38–42.

22. "Recruitment: How to Evaluate a Selection Test," *Personnel Journal,* March Issue Supplement, 1994, 1, 3. Originally adapted from Raymond M. Berger and Donna Tucker, "How to Evaluate a Selection Test," *Personnel Journal,* February 1987.

23. Michael A. McDaniel and Nhung T. Nguyen, "Situational Judgment Tests: A Review of Practice and Constraints Assessed," *International Journal of Selection and Assessment,* 9 (2001), 103–113.

24. Quentin Reade, "Assessment Centres Show Signs of Growth," *Personnel Today,* February 24, 2004, 47.

25. "How Assessment Centers Helped Energis Get Customer-Focused," *Strategic HR Review,* September/October, 2004, 10–11.

26. Barbara Rose, "Tests Help Decide If Personalities Fit Positions," *Omaha World-Herald,* May 1, 2005, CR1.

27. Steve Bates, "Personality Counts," *HR Magazine,* February 2002, 28–34.

28. Mitchell G. Rothstein and Richard D. Goffin, "The Use of Personality Measures in Personnel Selection: What Does Current Research Support?" *Human Resource Management Review,* 16 (2006), 155–180.

29. Arnold B. Bakker, Karen I. Van Der Zee, Kerry A. Lewig, and Maureen F. Dollard, "The Relationship Between the Big Five Personality Factors and Burnout: A Study of Volunteer Counselors," *Journal of Social Psychology,* 146 (2006), 31–50.

30. Sharon Clarke and Ivan T. Robertson, "A Meta-Analytic Review of the Big Five Personality Factors and Accident Involvement in Occupational and Non-Occupational Settings," *Journal of Occupational and Organizational Psychology,* 78 (2005), 355–376.

31. Lynn A. McFarland, "Warning Against Faking on a Personality Test for Faking," *International Journal of Selection and Assessment,* 11 (2003), 265–276.

32. Richard D. Goffin and Neil D. Christiansen, "Correcting Personality Tests for Faking," *International Journal of Selection and Assessment,* 11 (2003), 340–344.

33. Chris Piotowski and Terry Armstrong, "Current Recruitment and Selection Practices: A National Survey of Fortune 1000 Firms," *North American Journal of Psychology,* 8 (2006), 489–496.

34. Joseph Schmitt, "The Truth About Integrity Testing in Employment," *SHRM Legal Report,* July/August 2005, 3–8.

35. Matthew Heller, "Court Ruling that Employer's Integrity Test Violated ADA Could Open Door to Litigation," *Workforce Management,* September 2005, 74.

36. Ken Alder, "A Social History of Untruth: Lie Detection and Trust in Twentieth Century America," *Representations,* Fall 2002, 11–33.

37. "MSPB Calls for Use of Structured Interviews to Assess Candidates for

Federal Jobs," *PA Times*, May 2003, 13.

38. Derek S. Chapman, "Developing a Nomological Network for Interview Structure: Antecedents and Consequences of the Structured Selection Interview," *Personnel Psychology*, 58 (2005), 673–702.

39. Henryk T. Krajewski, Richard D. Goffin, Julie M. McCarthy, Mitchell G. Rothstein, and Norman Johnston, "Comparing the Validity of Structured Interviews for Managerial-Level Employees: Should We Look to the Past or Focus on the Future?" *Journal of Occupational & Organizational Psychology*, 79 (2006), 411–432.

40. "Interview Tips and Best Practice: Behavioral-Based Questions Help to Recruit Talent for Best Fit," *Healthcare Registration*, October 2006, 7–9.

41. Kathryn Tyler, "Train for Smarter Hiring," *HR Magazine*, May 2005, 89–93.

42. Michael A. Warech, "Competency Based Interviewing at the Buckhead Beef Company," *Cornell Hotel and Restaurant Administration Quarterly*, February 2002, 70–78.

43. "Find the Best Assistant by Asking Great Interview Questions," *Sales Leader*, October 23, 2006, 4.

44. Steven D. Maurer, "Using Situational Interviews to Assess Engineering Applicant Fit to Work Group, Job, and Organizational Requirements," *Engineering Management Journal*, 18 (2006), 27–35.

45. "Multiple Methods Needed to Assess Executive Applicants," *HR Magazine*, February 2006, 20.

46. Timothy Tran and Melinda C. Blackman, "The Dynamics and Validity of the Group Selection Interview," *Journal of Social Psychology*, 146 (2006), 183–201.

47. Jessica Mintz, "The Jungle," *The Wall Street Journal*, June 21, 2005, B4.

48. Erin White, "The Jungle," *The Wall Street Journal*, May 17, 2005, B8.

49. Sharon L. Segrest Purkiss, Pamela L. Perrewe, Treena L. Gillespie, Bronston T. Mayes, and Gerald R. Ferris, "Implicit Sources of Bias in Employment Interview Judgments and Decisions," *Organizational Behavior and Human Decision Processes*, 101 (2006), 152–167.

50. Steve Bates, "Research Confirms that Employers Choose Young Workers over Older Workers," *HR Magazine*, September 2005, 34.

51. Lynn A. McFarland et al., "Field Study Investigation of Applicant Use of Influence Tactics in a Selection Interview," *Journal of Psychology*, 136 (2002), 383–398.

52. "The Top 5 Resume Lies," *Netscape Careers & Jobs*, http://channels.netscape.com/ns/careers.

53. Gregory M. Davis, "Criminal Background Checks for Employment Purposes," *SHRM Legal Report*, July/August 2006, 1, 5–8.

54. Anne Zimmerman and Kortney Stringer, "As Background Checks Proliferate, Ex-Cons Face Jobs Lock," *The Wall Street Journal*, August 26, 2004, B1.

55. Kris Maher, "The Jungle," *The Wall Street Journal*, January 20, 2004, B8.

56. "Background Backfire," *Human Resource Executive*, February 2006, 20–28.

57. Based on Michelle Conlin, "You Are What You Post," *BusinessWeek*, March 27, 2006, 52–53; and Alan Finder, "Employers Watching MySpace," *Denver Post*, June 11, 2006, 6A.

58. Fay Hansen, "Taking 'Reasonable' Action to Avoid Negligent Hiring Claims," *Workforce Management*, December 11, 2006, 31.

59. Allen Smith, "EEOC Challenges Unnecessary Credit Checks," *HR News*, March 29, 2007, www.shrm.org/hrnews.

60. "Employers Opt for Shorter-Term Expatriate Assignments," *Newsline*, November 17, 2003, www.mercerhr.com.

61. Yaping Gong, "Subsidiary Staffing in Multinational Enterprises: Agency Resources, and Performance," *Academy of Management Journal*, 46 (2003), 728–739.

62. Brett Clegg and Sidney J. Gray, "Australian Expatriates in Thailand: Some Insights for Expatriate Management Policies," *International Journal of Human Resource Management*, 13 (2002), 598–623.

63. Mark Larson, "U.S. Employers International Expansion Raising Demand for Overseas Background Checks," *Workforce Management*, 85 (2006), 44–43.

64. Sheila D. Lafferty, "When Is a Job Candidate Actually an Applicant?" *Highlights*, October 2004, 7.

65. Allen Smith, "OFCCP Updates Guidance on Internet Applicant," *HR News*, November 17, 2006, www.shrm.org/news.

66. Aaron Dalton, "Hallmark's Quality-of-Hire Initiative," *Workforce Management*, May 2005, www.workforce.com/section/06/article/24/04/76.html.

67. Gina Ruiz, "UnitedHealth Group: A Two-Pronged Approach to Staffing has Enabled the Health Service Provider to Hire More People at a Cheaper Rate, Paving the Way for Rapid Growth," *Workforce Management*, March 13, 2006, 30, www.workforce.com.

SECTION 3

Developing Human Resources

CHAPTER

9

Training Human Resources

After you have read this chapter, you should be able to:

- Define training and discuss why a strategic approach is important.

- Discuss the four phases of the training process.

- Identify three types of analyses used to determine training needs.

- Explain different means of internal and external training delivery.

- Describe the importance of e-learning as part of current training efforts.

- Give an example for each of the four levels of training evaluation.

HR Headline

E-Learning Expands

The dramatic increase in the use of the Internet and Web-based links by industries has led to many employers significantly expanding their use of e-learning. Two examples include:

- *IBM:* Its Learning Suite is an on-demand e-learning system available through the IBM intranet. Numerous learning programs are available to employees on-demand, varying from simulations to best practices review.

- Nike: At the apparel and sports equipment firm, employees in Nike stores can access Sports Knowledge Underground, an e-learning program. This service provides product details, apparel technology specifics, and other types of information, which has helped Nike reduce employee turnover and increase sales and revenues of products and services.

But the excitement of e-learning has been moderated because employers have experienced problems. If e-learning is not part of a broader approach to training linked to strategic goals, it may become another "Internet game." This results in participants viewing training, but not using the information to enhance their job performances. Thus, e-learning must be integrated with other training means, especially including some face-to-face discussion. Overall then, e-learning must be part of effective training to produce organizational value.[1]

The competitive pressures facing organizations today require that staff members' knowledge and ideas be current and that they have skills and abilities that can deliver results. As organizations compete and change to increase organizational performance, training of employees and managers becomes even more critical than before. Employees who must adapt to the many changes facing organizations must be trained continually in order to maintain and update their capabilities. Also, managers must have training and development to enhance their managerial and leadership skills and abilities. Consequently, effective training is a crucial component of HR management.

NATURE OF TRAINING

Training Process whereby people acquire capabilities to perform jobs.

Training is the process whereby people acquire capabilities to perform jobs. Training provides employees with specific, identifiable knowledge and skills for use in their present jobs. Organizational usage of training may include "hard" skills such as teaching sales representatives how to use intranet resources, a branch manager how to review an income statement, or a machinist apprentice how to set up a drill press. "Soft" skills are critical in many instances and can be taught as well. They may include communicating, mentoring, managing a meeting, and working as part of a team.

Training Categories

Training can be designed to meet a number of objectives and can be classified in various ways. As Figure 9-1 indicates, some common groupings include the following:

■ *Required and regular training:* Complies with various mandated legal requirements (e.g., OSHA and EEO) and is given to all employees (e.g., new employee orientation).
■ *Job/technical training:* Enables employees to perform their jobs well (e.g., product knowledge, technical processes and procedures, and customer relations).
■ *Interpersonal and problem-solving training:* Addresses both operational and interpersonal problems and seeks to improve organizational working relationships (e.g., interpersonal communication, managerial/supervisory skills, and conflict resolution).
■ *Developmental and career training:* Provides longer-term focus to enhance individual and organizational capabilities for the future (e.g., business practices, executive development, organizational change, leadership).

It is common for a distinction to be drawn between *training* and *development,* with development being broader in scope and focusing on individuals' gaining new capabilities useful for both present and future jobs. Development is discussed in Chapter 10; training is the focus of this chapter.

Legal Issues and Training

A number of legal issues must be considered when designing and delivering training. One concern centers on the criteria and practices used to select individuals for inclusion in training programs, making sure that those criteria are job related and do not unfairly restrict the participation of protected-class members. Also, failure to accommodate the participation of individuals with disabilities in training exposes organizations to EEO lawsuits.

FIGURE 9-1	Types of Training

Required and Regular
- Safety compliance
- Driving provisions
- Wage and hour rules
- Employee orientation
- Benefits enrollment
- Sexual harassment prevention

Job and Technical
- Customer service
- Equipment operations
- Record-keeping needs
- Telecommunications
- IT systems
- Product details

Training

Interpersonal and Problem Solving
- Communications
- Writing skills
- Team relationships
- Coaching skills
- Problem analyses
- Conflict resolution

Developmental and Career
- Business trends
- Strategic thinking
- Leadership
- Change management
- Career planning
- Performance management

Another legal issue is employers' requiring employees to sign *training contracts* in order to protect the costs and time invested in specialized employee training. For instance, a telecommunications firm paid $17,000 each to train four network technicians and certify them in specialized equipment. The firm required that each of the technicians sign a training contract whereby one-fourth of the cost would be forgiven each year the employee stayed following the training. A technician who left sooner would be liable to the firm for the unforgiven balance. Health-care organizations, IT firms, and some other employers use training contracts especially for expensive external training.

TRAINING AND ORGANIZATIONAL STRATEGY

Training represents a significant HR expenditure for most employers. But it is too often viewed tactically rather than strategically, which means that training is seen as a short-term activity rather than one that has longer-term effects on organizational success. Fortunately, more and more employers have recognized that training must be increased. One survey found that about half of the firms surveyed planned to increase their yearly training budgets.[2]

Strategic Training

Strategic training is linked to how the organization accomplishes its organizational goals. It can have numerous organizational benefits. First, strategic training enables HR and training professionals to get intimately involved with the business, partner with operating managers to help solve their problems, and make significant contributions to organizational results. Additionally, a strategic training mind-set reduces the likelihood of thinking that training alone can solve most employee or organizational problems. It is not uncommon for operating managers and trainers to react to most important performance problems by saying "I need a training program on X." With a strategic training focus, the organization is more likely to assess such requests to determine what training and/or non-training approaches might address the most important performance issues.

The value of training can be seen at Walt Disney World where the company has established specific training plans. Implementing those training plans results in a distinct competitive advantage for the organization. For example, at the Disney Institute, employees (called "cast members") gain training experience from their guests' perspectives. As a part of their training, individuals taking hotel reservations stay at a resort as guests in order to gain greater understanding of what they are selling and to experience the services themselves.

Organizational Competitiveness and Training

Currently, U.S. employers spend at least $60 billion annually on training. For the typical employer, training expenditures are almost 2% of payroll expenses, and run over $800 per eligible employee, according to a study by the American Society for Training and Development (ASTD). Organizations that see training as especially crucial to business competitiveness average $1,400 in training expenditures per eligible employee.[3]

General Electric, Dell Computers, Motorola, Marriott, Cisco, FedEx, and Texas Instruments all emphasize the importance of training employees and managers. These companies and others recognize that training and HR development efforts are integral to business success. In a sense, for these companies, training is similar to the "continuous improvement" practiced by some manufacturing firms.

The nature of technological innovation and change is such that if employees are not trained all the time, they may fall behind and the company could become less competitive. For example, consider the telecommunications industry today compared with five years ago, with all the new technologies (wireless, Internet, and Web-based services, etc.) and the accompanying competitive shifts. Without continual training, organizations may not have staff members with the knowledge, skills, and abilities (KSAs) needed to compete effectively.

Training also can affect organizational competitiveness by aiding in the retention of employees. As emphasized in Chapter 3, one reason why many individuals stay or leave organizations is career training and development opportunities. Employers that invest in training and developing their employees may well enhance retention efforts.

Figure 9-2 shows how training may help accomplish certain organizational strategies. Ideally, the upper management group sees the training function as providing valuable intelligence about the necessary core skills.

Knowledge management
The way an organization identifies and leverages knowledge in order to be competitive.

Knowledge Management and Training For much of history, competitive advantage among organizations was measured in terms of physical capital. However, as the information age has evolved, "intelligence" has become the raw material that many organizations make and sell through their "knowledge workers." Knowledge management is the way an organization identifies and

FIGURE 9-2   Linking Organizational Strategies and Training

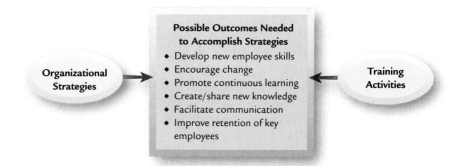

Source: Based on ideas from Lisa A. Burke and Joseph V. Wilson III.

leverages knowledge in order to be competitive. It is the art of creating value by using organizational intellectual capital, which is what the organization (or, more exactly, the people in the organization) knows. Knowledge management is a conscious effort to get the right knowledge to the right people at the right time so that it can be shared and put into action.

Training as a Revenue Source Some organizations have identified that training can be a source of business revenue. For instance, Microsoft, Ceridian, Cisco, Hewlett-Packard, and other technology firms bundle training with products and services sold to customers. Also, manufacturers of industrial equipment offer customers training on machine upgrades and new features. Customers of many of these firms pay for additional training either by course, by participant, or as part of equipment or software purchases. Not only are the costs of the trainers' salary, travel, and other expenses covered, but the suppliers make a profit on the training through the fees paid by customers. As a side benefit, customer satisfaction and loyalty increase if customers know how to use the products and services purchased. Thus, customer training aids customer retention and enhances future sales revenues. The HR Best Practices discussion (on the next page) illustrates how training can pay off for an employer.

Performance Consulting and Strategic Training

Performance consulting
Process in which a trainer and the organizational client work together to determine what needs to be done to improve organizational and individual results.

Training should result in improved organizational performance. For some companies, ensuring that it does requires a "performance consulting" approach. Performance consulting is a process in which a trainer (either internal or external to the organization) and the organizational client work together to decide how to improve organizational and individual results. That may or may not include training. Performance consulting takes a broad approach by:

- Focusing on identifying and addressing root causes of performance problems
- Recognizing that the interaction of individual and organizational factors influences employee performance
- Documenting the actions and accomplishments of high performers and comparing them with actions of more typical performers

Regardless of whether the trainer is an internal employee or an outside consultant, a performance consulting approach recognizes that training alone cannot automatically solve every employer performance problem. Instead, training is one piece of a larger "bundled solution." For instance, some

HR BEST PRACTICES

Randstad Ramps Up

Many professional service firms spend considerable time and money on training. But several years ago Randstad North America identified that it had to significantly improve its training of new employees. Randstad is part of a Netherlands-based firm that provides employment and staffing services to firms and individuals. With over 2,000 employees in almost 500 offices in the United States and Canada, the firm directs significant training efforts at both new and current employees.

About five years ago, Randstad had planned to open 100 new offices, which meant a large number of new employees to be trained. With a turnover rate of almost 50%, filling all of the new jobs and replacing workers who left required major attention.

Over a five-year period Randstad developed a centralized training program for both new and exist-

ing employees. The training evolved into a 16-week program. Specifically, new employees access different e-learning modules on the company intranet and receive class training on sales and use of company databases. Then they receive a week of training at the firm's Atlanta headquarters.

The training efforts have aided Randstad in reducing its turnover rates and resulted in newly trained employees generating significantly more productivity and performance. The firm documented that such training led to over $4 million in additional revenues and a return on investment of 338%. Its efforts resulted in Randstad receiving a *Workforce Management* "Optimas Award" for competitive advantage. It is obvious that the training efforts by Randstad have significantly enhanced organizational results through higher employee performance.[4]

Internet Research

International Society for Performance Improvement
This professional organization focuses on improving productivity and performance in the workplace. Visit their Website at:
http://thomsonedu.com/management/mathis.

employee performance issues might be resolved by creating a training program for employees, and others might call for compensation or job design changes.

Integration of Performance and Training Job performance, training, and employee learning must be integrated to be effective, and HR plays a crucial role in this integration.[5] Organizations are seeking more authentic (and hence more effective) training experiences for their employees by using real business problems to advance employee learning. Rather than separating the training experience from the context of actual job performance, trainers incorporate everyday business issues as learning examples, thus increasing the realism of training exercises and scenarios. As part of management training at GE, managers are given actual business problems to solve, and they must present their solutions to the firm's business leaders. Using real situations for practice is yet another way of merging the lines between training, learning, and job performance.

Chief Learning Officers To emphasize the importance of training and to have internal performance consulting expertise, some organizations have created a position entitled *chief learning officer (CLO)* or *chief knowledge officer (CKO)*. The CLO is not just a training director with an inflated new title.[6] Instead, the CLO is a leader who designs knowledge through training for individual employees and the organization. CLOs must demonstrate a high level of comfort in working with boards of directors and the top management team, a track record of success in running some type of business unit, and an understanding of adult learning technologies and processes. If they possess these characteristics, then CLOs are likely to take the lead in developing strategic training plans for their organizations.[7]

Training and Global Strategies

For global firms the most brilliant strategies ever devised will not work unless they have well-trained employees throughout the world to carry them out. A global look at strategic training is becoming more crucial as firms establish and expand operations worldwide. For U.S. employers, the challenge is increased. According to a report, the number of U.S. job skills certifications declined 18% in one year, while there was a 47% increase in similar certifications in India. The conclusion of the study was that U.S. firms may not remain innovative and strategic leaders much longer, due to the decline in specialized skilled and technical workers.[8] Add this problem to the number of global employees with international assignments, and training must be seen as crucial to global strategic success.

Global Assignment Training The orientation and training that expatriates and their families receive before departure significantly affect the success of an overseas assignment. When such programs are offered, most expatriates participate in them, and the programs usually produce a positive effect on cross-cultural adjustment.[9] Also, training in various areas helps expatriates and their families adjust to and deal with host-country counterparts. Training in customs and practices can be especially valuable to individuals who will not live outside the home country but will travel to other countries on business.

A related issue is the promotion and transfer of foreign citizens to positions in the United States. For example, many Japanese firms operating in the United States conduct training programs to prepare Japanese for the food, customs, labor and HR practices, and other facets of working and living in the United States. As more global organizations start or expand U.S. operations, more cross-cultural training will be necessary for international employees relocated to the United States.

Intercultural Competence Training Growing numbers of global employers are providing intercultural competence training for their global employees. Intercultural competence incorporates a wide range of human social skills and personality characteristics. As noted in Figure 9-3 (on the next page), three components of intercultural competence require attention when training expatriates for global assignments:

- *Cognitive:* What does the person know about other cultures?
- *Emotional:* How does the person view other cultures, and how sensitive is the person to cultural customs and issues?
- *Behavioral:* How does the person act in intercultural situations?

Increasingly, global employers are using training methods that allow individuals to behave in international situations and then receive feedback. One method is the Culture Assimilator. Used worldwide, especially by European-based firms, the Culture Assimilator is a programmed training and learning method consisting of short case studies and critical incidents. The case studies describe intercultural interactions and potential misunderstandings involving expatriates and host-country nationals.

Regardless of the means used to do cross-cultural training, it is important to track and measure the costs and results. Doing so increases the likelihood that more effective global activities will occur. One example of the value of such training is that global decision times were reduced 25% and product development increased significantly, resulting in over $40 million in more cash flow.[10] Such results can be used to justify expanding global training as part of organizational strategic efforts.

FIGURE 9-3   **Intercultural Competence Training**

Component	Possible Training
Cognitive	• Culture-specific training (traditions, history, cultural customs, etc.) • Language course
Emotional	• *Uneasiness:* Social skills training focusing on new/unclear and intercultural situations • *Prejudices:* Coaching may be clarifying • *Sensitivity:* Communication skills course (active listening, verbal/nonverbal cues, empathy)
Behavioral	• Culture Assimilator • International projects • Social skills training focusing on intercultural situations

Source: Developed by Andrea Graf, PhD, and Robert L. Mathis, PhD, SPHR.

Training Components

Training plans allow organizations to identify what is needed for employee performance *before* training begins. It is at this stage that fit with strategic issues is ensured. Effective training efforts consider the following questions[11]:

- Is there really a need for the training?
- Who needs to be trained?
- Who will do the training?
- What form will the training take?
- How will knowledge be transferred to the job?
- How will the training be evaluated?

Training Process The way firms organize and structure their training affects the way employees experience the training, which in turn influences the effectiveness of the training. Effective training requires the use of a systematic training process. Figure 9-4 shows the four phases of such a process: assessment, design, delivery, and evaluation. Using such a process reduces the likelihood that unplanned, uncoordinated, and haphazard training efforts will occur. A discussion of each phase of the training process follows.

TRAINING NEEDS ASSESSMENT

Assessing organizational training needs represents the diagnostic phase of a training plan. This assessment considers issues of employee and organizational performance to determine if training can help. Needs assessment measures the competencies of a company, a group, or an individual as they relate to what is required in the strategic plan. It is necessary to find out what is happening and what should be happening before deciding if training will help, and if it

FIGURE 9-4   Systematic Training Process

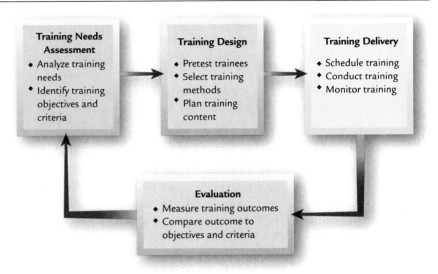

will help, what kind is needed.[12] For instance, suppose that in looking at the performance of clerks in a billing department, a manager identifies problems that employees have with their data-entry and keyboarding abilities, and she decides that they would benefit from instruction in these areas. As part of assessing the training needs, the manager has the clerks take a data-entry test to measure their current keyboarding skills. Then the manager establishes an objective of increasing the clerks' keyboarding speed to 60 words per minute without errors. The number of words per minute without errors is the criterion against which training success can be measured, and it represents the way in which the objective is made specific.

Analysis of Training Needs

The first step in training needs assessment is analyzing what training is needed. Figure 9-5 shows the three sources used to analyze training needs.

Organizational Analyses Training needs can be diagnosed by analyzing organizational outcomes and looking at future organizational needs. A part of planning for training is the identification of the KSAs that will be needed now and in the future as both jobs and the organization change. Both internal

FIGURE 9-5   Sources of Information Used in Training Needs Assessment

Organization-wide Sources
- Grievances
- Accidents
- Waste/scrap
- Training observations
- Observations
- Complaints
- Exit interviews
- Equipment use

Job/Task Sources
- Employee KSAs
- Job specifications

Individual Employee Sources
- Tests
- Records
- Assessment centers
- Questionnaires
- Surveys
- Job knowledge tools
- Performance appraisals

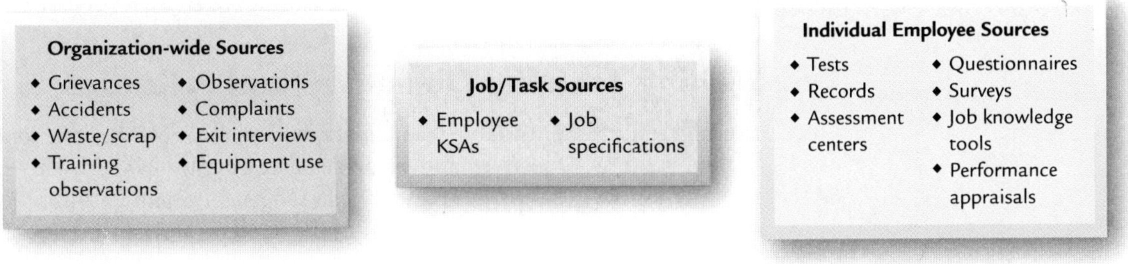

and external forces will influence training and must be considered when doing organizational analyses. For instance, the problems posed by the technical obsolescence of current employees and an insufficiently educated labor pool from which to draw new workers should be confronted before those issues become critical.

Organizational analyses comes from various operational measures of organizational performance. On a continuing basis, detailed analyses of HR data reveal training weaknesses. Departments or areas with high turnover, high absenteeism, low performance, or other deficiencies can be pinpointed. Following an analysis of such problems, training objectives then can be developed.

Job/Task Analyses The second way of doing training needs analysis is to review the jobs involved and the tasks performed in those jobs. By comparing the requirements of jobs with the KSAs of employees, training needs can be identified. Current job specifications can be a source for such an analysis. For example, at a manufacturing firm, analyses identified the tasks performed by engineers who served as technical instructors for other employees. By listing the tasks required of a technical instructor, management established a program to teach specific instructional skills; thus, the engineers were able to become more successful instructors.

Individual Analyses The third means of diagnosing training needs focuses on individuals and how they perform their jobs. The following sources are examples that are useful for individual analyses:

- Performance appraisals
- Skill tests
- Individual assessment tests
- Records of critical incidents
- Assessment center exercises
- Questionnaires and surveys
- Job knowledge tools
- Internet input

The most common approach for making these individual analyses is to use performance appraisal data. In some instances, a good HR information system can be used to identify individuals who require training in specific areas in order to be eligible for promotion. To assess training needs through the performance appraisal process, the organization first determines an employee's performance strengths and inadequacies in a formal review. Then, it can design some type of training to help the employee overcome the weaknesses and enhance the strengths.

Another way of assessing individual training needs is to use both managerial and non-managerial input about what training is needed. Obtaining such input can also be useful in building support from those who will be trained who have provided input for identifying training needs. A training needs survey can take the form of questionnaires or interviews with supervisors and employees individually or in groups.[13] The growth of the Internet has resulted in firms using web-based surveys, requests, and other inputs from managers and employees to identify training needs.[14]

Establishing Training Objectives and Priorities

Once training requirements have been identified using appropriate needs analyses, then training objectives and priorities can be established by a "gap analysis," which indicates the distance between where an organization is with its employee capabilities and where it needs to be. Training objectives and priorities are then determined to close the gap. Three types of training objectives can be set:

- *Knowledge:* Impart cognitive information and details to trainees.
- *Skill:* Develop behavior changes in how jobs and various task requirements are performed.
- *Attitude:* Create interest in and awareness of the importance of training.

The success of training should be measured in terms of the objectives set. Useful objectives are measurable. For example, an objective for a new sales clerk might be to "demonstrate the ability to explain the function of each product in the department within two weeks." This objective checks *internalization;* that is, whether the person really learned and is able to use the training.

Because training seldom is an unlimited budget item and because organizations have multiple training needs, prioritization is necessary. Ideally, management looks at training needs in relation to strategic organizational plans and as part of the organizational change process.[15] Then the training needs can be prioritized based on organizational objectives.[16] Conducting the training most needed to improve the performance of the organization will produce visible results more quickly.

TRAINING DESIGN

Once training objectives have been determined, training design can start. Whether job specific or broader in nature, training must be designed to address the assessed specific needs. Effective training design considers learning concepts and a wide range of different approaches to training.

Working in organizations should be a continual learning process, and learning is the focus of all training activities. Different approaches are possible because learning is a complex psychological process. There are three primary considerations when designing training: (1) determining learner readiness, (2) understanding different learning styles, and (3) designing training for transfer. Each of these elements must be considered for the training design to mesh and produce effective learning.

Learner Readiness

For training to be successful, learners must be ready to learn. Learner readiness means individuals having the ability to learn, which many people have. However, if effective learning is to occur, individuals must also have the motivation to learn and self-efficacy.

Ability to Learn Learners must possess basic skills, such as fundamental reading and math proficiency, and sufficient cognitive abilities. Companies may discover that some workers lack the requisite skills to comprehend their training effectively. Various firms have found that a significant number of job applicants and current employees lack the reading, writing, and math skills needed to do the jobs. Employers might deal with the lack of basic employee skills in several ways:

- Offer remedial training to people in their current workforce who need it.
- Hire workers who are deficient and then implement specific workplace training.
- Work with local schools to help better educate potential hires for jobs.

Motivation to Learn A person's desire to learn training content is referred to as "motivation to learn" and is influenced by multiple factors. For example, differences in gender and ethnicity and the resulting experiences may affect the motivation of adult learners.[17] The student's motivation level may also be influenced by the instructor's motivation and ability, friends' encouragement to do well, classmates' motivation levels, the physical classroom environment, and the training methods used. Regardless of what the motivation is, without it, the student will not learn the material. This example also reflects that a person's performance training has a significant effect on the motivation to learn.[18]

Self-efficacy Person's belief that he or she *can* learn the training program content.

Self-Efficacy Learners must also possess self-efficacy, which refers to a person's belief that he or she *can* successfully learn the training program content. For learners to be ready for and receptive to the training content, they must feel that it is possible for them to learn it. As an example, some college students' levels of self-efficacy diminish in math or statistics courses when they do not feel adequately able to grasp the material. These perceptions may have nothing to do with their actual ability to learn, but rather reflect the way they see themselves and their abilities. Instructors and trainers must find appropriate ways to boost the confidence of trainees who are unsure of their learning abilities. For instance, people with a high level of belief that they can learn certain content perform better and are more satisfied with the training they receive.[19]

Learning Styles

Once learning readiness has been considered, then learning styles and learning transfer become a focus, as Figure 9-6 indicates. The combination of these components can result in effective learning.

In designing training interventions, trainers also should consider individual learning styles. For example, *auditory* learners learn best by listening to

FIGURE 9-6   Elements of Training Design

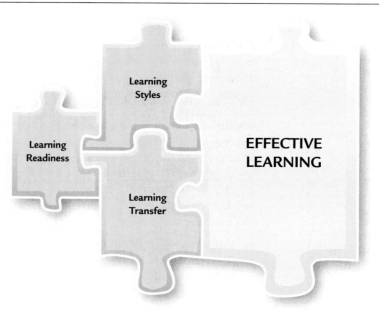

someone else tell them about the training content. *Tactile* learners must "get their hands on" the training resources and use them. *Visual* learners think in pictures and figures and need to see the purpose and process of the training. Trainers who address all these styles by using multiple training methods can design more effective training.[20]

Training many different people from diverse backgrounds poses a significant challenge in today's work organizations. In addition to considering cultural, gender, and race/ethnicity diversity, training design sometimes must address some special issues presented by adult learning. Certainly, the training design must consider that all the trainees are adults, but they come with widely varying learning styles, experiences, and personal goals.

Internet Research

Ageless Learner
For resources and Web links to information on how adults learn, link to this site at: http://thomsonedu.com/ management/mathis.

Training older adults in technology may require greater attention to explaining the need for changes and to enhancing the older trainees' confidence and abilities when learning new technologies. In contrast, younger adults are likely familiar with new technology because of their earlier exposure to computers and technology. As a consequence of differences such as these, a variety of training designs and delivery considerations must be assessed when developing training for adults of various ages.

Adult Learning Malcolm Knowles's classic work on adult learning suggests five principles for designing training for adults.[21] That and subsequent work by others suggests that adults:

- Have the need to know why they are learning something.
- Have a need to be self-directed.
- Bring more work-related experiences into the learning process.
- Enter into a learning experience with a problem-centered approach to learning.
- Are motivated to learn by both extrinsic and intrinsic factors.

Adult learners in work organizations present different issues for training design based on Knowles's principles.[22] For instance, trainers cannot expect to do a "brain dump" of material without giving trainees the context or bigger picture of why participants need the training information. This concept is referred to as *whole learning* or *Gestalt learning*. As applied to job training, this means that instructions should be divided into small elements *after* employees have had the opportunity to see how all the elements fit together—that trainers should present the big picture first.

Part of this need is because adult learners often have broad experiences and "world views."[23] Travel, family concerns, health issues, political involvement, and many more factors are in play as adult learners have aged. Such recognition illustrates why adult learners should be encouraged to bring work-related problems to training as a way to make the material more relevant to them.[24] Effective training should involve participants in learning by actively engaging them in the learning and problem-solving process. Active practice occurs when trainees perform job-related tasks and duties during training. It is more effective than simply reading or passively listening.[25] For instance, assume a person is being trained as a customer service representative. After being given some basic selling instructions and product details, the trainee calls a customer and uses the knowledge received.

Active practice
Performance of job-related tasks and duties by trainees during training.

Spaced practice Practice performed in several sessions spaced over a period of hours or days.

Massed practice Practice performed all at once.

Active practice can be structured in two ways. The first, spaced practice, occurs when several practice sessions are spaced over a period of hours or days. The second, massed practice, occurs when a person performs all the practice at once. Spaced practice works better for some types of skill or physical learning that requires muscle memory, whereas for other kinds of learning, such as memorizing tasks, massed practice is usually more effective. Imagine the difficulty of trying to memorize the lists of options for 20 dishwasher models, one model a day for 20 days. By the time an appliance distribution salesperson learned the last option, the person likely would have forgotten the first one.

Behavior modeling
Copying someone else's behavior.

Behavior Modeling The most elementary way in which people learn—and one of the best—is through behavior modeling, or copying someone else's behavior. The use of behavior modeling is particularly appropriate for skill training in which the trainees must use both knowledge and practice. It can aid in the transfer and usage of those skills by those trained.[26] For example, a new supervisor can receive training and mentoring on how to handle disciplinary discussions with employees by observing as the HR director or department manager deals with such problems.

Behavior modeling is used extensively as the primary means for training supervisors and managers in interpersonal skills. Fortunately or unfortunately, many supervisors and managers end up modeling the behavior they see their bosses use. For that reason, effective training should include good examples of how to handle interpersonal and other issues and problems.

Reinforcement Based on the idea that people tend to repeat responses that give them some type of positive reward and avoid actions associated with negative consequences.

Immediate confirmation Based on the idea that people learn best if reinforcement and feedback are given as soon as possible after training.

Reinforcement and Immediate Confirmation The concept of reinforcement is based on the *law of effect*, which states that people tend to repeat responses that give them some type of positive reward and to avoid actions associated with negative consequences. Closely related is a learning concept called immediate confirmation, which is based on the idea that people learn best if reinforcement and feedback are given as soon as possible after training. Immediate confirmation corrects errors that, if made throughout the training, might establish an undesirable pattern that would need to be unlearned. It also aids with the transfer of training to the actual work done.

Transfer of Training

Finally, trainers should design training for the highest possible transfer from the class to the job. Transfer occurs when trainees actually use on the job what knowledge and information they learned in training.[27] How much training effectively gets transferred to the job is estimated to be relatively low, given all of the time and money spent on training. A review of 150 organizations found that as few as 34% of employees apply training to their jobs within the first year after training. That study showed that employees may use the training immediately, but then decrease its use over time.[28]

Certain variables affect the continuation of training transfer, depending on the nature and type of training.[29] Verifying the effectiveness of training transfer is part of training evaluation and HR metrics, discussed later in this chapter. Effective transfer of training meets two conditions. First, the trainees can take the material learned in training and apply it to the job context in which they work. Second, employees maintain their use of the learned material over time.

A number of approaches can increase the transfer of training. Offering trainees an overview of the training content and process before the actual training seems to help with both short-term and longer-term training transfer. Another specific way to aid transfer of training to job situations is to ensure that the training mirrors the job context as much as possible. For example, training managers to be better selection interviewers should include role-playing with "applicants" who respond in the same way that real applicants would.

TRAINING DELIVERY

Once training has been designed, then the actual delivery of training can begin. Regardless of the type of training done, a number of approaches and methods can be used to deliver it. The growth of training technology continues to expand the available choices, as Figure 9-7 shows.

Whatever the approach used, a variety of considerations must be balanced when selecting training delivery methods. The common variables considered are:

- Nature of training
- Subject matter
- Number of trainees
- Individual vs. team
- Self-paced vs. guided

- Training resources/costs
- E-learning vs. traditional learning
- Geographic locations
- Time allotted
- Completion timeline

To illustrate, a large firm with many new hires may be able to conduct employee orientation using the Internet, videotapes, and specific HR staff members. However, a small firm with few new hires may have an HR staff member meet individually with the new hires for several hours. Or a medium-sized company with three locations in a geographic area may bring supervisors together for a two-day training workshop once a quarter. However, a large, global firm may use Web-based courses to reach supervisors throughout the world, with content available in several languages. Frequently, training is conducted internally, but some types of training use external or technological training resources.

FIGURE 9-7   **Methods Companies Use to Deliver Training**

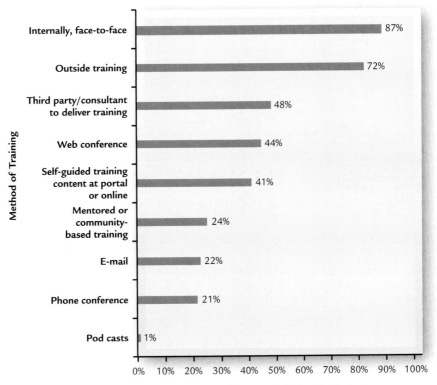

Source: *Employee Benefit News,* November 2006, 22.

Internal Training

Internal training generally applies very specifically to the organization and its jobs. It is popular because it saves the cost of sending employees away for training and often avoids the cost of outside trainers. Skills-based technical training is conducted inside organizations. Due to rapid changes in technology, the building and updating of technical skills may become crucial training needs. Basic technical skills training is also being mandated by federal regulations in areas where the Occupational Safety and Health Administration (OSHA), the Environmental Protection Agency (EPA), and other agencies have jurisdiction.

Informal Training One internal source of training is informal training, which occurs through interactions and feedback among employees. Much of what the employees know about their jobs they learn informally from asking questions and getting advice from other employees and their supervisors, rather than from formal training programs.

> **Informal training** Training that occurs through interactions and feedback among employees.

On-the-Job Training The most common type of training at all levels in an organization is *on-the-job training (OJT)* because it is flexible and relevant to what employees do. In contrast with informal training, which often occurs spontaneously, OJT should be planned. The supervisor or manager conducting the training must be able to both teach and show the employees what to do.

However, OJT has some problems. Often, those doing the training may have no experience in training, no time to do it, and no desire to participate in it. Under such conditions, learners essentially are on their own, and training likely will not be effective. Another problem is that OJT can disrupt regular work. Unfortunately, OJT can amount to no training at all in some circumstances, especially if the trainers simply abandon the trainees to learn the job alone. Also, bad habits or incorrect information from the supervisor or manager can be transferred to the trainees.

Well-planned and well-executed OJT can be very effective. Based on a guided form of training known as *job instruction training (JIT),* on-the-job training is most effective if a logical progression of stages is used, as shown in Figure 9-8.

FIGURE 9-8   Stages for On-the-Job Training (OJT)

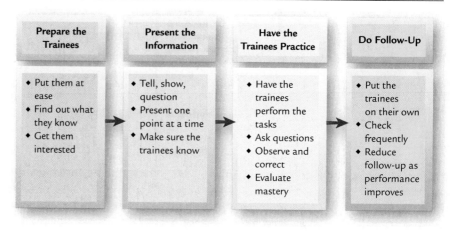

Cross training Training
people to do more than
one job.

Cross Training A variety of on-the-job training is cross training, which occurs when people are trained to do more than one job—theirs and someone else's. For the employer, the advantages of cross training are flexibility and development. However, although cross training is attractive to the employer, it is not always appreciated by employees, who often feel that it requires them to do more work for the same pay. To counteract such responses, learning "bonuses" can be awarded for successfully completing cross training to make it more appealing to employees.

In some organizations, the culture may be such that people seek cross-training assignments to grow or prepare for a promotion, but that is not the case in all organizations. Unions typically are not in favor of cross training because it threatens job jurisdiction and broadens jobs. Cross training may require scheduling work differently during training, and temporarily decreased productivity may result from it as people learn. Overall, an effective cross training program can overcome the concerns mentioned and has the potential to be good for both employer and employee.

External Training

External training, or training that takes place outside the employing organization, is used extensively by organizations of all sizes. Large organizations use external training if they lack the capability to train people internally or when many people need to be trained quickly. External training may be the best option for training in smaller firms due to limitations in the size of their HR staffs and in the number of employees who need various types of specialized training. Whatever the size of the organization, external training occurs for several reasons:

- It may be less expensive for an employer to have an outside trainer conduct training in areas where internal training resources are limited.
- The organization may have insufficient time to develop internal training materials.
- The HR staff may not have the necessary level of expertise for the subject matter in which training is needed.
- There are advantages to having employees interact with managers and peers in other companies in training programs held externally.

Outsourcing of Training Many employers of all sizes outsource training to external training firms, consultants, and other entities. According to data from ASTD, approximately 25% to 30% of training expenditures go to outside training sources. Interestingly, over a recent three-year period, the outsourcing of training has not increased dramatically.[30] The reasons may be cost concerns, a greater emphasis on internal linking of training to organizational strategies, and other issues. However, outsourcing of training is used more frequently when mergers and acquisition occur.[31]

A popular route for some employers is to use vendors and suppliers to train employees. Several computer software vendors offer employees technical certifications on their software. For example, being a Microsoft Certified Product Specialist gives employees credentials that show their level of technical expertise. Such certifications provide employees with items to put on their résumés should they decide to change jobs. These certifications also benefit employers, who can use them as job specifications for hiring and promotion.

Many suppliers host users' conferences, where employees from a number of firms receive detailed training on using products, services, and features that are new to the employees. Some vendors will conduct the training inside an organization as well if sufficient numbers of employees are to be trained.

Government-Supported Job Training Federal, state, and local governments provide a wide range of external training assistance and funding. The Workforce Investment Act (WIA) provides states with block grant programs that target adult education, disadvantaged youth, and family literacy. Employers hiring and training individuals who meet the WIA criteria receive tax credits and other assistance for six months or more, depending on the program regulations.

At state and local levels, employers who add to their workforces can take advantage of a number of programs that provide funding assistance to offset training costs. As examples, a number of states offer workforce training assistance for employers. Quick Start (Georgia), Smart Jobs (Texas), and Partnership (Alabama) are three well-known training support efforts. Often, such programs are linked to two-year and four-year colleges throughout the state.

Educational Assistance Programs Some employers pay for additional education for their employees. Typically, the employee pays for courses that apply to a college degree and is reimbursed upon successful completion of a course. The amounts paid by the employer are considered non-taxable income for the employee up to amounts set by federal laws. But one concern is that traditional forms of employee educational programs pose risks for the employer. Upon completion of the degree, the employee may choose to take the new skills and go elsewhere. Employers must plan to use these skills upon employee graduation to improve the retention of those employees.

Combination Training Approaches

Whether training is delivered internally or externally, appropriate training must be chosen. The following overview identifies two common training approaches that often integrate internal and external means. Some are used more for job-based training, while others are used more for development.

Cooperative Training Cooperative training approaches mix classroom training and on-the-job experiences. This training can take several forms. One form, generally referred to as *school-to-work transition*, helps individuals move into jobs while still in school or on completion of formal schooling. Such efforts may be arranged with high schools or with community colleges.

One form of cooperative training used by employers, trade unions, and government agencies is *apprentice training*. An apprenticeship program provides an employee with on-the-job experience under the guidance of a skilled and certified worker. Certain requirements for training, equipment, time length, and proficiency levels may be monitored by a unit of the U.S. Department of Labor. Figure 9-9 indicates the most common areas that use apprenticeships to train people for jobs. Apprenticeships usually last two to five years, depending on the occupation. During this time, the apprentice usually receives lower wages than the certified individual.

Another form of cooperative training called *internship* usually combines job training with classroom instruction from schools, colleges, and universities. Internships benefit both employers and interns. Interns get "real-world"

| FIGURE 9-9 | Most Common Apprenticeship Occupations |

- ◆ Electrician (construction)
- ◆ Carpenter
- ◆ Plumber
- ◆ Pipe fitter
- ◆ Sheet metal worker
- ◆ Structural-steel worker

- ◆ Elevator constructor
- ◆ Roofer
- ◆ Sprinkler fitter
- ◆ Bricklayer
- ◆ Construction craft laborer
- ◆ Painter

Source: U.S. Department of Labor, 2006, *www.dol.gov.*

exposure, a line on their résumés, and a chance to closely examine a possible employer. Employers get a cost-effective source of labor and a chance to see an intern at work before making a final hiring decision.

Instructor-Led Classroom and Conference Training Instructor-led training is still the most prevalent approach to training. Employer-conducted short courses, lectures, and meetings usually consist of classroom training, whereas numerous employee development courses offered by professional organizations, trade associations, and educational institutions are examples of conference training. A particularly important aspect of classroom training is the need to recognize that adults in a classroom setting have different expectations and learning styles from those of younger students. A number of large firms have established their own "universities" to offer classroom and other training as part of curricula for employees. Because these corporate universities generally offer both training and development courses, they are discussed in Chapter 10.

Orientation: On-Boarding for New Employees

Orientation Planned introduction of new employees to their jobs, co-workers, and the organization.

The most important and widely conducted type of regular training is done for *new* employees. Orientation is the planned introduction of new employees to their jobs, co-workers, and the organization, and is offered by most employers. It requires cooperation between individuals in the HR unit and operating managers and supervisors. In a small organization without an HR department, the new employee's supervisor or manager usually assumes most of the responsibility for orientation.[32] In large organizations, managers and supervisors, as well as the HR department, generally work as a team to orient new employees. Unfortunately, many new employee orientation sessions still come across as boring, irrelevant, and a waste of time to both new employees and their department supervisors and managers.

The term *on-boarding* is being used increasingly to describe orientation. This usage reflects that getting new employees, including executives, to immediately begin performing successfully is crucial.[33] Estimates are that about 75% of employers have implemented on-boarding activities to improve their employee orientation efforts. Many of them are using electronic technology as part of their on-boarding efforts.[34] Effective orientation achieves several key purposes:

- ■ Establishes a favorable employee impression of the organization and the job.
- ■ Provides organization and job information.

- Enhances interpersonal acceptance by co-workers.
- Accelerates socialization and integration of the new employee into the organization.
- Ensures that employee performance and productivity begin more quickly.

On-boarding through orientation efforts contributes to both short-term and long-term success for employees. The HR On-the-Job discussion contains some suggestions on how to make employee orientations more effective. The socialization of new employees and their initial commitment to the organization are positively affected by orientation. This socialization enhances the person/organization fit, which reinforces the employee's positive view of the job, co-workers, and the organization. Additionally, employers have found that higher employee retention rates result when new employees receive effective orientation.

Orientation also contributes to overall organizational performance. By helping employees to more quickly feel that they are a part of the organization, they can begin contributing more quickly to organizational work efforts.

One way of expanding the efficiency of orientation is to use electronic resources. A number of employers place general employee orientation information on company intranets or corporate Websites. New employees log on and go through much of the general material on organizational history, structure, products and services, mission, and other background, instead of sitting in a classroom where the information is delivered in person or by videotape.[35] Specific questions and concerns can be addressed by HR staff and others after employees review the Web-based information.

HR ON-THE-JOB

Effective New Employee Orientation

Effective new employee orientation requires planning and preparation. Unfortunately, orientation often is conducted rather haphazardly. To make orientation more effective, the following suggestions are useful:

- *Prepare for new employees.* New employees must feel that they belong and are important to the organization. The supervisor, HR unit, and co-workers should be prepared for a new employee's arrival.
- *Consider using mentors.* Some organizations assign co-workers or peers to serve as buddies or mentors as part of the new employees' orientation.
- *Use an orientation checklist.* An orientation checklist can be used to identify what the new employee needs to know now.
- *Cover needed information.* It is important to give employees information on the policies, work rules, and benefits of the company

- *Present orientation information effectively.* Managers and HR representatives should determine the most appropriate ways to present orientation information both in person and using technological means.
- *Avoid information overload.* One common failing of many orientation programs is information overload. New workers presented with too many facts may ignore or inaccurately recall much of the information.
- *Evaluate and follow up.* An HR representative or manager can evaluate the effectiveness of the orientation by conducting follow-up interviews with new employees a few weeks or months after the orientation.

E-Learning: On-Line Training

E-learning Use of the Internet or an organizational intranet to conduct training on-line.

E-learning is use of the Internet or an organizational intranet to conduct training on-line. E-learning is growing in popularity with employers. The major advantages are cost savings and access to more employees. Estimates are that corporate training conducted through learning technology today will be doubled in the next few years. Almost 30% of learning hours are totally technology based, according to an ASTD report. Also, e-learning is seen as more highly preferred by workers under the age of 30 years.[36] A number of e-learning methods are used for workers, regardless of age or location, some of which are discussed next.

Distance Training/Learning A growing number of college and university classes use some form of Internet-based course support. Blackboard and WebCT are two popular support packages that thousands of college professors use to make their lecture content available to students. These packages enable virtual chat and electronic file exchange among course participants, and also enhance instructor/student contact. Many large employers, as well as colleges and universities, use interactive two-way television to present classes. The medium allows an instructor in one place to see and respond to a "class" in any number of other locations. With a fully configured system, employees can take courses from anywhere in the world.

Internet Research

E-Learning Guild
The E-Learning Guild provides members with learning opportunities, networking services, resources, and publications on e-learning. Visit their site at:
http://thomsonedu.com/management/mathis.

Simulations and Training The explosive growth in information technology in the past few years has revolutionized the way all individuals work, including how they are trained. Today, computer-based training involves a wide array of multimedia technologies—including sound, motion (video and animation), graphics, and hypertext—to tap multiple learner senses.

Computer-supported simulations within organizational training can replicate the psychological and behavioral requirements of a task, often in addition to providing some amount of physical resemblance to the trainee's work environment. From highly complicated systems that replicate difficult landing scenarios for pilots to programs that help medical trainees learn to sew sutures, simulations allow for safe training when the risks associated with failure are high. Virtual reality is also used to create an artificial environment for trainees so that they can participate in the training. On-line gaming is a growing e-learning tool, as the HR On-Line feature (on the next page) describes.

The new technologies incorporated into training delivery also affect the design, administration, and support of training. Some companies have invested in electronic registration and record-keeping systems that allow trainers to register participants, record exam results, and monitor learning progress.

Generally, technology is moving from center stage to becoming embedded in the learning and training processes. As learning and work merge even closer in the future, technology is likely to integrate seamlessly into the work environment of more employees. This integration will allow employees to spend less time in the future learning how to use technology, and more time on learning the desired content.

Blended Learning E-learning alone cannot be the sole method of training, according to the findings of a significant number of employers. Therefore,

HR ONLINE

Gaming Grows in E-Training

A large number of Internet users play on-line games of all types. But games also are an important part of employer training initiatives. Estimates are that up to $150 million annually is being spent by employers on work-related games.

For years military and government workers have used games and simulations to prepare for combat exercises, improve use of military equipment, and prepare for natural and human-caused disasters. However, many private employers of all types are using gaming situations for both new and existing employees.

■ A technology company, Borland Software, uses games for training sales staff on its software products. Various games, including hangman and other simple ones, are combined to evalu-

ate trainees' knowledge of products and services. The individuals who meet the time limit and get perfect scores are eligible for drawings for cash incentives, free iPods, and other rewards.

■ Cold Stone Creamery, a California-based ice cream firm, has a game where employees scoop ice cream cones. Both timing and the amount of ice cream are part of the game scores. The excitement for this game led to over 8,000 persons downloading the game in one week.

Railroads, trucking companies, banks, retailers, technology firms, hotels, and many others are using gaming simulations. Doing so appears to increase employee interest in training, promises better training transfer, and improves performance and organizational results.[37]

Blended learning
Learning approach that combines short, fast-paced, interactive computer-based lessons and teleconferencing with traditional classroom instruction and simulation.

the solution seems to be blended learning, which combines short, fast-paced, interactive computer-based lessons and teleconferencing with traditional classroom instruction and simulation.[38] Deciding which training is best handled by which medium is important too. A blended learning approach uses e-learning for building knowledge of certain basics, a Web-based virtual classroom for building skills, and significant in-person traditional instructor-led training sessions and courses. Use of blended learning provides greater flexibility in the use of multiple training means and enhances the appeal of training activities to different types of employees.[39]

Advantages and Disadvantages of E-Learning The rapid growth of e-learning makes the Internet or an intranet a viable means for delivering training content. But e-learning has both advantages and disadvantages that must be considered.[40] In addition to being concerned about employee access to e-learning and desire to use it, some employers worry that trainees will use e-learning to complete courses quickly but will not retain and use much of what they learned. Taking existing training materials, putting them on the Internet, and cutting the training budget is not the way to succeed with e-learning. An important question is: Can this material be learned just as well on-line as through conventional methods?

In sum, e-learning is the latest development in training delivery. Some of the biggest obstacles to using it will continue to be keeping up with the rapid change in technological innovation, knowing when and how much to invest, and designing e-courses appropriately. Undoubtedly, e-learning will have a major impact on HR and training, but there are no "ten easy steps" to making e-learning successful. Figure 9-10 presents a listing of e-learning's most commonly cited advantages and disadvantages.

FIGURE 9-10   Advantages and Disadvantages of E-Learning

Advantages	Disadvantages
• Is self-paced; trainees can proceed on their own time • Is interactive, tapping multiple trainee senses • Enables scoring of exercises/assessments and the appropriate feedback • Incorporates built-in guidance and help for trainees to use when needed • Allows trainers to update content relatively easily • Can enhance instructor-led training • Is good for presenting simple facts and concepts	• May cause trainee anxiety • Some trainees may not be interested in how it is used • Requires easy and uninterrupted access to computers • Is not appropriate for some training (leadership, cultural change, etc.) • Requires significant up-front investment, both time and cost-wise • Requires significant support from top management to be successful

Source: Developed by Lisa A. Burke and Robert L. Mathis.

Developing E-Learning Rather than being adopted just for its efficiency, e-learning should meet strategic training needs.[41] Certain criteria to consider before adopting e-learning include the following:

- Sufficient top management support and funding must be committed to developing and implementing e-learning.
- Managers and HR professionals must be "re-trained" to accept the idea that training is being decentralized and individualized.
- Current training methods (compared with e-learning) are not adequately meeting organizational training needs.
- Potential learners are adequately computer literate and have ready access to computers and the Internet.
- Trainees attending training programs are geographically separated, and travel time and costs are concerns.
- Sufficient numbers of trainees exist, and many trainees are self-motivated enough to direct their own learning.

TRAINING EVALUATION

Evaluation of training compares the post-training results to the pre-training objectives of managers, trainers, and trainees. Too often, training is conducted with little thought of measuring and evaluating it later to see how well it worked. Because training is both time consuming and costly, it should be evaluated.[42]

Levels of Evaluation

It is best to consider how training is to be evaluated before it begins. Donald L. Kirkpatrick identified four levels at which training can be evaluated. As Figure 9-11 shows, the evaluation of training becomes successively more

FIGURE 9-11   **Levels of Training Evaluation**

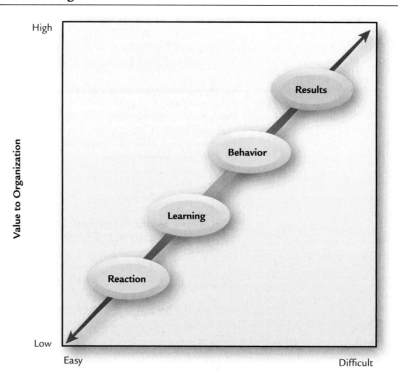

difficult as it moves from measuring reaction to measuring learning to measuring behavior and then to measuring results. But the training that affects behavior and results versus reaction and learning provides greater value in viewing training as a strategic performance contributor.

Reaction Organizations evaluate the reaction levels of trainees by conducting interviews with or administering questionnaires to the trainees. Assume that 30 managers attend a two-day workshop on effective interviewing skills. A reaction-level measure could be gathered by having the managers complete a survey that asked them to rate the value of the training, the style of the instructors, and the usefulness of the training to them. If the survey were administered immediately after the workshop, it might measure only how much the managers liked the training rather than how the training benefited them or how it affected the way they conduct interviews.

Learning Learning levels can be evaluated by measuring how well trainees have learned facts, ideas, concepts, theories, and attitudes. Tests on the training material are commonly used for evaluating learning, and they can be given both before and after training to provide scores that can be compared. If test scores indicate learning problems, then instructors get feedback and courses can be re-designed so that the content can be delivered more effectively. Of course, learning enough to pass a test does not guarantee that trainees will remember the training content months later or will change job behaviors.[43]

Behavior Evaluating training at the behavioral level means: (1) measuring the effect of training on job performance through interviews of trainees and their co-workers, and (2) observing job performance. But the evaluation should be broadly based and consider performance management improvements, not just be on the training events.[44] For instance, the managers who participated in the interviewing workshop might be observed conducting actual interviews of applicants for jobs in their departments. If the managers asked questions as they had been trained to and used appropriate follow-up questions, then behavioral indicators of the interviewing training exist. Behaviors are more difficult to measure than are reaction and learning. Even if behaviors do change after training, the results that management desires may not be obtained.

Results Employers evaluate results by measuring the effect of training on the achievement of organizational objectives. Because results such as productivity, turnover, quality, time, sales, and costs are relatively concrete, this type of evaluation can be done by comparing records before and after training. For the managers who attended the interviewing training, evaluators could gather records of the number of individuals hired compared with the number of employment offers made before and after the training.

The difficulty with measuring results is pinpointing whether changes were actually the result of training or of other major factors. For example, managers who completed the interviewing training program can be measured on employee turnover before and after the training. But turnover also depends on the current economic situation, the demand for workers, and many other variables.

Training Evaluation Metrics

Training is expensive, and it is an HR function that requires measurement and monitoring. Cost-benefit analysis and return on investment (ROI) analysis are commonly used to do so, as are various benchmarking approaches.

Cost-benefit analysis
Comparison of costs and benefits associated with training.

Cost-Benefit Analysis Training results can be examined through cost-benefit analysis, which is comparison of costs and benefits associated with training. There are four stages in calculating training costs and benefits[45]:

1. *Determine training costs.* Consider direct costs such as design, trainer fees, materials, facilities, and other administration activities.
2. *Identify potential savings results.* Consider employee retention, better customer service, fewer work errors, quicker equipment production, and other productivity factors.
3. *Compute potential savings.* Gather data on the performance results and assign dollar costs to each of them.
4. *Conduct costs and savings benefits comparisons.* Evaluate the costs per participant, the savings per participant, and how the cost-benefits relate to business performance numbers.

Internet Research

Workplace Basic Skills
For free tools to design, manage, and assess workplace education programs, visit this site at: http://thomsonedu .com/management/mathis.

One firm that has done cost-benefit analyses is the Cheesecake Factory restaurant chain. The firm uses HR metrics for many aspects of evaluating how over 100 general managers and their stores are performing. Scoring results are produced annually, quarterly, and monthly.[46]

Figure 9-12 shows some costs and benefits that may result from training. Even though some benefits (such as attitude changes) are hard to quantify, comparison of costs and benefits

FIGURE 9-12   Balancing Costs and Benefits of Training

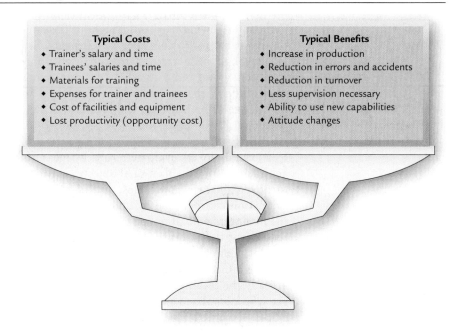

Typical Costs
- Trainer's salary and time
- Trainees' salaries and time
- Materials for training
- Expenses for trainer and trainees
- Cost of facilities and equipment
- Lost productivity (opportunity cost)

Typical Benefits
- Increase in production
- Reduction in errors and accidents
- Reduction in turnover
- Less supervision necessary
- Ability to use new capabilities
- Attitude changes

associated with training remains a way to determine whether or not training is cost effective. For example, one firm evaluated a traditional safety training program and found that the program did not lead to a reduction in accidents. Therefore, the safety training was re-designed, and better safety practices resulted. However, measurement of both the costs and the benefits listed in Figure 9-12 may be difficult.

Return on Investment Analysis In organizations, training is often expected to produce an ROI.[47] Still, in too many circumstances, training is justified because someone liked it, rather than on the basis of resource accountability. According to one study, firms that measure ROI on training spend 1% to 3% of payroll on training. But higher performing firms spend even more. The ROI of these companies has been determined to be 137% over five years, which is much more than the ROI at organizations spending less on training.[48] This study reveals that training can produce significant financial results for employers.

Benchmarking In addition to evaluating training internally, some organizations use benchmark measures to compare it with training done in other organizations. To do benchmarking, HR professionals gather data on training in their organization and compare them with data on training at other organizations in the same industry and of a similar size. Comparison data are available through the American Society for Training and Development and its Benchmarking Service. This service has training-related data from more than 1,000 participating employers who complete detailed questionnaires annually. Training also can be benchmarked against data from the American Productivity & Quality Center and the Saratoga Institute.

Training Evaluation Designs

With or without benchmarking data, internal evaluations of training programs can be designed in a number of ways. The rigor of the three designs discussed next increases with each level.

Post-Measure The most obvious way to evaluate training effectiveness is to determine after the training whether the individuals can perform the way management wants them to perform. Assume that a customer service manager has 20 representatives who need to improve their data-entry speeds. After a one-day training session, they take a test to measure their speeds. If the representatives can all type the required speed after training, was the training beneficial? It is difficult to say; perhaps most of them could have done as well before training. Tests after training do not always clearly indicate whether a performance is a result of the training or could have been achieved without the training.

Pre-/Post-Measure By differently designing the evaluation just discussed, the issue of pre-test skill levels can be considered. If the manager had measured the data-entry speed before and after training, she could have known whether the training made any difference. However, a question would have remained: Was any increase in speed a response to the training, or did these employees simply work faster because they knew they were being tested? People often perform better when they know their efforts are being evaluated.

Pre-/Post-Measure with a Control Group Another evaluation design can address the preceding problem. In addition to testing the 20 representatives who will be trained, the manager can test another group of representatives who will not be trained, to see if they do as well as those who are to be trained. This second group is called a control group. After training, if the trained representatives work significantly faster than those who were not trained, the manager can be reasonably sure that the training was effective.

SUMMARY

- Training is the process that provides people with the capabilities they need to do their jobs.
- Four types of training are regular/required, job/technical, interpersonal/problem solving, and developmental/career in nature.
- A strategic approach to training links organizational strategies and HR planning to various training efforts.
- Training affects factors such as organizational competitiveness, knowledge management, revenue, and performance.
- Performance consulting compares desired and actual results in order to identify needed training and non-training actions.
- Global strategies must consider training as a key component, including intercultural competence training to prepare employees to respond more appropriately to situations encountered during global assignments.
- The training process consists of four phases: assessment, design, delivery, and evaluation.
- Training needs can be assessed using organizational, job/task, and individual analyses, and then training objectives can be set to help the organization meet those needs.
- Training design must consider learner readiness, learning styles, and learning transfer.
- Training can be delivered internally through classes, informally, and on-the-job, or using different external means.
- Common training approaches include cooperative training and classroom/conference training.

- Orientation is a form of on-boarding designed to help new employees learn about their jobs.
- E-learning is training conducted using the Internet or an intranet, and its development must consider both its advantages and its disadvantages.
- Various organizations are taking advantage of training that uses technology, such as Web-based multimedia, video streaming, simulation, and virtual reality.
- Training can be evaluated at four levels: reaction, learning, behavior, and results.
- Training evaluation metrics may include cost-benefit analysis, return-on-investment analysis, and benchmarking.
- A pre-/post-measure with a control group is the most rigorous design for training evaluation; other, less rigorous designs can be used as well.

REVIEW AND APPLICATION QUESTIONS

1. Assume that you want to identify training needs for a group of sales employees in a luxury-oriented jewelry store. What would you do?
2. Discuss why evaluating training is an important part of strategic training.
3. Develop a briefing for division managers that shows the advantages and disadvantages of e-learning. Use various Web sources, including the following Website: *www.astd.org*.

CASE

Training Crucial for Hotels

In the United States and worldwide, there are many different hotels for guests to select. Some are part of high-end, luxury hotel chains such as Ritz-Carlton and Four Seasons. Other chains have multiple levels such as Starwood with Sheraton, Four Points, and others, and Marriott Corporation with a range of brands from Marriott resorts to Fairfield Inns.

One common characteristic that all of these hotels have identified is how crucial training is. Hotel executives have learned that high-quality service is usually what determines if guests will return to their facilities, even more so than price. Consequently, having a well-trained hotel staff is crucial to delivering the high-quality customer service guests expect. The focus of much of the training is on creating positive organizational cultures through all facilities and with all managers and employees. Many of these chains have expanded their training commitments by hiring more full-time trainers to work throughout all locations and areas. Several different types of training illustrate these efforts.

The Starwood collection of hotels (St. Regis, Westin, Sheraton, Four Points, W Hotels) sees a specific focus on training as a contributor to competitive success. Over a recent six-month period, Starwood trained its 185,000 workers on areas such as social skills, handling worker emotions, and conflict/problem solving. These elements are seen as crucial to providing successful customer service. The focus of the training is for employees to know more about the types of guests in the hotels and how to respond to different situations that occur. Managers and others at hotels are trained on such factors as ensuring eye contact, evaluating customer and employee body language signals, and flexibility in resolving problems.

Choice Hotels and other chains use role-playing as part of their training for hotel staff members. Handling families with kids, tired business travelers, and other types of individuals enhances the customer services culture in a facility. Another side benefit is that employees become less frustrated and stressed, which has reduced turnover and increased employee satisfaction.

The upscale Ritz-Carlton group has established the Mystique technology program. Individual guests' preferences can be entered and accessed by employees. This system can track what individual clients' preferences are for types of rooms, service that they have experienced, and even personal allergies. To implement this system and its use, the firm held train-the-trainer conferences. Then those trainers spread out and conducted training for hotel managers, local HR and training managers, and marketing/guest relations managers.

However, training just existing employees can be too limited. So Ritz-Carlton and other chains have revised their new employee orientation training. Integrating job-related details and how to use the Mystique system with customers is now part of the on-boarding process for employees at all levels, including housekeepers, desk clerks, restaurant servers, supervisors, and managers.

From these examples, it is evident that many hotels are investing significantly in training. The payoffs of the training are likely to be seen in more satisfied guests, better-performing employees, and increased organizational revenues and profits.[49]

Questions

1. Discuss how these hotels are using a strategic and performance consulting approach to developing training efforts.

2. Identify how the effectiveness of Ritz-Carlton's Mystique program might be measured several years later.

SUPPLEMENTAL CASE

The New Payroll Clerk

This case identifies the frustration that often accompanies the first day at work and why orientation often is important in aiding employee retention. (For the case, go to http://thomsonedu.com/management/mathis.)

NOTES

1. Based on Margery Weinstein, "IBM: Suite Success," *Training*, March 2006, 18–22; and Jessica Marquez, "Faced with High Turnover, Retailers Boot Up E-Learning for Quick Training," *Workforce Management*, August 2005, 74–75.
2. Kathryn Tyler, "Training Revs Up," *HR Magazine*, April 2005, 58–63.
3. *ASTD State of the Industry Report*, 2006, www.astd.org.
4. Based on Jessica Marquez, "Randstad North America," *Workforce Management*, March 13, 2006, 18.
5. S. P. Lopez, J. M. M. Peon, and C. J. V. Ordas, "Human Resource Management as a Determining Factor in Organizational Learning," *Management Learning*, 37 (2006), 215.
6. Robert Rodriguez, "Meet the New Learning Executive," *HR Magazine*, April 2005, 64.
7. Nick van Dam, "The New CLO," *Chief Learning Officer*, August 2006, 13.
8. J. J. Smith, "U.S. Workers Tech Skills Decline While India, Eastern Europe Grew," *SHRM Global HR News*, September 2006, www.shrm.org/global.
9. Yoshitaka Yamazaki and D. Christopher Hayes, "An Experiential Approach to Cross Cultural Learning. . . ." *Academy of Management Learning and Education*, 3 (2004), 362–379.
10. John G. Schieman, "Establishing an Effective Cross-Cultural Training Program and Measuring Benefits," *ASTD Links*, July 2006, www.astd.org.
11. Sharon Daniels, "Employee Training: A Strategic Approach to Better Return on Investment," *Journal of Business Strategy*, 24 (2003), 1–4.
12. John O'Connor, "Shifting Mindsets," *E-Learning Age*, April 2006, 14–17.
13. Sarah Cook, "Assessing Learning Needs," *Training Journal*, September 2005, 32.
14. Yu-Hui Tao, C. R. Yeh, and S. I. Sun, "Improving Training Needs Assessment Via the Internet: System Design and Qualitative Study," *Internet Research*, 16 (2006), 427.
15. Jacqueline Red and Maria Vakola, "What Role Can a Training Needs Analysis Play in Organizational Change?" *Journal of Organizational Change Management*, 19 (2006), 393.
16. Nicholas Clarke, "The Politics of Training Needs Assessment," *Journal of Workplace Learning*, 15 (2003), 141–153.
17. Sara B. Kimmel and Mary N. McNeese, "Barriers to Business Education: Motivating Adult Learners," *Journal of Behavioral and Applied Management*, 7 (2006), 292.
18. Gerard H. Seijts and Gary P. Latham, "Learning Versus Performance Goals: When Should Each Be Used?" *Academy of Management Executive*, February 2005, 124–131.
19. Gary P. Latham and Trevor C. Brown, "The Effect of Learning vs. Outcome Goals on Self-Efficacy, Satisfaction, and Performance in an MBA Program," *Applied Psychology*, 55 (2006), 606.
20. Gary L. Karns, "Learning Style Differences in the Perceived Effectiveness of Learning Activities," *Journal of Marketing Education*, 28 (2006), 56.
21. Malcolm S. Knowles, Elwood F. Holton III, and Richard A. Swanson, *The Adult Learner*, 6th ed. (New York: Elsevier, 2005).

22. Paul Hager, "Lifelong Learning in the Workplace? Challenges and Issues," *Journal of Workplace Learning*, 16 (2004), 22–32.

23. Gary N. McLean, "Rethinking Adult Learning in the Workplace," *Advances in Developing Human Resources*, August 2006, 416.

24. Karen Evans et al., "Recognition of Tacit Skills: Sustained Learning Outcomes in Adult Learning," *International Journal of Training and Development*, 8 (2004), 54–72.

25. Mel Siberman, *Active Training* (New York: Pfeffer, 2006).

26. P. J. Taylor, D. F. Russ-Eft, and D. W. L. Chan, "A Meta-Analytic Review of Behavior Modeling," *Journal of Applied Psychology*, 90 (2005), 692–709.

27. James P. Cavanaugh, "Training Versus Knowledge Transfer," *Emergency Number Professional Magazine*, September 2006, 26–30.

28. Alan M. Saks and Monica Belcourt, "An Investigation of Training Activities and Transfer of Training in Organizations," *Human Resource Management*, 45 (2006) 629.

29. Doo Hun Lim and Michael Lane Morris, "Influence of Trainee Characteristics, Instructional Satisfaction, and Organizational Climate on Perceived Learning and Training Transfer," *Human Resource Development Quarterly*, 17 (2006) 85.

30. Mark E. Van Buren, *ASTD State of the Industry Report, 2003* (Alexandria, VA: American Society of Training and Development, 2005), 11–12, *www.astd.org*.

31. "Mergers Transforming Outsourced Training," *Workforce Management*, May 22, 2006, 28.

32. "How 3 Companies Make New-Hire Training Mean Business," *Managing Training and Development*, September 2002, 1–3.

33. "That Tricky First 100 Days," *The Economist*, July 15, 2006, 65.

34. *Onboarding Benchmark Report* (Boston, MA: Aberdeen Group, Inc., 2006).

35. Margaret O. Kirk, "E-Orientation," *Human Resource Executive*, October 16, 2005, 40–43.

36. American Society of Training and Development, *www.astd.org*.

37. Based on Kim Fernandez, "Purposeful Playing," *Human Resource Executive*, October 2, 2006, 43–47; Reena Jana, "On-the-Job Video Gaming," *Business Week*, March 27, 2006, 43; and Michael Totty, "Better Training Through Gaming," *The Wall Street Journal*, April 25, 2005, R6.

38. Allison Rossett, "How Blended Learning Changes What We Do," *ASTD Learning Circuits*, 2006, *www.learningcircuits.org*.

39. Hemant Mirocha, "Learning Strategies: Blended Instruction," *Chief Learning Officer*, June 2005, 20–23.

40. Michael A. Tucker, "E-Learning Evolves," *HR Magazine*, October 2005, 75–78.

41. Andrew E. Hinger, Viki Holten, and Eddie Blass, "E-Learner Experiences: Key Questions to Ask When Considering Implementing E-Learning," *Industrial and Commercial Training*, 38 (2006), 143.

42. Gregg G. Wang and Diane Wilcox, "Training Evaluation: Knowing More Than Is Practiced," *Advances in Developing Human Resources*, 4 (2006), 528.

43. Mark A. Davis, "Evaluating Cognitive Training Outcomes," *Journal of Business and Psychology*, 18 (2003), 191–206.

44. Robert O. Brinkerhoff, "Increasing Impact of Training Investments: An Evaluation Strategy for Building Organizational Learning Capability," *Industrial and Commercial Training*, 38 (2006), 302.

45. "Calculate the Cost and Benefits of Training," *Workforce Management*, 2005, *www.workforce.com*.

46. Guna Ruiz, "A Heaping Help of Metrics," *Workforce Management*, April 24, 2006, 26.

47. For an extensive discussion of ROI on training, see Michael E. Echols, *ROI on Human Capital Investment* (Lincoln, NE: iUniverse, Inc., 2006).

48. Tom Casey and Carey Guggenheim, *Buch Consultants*, June 6, 2005, *www.workforce.com*.

49. Based on Jacqueline Dunett, "Ritz-Carlton: Plug In and Perform," *Training*, March 2006, 30–34; and Barbara DeLollis, "Hotels Train Employees to Think Fast," *USA Today*, November 29, 2006, 1B.

CHAPTER 10

Talent Management and Development

After you have read this chapter, you should be able to:

- Identify the importance of talent management and discuss two issues it addresses.

- Differentiate between organization-centered and individual-centered career planning.

- Discuss three career issues that organizations and employees must address.

- List options for development needs analyses.

- Identify several management development methods.

- Explain what succession planning is and its components.

HR Headline

The Importance of Talent Management

Recently the emphasis on talent management has appeared on the HR scene in organizations of all sizes and industries. Some forces behind the emphasis on talent management have included:

- The impending retirement of "baby boomers" worldwide
- Shortages of skilled workers of all types and levels
- Increasing global competition for human resource talent
- Growth in technology capable of automating talent management processes

These and other factors have forced organizations to develop a more strategic, integrated, and automated approach to talent management. For example, TNS North America, a market research firm, has automated the use of individual employee competency assessment and development and linked these assessments to their performance management processes. In the U.S. federal government, the Office of Personnel Management has developed requirements and guidelines. Called the "Human Capital Standards for Success," they are designed to increase talent management practices such as training, development, and career planning across the entire federal civilian workforce of approximately 1.8 million workers.

As these examples illustrate, talent management has escalated in importance. Hence, additional organizations are likely to focus on it the near future.[1]

Traditionally, employee training and development activities have been the responsibility of HR. However, a broader look has led to a more integrated effort labeled talent management, as the HR Headline identifies. **Talent management** is concerned with enhancing the attraction, development, and retention of key human resources. Over half of all HR professionals reported that their organizations recently had established talent management initiatives.[2]

Talent management must be linked to strategic organizational plans.[3] Key areas that are important in talent management as part of strategic HR planning are:

- Creating and maintaining an organizational culture that values individuals
- Identifying the future needs of the organization and how to develop individuals to fill those needs
- Developing a pool of talented people who can supply future job needs
- Establishing ways to conduct and manage HR activities to support talent development

Talent management is seen as more crucial than ever as the demographics of workforces change. For example, estimates are that manufacturers will need up to 10 million new highly skilled workers in the next decade. Also, U.S. employers are anticipated to lose over 10% of their current workforce by 2010 due to retirements of baby boomers.[4]

Global employers are also facing talent management issues. One survey of companies in 16 countries found that having qualified individuals to fill future jobs is a major concern. In some countries, such as the United States, France, and Japan, replacing experienced individuals who retire is a major challenge. In other countries with rapidly growing populations, such as China and Brazil, having adequately trained individuals who can perform additional jobs is a concern. Therefore, building talent and retaining it should be a priority worldwide.[5]

NATURE OF TALENT MANAGEMENT

Talent management can be seen as a bridge. As illustrated in Figure 10-1, talent management activities provide the means to ensure that individuals who have been recruited and selected are retained as well-performing human

FIGURE 10-1   Talent Management Bridge

resources. Talent management activities include training, individual career planning, and HR development efforts. Additionally, succession planning involves identifying future workforce needs and what candidates will be available to fill them. Throughout the talent management process, effective performance management activities are vital, as discussed in the next chapter.

One firm that has developed a talent management system is Pitney-Bowes (PB). For years PB had training, development, succession planning, and performance management efforts. However, these activities were not linked well. Now, use of integrated software systems means that PB is more engaged in talent management efforts, not just having a collection of uncoordinated HR activities.[6]

Talent Management Information Systems

A vital part of talent management is the implementation and use of electronic, Web-based, computer software. Vendors have developed software for various parts of talent management, such as tracking training, providing succession planning replacement charts, or online performance appraisal systems. But these systems must be integrated, rather than run as separate programs. The need for such integration is seen in a survey that concluded that 40% of all talent management systems have little or no integration of the various elements.[7] The HR On-Line illustrates how one firm has benefited from a better e-development system.

HR ONLINE

E-Development at Linens-n-Things

As talent management and development needs are changing HR practices, more and more organizations are automating phases of their development processes. One company doing this is Linens-n-Things, the home furnishings retailer. Linens-n-Things has more than 500 stores throughout the United States and Canada and more than 27,000 employees. Several years ago, Linens-n-Things started working with Learn.com to automate training and development to a wider audience of employees. Some of the activities that have been successful components of e-learning have included:

- Documenting new employee orientations and the on-boarding training regardless of how and where it is done
- Tracking classroom training and certifications completed by all store employees
- Automating registration of participants for training and development activities

- Reporting on completions of training certifications for store employees
- Compiling and reporting the training and development history of individuals for use with career planning and development

Once the system was automated and training implemented, Linens-n-Things began to see results. At any time, HR can access a "snapshot" of who and how many have completed development opportunities and who did not. When store sales and employee retention were subsequently measured, a direct correlation was found between new hire certifications and store results and customer effectiveness. Results like these epitomize the reason why an increasing number of organizations are automating many facets of their development processes.[8]

Scope of Talent Management

As talent management has evolved, some design issues have been identified. Each of these issues reflects differences in how talent management is viewed and the organizational priorities that exist.[9]

Targeting Jobs The first issue is to identify the types of jobs that will be the focus of talent management. In some organizations talent management focuses on the CEO and other executive jobs, rather than more broadly. Other organizations target primarily senior-management jobs, mid-level managers, and other key jobs. One study found that of the groups and individuals seen as "talent," 86% were senior leaders, 82% were mid-managers, and 75% were key technical and other contributors. However, those three groups only represent about one-third of the total workforces of many employers.[10]

Targeting High-Potential Individuals Another issue associated with talent management is how it is used with individuals in organizations. One problem identified with fulfilling effective talent management needs is that managers at all levels are not committed to the time and effort required, which can limit successful activities.[11]

Some organizations focus talent management efforts primarily on "high-potential" individuals, often referred to as "high-pos." Attracting, retaining, and developing high-pos have become emphases of senior managers and HR efforts. Some firms classify individuals as being in the top 10% and then set limits on the number of people who can participate in intensive talent management efforts. For instance, IBM limited participation in its leadership development programs to only those who were likely to become executives within 18 months.[12]

Other organizations view talent management more broadly. Targeting primarily high-pos may lead to many of the other employees seeing their career opportunities as being limited. Thus, talent management may need to include more than the top 10%.

Regardless of the focus, effective talent management must be linked to HR planning. This means having the *right number of human resources*, with the *right capabilities*, at the *right times*, and in the *right places*, both short term and longer term, as Figure 10-2 indicates.

FIGURE 10-2   **Effective Talent Management**

CAREERS AND CAREER PLANNING

Career Series of work-related positions a person occupies throughout life.

A career is the series of work-related positions a person occupies throughout life. People pursue careers to satisfy individual needs. Careers are an important part of talent managment, but both individuals and organizations view careers in distinctly different ways.

Changing Nature of Careers

The old model of a career in which a person worked his or her way up the ladder in one organization is becoming rarer. Indeed, in a few industries, changing jobs and companies every year or two is becoming more common. U.S. workers in high-demand jobs, such as information technologists and pharmacists, often dictate their own circumstances to some extent. For instance, the average 30- to 35-year-old in the United States typically may have already worked for up to seven different firms. However, physicians, teachers, economists, and electricians do not change jobs as frequently. As would be expected, valuable employees even in some of these professions who are deluged with job offers switch jobs at a higher rate than in the past.

Careers and Work–Life Balance Various signs indicate that the patterns of individuals' work lives are changing in many areas: more freelancing, more working at home, more frequent job changes, more job opportunities but less security. Rather than letting jobs define their lives, more people set goals for the type of lives they want and then use jobs to meet those goals. However, for dual-career couples and working women, balancing work demands with personal and family responsibilities is difficult to do.

For employers, career issues have changed too. The best people will not go to workplaces viewed as undesirable, because they do not have to do so. Employers must focus on retaining and developing talented workers by providing coaching, mentoring, and appropriate assignments.

Global Evolution of Careers Insecurity caused by layoffs and downsizings marks a trend that contrasts with the trend toward personal control over career goals. A number of older male American workers express fear of losing their jobs. This situation is not just a U.S. phenomenon. Many Japanese workers who have typically worked for the same company their entire lives are experiencing similar job insecurity. In Europe, employers are pressuring different governments to dismantle outmoded labor rules that make eliminating employees difficult, while workers are pressuring the same governments to alleviate high unemployment rates. As a result worldwide, careers for many individuals contain both more flexibility and more insecurity.

Organization-Centered Career Planning

Careers are different from before, and their evolution puts a premium on career development by both the employers and the employees. Effective career planning considers both organization-centered and individual-centered perspectives. Figure 10-3 summarizes the perspectives and interaction between the organizational and individual approaches to career planning.

FIGURE 10-3   Organizational and Individual Career Planning Perspectives

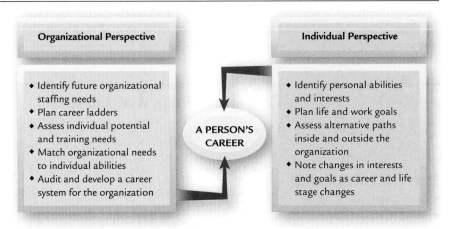

Organizational Perspective

- Identify future organizational staffing needs
- Plan career ladders
- Assess individual potential and training needs
- Match organizational needs to individual abilities
- Audit and develop a career system for the organization

A PERSON'S CAREER

Individual Perspective

- Identify personal abilities and interests
- Plan life and work goals
- Assess alternative paths inside and outside the organization
- Note changes in interests and goals as career and life stage changes

Organization-centered career planning Career planning that focuses on identifying career paths that provide for the logical progression of people between jobs in an organization.

Organization-centered career planning focuses on identifying career paths that provide for the logical progression of people between jobs in an organization. Individuals follow these paths as they advance in organizational units. For example, a person might enter the sales department as a sales representative, then be promoted to account director, to sales manager, and finally to vice president of sales.

Top management and HR professionals are responsible for developing career planning programs. A good program includes many elements of talent management, such as performance appraisal, development activities, opportunities for transfer and promotion, and some planning for succession. To communicate with employees about opportunities and to help with planning, employers frequently use career workshops, a career "center" or newsletter, and career counseling. Individual managers frequently play the role of coach and counselor in their direct contact with individual employees and within an HR-designed career management system.

The systems that an employer uses should be planned and managed in an integrated fashion to guide managers in developing employees' careers. One such system is the career path, or "map," which is created and shared with the individual employee.

Career Paths Employees need to know their strengths and weakness, and they often discover those through company-sponsored assessments. Then, career paths to develop the weak areas and fine-tune the strengths are developed. Career paths represent employees' movements through opportunities over time. Although most career paths are thought of as leading upward, good opportunities also exist in cross-functional or horizontal directions.

Career paths Represent employees' movements through opportunities over time.

Working with employees to develop career paths has aided employers in retaining key employees. At EchoStar Communications, use of a career path program has led to greater retention of entry-level call center employees. Career progression opportunities are identified to employees who perform well and who see EchoStar as a place to stay and grow career-wise.[13]

Employer Websites and Career Planning Many employers have careers sections on their Websites. Such sections can be used to list open jobs for current employees looking to change jobs. An employer's Website is a link to the external world, but should also be seen as a link to existing employee development. Sites also can be used for career assessment, information, and instruction. When designing Websites, firms should consider the usefulness of the careers section for development as well as recruitment.

Individual-Centered Career Planning

Organizational changes have altered career plans for many people. Individuals have had to face "career transitions"—in other words, they have had to find new jobs. These transitions have identified the importance of individual-centered career planning, which focuses on an individual's responsibility for a career rather than on organizational needs. It is done by the employees themselves when they analyze their individual goals and capabilities. Such efforts might consider situations both inside and outside the organization that could expand a person's career. Individuals are the only ones who can know for certain what they consider to be successful careers, but they do not always act to that end. For example, few college students enrolled in business programs know exactly what they want to do upon graduation; many can eliminate some types of jobs but might be interested in any of several others.

Individual Career Planning Components For individuals to successfully manage their own careers, they should perform several activities. The three key ones are as follows:

- *Self-assessment:* Individuals need to think about what interests them, what they do not like, what they do well, and their strengths and weaknesses. Career advisors use a number of tools to help people understand themselves. Common professional tests include the Strong Interest Inventory to determine preferences among vocational occupations, and the Allport-Vernon-Lindzey Study of Values to identify a person's dominant values.
- *Feedback on reality:* Employees need feedback on how well they are doing, how their bosses see their capabilities, and where they fit in organizational plans for the future. One source of this information is through performance appraisal feedback and career development discussions.
- *Setting of career goals:* Deciding on a desired path, setting some timetables, and writing down these items all set the stage for a person to pursue the career of choice. These career goals are supported by short-term plans for the individual to get the experience or training necessary to move forward toward the goals.

Individual Career Choices Four general individual characteristics affect how people make career choices:

- *Interests:* People tend to pursue careers that they believe match their interests. But over time, interests change for many people, and career decisions eventually are made based on special skills, abilities, and career paths that are realistic for them.
- *Self-image:* A career is an extension of a person's self-image, as well as a molder of it. People follow careers they can "see" themselves in and avoid those that do not fit with their perceptions of their talents, motives, and values.
- *Personality:* An employee's personality includes her or his personal orientation (for example, inclination to be realistic, enterprising, or artistic) and personal needs (including affiliation, power, and achievement needs). Individuals with certain personality types gravitate to different clusters of occupations.

Individual-centered career planning Career planning that focuses on an individual's responsibility for a career rather than on organizational needs.

■ *Social backgrounds:* Socioeconomic status and the educational levels and occupations of a person's parents are included in that person's social background. Children of a physician or a welder know from a parent what that job is like and may either seek or reject it based on how they view the parent's job.

Less is known about how and why people choose specific organizations than about why they choose specific careers. One obvious factor is timing—the availability of a job when the person is looking for work. The amount of information available about alternatives is an important factor as well. Beyond these issues, people seem to pick an organization on the basis of a "fit" of the climate of the organization as they view it and their own personal characteristics, interests, and needs.

Career Progression Considerations

The typical career of many individuals today includes more positions, transitions, and organizations—more so than in the past, when employees were less mobile and organizations were more stable as long-term employers. Therefore, it is useful to think about general patterns in people's lives and the effects on their careers.

Theorists in adult development describe the first half of life as the young adult's quest for competence and for a way to make a mark in the world. According to this view, a person attains happiness during this time primarily through achievement and the acquisition of capabilities.

The second half of life is different. Once the adult starts to measure time from the expected end of life rather than from the beginning, the need for competence and acquisition changes to the need for integrity, values, and well-being. For many people, internal values take precedence over external scorecards or accomplishments such as wealth and job title status. In addition, mature adults already possess certain skills, so their focus may shift to interests other than skills acquisition. Career-ending concerns, such as life after retirement, reflect additional shifts. Figure 10-4 shows a model that identifies general career and life periods.

Contained within this life pattern is the idea that careers and lives are not predictably linear but cyclical. Individuals experience periods of high stability followed by transition periods of less stability, and by inevitable discoveries,

---

FIGURE 10-4   **General Career Periods**

CAREER STAGE

Characteristics	Early Career	Mid-Career	Late Career	Career End
Age group	+/− 20 years	30–40 years	+/− 50 years	60–70 years
Needs	Identifying interests, exploring several jobs	Advancing in career; lifestyle may limit options, growth, opportunities	Updating skills; individual is settled in; individual is a leader whose opinions are valued	Planning for retirement, examining non-work interests
Concerns	External rewards, acquiring more capabilities	Values, contribution, integrity, well-being	Mentoring, disengaging, organizational continuance	Retirement, part-time employment

disappointments, and triumphs. These cycles of structure and transition occur throughout individuals' lives and careers. This cyclical view may be an especially useful perspective for individuals affected by downsizing or early career plateaus in large organizations. Such a perspective argues for the importance of flexibility in an individual's career. It also emphasizes the importance of individuals' continuing to acquire more and diverse knowledge, skills, and abilities.

Late-Career/Retirement Issues Whether retirement comes at age 50 or age 70, it can require a major adjustment for many people. Some areas of emotional adjustment faced by many retirees include self-direction, a need to belong, sources of achievement, personal space, and goals. To help address concerns over these issues, as well as anxieties about finances, some employers offer pre-retirement planning seminars for employees.

U.S. companies will face a severe shortage of badly needed skills in the coming decade unless they act now to convince top-performing older employees to delay or phase in their retirement.[14] Career development for people toward the ends of their careers may be managed in a number of ways.[15] Phased-in retirement, consulting arrangements, and callback of some retirees as needed all act as means for gradual disengagement between the organization and the individual. However, phased-in retirement (which is widely seen as a good situation for all involved) faces major obstacles in current pension laws. Under many pension plans, employees who are working may not receive pension benefits until they reach a normal retirement age.

Forced early retirement often occurs as a result of downsizings and organizational restructurings. These events have required thousands of individuals, including many managers and professionals, to determine what is important to them while still active and healthy. As a result, some of these people begin second careers rather than focusing primarily on leisure activities or travel. To be successful with early retirement, management must avoid several legal issues, such as forced early retirement and pressuring older workers to resign.

Career Plateaus Those who do not change jobs may face another problem: career plateaus. Many workers define career success in terms of upward mobility. As the opportunities to move up decrease, some employers try to convince employees they can find job satisfaction in lateral movement. Such moves can be reasonable if employees learn new skills that increase individual marketability in case of future layoffs, termination, or organizational re-structurings.[16]

One strategy for individuals to get off career plateaus is to take seminars and university courses. This approach may reveal new opportunities for plateaued employees. Rotating workers to other departments is another way to deal with career plateaus. A computer chip manufacturer instituted a formal "poaching" program that encouraged managers to recruit employees from other departments, thereby giving employees greater opportunities to experience new challenges without having to leave the employer. Some plateaued individuals change careers and go into other lines of work altogether. Figure 10-5 shows a portable career path that one might encounter under those career situations. In summary, plateaued employees present a particular challenge for employers. They can affect morale if they become negative, but they may also represent valuable resources that are not being well used.

FIGURE 10-5   Portable Career Path

Beginning	Expanding	Changing	Sustaining	Concluding
Spend several years at large company to learn skills and build network	Use networking to develop broader skills and make contacts; establish good reputation	Change industries, or go to work for smaller companies; start a company	Refresh skills; take a sabbatical; go back to school; gain experience in non-profit organizations	Move to projects as a temporary employee or subcontractor

Career Transitions and HR

Career transitions can be stressful for individuals who change employers and jobs.[17] Three career transitions are of special interests to HR: organizational entry and socialization, transfers and promotions, and job loss.

Starting as a new employee can be overwhelming. "Entry shock" is especially difficult for younger new hires who find the work world very different from school. Entry shock includes the following concerns:

- *Supervisors:* The boss/employee relationship is different from the student/teacher relationship.
- *Feedback:* In school, feedback is frequent and measurable, but that is not true of most jobs.
- *Time:* School has short (quarter/semester) time cycles, whereas time horizons are longer at work.
- *The work:* Problems are more tightly defined at school; at work, the logistical and political aspects of solving problems are less certain.

Transfers and promotions offer opportunities for employees to develop. However, unlike new hires, employees who have moved to new positions are often expected to perform well immediately, though that may not be realistic. International transfers cause even more difficulties than in-country transfers for many.

Job loss as a career transition has been most associated with downsizing, mergers, and acquisitions. Losing a job is a stressful event in one's career, frequently causing depression, anxiety, and nervousness. The financial implications and the effects on family can be extreme as well. Yet the potential for job loss continues to increase for many individuals, and effectively describing their concerns should be considered in career transition decision making.[18]

SPECIAL INDIVIDUAL CAREER ISSUES

The goals and perspectives in career planning may differ for organizations and individuals, but three issues can be problematic. Those issues are highlighted next.

Technical and Professional Workers

Technical and professional workers, such as engineers, scientists, physical therapists, and IT systems experts, present a special challenge for organizations. Many of these individuals want to stay in their technical areas rather than enter management; yet advancement in many organizations frequently requires a move into management. Most of these people like the idea of the responsibility and opportunity associated with professional advancement, but they do not want to leave the professional and technical puzzles and problems at which they excel.

Dual-career ladder
System that allows a person to advance up either a management or a technical/professional ladder.

An attempt to solve this problem, a dual-career ladder, is a system that allows a person to advance up either a management or a technical/professional ladder. Dual-career ladders are now used at many firms, most commonly in technology-driven industries such as pharmaceuticals, chemicals, computers, and electronics. For instance, a telecommunications firm created a dual-career ladder in its IT department to reward talented technical people who do not want to move into management. Different tracks, each with attractive job titles and pay opportunities, are provided. Some health-care organizations are using "master" titles for senior experienced specialists such as radiologists and neonatal nurses who do not want to be managers. The masters often are mentors and trainers for younger specialists. Unfortunately, the technical/professional ladder may be viewed as "second-class citizenship" within some organizations.

Women and Careers

According to the U.S. Bureau of Labor Statistics, the percentage of women in the workforce has more than doubled since 1970, and will reach almost 50% by 2010. Women are found in all occupations and jobs, but their careers may have a different element than those of men. Women give birth to children, and in most societies they are also primarily responsible for taking care of their children. The effect of this biology and sociology is that women's careers are often interrupted for childbirth and child rearing.

Work, Family, and Careers The career approach for women frequently is to work hard before children arrive, plateau or step off the career track when children are younger, and go back to career-focused jobs that allow flexibility when they are older. This approach is referred to as *sequencing*. But some women who sequence are concerned that the job market will not welcome them when they return, or that the time away will hurt their advancement chances. Thus, many women's careers are stifled due to their career interruptions.[19]

The interaction and conflicts among home, family, and a career affect the average woman differently than they do men.[20] By the time men and women have been out of school for six years, many women may have worked on average 30% less time than men.[21] These and other career differences provide different circumstances for many females. Employers can tap into the female labor market to a greater extent with child-care assistance, flexible work policies, and a general willingness to be accommodating.

Glass Ceiling Another concern specifically affecting women is the "glass ceiling." This issue describes the situation in which women fail to progress into top and senior management positions. Nationally, women hold about half of managerial/professional positions but only 10% to 15% of corporate officer positions.[22] Some organizations provide leaves of absence, often under FMLA provisions, but take steps to keep women who are away from work involved in their companies. Some have used e-mentoring for women temporarily off their jobs. Other firms use "phased returns" whereby women employees return to work part-time and then gradually return to full-time schedules. Consequently, in the United States, women are making slow but steady strides into senior management and executive positions.

Dual-Career Couples

As the number of women in the workforce continues to increase, particularly in professional careers, so does the number of dual-career couples. The U.S. Bureau of Labor Statistics estimates that over 80% of all couples are dual-career couples. Marriages in which both mates are managers, professionals, or technicians have doubled over the past two decades.[23] Problem areas for dual-career couples include family issues and job transfers that require relocations.

Family-Career Issues For dual-career couples with children, family issues may conflict with career progression. Thus, one partner's flexibility may depend on what is "best" for the family. Additionally, it is important that the career development problems of dual-career couples be recognized as early as possible. Whenever possible, having both partners involved in planning, even when one is not employed by the company, may enhance the success of such efforts.

Relocation of Dual-Career Couples Traditionally, employees accepted transfers as part of upward mobility in organizations. However, for some dual-career couples, the mobility required because of one partner's transfer often interferes with the other's career. In addition to having two careers, dual-career couples often have established support networks of co-workers, friends, and business contacts to cope with both their careers and their personal lives. Relocating one partner in a dual-career couple may mean upsetting this carefully constructed network for the other person or creating a "commuting" relationship. Recruiting a member of a dual-career couple to a new location may mean HR assistance in finding an equally attractive job available for the candidate's partner at the new location or offering HR assistance in finding a job for the non-employee person. The HR On-the-Job highlights the global relocation issues faced by firms with employees having dual-career jobs. That is one common global career concern.

Global Career Concerns

Many global employees experience anxiety about their continued career progression. Therefore, the international experiences of expatriates must offer benefits both to the employer and to expatriates' careers as well. Firms sometimes address this issue by bringing expatriates back to the home country for development programs and interaction with other company managers and professionals. Another useful approach is to establish a mentoring system that matches an expatriate with a corporate executive at the headquarters.

Repatriation Another global HR issue is repatriation, which involves planning, training, and reassignment of global employees to their home countries.

Repatriation Planning, training, and reassignment of global employees to their home countries.

HR ON-THE-JOB

Handling Global Dual-Career Situations

Special difficulties exist when individuals transfer to overseas jobs. For example, a spouse who wants to work may not be able to get a work permit, may find that local residents have priority in the job market, or may find incompatible certification/licensing. In particular, women partners may have difficulty finding employment opportunities in certain countries due to cultural and religious considerations. According to one survey, only 21% of spouses and partners of expatriates are employed during their partners' international assignments. That is a significant drop from the 61% who are working prior to the international move. This disparity is one reason why a number of expatriates do not complete the full term of their overseas jobs.[24]

When setting HR policies for global employee relocation assistance, organizations must consider the concerns of dual-career couples. The following approaches can help them reduce the problems faced in such situations:

- Pay employment agency fees for the relocating partner.
- Compensate for a designated number of trips for the partner to look for a job in the proposed new location.
- Help the partner find a job in the same company or in another division or subsidiary of the company in the new geographic location.
- Develop computerized job banks to share with other global companies and employers in the new area that list partners available for job openings.

For example, after expatriates are brought home, they no often longer receive special compensation packages available to them during their assignments. The result is that they experience a net decrease in total income, even if they receive promotions and pay increases. In addition to dealing with concerns about personal finances, returning expatriates must often re-acclimate to U.S. lifestyles, transportation services, and other cultural circumstances, especially if they have been living in less-developed countries.

Back in the home organization, repatriated employees must re-adjust to closer working and reporting relationships with other corporate employees. Often, expatriates have had a greater degree of flexibility, autonomy, and independent decision making than their counterparts in the United States.

Another major concern focuses on the organizational status of expatriates upon return.[25] Many expatriates wonder what jobs they will have, whether their international experiences will be valued, and how they will be accepted back into the organization. Unfortunately, many global employers do a poor job of repatriation. To counter this problem, some companies provide career planning, the mentoring programs mentioned earlier, and even guarantees of employment on completion of foreign assignments.

Global Development Issues Global managers are more expensive than home-country managers, and more problematic as well. Most global firms have learned that it is often a mistake to staff foreign operations with only personnel from headquarters, and they quickly hire nationals to work in a country. For this reason, global management development must focus on developing local managers as well as global executives. Development areas typically include such items as cultural issues, running an international business, leadership/management skills, handling problematic people, and personal qualities.[26]

DEVELOPING HUMAN RESOURCES

Development Efforts to improve employees' abilities to handle a variety of assignments and to cultivate employees' capabilities beyond those required by the current job.

Development represents efforts to improve employees' abilities to handle a variety of assignments and to cultivate employees' capabilities beyond those required by the current job. Development benefits both organizations and individuals. Employees and managers with appropriate experiences and abilities may enhance organizational competitiveness and the ability to adapt to a changing environment. In the development process, individuals' careers also may evolve and gain new or different focuses.

Because development differs from training, in many organizations greater focus is being placed on development rather than simply on training.[27] It is possible to train many people to answer customer service questions, drive a truck, enter data in a computer system, or assemble a television. However, development in areas such as judgment, responsibility, decision making, and communication presents a bigger challenge. These areas may or may not develop through life experiences of individuals. As a key part of talent management, a planned system of development experiences for all employees, not just managers, can help expand the overall level of capabilities in an organization. Figure 10-6 profiles development and compares it with training.

Internet Research

Academy of Human Resource Development

For research resources on human resource development, theories, processes, and practices, link to this site at: http://thomsonedu .com/management/mathis.

At the organizational level of analysis, executives craft the broader organizational strategies and should establish a system for developing the people to manage and achieve those identified strategies. Development must be tied to this strategic planning because the firm needs to develop appropriate talents to carry out the plans. Successful HR development focuses on employee and managerial succession on several levels and in several different pathways as part of that development.

Developing Specific Capabilities/Competencies

Exactly what kind of development individuals might require to expand their capabilities depends on both the individuals and the capabilities needed. As

FIGURE 10-6   Development vs. Training

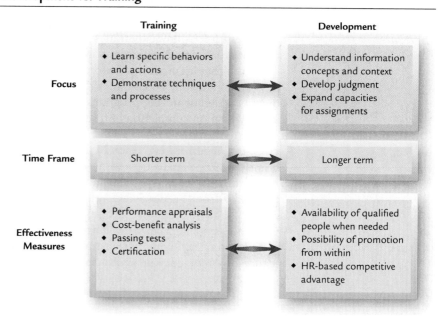

a result, development is more difficult in certain areas than in others.[28] Some important and common management capabilities often include an action orientation, quality decision-making skills, ethical values, and technical skills. Ability to build teams, develop subordinates, direct others, and deal with uncertainty are equally important but much less commonly developed capabilities for successful managers. For some tech specialties (tech support, database administration, network design, etc.), certain non-technical abilities must be developed as well: ability to work under pressure, to work independently, to solve problems quickly, and to use past knowledge in a new situation.

One point about development is clear: in numerous studies that asked employees what they want out of their jobs, training and development ranked at or near the top. Because the primary assets that individuals have are their knowledge, skills, and abilities (KSAs), many people view the development of their KSAs as an important part of the organizational package that affects retention and performance.

Lifelong Learning Learning and development are closely linked. For most people, lifelong learning and development are likely and desirable. For many professionals, lifelong learning may mean meeting continuing education requirements to retain certificates. For example, lawyers, CPAs, teachers, dentists, and nurses must complete continuing education requirements in most states to keep their licenses to practice. For other employees, learning and development may involve training to expand existing skills and to prepare for different jobs, for promotions, or even for new jobs after retirement.

Assistance from employers for needed lifelong development typically comes through programs at work, including tuition reimbursement programs. However, much of lifelong learning is voluntary, takes place outside work hours, and is not always formal. Although it may have no immediate relevance to a person's current job, learning often can enhance the individual's confidence, ideas, or enthusiasm.

Re-Development Whether due to a desire for career change or because the employer needs different capabilities, people may shift jobs in mid-life or mid-career. Re-developing people in the capabilities they need is logical and important. In the last decade, the number of college enrollees over the age of 35 has increased dramatically. But helping employees go back to college is only one way of re-developing them. Some companies offer re-development programs to recruit experienced workers from other fields. For example, different firms needing truck drivers, reporters, and IT workers have sponsored second-career programs. Public-sector employers have been using re-development opportunities as a recruiting tool as well.

Development Needs Analyses

Like employee training, employee development begins with analyses of the needs of both the organization and the individuals. Either the company or the individual can analyze what a given person needs to develop. The goal, of course, is to identify strengths and weaknesses. Methods that organizations use to assess development needs include assessment centers, psychological testing, and performance appraisals.

Assessment centers
Collections of instruments and exercises designed to diagnose individuals' development needs.

Assessment Centers Assessment centers are collections of instruments and exercises designed to diagnose individuals' development needs. Organizational leadership uses assessment centers for both developing and selecting managers. Many types of employers use assessment centers for a wide variety of jobs.

In a typical assessment-center experience, an individual spends two or three days away from the job performing many assessment activities. These activities might include role-playing, tests, cases, leaderless-group discussions, computer-based simulations, and peer evaluations. Frequently, they also include in-basket exercises, in which the individual handles typical work and management problems. For the most part, the exercises represent situations that require the use of individual skills and behaviors. During the exercises, several specially trained judges observe the participants.

Assessment centers provide an excellent means for determining individual potential. Management and participants often praise them because they are likely to overcome many of the biases inherent in interview situations, supervisor ratings, and written tests. Experience shows that key variables such as leadership, initiative, and supervisory skills cannot be measured with tests alone. Assessment centers also offer the advantage of helping identify employees with potential in large organizations. Supervisors may nominate people for the assessment center, or employees may volunteer. For talented people, the opportunity to volunteer is invaluable because supervisors may not recognize their potential interests and capabilities.

Assessment centers can also raise concerns.[29] Some managers may use the assessment center to avoid making difficult promotion decisions. Suppose a plant supervisor has personally decided that an employee is not qualified for promotion. Rather than being straightforward and informing the employee, the supervisor sends the employee to the assessment center, hoping the report will show that the employee is unqualified for promotion. Problems between the employee and the supervisor may worsen if the employee earns a positive report. Using the assessment center for this purpose does not aid the development of the employee but does occur.

Psychological Testing Psychological tests have been used for several years to determine employees' development potential and needs. Intelligence tests, verbal and mathematical reasoning tests, and personality tests are often given. Psychological testing can furnish useful information on individuals about such factors as motivation, reasoning abilities, leadership style, interpersonal response traits, and job preferences.

The biggest problem with psychological testing lies in interpretation, because untrained managers, supervisors, and workers usually cannot accurately interpret test results. After a professional scores the tests and reports the scores to someone in the organization, untrained managers may attach their own meanings to the results. Also, some psychological tests are of limited validity, and test takers may fake desirable responses. Thus, psychological testing is appropriate only when the testing and feedback processes are closely handled by a qualified professional.

Performance Appraisals Well-done performance appraisals can be a source of development information. Performance data on productivity, employee relations, job knowledge, and other relevant dimensions can be gathered in such assessments. As noted in Chapter 11, appraisals designed for development purposes may be different and more useful in aiding individual employee development than appraisals designed strictly for administrative purposes.

HR DEVELOPMENT APPROACHES

The most common development approaches can be categorized under three major headings, as Figure 10-7 depicts. Investing in human intellectual capital, whether on or off the job or in learning organizations, becomes imperative as "knowledge work," such as research skills and specialized technology expertise, increases for almost all employers. But identifying the right mix and approaches for development needs for different individuals requires analyses and planning.

Job-Site Development Approaches

All too often, unplanned and perhaps useless activities pass as development on the job. To ensure that the desired development actually occurs, managers must plan and coordinate their development efforts.[30] Managers can choose from various job-site development methods.

Coaching Training and feedback given to employees by immediate supervisors.

Coaching The oldest on-the-job development technique is coaching, which is the training and feedback given to employees by immediate supervisors. Coaching involves a continual process of learning by doing. For coaching to be effective, employees and their supervisors or managers must have a healthy and open relationship. Many firms conduct formal courses to improve the coaching skills of their managers and supervisors.

The use of coaching is increasing, and its success is being seen in companies throughout the world.[31] One type of coaching that is growing is *team coaching*. This approach focuses on coaching groups of individual employees on how to work more effectively as parts of workforce teams. Such team efforts may utilize outside consultants and cover many different areas. Group coaching on leadership may help create high-performance teams.[32]

Unfortunately, organizations may be tempted to implement coaching without sufficient planning. Even someone who is good at a job or a particular part of a job will not necessarily be able to coach someone else to do it well. "Coaches" can easily fall short in guiding learners systematically, even if they know

Internet Research

Feroce Coaching
For information about this consulting firm's coaching techniques and services, visit their Website at:
http://thomsonedu.com/management/mathis.

FIGURE 10-7   HR Development Approaches

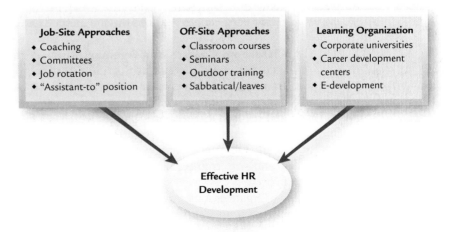

which experiences are best. Often the coach's job responsibilities take priority over learning and coaching of subordinates. Also, the intellectual component of many capabilities might be better learned from a book or a course before coaching occurs. Therefore, outside consultants often are used as coaches.

Committee Assignments Assigning promising employees to important committees may broaden their experiences and help them understand the personalities, issues, and processes governing the organization. For instance, employees on a safety committee can gain a greater understanding of safety management, which would help them to become supervisors. They may also experience the problems involved in maintaining employee safety awareness. However, managers need to guard against committee assignments that turn into time-wasting activities.

Job rotation Process of shifting a person from job to job.

Job Rotation The process of shifting a person from job to job is called job rotation, which is widely used as a development technique. For example, a promising young manager may spend three months in the plant, three months in corporate planning, and three months in purchasing. When properly handled, such job rotation fosters a greater understanding of the organization and aids with employee retention by making individuals more versatile, strengthening their skills, and reducing boredom.[33] When opportunities for promotion within a smaller or medium-sized organization are scarce, job rotation through lateral transfers may help rekindle enthusiasm and develop employees' talents. A disadvantage of job rotation is that it can be expensive because a substantial amount of time is required to acquaint trainees with the different people and techniques in each new unit.

"Assistant-To" Positions Some firms create "assistant-to" positions, which are staff positions immediately under a manager. Through such jobs, trainees can work with outstanding managers they might not otherwise have met. Some organizations set up "junior boards of directors" or "management cabinets" to which trainees may be appointed. These assignments provide useful experiences if they present challenging or interesting assignments to trainees.

Off-Site Development Approaches

Off-the-job development techniques give individuals opportunities to get away from their jobs and concentrate solely on what is to be learned. Moreover, contact with others who are concerned with somewhat different problems and come from different organizations may provide employees with new and different perspectives. Various off-site methods are used.

Classroom Courses and Seminars Most off-the-job development programs include some classroom instruction. Most people are familiar with classroom training, which gives it the advantage of being widely accepted. But the lecture system sometimes used in classroom instruction encourages passive listening and reduced learner participation, which is a distinct disadvantage. Sometimes trainees have little opportunity to question, clarify, and discuss the lecture material. The effectiveness of classroom instruction depends on multiple factors: group size, trainees' abilities, instructors' capabilities and styles, and subject matter.

Organizations often send employees to externally sponsored seminars or professional courses, such as those offered by numerous professional and consulting entities. Many organizations also encourage continuing education by reimbursing employees for the costs of college courses. Tuition reimbursement programs provide incentives for employees to study for advanced degrees through evening and weekend classes that are outside their regular workdays and hours.

Outdoor Development Experiences Some organizations send executives and managers off to ordeals in the wilderness, called *outdoor training* or *outdoor development*. The rationale for using these wilderness excursions, which can last one day or even seven days or longer, is that such experiences can increase self-confidence and help individuals re-evaluate personal goals and efforts. For individuals in work groups or teams, shared risks and challenges outside the office environment can create a sense of teamwork. The challenges may include rock climbing in the California desert, whitewater rafting on a river, backpacking in the Rocky Mountains, or handling a longboat off the coast of Maine.

Survival-type management development courses may have more impact than many other management seminars. But companies must consider the inherent perils. Some participants have been unable to handle the physical and emotional challenges associated with rappelling down a cliff or climbing a 40-foot tower. The decision to sponsor such programs should depend on the capabilities of the employees involved.[34]

Sabbatical Time off the job to develop and rejuvenate oneself.

Sabbaticals and Leaves of Absence A sabbatical is time off the job to develop and rejuvenate oneself. Some employers provide paid sabbaticals while others allow employees to take unpaid sabbaticals. Popular for many years in the academic world, sabbaticals have been adopted in the business community as well. About 17% of U.S. corporations offer unpaid sabbaticals, while only 6% provide paid sabbaticals.[35] Some firms give employees three to six months off with pay to work on "socially desirable" projects.[36] Such projects have included leading training programs in urban ghettos, providing technical assistance in foreign countries, and participating in corporate volunteer programs to aid non-profit organizations.

Companies that offer sabbaticals speak well of the results. Positive reasons for sabbaticals are to help prevent employee burnout, offer advantages in recruiting and retention, and boost individual employee morale. Women employees have made use of sabbaticals or leaves for family care reasons. The value of this time off to employees is seen in better retention of key women, who also often return more energized and enthusiastic about their work–life balancing act.[37] One obvious disadvantage of paid sabbaticals is the cost.[38] Also, the nature of the learning experience generally falls outside the control of the organization, leaving it somewhat to chance.

Learning Organization Development Efforts

As talent management becomes more important, employers may attempt to become *learning organizations*. These organizations encourage development efforts through shared information, culture, and leadership that stresses the importance of individual learning. This approach focuses on employees who want to develop new capabilities. A learning mindset is probably difficult to introduce into an organization where it does not exist. But where it does exist, it represents a significant potential for development. Figure 10-8 depicts some possible means for developing employees in a learning organization.

FIGURE 10-8   Possible Means for Developing Employees in a Learning Organization

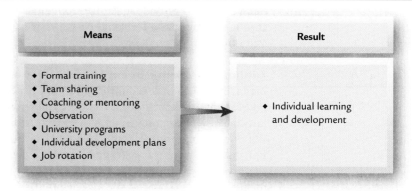

Means	Result
◆ Formal training ◆ Team sharing ◆ Coaching or mentoring ◆ Observation ◆ University programs ◆ Individual development plans ◆ Job rotation	◆ Individual learning and development

Knowledge-based organizations that deal primarily with ideas and information must have employees who are experts at one or more conceptual tasks. These employees continuously learn and solve problems in their areas of expertise. Developing such employees requires an "organizational learning capacity" based on solving problems and learning new ways not previously used.

Corporate Universities and Career Development Centers Large organizations may use corporate universities to develop managers or other employees. Corporate universities take various forms. Sometimes regarded as little more than fancy packaging for company training, they may not provide a degree, accreditation, or graduation in the traditional sense. A related alternative, partnerships between companies and traditional universities, can occur where the universities design and teach specific courses for employers.

Career development centers are often set up to coordinate in-house programs and programs provided by suppliers. They may include assessment data for individuals, career goals and strategies, coaching, seminars, and on-line approaches.

E-Development The rapid growth in technology has led to more use of e-development. On-line development can take many forms, such as video conferencing, live chat rooms, document sharing, video and audio streaming, and Web-based courses. HR staff members can facilitate on-line development by providing a *learning portal,* which is a centralized Website for news, information, course listings, business games, simulations, and other materials.

On-line development allows participation in courses previously out of reach due to geographic or cost considerations. It allows costs to be spread over a larger number of people, and it can be combined with virtual reality and other technological tools to make presentations more interesting. It can eliminate travel costs as well. When properly used, e-development is a valuable HR development tool. However, the lack of realism can diminish the learning experience. The focus must be learning, not just "using the technology."

MANAGEMENT DEVELOPMENT

Although development is important for all employees, it is essential for managers. Without appropriate development, managers may lack the capabilities to best deploy and manage resources (including employees) throughout the organization.

Experience plays a central role in management development. Indeed, experience often contributes more to the development of senior managers than does classroom training, because much of it occurs in varying circumstances on the job over time. Yet, in many organizations it is difficult to find managers for middle-level jobs. Some individuals refuse to take middle-management jobs, feeling that they are caught between upper management and supervisors. Similarly, not all companies take the time to develop their own senior-level managers. Instead, senior managers and executives often are hired from the outside. Figure 10-9 shows experience-based sources of managers' learning and lists some lessons important in effectively developing supervisors, middle managers, and senior-level executives.

Internet Research

Management Resource Group
For free publications on management and leadership development, link to this site at: http://thomsonedu.com/management/mathis.

A number of approaches are used to mold and enhance the experiences that managers need to be effective. The most widely used methods are supervisor development, leadership development, management modeling, management coaching, management mentoring, and executive education.

Supervisor Development

At the beginning level for managerial development is the first-line supervisory job. It is often difficult to go from being a member of the work group to being the boss. Therefore, the new supervisors who are used to functioning as individual contributors often require new skills and mindsets to be successful supervisors.

A number of employers conduct *pre-supervisor training*. This effort is done to provide realistic job previews of what supervisors will face and to convey to individuals that they cannot just rely on their current job skills and experience in their new positions.

FIGURE 10-9   **Management Lessons Learned from Job Experience**

SOURCES OF MANAGERS' LEARNING

Job Transitions	**Challenges**	**Obstacles**
◆ New jobs ◆ Problems ◆ New people ◆ Changes in responsibilities	◆ Starting or changing some major organizational feature ◆ Having decision-making responsibility ◆ Influencing others without formal authority	◆ A bad job situation ◆ A difficult boss ◆ Demanding clients ◆ Unsupportive peers ◆ Negative economic circumstances

LESSONS MANAGERS NEED TO LEARN

- *Setting agendas:* Developing technical/business knowledge, taking responsibility, setting goals
- *Handling relationships:* Dealing successfully with people
- *Management values:* Understanding successful management behavior
- *Personality qualities:* Having the temperament necessary to deal with the chaos and ambiguity of executive life
- *Self-awareness:* Understanding oneself and how one affects others

Development for supervisors may vary but usually contains common elements. The usual materials for supervisor training and development include several topics: basic management responsibilities, time management, and human relations topics.

Human Relations Training This type of training attempts to prepare supervisors to deal with "people problems" brought to them by their employees. The training focuses on the development of the human relations skills a person needs to work well with others. Most human relations programs typically are aimed at new or relatively inexperienced first-line supervisors and middle managers. They cover motivation, leadership, employee communication, conflict resolution, team building, and other behavioral topics.

The most common reason employees fail after being promoted to management is poor teamwork with subordinates and peers. Other common reasons for management failure include not understanding expectations, failure to meet goals, difficulty adjusting to management responsibilities, and inability to balance work and home lives.

Leadership Development

Organizations are aware that effective leaders create positive change and are important for organizational success. Firms such as Johnson & Johnson, General Electric, and 3M Company are among the top firms in leadership development.[39] An SHRM survey found that 80% of organizations use multiple types of leadership development efforts. Activities include seminars, coaching, job rotation, mentoring, and other means. Firms often target "high-potential" individuals for leadership development as part of meeting future staffing needs.[40]

Management Modeling

A common adage in management development says that managers tend to manage as they were managed. In other words, managers learn by behavior modeling, or copying someone else's behavior. This tendency is not surprising, because a great deal of human behavior is learned by modeling. Children learn by modeling the behaviors of parents and older children. Management development efforts can take advantage of natural human behavior by matching young or developing managers with appropriate models and then reinforcing the desirable behaviors exhibited by the learners. The modeling process involves more than straightforward imitation or copying. For example, one can learn what not to do by observing a model who does something wrong. Thus, exposure to both positive and negative models can benefit a new manager as part of leadership development efforts.

Management Coaching

In the context of management development, coaching involves a relationship between two individuals for a period of time as they perform their jobs. Effective coaching requires patience and good communication skills. Coaching combines observation with suggestions. Like modeling, it complements the natural way humans learn. A brief outline of good coaching pointers often includes the following:

- Explaining appropriate behaviors
- Making clear why actions were taken
- Accurately stating observations

- Providing possible alternatives/suggestions
- Following up and reinforcing behaviors used

A specific application of coaching is use of *leadership coaching*.[41] Companies use outside experts as executive coaches to help managers improve interpersonal skills or decision-making skills. In some cases they are used to help deal with problematic management styles. Consultants as executive coaches predominantly come from a psychology or counseling background and can serve many roles for a client by providing key questions and general directions. Sometimes they meet in person, but many do their coaching by phone. Research on the effectiveness of coaching suggests that coaching can be beneficial in dealing with chronic stress, psychological, and even physiological problems faced by executives and managers.[42]

Management Mentoring

Management mentoring
Relationship in which experienced managers aid individuals in the earlier stages of their careers.

A method called **management mentoring** is a relationship in which experienced managers aid individuals in the earlier stages of their careers. Such a relationship provides an environment for conveying technical, interpersonal, and organizational skills from the more-experienced person to a designated less-experienced person. Not only does the inexperienced employee benefit, but the mentor may enjoy the challenge of sharing his or her wisdom.

Fortunately, many individuals have a series of advisors or mentors during their careers and may find advantages in learning from the different mentors. For example, the unique qualities of individual mentors may help less-experienced managers identify key behaviors in management success and failure. Additionally, those being mentored may find previous mentors to be useful sources for networking. Figure 10-10 describes the four stages in most successful mentoring relationships.

FIGURE 10-10   **Stages in Management Mentoring Relationships**

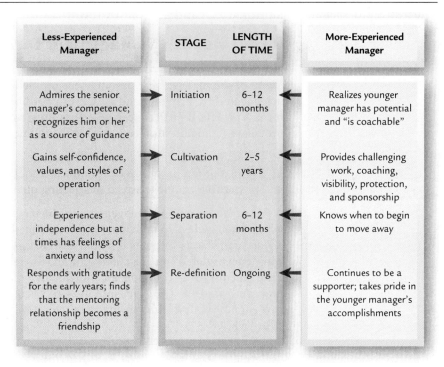

Less-Experienced Manager	STAGE	LENGTH OF TIME	More-Experienced Manager
Admires the senior manager's competence; recognizes him or her as a source of guidance	Initiation	6–12 months	Realizes younger manager has potential and "is coachable"
Gains self-confidence, values, and styles of operation	Cultivation	2–5 years	Provides challenging work, coaching, visibility, protection, and sponsorship
Experiences independence but at times has feelings of anxiety and loss	Separation	6–12 months	Knows when to begin to move away
Responds with gratitude for the early years; finds that the mentoring relationship becomes a friendship	Re-definition	Ongoing	Continues to be a supporter; takes pride in the younger manager's accomplishments

Management Mentoring for Women and Minorities In virtually all countries in the world, the proportion of women holding management jobs is lower than the proportion of men holding such jobs. Similarly, the number of minorities who fill senior management positions is less than 10%. Unfortunately, younger minority employees and managers have difficulty finding mentors. Company mentoring programs that focus specifically on women and individuals of different racial/ethnic backgrounds have been successful in a number of larger firms. Based on various narratives of successful women executives, breaking the glass ceiling requires developing political sophistication, building credibility, and refining management styles aided by mentoring.

Reverse Mentoring An interesting shift in mentoring has been called *reverse mentoring*. This type occurs when younger, less-experienced employees mentor older higher-level managers and executives. Using Generation X workers who are more adept at technology to train the baby boomers is one key use of reverse mentoring. Such efforts also can be beneficial for the younger workers who can learn about the organizational culture and leadership experiences from the older workers. Also, the older worker gets updated on new technology, marketing ideas, and other current trends. For instance, a key higher-level manager knew nothing about blogs and wikis, but was shown by a younger professional how those technology tools can be used.[43]

Executive Education

Executives in an organization often face difficult jobs due to changing and unknown circumstances. "Churning" at the top of organizations and the stresses of executive jobs contribute to increased turnover in these positions. In an effort to decrease turnover and increase management development capabilities, organizations are using specialized education for executives. This type of training includes executive education traditionally offered by university business schools and adds strategy formulation, financial models, logistics, alliances, and global issues. Enrollment in Executive Masters of Business Administration (EMBA) degree programs is popular also.

Problems with Management Development Efforts

Development efforts are subject to certain common mistakes and problems. Many of the management development problems in firms have resulted from inadequate HR planning and a lack of coordination of HR development efforts. The HR Best Practices describes how Mattel has counteracted these problems. Common problems include the following:

- Failing to conduct adequate needs analysis
- Trying out fad programs or training methods
- Substituting training instead of selecting qualified individuals

Another common management problem is *encapsulated development,* which occurs when an individual learns new methods and ideas, but returns to a work unit that is still bound by old attitudes and methods. The development was "encapsulated" in the classroom and is essentially not used on the job. Consequently, it is common for individuals who participate in development programs paid for by their employers to become discouraged and move to new employers that allow them to use their newly developed capabilities more effectively.

HR BEST PRACTICES

Mattel Develops

Mattel is well known in the toy and game industry. With 25,000 employees globally, the need for coordinated development efforts has been recognized. The first part of Mattel's effort has been led by its CEO, who recognized the need to change the Mattel culture and develop a broad-based strategy. At the heart of Mattel's efforts are having development programs that create a more skilled and productive workforce and a succession plan to help retain HR talent. Implementing these efforts resulted in Mattel receiving an Optimas Award from *Workforce Management.*

Some efforts have led to creating a more integrated corporate culture. For instance, the "Barbie" girls groups and the boys "Hot Wheels" groups did not interact and work together effectively. Putting these employees together under the same division required extensive training in areas such as marketing, design, product development, and other topics. Development facilitators met with groups of 10 to 12 employees throughout the world to reinforce the culture change efforts.

Another part of Mattel's talent management has been expanding its learning efforts. A digital training center offers over 200 e-development courses to Mattel employees worldwide. For continuing development, managers are expected to identify potential leaders and develop succession plans for key positions. Such efforts have led to increased employee retention, and the company and its workforce are better positioned for the intensive competitive nature of its industry and markets.[44]

SUCCESSION PLANNING

Succession planning
Process of identifying a long-term plan for the orderly replacement of key employees.

Planning for the succession of key executives, managers, and other employees is an important part of talent management. Succession planning is the process of identifying a long-term plan for the orderly replacement of key employees. In many industries succession planning is increasingly seen as a major concern. The primary cause is the huge workforce changes and shortages that are expected to occur as the baby-boomer generation continues to retire. The U.S. Census Bureau has estimated that over 75 million baby boomers will retire or be planning retirement transitions by 2010.[45]

Often the employees in the firms tapped to take the boomers' jobs are currently in their 30s and 40s and have 10 to 15 years of work experience. But these employees often have work–family issues that impact their careers. For instance, with women composing almost half of the U.S. workforce, some women in this group may have small children and may want to work part-time or shorter weeks. However, their jobs may not be compatible with such flexibility, which may affect succession planning and leadership development opportunities for them.

Internet Research

SCORE–Counselors to America's Small Business
For an overview of how to develop a succession plan, visit this site at:
http://thomsonedu.com/management/mathis.

Succession Planning Process

Whether in small or large firms, succession planning is linked to strategic HR planning through the process shown in Figure 10-11. In that process, both the quantity and the capabilities of potential successors must be linked to organizational strategies and plans.[46]

FIGURE 10-11   Succession Planning Process

Two coordinated activities begin the actual process of succession planning. First, the development of preliminary replacement charts ensures that the right individuals with sufficient capabilities and experience to perform the targeted jobs are available at the right time. Replacement charts (similar to depth charts used by football teams) both show the backup "players" at each position and identify positions without current qualified backup players. The charts identify who could take over key jobs if someone leaves, retires, dies unexpectedly, or otherwise creates a vacancy. Second, assessment of the capabilities and interests of current employees provides information that can be placed into the preliminary replacement charts.

With that information, a formal succession plan is prepared as a guide for future use. Next, HR development and career planning efforts should be linked to the succession plans. Finally, the succession plan should be reviewed and revised regularly.

HR's Role in Succession Planning Often HR has the primary responsibility for succession planning organization-wide. However, for CEO and senior management succession efforts, top executives and board members often have major involvement. Because of this, HR often performs the following actions[47]:

- Identifying development needs of the workforce
- Assisting executives/managers in identifying needed future job skills
- Participating in noting employees who might fill future positions
- Communicating succession planning process to employees
- Aiding in tracing and regularly updating succession plan efforts

Global Succession Planning Succession planning is not just a U.S. issue. In fact, the percentage of aging population in the workforce is even higher in countries such as Japan, Germany, Italy, and England. In those countries, as well as the United States, the growth of immigrants has added to the population, which also means that both legal and workforce diversity issues are facing employers. Even in countries with growing workforces, such as China and India, succession planning is important. Having younger workers who can replace senior managers with international experiences and contacts is a growing concern faced worldwide by employers of different sizes and industries.

Succession in Small and Closely Held Organizations Succession planning can be especially important in small and medium-sized firms, but studies show that few of these firms formalize succession plans.[48] In fact, more than half of the respondents in one study named lack of succession planning as the biggest threat facing small businesses.[49] In closely held family firms (those that are not publicly traded on stock exchanges), multiple family members often are involved. But in others, the third- and fourth-generation family members are not employees and many do not want to be involved, other than as owners or as members of the Board of Directors.[50]

Even if many CEOs plan to pass the business leadership on to a family member, most of these firms would benefit from planning for orderly succession, particularly if non-family members or owners are involved. Addressing the development needs of the successor also helps to avoid a host of potential problems for both the organization and family-member relationships. One survey found that in about one-third of family businesses in Australia, the CEOs have not identified who would replace them upon retirement or for personal reasons (health problems, death, etc.).[51] Similar results are common in smaller U.S. firms also.

Succession Planning Considerations

A number of areas should be considered as part of succession planning. One is succession for different types of jobs and how to anticipate filling those jobs.

"Make or Buy" Talent? To some extent, employers face a "make-or-buy" choice: develop ("make") competitive human resources, or hire ("buy") them already developed from somewhere else.[52] Many organizations show an apparent preference for buying rather than making scarce employees in today's labor market. Current trends indicate that technical and professional people usually are "bought" because of the amount of skill development already achieved, rather than internal individuals being picked because of their ability to learn or their behavioral traits. However, hiring rather than developing internal human resource capabilities may not fit certain industry competitive environments.

Other organizations are focusing on growing their own leaders. Wachovia, the large financial firm, has created a leadership program for its 1,500 HR professionals that has been successful. That program is now being expanded to other professional groups in Wachovia.[53] Like any financial decision, the make-or-buy decision can be quantified and calculated when some assumptions are made about time and costs.

Succession Planning Skill Areas Another focus of succession planning is shown in Figure 10-12. Note that when developing succession plans for jobs and identifying candidates, focusing only on management skills may be too narrow. For example, assume that succession planning for a Vice President of Operations at a hospital is being done. That position must have candidates who have industry contacts, community involvement, leadership and management capabilities, and other competencies. These items are especially important if the current VP has extensive experience and numerous internal and external capabilities.

Electronic/Web-Based Succession Planning The expansion of information technology capabilities has resulted in employers being able to have succession planning components available electronically to staff members. HR departments have skills tracking systems and databases that can be linked to succession plans. As employees complete training and development activities, their data can be updated and viewed as career openings occur in the company.

Via intranet systems, employees can access and update their databases, review job and career opportunities, and complete skill and career interest self-surveys and numerous other items. Also online, 360° reviews of managers by others can be useful for aiding with leadership development. Such a system has been used successfully by Pep Boys, the large retail automotive chain.[54] The Pep Boys system creates a grid that managers can review that links employee performance ratings and results to potential career movements.[55]

FIGURE 10-12   Areas for Planning "Succession"

Values of Succession Planning

Many employers are doing succession planning formally or informally. But to justify these efforts, it is important that determinations be made to identify the benefits and value of succession planning.[56] Key benefits include:

- Having an adequate supply of employees to fill future key openings
- Providing career paths and plans for employees, which aids in employee retention and performance motivation
- Continually reviewing the need for individuals as organizational changes occur more frequently
- Enhancing the organizational "brand" and reputation as a desirable place to work

Metrics and Succession Planning Some organizations measure the impact of succession planning. A wide range of metrics are used depending on the company plans.[57] One key measure is identifying the reduced costs of turnover, which is related to employee retention. For instance, a mid-sized bank's turnover of "high-potential" employees declined significantly after conducting an organization-wide succession plan. Estimates of the turnover savings were done by the HR Director, and the median cost per key employee "saved" was over $15,000 per person.

Another factor to consider is how succession planning and its follow-up may lead to higher performance and organizational profitability.[58] A study of organizations such as Apple Computers, General Electric, Merck, Hewlett-Packard, Motorola, Verizon, and other major companies was done. The study used benchmark and quantitative measures to show that succession planning provided significant financial returns.[59]

Common Succession Planning Mistakes The greatest succession focus of Boards of Directors is on CEO succession.[60] The reasons why boards have increased the priority of CEO succession have become more complex due to regulatory and other changes. Specifically, Sarbanes-Oxley Act provisions have added more demands on boards to do CEO succession planning.[61] However, one survey found that about half of board members of firms felt their CEO succession planning efforts were less effective than needed.[62]

Focusing only on CEO and top management succession is one of the most common mistakes made.[63] Other mistakes include:

- Starting too late, when openings are occurring
- Not linking well to strategic plans
- Allowing the CEO to direct the planning and make all succession decisions
- Looking only internally for succession candidates

All of these mistakes are caused by lack of preparation for succession planning. A study found that about 50% of corporations have insufficient preparation, which results in less effective succession planning.[64] An example of the importance of succession planning is seen in the banking industry. Regulatory provisions and auditors are requiring banks to have succession plans identified for top management jobs. Also, law firms are recognizing the importance of succession planning as more senior partners retire.[65]

Longer-term succession planning should include mid-level and lower-level managers, as well as other key non-management employees.[66] Some firms target key technical, professional, and sales employees as part of succession planning. Others include customer service representatives, warehouse specialists, and additional hourly paid employees who may be able to move up into other jobs or departments.

Succession planning is an important part of employers seeing talent management strategically. Actions such as career planning, HR development efforts, and succession planning are aiding in fulfilling the expectations and goals important for future workforce needs.

SUMMARY

- Talent management is growing in importance, because it is concerned with attraction, development, and retention of human resources.
- Training, career planning, succession planning, and performance management are crucial parts of talent management.
- The nature of careers is changing as retention of employees and work–life balance have become more important.
- Career planning may focus on organizational needs, individual needs, or both, and career paths and employer Websites are part of career planning.
- A person chooses a career according to interests, self-image, personality, social background, and other factors.
- Several special individual career issues must be addressed, including those related to technical and professional workers.
- Career issues for women may include work–family balancing and glass ceiling concerns, as well as being part of dual-career couples.
- Global career development has special challenges, including relocations of dual-career couples, global development, and repatriation.
- Development differs from training because it focuses on less tangible aspects of performance, such as attitudes and values.
- Developing specific competencies may require lifelong learning and re-development of employees.

- Needs analyses for development may include assessment centers, psychological testing, and performance appraisals.
- HR development approaches can involve job-site, off-site, and learning organization activities.
- On-the-job development methods include coaching, committee assignments, job rotation, and "assistant-to" positions.
- Off-site development means often include classroom courses, seminars, and degrees, outdoor experiences, sabbaticals, and leaves of absences.
- Learning organization development efforts reflect knowledge-based means, such as corporate universities and centers and e-development efforts.
- Management development is a special focus in many organizations, including supervisor development and leadership development.
- Management modeling, coaching, and mentoring are valuable parts of management development efforts.
- Succession planning is the process that identifies how key employees are to be replaced and includes whether to make or buy talent and electronic and Web-based succession planning.
- A number of different mistakes can occur in succession planning, including focusing only on CEO and senior management succession.

REVIEW AND APPLICATION QUESTIONS

1. Discuss what talent management is and why it is a consideration being addressed by a growing number of employers.
2. Why is succession planning important in businesses of all sizes today?
3. Describe the broad range of talent management efforts that use software applications by going to *www.learn.com*. Then give some examples of firms that have successfully used these applications.

CASE

Equipping for the Future

Many employers facing industry job shifts also are confronted by workforce changes due to retirement of key executives and employees. One firm that has "drilled" well in the oil equipment and services industry is National Oilwell Varco (NOV). Based in Houston, Texas, the firm has over 20,000 employees working in manufacturing, selling, and servicing oil and gas equipment.

Several years ago the CEO at NOV, Pete Miller, recognized that all of the senior management executives were baby boomers. The CEO realized that many of these executives would be retiring about the same time, so NOV would face a significant vacuum of talent to be replaced. Two senior executives were given the assignment to prepare for the changes, resulting in a plan labeled "Next Generation."

To generate a supply of potential leaders, technical professionals, and others, NOV had to broaden its recruiting process beyond the normal oil-based states, such as Texas, Louisiana, and Oklahoma. Miller also demanded that foreign candidates be considered, because of the expanding global oil market.

A specific focus of NOV recruiting efforts included foreign students at U.S. universities who had high English communication skills and other relevant capabilities. Up to 40 individuals at 10 universities were interviewed, and then the primary candidates went through two more interviews by NOV middle managers. Those candidates who "passed" this phase spent two days in Houston going through additional interviews and selection means. Finally, the individuals selected were offered jobs at NOV. This process has continued during the past several years.

Once the selected individuals go to work at NOV, they spend one year in job rotation, with four assignments of three months each in different business areas. This rotation provides the individuals with a broader view of NOV and its operations. During the rotation, candidates participate in various efforts, including development programs and mentoring by various division managers.

A unique part of NOV's talent management process is that after the individuals complete their one-year job rotation, they become "draft candidates." Modeled after the National Football League draft, each business unit identifies which individuals they want on their "team." After completing the draft, individuals get jobs in the different business units.

NOV's "Next Generation" program has been successful. The retention rate for the drafted candidates is over 90%, higher than normal in the industry. Also, its recruiting costs have declined. So there has been a payoff for both NOV and its employees. [67]

Questions

1   Discuss how NOV's efforts combine different phases of talent management to reach a successful result.

2. What are some of the possible advantages and disadvantages of the "draft approach" to placing candidates in business units?

SUPPLEMENTAL CASE

Developed Today, Gone Tomorrow

This case illustrates a serious concern that some employers have about developing employees only to have them leave. (For the case, go to http://thomsonedu .com/management/mathis.)

NOTES

1. Based on interviews and information provided by Michael Sabbag, 2007, at Learn.com, *www.learn.com.*

2. "2006 Talent Management Survey Report," *SHRM Research,* 2006, *www.shrm.org.*

3. Nancy R. Lockwood, "Talent Management: Driver for Organizational Success," *SHRM Research Quarterly,* Second Quarter 2006, 1–11.

4. Molly Bernhart, "Preparing for a Skills Shortage, Work Intensification," *Employee Benefit News,* November 2006, 20.

5. Sandra O'Neal and Julie Gebauer, "Talent Management in the 21st Century: Attracting, Retaining, and Engaging Employees of Choice," *WorldatWork Journal,* First Quarter 2006, 6–17.

6. Michelle V. Rafter, "Talent Management Systems Make Inroads with Employers," *Workforce Management,* January 30, 2006, 44.

7. "Talent Management Software Is Bundling Up," *Workforce Management,* October 9, 2006, 35.

8. Based on case example details from Learn.com, 2007, *www.learn.com.*

9. Robert E. Lewis and Robert J. Heckman, "Talent Management: A Critical Review," *Human Resource Management Review,* 15 (2006), 139–154.

10. *Talent Management: The State of the Art* (New York: Towers Perrin, 2005).

11. Matthew Gulteridge, Asmus B. Komm, and Emily Lawson, "The People Problem in Talent Management," *The McKinsey Quarterly,* Second Quarter 2006, *www.mckinseyquarterly.com.*

12. Ed Frauenheim, "Firms Walk Fine Line with 'High-Potential' Programs," *Workforce Management,* September 25, 2006, 44.

13. Jaclyne Badal, "Career-Path Programs Help Retain Workers," *The Wall Street Journal,* July 24, 2006, B1.

14. Toddi Gutner, "Still Working and Loving It," *Business Week,* October 16, 2006, 108.

15. Lyle C. Bridgeford, "Educating Workers About Delayed Retirement," *Employee Benefit News,* November 2006, *www.benefitnews.com.*

16. Patrick Chang Boon Lee, "Going Beyond Career Plateaus," *Journal of Management Development,* 22 (2003), 538–551.

17. Sheila Delargy and Mike Smith, "Why Employee Involvement Can Limit the Trauma of Career Transitions," *People Management,* April 20, 2006, 38.

18. Herminica Ibarra and Kent Lineback, "What's Your Story?" *Harvard Business Review,* January 2005, 64–71.

19. Anne Freedman, "Women Pay a Price for Taking Time Off," *Human Resource Executive,* November 2005, 18.

20. L. B. Hammer et al., "Work–Family Conflict and Work-Related Withdrawal Behaviors," *Journal of Business and Psychology,* 17 (2003), 419–436.

21. Anne M. Alexander et al., "A Study of the Disparity in Wages and Benefits Between Men and Women in Wyoming," Research Paper (University of Wyoming, College of Business, 2003), 10.

22. Nancy Lockwood, "The Glass Ceiling," *SHRM Research Quarterly,* Second Quarter 2004, 1–11.

23. *www.bls.gov,* 2006.

24. "Global Labor Mobility," *SHRM Workplace Visions,* Second Quarter 2006, 1–8.

25. David C. Martin and John J. Anthony, "The Repatriation and Retention of Employees: Factors Leading to Successful Programs," *International Journal of Management,* 23 (2006), 620.

26. Paula Caligiuri, "Developing Global Leaders, *Human Resource Management Review,* 16 (2006), 219–228.

27. Stephanie Sparrow, "Talent Spotting," *Utility Week,* April 7, 2006, 20.

28. "Competitive Intelligence Education: Competencies, Sources, and Trends," *Information Management Journal,* 38 (2004), 56–64.

29. Cam Caldwell et al., "Ten Classic Assessment Center Errors," *Public Personnel Management,* 32 (2003), 73–88.

30. Robert L. Grossman, "Developing Talent," *HR Magazine,* January 2006, 40.

31. Caroline Homer, "Coaching for the Better," *Training & Management Development Methods,* 20 (2006), 535.

32. M. F. R. Kets de Vries, "Leadership Group Coaching in Action," *Academy of Management Executive,* February 2005, 61–76.

33. Tor Erickson and Jaime Ortega, "The Adoption of Job Rotation: Testing the Theories," *Industrial & Labor Relations Review,* 59 (2006), 653.

34. John P. Meyer, "Four Territories of Experience," *Academy of Management Learning and Education,* 2 (2003), 352–263.

35. Frank Giancolo, "Making Sense of Sabbaticals," *Workspan,* July 2006, 38–41.

36. Loretta Chao, "Sabbaticals Can Offer Dividends for Employers," *The Wall Street Journal,* July 17, 2006, B1.

37. Leah Carlson, "Keeping Top Performers," *Employee Benefit,* January 2005, *www.benefitnews.com.*

38. Ed Silverman, "Taking Leave," *Human Resource Executive,* June 2, 2006, *www.hreonline.com.*

39. Ann Pomeroy, "Developing Leaders Is Key to Success," *HR Magazine,* June 2005, 20.

40. Nancy R. Lockwood, "Leadership Development: Optimizing Human Capital for Business Success," *SHRM Research Quarterly,* Fourth Quarter 2006, 1–11.

41. Douglas P. Shuit, "Huddling with the Coach," *Workforce Management,* February 2005, 53–57.

42. R. E. Boyatzis, M. L. Smith, and Nancy Blaize, 'Developing Sustainable Leaders Through Coaching and Compassion," *Academy of Management Learning & Education,* 5 (2006), 8–24.

43. "Some See Reverse Mentoring as Forward Thinking," *Omaha World-Herald,* May 1, 2006, D1.

44. Based on Gina Ruiz, "Playing Together," *Workforce Management,* June 26, 2006, 27–34.

45. *www.census.gov,* 2006.

46. William J. Rothwell, *Effective Succession Planning: Ensuring Leadership Continuity and Building Talent Within,* 3rd ed. (New York: AMACOM, 2005).

47. Shawn Fegley, "2006 Succession Planning Survey Report," *SHRM Research Quarterly*, Second Quarter 2006, *www.shrm.org*.

48. Barry Ip and Gabriel Jacobs, "Business Succession Planning: A Review of the Evidence," *Journal of Small Business and Enterprise Development*, 13 (2006), 326.

49. Khai Sheang Lee et al., "Family Business Succession: Appropriate Risk and Choice of Successor," *Academy of Management Review*, 28 (2003), 657–666.

50. Jill Carlson, "Succession Plan: A Must for Long-Term Success," *Capital Region Business Journal*, December 1, 2005, 22.

51. Claire Heaney, "Families Fail Future Planning," *Perth Sunday Times*, August 28, 2005, 1.

52. Carol Henriques, "Build or Buy," *Workspan*, August 2005, 24.

53. Carolyn Hirschman, "Growing Their Own," *Human Resource Executive*, January 2007, 1+.

54. "Pep Boys Jump Starts Succession Planning Initiative with Success Factors," *Business Wire*, September 1, 2005, *www.businesswire.com*.

55. Drew Robb, "Succeeding with Succession," *HR Magazine*, January 2006, 89.

56. "The Case for Succession Planning," *Succession Planning*, 2005, *www.jacobsononline.com*.

57. "Succession Planning: Tools for Execution," *Cutting Edge Information*, 2005, *www.cuttingedgeinfo.com*.

58. "Succession Planning and Profitability," *Leadership Solutions*, May/June 2006, *www.perthleadership.com*.

59. For more details, go to "Human Resources Strategies Identified: Effective Succession Planning Delivers Real Returns," *PR Newswire*, March 28, 2005, *www.best-in-class.com*.

60. Ram Charan, "Ending the CEO Succession Crisis," *Harvard Business Review*, February 2005, 72–81.

61. Dan R. Dalton and Catherine M. Dalton, "CEO Succession: The Times They Are A-Changing," *Journal of Business Strategy*, 28 (2007), 5.

62. Jeff Nash, "Report Finds CEO Succession Is Directors' Top Concern," *Workforce Management*, January 12, 2007, *www.workforce.com*.

63. "Ten Ways to Take the 'Success' Out of Succession Planning," *Workforce Management*, February 2005, *www.workforce.com*.

64. Jill Schildhouse, "The Plan to Succeed," *Inside Supply Management*, November 2006, 20–23.

65. "Succession Planning: Key to Assuring Your Law Firm's Continuity and Prosperity," *Partner's Report for Law Firm Owners*, July 2005, *www.ioma.com*.

66. Jeff Cooper, "Succession Planning: It's Not Just for Executives Anymore," *Workspan*, February 2006, 44–47.

67. Based on Bridget Mintz Testa, "Building a Strong Bench," *Workforce Management*, June 12, 2006, 24–31.

CHAPTER

11

Performance Management and Appraisal

After you have read this chapter, you should be able to:

- Identify the components of performance management systems.

- Distinguish between performance management and performance appraisal.

- Explain the differences between administrative and developmental uses of performance appraisal.

- Describe the advantages and disadvantages of multisource (360°) appraisals.

- Discuss the importance of training managers and employees about performance appraisal and give examples of rater errors.

- Identify several concerns about appraisal feedback and ways to make it more effective.

(HR) Headline

Welch says: "Ranking Workers Pays 20/70/10!"

Legendary manager Jack Welch, retired chairman and CEO of General Electric, is identified with a performance system for employees he calls *differentiation*. On the street, it is known as "Rank and Yank."

The system identifies the top 20% of employees at all levels, and they are nurtured and rewarded for excelling in performing their jobs. The middle 70% who make up the majority and are putting forth acceptable job performances are rewarded too, but at a lower level. The bottom 10% are identified, told they are not measuring up, and that if they do not improve, it would be best for them to find another place to work. Welch contends that letting people know where they stand, how far they can advance, and what their performance improvement needs are components of a good performance system.

This approach certainly is not universally accepted and has been condemned by some on the basis that it is "mean spirited" and "encourages politics." However, Welch asks if it is better to fail to tell people that they are not measuring up. "How can you have a system where people never know where they stand?" He contends that there is politics everywhere and that there is no system for appraising performance that eliminates politics. An evaluation system can restrict politics only if it is rigorous, as Welch argues.[1] The effectiveness of this approach is likely to continue to be debated.

Employers want employees who perform their jobs well. Performance management is used to identify, communicate, measure, and reward employees who do just that. Performance management system design is one of the key methods HR management uses to contribute to organizational performance.

THE NATURE OF PERFORMANCE MANAGEMENT

Performance management should originate with what the organization needs to accomplish to meet its strategic objectives. Each employee has some contribution to make to those greater objectives through his or her job. In a sense, the sum of all performances in all jobs in the organization should equal the strategic plan for the organization.

As Figure 11-1 shows, performance management links strategy to results. The figure shows how performance management facilitates turning an organization's strategy into results. However, just having a strategic plan does not guarantee that any action will occur on the plan. When organizational

FIGURE 11-1   Performance Management Linkage

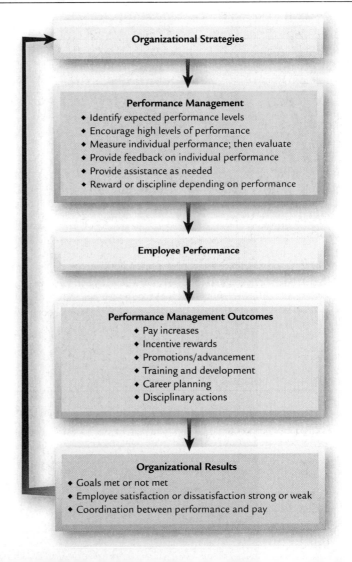

Performance management
Series of activities designed to ensure that the organization gets the performance it needs from its employees.

Performance appraisal
Process of determining how well employees do their job relative to a standard and communicating that information to the employee.

strategies have been defined, they must be translated to department or unit level actions. Then those actions must be assigned to individuals who must be held responsible and measured on whether the actions occurred and how well they were done.[2]

In some situations performance management is confused with one of its component parts—performance appraisal. **Performance management** is a series of activities designed to ensure that the organization gets the performance it needs from its employees. **Performance appraisal** is the process of determining how well employees do their job relative to a standard and communicating that information to the employee.

An effective performance management system should do the following:

- Make clear what the organization expects.
- Provide performance information to employees.
- Identify areas of success and needed development.
- Document performance for personnel records.

For example, Textron (with more than $10 billion in revenue and 43,000 employees) lets employees know within 30 days of hire specifically what their goals and objectives are and how they will be measured. Managers start with the company's goals and work with employees to make their goals support the company's. This results in a set of deliverables used to determine employee performance and pay.[3]

Even well-intentioned employees do not always know what is expected or how to improve their performance. That also makes performance management necessary. Additionally, dismissal of an employee may become necessary, and without evidence that the employee has been advised of the performance issues, legal problems may result.

Global Cultural Differences in Performance Management

Performance management systems and performance appraisal processes are very common in the United States and some other countries. When they are transported for use in other countries where multi-national organizations have operations, or when they are used with employees having non-American cultural backgrounds, problems can arise.

In some countries and cultures, it is uncommon for managers to rate employees or to give direct feedback, particularly if some points are negative. For instance, in several countries, including China and Japan, there is a high respect for authority and age. Consequently, expecting younger subordinates to engage in joint discussions with their managers through a performance appraisal process is uncommon. Use of such programs as multisource/360° feedback (discussed later in this chapter) would be culturally inappropriate.

In various other cultures, employees may view criticism from superiors as personally devastating rather than as useful feedback indicating training and development needs. Therefore, many managers do not provide feedback, nor do employees expect it.

Even in the physical settings for the appraisal discussions, "cultural customs" associated with formal meetings may need to be observed. In some Eastern European countries, it is common to have coffee and pastries or an alcoholic drink before beginning any formal discussion. These examples illustrate that the performance management processes may need to be adapted or maybe even not used in certain global settings.

Internet Research

Management Help
This Website is an integrated on-line library of resources for profit and non-profit entities regarding performance management. Visit their Website at: http://thomsonedu.com/management/mathis.

Performance-Focused Organizational Cultures

Organizational cultures vary on many dimensions, one of which is the emphasis on performance. Some corporate cultures are based on *entitlement*, meaning that *adequate* performance and stability dominate the organization. Employee rewards vary little from person to person and are not based on individual performance differences. As a result, performance appraisal activities are seen as having little tie to performance and as being primarily a "bureaucratic exercise."

At the other end of the spectrum is a *performance-driven* organizational culture that is focused on results. Performance appraisals link results to employee compensation and development. The importance of a performance-focused culture can be seen in the results of studies. One longitudinal study of 207 companies in 22 industries found that firms with performance-focused cultures had significantly higher growth in company revenue, employment, net income, and stock prices than did companies with different cultures. Another study, by Becker, Huselid, and Ulrich, found that firms with strong performance cultures had dramatically better results as well.[4] Figure 11-2 shows components of a successful performance-focused culture for an organization.

One study found that 33% of managers and 43% of non-managers feel their company is not doing enough about poor performers. The non-managers felt that failure to deal with poor performance was unfair to those who work hard.[5] An example of a company that dealt with this issue is a financial services company whose culture included not wanting to give anyone poor

Internet Research

Performance Management Technical Assistance Center
Information on managing performance, including a Performance Management Handbook, is available by visiting their Website at: http://thomsonedu.com/management/mathis.

FIGURE 11-2   Components of a Performance-Focused Culture

performance reviews. A new CEO brought in a new performance system when he came. Star performers got raises as high as 20%, and poor performers got nothing. The tougher performance system has been credited with weeding out poor performers voluntarily, bringing even better performance from many employees and better company profitability.[6]

IDENTIFYING AND MEASURING EMPLOYEE PERFORMANCE

The most critical performance criteria vary from job to job, but the employee performance measures common to *most* jobs include the following:

- Quantity of output
- Quality of output
- Timeliness of output
- Presence at work

Job duties Important elements in a given job.

Specific job duties identify the most important elements in a given job. For example, a college professor's job often includes the job duties of teaching, research, and service. Duties are identified from job descriptions that contain the most important parts of individual jobs. They define what the organization pays employees to do. Therefore, the performance of individuals on those important job duties should be measured and compared against appropriate standards and the results communicated to the employee. To complicate matters, multiple job duties are the rule rather than the exception in most jobs. A given individual might demonstrate better performance on some duties than others. Additionally, some duties might be more important than others to the organization.

Weights can be used to show the relative importance of several job duties in one job. For example, in a management job at a company that has a strategy of increasing revenue, cost control, and employee development, weights might be assigned as follows:

Weighting of Management Duties at Sample Firm	Weight
Revenue increase	50%
Cost control	30%
Employee development	20%
Total Management Performance	**100%**

Types of Performance Information

Managers can use three different types of information about how employees are performing their jobs, as Figure 11-3 shows. *Trait-based information* identifies a character trait of the employee—such as attitude, initiative, or creativity—and may or may not be job related. Because traits tend to be ambiguous, and favoritism of raters can affect how traits are viewed, court decisions have generally held that trait-based performance appraisals are too vague to use when making performance-based HR decisions such as promotions or terminations.

Behavior-based information focuses on specific behaviors that lead to job success. For a salesperson, the behavior "verbal persuasion" can be observed

FIGURE 11-3   Types of Performance Information

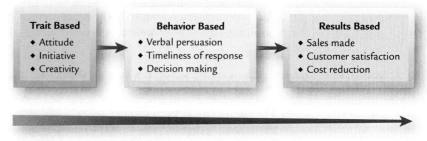

Trait Based	Behavior Based	Results Based
◆ Attitude	◆ Verbal persuasion	◆ Sales made
◆ Initiative	◆ Timeliness of response	◆ Customer satisfaction
◆ Creativity	◆ Decision making	◆ Cost reduction

Less Useful   More Useful

and used as information on performance. Behavioral information clearly specifies the behaviors management wants to see. A potential problem arises when any of several behaviors can lead to successful performance in a given situation. For example, identifying successful use of verbal persuasion for a salesperson might be difficult because an approach that is successful when used by one salesperson may not be successful when used by another. For a study on behavior-based information, see the HR Perspective.

Results-based information considers employee accomplishments. For jobs in which measurement is easy and obvious, a results-based approach works well. However, that which is measured tends to be emphasized, and that emphasis may leave out equally important but unmeasurable parts of the job. For example, a car sales representative who gets paid *only* for sales may be unwilling to do paperwork or other work not directly related to selling cars. Further, ethical or even legal issues may arise when only results are emphasized and *how* the results were achieved is not considered.

HR PERSPECTIVE

Effective Behaviors for a Project Manager

The behaviors associated with successful performance as a project manager have been identified in a research study. Many industries, such as construction, product design, information technology, and publishing, are project based. Different groups of individuals are brought together for a short period of time to accomplish a project. This unpredictable situation requires special behaviors for a manager to be successful. The study found that these top four behaviors are necessary to be a successful project manager:

■ Achievement orientation (improving performance, innovation, entrepreneurial actions)
■ Initiative (proactive behaviors to avert problems)
■ Information seeking (looking elsewhere for solutions to issues)

■ Focus on client's needs (efforts to fulfill client's requirements)

Of all the behaviors identified as important to the project manager's job performance, two were most predictive of success. *Self-control* and *team leadership,* when present, suggest the presence of other important characteristics or the capacity to develop them.

There were other behaviors that were important as well, but all share the common characteristic of behavioral performance information—it can be *observed.*[7] Observing self-control and leadership in a potential project manager may be the basis for predicting success if that person is promoted.

Performance measures can also be viewed as objective or subjective. The *objective measures* can be observed—for example, the number of cars sold or the number of invoices processed can be counted. *Subjective measures* require judgment on the part of the evaluator and are more difficult to determine. One example of a subjective measure is a supervisor's ratings of an employee's "attitude," which cannot be seen directly. Consequently, both objective and subjective measures should be used carefully.

Relevance of Performance Criteria

Measuring performance requires focusing on the most important aspects of employees' jobs. For example, measuring the *initiative* of customer service representatives in an insurance claims center may be less relevant than measuring the number of calls they handle properly. This example stresses that the most important job criteria or duties should be identified in the employees' job descriptions.

Performance measures that leave out some important job duties are considered *deficient*. For example, measurement of an employment interviewer's performance is likely to be deficient if it evaluates only the number of applicants hired and not the quality of those hired or how long those hired stay at the company. On the other hand, including some irrelevant criteria *contaminates* the measure. For example, appearance might be a contaminating criterion in measuring the performance of a telemarketing sales representative whom customers never see. Managers need to guard against using deficient or contaminated performance measures.

Additionally, *overemphasis* on one or two criteria can lead to problems. For example, overstressing the number of traffic tickets written by a police officer or the revenue generated by a sales representative may lead to ignoring other important performance areas. Ethical issues can arise because employees may falsify results in order to meet the one or two criteria that are overemphasized.[8] The corporate scandals involving Enron, Qwest, Tyco, and other large firms illustrate this concern.

Performance Standards

Performance standards
Define the expected levels of performance.

Performance standards define the expected levels of performance, and are labeled *benchmarks* or *goals* or *targets*—depending on the approach taken. Realistic, measurable, clearly understood performance standards benefit both organizations and employees. In a sense, performance standards define what satisfactory job performance is. It is recommended that they be established *before* the work is performed. Well-defined standards ensure that everyone involved knows the levels of accomplishment expected.

Both numerical and non-numerical standards can be established. Sales quotas and production output standards are familiar numerical performance standards. A standard of performance can also be based on non-numerical criteria. Assessing whether someone has met a performance standard, especially a non-numerical one, can be difficult, but usually can be done. For example, how would you correctly measure someone's ability to speak a foreign language before they were sent overseas? Figure 11-4 shows performance standards that help do that. Establishing performance standards such as those listed in Figure 11-4 makes assessing a person's performance level, even non-numerical performance, much more accurate.

FIGURE 11-4   ACTFL Performance Standards for Speaking Proficiency

Performance Level	Demonstrated Ability
Superior	• Participates fully in conversations relating to needs and professional interests • Discusses topics both concretely and abstractly • Can deal effectively with unfamiliar speaking situations
Intermediate	• Can participate in simple conversations on predictable topics • Can satisfy simple needs to survive in the language's culture • Can ask and answer questions
Novice	• Can respond to simple questions • Can convey minimal meaning by using isolated words or memorized phrases • Can satisfy a limited number of immediate needs

Source: Adapted from American Counsel on the Teaching of Foreign Languages (ACTFL) *Oral Proficiency Interview Tester Training Manual* (Stamford, CT: ACTFL Inc., 2006), 81–109.

Performance Metrics in Service Businesses

Measuring performance in service businesses is difficult, but just as important as in product businesses. It is difficult because services are very individualized for customers. Yet the performance of people is commonly the basic productivity measure in services. Some of the most useful sources of performance differences among managers in service businesses are:

- Regional differences in labor costs
- Service agreement differences
- Equipment/infrastructure differences
- Work volume

On an individual level, cost per employee, incidents per employee per day, number of calls per product, cost per call, sources of demand for services, and service calls per day are common measures. Once managers have determined appropriate measures of the variance in their company, they can deal with waste and service delivery. *Performance that is measured can be managed.*[9]

PERFORMANCE APPRAISALS

Performance appraisals are used to assess an employee's performance and to communicate that performance to the employee. Performance appraisal is variously called *employee rating, employee evaluation, performance review, performance evaluation,* or *results appraisal.*

Performance appraisals are widely used for administering wages and salaries, giving performance feedback, and identifying individual employee strengths and weaknesses. Most U.S. employers use performance appraisal systems for office, professional, technical, supervisory, middle management, and non-union production workers.

Poorly done performance appraisals lead to disappointing results for all concerned. But to have no formal performance appraisal done may limit an employer's options regarding discipline and dismissal. Performance appraisals can answer questions about whether the employer acted fairly or how the employer actually knew that the employee's performance did not meet standards. Even though an employer technically may not need a reason to terminate an employee, as a practical matter, appraisals can provide justification for such actions should they become necessary. Employees also benefit if appraisals help them determine how they can improve their performance, even after a positive appraisal.

Uses of Performance Appraisals

Organizations generally use performance appraisals in two potentially conflicting ways. One use is to provide a measure of performance for consideration in making pay or other administrative decisions about employees. This *administrative* role often creates stress for managers doing the appraisals. The other use focuses on the *development* of individuals. In this role, the manager acts more as counselor and coach than as a judge, which may change the tone of the appraisal. The developmental performance appraisal emphasizes identifying current training and development needs, as well as planning employees' future opportunities and career directions. Figure 11-5 shows both uses for performance appraisal.

Administrative Uses of Appraisals Three administrative uses of appraisal impact managers and employees the most: (1) determining pay adjustments; (2) making job placement decisions on promotions, transfers, and demotions; and (3) choosing employee disciplinary actions up to and including termination of employment.

A performance appraisal system is often the link between additional pay and rewards that employees receive and their job performance. Performance-based compensation affirms the idea that pay raises are given for performance accomplishments rather than based on length of service (seniority) or granted automatically to all employees at the same percentage levels. In pay-for-performance compensation systems, historically supervisors and managers have evaluated the performance of individual employees and also made compensation recommendations for the same employees. If any part of the appraisal process fails, better-performing employees may not receive larger pay increases, and the result is perceived inequity in compensation.

FIGURE 11-5   Conflicting Uses for Performance Appraisal

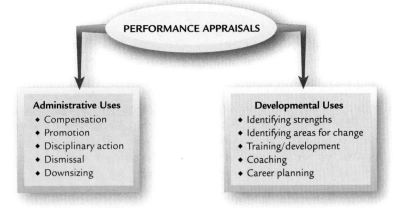

Many U.S. workers say that they see little connection between their performance and the size of their pay increases due to flaws in the performance appraisal processes.[10] However, the use of performance appraisals to determine pay is common. Consequently, many people argue that performance appraisals and pay discussions should be separated. Two major realities support this view. One is that employees often focus more on the pay amount received than on the appraisal feedback that identifies what they have done well or need to improve. The other is that managers sometimes manipulate performance appraisal ratings to justify the pay treatment they wish to give specific individuals. As a result of the second circumstance, many employees view the appraisal process as a "game," because compensation increases have already been determined before the appraisal decision.

To address these issues, numerous organizations have managers first conduct performance appraisals and discuss the results with employees, then several weeks later hold a shorter meeting in which pay is discussed. With this approach, the results of the performance appraisal can be considered before the amount of the pay adjustment is determined. Also, the performance appraisal discussions between managers/supervisors and employees can focus on the developmental uses of appraisals.

Employers are interested in the other administrative uses of performance appraisal as well, such as decisions about promotions, terminations, layoffs, and transfer assignments. Promotions and demotions based on performance must be documented through performance appraisals; otherwise, legal problems can result.

To improve the administrative processes of performance appraisals, many employers have implemented software so that managers can prepare appraisals electronically. As the HR On-Line indicates, even smaller firms are using such HR technology.

Developmental Uses of Appraisals For employees, a performance appraisal can be a primary source of information and feedback, which are often key to

HR ONLINE

Automating Performance Appraisal

An automated performance appraisal system can provide some advantages. Often performance management processes, such as manually collecting annual evaluations, are labor and paper intensive. Automated systems offered by several vendors provide common formats, integration with compensation, and development and succession planning. They can provide information on individuals, units, or whole organizations performance.

Such systems may help a manager identify which of the company's thousands of employees are its top performers, or a breakdown of workers with certain competencies and the best performers among them.

The systems may use "dashboards," which are technologies that work like the dashboard of a car to provide indicators of how the organization's performance is proceeding. Aggregating performance information can provide big picture perspectives that are difficult to get otherwise. Further, on-line performance assessment can minimize face-to-face meetings and reduce time—perhaps allowing for more frequent appraisals.

One survey found that about 28% of organizations surveyed have automated their performance systems. Those that had done so confirmed that ease of use, time savings, and ability to track performance had improved.[11]

their future development. In the process of identifying employee strengths, weaknesses, potentials, and training needs through performance appraisal feedback, supervisors can inform employees about their progress, discuss areas where additional training may be beneficial, and outline future development plans. The manager's role in such a situation parallels that of a coach, discussing good performance, explaining what improvement is necessary, and showing employees how to improve. It is clear employees do not always know where and how to improve, and managers should not expect improvement if they are unwilling to provide developmental feedback.

Internet Research

HR.com

For a Website with free registration to access resources on best practices and performance management, link to their site at: http://thomsonedu.com/management/mathis.

The purpose of such feedback is both to reinforce satisfactory employee performance and to address performance deficiencies. Positive reinforcement for desired behaviors contributes to both individual and organizational development. The development function of performance appraisal also can identify areas in which the employee might wish to grow. For example, in a performance appraisal interview targeted exclusively to development, an employee found out that the only factor keeping her from being considered for a management job in her firm was the lack of a working knowledge of cost accounting. Her supervisor suggested that she consider taking some night courses at the local college.

The use of teams provides a different set of circumstances for developmental appraisal. The manager may not see all of an employee's work, but the employee's team members do. Teams can provide developmental feedback. However, it is still an open question whether teams can handle administrative appraisals. When teams are allowed to design appraisal systems, they tend to "get rid of judgment" and avoid differential rewards. Thus, group appraisal may be best suited to developmental purposes, not administrative uses.

Decisions About the Performance Appraisal Process

A number of decisions must be made when designing performance appraisal systems. Some important ones are identifying the appraisal responsibilities of the HR unit and of the operating managers, the type of appraisal system to use, the timing of appraisals, and who conducts appraisals.

Appraisal Responsibilities The appraisal process can benefit both the organization and the employees, if done properly. As Figure 11-6 (on the next page) shows, the HR unit typically designs a performance appraisal system. The operating managers then appraise employees using the appraisal system. During development of the formal appraisal system, managers usually offer input as to how the final system will work.

It is important for managers to understand that appraisals are *their* responsibility. Through the appraisal process, effective employee performance can be developed to be even better, and poor employee performance can be improved or poor performers can be removed from the organization. Performance appraisal is not simply an HR requirement; it must also be a management process, because guiding employees' performance is among the most important responsibilities of managers.

Informal vs. Systematic Appraisal Processes Performance appraisals can occur in two ways: informally and/or systematically. A supervisor conducts an *informal appraisal* whenever necessary. The day-to-day working relationship

FIGURE 11-6   Typical Division of HR Responsibilities: Performance Appraisal

HR Unit	Managers
• Designs and maintains appraisal system • Trains raters • Tracks timely receipt of appraisals • Reviews completed appraisals for consistency	• Typically rate performance of employees • Prepare formal appraisal documents • Review appraisals with employees • Identify development areas

between a manager and an employee offers an opportunity for the employee's performance to be evaluated. A manager communicates this evaluation through conversation on the job, over coffee, or by on-the-spot discussion of a specific occurrence. Although informal appraisal is useful and necessary, it should not take the place of formal appraisal.

Frequent informal feedback to employees can prevent "surprises" during a formal performance review. However, informal appraisal can become *too* informal. For example, a senior executive at a large firm so dreaded face-to-face evaluations that he recently delivered one manager's review while both sat in adjoining stalls in the men's room.

A *systematic appraisal* is used when the contact between a manager and employee is formal, and a system is in place to report managerial impressions and observations on employee performance. One survey found that almost 90% of employers have a formal performance management system or process.[12]

Systematic appraisals feature a regular time interval, which distinguishes them from informal appraisals. Both employees and managers know that performance will be reviewed on a regular basis, and they can plan for performance discussions.

Timing of Appraisals Most companies require managers to conduct appraisals once or twice a year, most often annually. Employees commonly receive an appraisal 60 to 90 days after hiring, again at six months, and annually thereafter. *Probationary* or *introductory employees,* who are new and in a trial period, should be informally evaluated often—perhaps weekly for the first month, and monthly thereafter until the end of the introductory period. After that, annual reviews are typical. For employees in high demand, some employers use accelerated appraisals—every six months instead of every year. This is done to retain those employees so that more feedback can be given and pay raises may occur more often.

To separate the administrative and developmental uses of appraisals, some employers implement the following appraisal schedule: First there is a performance review and discussion. Some time after that a separate training, development, and objective-setting session is held. Within two weeks, a compensation adjustment discussion takes place. Having three separate discussions provides both the employee and the employee's manager with opportunities to focus on the administrative, developmental, and compensation issues. Using this framework is generally better than addressing all three areas in one discussion of an hour or less, once a year.

Legal Concerns and Performance Appraisals

Because appraisals are supposed to measure how well employees are doing their jobs, it may seem unnecessary to emphasize that performance appraisals must be job related. HR On-the-Job shows the elements of a legal performance appraisal system.

Yet courts have ruled in numerous cases that performance appraisals were discriminatory and not job related.[13] For instance, in a case involving an African American computer engineer at Hewlett-Packard, performance appraisals commended his technical skills and work efforts, but criticized his taking too much time analyzing problems. A few months after those appraisals were issued, the employee helped start a diversity group at the company. Shortly after that, his performance appraisal ratings declined, and his supervisor "encouraged" him to leave the company. The court ruled that there appeared to be enough irregularities in the performance appraisal documentation to raise questions about the fairness of the appraisal system. One concern was that the ratings were viewed as being overly subjective.[14]

Legal concerns have also arisen with the use of forced distribution rating systems. In these systems, managers are forced to rate a certain percentage of employees as "outstanding," another percentage as "satisfactory," and still another percentage as "needing improvement." For example, Ford, Goodyear Tire & Rubber, and Capital One have been sued and/or have settled lawsuits related to forced distribution ranking in performance appraisals. Ford paid $10.5 million to settle a lawsuit based on an employee's claim that the Ford appraisal system disproportionally and negatively affected the pay raises of older workers. Goodyear dropped its forced ranking appraisal system because of legal complaints that it discriminated on the bases of race and gender.[15]

A number of court decisions over 30 years have focused attention on performance appraisals, particularly on equal employment opportunity (EEO)

HR ON-THE-JOB

Elements of a Legal Performance Appraisal System

The elements of a performance appraisal system that can survive court tests can be determined from existing case law. It is generally agreed that a legally defensible performance appraisal should include the following:

- Performance appraisal criteria based on job analysis
- Absence of disparate impact
- Formal evaluation criteria that limit managerial discretion
- A rating instrument linked to job duties and responsibilities

- Documentation of the appraisal activities
- Personal knowledge of and contact with each appraised individual
- Training of supervisors in conducting appraisals
- A review process that prevents one manager, acting alone, from controlling an employee's career
- Counseling to help poor performers improve

Of course, having all of these components is no guarantee against lawsuits. However, they do improve the chance of winning lawsuits that might be filed.

concerns.[16] The uniform guidelines issued by the Equal Employment Opportunity Commission (EEOC) and various court decisions make it clear that performance appraisals must be job related, non-discriminatory, and documented.[17]

Clearly, employers should have fair and non-discriminatory performance appraisals. They should design their appraisal systems to satisfy the courts as well as performance management needs.[18]

WHO CONDUCTS APPRAISALS?

Performance appraisals can be conducted by anyone familiar with the performance of individual employees. Possible combinations include the following:

- Supervisors rating their employees
- Employees rating their superiors
- Team members rating each other
- Employees rating themselves
- Outside sources rating employees
- A variety of parties providing multisource, or 360°, feedback

Supervisory Rating of Subordinates

The most widely used means of rating employees is based on the assumption that the immediate supervisor is the person most qualified to evaluate an employee's performance realistically and fairly. To help themselves provide accurate evaluations, some supervisors keep performance logs noting their employees' accomplishments. These logs provide specific examples to use when rating performance. Figure 11-7 shows the traditional review process by which supervisors conduct performance appraisals on employees.

Employee Rating of Managers

A number of organizations today ask employees or group members to rate the performance of supervisors and managers. A prime example of this type of rating takes place in colleges and universities, where students evaluate the performance of professors in the classroom. Performance appraisal ratings also are used for management development purposes.

Having employees rate managers provides three primary advantages. First, in critical manager/employee relationships, employee ratings can be quite useful for identifying competent managers. The rating of leaders by combat soldiers is one example of such a use. Second, this type of rating program can help make a manager more responsive to employees. This advantage can quickly become a disadvantage if the manager focuses on being "nice" rather than on managing; people who are nice but have no other qualifications may not be good managers in many situations. Finally, employee appraisals can contribute to career development efforts for managers by identifying areas for growth.

A major disadvantage of having employees rate managers is the negative reaction many superiors have to being evaluated by employees. Also, the fear of reprisals may be too great for employees to give realistic ratings. This may prompt workers to rate their managers only on the way the managers treat them, not on critical job requirements. The problems associated with this appraisal approach limit its usefulness to certain situations, including managerial development and improvement efforts.[19]

| FIGURE 11-7 | Traditional Performance Appraisal Process |

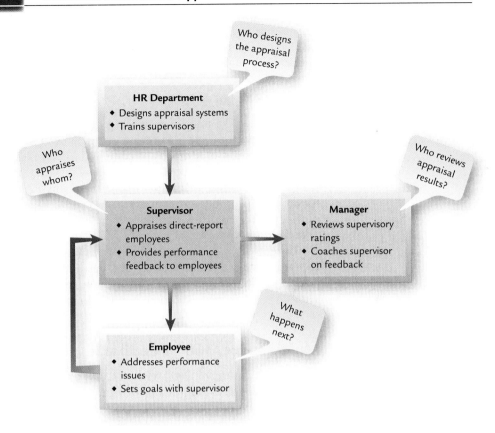

Team/Peer Rating

Having employees and team members rate each other is another type of appraisal with potential both to help and to hurt. Peer and team ratings are especially useful when supervisors do not have the opportunity to observe each employee's performance but other work group members do. One challenge of this approach is how to obtain ratings with virtual or global teams, in which the individuals work primarily through technology, not in person. Another challenge is how to obtain ratings from and for individuals who are on different special project teams throughout the year.

Some contend that any performance appraisal, including team/peer ratings, can negatively affect teamwork and participative management efforts. Although team members have good information on one another's performance, they may not choose to share it. They may unfairly attack, or "go easy" to spare feelings. Some organizations attempt to overcome such problems by using anonymous appraisals and/or having a consultant or HR manager interpret team/peer ratings. Despite the problems, team/peer performance ratings are probably inevitable, especially where work teams are used extensively.[20]

Self-Rating

Self-appraisal works in certain situations. As a self-development tool, it forces employees to think about their strengths and weaknesses and set goals for improvement. Employees working in isolation or possessing unique skills may be the only ones qualified to rate themselves. However, employees may not rate themselves as supervisors would rate them; they may use quite different standards. Evidence showing whether people tend to be more lenient or more demanding when rating themselves is mixed, with self-rating frequently higher than supervisory ratings. Still, employee self-ratings can be a useful source of performance information for development.[21]

Outsider Rating

People outside the immediate work group may be called in to conduct performance reviews. This field review approach can include someone from the HR department as a reviewer, or completely independent reviewers from outside the organization. Examples include a review team evaluating a college president or a panel of division managers evaluating a supervisor's potential for advancement in the organization. A disadvantage of this approach is that outsiders may not know the important demands within the work group or organization.

The customers or clients of an organization are obvious sources for outside appraisals. For sales and service jobs, customers may provide very useful input on the performance behaviors of employees. One firm measures customer service satisfaction to determine bonuses for top marketing executives. Use of such input has led to multisource ratings.

Multisource/360° Feedback

Multisource rating, or 360° feedback, has grown in popularity. Multisource feedback recognizes that for a growing number of jobs, employee performance is multi-dimensional and crosses departmental, organizational, and even global boundaries. The major purpose of 360° feedback is *not* to increase uniformity by soliciting like-minded views. Instead, it is designed to capture evaluations of the individual employee's different roles. Figure 11-8 shows graphically some of the parties who may be involved in 360° feedback. For example, an HR manager for an insurance firm deals with seven regional sales managers, HR administrators in five claims centers, and various corporate executives in finance, legal, and information technology. The Vice President of HR uses

FIGURE 11-8   Multisource Appraisal

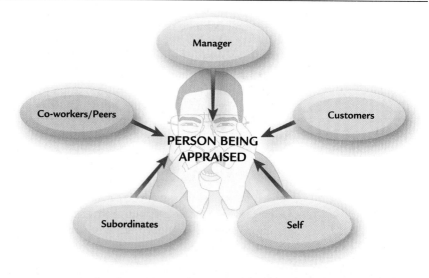

360° feedback to gather data on all facets of the HR manager's job before completing a performance appraisal on the manager. Similar examples can be cited in numerous managerial, professional, technical, operational, and administrative jobs.

Significant administrative time and paperwork are required to request, obtain, and summarize feedback from multiple raters. Use of Web-based systems can significantly reduce the administrative demands of multisource ratings.

Developmental Use of Multisource Feedback As originally designed and used, multisource feedback focuses on the use of appraisals for future development of individuals. Conflict resolution skills, decision-making abilities, team effectiveness, communication skills, managerial styles, and technical capabilities are just some of the developmental areas that can be examined. Even in a multisource system, the manager remains a focal point, both to receive the feedback initially and to follow up with the employee appropriately.

Administrative Use of Multisource Feedback The popularity of 360° feedback systems has led to the results being used for making compensation, promotion, termination, and other administrative decisions. When using 360° feedback for administrative purposes, managers must anticipate potential problems. Differences among raters can present a challenge, especially in the use of 360° ratings for discipline or pay decisions. Bias can just as easily be rooted in customers, subordinates, and peers as in a boss, and the lack of accountability of those sources can affect the ratings. "Inflation" of ratings is common when the sources know that their input will affect someone's pay or career. Also, issues of the confidentiality of the input and whether it is truly kept anonymous have led to lawsuits. Even though multisource approaches to performance appraisal offer possible solutions to the well-documented dissatisfaction with performance appraisal, a number of questions have arisen as multisource appraisals have become more common.

Evaluating Multisource Feedback Research on multisource/360° feedback has revealed both positives and negatives. More variability than expected may be seen in the ratings given by the different sources. Thus, supervisor ratings must carry more weight than peer or subordinate input to resolve the differences. One concern is that those peers who rate poor-performing co-workers tend to inflate the ratings of those people so that the peers themselves can get higher overall evaluation results.[22]

One concern is whether 360° appraisals improve the process or simply multiply the number of problems by the total number of raters. Also, some wonder whether multisource appraisals really create better decisions that offset the additional time and investment required. These issues appear to be less threatening when the 360° feedback is used *only for development*. But they may effectively reduce the use of multisource appraisals as an administrative tool in many situations.

TOOLS FOR APPRAISING PERFORMANCE

Performance can be appraised by a number of methods. Some employers use one method for all jobs and employees, some use different methods for different groups of employees, and others use a combination of methods. The following discussion highlights different tools that can be used and some of the pluses and minuses of each.

Category Scaling Methods

The simplest methods for appraising performance are category scaling methods, which require a manager to mark an employee's level of performance on a specific form divided into categories of performance. A *checklist* uses a list of statements or words from which raters check statements most representative of the characteristics and performance of employees. Often, a scale indicating perceived level of accomplishment on each statement is included, which becomes a type of graphic rating scale.

Graphic Rating Scales The graphic rating scale allows the rater to mark an employee's performance on a continuum. Because of its simplicity, this method is used frequently. Figure 11-9 shows a sample appraisal form that combines graphic rating scales with essays. Three aspects of performance are appraised using graphic rating scales: *descriptive categories* (such as quantity of work, attendance, and dependability), *job duties* (taken from the job description), and *behavioral dimensions* (such as decision making, employee development, and communication effectiveness).

Each of these types can be used for different jobs. How well employees meet established standards is often expressed either numerically (e.g., 5, 4, 3, 2, 1) or verbally (e.g., "outstanding," "meets standards," "below standards"). If two or more people are involved in the rating, they may find it difficult to agree on the exact level of performance achieved relative to the standard in evaluating employee performance. Notice that each level specifies performance standards or expectations in order to reduce variation in interpretations of the standards by different supervisors and employees.

Concerns with Graphic Rating Scales Graphic rating scales in many forms are widely used because they are easy to develop; however, they encourage errors on the part of the raters, who may depend too heavily on the form to define performance. Also, graphic rating scales tend to emphasize the rating instrument itself and its limitations. If they fit the person and the job, the scales work well. However, if they fit poorly, managers and employees who must use them frequently complain about "the rating form."

A key point must be emphasized. Regardless of the scales used, the focus should be on the job duties and responsibilities identified in job descriptions. The closer the link between the scales and what people actually do, as identified in current and complete job descriptions, the stronger the relationship between the ratings and the job, as viewed by employees and managers. Also, should the performance appraisal results be challenged by legal actions, the more performance appraisals are tied to what people actually do, the more likely employers are to prevail in those legal situations.

An additional drawback to graphic rating scales is that often, separate traits or factors are grouped together, and the rater is given only one box to check. For example, "dependability" could refer to meeting deadlines for reports, or it could refer to attendance and tardiness. If a supervisor gives an employee a rating of 3, which aspect of "dependability" is being rated? One supervisor might rate her employees on meeting deadlines, while another supervisor rates his employees on attendance.

Another drawback is that the descriptive words sometimes used in scales may have different meanings to different raters. Terms such as *initiative* and

Graphic rating scale
Scale that allows the rater to mark an employee's performance on a continuum.

Internet Research
Performance Review Guide
This Website contains links to numerous resources on performance appraisals. Visit their site at: http://thomsonedu.com/management/mathis.

| FIGURE 11-9 | Sample Performance Appraisal Form |

Date sent: 4/19/08

Name: Joe Hernandez

Department: Receiving

Employment status (check one): Full-time __X__ Part-time _____

Rating period: From: 4/30/07   To: 4/30/08

Reason for appraisal (check one): Regular interval __X__   Introductory ____   Counseling only ____   Discharge ____

Return by: 5/01/08

Job title: Receiving Clerk

Supervisor: Marian Williams

Date of hire: 5/12/00

Using the following definitions, rate the performance as I, M, or E.

I—Performance is below job requirements and **improvement is needed.**

M—Performance **meets** job requirements and standards.

E—Performance **exceeds** job requirements and standards **most** of the time.

SPECIFIC JOB RESPONSIBILITIES: List the prinicipal activities from the job summary, rate the performance on each job duty by placing an X on the rating scale at the appropriate location, and make appropriate comments to explain the rating.

I ——————————————— M ——————————— E

Job Duty #1: Inventory receiving and checking
Explanation: _____

_____

I ——————————————— M ——————————— E

Job Duty #2: Accurate recordkeeping
Explanation: _____

_____

I ——————————————— M ——————————— E

Attendance (including absences and tardies):   Number of absences ____   Number of tardies ____
Explanation: _____

_____

Overall rating: In the box provided, place the letter—**I, M, or E**—that best describes the employee's overall performance.

Explanation: _____

_____

FIGURE 11-10   Sample Terms for Defining Standards

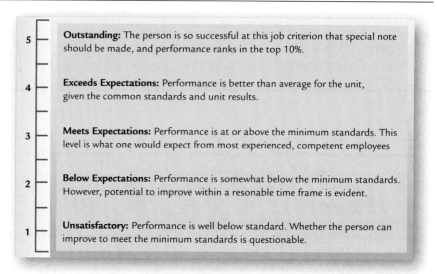

5 — **Outstanding:** The person is so successful at this job criterion that special note should be made, and performance ranks in the top 10%.

4 — **Exceeds Expectations:** Performance is better than average for the unit, given the common standards and unit results.

3 — **Meets Expectations:** Performance is at or above the minimum standards. This level is what one would expect from most experienced, competent employees

2 — **Below Expectations:** Performance is somewhat below the minimum standards. However, potential to improve within a resonable time frame is evident.

1 — **Unsatisfactory:** Performance is well below standard. Whether the person can improve to meet the minimum standards is questionable.

cooperation are subject to many interpretations, especially if used in conjunction with words such as *outstanding, average,* and *poor*. Also, as Figure 11-10 shows, the number of scale points can be defined differently.

Behavioral Rating Scales In an attempt to overcome some of the concerns with graphic rating scales, employers may use behavioral rating scales, which are designed to assess an employee's *behaviors* instead of other characteristics. Different approaches are used, but all describe specific examples of employee job behaviors. In a behaviorally anchored rating scale (BARS), these examples are "anchored" or measured against a scale of performance levels.

When creating a BARS, identifying important *job dimensions,* which are the most important performance factors in a job description, is done first. Short statements describe both desirable and undesirable behaviors (anchors). These are then "translated," or assigned, to one of the job dimensions. Anchor statements are usually developed by a group of people familiar with the job. Assignment to a dimension usually requires the agreement of 60% to 70% of the group. The group then assigns each anchor a number that represents how good or bad the behavior is, and the anchors are fitted to a scale. Figure 11-11 contains an example that rates customer service skills for individuals taking orders for a national catalog retailer. Spelling out the behaviors associated with each level of performance helps minimize some of the problems noted for the graphic rating scale.

Several problems are associated with the behavioral approaches. First, developing and maintaining behaviorally anchored rating scales require extensive time and effort. In addition, various appraisal forms are needed to accommodate different types of jobs in an organization. For instance, because nurses, dietitians, and admissions clerks in a hospital all have distinct job descriptions, a separate BARS form needs to be developed for each.

Comparative Methods

Comparative methods require that managers directly compare the performance levels of their employees against one another. For example, the information systems supervisor would compare the performance of a programmer

FIGURE 11-11   Behaviorally-Anchored Rating Scale for Customer Service Skills

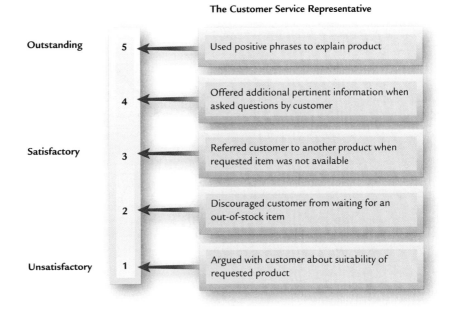

The Customer Service Representative

Outstanding	5	Used positive phrases to explain product
	4	Offered additional pertinent information when asked questions by customer
Satisfactory	3	Referred customer to another product when requested item was not available
	2	Discouraged customer from waiting for an out-of-stock item
Unsatisfactory	1	Argued with customer about suitability of requested product

with that of other programmers. Comparative techniques include ranking and forced distribution.

Ranking Performance appraisal method in which all employees are listed from highest to lowest in performance.

Ranking The ranking method lists all employees from highest to lowest in performance. The primary drawback of the ranking method is that the sizes of the differences between individuals are not well defined. For example, the performances of individuals ranked second and third may differ little, while the performances of those ranked third and fourth differ a great deal. This drawback can be overcome to some extent by assigning points to indicate the sizes of the gaps. Ranking also means someone must be last, which ignores the possibility that the last-ranked individual in one group might be equal to the top-ranked employee in a different group. Further, the ranking task becomes unwieldy if the group to be ranked is large.

Forced distribution Performance appraisal method in which ratings of employees' performance are distributed along a bell-shaped curve.

Forced Distribution Forced distribution is a technique for distributing ratings that are generated with any of the other appraisal methods and comparing the ratings of people in a work group. With the forced distribution method, the ratings of employees' performance are distributed along a bell-shaped curve. For example, a medical clinic administrator ranking employees on a five-point scale would have to rate 10% as a 1 ("unsatisfactory"), 20% as a 2 ("below expectations"), 40% as a 3 ("meets expectations"), 20% as a 4 ("above expectations"), and 10% as a 5 ("outstanding").

Forced distribution is used in some form by an estimated 30% of all firms with performance appraisal systems. At General Electric, in the "20/70/10" program, managers identify the top 20% and reward them richly so that few will leave. The bottom 10% are given a chance to improve or leave. The forced distribution system is controversial because of both its advantages and its disadvantages, which are discussed next.[23]

Advantages and Disadvantages of Forced Distribution One reason why firms have mandated the use of forced distributions for appraisal ratings is to

FIGURE 11-12   **Forced Distribution on a Bell-Shaped Curve**

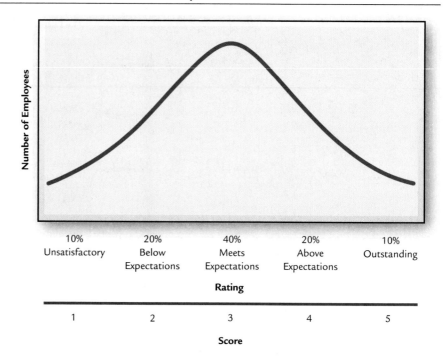

deal with "rater inflation." If employers do not require a forced distribution, performance appraisal ratings often do not approximate the normal distribution of the bell-shaped curve (see Figure 11-12).

The use of a forced distribution system makes managers identify high, average, and low performers. Thus, high performers can be rewarded and developed, while low performers can be "encouraged" to improve or leave. Advocates of forced ranking also state that forced distribution ensures that compensation increases truly are differentiated by performance rather than being spread somewhat equally among all employees.

But the forced distribution method suffers from several drawbacks. One problem is that a supervisor may resist placing any individual in the lowest (or the highest) group. Difficulties also arise when the rater must explain to an employee why she or he was placed in one group and others were placed in higher groups. Further, with small groups, the assumption that a bell-shaped or other distribution of performance occurs may be faulty. Finally, in some cases, the manager may make false distinctions between employees. By comparing people against each other, rather than against a standard of job performance, supervisors trying to fill the percentages may end up giving employees subjective ratings.

As a result of such drawbacks, forced distribution systems have been challenged legally.[24] As mentioned earlier, Ford and Goodyear Tire & Rubber, among other firms, have settled similar lawsuits and agreed to modify their performance appraisal processes.[25]

A number of actions are recommended to address these problems if a forced distribution system is to be used. They include many that are similar to those for making other methods of appraisals more legal and effective[26]:

■ Use specific, objective criteria and standards.
■ Involve employees in planning and designing the programs.

- Ensure that sufficient numbers of people are rated, so that statistical rankings are relevant.
- Train managers, and review their ratings to ensure that they are job related, not based on favoritism.

Narrative Methods

Managers and HR specialists often are required to provide written appraisal information. However, some appraisal methods are entirely written. Documentation and description are the essence of the critical incident method and the essay method.

Critical Incident In the critical incident method, the manager keeps a written record of both highly favorable and unfavorable actions performed by an employee during the entire rating period. When a "critical incident" involving an employee occurs, the manager writes it down. The critical incident method can be used with other methods to document the reasons why an employee was given a certain rating.

Essay The essay method requires a manager to write a short essay describing each employee's performance during the rating period. Some "free-form" essays are without guidelines; others are more structured, using prepared questions that must be answered. The rater usually categorizes comments under a few general headings. The essay method allows the rater more flexibility than other methods do. As a result, appraisers often combine the essay with other methods.

The effectiveness of the essay approach often depends on a supervisor's writing skills. Some supervisors do not express themselves well in writing and as a result produce poor descriptions of employee performance, whereas others have excellent writing skills and can create highly positive impressions.

Management by Objectives

Management by objectives (MBO) Performance appraisal method that specifies the performance goals that an individual and manager mutually identify.

Management by objectives (MBO) specifies the performance goals that an individual and manager mutually identify. Each manager sets objectives derived from the overall goals and objectives of the organization; however, MBO should not be a disguised means for a superior to dictate the objectives of individual managers or employees. Other names for MBO include *appraisal by results, target coaching, work planning and review, performance objective setting,* and *mutual goal setting.*

MBO Process Implementing a guided self-appraisal system using MBO is a four-stage process. The stages are as follows:

1. *Job review and agreement:* The employee and the superior review the job description and the key activities that constitute the employee's job. The idea is to agree on the exact makeup of the job.
2. *Development of performance standards:* Together, the employee and his or her superior develop specific standards of performance and determine a satisfactory level of performance that is specific and measurable. For example, a quota of selling five cars a month may be an appropriate performance standard for a salesperson.
3. *Setting of objectives:* Together, the employee and the superior establish objectives that are realistically attainable.

4. *Continuing performance discussions:* The employee and the superior use the objectives as bases for continuing discussions about the employee's performance. Although a formal review session may be scheduled, the employee and the supervisor do not necessarily wait until the appointed time to discuss performance. Objectives can be mutually modified as warranted.

The MBO process seems to be most useful with managerial personnel and employees who have a fairly wide range of flexibility and control over their jobs. When imposed on a rigid and autocratic management system, MBO often has failed. Emphasizing penalties for not meeting objectives defeats the development and participative nature of MBO.

Combinations of Methods

No single appraisal method is best for all situations. Therefore, a performance measurement system that uses a combination of methods may be sensible in certain circumstances. Using combinations may offset some of the advantages and disadvantages of individual methods. Category scaling methods sometimes are easy to develop, but they usually do little to measure strategic accomplishments. Further, they may make interrater reliability problems worse. Comparative approaches help reduce leniency and other errors, which makes them useful for administrative decisions such as determining pay raises. But comparative approaches do a poor job of linking performance to organizational goals, and they do not provide feedback for improvement as well as other methods do.

Narrative methods work well for development because they potentially generate more feedback information. However, without good definitions of criteria or standards, they can be so unstructured as to be of little value. Also, these methods work poorly for administrative uses. The MBO approach works well to link performance to organizational goals, but it can require much effort and time for defining expectations and explaining the process to employees. Narrative and MBO approaches may not work as well for lower-level jobs as for jobs with more varied duties and responsibilities.

When managers can articulate what they want a performance appraisal system to accomplish, they can choose and mix methods to realize those advantages. For example, one combination might include a graphic rating scale of performance on major job criteria, a narrative of developmental needs, and an overall ranking of employees in a department. Different categories of employees (e.g., salaried exempt, salaried non-exempt, and maintenance) might require different combinations of methods.

TRAINING OF MANAGERS AND EMPLOYEES IN PERFORMANCE APPRAISAL

Court decisions on the legality of performance appraisals and research on appraisal effectiveness both stress the importance of training managers and employees on performance management and conducting performance appraisals. Managers with positive views of the performance appraisal system are more likely to use the system effectively. Unfortunately, such training occurs only sporadically or not at all in many organizations. One survey found that over half of all employers provide employees with little or no performance management training, and a third provide managers with little or no such training.[27]

Internet Research

HR-Software.net

For links to numerous on-line performance appraisal software systems, visit their Website at: http://thomsonedu .com/management/mathis.

For employees, performance appraisal training focuses on the purposes of appraisal, the appraisal process and timing, and how performance criteria and standards are linked to job duties and responsibilities. Some training also discusses how employees should rate their own performance and use that information in discussions with their supervisors and managers.

Most systems can be improved by training supervisors in how to do performance appraisals.[28] Because conducting the appraisals is critical, training should center around minimizing rater errors and providing raters with details on documenting performance information.

Training is especially essential for those who have recently been promoted to jobs in which conducting performance appraisals is a new experience for them. Without training, managers and supervisors often "repeat the past." This repeat means they appraise others much as they have been appraised in the past, which often will have been done inaccurately. The following list is not comprehensive, but it does identify some topics covered in appraisal training:

- Appraisal process and timing
- Performance criteria and job standards that should be considered
- How to communicate positive and negative feedback
- When and how to discuss training and development goals
- Conducting and discussing the compensation review
- How to avoid common rating errors

Rater Errors

There are many possible sources of error in the performance appraisal process. One of the major sources is mistakes made by raters. Although completely eliminating these errors is impossible, making raters aware of them through training is helpful. Figure 11-13 (on the next page) lists some common rater errors.

Recency effect Occurs when a rater gives greater weight to recent events when appraising an individual's performance.

Primacy effect Occurs when a rater gives greater weight to information received first when appraising an individual's performance.

Central tendency error Occurs when a rater gives all employees a score within a narrow range in the middle of the scale.

Leniency error Occurs when ratings of all employees fall at the high end of the scale.

Strictness error Occurs when ratings of all employees fall at the low end of the scale.

Varying Standards When appraising employees, a manager should avoid applying different standards and expectations for employees performing similar jobs. Such problems often result from the use of ambiguous criteria and subjective weightings by supervisors.

Recency and Primacy Effects The recency effect occurs when a rater gives greater weight to recent events when appraising an individual's performance. Giving a student a course grade based only on his performance in the last week of class and giving a drill press operator a high rating even though she made the quota only in the last two weeks of the rating period are examples. The opposite is the primacy effect, which occurs when a rater gives greater weight to information received first.

Central Tendency, Leniency, and Strictness Errors Ask students, and they will tell you which professors tend to grade easier or harder. A manager may develop a similar *rating pattern*. Appraisers who rate all employees within a narrow range in the middle of the scale (i.e., rate everyone as "average") commit a central tendency error, giving even outstanding and poor performers an "average" rating.

Rating patterns also may exhibit leniency or strictness. The leniency error occurs when ratings of all employees fall at the high end of the scale. The strictness error occurs when a manager uses only the lower part of the scale to

FIGURE 11-13   Common Rater Errors

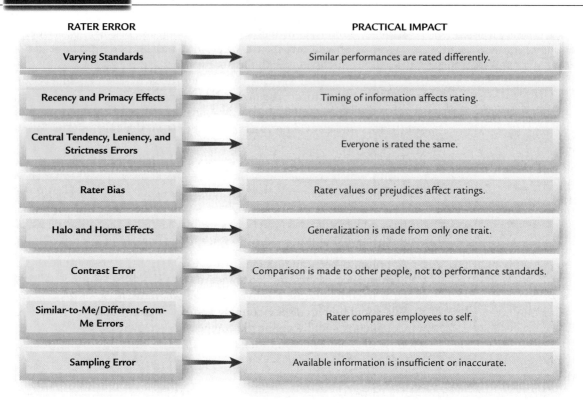

RATER ERROR	PRACTICAL IMPACT
Varying Standards	Similar performances are rated differently.
Recency and Primacy Effects	Timing of information affects rating.
Central Tendency, Leniency, and Strictness Errors	Everyone is rated the same.
Rater Bias	Rater values or prejudices affect ratings.
Halo and Horns Effects	Generalization is made from only one trait.
Contrast Error	Comparison is made to other people, not to performance standards.
Similar-to-Me/Different-from-Me Errors	Rater compares employees to self.
Sampling Error	Available information is insufficient or inaccurate.

rate employees. To avoid conflict, managers often rate employees higher than they should. This "ratings boost" is especially likely when no manager or HR representative reviews the completed appraisals.

Rater bias Occurs when a rater's values or prejudices distort the rating.

Rater Bias Rater bias occurs when a rater's values or prejudices distort the rating. Such bias may be unconscious or quite intentional. For example, a manager's dislike of certain ethnic groups may cause distortion in appraisal information for some people. Use of age, religion, seniority, sex, appearance, or other "classifications" also may skew appraisal ratings if the appraisal process is not properly designed. A review of appraisal ratings by higher-level managers may help correct this problem.

Halo effect Occurs when a rater scores an employee high on all job criteria because of performance in one area.

Halo and Horns Effects The halo effect occurs when a rater scores an employee high on all job criteria because of performance in one area. For example, if a worker has few absences, her supervisor might give her a high rating in all other areas of work, including quantity and quality of output, without really thinking about the employee's other characteristics separately. The opposite is the *horns effect,* which occurs when a low rating on one characteristic leads to an overall low rating.

Contrast error Tendency to rate people relative to others rather than against performance standards.

Contrast Error Rating should be done using established standards. One problem is the contrast error, which is the tendency to rate people relative to others rather than against performance standards. For example, if everyone else performs at a mediocre level, then a person performing somewhat better may be rated as "excellent" because of the contrast effect. But in a group where many employees are performing well, the same person might receive a lower rating. Although it may be appropriate to compare people at times, the performance rating usually should reflect comparison against performance standards, not against other people.

Similar-to-Me/Different-from-Me Errors Sometimes, raters are influenced by whether people show characteristics that are the same as or different from their own. For example, if a manager has an MBA degree, he might give subordinates with MBAs higher appraisals than those with only bachelor's degrees. The error comes in measuring an individual against another person rather than measuring how well the individual fulfills the expectations of the job.

Sampling Error If the rater has seen only a small sample of the person's work, an appraisal may be subject to sampling error. For example, assume that 95% of the reports prepared by an employee have been satisfactory, but a manager sees only the 5% that has had errors. If the supervisor rates the person's performance as "poor," then a sampling error has occurred. Ideally, the work being rated should be a broad and representative sample of all the work done by the employee.

APPRAISAL FEEDBACK

After completing appraisals, managers need to communicate results in order to give employees a clear understanding of how they stand in the eyes of their immediate superiors and the organization. Organizations commonly require managers to discuss appraisals with employees. The appraisal feedback interview provides an opportunity to clear up any misunderstandings on both sides. In this interview, the manager should focus on coaching and development, and not just tell the employee, "Here is how you rate and why." Emphasizing development gives both parties an opportunity to consider the employee's performance as part of appraisal feedback.[29]

Appraisal Interview

The appraisal interview presents both an opportunity and a danger. It can be an emotional experience for the manager and the employee because the manager must communicate both praise and constructive criticism. A major concern for managers is how to emphasize the positive aspects of the employee's performance while still discussing ways to make needed improvements. If the interview is handled poorly, the employee may feel resentment, which could lead to conflict in future working relationships.

Employees usually approach an appraisal interview with some concern. They may feel that discussions about performance are both personal and important to their continued job success. At the same time, they want to know how their managers feel about their performance. Figure 11-14 summarizes hints for an effective appraisal interview for supervisors and managers.

Feedback as a System

The three commonly recognized components of a feedback system are data, evaluation of that data, and some action based on the evaluation. *Data* are factual pieces of information regarding observed actions or consequences. Most often, data are facts that report what happened, such as "Charlie solved

FIGURE 11-14   Appraisal Interview Hints for Supervisors and Managers

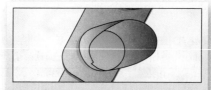
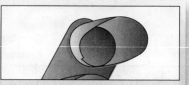

DO	DO NOT
◆ Prepare in advance	◆ Do all the talking
◆ Focus on performance and development	◆ Lecture the employee
◆ Be specific about reasons for ratings	◆ Mix performance appraisal and salary
◆ Decide on specific steps to be taken for improvement	or promotion issues
◆ Consider the supervisor's role in the subordinate's performance	◆ Concentrate only on the negative
◆ Reinforce desired behaviors	◆ Be overly critical or "harp on" a failing
◆ Focus on future performance	◆ Feel it is necessary for both parties to agree in all areas
	◆ Compare the employee with others

an engineering problem" or "Mary spoke harshly to an engineer." Data alone rarely tell the whole story. For instance, Mary's speaking harshly may have been an instance of poor communication and reflective of a lack of sensitivity, or it may have been a proper and necessary action. Someone must evaluate the meaning or value of the data.

Evaluation is the way the feedback system reacts to the facts, and it requires performance standards. Managers might evaluate the same factual information differently than would customers (for example, regarding merchandise exchange or credit decisions) or co-workers. Evaluation can be done by the person supplying the data, by a supervisor, or by a group.

For feedback to cause change, some decisions must be made regarding subsequent *action*. In traditional appraisal systems, the manager makes specific suggestions regarding future actions the employee might take. Employee input often is encouraged as well. In 360° feedback, people from whom information was solicited might also suggest actions that the individual may consider. It may be necessary to involve those providing information if the subsequent actions are highly interdependent and require coordination with the information providers.[30] Regardless of the process used, the feedback components (data, evaluation, and action) are necessary parts of a successful performance appraisal feedback system.

Reactions of Managers

Managers and supervisors who must complete appraisals of their employees often resist the appraisal process.[31] Many managers feel that their role calls on them to assist, encourage, coach, and counsel employees to improve their performance. However, being a judge on the one hand and a coach and a counselor on the other hand may cause internal conflict and confusion for managers.

Knowing that appraisals may affect employees' future careers also may cause altered or biased ratings. This problem is even more likely when managers know that they will have to communicate and defend their ratings to the employees, their bosses, or HR specialists. Managers can easily avoid providing negative feedback to an employee in an appraisal interview and thus avoid unpleasantness in an interpersonal situation by making the employee's ratings positive. But avoidance helps no one. A manager owes an employee a well-done appraisal, as the HR Practice indicates.

Reactions of Appraised Employees

Employees may well see the appraisal process as a threat and feel that the only way for them to get a higher rating is for someone else to receive a low rating. This win/lose perception is encouraged by comparative methods of rating. Emphasis on the self-improvement and developmental aspects of appraisal appears to be the most effective means to reduce these reactions from those participating in the appraisal process.[33]

Another common employee reaction resembles students' reactions to tests. A professor may prepare a test he or she feels is fair, but it does not necessarily follow that students will feel the test is fair; they simply may see it differently. Likewise, employees being appraised may not necessarily agree with the manager doing the appraising. However, in most cases, employees will view appraisals done well as what they are meant to be—constructive feedback.

Effective Performance Management

Regardless of the approach used, managers must understand the intended outcome of performance management.[34] When performance management is used to develop employees as resources, it usually works. When one key part of performance management, a performance appraisal, is used to punish employees, performance management is less effective. In its simplest form as part of

HR BEST PRACTICES

Lessons from Two Different Performances: A Supervisor's Story

My employees who do the best work are usually easy to get along with, but not always. I worked with one employee who alienated me and all his colleagues with his fierce competitiveness. He was quick to point out our mistakes, never spoke positively, and usually whined when someone else had a good project that he thought should have been his instead. I tried praising him and sought out his counsel to ease his obvious insecurities, but he was no fun to be around. However, he was productive. He got to work early and left late, was always eager to do more, and frequently worked overtime. He always did good work, could be counted on, and never missed a deadline. When he finally left, I realized I had come to rely on him, even though I did not miss his sour jealousy. He would not change.

Another employee and I shared common interests: some hobbies, the same work values and goals, and other interests. He was generous and willing to help, and his colleagues liked and appreciated him. Early on, he was a good producer, but later, he began procrastinating and often turned in incomplete work. I discussed it with him, and he promised to do better. But he did not. Project after project either flopped or was not done properly. Finally, I told him he would have to improve or find another job. The fact that I considered him a friend made that conversation painful, and I put it off longer than I should have. He told me he felt betrayed, and quit. Yet, when he got a new job, he called to say he had been unhappy but had been unable to move until I had pushed.[32]

What conclusions about performance management and performance appraisal can you draw from these two real-world examples?

performance management, performance appraisal is a manager's observation: "Here are your strengths and weaknesses, and here is a way to develop for the future."

Done well, performance management can lead to higher employee motivation and satisfaction. To be effective, a performance management system, including the performance appraisal processes, should be:

- Consistent with the strategic mission of the organization
- Beneficial as a development tool
- Useful as an administrative tool
- Legal and job related
- Viewed as generally fair by employees
- Effective in documenting employee performance

SUMMARY

- Performance management systems attempt to identify, measure, communicate, develop, and reward employee performance.
- Performance management has a broad organizational focus, whereas performance appraisals are the processes used to evaluate how employees perform their jobs and then communicate that information to employees.
- Effective performance management has a number of components, beginning with a performance-focused organizational culture.
- Job criteria identify important elements of a job, and the relevance of job criteria affects the establishment of performance standards.
- Federal employment guidelines and numerous court decisions affect the design and use of the performance appraisal process.
- Appraising employee performance serves both administrative and developmental purposes.
- Performance appraisals can be done either informally or systematically.
- Appraisals can be conducted by superiors, employees (rating superiors or themselves), teams, outsiders, or a variety of sources.

- Appraisal methods include: category scaling, comparative, narrative, and management by objectives.
- Category scaling methods, especially graphic rating scales and behavioral rating scales, are widely used.
- Comparative methods include ranking and forced distribution, which both raise methodological and legal concerns.
- Narrative methods include the critical incident technique and the essay approach.
- Training managers and employees on how to conduct performance appraisals can contribute to the effectiveness of a performance management system.
- Many performance appraisal problems are caused by a number of different rater errors.
- The appraisal feedback interview is a vital part of any appraisal system, and the reactions of both managers and employees must be considered when evaluating the system.

REVIEW AND APPLICATION QUESTIONS

1. Describe how an organizational culture and the use of performance criteria and standards affect the remaining components of a performance management system.
2. Suppose you are a supervisor. What errors might you make when preparing the performance appraisal on a clerical employee? How might you avoid those errors?
3. Review the performance appraisal process and appraisal form used by a current or former employer, and compare them with those provided by other students. Also review other appraisal issues by going to *www.workforce.com* and search for articles on *performance appraisals*. Develop a report suggesting changes to make the performance appraisal form and process you reviewed more effective.

CASE

Performance Management Improvements for Bristol-Myers Squibb

Bristol-Myers Squibb (BMS) is one of the world's largest pharmaceutical firms and is widely known for its innovative research. But the firm has not limited its innovations to products. Several years ago, BMS leaders decided that the company's performance management system needed to be re-invented. Specifically, they determined that the existing performance appraisal process was not working. Managers were "form focused," meaning that they were so concentrated on filling out the performance review forms, the content of the forms was not being used for employee coaching and based on development. Also, most of the attention of managers and employees was historical and based on what employees had done in the past. Little attention was being given to how employees could develop and improve in the future.

The most radical steps taken were to totally eliminate the appraisal forms and their rating scales and to request that managers not discuss pay increases during performance review sessions. Instead, a new "performance partnership" became the focus. At all levels of BMS, managers were trained to hold regular meetings with their employees. At these meetings managers and employees review performance goals expectations. Together they set expectations and timelines for accomplishing the goals. Rather than meeting just once a year, the performance partnership update occurs throughout the year.

The changes in the performance management system have led to several positive results. First, employees are more active participants, rather than just getting their ratings on forms and then passively listening to the managers. Also, a greater amount of time is spent on coaching because managers were trained on use of a guided feedback approach. This approach has led to more discussions in which employees and managers emphasize joint problem solving and goal achievements. Although the system takes more managerial and employee time, the coaching and employee involvement have created a more positive relationship and improved individual and managerial performance.[35]

Questions

1. Discuss how this case illustrates the contrasts between the administrative use and developmental use of appraisals.

2. Identify some of the advantages and disadvantages of eliminating the use of appraisal forms and ratings.

SUPPLEMENTAL CASE

Unequal/Equal Supervisors

This case identifies the consequences of giving appraisal ratings that may not be accurate. (For the case, go to http://thomsonedu.com/management/mathis.)

NOTES

1. Based on "Let People Know Where They Stand, Welch Says," *USA Today,* April 18, 2005, 5B.
2. Herman Aguinis, *Performance Management* (Upper Saddle River, NJ: Pearson/Prentice Hall, 2007), 50–51.
3. Mark Albrecht, "Breaking the Performance Management Myths," September 22, 2004, *workindex.com.*
4. Brian E. Becker, Mark A. Huselid, and Dave Ulrich, *The HR Scorecard: Linking People, Strategy, and Performance* (Boston, MA: Harvard Business School Press, 2001).
5. "Survey: Failure to Deal with Poor Performers May Decrease Engagement of Other Employees," *Newsline,* June 22, 2006.
6. Susan J. Wells, "No Results, No Raise," *HR Magazine,* May 2005, 76–80.
7. Based on Mei-I Cheng and Andrew Dainty, "What Makes a Good Project Manager?" *Human Resource Management Journal,* 15 (2005), 25–37.
8. Inge C. Kerssens-von Dronghen and Olaf Fisscher, "Ethical Dilemmas in

Performance Management," *Journal of Business Ethics*, June 2003, 51.

9. Eric Harmon, Scott Hensel, and T. E. Lukes, "Measuring Performance in Services," *The McKinsey Quarterly*, 2006, 2–7.

10. "Communicating Beyond Ratings Can Be Difficult," *Workforce Management*, April 24, 2006, 35.

11. "Performance Management," *HR Magazine*, November 2005, 135; Dawn S. Onley, "Using Dashboards to Drive HR," *HR Magazine*, April 2006, 109–115; Erin White, "For Relevance Firms Revamp Worker Reviews," *The Wall Street Journal*, July 17, 2006, B1; and Anne Freedman, "Balancing Values, Results in Reviews," *Human Resource Executive*, August 2006, 62.

12. "Performance Management Practices," *www.ddi.com*.

13. Stuart Buttrick, "How to Do Appraisals," *Indiana Employment Law Letter*, December 2003.

14. *Garrett v. Hewlett-Packard Company*, 305 F. 3d 1210 (10th Cir. 2002).

15. Andy Meisler, "Dead Man's Curve," *Workforce Management*, July 2003, 44–49.

16. *Britov v. Zia Co.*, 478 F. 2d 1200 (10th Cir. 1973).

17. John Goemaat, "Documentation Makes the Difference," *Security Management*, September 2003, 94–102.

18. Gerard P. Panaro, "The Two-Edged Sword of Employee Job Evaluations," *HR Advisor*, May/June 2005, 39–43.

19. Clinton Longnecker, "Managerial Performance Appraisals: The Good, The Bad, and The Ugly," *HR Advisor*, May/June 2005, 19–26.

20. Aguinis, *Performance Management*, 256–265.

21. W. H. Berman, J. C. Scott, and D. Finch, "Assessments: Connecting Employees with the Performance Improvement Process," *Workforce Performance Solutions*, June 2005, 20–24.

22. "360° Evaluation of Managers," *Omaha World-Herald*, May 9, 2005, D1.

23. Jena McGregor, "The Struggle to Measure Performance," *Business Week*, January 9, 2006, 26–28.

24. Kristen B. Frasch, "Lawsuit Ties Performance Rankings to Age Discrimination," *Human Resource Executive*, July 2003, 13.

25. Dick Grote, "Making Forced Rankings Work," *Workforce Management Online*, November 2005, *www.workforce.com*.

26. Steve Scullen, Paul Bergey, and Lynda Aiman-Smith, "Forced Distribution Rating Systems and the Improvement of Workforce Potential," *Personnel Psychology*, 58 (2005), 1–31.

27. Colleen O'Neill and Lori Holsinger, "Effective Performance Management Systems," *WorldatWork Journal*, Second Quarter 2003, 61–67.

28. Aguinis, *Performance Management*, 155–162.

29. Steve Hamm, "Motivating the Troops," *Business Week*, November 21, 2005, 88–92.

30. D. Van Fleet, T. Peterson, and E. Van Fleet, "Closing the Performance Feedback Gap with Expert Systems," *The Academy of Management Executive*, August 2005, 38–53.

31. G. Adler and M. Ambrose, "Toward Understanding Fairness Judgments Associated with Computer Performance Monitoring," *Human Resource Management Review*, 15 (2005), 43–67.

32. Adapted from Carol Hymowitz, "What to Do When Your Favorite Workers Don't Make the Grade," *The Wall Street Journal*, April 11, 2000, B1.

33. Laura Roberts et al., "How to Play to Your Strengths," *Harvard Business Review*, January 2005, 74–80; and Peter Drucker, "Managing Oneself," *Harvard Business Review*, January 2005, 100–109.

34. Aileen MacMillan, "Raising the Bar on Performance Management Practices to Optimize Performance Reviews and Goal Management," *HR.com*, April 2006, 2–12.

35. Based on "Adding New Life to Performance Reviews Keeps Employees, Managers Rejuvenated," *Bulletin to Management*, February 7, 2002, 41–42.

SECTION 4

Compensating Human Resources

CHAPTER

12

Total Rewards and Compensation

After you have read this chapter, you should be able to:

- Identify the three general components of total rewards and examples of each.

- Discuss four compensation system design issues.

- List the basic provisions of the Fair Labor Standards Act (FLSA).

- Outline the process of building a base pay system.

- Describe the two means of valuing jobs.

- Explain two ways individual pay increases are determined.

 McDonald's Global Rewards Strategy

Many people worldwide know McDonald's because it has restaurants in over 100 countries. But, for McDonald's, attracting and retaining more than 400,000 managers and senior-level employees has been a continuing challenge.

Beginning in 2004, a new global rewards program was developed and implemented. The program, called Plan to Win, focuses on key business success areas such as customer service and marketing. In each country, managers select three to five factors to ensure success in their local markets, such as implementing a new menu, changing customer service hours, or redesigning restaurants.

The rewards program includes base pay and benefits. In addition, annual incentive pools are linked to meeting regional, country, business unit, and operating income targets. The incentive program also considers individual performance based on annual performance ratings.

The Plan to Win program has led to decreases in managerial and employee turnover. The program has also helped managers and senior employees understand how they contribute to McDonald's global success. Thus, McDonald's global rewards strategy appears to pay off for both the company and key employees.[1]

Total rewards in organizations, including compensation systems, must be linked to organizational objectives and strategies, as McDonald's has done. Total rewards are the monetary and non-monetary rewards provided to employees in order to attract, motivate, and retain them. Critical to an effective total rewards approach is the need to balance the interests and costs of the employers with the needs and expectations of employees. In some industries, such as financial services, health care, education, and hospitality, employee payroll and benefits compose more than 60% of all operating costs. Although actual costs can be easily calculated, the value derived by employers and employees may prove more difficult to identify.

Total rewards Monetary and non-monetary rewards provided to employees in order to attract, motivate, and retain them.

NATURE OF TOTAL REWARDS AND COMPENSATON

Because so many organizational funds are spent on employees, it is critical for top management and HR executives to match total rewards systems and practices with what the organization is trying to accomplish. A number of important decisions must be made to achieve the following objectives:

- Legal compliance with all appropriate laws and regulations
- Cost effectiveness for the organization
- Internal, external, and individual equity for employees
- Performance enhancement for the organization
- Performance recognition and talent management for employees

Employers must balance their costs at a level that rewards employees sufficiently for their knowledge, skills, abilities, and performance accomplishments. During the past several years, total rewards have been a significant focus in HR and different frameworks have been developed.[2] One prominent approach has been developed by *WorldatWork,* a leading professional association.[3] To combine the leading approaches into a simplified view, Figure 12-1 identifies three primary groups. What the figure illustrates is that total rewards

---

FIGURE 12-1   **Total Rewards Components**

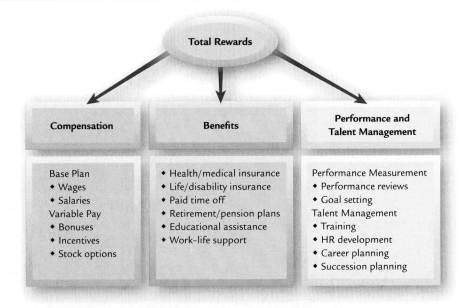

must be seen more broadly than just compensation and benefits. Although the importance of performance management and talent management have been discussed in detail in the previous two chapters, the focus of the next three chapters is on compensation, variable pay, and benefits.

Types of Compensation

One of the distinctions not formally a part of Figure 12-1 is that rewards can be both intrinsic and extrinsic. *Intrinsic rewards* may include praise for completing a project or meeting performance objectives. Other psychological and social forms of compensation also reflect intrinsic type of rewards. *Extrinsic rewards* are tangible and take both monetary and non-monetary forms. One tangible component of a compensation program is *direct compensation*, whereby the employer exchanges monetary rewards for work done and performance results achieved. *Base pay* and *variable pay* are the most common forms of direct compensation. Indirect compensation commonly consists of employee *benefits*.

Base pay Basic compensation that an employee receives, usually as a wage or a salary.

Base Pay The basic compensation that an employee receives, usually as a wage or a salary, is called base pay. Many organizations use two base pay categories, *hourly* and *salaried,* which are identified according to the way pay is distributed and the nature of the jobs. Hourly pay is the most common means and is based on time. Employees paid hourly receive wages, which are payments directly calculated on the amount of time worked. In contrast, people paid salaries receive consistent payments each period regardless of the number of hours worked. Being paid a salary has typically carried higher status for employees than has being paid a wage. However, overtime may have to be paid to certain salaried employees as defined by federal and state laws.

Wages Payments directly calculated on the amount of time worked.

Salaries Consistent payments made each period regardless of the number of hours worked.

Variable Pay Another type of direct pay is variable pay, which is compensation linked directly to individual, team, or organizational performance. The most common types of variable pay for most employees are bonuses and incentive program payments. Executives often receive longer-term rewards such as stock options. Variable pay, including executive compensation, is discussed in Chapter 13.

Variable pay Compensation linked directly to individual, team, or organizational performance.

Benefits Many organizations provide numerous extrinsic rewards in an indirect manner. With indirect compensation, employees receive the tangible value of the rewards without receiving actual cash. A benefit is an indirect reward—for instance, health insurance, vacation pay, or a retirement pension—given to an employee or a group of employees for organizational membership, regardless of performance. Often employees do not directly pay for all of the benefits they receive. Benefits are discussed in Chapter 14.

Benefit Indirect reward given to an employee or a group of employees for organizational membership.

Compensation Philosophies

Two basic compensation philosophies lie on opposite ends of a continuum, as shown in Figure 12-2. At one end of the continuum is the *entitlement* philosophy; at the other end is the *performance* philosophy. Most compensation systems fall somewhere in between.

Entitlement philosophy Assumes that individuals who have worked another year are entitled to pay increases, with little regard for performance differences.

Entitlement Philosophy The entitlement philosophy assumes that individuals who have worked another year are entitled to pay increases, with little regard for performance differences. Many traditional organizations

---

FIGURE 12-2   **Continuum of Compensation Philosophies**

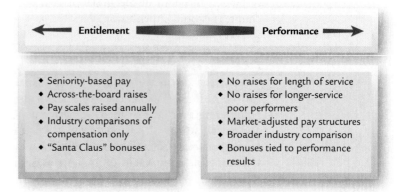

that give automatic increases to their employees every year are practicing the entitlement philosophy. These automatic increases may be referred to as *cost-of-living raises,* even if they are not tied specifically to economic indicators. Further, most of those employees receive the same or nearly the same percentage increase each year. Bonuses in many entitlement-oriented organizations are determined in a manner that often fails to reflect operating results. Therefore, employees "expect" the bonuses, which become another form of entitlement.

Pay-for-performance philosophy Requires that compensation changes reflect performance differences.

Performance Philosophy The pay-for-performance philosophy requires that compensation changes reflect performance differences. Organizations operating under this philosophy do not guarantee additional or increased compensation simply for completing another year of organizational service. Instead, they structure pay and incentives to reflect performance differences among employees. Thus, employees who perform satisfactorily maintain or advance their compensation levels more than marginal performers. Also, the bonuses and incentives are based on individual, group, and/or organizational performance.

Few organizations totally follow performance-oriented compensation practices, but the overall trend is toward greater use of pay-for-performance systems. A survey of *Fortune 1000* firms found that over 80% of the firms use some types of performance-based compensation plans. The study found that recent growth had been greater in individual incentive plans and team/group reward systems than organization-wide gainsharing, profit sharing, and stock option plans.[4] Such plans may help reduce employee turnover and increase employee commitment and retention.[5] The HR Best Practices illustrates the effectiveness at one firm.

The total rewards approach reflects a more performance-oriented philosophy because it tries to place more value on individuals and their performance rather than just on paying for having a job. When determining compensation, managers factor in elements such as how much an employee knows or how competent an employee is. Some organizations use compensation and variable pay programs as part of a total rewards approach for all levels of employees. Widespread use of various incentive plans, team bonuses, organizational gainsharing programs, and other designs links growth in compensation and variable pay to results. Regularly communicating to employees and managers the compensation philosophy helps reinforce the organizational commitment to it.[6]

HR BEST PRACTICES

Pay-for-Performance at First Merit Bank

The effectiveness of a pay-for-performance approach is illustrated in the experience at First Merit Bank based in Akron, Ohio. With over 3,400 employees, employee turnover and retention are ongoing issues. But focusing on reducing turnover of proof operators has paid off. Proof operators perform repetitive tasks at keyboards by entering amounts of customer checks into the computer system. At many banks the turnover rate of proof operators is among the highest for any job group.

First Merit developed a pay-for-performance system based on two metrics: speed and accuracy. Using the computer system to provide measurements, operators are rewarded on key strokes per hour and accuracy rates. Additionally, the amount of money that employees could earn was uncapped. Thus, while the base rate was $9 per hour, 22 of 27 employees at one location earned over $15 per hour, depending on performance and productivity. As would be expected, proof operator turnover rates declined significantly. The success of the system has been extended to other jobs throughout the bank using different performance metrics and pay amounts. This program illustrates the potential value of using a total rewards approach and a pay-for-performance philosophy.[7]

HR Metrics and Compensation

Employers spend huge amounts of money for employee compensation. Just like any other area of expenditures, compensation expenditures should be evaluated to determine their effectiveness. Many measures can be used for this evaluation.[8] Employee turnover/retention is one widely used factor. This usage assumes that how well compensation systems operate affects employees' decisions about staying or leaving the organization. Other more specific measures are used as well, such as the ones shown in Figure 12-3.[9]

The numbers for calculating these measures are readily available to most HR professionals and Chief Financial Officers, but such calculations are not made in many firms. Often the importance of using these numbers is not a priority for managers or CFOs. Ideally, compensation metrics should be computed each year, and then compared with metrics from past years to show how the rate of compensation changes compares with the rate of changes in the organization overall (revenues, expenses, etc.).

FIGURE 12-3   HR Metrics for Compensation

HR Performance Area	Method of Calculation
1. Pay and benefits as percentage of operating expense	Total pay and benefits expenditures ÷ Total operating expenses
2. Human value added	Revenue − Operating expense − Pay and benefits = Adjusted profit ÷ Full-time-equivalent employees (FTEs)
3. Return on human capital invested	Revenue − Operating expense − Pay and benefits = Adjusted profit ÷ Pay and benefits
4. Employee cost factor	Total compensation and benefits ÷ FTEs

FIGURE 12-4   Typical Division of HR Responsibilities: Compensation

HR Unit	Managers
• Develops and administers the compensation system • Evaluate jobs and analyzes pay surveys • Develops wage/salary structures and policies	• Identify job descriptions and compensation concerns • Recommend pay rates and increases according to HR guidelines • Evaluate employee performance for compensation purposes

Compensation Responsibilities

To administer compensation expenditures wisely, HR specialists and operating managers must work together. A typical division of compensation responsibilities is illustrated in Figure 12-4. HR specialists guide the development and administration of an organizational compensation system and conduct job evaluations and wage surveys. Also, because of the technical complexity involved, HR specialists typically assume responsibility for developing base pay programs and salary structures and policies. HR specialists may or may not do actual payroll processing. This labor-intensive responsibility is typically among the first to be outsourced. Operating managers evaluate the performance of employees and consider their performance when deciding compensation increases within the policies and guidelines established by the HR unit and upper management.

Internet Research

Compensation Resources, Inc.
The development, design, and implementation of compensation plans are the specialty services provided by this consulting firm. Visit their Website at: http://thomsonedu .com/management/mathis.

COMPENSATION SYSTEM DESIGN ISSUES

Depending on the compensation philosophies, strategies, and approaches identified for an organization, a number of decisions are made that affect the design of the compensation system. Some important ones are highlighted next.

Compensation Fairness and Equity

Most people in organizations work in order to gain rewards for their efforts. Whether employees are considering base pay or variable pay, the extent to which they perceive their compensation to be fair often affects their performance, how they view their jobs, and their employers. This factor may lead to lower or higher turnover rates. Also pay satisfaction has been found to be linked to organizational-level performance outcomes.[10]

Equity Perceived fairness between what a person does and what the person receives.

Equity Equity is the perceived fairness between what a person does (inputs) and what the person receives (outcomes). Individuals judge equity in compensation by comparing their input (effort and performance) against the effort and performance of others and against the outcomes (the rewards received).

These comparisons are personal and are based on individual perceptions, not just facts. A study by Salary.com found that almost 60% of the workers surveyed believed they were underpaid. But according to reviews of compensation databases, less than 20% were actually underpaid.[11] These findings illustrate how the perceptions of individuals are critical in how equity is viewed.

External Equity If an employer does not provide compensation that employees view as equitable in relation to the compensation provided to other employees performing similar jobs in other organizations, that employer is likely to experience higher turnover. Other drawbacks include greater difficulty in recruiting qualified and high-demand individuals. Also, by not being competitive, the employer is more likely to attract and retain individuals with less knowledge and fewer skills and abilities, resulting in lower overall organizational performance. Organizations track external equity by using pay surveys, which are discussed later in this chapter, and by looking at the compensation policies of competing employers.

Internal Equity in Compensation Equity internally means that employees receive compensation in relation to the knowledge, skills, and abilities (KSAs) they use in their jobs, as well as their responsibilities and accomplishments. Two key issues—procedural justice and distributive justice—relate to internal equity.

Procedural justice
Perceived fairness of the process and procedures used to make decisions about employees.

Procedural justice is the perceived fairness of the process and procedures used to make decisions about employees, including their pay. As it applies to compensation, the entire process of determining base pay for jobs, allocating pay increases, and measuring performance must be perceived as fair.

Distributive justice
Perceived fairness in the distribution of outcomes.

A related issue that must be considered is distributive justice, which is the perceived fairness in the distribution of outcomes. As one example, if a hardworking employee whose performance is outstanding receives the same across-the-board raise as an employee with attendance problems and mediocre performance, then inequity may be perceived. Likewise, if two employees have similar performance records but one receives a significantly greater pay raise, the other may perceive an inequity due to supervisory favoritism or other factors not related to the job.

To address concerns about both types of justice, some organizations establish compensation appeals procedures. Typically, employees are encouraged to contact the HR department after discussing their concerns with their immediate supervisors and managers.

Pay Secrecy vs. Openness Another equity issue concerns the degree of secrecy or openness that organizations have regarding their pay systems. Pay information kept secret in "closed" systems includes how much others make, what raises others have received, and even what pay grades and ranges exist in the organization. Some firms have policies that prohibit employees from discussing their pay with other employees, and violations of these policies can lead to disciplinary action.[12] However, several court decisions have ruled that these policies violate the National Labor Relations Act.

A number of organizations are opening up their pay systems to some degree by providing employees with more information on compensation policies, pay structures, and other general details. Having a more open pay system has been found to have positive effects on employee retention and organizational effectiveness.[13]

Market Competitiveness and Compensation

The market competitiveness of compensation has a significant impact on how equitably employees view compensation. Providing competitive compensation to employees, whether globally, domestically, or locally, is a concern for all employers.[14] Some organizations establish specific policies about where they wish to be positioned in the labor market. These policies use a *quartile strategy*, as illustrated in Figure 12-5. Data in pay surveys reveal that the dollar differential between quartiles is generally 15% to 20%.

"Meet the Market" Strategy Most employers choose to position themselves in the *second quartile* (median), in the middle of the market, as identified by pay data from surveys of other employers' compensation plans. Choosing this level attempts to balance employer cost pressures and the need to attract and retain employees, by providing mid-level compensation scales that "meet the market" for the employer's jobs.

"Lag the Market" Strategy An employer using a *first-quartile* strategy may choose to "lag the market" by paying below market levels, for several reasons. If the employer is experiencing a shortage of funds, it may be unable to pay more. Also, when an abundance of workers is available, particularly those with lower skills, a below-market approach can be used to attract sufficient workers at a lesser cost. Some employers hire illegal immigrants at below-market rates because of the large numbers of those individuals who want to work in the United States. The downside of this strategy is that it increases the likelihood of higher worker turnover. If the labor market supply tightens, then attracting and retaining workers becomes more difficult.

"Lead the Market" Strategy A *third-quartile* strategy uses an aggressive approach to "lead the market." This strategy generally enables a company to attract and retain sufficient workers with the required capabilities and to be more selective when hiring. Because it is a higher-cost approach, organizations often look for ways to increase the productivity of employees receiving above-market wages.

FIGURE 12-5   **Compensation Quartile Strategies**

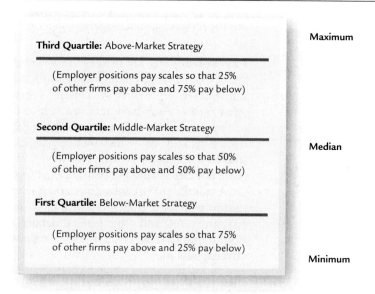

Maximum

Third Quartile: Above-Market Strategy

(Employer positions pay scales so that 25% of other firms pay above and 75% pay below)

Second Quartile: Middle-Market Strategy

Median

(Employer positions pay scales so that 50% of other firms pay above and 50% pay below)

First Quartile: Below-Market Strategy

(Employer positions pay scales so that 75% of other firms pay above and 25% pay below)

Minimum

Selecting a Quartile The pay levels and pay structures used can affect organizational performance.[15] Individual employee pay levels will vary around the quartile level, depending on experience, performance, and other individual factors. Deciding in which quartile to position pay structures is a function of a number of considerations. The financial resources available, competitiveness pressures, and the market availability of employees with different capabilities are external factors. For instance, some employers with extensive benefits programs or broad-based incentive programs may choose a first-quartile strategy so that their overall compensation costs and levels are competitive.

Competency-Based Pay

The design of most compensation programs rewards employees for carrying out their tasks, duties, and responsibilities. The job requirements determine which employees have higher base rates. Employees receive more for doing jobs that require a greater variety of tasks, more knowledge and skills, greater physical effort, or more demanding working conditions. However, the design of some compensation programs emphasizes competencies rather than tasks performed.

Competency-based pay
Rewards individuals for the capabilities they demonstrate and acquire.

Competency-based pay rewards individuals for the capabilities they demonstrate and acquire. In knowledge-based pay (KBP) or skill-based pay (SBP) systems, employees start at a base level of pay and receive increases as they learn to do other jobs or gain additional skills and knowledge and thus become more valuable to the employer.[16] For example, a printing firm operates two-color, four-color, and six-color presses. The more colors, the more skills required of the press operators. Under a KBP or SBP system, press operators increase their pay as they learn how to operate the more complex presses, even though sometimes they may be running only two-color jobs.

When an organization moves to a competency-based system, considerable time must be spent identifying the required competencies for various jobs. Reliance on items such as relevant college diplomas and degrees may need to change such that more emphasis is placed on demonstrated knowledge and competencies.[17] *Progression* of employees must be possible, and employees must be paid appropriately for all their competencies. Any *limitations* on the numbers of people who can acquire more competencies should be clearly identified. *Training* in the appropriate competencies is particularly critical. Also, a competency-based system needs to acknowledge or certify employees as they acquire certain competencies, and then to verify the maintenance of those competencies. In summary, use of a competency-based system requires significant investment of management time and commitment.

Individual vs. Team Rewards

As some organizations have shifted to using work teams, they have faced the logical concern of how to develop compensation programs that build on the team concept. At issue is how to compensate the individuals whose performance may also be evaluated on team achievements.[18] For base pay, employers often compensate individuals on the basis of competencies, experience, and other job factors. Then many organizations use team incentive rewards on top of base pay. Variable pay rewards for teams are most frequently distributed annually as specified dollar amounts, not as percentages of base pay. Discussion of team-based incentives is contained in Chapter 13.

Global Compensation Issues

All of the previous issues can become more complex when dealing with global compensation. The growing world economy has led to many more employees working internationally. Some are located and work in multiple countries, while others may be based in a home country such as the United States or Germany, but have international responsibilities. Therefore, organizations with employees working throughout the world face some special compensation issues for employees. The components of a global compensation package that may be used are illustrated in Figure 12-6. Variations in laws, living costs, tax policies, and other factors all must be considered in establishing the compensation for local employees and managers, as well as managers and professionals brought in from other countries. Even fluctuations in the values of various monetary currencies must be tracked and adjustments made as the currencies rise or fall in relation to currency rates in other countries. With these and numerous other concerns, developing and managing a global compensation system becomes extremely complex.[19]

One significant global issue in compensation design is how to compensate the employees from different countries. In many countries, the local wage scales vary significantly. For instance, in some less-developed countries, pay levels for degreed professionals may range from $15,000 to $30,000 a year, whereas in Europe and the United States, individuals with the same qualifications are paid $50,000 to $80,000 a year. Lower-skilled local workers may make as little as $300 a month in less-developed countries, whereas comparable employees make $1,800 to $2,500 a month in the United States and Europe. These large compensation differences have led to significant "international outsourcing" of jobs to lower-wage countries. The movement

FIGURE 12-6   Possible Components of Global Employee Compensation

Internet Research

of call-center and information technology jobs to India and manufacturing jobs to China, the Philippines, and Mexico are examples.

Compensating Expatriates Expatriates are citizens of one country who are working in a second country and employed by an organization headquartered in the first country. It has been estimated that the aggregate employer costs for an expatriate, including all allowances, is three to four times the expatriate's salary. Thus, if an expatriate's salary is $200,000, the actual cost of employing that person is likely $600,000 to $800,000. The overall costs for many senior-level expatriates can be near $1 million.[20]

The two primary approaches to international compensation for expatriates are the balance-sheet approach and the global market approach. The balance-sheet approach is a compensation plan that equalizes cost differences between the international assignment and the same assignment in the home country of the individual or the corporation. Reviews have found that the balance-sheet approach can result in higher employer costs and more administrative complexity than other plans.[21] These considerations have led more multinational firms to use a different means.

Unlike the balance-sheet approach, the global market approach attempts to be more comprehensive in providing base pay, incentives, benefits, and relocation expenses regardless of the country to which the employee is assigned. This approach to compensation requires significant flexibility, detailed analyses, and extensive administrative effort. Almost 60% of multinational firms use this approach.[22]

Many international compensation plans attempt to protect expatriates from negative tax consequences by using a tax equalization plan. Under such a plan, the company adjusts an employee's base income downward by the amount of estimated home-country tax to be paid for the year. Thus, the employee pays only the foreign-country tax. For instance, a tax equalization plan attempts to ensure that U.S. expatriates will not pay any more or less in taxes than if they were working in the United States. Major changes in the U.S. tax law in 2006 increased the tax provisions that may affect the 300,000 U.S. expatriates working abroad.[23] Because of the variation in tax laws and rates from country to country, tax equalization is very complex to determine.

Balance-sheet approach
Compensation plan that equalizes cost differences between the international assignment and the same assignment in the home country.

Global market approach
Compensation plan that attempts to be more comprehensive in providing base pay, incentives, benefits, and relocation expenses regardless of the country to which the employee is assigned.

Tax equalization plan
Compensation plan used to protect expatriates from negative tax consequences.

LEGAL CONSTRAINTS ON PAY SYSTEMS

Compensation systems must comply with many government constraints. The important areas addressed by the laws include minimum-wage standards and hours of work. The following discussion examines the laws and regulations affecting base compensation; laws and regulations affecting incentives and benefits are examined in later chapters.

Fair Labor Standards Act (FLSA)

The major federal law affecting compensation is the Fair Labor Standards Act (FLSA), which was originally passed in 1938. Compliance with FLSA provisions is enforced by the Wage and Hour Division of the U.S. Department of Labor. To meet FLSA requirements, employers must keep accurate time records and maintain those records for three years. Penalties for wage and

HR PERSPECTIVE

Wal-Mart Pays for Violations of Compensation Laws

Wal-Mart, the largest retailer in the United States with 1.4 million workers in 1,500 stores, has faced numerous lawsuits for violating FLSA and state compensation legal regulations. At one point, more than 70 class action lawsuits were pending, and large payments had been made to settle others.

Several cases illustrate Wal-Mart's problems. A Colorado case was settled for $50 million, and Wal-Mart is facing a more than $100 million fine in a California case. An example of some of the alleged violations is illustrated in a Pennsylvania case involving 187,000 workers who were denied meal breaks and were working unpaid hours over breaks and before clocking in.

Additionally, a federal case found that Wal-Mart violated child labor laws in a number of states. Teenage workers 16 and 17 years of age operated hazardous equipment, such as forklifts, and did other prohibited work. Consequently, Wal-Mart paid $135,000 to settle these violations.

To prevent and reduce such compensation law violations, Wal-Mart has used expanded management training. Also, specific systems have been established to improve compliance with the various regulations on non-exempt employees regarding unpaid hours worked, required breaks, child labor compliance, and other provisions. The future extent of the success of these efforts will be judged by the scope and number of additional lawsuits and legal settlements that Wal-mart may continue to face.[24]

hour violations often include awards of up to two years of back pay for affected current and former employees. The HR Perspective describes the cost of FLSA and related violations by Wal-Mart.

To update and modernize the provisions of the FLSA, the U.S. Department of Labor made some changes in 2004. The provisions of both the original act and subsequent revisions focus on the following major areas:

- Establish a minimum wage.
- Discourage oppressive use of child labor.
- Encourage limits on the number of hours employees work per week, through overtime provisions (exempt and non-exempt statuses).

Minimum Wage The FLSA sets a minimum wage to be paid to the broad spectrum of covered employees. The actual minimum wage can be changed only by congressional action. A lower minimum wage is set for "tipped" employees, such as restaurant workers, but their compensation must equal or exceed the minimum wage when average tips are included. Minimum wage levels have sparked significant political discussions and legislative maneuvering at both the federal and state levels for the past decade. Consequently, a three-stage increase in the federal minimum wage occurred beginning in 2007. Note that if a state's minimum wage is higher, employers must meet the state level rather than the federal level.

Debate also surrounds the payment of a living wage versus the minimum wage. A living wage is one that is supposed to meet the basic needs of a worker's family. In the United States, the living wage typically aligns with the amount needed for a family of four to be supported by one worker so that family income is above the officially identified "poverty" level. Without waiting for U.S. federal laws to change, over 80 cities have passed local living-wage laws. Ethical, economic, and employment implications affect both sides of this issue.[25]

Living wage One that is supposed to meet the basic needs of a worker's family.

Child Labor Provisions The child labor provisions of the FLSA set the minimum age for employment with unlimited hours at 16 years. For hazardous occupations (see Chapter 15), the minimum is 18 years of age. Individuals 14 to 15 years old may work outside school hours with certain limitations. Many employers require age certificates for employees because the FLSA makes the employer responsible for determining an individual's age. A representative of a state labor department, a state education department, or a local school district generally issues such certificates.

Exempt and Non-Exempt Statuses Under the FLSA, employees are classified as exempt or non-exempt. Exempt employees hold positions for which employers are not required to pay overtime. Non-exempt employees must be paid overtime. The current FLSA regulations used to identify whether or not a job qualifies for exempt status identifies five categories of exempt jobs:

Exempt employees
Employees to whom employers are not required to pay overtime.

Non-exempt employees
Employees who must be paid overtime.

- Executive
- Administrative
- Professional (learned or creative)
- Computer employees
- Outside sales

As Figure 12-7 indicates the regulations identify factors related to salaried pay levels per week, duties and responsibilities, and other criteria that must exist for jobs to be categorized as exempt. To review the details for each exemption, go to the U.S. Department of Labor's Website at *www.dol.gov*.

In base pay programs, employers often categorize jobs into groupings that tie the FLSA status and the method of payment together. Employers are required to pay overtime for *hourly* jobs in order to comply with the FLSA. Employees in positions classified as *salaried non-exempt* are covered by the overtime provisions of the FLSA and therefore must be paid overtime. Salaried non-exempt positions sometimes include secretarial, clerical, and salaried blue-collar positions. A common mistake made by employers is to avoid paying overtime to any salaried employees, even though some do not qualify for exempt status. Misclassifying certain assistant managers is one example.[26]

The FLSA does not require employers to pay overtime for *salaried exempt* jobs, although some organizations have implemented policies to pay a straight rate for extensive hours of overtime. For instance, some electric utilities pay first-line supervisors extra using a special rate for hours worked over 50 a week during storm emergencies. A number of salaried exempt professionals in various information technology jobs also receive additional compensation for working extensively more than 40 hours per week.

Internet Research

Wage and Hour Division
This government Website from the Wage and Hour Division of the U.S. Department of Labor provides an overview of the exemptions under the Fair Labor Standards Act. Visit the site at: http://thomsonedu.com/management/mathis.

FIGURE 12-7   Determining Exempt Status Under the FLSA

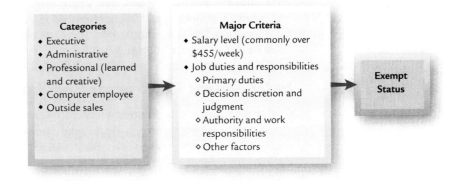

Categories	Major Criteria	
• Executive	• Salary level (commonly over $455/week)	
• Administrative	• Job duties and responsibilities	
• Professional (learned and creative)	◇ Primary duties	**Exempt Status**
• Computer employee	◇ Decision discretion and judgment	
• Outside sales	◇ Authority and work responsibilities	
	◇ Other factors	

Overtime The FLSA establishes overtime pay requirements. Its provisions set overtime pay at one and one-half times the regular pay rate for all hours over 40 a week, except for employees who are not covered by the FLSA. Overtime provisions do not apply to farm workers, who also have a lower minimum-wage schedule.

The workweek is defined as a consecutive period of 168 hours (24 hours × 7 days) and does not have to be a calendar week. If they wish to do so, hospitals and nursing homes are allowed to use a 14-day period instead of a 7-day week, as long as overtime is paid for hours worked beyond 8 in a day or 80 in a 14-day period. No daily number of hours requiring overtime is set, except for special provisions relating to hospitals and other specially designated organizations. Thus, if a manufacturing firm operates on a 4-day/10-hour schedule, no overtime pay is required by the act.

The most difficult part is distinguishing who is and is not exempt.[27] Some recent costly settlements have prompted more white-collar workers to sue for overtime pay. Retail managers, reporters, sales reps, personal bankers, engineers, computer programmers, and claims adjusters have won in some cases as being non-exempt workers.

Common Overtime Issues For individuals who are non-exempt, there are a number of issues that employers must consider. A few of them include the following:

■ *Compensatory time off:* "Comp" hours are given to an employee in lieu of payment for extra time worked. Unless it is given to non-exempt employees at the rate of one and one-half times the number of hours over 40 that are worked in a week, comp-time is illegal in the private sector. Also, comp-time cannot be carried over from one pay period to another. The only major exception to these provisions is for public-sector employees, such as fire and police officers, and a limited number of other workers.

■ *Incentives for non-exempt employees:* Employers must add the amount of direct work-related incentives to a person's base pay. Then overtime pay should be calculated as one and one-half times the higher (adjusted) rate of pay.

■ *Training time:* Must be counted as time worked by non-exempt employees unless it is outside regular work hours, not directly job related, and other aspects. College degree programs may not be affected by these provisions.

■ *Travel time:* Must be counted as work time if it occurs during normal work hours, even on non-working days, unless the non-exempt person is a passenger in a car, bus, train, airplane, etc. Other complex clarifications regarding travel regulations affecting overtime should be reviewed by HR specialists to ensure compliance.

The complexity of overtime determination regulations can be confusing for managers, employees, and HR professionals. To review the above areas and additional ones, examine Sections 541, 775, 785, and others listed on the following U.S. Department of Labor Website: *www.dol.gov/dol/allcfr/ ESA/Title_29/Chapter_V.htm.*

Independent Contractor Regulations

The growing use of contingent workers by many organizations has focused attention on another group of legal regulations—those identifying the criteria that independent contractors must meet.[28] For an employer, classifying someone as an independent contractor rather than an employee offers a major advantage. The employer does not have to pay Social Security, unemployment, or workers' compensation costs. These additional payroll levies may add 10% or more to the costs of hiring the individual as an employee. Most other federal and state entities rely on the criteria for independent contractor status identified by the IRS. Firms such as Wal-Mart, Allstate, Microsoft, and FedEx have settled lawsuits for misclassifying individuals as independent contractors.[29]

Behavioral Control Some key differences between an employee and an independent contractor have been identified by the Internal Revenue Service. The first set of factors are behavioral control factors, which indicate the extent to which an employer can control what and how a worker performs. One key area includes *business instructions given to the worker,* such as where and when to do work, in what sequences, what tools and equipment to use, and how to purchase supplies and services. The other area is *business training given to the worker,* such as when someone must be trained to perform in a specific manner, rather than accomplishing results.

Financial Control This factor focuses on the extent an employer can control the business facets of a worker's job. Considerations include how much *unreimbursed business expenses* a worker has and what investments a worker makes independently to do the job. Other financial factors include whether a worker *provides services to other firms,* how the *business pays the worker,* and if the worker can make a *profit or loss.*

Relationship-Type Factors A number of items can help clarify whether a relationship is independent or not, such as having *written contracts* and the *extent of services provided.* Also, if the employer *provides benefits,* such as insurance or pensions, then it is more likely that the person is an employee, not an independent contractor. For additional details, go to *www.irs.gov.*

Acts Affecting Government Contractors

Several compensation-related acts apply to firms having contracts with the U.S. government. The Davis-Bacon Act of 1931 affects compensation paid by firms engaged in federal construction projects valued at over $2,000. It deals only with federal construction projects and requires that the "prevailing" wage be paid on all federal construction projects. The *prevailing wage* is determined by a formula that considers the rate paid for a job by a majority of the employers in the appropriate geographic area.

Two other acts require firms with federal supply or service contracts exceeding $10,000 to pay a prevailing wage. Both the Walsh-Healy Public Contracts Act and the McNamara-O'Hara Service Contract Act apply only to those who are working directly on a federal government contract or who substantially affect its performance.

Legislation on Equal Pay and Pay Equity

Various legislative efforts have addressed the issue of wage discrimination on the basis of gender. The Equal Pay Act of 1963 applies to both men and women and prohibits using different wage scales for men and women performing substantially the same jobs.[30] Pay differences can be justified on the basis of merit (better performance), seniority (longer service), quantity or quality of work, experience, or factors other than gender. Similar pay must be given for jobs requiring equal skills, equal responsibilities, equal efforts, or jobs done under similar working conditions.

Pay equity is not the same as equal pay for equal work; instead, it is similar to comparable worth. **Pay equity** is the concept that the pay for all jobs requiring comparable KSAs should be the same even if actual job duties and market rates differ significantly. A number of states and the Canadian province of Ontario have laws requiring pay equity for public-sector jobs. However, simply showing the existence of pay disparities for jobs that are significantly different has not been sufficient to prove discrimination in many court cases.

Pay equity Similarity in pay for all jobs requiring comparable knowledge, skills, and abilities, even if actual job duties and market rates differ significantly.

State and Local Laws

Many states and municipalities have enacted modified versions of federal compensation laws. If a state has a higher minimum wage than that set under the Fair Labor Standards Act, the higher figure becomes the required minimum wage in that state. On the other end of the spectrum, many states once limited the number of hours women could work. However, these laws have generally been held to be discriminatory in a variety of court cases, and states have dropped such laws.

Garnishment Laws

Garnishment A court order that directs an employer to set aside a portion of an employee's wages to pay a debt owed a creditor.

Garnishment occurs when a creditor obtains a court order that directs an employer to set aside a portion of an employee's wages to pay a debt owed a creditor. Regulations passed as a part of the Consumer Credit Protection Act established limitations on the amount of wages that can be garnished. Also, the act restricted the right of employers to discharge employees whose pay is subject to a single garnishment order. All 50 states have laws applying to wage garnishments.

DEVELOPMENT OF A BASE PAY SYSTEM

As Figure 12-8 shows, a base compensation system is developed using current job descriptions and job specifications. These information sources are used when *valuing jobs* and analyzing *pay surveys*. These activities are designed to ensure that the pay system is both internally equitable and externally competitive. The data compiled in these two activities are used to design *pay structures*, including *pay grades* and minimum-to-maximum *pay ranges*. After pay structures are established, individual jobs must be placed in the appropriate pay grades and employees' pay must be adjusted according to length of service and performance. Finally, the pay system must be monitored and updated.

Employers want their employees to perceive their pay levels as appropriate in relation to pay for jobs performed by others inside the organization. Frequently, employees and managers make comments such as "This job is more important than that job in another department, so why are the two jobs paid about the same?" Two general approaches for valuing jobs are available: job evaluation and market pricing. Both approaches are used to determine initial values of jobs in relation to other jobs in an organization, and they are discussed next.

FIGURE 12-8	Compensation Administration Process

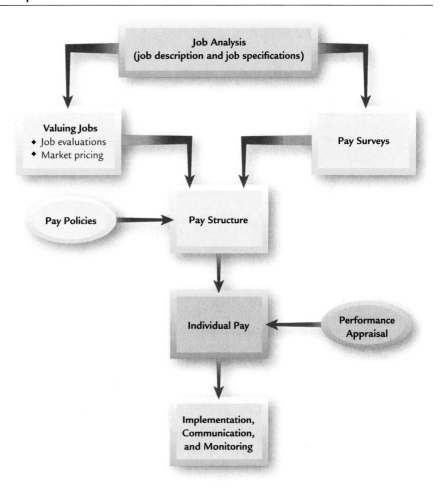

Valuing Jobs with Job Evaluation Methods

Job evaluation Formal, systematic means to identify the relative worth of jobs within an organization.

Job evaluation is a formal, systematic means to identify the relative worth of jobs within an organization. Several job evaluation methods are available for use by employers of different sizes.[31]

Point Method The most widely used job evaluation method, the point method, breaks jobs down into various compensable factors and places weights, or *points*, on them. A compensable factor identifies a job value commonly present throughout a group of jobs. Compensable factors are derived from the job analysis and reflect the nature of different types of jobs, as illustrated in Figure 12-9.

Compensable factor Job value commonly present throughout a group of jobs.

A special type of point method, the *Hay system*, uses three factors and numerically measures the degree to which each of these factors is required in a job. The three factors are *know-how, problem-solving ability,* and *accountability*.

The point method is the most popular because it is relatively simple to use and it considers the components of a job rather than the total job. However, point systems have been criticized for reinforcing traditional organizational

FIGURE 12-9   Examples of Compensable Factors for Different Job Families

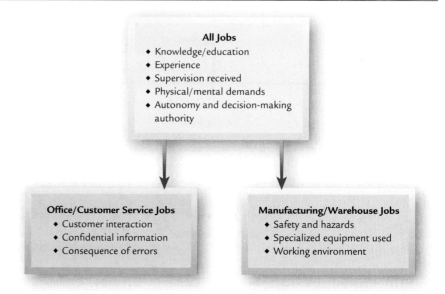

structures and job rigidity. Although not perfect, the point method of job evaluation is generally better than the ranking and classification methods because it quantifies job elements.

Other Job Evaluation Methods Several job evaluation methods are available that are used for different reasons. Common ones include the following:

■ The *ranking method* is a simple system that places jobs in order, from highest to lowest, by their value to the organization. The entire job is considered rather than the individual components. The ranking method generally is more appropriate in a small organization having relatively few jobs.

■ In the *classification method* of job evaluation, descriptions of each class of jobs are written, and then each job in the organization is put into a grade according to the class description it best matches. The major difficulty with the classification method is that subjective judgments are needed to develop the class descriptions and to place jobs accurately in them.

■ The *factor-comparison method* is a quantitative complex combination of the ranking and point methods. Each organization must develop its own key jobs and its own factors. The major disadvantages of the factor-comparison method are that it is difficult to use and time consuming to establish and develop.

Legal Issues and Job Evaluation Because job evaluation affects the employment relationship, specifically the pay of individuals, some legal issues are a concern.[32] Critics have charged that traditional job evaluation programs place less weight on knowledge, skills, and working conditions for many female-dominated jobs in office and clerical areas than on the same factors for male-dominated jobs in craft and manufacturing areas. Employers counter that because they base their pay rates heavily on external equity comparisons in the labor market, they are simply reflecting rates the "market economy" sets for jobs and workers, rather than discriminating on the basis of gender.

Valuing Jobs Using Market Pricing

Market pricing Use of market pay data to identify the relative value of jobs based on what other employers pay for similar jobs.

A growing number of employers have scaled back their use of "internal valuation" through traditional job evaluation methods. They have instead switched to **market pricing**, which uses market pay data to identify the relative value of jobs based on what other employers pay for similar jobs. Jobs are arranged in groups tied directly to similar survey data amounts.

Key to market pricing is identifying relevant market pay data for jobs that are good "matches" with the employer's jobs, geographic considerations, and company strategies and philosophies about desired market competitiveness levels. That is why some firms have used market pricing as part of strategic decisions in order to ensure market competitiveness of their compensation levels and practices.

Advantages of Market Pricing The primary advantage cited for the use of market pricing is that it closely ties organizational pay levels to what is actually occurring in the market, without being distorted by "internal" job evaluation. An additional advantage of market pricing is that it allows an employer to communicate to employees that the compensation system is truly "market linked," rather than sometimes being distorted by internal issues. Employees often see a compensation system that was developed using market pricing as having "face validity" and as being more objective than a compensation system that was developed using the traditional job evaluation methods.[33]

Disadvantages of Market Pricing The foremost disadvantage of market pricing is that for numerous jobs, pay survey data are limited or may not be gathered in methodologically sound ways. A closely related problem is that the responsibilities of a specific job in a company may be somewhat different from those of the "matching" job identified in the survey.[34]

Finally, tying pay levels to market data can lead to wide fluctuations based on market conditions. For evidence of this, one has only to look back at the extremes of the information technology job market during the past decade, when pay levels varied significantly. For these and other types of jobs, the debate over the use of job evaluation versus market pricing is likely to continue because both approaches have pluses and minuses associated with them.

Pay Surveys

Pay survey Collection of data on compensation rates for workers performing similar jobs in other organizations.

Benchmark jobs Jobs found in many organizations.

A **pay survey** is a collection of data on compensation rates for workers performing similar jobs in other organizations. Both job evaluation and market pricing are tied to surveys of the pay that other organizations provide for similar jobs.

Because jobs may vary widely in an organization, it is particularly important to identify **benchmark jobs**—ones that are found in many other organizations. Often these jobs are performed by individuals who have similar duties that require similar KSAs. For example, benchmark jobs commonly used in clerical/office situations are accounts payable processor, customer service representative, and receptionist. Benchmark jobs are used because they provide "anchors" against which individual jobs can be compared.

An employer may obtain surveys conducted by other organizations, access Internet data, or conduct its own survey. Many different surveys are available from a variety of sources.

Internet Research

Economic Research Institute

For resources on salary surveys, link to this site at: http://thomsonedu.com/management/mathis.

HR ONLINE

Responding to Internet Pay Survey Data Questions

Employees who are dissatisfied with their pay may bring Internet data to HR professionals or their managers and ask why their current pay is different from the pay reported in the Internet data. Responding to such questions from employees requires addressing a number of areas. Salary.com, for example, includes explanations on its Website. Points to be made in discussing employee concerns include the following:

■ *Job titles and responsibilities:* Comparison should be made against the employee's full job description, not just job titles and the brief job summaries on the Websites.
■ *Experience, KSAs, and performance:* Most pay survey data on the Internet are averages of multiple

companies and of multiple employees in those companies with varying experience and KSA levels.
■ *Geographic differences:* Many pay survey sites on the Internet use geographic index numbers, not the actual data from employers in a particular area.
■ *Company size and industry:* Pay levels may vary significantly by company size, with smaller firms often having lower pay. Also, pay levels may be lower in certain industries, such as retail and non-profits.
■ *Base pay vs. total compensation:* Employers have different benefits and incentive compensation programs. However, Internet data usually reflect only base pay amounts.

National surveys on many jobs and industries come from the U.S. Department of Labor's Bureau of Labor Statistics, professional and national trade associations, and various management consulting companies. In many communities, employers participate in wage surveys sponsored by the local chamber of commerce or local HR associations to provide information relevant to jobs in the community.

Internet-Based Pay Surveys HR professionals can access a wide range of pay survey data on-line. In many cases, pay survey questionnaires are distributed electronically rather than as printed copies, and HR staff members complete the questionnaires electronically. It is anticipated that during the next five years, most pay surveys will be conducted using electronic, Web-based technology.

The Internet provides a large number of pay survey sources and data. However, use of these sources requires caution because their accuracy and completeness may not be verifiable or may not be applicable to individual firms and employees. The HR On-Line discusses how to address employee questions regarding pay survey data that are accessible from the Internet.

Using Pay Surveys The proper use of pay surveys requires evaluating a number of factors to determine if the data are relevant and valid. The following questions should be answered for each survey:

■ *Participants:* Does the survey cover a realistic sample of the employers with whom the organization competes for employees?
■ *Broad-based:* Does the survey include data from employers of different sizes, industries, and locales?

■ *Timeliness:* How current are the data (determined by the date the survey was conducted)?

■ *Methodology:* How established is the survey, and how qualified are those who conducted it?

■ *Job matches:* Does the survey contain job summaries so that appropriate matches to job descriptions can be made?

Pay Surveys and Legal Issues One reason for employers to use outside sources for pay surveys is to avoid charges that the employers are attempting "price fixing" on wages. One such case involved an HR group and nine hospitals in the Salt Lake City area. The consent decree that resulted prohibited health-care facilities in Utah from cooperating when developing or conducting a wage survey. The hospitals can participate in surveys conducted by independent third-party firms only if privacy safeguards are met. Cases in other industries have alleged that by sharing wage data, the employers attempted to hold wages down artificially in violation of the Sherman Antitrust Act.[35]

PAY STRUCTURES

Job family Group of jobs having common organizational characteristics.

Once job valuations and pay survey data are gathered, pay structures can be developed using the process identified in Figure 12-10. Data from the valuation of jobs and the pay surveys may lead to the establishment of several different pay structures for different job families, rather than just one structure for all jobs. A job family is a group of jobs having common organizational characteristics. Organizations can have a number of different job families. Examples of some common pay structures based on different job families include: (1) hourly and salaried; (2) office, plant, technical, professional, and managerial; and (3) clerical, information technology, professional, supervisory, management, and executive. The nature, culture, and structure of the organization are considerations for determining how many and which pay structures to have.

Pay Grades

Pay grades Groupings of individual jobs having approximately the same job worth.

In the process of establishing a pay structure, organizations use pay grades to group individual jobs having approximately the same job worth. Although no set rules govern the establishment of pay grades, some overall suggestions can be useful. Generally, 11 to 17 grades are used in small and medium-sized companies, such as companies with fewer than 500 to 1,000 employees. Two methods are commonly used to establish pay grades: job evaluation data and use of job market banding.

Market line Graph line that shows the relationship between job value as determined by job evaluation points and job value as determined by pay survey rates.

Setting Pay Grades Using Job Evaluation Points The second approach to determining pay grades uses job evaluation points or other data generated from the traditional job evaluation methods discussed earlier in the chapter. This process ties pay survey information to job evaluation data by plotting a market line that shows the relationship between job value as determined by job evaluation points and job value as determined by pay survey rates. The statistical analysis done when determining market lines particularly focuses on the r^2 levels from the regression when the data are analyzed by different job families and groups. Generally, an r^2 of 0.85 or higher is desired.

FIGURE 12-10   Establishing Pay Structures

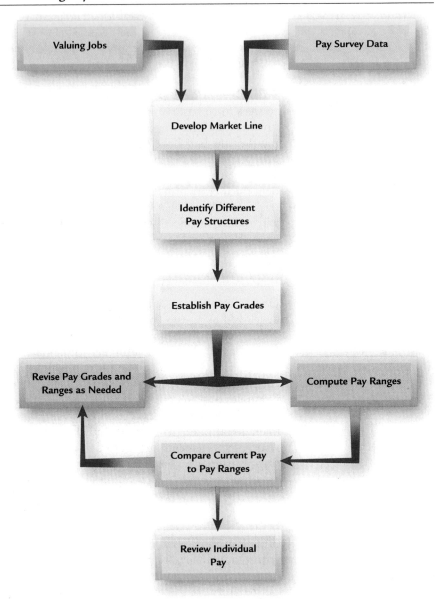

(Details on the methods and statistical analyses can be found in compensation texts.)[36]

A market line uses data to group jobs having similar point values into pay grades. Pay ranges can then be computed for each pay grade.

Setting Pay Grades Using Market Banding Closely linked to the use of market pricing to value jobs, **market banding** groups jobs into pay grades based on similar market survey amounts. Figure 12-11 shows two "bands" for jobs in a community bank. The midpoint of the survey average is used to develop pay range minimums and maximums, the methods of which are discussed later in this chapter.

Market banding Grouping jobs into pay grades based on similar market survey amounts.

| FIGURE 12-11 | Market-Banded Pay Grades for Community Bank |

Grade	Job	Pay Survey Summary	Pay Grade		
			Minimum	Midpoint*	Maximum
1	Bookkeeper	$22,913			
	Loan Clerk	$22,705			
	Customer Service Representative	$22,337			
	Data Entry / Computer Operator	$22,309	$17,966	$22,458	$26,950
	Head Teller	$22,305			
	Special Teller	$22,179			
2	Mail Clerk / Messenger	$19,167			
	Proof Machine Operator	$18,970			
	General Office Clerk	$18,594	$14,962	$18,703	$22,444
	Receptionist	$18,184			

*Computed by averaging the pay survey summary data for the jobs in each pay grade.

Pay Ranges

The pay range for each pay grade also must be established. Using the market line as a starting point, the employer can determine minimum and maximum pay levels for each pay grade by making the market line the midpoint line of the new pay structure (see Figure 12-12). For example, in a particular pay grade, the maximum value may be 20% above the midpoint located on the market line, and the minimum value may be 20% below it. Once pay grades and ranges have been computed, then the current pay of employees must be compared with the draft ranges. A growing number of employers are reducing the number of pay grades and expanding pay ranges by broadbanding.

Broadbanding Broadbanding is the practice of using fewer pay grades with much broader ranges than in traditional compensation systems. Combining many grades into these broadbands is designed to encourage horizontal movement and therefore more skill acquisition. About one-quarter of all employers in one survey are using broadbanding.[37] The main advantage of broadbanding is that it is more consistent with the flattening of organizational levels and the growing use of jobs that are multi-dimensional. The primary reasons for using broadbanding are: (1) to create more flexible organizations, (2) to encourage competency development, and (3) to emphasize career development.

A problem with broadbanding is that many employees expect a promotion to be accompanied by a pay raise and movement to a new pay grade. As a result of removing this grade progression, the organization may be seen as offering fewer upward promotion opportunities. An additional concern identified by a research study on broadbanding of information technology (IT) jobs is that it can significantly impact salary levels and costs. Therefore, HR must closely monitor the effects of broadbanding.[38] Despite these and other problems, it is likely that broadbanding will continue to grow in usage.

Broadbanding Practice of using fewer pay grades with much broader ranges than in traditional compensation systems.

FIGURE 12-12   Example of Pay Grades and Pay Ranges

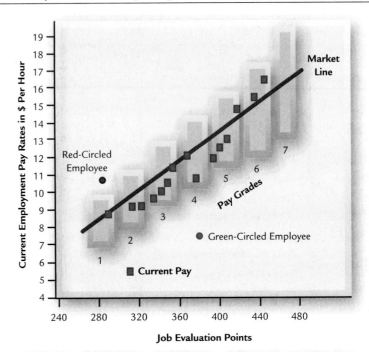

Grade	Point Range	Minimum Pay	Midpoint Pay	Maximum Pay
1	Below 300	6.94	8.50	10.06
2	300–329	7.96	9.75	11.54
3	330–359	8.98	11.00	13.02
4	360–389	10.00	12.25	14.50
5	390–419	11.01	13.49	15.97
6	420–449	11.79	14.74	17.69
7	Over 450	12.79	15.99	19.18

Individual Pay

Once managers have determined pay ranges, they can set the pay for specific individuals. Setting a range for each pay grade gives flexibility by allowing individuals to progress within a grade instead of having to move to a new grade each time they receive a raise. A pay range also allows managers to reward the better-performing employees while maintaining the integrity of the pay system. Regardless of how well a pay structure is constructed, there usually are a few individuals whose pay is lower than the minimum or higher than the maximum due to past pay practices and different levels of experience and performance. Two types are discussed next.

Red-Circled employee
Incumbent who is paid above the range set for the job.

Red-Circled Employees A red-circled employee is an incumbent who is paid above the range set for the job. For example, assume that an employee's current pay is $10.92 an hour, but the pay range for that person's pay grade is $6.94 to $10.06 an hour. The person would be red circled. Management would try over a year or so to bring the employee's rate into grade.

Several approaches can be used to bring a red-circled person's pay into line. Although the fastest way would be to cut the employee's pay, that approach is not recommended and is seldom used. Instead, the employee's pay may be frozen until the pay range can be adjusted upward to get the employee's pay rate back into the grade. Another approach is to give the employee a small lump-sum payment but not adjust the pay rate when others are given raises.

Green-Circled Employees An individual whose pay is below the range is a green-circled employee. Promotion is a major contributor to this situation. Generally, it is recommended that the green-circled individual receive fairly rapid pay increases to reach the pay grade minimum. More frequent increases can be used if the minimum is a large amount above the incumbent's current pay.

Green-circled employee
Incumbent who is paid below the range for the job.

Pay Compression One major problem many employers face is pay compression, which occurs when the pay differences among individuals with different levels of experience and performance become small. Pay compression occurs for a number of reasons, but the major one involves situations in which labor market pay levels increase more rapidly than current employees' pay adjustments.[39]

Pay compression
Occurs when the pay differences among individuals with different levels of experience and performance become small.

In response to shortages of particular job skills in a highly competitive labor market, managers may occasionally have to pay higher amounts to hire people with those scarce skills. For example, suppose the job of specialized information systems analyst is identified as a $48,000 to $68,000 salary range in one company, but qualified individuals are in short supply and other employers are paying $70,000. To fill the job, the firm likely will have to pay the higher rate. Suppose also that several analysts who have been with the firm for several years started at $55,000 and have received 4% increases each year. These current employees may still be making less than the $70,000 paid to attract and retain new analysts from outside with less experience. One partial solution to pay compression is to have employees follow a step progression based on length of service, assuming performance is satisfactory or better. Other approaches are to provide better performers with higher raises, use project incentives, and adjust pay ranges more often.[40]

DETERMINING PAY INCREASES

Decisions about pay increases are often critical ones in the relationships between employees, their managers, and the organization. Individuals express expectations about their pay and about how much of an increase is "fair," especially in comparison with the increases received by other employees. There are several ways to determine pay increases: performance, seniority, cost-of-living adjustments, across-the-board increases, and lump-sum increases. These methods can be used separately or in combination.

Performance-Based Increases

As mentioned earlier, a growing number of employers have shifted to more pay-for-performance philosophies and strategies. Consequently, they have adopted various means to provide employees with performance-based increases.

Targeting High Performers This approach focuses on providing the top performing employees with significantly higher pay raises. Some organizations target the top 10% of employees for significantly greater increases while providing more standard increases to the remaining satisfactory performers. According to a survey by Hewitt Associates in a recent year, average raises for the best performers were 9.9%, satisfactory performers got 3.6%, and low performers got 0% to 1.3%.[41]

The primary reason for having such significant differentials focuses on rewarding and retaining the critical high-performing individuals.[42] Key to rewarding exceptional performers is identifying what their accomplishments have been above the normal work expectations. The more "standard" increases for the average performers are usually aligned with labor market pay adjustments, so that those individuals are kept competitive. The lower performers are given less because of their performance issues, which "encourages" them to leave their organizations.

Pay Adjustment Matrix Some system for integrating appraisals and pay changes must be developed and applied equally. Often, this integration is done through the development of a *pay adjustment matrix,* or *salary guide chart*. Use of pay adjustment matrices bases adjustments in part on a person's compa-ratio, which is the pay level divided by the midpoint of the pay range. To illustrate, the compa-ratio for an employee would be:

$$\text{Employee } J = \frac{\$13.35 \text{ (current pay)}}{\$15.00 \text{ (midpoint)}} \times 100 = 89 \text{ (Compa-ratio)}$$

> **Compa-ratio** Pay level divided by the midpoint of the pay range.

Salary guide charts reflect a person's upward movement in an organization. That movement often depends on the person's performance, as rated in an appraisal, and on the person's position in the pay range, which has some relation to experience as well. A person's placement on the chart determines what pay raise the person should receive. According to the chart shown in Figure 12-13, if employee *J* is rated as exceeding expectations (3) with a compa-ratio of 89, that person is eligible for a raise of 7% to 9%.

Two interesting facets of the sample matrix illustrate the emphasis on paying for performance. First, individuals whose performance is below expectations receive small to no raises. This approach sends a strong signal that poor performers will not continue to receive increases just by completing another year of service.

Second, as employees move up the pay range, they must exhibit higher performance to obtain the same percentage raise as those lower in the range performing at the "Meets Performance Expectations" level (see Figure 12-13). This approach is taken because the firm is paying above the market midpoint but receiving only satisfactory performance rather than above-market performance. Charts can be constructed to reflect the specific pay-for-performance policies and philosophy in an organization.

Standardized Pay Adjustments

Several different methods are used to provide standardized pay increases to employees. The most common ones are discussed next.

> **Seniority** Time spent in the organization or on a particular job.

Seniority Seniority, or time spent in the organization or on a particular job, can be used as the basis for pay increases. Many employers have policies that require a person to be employed for a certain length of time before being eligible for pay increases. Pay adjustments based on seniority often are set

FIGURE 12-13   Pay Adjustment Matrix

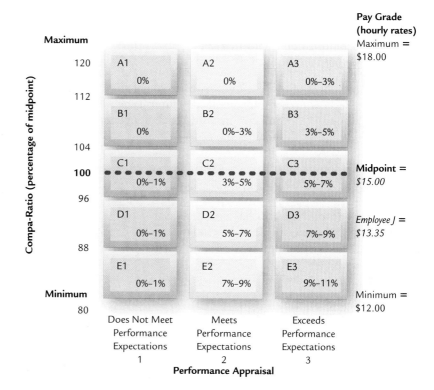

Performance Appraisal

as automatic steps once a person has been employed the required length of time, although performance must be at least satisfactory in many non-union systems.

Cost-of-Living Adjustments A common pay-raise practice is the use of a *cost-of-living adjustment (COLA)*. Often, these adjustments are tied to changes in the Consumer Price Index (CPI) or some other general economic measure. However, numerous studies have revealed that the CPI overstates the actual cost of living.

Across-the-Board Increases Unfortunately, some employers give across-the-board raises and call them *merit raises,* which they are not. Usually the percentage raise is based on standard market percentage changes, or financial budgeting determinations not specifically linked to the COLA. If all employees get the same percentage pay increase, it is legitimately viewed as having little to do with merit or good performance. For this reason, employers should reserve the term *merit* for any amount above the standard raise, and they should state clearly which amount is for performance and which is the "automatic" amount.

Lump-Sum Increases Most employees who receive pay increases, either for merit or for seniority, first receive an increase in the amount of their regular monthly or weekly paycheck. For example, an employee who makes $12.00 an hour and then receives a 3% increase will move to $12.36 an hour.

Lump-sum increase (LSI)
One-time payment of all or part of a yearly pay increase.

In contrast, a lump-sum increase (LSI) is a one-time payment of all or part of a yearly pay increase. The pure LSI approach does not increase the base pay. Therefore, in the example of a person making $12.00 an hour, if an LSI of 3% is granted, the person receives a lump sum of $748.80 ($0.36 an hour × 2,080 working hours in the year). However, the base rate remains at $12.00 an hour, which slows down the progression of the base wages.

An LSI plan offers advantages and disadvantages.[43] The major advantage of an LSI plan is that it heightens employees' awareness of what their performance levels "merited." Another advantage is that the firm can use LSIs to slow down the increase of base pay and thus reduce or avoid the compounding effect on succeeding raises. One disadvantage of LSI plans is that workers who take a lump-sum payment may become discouraged because their base pay has not changed. Unions generally resist LSI programs because of their impact on pensions and benefits, unless the total amount used in those computations includes the LSI.

SUMMARY

- The concept of *total rewards* has become a crucial part of HR management, and includes compensation, benefits, and performance and talent management.
- Compensation provided by an organization can come directly through base pay and variable pay and indirectly through benefits.
- A continuum of compensation philosophies exists, ranging from an entitlement philosophy to a performance philosophy.
- HR metrics can and should be used to measure the effectiveness of compensation.
- For compensation expenditures to be administered effectively, compensation responsibilities of both HR specialists and managers must be performed well.
- When designing and administering compensation programs, internal and external equity, organizational justice, and pay openness all must be considered.
- Decisions about compensation must always consider market competitiveness and positioning, use of competency-based pay, and team rewards.
- Compensation practices for international employees are much more complex than those for domestic employees, because they are affected by many more factors.
- The Fair Labor Standards Act (FLSA), as amended, is the major federal law that affects

pay systems. It requires most organizations to pay a minimum wage and to comply with overtime provisions, including appropriately classifying employees as exempt or non-exempt and as independent contractors or employees.
- A base pay system is developed using information from valuations of jobs and pay surveys, both of which are designed to ensure that the pay system is internally equitable and externally competitive.
- The valuation of jobs can be determined using either job evaluation or market pricing.
- Once a firm has collected pay survey data, it can develop a pay structure, which is composed of pay grades and pay ranges.
- Broadbanding, which uses fewer pay grades with wider ranges, has grown in popularity.
- Individual pay must take into account the placement of employees within pay grades.
- Problems involving "red-circled" jobs, whose rates are above the applicable pay range, and "green-circled" jobs, whose rates are below the applicable pay range, can be addressed in a number of ways.
- Individual pay increases can be based on performance, seniority, cost-of-living adjustments, across-the-board increases, lump-sum increases, or a different combination of approaches.

REVIEW AND APPLICATION QUESTIONS

1. Discuss the compensation philosophies and approaches that have been used at organizations where you have worked. What have been the consequences of those philosophies and approaches?

2. You have been named Human Resources Manager for a company that has 180 employees and no formal base pay system. What steps will you take to develop such a coordinated system?

3. You are the HR Director for an insurance company with regional offices in several states. For each office, you want to be sure that the administrative assistants reporting to the regional manager are paid appropriately. Go to *www.Salary.com* to find geographic pay survey data for this job in Hartford, Connecticut; Atlanta, Georgia; Omaha, Nebraska; and Phoenix, Arizona. Then, recommend pay ranges; identify the low, median, and high rate for each pay range. To present the data, list each of the offices in order from lowest median pay to highest median pay.

CASE

Compensation Changes at JC Penney

Having been in business for over 100 years, JC Penney has experienced highs and lows in organizational performance. In the past decade the firm has faced a dramatically changing retail environment from competitors such as Target, Wal-Mart, the Gap, and others. As a result, JC Penney was increasingly viewed by customers and analysts of the retail industry as lagging in its merchandising strategies.

Even the compensation system at JC Penney was viewed as traditional and paternalistic in nature because it emphasized rewarding employees primarily for their length of service. Also, most promotions were made internally, which created a more static organizational culture. The traditional pay structure at the firm contained many pay grades and was based on job evaluations to establish those grades. Its performance review system emphasized employee tenure and effort to a greater degree than performance results.

To respond to the competitive environment, the firm's executives decided that JC Penney had to become more dynamic and able to change more quickly. One of the changes identified was that a new compensation system was needed. The restructured compensation system that was developed and implemented focused heavily on market value, using pay survey data that specifically matched job responsibilities. The greatest change was the development of "career bands." These career bands grouped jobs together based on survey data and job responsibilities and resulted in fewer grades with wider ranges. The career bands represented a broadbanding approach that was based on benchmark jobs for which market pricing data were available. Jobs for which market data could not be found were analyzed using a job evaluation system.

Use of the career bands was designed to identify career paths for employees throughout the company and to better link compensation to all of the jobs. By having career bands, greater flexibility was provided for employees to be rewarded for both current performance and continuing career growth. To support this new compensation system, a revised performance management system was developed. This system used performance goals and measures more closely tied to business strategies and objectives. Important to implementing the new performance management system was managerial training. This training was needed so that the managers could use the new system effectively and to describe to employees the importance of performance and its link to compensation.

Implementation of the new compensation system required extensive communication. Newsletters were prepared for all managers explaining the new compensation system. Then departmental and store meetings were held with managers and employees to describe the new system. A number of printed materials and videos discussing the importance of the new compensation plan were prepared and utilized. A final part of communications was to prepare letters for individual employees that informed them about their job band and market pay range.[44]

Questions

1. How do the JC Penney changes reflect a total rewards approach?

2. Discuss why JC Penney's shift to a more performance-oriented compensation system had to be linked to market pricing.

SUPPLEMENTAL CASE

Scientific Turmoil

This case discusses the concerns associated with having a formal base pay system, and communication issues that occur. (For the case, go to http://thomsonedu.com/management/mathis.)

NOTES

1. Adapted from Jessica Marquez, "McDonald's Rewards Program Leaves Room for Local Flavor," *Workforce Management,* April 10, 2006, 26.

2. Richard Kantor and Tina Kao, "Total Rewards: Clarity from Confusion and Chaos," *Worldat Work Journal,* Third Quarter 2004, 7–15.

3. To view this model, go to *World-atWork Total Rewards Model; Strategies to Attract, Motivate, and Retain Employees, www.worldatwork.org.*

4. Edward E. Lawler III, "Pay Practices in *Fortune 1000* Corporations," *Worldat Work Journal,* Fourth Quarter 2003, 45–54.

5. Brad Hill and Christine Tande, "Total Rewards: The Employment Value Proposition," *Workspan,* October 2006, 18–22.

6. Charlotte Garvey, "Philosophizing Compensation," *HR Magazine,* January 2005, 73–76.

7. Based on Aaron Dalton, "Pay-for-Performance Plan Helps Shrink Bank's Turnover," *Workforce Management,* April 27, 2005, www.workforce.com.

8. For examples, see Dow Scott, Dennis Morajda and Thomas D. McMillien, "Evaluating Pay Program Effectiveness," *Worldat Work Journal,* Second Quarter 2006, 50–59.

9. Jac Fitz-Enz and Barbara Davison, *How to Measure Human Resources Management,* 3rd ed. (New York: McGraw-Hill, 2002); and *www.shrm.org/hrtools.*

10. S. C. Currell et al., "Pay Satisfaction and Organizational Outcomes," *Personnel Psychology,* 58 (2005), 613–640.

11. For details of various compensation surveys and studies, go to *www.salary.com.*

12. Jonathan A. Segal, "Labor Pains for Union-Free Employers," *HR Magazine,* March 2004, 113–118.

13. Paul W. Mulvey et al., "Study Finds that Knowledge of Pay Processes Can Beat Out Amount of Pay in Employee Retention, Organizational Effectiveness," *Journal of Organizational Excellence,* Autumn 2002, 29.

14. Mark Reilly and Lisa Audi, "Does It Still Make Sense to Use Geographic Pay Rates?" *Workspan,* December 2006, 52–56.

15. Mark P. Brown, Michael C. Sturman, and Marcia J. Simmering, "Compensation Policy and Organizational Performance: The Efficiency, Operational, and Financial Implications of Pay Levels and Pay Structures," *Academy of Management Journal,* 46 (2003), 752–762.

16. Carri Baca and Gary Starzmann, "Clarifying Competencies: Powerful Tools for Driving Business Success," *Workspan,* March 2006, 44–47.

17. R. Eugene Hughes, "Skill or Diploma? The Potential Influence of Skill-Based Pay Programs on Sources of Skills Acquisition and Degree Programs," *WorkStudy,* 45 (2003), 179.

18. Larry S. Carlton, "Finding the Right Method of Team Compensation," *SHRM White Paper,* December 2004, www.shrm.org.

19. Geoffrey W. Latta, "The Future of Expatriate Compensation," *Worldat Work Journal,* Second Quarter 2006, 42–49.

20. T. T. Runnion, "Expatriate Programs from Preparation to Success," *Workspan,* July 2005, 21.

21. B. W. Watson and G. Singh, "Global Pay Systems in Support of a Multinational Strategy," *Compensation and Benefits Review,* January/February 2005, 33–37.

22. Fay Hansen, "Many Countries, One Compensation System," *Workforce Management,* October 23, 2006, 28.

23. Kelley M. Butler, "Foreign Income Tax Hikes Squeeze Expats, Employers," *Employee Benefit News,* October 2006, 18.

24. Based on Allen Smith, "Wal-Mart Attorney: Adopt Policies to Comply with FLSA," *HR News,* October 25, 2006, www.shrm.org/hr.news; "Wal-Mart Agrees to Pay Fine for Violating Child Labor Laws," *U.S. Department of Labor News Release,* February 14, 2005; and Mary Claire Dale, "Jury Weighs Award in Wal-Mart Labor Case," *YahooNews,* October 13, 2006, www.yahoo.com.

25. David Neumark, "Detecting Effects of Living Wage Laws," *Industrial Relations,* 42 (2003), 531–565.

26. Steven Siegel, "Top Five Employer Mistakes Under the FLSA," *Workforce Management,* September 2006, www.workforce.com.

27. "The Overtime Rules: Are You Truly in Compliance?" *The HR Specialist,* December 2006, 1–2.

28. Andrew E. Schultz, "Are Your Independent Contractors Really Employees in Disguise? *Workspan,* April 1, 2006, 57–60.

29. Dean Faust, "The Ground War at FedEx," *Business Week,* November 28, 2005, 42–43.

30. For example, see Norman L. Tolle, "Court Affirms Decision Holding Employer Liable for Violating Equal Pay Act," *Employee Benefit Plan Review,* July 2006, 24.

31. For additional details on different methods, see *Job Evaluation: Methods to the Process* (Scottsdale, AZ: WorldatWork), 2005, 159 pp.

32. Kay Gilbert, "The Role of Job Evaluation in Determining Equal Value in Tribunals: Tool, Weapon, or Cloaking Device?" *Employee Relations,* 27 (2005), 7–20.

33. Kimberly Merriman, "A Fairness Approach to Market-Based Pay," *Workspan,* March 2006, 48–50.

34. Charles H. Fay and Madhura Tare, "Market Pricing Concerns," *WorldatWork Journal,* Second Quarter 2007, 61–69.

35. *District of Utah, U.S. District Court v. Utah Society for Healthcare Human Resources Administration et al., Federal Register,* March 1994, No. 14203.

36. For example, see Richard I. Henderson, *Compensation Management in a Knowledge-Based World,* 10th ed. (Upper Saddle River, NJ: Prentice Hall, 2006).

37. Mercer Human Resource Consulting, *2006 Compensation Planning Survey* (New York: Mercer Corporation, 2006).

38. C. H. Fay et al., "Broadbanding-Pay Ranges and Labor Costs," *WorldatWork Journal,* Second Quarter 2004, 8–23.

39. Susan Ladika, "Decompressing Pay," *HR Magazine,* December 2005, 79–82.

40. Andrew L. Klein, Kimberly M. Keating, and Lisa M. Ruggerio, "The Perils of Pay Inequity: Addressing the Problems of Compression," *WorldatWork Journal,* Fourth Quarter 2002, 56–62.

41. Erin White, "The Best vs. the Rest," *The Wall Street Journal,* January 30, 2006, B1.

42. Jessica Marquez, "Raising the Performance Bar," *Workforce Management,* April 24, 2006, 31–32.

43. Bob Fulton, "What Are the Pro's and Con's of Switching to Lump-Sum Payments as Compensation?" *Workforce Management Research Center,* January 12, 2004, *www.workforce.com.*

44. Based on Donna R. Graebner and Kevin A. Seward, "Bringing It All Inside," *Workspan,* August 2004, 30–35.

CHAPTER

13

Variable Pay and Executive Compensation

After you have read this chapter, you should be able to:

■ Define variable pay and identify three elements of successful pay-for-performance plans.

■ Discuss three types of individual incentives.

■ Identify key concerns that must be addressed when designing group/team variable pay plans.

■ Discuss why profit sharing and employee stock ownership are common organizational incentive plans.

■ Explain three ways that sales employees are typically compensated.

■ Identify the components of executive compensation and discuss criticisms of executive compensation levels.

HR Headline

Pay for Performance in Public Schools

Incentive pay or *pay for performance* has made inroads in business but has remained a hard sell in public school systems. Teachers' unions have resolutely resisted the idea, saying these programs expose members to arbitrary benchmarks set by school administrators. But that is changing in several places.

In Lake Charles, Louisiana, a performance bonus of $2,600 for improvement in student test scores and information on how to improve scores even more were given to a high-performing first-grade teacher. School districts in Florida and Houston link student test scores and teacher pay. In Minnesota some districts have stopped giving automatic raises for seniority and base 60% of all pay increases on performance. In Denver, Colorado, unions and school districts worked together to design a program that uses bonuses for student achievement and $3,000 boosts to teachers for earning national teaching certificates.

Such plans have not worked everywhere, however. Cincinnati teachers voted against their district's merit pay proposal, and in a district outside Philadelphia, teachers gave their bonus checks to charity rather than cash them. Apparently, being successful in ending compensation that traditionally has been based only on seniority and degrees, and instead tying more compensation to student achievement, requires that teachers be involved in planning the incentive system.[1] The same can be said for all incentive plans—if the employees don't buy into them, they will not work. But if they do, both employers and employees can be rewarded.

Tying pay to performance holds a promise that employers and employees both find attractive. For employees it can mean more pay and for employers it can mean more output per employee and therefore more productivity. However, it is much more difficult to design a successful incentive system than to simply pay employees hourly or with a set salary.

Pay for performance is being utilized by a growing number of employers. In today's competitive global economy, many employers believe that people become more productive if compensation varies directly according to their performance. Employers are adding to their traditional base pay programs by offering employees additional compensation tied to performance. The amount of payment varies based on the degree to which individual, group/team, and organizational performance goals are attained.

VARIABLE PAY: INCENTIVES FOR PERFORMANCE

Variable pay
Compensation linked to individual, group/team, and/or organizational performance.

Variable pay is compensation linked to individual, group/team, and/or organizational performance. Traditionally also known as *incentives,* variable pay plans attempt to provide tangible rewards to employees for performance beyond normal expectations. The philosophical foundation of variable pay rests on several basic assumptions:

- Some people perform better and are more productive than others.
- Employees who perform better should receive more compensation.
- Some of employees' total compensation should be tied directly to performance and results.
- Some jobs contribute more to organizational success than others.

Pay for performance has a different philosophical base than does the traditional compensation system, in which differences in job responsibilities are recognized through different amounts of base pay. In many organizations, length of service is a primary differentiating factor. However, giving additional rewards to some people and not others is seen as potentially divisive and as hampering employees' working together. These thoughts are part of the reason why many labor unions oppose pay-for-performance programs. In contrast, however, high-performing workers expect extra rewards for outstanding performance that increases organizational results.

Incentives can take many forms from simple praise, to "recognition and reward" programs that award trips and merchandise, to bonuses for performance accomplishments or for successful results for the company. Forty-nine percent of organizations have incentive programs for their employees.[2] The variety of possibilities, shown in Figure 13-1, are discussed later.

How well do incentive programs work? It varies from employer to employer, but one study found that 55% of employees are unhappy with their company's incentive program. As a result employers change the programs by revising metrics, increasing goals, increasing awards, etc.

Developing Successful Pay-for-Performance Plans

Employers adopt variable pay or incentive plans for a number of reasons. The main ones include desires to do the following:

- Link strategic business goals and employee performance.
- Enhance organizational results and reward employees financially for their contributions.

FIGURE 13-1   Examples of Incentives

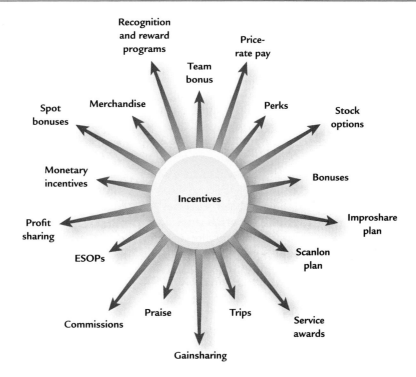

- Reward employees and recognize different levels of employee performance.
- Achieve HR objectives, such as increasing retention, reducing turnover, recognizing training, or rewarding safety.

Variable pay plans can be considered successful if they meet the objectives the organization had for them when they were initiated. Three elements that affect the success of variable pay systems are discussed next.

Does the Plan Fit the Organization? In the case of pay-for-performance plans, one size does not fit all. A plan that has worked well for one company will not necessarily work well for another. For a plan to work, it must be linked to the objectives of the organization. For example, a distribution company based in New Jersey used a teamsharing compensation plan as part of efforts to create an organizational culture within the firm that allowed it to respond to competitive changes more easily. One indication of success was a sales increase of 700% in target markets over several years following implementation of the teamsharing program. In this program, all employees, whether sales, warehouse, office, or managerial, were rewarded if the company's sales goals were met.[3]

However, not all incentive plans do fit the organization. For example, Boeing found that its "rewards and recognition" program was complex, confusing, expensive, and was not motivating employees. It revamped the program around the goals of encouraging financial performance, customer satisfaction, and good corporate citizenship. The results were successful.[4]

The success of any variable pay program relies on its consistency with the culture of the organization. For example, if an organization is autocratic and adheres to traditional rules and

HR PERSPECTIVE

Using Slot Machines as Incentives

The "Snowfly System" is an incentive program in which employees can win money by playing Las Vegas–style games. It is one of a new wave of programs aimed at front-line workers that offer smaller rewards more frequently so employees can see the link between their performance and reward.

Managers give employees electronic tokens when they display the desired behaviors or achieve goals. The tokens can then be used in special slot machines (or other games) to win "points." The game is set up so that employees always win something, although the winnings may vary from 2 points to 5,000. The points can then be valued by the company for whatever is appropriate and cashed in for money or other prizes. LDF Sales and Distributing in Wichita, Kansas, used Snowfly to cut inventory losses. Managers gave employees tokens every time they double checked a shipment. Inventory losses fell by half, saving $31,000 per year.

At First Interstate Bank, the president tried to encourage employees to sign up customers for credit cards. Offering a chance to win a Las Vegas vacation to the person who signed up the most customers did not work as hoped. He switched to Snowfly with employees getting tokens for opening credit card accounts. This cost was $12,000 per year rather than $4,000, but more profits were generated.[5]

procedures, an incentive system that rewards flexibility and teamwork is likely to fail. In such a case, the incentive plan has been "planted" in the wrong growing environment.

Does the Plan Reward the Appropriate Actions? Variable pay systems should be tied as much as possible to desired performance. Employees must see a direct relationship between their efforts and their financial rewards, as the HR Perspective illustrates.

Because people tend to produce what is measured and rewarded, organizations must make sure that what is being rewarded links with organizational objectives. Use of multiple measures helps ensure that various performance dimensions are not omitted. For example, assume a hotel reservation center wants to set incentives for employees to increase productivity by lowering the time they spend on each call. If that reduction is the only measure, the quality of customer service and the number of reservations made might drop as employees rush callers in order to reduce talk time. Therefore, the center should consider basing rewards on multiple measures, such as talk time, reservations booked, and the results of customer satisfaction surveys.

Linking pay to performance may not always be appropriate. For instance, if the output cannot be measured objectively, management may not be able to correctly reward the higher performers with more pay. Managers may not even be able to accurately identify the higher performers. For example, in an office where tasks are to provide permits for building renovations, individual contributions may not be identifiable or appropriate.

Is the Plan Administered Properly? A variable pay plan may be complex or simple, but it will be successful only if employees understand what they have to do to be rewarded. The more complicated a plan is, the more difficult it will be to communicate it meaningfully to employees. Experts generally recommend that a variable pay plan include several performance criteria. Having multiple areas of focus should not overly complicate the calculations necessary for employees to determine their own incentive amounts. Managers also need to be able to explain clearly what future performance targets need to be met and what the rewards will be.

While administering an incentive plan can be difficult, global incentive programs can be especially complex. Although a company may have an overarching strategy, such as growing market share or increasing the bottom line, that strategy frequently works out to different goals in different geographical regions. Global programs must be able to accommodate cultural differences as well.[6]

Metrics for Variable Pay Plans

The results of variable pay plans, like those in other areas of HR, should be measured to determine the success of the programs. Different measures of success can be used, depending on the nature of the plan and the goals set for it. An employer can start by deciding what it wants an incentive program to accomplish and then devise measures against which to check the outcomes. A common metric for incentive plans is return on investment (ROI).[7] For example, a company may feel that using a program that provides rewards in the form of chances on a lottery drawing each month for those employees who were not absent during that month will reduce absenteeism. An ROI metric would look at the dollar value of the improvement minus the cost of the program divided by the total cost. So if the reduction in absenteeism cost was $100,000 per year, but the program costs were $85,000, calculations would be $(100,000 - 85,000) \div 85,000$, or a bit more than a 17% return on the investment of $85,000 in the program. Figure 13-2 (on the next page) shows some examples of different metrics that can be used to evaluate variable pay plans.

Regardless of the plan, the critical decision is to gather and evaluate data to determine if the expenditures are justified by increased performance and results. If the measures show positive analyses, then the plan is truly a pay-for-performance plan in nature.

Successes and Failures of Variable Pay Plans

Even though variable pay has grown in popularity, some attempts to implement it have succeeded and others have not. Incentives *do* work, but they are not a panacea because their success depends on multiple factors.[8]

The positive view that many employers have of variable pay is not shared universally by all employees. If individuals see incentives as desirable, they are more likely to put forth the extra effort to attain the performance objectives that trigger the incentive payouts. Not all employees believe that they are rewarded when doing a good job; nor are some employees motivated by their employers' incentive plans. One problem is that some employees prefer that performance rewards increase their base pay, rather than be given as a one-time, lump-sum payment. Further, many employees prefer individual rewards to group/team or organizational incentives.

Given these underlying dynamics, providing variable pay plans that are successful can be complex and requires significant, continuing efforts. Some suggestions that appear to contribute to successful incentive plans are as follows:

- Develop clear, understandable plans that are continually communicated.
- Use realistic performance measures.
- Keep the plans current and linked to organizational objectives.
- Clearly link performance results to payouts that truly recognize performance differences.
- Identify variable pay incentives separately from base pay.

FIGURE 13-2   Metric Options for Variable Pay Plans

* Actual change vs. planned change
* Revenue growth
* Return on investment
* Average employee productivity change

* Increase in market share
* Customer acquisition rate
* Growth of existing customer sales
* Customer satisfaction

Production Performance Variable Pay Plans

Sales Programs

Variable Pay Program

HR-Related Program Measures

* Employee satisfaction
* Turnover costs
* Absenteeism cost
* Workers' comp claims
* Accident rates

Three Categories of Variable Pay

Individual incentives are given to reward the effort and performance of individuals. Some common means of providing individual variable pay are piece-rate systems, sales commissions, and bonuses. Others include special recognition rewards such as trips or merchandise. With individual incentives, however, employees may focus on what is best for them personally and may inhibit the performance of other individuals with whom they are competing. That is one reason group/team incentives have been developed.

When an organization rewards an entire group/team for its performance, cooperation among the members may increase. The most common *group/team incentives* are gainsharing or goalsharing plans, in which employee teams that meet certain goals share in the gains measured against performance targets. Often, those programs focus on quality improvement, cost reduction, and other measurable results.

Organizational incentives reward people according to the performance results of the entire organization. This approach assumes that all employees working together can generate greater organizational results that lead to better financial performance. These programs often share some of the financial gains made by the firm with employees through payments calculated as a percentage of the employees' base pay. The most prevalent forms of organization-wide incentives are profit-sharing plans and employee stock plans. Figure 13-3 shows some of the programs under each type of incentive or variable pay plan. These programs are discussed in detail in the following sections.

FIGURE 13-3   Categories of Variable Pay Plans

Individual	Group/Team	Organizational
◆ Piece-rate systems ◆ Bonuses ◆ Special incentive programs (trips, merchandise, awards) ◆ Sales compensation	◆ Group team results ◆ Gainsharing/goalsharing ◆ Quality improvement ◆ Cost reduction	◆ Profit sharing ◆ Employee stock plans ◆ Executive stock options ◆ Deferred compensation

INDIVIDUAL INCENTIVES

Individual incentive systems try to tie individual effort to additional rewards. Conditions necessary for the use of individual incentive plans are as follows:

- *Individual performance must be identified.* The performance of each individual must be measured and identified because each employee has job responsibilities and tasks that can be separated from those of other employees.
- *Individual competitiveness must be desired.* Because individuals generally pursue the incentives for themselves, competition among employees often occurs. Therefore, independent competition in which some individuals "win" and others do not must be something the employer can tolerate.
- *Individualism must be stressed in the organizational culture.* The culture of the organization must be one that emphasizes individual growth, achievements, and rewards. If an organization emphasizes teamwork and cooperation, then individual incentives may be counterproductive.

Piece-Rate Systems

Straight piece-rate system
Pay system in which wages are determined by multiplying the number of units produced by the piece rate for one unit.

The most basic individual incentive systems are piece-rate systems, whether straight or differential. Under a straight piece-rate system, wages are determined by multiplying the number of units produced (such as garments sewn or service calls handled) by the piece rate for one unit. Because the cost is the same for each unit, the wage for each employee is easy to figure, and labor costs can be accurately predicted.

A *differential piece-rate system* pays employees one piece-rate wage for units produced up to a standard output and a higher piece-rate wage for units produced over the standard. Managers often determine the quotas or standards by using time and motion studies. For example, assume that the standard quota for a worker is set at 300 units per day and the standard rate is 14 cents per unit. For all units over the standard, however, the employee receives 20 cents per unit. Under this system, the worker who produces 400 units in one day would get $62 in wages (300 × 14¢) + (100 × 20¢). Many possible combinations of straight and differential piece-rate systems can be used, depending on situational factors.

Despite their incentive value, piece-rate systems are difficult to apply because determining standards is a complex and costly process for many types of jobs. In some instances, the cost of determining and maintaining the standards may be greater than the benefits derived. Also, jobs in which individuals have limited control over output or in which high standards of quality are necessary may be unsuited to piecework.

Bonuses

Individual employees may receive additional compensation in the form of a bonus, which is a one-time payment that does not become part of the employee's base pay. Growing in popularity, individual bonuses are used at all levels in some firms.

A bonus can recognize performance by an employee, a team, or the organization as a whole. When performance results are good, bonuses go up. When performance results are not met, bonuses go down. Most employers base part of an employee's bonus on individual performance and part on company results, as appropriate.

Bonuses can also be used to reward employees for contributing new ideas, developing skills, or obtaining professional certifications. When helpful skills or certifications are acquired by an employee, a pay increase or a one-time bonus may follow. For example, a financial services firm provides the equivalent of two weeks' pay to employees who master job-relevant computer skills. Another firm gives one week's additional pay to members of the HR staff who obtain professional certifications such as Professional in Human Resources (PHR), Senior Professional in Human Resources (SPHR), or Certified Compensation Professional (CCP).

"Spot" Bonuses A special type of bonus used is a "spot" bonus, so called because it can be awarded at any time. Spot bonuses are given for a number of reasons, perhaps for extra time worked, extra efforts, or an especially demanding project. For instance, a spot bonus may be given to an information technology employee who installed a computer software upgrade that required extensive time and effort. Other examples are to compensate a nurse who dealt successfully with a difficult patient or to pay a customer service employee who resolved an unusual problem of a major client.

Often, spot bonuses are given in cash, although some firms provide managers with gift cards, travel vouchers, or other rewards. The keys to successful use of spot bonuses are to keep the amounts reasonable and to provide them for exceptional performance accomplishments.[9] The downside to their use is that it can create jealousy and resentment from other employees, who may feel that they were deserving but did not get a spot bonus.

Special Incentive Programs

Numerous special incentive programs can be used to reward individuals, ranging from one-time contests for meeting performance targets to awards for performance over time. For instance, safe-driving awards are given to truck drivers with no accidents or violations on their records during a year. Although special programs can be developed for groups and for entire organizations, they often focus on rewarding high-performing individuals. Special incentives are used for several purposes, as noted in Figure 13-4.

Performance Awards Cash, merchandise, gift certificates, and travel are the most frequently used incentive rewards for significant performance. Cash is still highly valued by many employees because they can decide how to spend it. However, travel awards appeal to many employees, particularly ones to popular destinations such as Disney World, Las Vegas, Hawaii, and international locations.

The most effective incentives for sales employees are travel, cash, merchandise, or a combination of these means. Generally, employees appreciate the "trophy" value of such awards as much as the actual monetary value.[10]

| **FIGURE 13-4** | **Purposes of Special Incentives** |

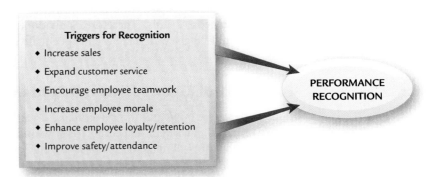

Triggers for Recognition

- Increase sales
- Expand customer service
- Encourage employee teamwork
- Increase employee morale
- Enhance employee loyalty/retention
- Improve safety/attendance

PERFORMANCE RECOGNITION

Recognition Awards Another type of program recognizes individual employees for their performance or service. Global employers are using recognition awards in different countries that reflect cultural differences.[11] For instance, many organizations in industries such as hotels, restaurants, and retailers have established "employee of the month" and "employee of the year" awards. Hotels often use favorable guest comment cards as the basis for providing recognition awards to front desk representatives, housekeepers, and other hourly employees.

Recognition awards often work best when given to acknowledge specific efforts and activities that the organization has targeted as important. The criteria for selecting award winners may be determined subjectively in some situations; however, formally identified criteria provide greater objectivity and are more likely to be seen as rewarding performance rather than as favoritism. When giving recognition awards, organizations should use specific examples to describe clearly how those receiving the awards were selected.

Service Awards Another type of reward given to individual employees is the *service award*. Although service awards may often be portrayed as rewarding performance over a number of years, in reality, they recognize length of service and have little to do with employees' actual performance.

GROUP/TEAM INCENTIVES

The use of groups/teams in organizations has implications for compensation. Although the use of groups/teams has increased substantially in the past few years, the question of how to compensate their members equitably remains a significant challenge. According to several studies, about 80% of large firms provide rewards for work groups or teams in some different ways.[12]

Organizations may establish variable pay plans for teams or groups to:

- Improve productivity.
- Tie pay to team performance.
- Improve customer service or production quality.
- Increase employee retention.

Team incentives can be cash bonuses for the team or they can take a form other than money, such as merchandise or trips. But group incentive situations may place social pressure on members of the group.[13] Everyone in the group succeeds or fails. Therefore, individuals could argue that team incentives should be given to team members equally, although not everyone would agree.

Design of Group/Team Incentive Plans

In designing group/team incentive plans, organizations must consider a number of issues. The main concerns are how and when to distribute the incentives, and who will make decisions about the incentive amounts.

Distribution of Group/Team Incentives Several decisions about how to distribute and allocate group/team rewards must be made. The two primary ways for distributing those rewards are as follows:

1. *Same-size reward for each member:* With this approach, all members receive the same payout, regardless of job level, current pay, seniority, or individual performance differences.
2. *Different-size reward for each member:* With this approach, employers vary individual rewards depending on such factors as contribution to group/team results, current pay, years of experience, and skill levels of jobs performed.

Generally, more organizations use the first approach in addition to different levels of individual pay. The combination rewards performance by making the group/team incentive equal, while still recognizing that individual pay differences exist and are important to many employees. The size of the group/team incentive can be determined either by using a percentage of base pay for the individuals or the group/team as a whole, or by offering a specific dollar amount. For example, one firm pays members individual base rates that reflect years of experience and any additional training that they have. Additionally, the group/team reward is distributed to all as a flat dollar amount.

Timing of Group/Team Incentives How often group/team incentives are paid out is another important consideration. Some of the choices seen in firms with group/team incentives are monthly, quarterly, semiannually, and annually. The most common period used is annually. However, the shorter the time period, the greater the likelihood that employees will see a closer link between their efforts and the performance results that trigger the award payouts. Employers may limit the group/team rewards to $1,000 or less, allowing them to pay out rewards more frequently. The nature of the teamwork, measurement criteria, and organizational results must all be considered when determining the appropriate time period.

Decision Making About Group/Team Incentive Amounts To reinforce the effectiveness of working together, some group/team incentive programs allow members to make decisions about how to allocate the rewards to individuals. In some situations, members vote; in some, a group/team leader decides. In other situations, the incentive "pot" is divided equally, thus avoiding conflict and recognizing that all members contributed to the team results. However, many companies have found group/team members unwilling to make incentive decisions about co-workers.

Group/Team Incentives Challenges

The difference between rewarding team members *equally* and rewarding them *equitably* triggers many of the problems associated with group/team incentives. Rewards distributed in equal amounts to all members may be perceived as "unfair" by employees who work harder, have more capabilities, or perform more difficult jobs. This problem is compounded when an individual who is performing poorly prevents the group/team from meeting the goals needed to trigger the incentive payment. Also, employees working in groups/teams have shown a relatively low level of satisfaction with rewards that are the same for all, versus rewards based on performance, which often may be viewed as more equitable.

Generally, managers view the concept of people working in groups/teams as beneficial. But to a large extent, many employees still expect to be paid according to individual performance. Until this individualism is recognized and compensation programs that are viewed as more equitable by more "team members" are developed, caution should be used when creating and implementing group/team incentives.

Group size is another consideration in team incentives. If a group becomes too large, employees may feel that their individual efforts will have little or no effect on the total performance of the group and the resulting rewards. But group/team incentive plans may encourage cooperation in small groups where interdependence is high. Therefore, in those groups, the use of group/team performance measures is recommended. Such plans have been used in many industries. Conditions for successful team incentives are shown in Figure 13-5. If these conditions cannot be met, then either individual or organizational incentives may be more appropriate.

FIGURE 13-5   Conditions for Successful Group/Team Incentives

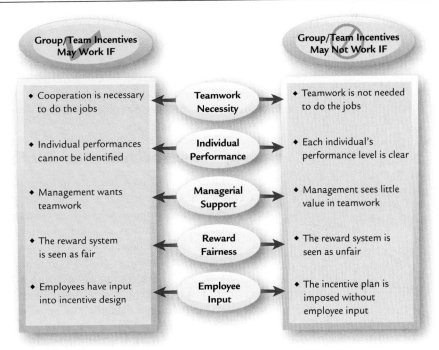

Types of Group/Team Incentives

Group/team reward systems use various ways of compensating individuals. The components include individual wages and salaries in addition to the other rewards. Most organizations that use group/team incentives continue to pay individuals based either on the jobs performed or the individuals' competencies and capabilities. The two most frequently used types of group/team incentives situations are work team results and gainsharing.

Group/Team Results Pay plans for groups/teams may reward all members equally on the basis of group output, cost savings, or quality improvement. The design of most group/team incentives is based on a "self-funding" principle, which means that the money to be used as incentive rewards is obtained through improvement of organizational results. A good example is gainsharing, which can be extended within a group or plantwide.

Gainsharing The system of sharing with employees greater-than-expected gains in profits and/or productivity is gainsharing. Also called *teamsharing* or *goalsharing*, the focus is to increase "discretionary efforts," that is, the difference between the maximum amount of effort a person can exert and the minimum amount of effort that person needs to exert to keep from being fired. Workers in many organizations are not paid for discretionary efforts, but are paid to meet the minimum acceptable level of effort required. When workers do demonstrate discretionary efforts, the organization can afford to pay them more than the going rate, because the extra efforts produce financial gains over and above the returns of minimal efforts. Some organizations have labeled their programs *goalsharing* to emphasize the attainment of results based on business strategy objectives.

> **Gainsharing** System of sharing with employees greater-than-expected gains in profits and/or productivity.

To develop and implement a gainsharing or goalsharing plan, management must identify the ways in which increased productivity, quality, and financial performance can occur and decide how some of the resulting gains should be shared with employees. Often, measures such as labor costs, overtime hours, and quality benchmarks are used. Both organizational measures and departmental measures may be used, with the weights for gainsharing split between the two categories. Plans frequently require that an individual must exhibit satisfactory performance to receive the gainsharing payments.

Two older approaches similar to gainsharing exist. One, called Improshare, sets group piece-rate standards and pays weekly bonuses when the standard is exceeded. The other, the Scanlon plan, uses employee committees and passes on savings to the employees.

Group/Team Incentives and Information Sharing

Team incentives such as gainsharing can have a benefit that might not be obvious, according to research studies. Gainsharing programs provide money to be used as a bonus for employees based on cost savings from implementing employee ideas. The articulation and accumulation of employee-based knowledge due to the program have been shown to be related to lower production costs.[14]

For example, at one time, IBM's bonuses were based primarily on individual performance. The result was a number of "fiefdoms" that paralyzed information exchange. People would not share valuable information because "knowledge is power," so executive management changed compensation to a team-based model. The result was improved information flow, which contributed to IBM's growth for the decade that followed.[15]

ORGANIZATIONAL INCENTIVES

An organizational incentive system compensates all employees in the organization according to how well the organization as a whole performs during the year. The basic concept behind organizational incentive plans is that overall results may depend on organization-wide or plantwide cooperation. The purpose of these plans is to produce better results by rewarding cooperation throughout the organization. For example, conflict between marketing and production can be overcome if management uses an incentive system that emphasizes organization-wide profit and productivity. To be effective, an organizational incentive program should include everyone from non-exempt employees to managers and executives. Two common organizational incentive systems are profit sharing and employee stock plans.

Profit Sharing

Profit sharing System to distribute a portion of the profits of an organization to employees.

As the name implies, profit sharing distributes some portion of organizational profits to employees. The primary objectives of profit-sharing plans include the following:

- Increase productivity and organizational performance.
- Attract or retain employees.
- Improve product/service quality.
- Enhance employee morale.

Typically, the percentage of the profits distributed to employees is set by the end of the year before distribution. In some profit-sharing plans, employees receive portions of the profits at the end of the year; in others, the profits are deferred, placed in a fund, and made available to employees on retirement or on their departure from the organization. Figure 13-6 shows how profit-sharing plans can be funded and allocated. Unions sometimes are skeptical of profit-sharing plans. Often, the level of profits is influenced by factors not under the employees' control, such as accounting decisions, marketing efforts, competition, and elements of executive compensation. However, in recent years, some unions have supported profit-sharing plans that tie employees' pay increases to improvements against organizational performance measures, not just the "bottom-line" numbers.

Drawbacks of Profit-Sharing Plans When used throughout an organization, including with lower-echelon workers, profit-sharing plans can have some drawbacks. First, employees must trust that management will disclose accurate

FIGURE 13-6   **Framework Choices for a Profit-Sharing Plan**

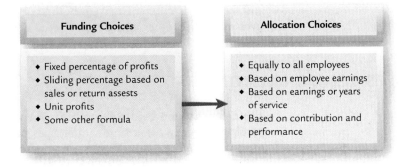

financial and profit information. As many people know, both the definition and level of profit can depend on the accounting system used and on decisions made. To be credible, management must be willing to disclose sufficient financial and profit information to alleviate the skepticism of employees, particularly if profit-sharing levels fall from those of previous years. Second, profits may vary a great deal from year to year, resulting in windfalls or losses beyond the employees' control. Third, payoffs are generally far removed by time from employees' efforts and, therefore, higher rewards may not be strongly linked to better performance.

Employee Stock Plans

Two types of organizational incentive plans use employer stock ownership to reward employees. The goal of these plans is to get employees to think and act like "owners."[16]

A stock option plan gives employees the right to purchase a fixed number of shares of company stock at a specified exercise price for a limited period of time. If the market price of the stock exceeds the exercise price, employees can then exercise the option and buy the stock. The number of firms giving stock options to non-executives has declined some in recent years, primarily due to changing laws and accounting regulations.

Employee Stock Ownership Plans An employee stock ownership plan (ESOP) is designed to give employees significant stock ownership in their employers. According to the National Center for Employee Ownership, an estimated 9,000 firms in the United States offer broad employee-ownership programs covering about 10 million workers. Well-known supermarket firms that offer ESOPs include Publix, Hy-Vee, Price Chopper, and Houtchens. Firms in many other industries have ESOPs as well.[17]

Establishing an ESOP creates several advantages. The major one is that the firm can receive favorable tax treatment on the earnings earmarked for use in the ESOP. Another is that an ESOP gives employees a "piece of the action" so that they can share in the growth and profitability of their firm. Employee ownership may motivate employees to be more productive and focused on organizational performance.

Many people approve of the concept of employee ownership as a kind of "people's capitalism." However, the sharing can also be a disadvantage for employees because it makes both their wages/salaries and their retirement benefits dependent on the performance of their employers. This concentration poses even greater risk for retirees because the value of pension fund assets is also dependent on how well the company does. The financial bankruptcy and travails of several airlines illustrate that an ESOP does not necessarily guarantee success for the employees who become investors.[18]

Salespeople and executives are unique in many ways from other employees and their pay is different as well. Both are typically tied to variable pay incentives more than other employees. A consideration of sales and executive pay follows.

SALES COMPENSATION

The compensation paid to employees involved with sales and marketing is partly or entirely tied to individual sales performance. Salespeople who sell more receive more total compensation than those who sell less. Sales incentives

Stock option plan Plan that gives employees the right to purchase a fixed number of shares of company stock at a specified exercise price for a limited period of time.

Employee stock ownership plan (ESOP) Plan whereby employees have significant stock ownership in their employers.

are perhaps the most widely used individual incentives. The intent is to stimulate more effort from salespeople to earn more money.

Jobs in sales in many organizations have changed greatly in the last 20 years. Certainly sales is still responsible for bringing in revenue for the company. But today's customers have more choices, more information, and the distribution of power has changed.[19] Because of the pressure to make sales and the international environment in which competition is taking place, ethical issues have arisen in the sales area.

A number of legal experts and academics express concerns that some sales incentives programs encourage unethical behavior, particularly if compensation is based solely on commissions. For instance, there have been consistent reports that individuals in other countries buying major industrial equipment have received bribes or kickbacks from sales representatives. The bribes are paid from the incentives received by the sales representatives. This criticism applies especially with major transactions such as large industrial machines, aircraft contracts, and even large insurance policies.

One way of addressing these ethical issues uses a mixture of guaranteed base salary and lowered commission rates. Other approaches use other sales-related dimensions, such as customer service, repeat business, and customer satisfaction.

Types of Sales Compensation Plans

Sales compensation plans can be of several general types, depending on the degree to which total compensation includes some variable pay tied to sales performance. A look at three general types of sales compensation and some challenges to sales compensation follows.

Salary Only Some companies pay salespeople only a salary. The *salary-only approach* is useful when an organization emphasizes serving and retaining existing accounts, over generating new sales and accounts. This approach is frequently used to protect the income of new sales representatives for a period of time while they are building up their sales clientele. Generally, the employer extends the salary-only approach for new sales representatives to no more than six months, at which point it implements a salary-plus-commission or salary-plus-bonuses system (discussed later in this section). Salespeople who want extrinsic rewards function less effectively in salary-only plans because they are less motivated to sell without additional performance-related compensation.

Straight Commission An individual incentive system that is widely used in sales jobs is the commission, which is compensation computed as a percentage of sales in units or dollars. Commissions are integrated into the pay given to sales workers in three common ways: straight commission, salary-plus-commission, and bonuses.

Commission
Compensation computed as a percentage of sales in units or dollars.

In the *straight commission system,* a sales representative receives a percentage of the value of the sales she has made. Consider a sales representative working for a consumer products company. She receives no compensation if she makes no sales, but she receives a percentage of the total amount of all sales revenues she has generated. The advantage of this system is that it requires sales representatives to sell in order to earn. The disadvantage is that it offers no security for the sales staff.

To offset this insecurity, some employers use a draw system, in which sales representatives can draw advance payments against future commissions. The amounts drawn are then deducted from future commission checks. Arrangements must be made for repayment of drawn amounts if individuals leave the organization before earning their draws in commissions.

Salary-Plus-Commission or Bonuses The form of sales compensation used most frequently is the *salary-plus-commission,* which combines the stability of a salary with the performance aspect of a commission. A common split is 70% salary to 30% commission, although the split varies by industry and based on numerous other factors. Many organizations also pay salespeople salaries and then offer bonuses that are a percentage of the base pay, tied to how well the employee meets various sales targets or other criteria.

Sales Compensation Challenges

Sales incentives work well, especially when they are tied to the strategic initiatives of the organization. However, they do present many challenges—from calculating total pay correctly, to dealing with sales in e-business, to causing competition among salespeople. Often, sales compensation plans become quite complex, and tracking individual incentives can be demanding. Internet-based software has helped because companies can use it to post results daily, weekly, or monthly, and salespeople can use it to track their results.

Administering incentives globally is difficult, but HR technology can help. Use of incentive management software has become widespread. These systems are advantageous because they can track the performance of numerous employees worldwide who may be covered by different incentive plans. Consider a company that has different product lines, geographic locations, and company subsidiaries, and imagine tracking the performance of hundreds or thousands of sales representatives for a sales incentive program. Or imagine manually tracking attendance, safety, and training incentives for firms with many employees worldwide. Overall, it is evident that the data provided by the software systems are helping executives and managers worldwide to support and manage their sales forces more effectively.[20]

The last few years have seen the growth of sales compensation plans with different design features. Many of them are multi-tiered and can be rather complex. Selling over the Internet brings challenges to incentive compensation as well. Some sales organizations combine individual and group sales bonus programs. In these programs, a portion of the sales incentive is linked to the attainment of group sales goals. This approach is supposed to encourage cooperation and teamwork among the salespeople, but that may not always occur.[21]

Sales Performance Metrics Successfully using variable sales compensation requires establishing clear performance criteria and measures. Figure 13-7 shows some of the possible sales metrics. Generally, no more than three sales performance measures should be used in a sales compensation plan. Consultants criticize many sales commission plans as being too complex to motivate sales representatives. Other plans may be too simple, focusing only on the salesperson's pay, not on organizational objectives. Many companies measure performance primarily by comparing an individual's sales revenue against established quotas. The plans would be better if the organizations used a variety of criteria, including obtaining new accounts and selling high-value versus low-value items that reflect marketing plans. A number of different criteria are commonly used to determine incentive payments for salespeople and how they are part of determining sales effectiveness.[22]

FIGURE 13-7   Sales Metric Possibilities

- Revenue growth
- Margin growth
- New customer revenue
- Average sales revenue per salesperson
- Sales from new products
- Customer satisfaction
- Account retention
- Return on sales compensation
- Return on sales investment
- Increase in average sale
- Control of sales expenses

Effectiveness of Sales Incentive Plans So many organizations have sales incentive plans that it would be logical to think those plans are effective. However, many sales compensation plans are not seen as effective by either sales-people or managers and executives. One study found that sales productivity was not above targets in over half of all the surveyed firms and that the respondents were dissatisfied with their sales incentive plans. Consequently, almost 80% of the firms had made at least six changes in those plans in a two-year period.[23] Such frequent changes reduce the effectiveness of plans and create concerns and frustrations with the sales representatives and managers. HR professionals may be involved in designing, revising, and communicating sales incentive plans, as well as in responding to the complaints and concerns of sales representatives.

Effective sales incentives should be extra compensation for sales. Practicing sales managers warn that sales incentive systems will fail when such an "entitlement culture" takes hold in the sales force. An entitlement culture is the idea that bonuses are *deferred salary* rather than extra pay for extra sales performance. When sales incentive pay that was designed to be extra pay for top performers becomes a reliable paycheck on which everyone can count, entitlement has taken root and motivation drops.[24] Failure to deal with incentive programs that no longer motivate causes variable costs (pay for performance) to in effect become fixed costs (salary) from the perspective of the employer. Pay without performance, poor quota setting, and little difference in pay between top and bottom performers can cause the problem. Not all sales incentives must focus on just the very top performers, as the HR Best Practices (on the next page) shows.

EXECUTIVE COMPENSATION

Many organizations, especially large ones, administer compensation for executives differently from compensation for lower-level employees. At the heart of most executive compensation plans is the idea that executives should be rewarded if the organization grows in profitability and value over a period of years.[26] Therefore, variable pay distributed through different types of incentives is a significant part of executive compensation.

HR BEST PRACTICES

T-Mobile and Rewards/Recognition

T-Mobile, a cellular telephone provider based in Bellevue, Washington, targeted the company's employees who deal with the customers to increase customer satisfaction and reduce turnover. This group included 11,000 customer service employees. Not surprisingly, the group was quite varied in terms of age, gender, racial makeup, and geography.

Extensive surveys were conducted and focus groups were used to find out what would motivate the entire target group, not just a small segment of it. T-Mobile management saw that most incentive programs rewarded the top 10% to 20% of the workforce, but they wanted to increase the efforts of the middle 60%. They felt that if this group could consistently exceed their key performance indicators (KPIs), customer service would significantly improve. The incentive program that was designed included travel and activity rewards and the company promoted the program using national events, conference calls, meetings, and newsletters. After implementation of the program, T-Mobile saw marked improvement in KPI scores, *especially* for the targeted mid-level 60%.

A national study later that year ranked T-Mobile as the top provider of customer service in the cellular telephone industry. Additionally, the firm benefited because employee attrition rates decreased by 50%. The incentive program achieved improvement throughout the company.[25]

Global Executive Compensation

Senior executives in the United States earn the highest salaries and annual total cash of all countries. Successful global companies are increasing use of long-term incentives and bonuses, moving closer to the model used in the United States, in which variable pay is 95% of basic compensation.[27] The basic salaries of CEOs in Europe are much the same as in the United States, but variable pay adds 150% to that in Europe and adds 400% in America.[28]

The most important reason for giving pay as incentives is that it is thought to motivate effectiveness to increase corporate performance and stock values, but a survey suggests that incentives only improve performance slightly. A more likely explanation may have to do with the ability to attract and keep executives. Experienced CEOs have an advantage when boards of directors want to replace a poor performing CEO with a seasoned replacement.[29]

In comparably sized firms in Europe and the United States, total cash compensation for CEOs is similar. But long-term incentives are used more in French and German companies than in the United Kingdom. Scandinavian firms pay their CEOs less than do other European firms. Also, Japanese CEOs are paid less than what U.S. CEOs in comparably sized firms are paid. Critics of executive pay levels point out that in the United States, many corporate CEOs make almost 370 times more than do average workers in their firms, up from 35 times more in the 1970s. In Japan, the ratio is 15:1, and in Europe, 20:1.[30]

Internet Research

The Riley Guide

For a directory of information resources and services on executive compensation, link to their Website at: http://thomsonedu.com/management/mathis.

Elements of Executive Compensation

Because high-salaried executives are in higher tax brackets, many executive compensation packages are designed to offer significant tax savings. These savings occur through use of deferred compensation methods whereby taxes are not due until after the executives leave the firm.

Executive Salaries Salaries of executives vary by the type of job, size of organization, industry, and other factors. In some organizations, particularly non-profits, salaries often make up 90% or more of total compensation. In contrast, in large corporations, salaries may constitute a small part of the total package. Survey data on executive salaries are often reviewed by Boards of Directors to ensure that their organizations are competitive.

Executive Benefits Many executives are covered by *regular benefits plans* that are also available to non-executive employees, including traditional retirement, health insurance, and vacation plans. In addition, executives may receive *supplemental benefits* that other employees do not receive. For example, executive health plans with no co-payments and with no limitations on deductibles or physician choice are popular among small and middle-size businesses. Corporate-owned insurance on the life of the executive is also popular; this insurance pays both the executive's estate and the company in the event of death. One supplemental benefit that has grown in popularity is company-paid financial planning for executives. Trusts of various kinds may be designed by the company to help the executives deal with estate-planning and tax issues. Deferred compensation is another possible means of helping executives with tax liabilities caused by incentive compensation plans.

Executive Perquisites (Perks) In addition to the regular benefits received by all employees, executives often receive benefits called perquisites. Perquisites (perks) are special benefits—usually non-cash items—for executives. Many executives value the status enhancement of these visible symbols, which allow them to be seen as "very important people" both inside and outside their organizations. Perks can also offer substantial tax savings because some of them are not taxed as income. Some commonly used executive perks are company cars, health club and country club memberships, first-class air travel, use of private jets, stress counseling, and chauffeur services.

Perquisites (perks) Special benefits—usually non-cash items—for executives.

Annual Executive Incentives and Bonuses Annual incentives and bonuses for executives can be determined in several ways. One way is to use a discretionary system whereby the CEO and the Board of Directors decide bonuses; the absence of formal, measurable targets detracts significantly from this approach. Another way is to tie bonuses to specific measures, such as return on investment, earnings per share, and net profits before taxes. More complex systems create bonus pools and thresholds above which bonuses are computed. Whatever method is used, it is important to describe it so that executives attempting to earn additional compensation understand the plan; otherwise, the incentive effect will be diminished.

Performance Incentives: Long Term vs. Short Term Use of executive performance-based incentives tries to tie executive compensation to the long-term growth and success of the organization. However, whether these incentives really emphasize the long term or merely represent a series of short-term rewards is controversial. Short-term rewards based on quarterly or annual performance may not result in the kind of long-run-oriented decisions necessary for the company to perform well over multiple years.

As would be expected, the total amount of pay-for-performance incentives varies by management level, with CEOs receiving significantly more than subsidiary or other senior managers. The typical CEO gets about half of all the total incentives paid to all senior managers and executives.

HR ON-THE-JOB

Are They Worth It?

The large amounts of some annual compensation packages for executives have raised ethical questions. A primary question is whether any single CEO is really deserving of compensation totaling over $50 million when stock option profits, retirement bonuses, and other payments are included.

Of course, these compensation packages, as large as they are, provide little meaning unless put into context. If the company is doing well and performing better than competitors and above expectations, the huge packages might be justifiable to stockholders. Certainly, the opposite can be true as well.

The question that still must be addressed by Boards of Directors, stockholders, and executives is this: How realistic and ethical is it to provide such huge amounts to one person, when many other executives have contributed to organizational performance and do not receive such lavish payouts? Is company performance really dependent on one person's performance? What do you think?

The most widely used long-term incentives are stock option plans. A *stock option* gives employees the right to buy stock in a company, usually at an advantageous price. Despite the prevalence of such plans, research has found little relationship between providing CEOs with stock options and subsequent firm performance.[32] Because of the numerous corporate scandals involving executives at Enron, WorldCom, Tyco, and elsewhere who received outrageously high compensation due to stock options and the backdating of those options, the use of stock options has been changing. Instead, more firms with publicly traded stock are using means such as *restricted stock, phantom stock, performance shares,* and other specialized technical forms, which are beyond the scope of this discussion.

Another outcome of the recent corporate abuses by executives was the passage of the Sarbanes-Oxley Act. This act has numerous provisions that have affected the accounting and financial reporting requirements of different types of executive compensation.[33] Also, the Financial Accounting Standards Board (FASB) has adopted rules regarding the expensing of stock options.

"Reasonableness" of Executive Compensation

The notion that monetary incentives tied to performance result in improved performance makes sense to most people. However, there is an ongoing debate about whether executive compensation in the United States is truly linked to performance. This is particularly of concern given the astronomical amounts of some executive compensation packages, as highlighted in the HR On-the-Job feature.

The reasonableness of executive compensation is often justified by comparison to compensation market surveys, but these surveys usually provide a range of compensation data that requires interpretation. Various questions have been suggested for determining if executive pay is "reasonable," including the following useful ones:

- Would another company hire this person as an executive?
- How does the executive's compensation compare with that for executives in similar companies in the industry?
- Is the executive's pay consistent with pay for other employees within the company?
- What would an investor pay for the level of performance of the executive?

A final question is being tied to the customer loyalty dimension of CEO performance. Customers are asked "On a scale of 1 to 10 how likely is it that you would recommend us to your friends or colleagues?" The difference between the percentage of customers who give high responses and those who give low scores correlates highly with a company's revenue growth and can be used to measure one part of executive performance.[34]

Linkage Between Executive Compensation and Corporate Performance
Of all the executive compensation issues that are debated, the one discussed most frequently is whether or not executive compensation levels are sufficiently linked to organizational performance.[35] One key aspect of evaluating all the studies on this topic is the performance measures used. Numerous studies have examined different facets of this topic.[36] In many settings, financial measures such as return on equity, return to shareholders, earnings per share, and net income before taxes are used to measure performance. However, a number of firms also incorporate non-financial organizational measures of performance when determining executive bonuses and incentives. Customer satisfaction, employee satisfaction, market share, productivity, and quality are other areas measured for executive performance rewards.

Measurement of executive performance varies from firm to firm. Some executive compensation packages use a short-term focus of one year, which may lead to large rewards for executive performance in a given year even though corporate performance over a multi-year period is mediocre. This difference is especially pronounced if the yearly measures are carefully chosen. Executives can even manipulate earnings per share by selling assets, liquidating inventories, or reducing research and development expenditures. All of these actions may make organizational performance look better, but they may also impair the long-term growth of the organization.

A number of other executive compensation issues and concerns exist. Figure 13-8 highlights the criticisms and counter-arguments of some common points of contention.

FIGURE 13-8   **Common Executive Compensation Criticisms**

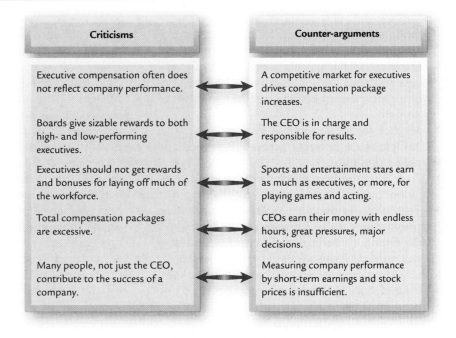

Criticisms	Counter-arguments
Executive compensation often does not reflect company performance.	A competitive market for executives drives compensation package increases.
Boards give sizable rewards to both high- and low-performing executives.	The CEO is in charge and responsible for results.
Executives should not get rewards and bonuses for laying off much of the workforce.	Sports and entertainment stars earn as much as executives, or more, for playing games and acting.
Total compensation packages are excessive.	CEOs earn their money with endless hours, great pressures, major decisions.
Many people, not just the CEO, contribute to the success of a company.	Measuring company performance by short-term earnings and stock prices is insufficient.

One of the more controversial issues is that some executives seem to get large awards for negative actions. It seems contradictory from an employee's perspective to reward executives who often improve corporate results by cutting staff, laying off employees, changing pension plans, or increasing the deductible on the health insurance. But sometimes cost-cutting measures are necessary to keep a company afloat. However, a sense of reasonableness may be appropriate too; if rank-and-file employees suffer, giving bonuses and large payouts to executives appears counterproductive and even hypocritical.

Executive Compensation and Boards of Directors In most organizations, the Board of Directors is the major policy-setting entity and must approve executive compensation packages. The compensation committee usually is a subgroup of the board, composed of directors who are not officers of the firm. Compensation committees generally make recommendations to the Board of Directors on overall pay policies, salaries for top officers, supplemental compensation such as stock options and bonuses, and additional perquisites for executives.

Increasingly, the independence of these committees has been criticized.[37] One major concern voiced by many critics is that the base pay and bonuses of CEOs are often set by the members of board compensation committees, many of whom are CEOs of other companies with similar compensation packages. Also, the compensation advisors and consultants to the CEOs often collect large fees, and critics charge that those fees distort the objectivity of the advice given.

To counter criticism, some corporations have changed the composition of the compensation committees by taking actions such as prohibiting "insider" company officers from serving on them. Also, some firms have empowered the compensation committees to hire and pay compensation consultants without involving executive management. Finally, a tool called a "tally sheet" can provide the board with a fuller picture of a chief's entire compensation package.[38]

Compensation committee Subgroup of the Board of Directors, composed of directors who are not officers of the firm.

SUMMARY

- Variable pay, also called incentives, is compensation that can be linked to individual, group/team, and/or organizational performance.
- Effective variable pay plans should fit both business strategies and organizational cultures, appropriately award actions, and be administered properly.
- Metrics for measuring the success of variable pay plans are different across HR-related and production plans.
- Piece-rate and bonus plans are the most commonly used individual incentives.
- The design of group/team variable pay plans must consider how the incentives are to be distributed, the timing of the incentive payments, and who will make decisions about the variable payout.
- Organization-wide rewards include profit sharing and stock ownership plans.

- Sales employees may have their compensation tied to performance on a number of sales-related criteria. Sales compensation can be provided as salary only, commission only, or salary-plus-commission or bonuses.
- Measuring the effectiveness of sales incentive plans is a challenge that may require the plans to be adjusted based on success metrics.
- Executive compensation must be viewed as a total package composed of salaries, bonuses, long-term performance-based incentives, benefits, and perquisites (perks).
- Performance-based incentives often represent a significant portion of an executive's compensation package.
- A compensation committee, which is a subgroup of the Board of Directors, generally has authority over executive compensation plans.

REVIEW AND APPLICATION QUESTIONS

1. Discuss why pay-for-performance plans have become popular and what elements are needed to make them successful.
2. Give examples of individual incentives used by an organization in which you were employed. Then describe why those plans were successful and/or unsuccessful.
3. Suppose you have been asked to lead a task force to develop a sales incentive plan at your firm. The task force is to generate a list of strategies and issues to be evaluated by upper management. Using details from *www.mercerhr.com* and various other Websites, identify and develop preliminary material for the task force.

CASE

Incentive Plans for Fun and Travel

For incentive plans to pay off for companies, the plans must stimulate employee interest and motivate them to perform well. Firms in several different industries have been creative in developing incentive plans, which have resulted in the companies receiving *Top Motivator Awards* from *Incentive* magazine. A look at two of the recent winners illustrates the variety of plans being used.

Houston-based Pappas Restaurants has over 10,000 employees working in restaurants such as Pappadeux Seafood Kitchen, Pappas Pizza, and others. As a key part of creating and maintaining a "fun culture," Pappas has created an unusual job as part of its management structure, a Director of Fun Stuff. This individual's role is to develop and conduct activities that reinforce the performance-oriented, fun culture that Pappas wants. By stressing this culture, the firm hopes to ensure that both customers and employees enjoy Pappas restaurants. One successful incentive program is called "Rising Stars." Employees working as bartenders, food servers, and in other customer contact jobs receive $20 gift certificates weekly for such actions as favorable customer comments, attendance, and working extra shifts as needed. But employees without primary customer roles are not forgotten, because Pappas has a "Kitchen Superstars" program for its dishwashers, cooks, and clean-up workers, who can receive gift certificates also. Purchased from well-known retailers such as Target, Blockbuster, and other retailers located near Pappas restaurants, the gift certificates provide immediate reinforcement for positive actions, as well as providing an easily used reward.

In a very different work setting, Washington Mutual, an insurance and financial services firm based in Seattle, has used sales incentive programs effectively. One successful program was called "Fresh Perspectives." To motivate sales employees to generate a greater number and volume of home loans, the company developed several different incentive plans. In the primary plan, the firm's sales representatives accumulated points for loan product sales. Sales results for employees were tracked and posted monthly so that everyone knew where they were in comparison to other sales representatives. The 400 top-producing salespeople became members of the President's Club. To provide special recognition of their accomplishments, the President's Club members were rewarded with a five-day trip to Cancun. Unique entertainment events, jungle safaris, and other activities were participated in by the club members and key executives. The Cancun trip was both an incentive to encourage performance and a reward for the top sales performers.

Numerous other firms spend considerable time and money on various incentive programs. The key focus of those programs, as well as the ones used at Pappas Restaurants and Washington Mutual, are to motivate and reward performance.[39]

Questions

1. Why might the use of incentives in the form of gift certificates be better than just providing cash to employees?
2. What are some advantages and disadvantages of a sales incentive program in which the top performers receive a trip or other large reward, while other sales individuals receive lesser or different types of rewards?

SUPPLEMENTAL CASE

"Cash Is Good, Card Is Bad"

Both the positive and negative issues associated with the use of an incentive plan are discussed in this case. (For the case, go to http://thomsonedu.com/management/mathis.)

NOTES

1. Based on Robert Tomsho, "More Districts Pay Teachers for Performance," *The Wall Street Journal*, March 23, 2006, B1.
2. Kathy Gurchiek, "Incentive Programs Fall Short with Employees Survey Finds," *HR News*, December 16, 2004, *www.shrm.org/hrnews*; and Worldatwork Staff, "U.S. Companies Revise Variable Pay Plans for Non-Executive Workers," *Newsline*, November 3, 2004, *www.e-topics.com*.
3. Dorren Remmen, "Performance Pays Off," *Strategic Finance*, March 2003, 27–32.
4. "Boeing Awards Taking Off in a New Direction," *Workforce Management*, April 24, 2006, 37–39.
5. Based on Jaclyne Badal, "New Incentives for Workers Combine Cash and Fun," *The Wall Street Journal*, June 19, 2006, B3.
6. Leo Jakobson, "Incentives Without Borders," *Incentive*, March 2006, 12–17.
7. Chris Silva, "An Incentive to Provide Incentives," *Employee Benefit News*, May 2007, 11.
8. Ed Silverman, "Sending a Message," *Human Resource Executive*, May 16, 2005, 27–29.
9. Chris Taylor, "On-the-Spot Incentives," *HR Magazine*, May 2004, 80–84.
10. E. L. Ford, "Leveraging Recognition: Non-Cash Incentives to Improve Performance," *Workspan*, November 2006, 18–22.
11. Leo Jakobson, "The World Gets Smaller," *Incentive*, April 4, 2007, *www.incentivemag.com*.
12. Edward E. Lawler III, "Pay Practices in *Fortune 1000* Corporations,"

WorldatWork Journal, Fourth Quarter 2003, 45–54.
13. Tom Hajny, "Pay Increase or Financial Incentive?" *Health Care Collector*, November 2005, 6–7.
14. J. B. Arthur and C. L. Huntley, "Ramping Up the Organizational Learning Curve: Assessing the Impact of Deliberate Learning on Organizational Performance Under Gainsharing," *Academy of Management Journal*, 48 (2005), 1159–1170.
15. M. W. Van Alstyne, "Create Colleagues Not Competitors," *Harvard Business Review*, September 2005, 24–28.
16. Stephen H. Wagner, Christopher P. Parker, and Neil D. Christiansen, "Employees that Think and Act Like Owners," *Personnel Psychology*, 56 (2003), 847–871.
17. For current data, see the National Center for Employee Ownership, *www.nceo.org*.
18. Jason Kovac, "Stock Options," *Workspan*, August 2006, 23.
19. Jerone Colletti and Mary Fiss, "The Ultimately Accountable Job," *Harvard Business Review*, July/August 2006, 1–8.
20. Based on Peter Kurlander and Scott Barton, "Improving Your Odds: Successful Incentive Compensation Automation," *Workspan*, January 2004, 30–33; and Jakobson, "Incentives Without Borders."
21. Kenneth Hein, "Anatomy of an Online Incentive Program," *Incentive*, February 2006, 17–20.
22. Jerry Colletti and Mary Fiss, "Sales Force Productivity Metrics," *http://Collettifiss.com/shortc.aspx*.
23. "Pay-for-Performance Sales Comp Not Living Up to Expectations,"

Newsline, September 24, 2003, *www.deloite.com*.
24. D. Bello and S. Barnes, "The Sales-Incentive Entitlement Culture," *Workspan*, August 2006, 40–43.
25. Based on William Flanagan, "The Best Incentive Programs of 2005," *Incentive*, December 2005, 15–18.
26. Martin Conyon, "Executive Compensation and Incentives," *Academy of Management Perspectives*, February 2006, 25–44.
27. "Global Pay for Performance," *HR Magazine*, April 2006, 51, 18.
28. "CEO's and Their Indian Rope Trick," *The Economist*, December 11, 2004, 60.
29. Joann S. Lublin, "The Serial CEO," *The Wall Street Journal*, September 19, 2005, B1.
30. Joann S. Lublin and Scott Thurm, "Money Rules," *The Wall Street Journal*, October 12, 2006, 1.
31. Jean McGuire and Elie Matta, "CEO Stock Options: The Silent Dimension of Ownership," *Academy of Management Journal*, 46 (2003), 255–265.
32. For example, see Scott Thurm, "Extra Pay: Many CEO's Receive Dividends on 'Phantom' Stock," *The Wall Street Journal*, May 4, 2006, 1; and Joann S. Lublin, "Boards Tie CEO Pay More Tightly to Performance," *The Wall Street Journal*, February 21, 2006, A1.
33. Rodney K. Platt, "Sarbanes-Oxley Bane or Boon?" *Workspan*, March 2004, 22–27; and C. Forelle and K. Scannell, "Revisiting Executive-Pay Law," *The Wall Street Journal*, September 6, 2006, C1.

34. Jena McGregor, "Would You Recommend Us?" *Business Week*, January 30, 2006, 94–96.

35. Joann S. Lublin, "Ten Ways to Restore Investor Confidence in Compensation," *The Wall Street Journal*, April 9, 2007, 1; and Charles Elson, "What's Wrong with Executive Compensation?" *Harvard Business Review*, January 2003, 68.

36. For example, see James J. Corderio and Rajaram Viliyath, "Beyond Pay for Performance: A Panel Study of the Determinants of CEO Compensation," *American Business Review*, 21 (2003), 57–67; and Dan Dalton et al., "Meta-Analyses of Financial Performance and Equity: Fusion or Confusion?" *Academy of Management Journal*, 46 (2003), 13–26.

37. L. A. Bebchuk and J. M. Fried, "Pay Without Performance," *Academy of Management Perspectives*, February 2006, 5–24.

38. Joann S. Lublin, "Adding It All Up," *The Wall Street Journal*, April 10, 2006, R1.

39. Based on Kenneth Hein, "Motivators of the Year," *Incentive*, October 2003, 40–44.

CHAPTER

14

Managing Employee Benefits

After you have read this chapter, you should be able to:

- Define a benefit and identify four strategic benefits considerations.

- Summarize why benefits management and communications efforts are important.

- Distinguish between mandated and voluntary benefits and list three examples of each.

- Explain the importance of managing the costs of health benefits and identify some methods of doing so.

- Discuss the shift of retirement plans from defined-benefit to defined-contribution and cash balance programs.

- Describe the growth of financial, family-oriented, and time-off benefits and their importance to many employees.

HR Headline

Health Benefit Costs Concerns of Employers and Employees

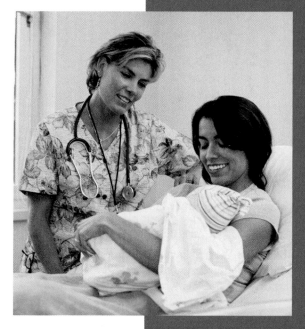

Health benefit costs for employers have been increasing significantly over the past two decades. During the past five years there has been a 75% growth in those costs. Total health benefits costs for employers are about $9,000 annually per employee, according to a Towers Perrin study.

Consequently, the costs of health-care benefits have become the number one issue of concern for employers, with over 60% of employers citing containing these costs as their highest HR priority. To counter the cost increases, employers are taking steps to reduce or even eliminate benefits. Actions that companies are taking include increasing the amount that employees and retirees have to pay for health insurance and implementing prescription drug management programs.

These actions have reduced employee satisfaction with their benefits, especially in smaller companies. Many employees voice concerns that their annual pay increases merely cover the extra benefits charges they must pay. About 60% of employees in one survey indicated that they likely would not be able to pay for unexpected medical expenses that are not covered by their employers. Thus, the pressures on health benefit costs is likely to continue, and employer/employee conflicts and concerns over health benefit costs probably will be ongoing as well.[1]

FIGURE 14-1   Employer Compensation and Benefits Costs per Hour, Private Industry

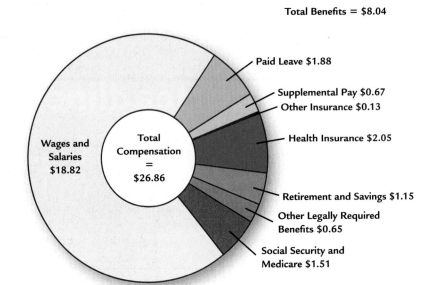

Total Benefits = $8.04

Paid Leave $1.88

Supplemental Pay $0.67
Other Insurance $0.13

Health Insurance $2.05

Wages and Salaries $18.82

Total Compensation = $26.86

Retirement and Savings $1.15

Other Legally Required Benefits $0.65

Social Security and Medicare $1.51

Source: U.S. Bureau of Labor Statistics, "Employer Costs for Compensation," News Release, June 21, 2006, *www.bls.gov.*

Benefit Indirect reward given to an employee or a group of employees for organizational membership.

An employer provides benefits to workers for being part of the organization. A benefit is an indirect reward given to an employee or a group of employees for organizational membership. Benefits often include retirement plans, vacations with pay, health insurance, educational assistance, and many more programs.

In the United States, employers often fill the role of major provider of benefits for citizens. In many other nations, citizens and employers are taxed to pay for government-provided benefits, such as health-care and retirement programs. Although federal regulations require U.S. employers to provide certain benefits, U.S. employers voluntarily provide many others.

Benefits are costly for the typical U.S. employer, averaging 30% to 40% of payroll expenses. In highly unionized manufacturing and utility industries, they may be over 70% of payroll. Figure 14-1 shows the per hour costs employers expend for average wages and salary amounts, as well as different types of benefits. Notice that of the average total compensation of $26.86, employers are paying $8.04 for benefits, 25% of which are for health insurance benefits. This area is the most costly for the average employer. These numbers illustrate why benefits have become a strategic concern in HR management.

BENEFITS AND HR STRATEGY

In the United States, a challenge for employers is how to best manage the balancing act between the growing costs of benefits and the use of those benefits in accomplishing organizational goals. For instance, organizations can choose to compete for or retain employees by providing different levels of base compensation, variable pay, and benefits. That is why benefits should be looked at as a vital part of the total rewards "package" when determining organizational strategies.

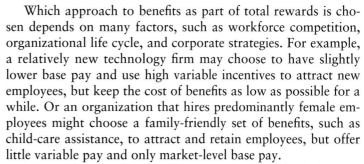

Which approach to benefits as part of total rewards is chosen depends on many factors, such as workforce competition, organizational life cycle, and corporate strategies. For example, a relatively new technology firm may choose to have slightly lower base pay and use high variable incentives to attract new employees, but keep the cost of benefits as low as possible for a while. Or an organization that hires predominantly female employees might choose a family-friendly set of benefits, such as child-care assistance, to attract and retain employees, but offer little variable pay and only market-level base pay.

The reasons why employers offer benefits are multi-faceted and tie into strategic considerations. As Figure 14-2 indicates, there are several aspects to looking at benefits strategically.

Benefits as Competitive Advantage

It is important that benefits be used to help create and maintain competitive advantages.[2] Benefits should not be viewed merely as cost factors because they positively affect HR efforts.

Employers may offer benefits to aid recruiting and retention, impact organizational performance, and meet legal requirements. Also, some employers see benefits as reinforcing the company philosophy of social and corporate citizenship. Employers that provide good benefits are viewed more positively within a community and the industry by customers, civic leaders, current employees, and workers in other firms. Conversely, the employers who are seen as skimping on benefits, cutting benefits, or taking advantage of workers may be viewed more negatively.

One company that has used benefits as part of a total rewards strategy is Jackson's Food Stores, based in Idaho, with 87 stores. The firm has expanded its

FIGURE 14-2   **Strategic Benefits Considerations**

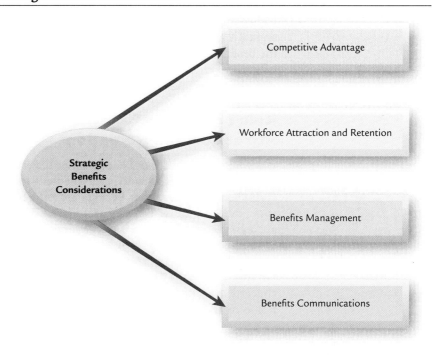

variable pay and benefits package for both full-time and part-time employees. Consequently, employee retention has increased, which has resulted in better customer service and enhanced organizational results.[3]

The primary reasons executives see for offering benefits is to attract and retain talent and meet responsibilities to employees. According to a survey by an international consulting firm, 48% of executives see benefits as extremely important to a company's competitive effectiveness and another 41% saw benefits as somewhat important.[4] This survey and others confirm that benefits are viewed by both employers and employees as a part of being an "employer of choice" when attracting and retaining individuals.[5]

Global Benefits Benefits vary from country to country. In many countries, retirement, health, and other benefits are provided as part of government services. Employers are taxed heavily to pay into government funds that cover the benefits. This model is very different from the one in the United States, where most benefits are provided by employers directly.

Retirement and pension systems are provided by the government in many countries as well. National pension programs in Germany, France, and Japan, among other countries, are facing significant financial pressures due to their aging workforces and populations. Such challenges also face the Social Security and Medicare systems in the United States.

Health-care benefits also differ significantly worldwide. Many countries, including Great Britain and Canada, have national health services. Some global firms require employees to use the medical services available from host countries, whereas other global employers provide special coverage that allows expatriates to receive health care from private providers. Arranging quality private coverage becomes an especially important issue for global employees located in various underdeveloped countries where the availability and quality of medical facilities and treatment vary widely.

The amount of leave and vacation time also vary significantly around the globe. Of all of the major countries, only the United States, Australia, and Ethiopia do not provide paid leave for new parents. Additionally, the annual leave/vacation in European countries averages 36 days per year, whereas the United States and Canada average about 10 to 12 days, the lowest amounts of annual vacation leave among developed countries. These examples illustrate the benefits challenges faced by firms that have employees located in different countries.[6] How these challenges are handled impacts global attraction of the international employers.

Role of Benefits for Workforce Attraction and Retention

It is well-established that benefits influence employees' decisions about which particular employer to work for, whether to stay with or leave an employer, and when to retire. What benefits are offered, the competitive level of benefits, and how those benefits are viewed by individuals all affect employee attraction and retention efforts of employers. An additional concern is that the composition of the U.S. workforce is changing, and expectations about benefits by different generations of employees are affecting benefit decisions.[7] For instance, many "baby boomers" who are approaching retirement age are concerned about retirement benefits and health care. The younger generation of workers, however, is more interested in flexible and portable benefits.

However, all generations have concerns about the nature of and changes in health insurance. Having benefits plans that appeal to the different groups is vital to attracting and retaining all different types of employees.

A major advantage of benefits is that they generally are not taxed as income to employees. For this reason, benefits represent a somewhat more valuable reward to employees than an equivalent cash payment. For example, assume that employee Clara Smith is in a 25% tax bracket. If Clara earns an extra $400, she must pay $100 in taxes on this amount (disregarding exemptions). But if her employer provides prescription drug coverage in a benefits plan, and she receives the $400 as payments for prescription drugs, she is not taxed on the amount, and she receives the value of the entire $400, not just $300. This feature makes benefits a desirable form of compensation to employees.

BENEFITS MANAGEMENT AND COMMUNICATIONS

Based on the strategic benefits decisions made, benefits programs must be designed, administered, measured, and communicated. Figure 14-3 highlights the key components of effective benefits management.

Benefits Design

Benefits plans can provide flexibility and choices for employees, or they can be standardized for all employees. Increasingly, employers are finding that providing employees with some choices and flexibility allows individuals to tailor

---

FIGURE 14-3   Benefits Management Components

their benefits to their own situations. However, the more choices available, the higher the administrative demands placed on organizations.[8] A number of key decisions are part of benefits design:

- How much total compensation, including benefits, can be provided?
- What part of the total compensation of individuals should benefits constitute?
- Which employees should be provided which benefits?
- What expense levels are acceptable for each benefit offered?
- What is being received by the organization in return for each benefit?
- How flexible should the package of benefits be?

Part-Time Employee Benefits Another key design issue is whether or not to provide benefits coverage to part-time employees. Many employers do not provide part-time employee benefits, except some time-off leave benefits. According to data from the U.S. Bureau of Labor Statistics, about one-fourth of part-time workers are in company retirement plans, and a minority of them are eligible for health-care benefits.[9] Part-time employees who do receive benefits usually do so in proportion to the percentage of full-time work they provide.

UPS, the package delivery firm, provides some health benefits to most part-time employees. Wegmans Food Markets and Starbucks also provide benefits to part-timers. All these firms indicate that providing benefits positively affects their ability to attract and retain part-time workers in tight labor markets.[10]

Flexible Benefits As mentioned, as part of both benefits design and administration, many employers offer employees choices for benefits. A flexible benefits plan allows employees to select the benefits they prefer from groups of benefits established by the employer. Sometimes called a *flex plan* or *cafeteria plan,* these plans have a variety of "dishes," or benefits, available so that each employee can select an individual combination of benefits within some overall limits.

As a result of the changing composition of the workforce, flexible benefits plans have grown in popularity. Flexible benefits systems recognize that individual employee situations differ because of age, family status, and lifestyle. For instance, dual-career couples may not want the same benefits from two different employers. Under a flex plan, one of them can forgo some benefits that are available in the partner's plan and take other benefits instead.

A problem with flexibility in benefits choice is that an *inappropriate benefits package* may be chosen by an employee. A young construction worker may not choose a disability benefit; however, if he or she is injured, the family may suffer financial hardship. Part of this problem can be overcome by requiring employees to select a core set of benefits (life, health, and disability insurance) and then offering options on other benefits.

Another problem can be adverse selection, whereby only higher-risk employees select and use certain benefits. For example, only employees with chronic illnesses might choose health insurance. Because many insurance plans are based on a group rate, the employer may face higher rates if insufficient numbers of employees select an insurance option.

Because many flexible plans have become so complex, they require more administrative time and information systems to track the different choices made by employees. Despite all these disadvantages, flex plans will likely continue to grow in popularity.

Flexible benefits plan
Program that allows employees to select the benefits they prefer from groups of benefits established by the employer.

Adverse selection
Situation in which only higher-risk employees select and use certain benefits.

FIGURE 14-4   Typical Division of HR Responsibilities: Benefits Administration

HR Unit	Managers
• Develops and administers benefits systems • Answers employees' technical questions on benefits • Monitors benefits usage • Suggests benefits cost-control approaches	• Answer simple questions on benefits • Maintain liaison with HR specialist on benefits • Maintain good communications with employees near retirement • Coordinate use of time-off benefits

HR and Benefits Administration

With the myriad of benefits, it is easy to see why many organizations must make coordinated efforts to administer benefits programs. Figure 14-4 shows how benefits administration responsibilities can be split between HR specialists and operating managers. HR specialists play the more significant role, but managers must assume responsibility for some of the communication aspects of benefits administration.

One significant trend affecting HR is that outsourcing of benefits administration may be necessary. A sizable majority of corporations in one study indicated that they were outsourcing more benefits functions. [11] The most frequently outsourced item is Employee Assistance Plans. Administrative activities related to retiree benefits, 401(k) plans, and flexible spending accounts are also often outsourced.

Internet Research

International Foundation of Employee Benefit Plans
Members have access to extensive databases of resources, research, and information on benefits programs. Link to their Website at: http://thomsonedu.com/management/mathis.

HR Technology and Benefits

The spread of HR technology, particularly Internet-based systems, has significantly changed the benefits administration time and activities for HR staff members. Internet-based systems are being used to communicate benefits information, conduct employee benefits surveys, and facilitate benefits administration.

Information technology also allows employees to change their benefits choices, track their benefits balances, and submit questions to HR staff members and external benefits providers. Use of the Internet for benefits enrollment has increased significantly in a three-year period. The greatest use has been to allow employees to sign up for, change, or update their benefits choices through Web-based systems.[12] Previously, HR departments had to send out paper forms, hold numerous benefits meetings, and answer many phone calls from employees. The switch to on-line enrollment and communications has led to reductions in HR staff and benefits administration costs.

Benefits Measurement

The significant costs associated with benefits require that analyses be conducted to determine the payoffs for the benefits. With the wide range of benefits that are offered, numerous HR metrics can be used.[13] Some examples are shown in Figure 14-5.

FIGURE 14-5	Common Benefits Metrics

- Benefits as a percentage of payroll (pattern over a multi-year period)
- Benefits expenditures per full-time equivalent (FTE) employee
- Benefits costs by employee group (full-time vs. part-time, union vs. non-union, office, management, professional, technical, etc.)
- Benefits administration costs (including staff time multiplied by the staff pay and benefits costs per hour)
- Health-care benefits costs per participating employee

Other metrics are used to measure the return on the expenditures for various benefits programs provided by employers. Some common benefits that employers track using HR metrics are workers' compensation, wellness programs, prescription drug costs, leave time, tuition aid, and disability insurance. The overriding point is that both benefits expenditures generally, as well as costs for individual benefits specifically, need to be measured and evaluated as part of strategic benefits management.

Benefits Cost Control

Because benefits expenditures have risen significantly in the past few years, particularly for health care, employers are focusing more attention on measuring and controlling benefits costs, even reducing or dropping benefits offered to employees.

The most common means of benefits cost control is cost sharing, which refers to having employees pay more of their benefits costs. Almost 60% of firms use this means. The next three means of health-care cost control are using wellness programs, adding employee health education efforts, and changing prescription drug programs.[14]

Benefits Communication

Employees generally do not know much about the values and costs associated with the benefits they receive from employers. This ignorance is illustrated by a survey in which only 5% of HR executives identified that their employees appreciated their total compensation package. Over one-third stated that the employees do not understand the value of benefits.[15]

Benefits communication and satisfaction of employees with their benefits are linked. Consequently, many employers have instituted special benefits communication systems to inform employees about the value of the benefits they provide. Employers can use various means, including videos, CDs, electronic alerts, newsletters, and employee meetings. All these efforts are done to ensure that employees are knowledgeable about their benefits. The HR On-Line describes the use of Internet communications. Some of the important information to be communicated includes the value of the plans offered, why changes have to be made, and the fundamental financial costs of the plans.[16] When planning benefits communication efforts, it is important to consider factors such as the timing and frequency, the communication sources, and the specialized content.[17]

Benefits Statements Some employers give individual employees a "personal statement of benefits" that translates benefits into dollar amounts. Increasingly,

HR ONLINE

Communicating About Benefits

The extensive use of the Internet is changing many facets of HR management, both positively and negatively. But for benefits communication, the Internet has become a major tool. The use of Web-based programs and e-mails to communicate regularly about benefits is widespread. For instance, many firms provide health plan and wellness information to employees on-line in weekly or monthly messages. Communicating such information is especially important as firms try to hold down health benefits costs through consumer-driven health plans.

Many large firms have Web portals where individuals can review health plan options, track the status of their medical claims, and locate medical providers. Other firms use Web sources for accessing health and wellness information. Employees can complete confidential personal health profiles, and in return get health and wellness analyses. These analyses suggest various wellness activities and direct employees to on-line resources they can review. Employers such as Intel, Wal-Mart, and Pitney Bowes have implemented systems whereby employees can access their personal health-care insurance information and other records.[18] These examples illustrate that both employers and employees gain from having access to on-line resources for employee benefits.

firms are using the Internet to provide statements, with estimates that 60% of employers are doing so.[19] These statements often are used as part of a total rewards education and communication effort. Federal regulations under the Employee Retirement Income Security Act (ERISA) require that employees receive an annual pension-reporting statement, which also can be included in the personal benefits statement.

TYPES OF BENEFITS

A wide range of benefits are offered by employers. Some are mandated by laws and government regulations, while others are offered voluntarily by employers as part of their HR strategies. Figure 14-6 (see next page) shows how the typical employer dollar is spent on different types of benefits.

Government-Mandated Benefits

There are many mandated benefits that employers in the United States must provide to employees by law. Social Security and unemployment insurance are funded through a tax paid by the employer based on the employee's compensation. Workers' compensation laws exist in all states. In addition, under the Family and Medical Leave Act (FMLA), employers must offer unpaid leave to employees with certain medical or family difficulties. Other mandated benefits are funded in part by taxes, through Social Security. The Consolidated Omnibus Budget Reconciliation Act (COBRA) mandates that an employer continue to provide health-care coverage—albeit paid for by the employees—for a time after they leave the organization. The Health Insurance Portability and Accountability Act (HIPAA) requires that most employees be able to obtain coverage if they were previously covered in a health plan and provides privacy rights for medical records.

Internet Research

Employee Benefits Institute of America, Inc.
For an e-mail newsletter with analysis of legal developments in a variety of benefit areas, link to this Website at:
http://thomsonedu.com/management/mathis.

FIGURE 14-6   How the Typical Benefits Dollar Is Spent

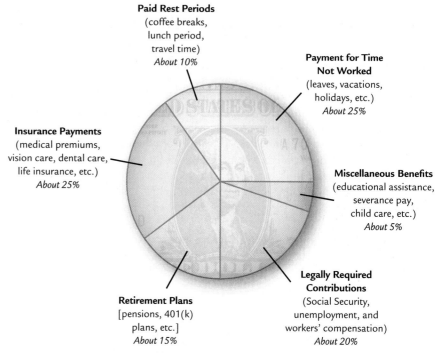

Paid Rest Periods
(coffee breaks,
lunch period,
travel time)
About 10%

**Payment for Time
Not Worked**
(leaves, vacations,
holidays, etc.)
About 25%

Insurance Payments
(medical premiums,
vision care, dental care,
life insurance, etc.)
About 25%

Miscellaneous Benefits
(educational assistance,
severance pay,
child care, etc.)
About 5%

Retirement Plans
[pensions, 401(k)
plans, etc.]
About 15%

**Legally Required
Contributions**
(Social Security,
unemployment, and
workers' compensation)
About 20%

Source: Based on data summarized from the U.S. Department of Labor, Bureau of Labor statistics, *National Compensation Survey: Employee Benefits in Private Industry in the United States,* 2006; and *Employee Benefits Study,* 2006 ed. (Washington, D.C.: U.S. Chamber of Commerce, 2007).

A major reason for additional mandated benefits proposals is that federal and state governments would like to shift many of the social costs for health care and other expenditures to employers. This shift would relieve some of the budgetary pressures facing government entities that otherwise might have to raise taxes and/or cut spending.

Additional mandated benefits have been proposed for many other areas. These possibilities for which mandated coverage has been proposed but not adopted are as follows:

■ Universal health-care benefits for all workers
■ Child-care assistance
■ Pension plan coverage that can be transferred by workers who change jobs
■ Core benefits for part-time employees working at least 500 hours a year
■ Paid time-off for family leave

Voluntary Benefits

Employers voluntarily offer other types of benefits to help them compete for and retain employees. By offering additional benefits, organizations are recognizing the need to provide greater security and benefits support to workers with widely varied personal circumstances. In addition, as jobs become more flexible and varied, both workers and employers recognize that choices among benefits are necessary, as evidenced by the growth in flexible benefits and cafeteria benefit plans. Figure 14-7 lists seven types of mandated and voluntary benefits. The following sections describe them by type.

FIGURE 14-7	Types of Benefits

Government mandated	Employer voluntary

Security Benefits	Health-Care Benefits	Family Benefits
◆ Workers' compensation ◆ Unemployment compensation	◆ COBRA and HIPAA provisions	◆ FMLA provisions

◆ Supplemental unemployment
  benefits (SUBs)
◆ Severance pay
	◆ Medical and dental
	◆ Prescription drugs
	◆ Vision
	◆ PPO, HMO, and CDH plans
	◆ Wellness programs
	◆ Flexible spending accounts
		◆ Adoption benefits and
		  dependent-care assistance
		◆ Domestic partner benefits

Retirement Benefits		Time-Off Benefits

◆ Social Security ◆ ADEA and OWBPA provisions	**Financial Benefits**	◆ Military reserve time off ◆ Election and jury leaves

◆ Early retirement options
◆ Health care for retirees
◆ Pension plans
◆ Individual retirement accounts
  (IRAs)
◆ Keogh plans
◆ 401(k), 403(b), and 457 plans
	◆ Financial services (e.g.,
	  credit unions and counseling)
	◆ Relocation assistance
	◆ Life insurance
	◆ Disability insurance
	◆ Long-term care insurance
	◆ Legal insurance
	◆ Educational assistance
		◆ Lunch and rest breaks
		◆ Holidays and vacations
		◆ Family leave
		◆ Medical and sick leave
		◆ Paid time off
		◆ Funeral and bereavement
		  leaves

Miscellaneous Benefits
◆ Social and recreational   programs and events ◆ Unique programs

SECURITY BENEFITS

A number of benefits provide employee security. These benefits include some mandated by laws and others offered by employers voluntarily. The primary benefits found in most organizations include workers' compensation, unemployment compensation, and severance pay.

Workers' Compensation

Workers' compensation
Security benefits provided to persons injured on the job.

Workers' compensation provides benefits to persons injured on the job. State laws require most employers to supply workers' compensation coverage by purchasing insurance from a private carrier or state insurance fund or by providing self-insurance. U.S. government employees are covered under the Federal Employees Compensation Act, administered by the U.S. Department of Labor.

The workers' compensation system requires employers to give cash benefits, medical care, and rehabilitation services to employees for injuries or illnesses occurring within the scope of their employment. In exchange, employees give up the right to pursue legal actions and awards. The costs to employers for workers' compensation average about 1.8% of total payroll, and cost about $0.47 per hour in wages per worker.[20] Workers' compensation is a part of HR risk management and worker protection, discussed further in the next chapter.

Unemployment Compensation

Another benefit required by law is unemployment compensation, established as part of the Social Security Act of 1935. Because each U.S. state operates its own unemployment compensation system, provisions differ significantly from state to state. The tax is paid to state and federal unemployment compensation funds. The percentage paid by individual employers is based on "experience rates," which reflect the number of claims filed by workers who leave.

An employee who is out of work and is actively looking for employment normally receives up to 26 weeks of pay, at the rate of 50% to 80% of normal pay. Most employees are eligible. However, workers fired for misconduct or those not actively seeking employment generally are ineligible. Only about 40% of eligible people use the unemployment compensation system. This underutilization may be due both to the stigma of receiving unemployment and the complexity of the system, which some feel is simply not worth the effort.

Supplemental unemployment benefits (SUBs) are closely related to unemployment compensation, but they are not required by law. A provision in some union contracts requires organizations to contribute to a fund that supplements the unemployment compensation available to employees from federal and/or state sources.

Criticisms of Unemployment Insurance Two problems explain changes in unemployment insurance laws proposed at state and federal levels: (1) abuses are estimated to cost billions each year, and (2) many state unemployment funds are exhausted during economic slowdowns. Also, some states allow striking union workers to collect unemployment benefits despite strike fund payments from the union. This provision is bitterly opposed by many employers.

Severance Pay

Severance pay Security benefit voluntarily offered by employers to individuals whose jobs are eliminated or who leave by mutual agreement with their employers.

As a security benefit, severance pay is voluntarily offered by employers to individuals whose jobs are eliminated or who leave by mutual agreement with their employers. Employer severance pay provisions often provide severance payments corresponding to an employee's level within the organization and the person's years of employment. The Worker Adjustment and Retraining Notification Act (WARN) of 1988 requires that many employers give 60 days' notice if a mass layoff or facility closing is to occur. The act does not require employers to give severance pay.

Some employers have offered reduced amounts of cash severance and replaced some of the severance value with continued health insurance and outplacement assistance. Through *outplacement assistance,* ex-employees receive résumé writing instruction, interviewing skills workshops, and career counseling.

HEALTH-CARE BENEFITS

Employers provide a variety of health-care and medical benefits, usually through insurance coverage. The most common plans cover medical, dental, prescription drug, and vision care expenses for employees and their dependents. Figure 14-8 notes the percentage of private industry workers receiving different types of health benefits. As the opening HR Headline identified, employers see controlling the increasing costs of health-care benefits as their most important concern.

FIGURE 14-8   Private Industry Workers with Health Benefits

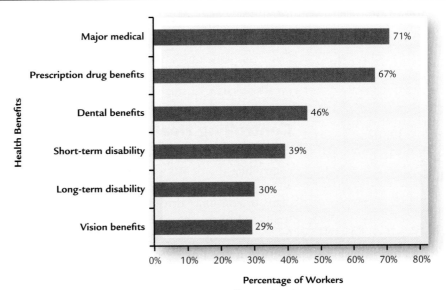

Source: U.S. Bureau of Labor Statistics, March 2006, *www.bls.gov/ncs/home.htm*.

Increases in Health Benefits Costs

For several decades, the costs of health care have escalated at rates well above those of inflation and changes in workers' earnings. As a result of these large increases, many employers find that dealing with health-care benefits is time consuming and expensive. This is especially frustrating for employers who have found that many employees seem to take their health benefits for granted. Consequently, a growing number of firms, particularly smaller ones, have asked, "Why are we offering these benefits anyway?" About 10% of employers have answered the question by discontinuing or dramatically cutting health benefits.[21] Two major groups of workers that have contributed to the increasing costs are uninsured workers and retirees.

Uninsured Workers Some of the health benefits cost pressures are due to health-care providers having to cover the costs for the rising number of individuals in the United States without health insurance coverage. A number of uninsured workers are illegal immigrants; others work for employers that do not provide benefits. About 15% to 20% of the U.S. population lacks health coverage, and covering those costs forces hospitals, pharmacies, and other health-care providers to raise their rates on all patient services. Thus, the costs are shifted to those with health insurance paid for by employers.

Retirees' Health Benefits Costs Another group whose benefits costs are rising is retirees whose former employers still provide health benefits coverage. For instance, at General Motors, there are 2.4 retired employees for every active employee. Increasing the problem at GM is that health-care usage rates for older retirees are significantly higher than those of current employees. GM has to add almost $1,500 per vehicle to cover employee and retiree health-care costs, which costs more than the steel used to build the cars.[22]

To control retiree health benefits costs, some firms are cutting their benefits or requiring retirees to pay higher rates for health benefits. Approximately

75% of employers in one survey have increased retirement premiums in recent years.[23] For instance, Ford Motor Company has frozen health-care benefits for thousands of its retirees. Future increased costs will be paid for by the individual retirees, not Ford Motor.[24] Naturally, such efforts by firms have faced resistance and even lawsuits from disgruntled retirees. At these and other firms, this issue raises troubling ethical concerns. Many of the retirees worked for their employers for 20, 30, or more years, yet the reward for their long and loyal service increasingly is a reduction in health-care benefits.

Controlling Health-Care Benefits Costs

Employers offering health-care benefits are taking a number of approaches to controlling their costs. The most prominent ones are changing co-payments and employee contributions, using managed care, switching to mini-medical plans or consumer-driven health plans, and increasing health preventive and wellness efforts.

Co-payment Strategy requiring employees to pay a portion of the cost of insurance premiums, medical care, and prescription drugs.

Changing Co-Payments and Employee Contributions The co-payment strategy requires employees to pay a portion of the cost of insurance premiums, medical care, and prescription drugs. Requiring new or higher co-payments and employee contributions is the most prevalent cost-control strategy identified by many employers surveyed. For instance, employers who raise the per person deductible from $50 to $250 realize significant savings in health-care expenses due to decreasing employee usage of health-care services and prescription drugs.

These changes are facing significant resistance by employees, especially those who have had *first-dollar coverage*. With this type of coverage, all expenses, from the first dollar of health-care costs, are paid by the employee's insurance. Experts claim that when first-dollar coverage is included in a basic health plan, many employees see a doctor for even minor illnesses, which results in an escalation of the benefits costs.

Managed care Approaches that monitor and reduce medical costs through restrictions and market system alternatives.

Using Managed Care Several other types of programs attempt to reduce health-care costs paid by employers. Managed care consists of approaches that monitor and reduce medical costs through restrictions and market system alternatives. Managed care plans emphasize primary and preventive care, the use of specific providers who will charge lower prices, restrictions on certain kinds of treatment, and prices negotiated with hospitals and physicians.

Preferred provider organization (PPO) A health-care provider that contracts with an employer or an employer group to supply health-care services to employees at a competitive rate.

The most prominent managed care approach is the preferred provider organization (PPO), a health-care provider that contracts with an employer or an employer group to supply health-care services to employees at a competitive rate. Employees have the freedom to go to other providers if they want to pay the differences in costs. *Point-of-service plans* are somewhat similar, offering financial incentives to encourage employees to use designated medical providers.

Health maintenance organization (HMO) Plan that provides services for a fixed period on a pre-paid basis.

Another managed care approach is a health maintenance organization (HMO), which provides services for a fixed period on a pre-paid basis. The HMO emphasizes both prevention and correction. An employer contracts with an HMO and its staff of physicians and medical personnel to furnish complete medical care, except for hospitalization. The employer pays a flat rate per enrolled employee or per enrolled family. The covered individuals may then go to the HMO for health care as often as needed. Supplemental policies for hospitalization are also provided. While HMOs remain widely used, a growing number of employers are focusing on other means to control the costs of health-care benefits.

Many employers have found that some of the health care provided by doctors and hospitals is unnecessary, incorrectly billed, or deliberately overcharged. Consequently, both employers and insurance firms often require that medical work and charges be audited through a utilization review. This process may require a second opinion, a review of the procedures done, and a review of charges for the procedures.

Utilization review Audit of the services and costs billed by health-care providers.

Mini-Medical Plans Another type of plan that has grown in usage in the past few years is the *mini-medical plan*. This type of plan provides limited health benefits coverage for employees. In the past, these plans have been used more with part-time and lower wage level employees. But more employers are using these plans for full-time employees of all types. A typical mini-medical plan limits the number of doctor visits paid per year to fewer than 10, covers only certain prescription drugs, provides very limited hospital coverage, and caps total annual health benefits costs at $10,000 or less. These limitations result in significantly fewer benefits for employees, but dramatically lower costs for employers.[25]

Consumer-Driven Health Plans

Some employers are turning to employee-focused health benefits plans. The most prominent is a consumer-driven health (CDH) plan, which provides financial contributions to employees to help cover their own health-related expenses. Various surveys of companies have identified that a growing number of employers have switched to CDH plans, and that others are actively considering switching to these plans.[26]

Consumer-driven health (CDH) plan Health plan that provides employer financial contributions to employees to help cover their own health-related expenses.

In these plans, which are also called *defined-contribution health plans*, an employer places a set amount into each employee's "account" and identifies a number of health-care alternatives that are available. Then individual employees select from those health-care alternatives and pay for part of the costs from their accounts.

There are two advantages to such plans for employers. One is that more of the increases in health-care benefits costs are shifted to employees, because the employer contributions need not increase as fast as health-care costs. Second, the focus of controlling health-care usage falls on employees, who may have to choose when to use and not use health-care benefits. Figure 14-9 (on the next page) highlights the components of CDH plans.

Health Savings Accounts Health savings accounts (HSAs) are often combined with high-deductible insurance to cut employer costs. Components of an HSA include the following:

Health Savings Accounts (HSAs) High-deductible health plans with federal tax advantages.

- Both employees and employers can make contributions to an account.
  - Individual employees can set aside pre-tax amounts for medical care into an HSA.
  - Unused amounts in an individual's account can be rolled over annually for future health expenses.
  - Incentives are included to encourage employees to spend less on health expenses.

The key component of HSA accounts is that employees may get more health benefits choices, but their insurance usually

FIGURE 14-9   **Components of Consumer-Driven Health Plans**

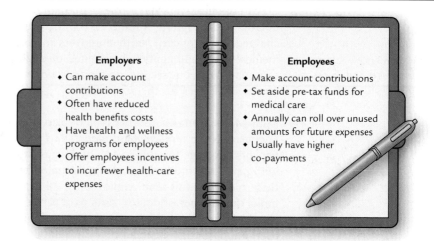

has higher annual deductibles. These plans often result in employers having lower overall expenditures because higher employee deductibles result in lower costs for the employers. For example, at one firm an employee has a $3,000 annual deductible to meet, compared with a $1,000 amount previously under a PPO plan. With the higher deductible amounts, employers often cut or limit their contributions, reducing their costs by 10% to 30%.[27] Because of these shifts in costs, less than 7% of employees are voluntarily switching to these plans, even though many employers have added HSAs to their benefits plan mix.[28]

Health Reimbursement Arrangements Closely related to an HSA is a health reimbursement arrangement. They also may be called *health reimbursement accounts* or *personal care accounts*. Under a health reimbursement arrangement (HRA), the employer sets aside money in a health reimbursement account to help employees pay for qualified medical expenses. The definition of "qualified medical expenses" can be determined by the employer within tax law limitations. A key difference from an HSA is that employees cannot contribute money to an HRA. The employer can also decide if employees must pay deductibles first or if they can utilize funds in their HRA to pay for first-dollar expenses. If an employee does not utilize all of the funds available in his or her HRA during the plan year, he or she may be allowed to roll all or a portion of the balance into the next plan year.

Health reimbursement arrangement (HRA)
Health plan in which the employer sets aside money in a health reimbursement account to help employees pay for qualified medical expenses.

Health-Care Preventive and Wellness Efforts

Preventive and wellness efforts can occur in a variety of ways. Many employers offer programs to educate employees about health-care costs and how to reduce them.[29] Newsletters, formal classes, and many other approaches are all designed to help employees understand why health-care costs are increasing and what they can do to control them. Many employers have programs that offer financial incentives to improve health habits. These wellness programs, discussed more in Chapter 15, reward employees who stop smoking, lose weight, and participate in exercise programs, among other activities.

HR BEST PRACTICES

Reducing Health Benefits Costs

The global aviation and defense firm Textron has 37,000 employees and, as would be expected, large health-care benefits costs. To counteract these rising costs, Textron has established both HSA and HRA plans for its employees. These plans replaced over 100 different health plans throughout the firm's locations and business units.

To make these plans successful, significant efforts have been made to communicate the importance of these plans to employees. These communications efforts have been quite varied, including numerous Internet-related efforts. The value of the expanded communications on benefits costs, values, and alternatives has been a key part of Textron's changes in benefits plans.

Both Textron and employees have seen results. For the company, over three years there was a decrease in employee medical utilization by more than 15%. This decrease has resulted in significantly lower expenditures by Textron. Interestingly, employees throughout Textron's locations and business units have increased their usage of preventive health-care efforts by over 20%. This increase indicates that employees are viewing their health as more important and taking steps to discover problems before they occur. The ultimate goal of these efforts is to contribute to the decreasing costs noted at Textron.

Even more important is that employee satisfaction with health benefits overall has increased, which indicates the success of the Textron changes. This firm's experience provides one illustration of why CDH plans are becoming more popular with employers, and are being used by more employees.[31]

Employee Reactions to Cost-Control Efforts As would be expected, many employees are skeptical about or even hostile to employer efforts to reduce health benefits costs and raise employees' contributions. Surveys of employees have found that they are more dissatisfied with changes to their health benefits than with the moderation of base pay increases. In fact, about 75% of the employees in one survey said that they would forgo any pay increase to keep their health benefits unchanged.[30]

For cost-control efforts to work for employers, the gap between employees' and employers' views on benefits must be bridged, which requires significant communications and education of employees to counter their negative reactions. Key in communicating about controlling health benefits costs is sharing information and having a continuing and effective benefits communications plan. The HR Best Practices describes how one firm has been successful with reducing health benefits costs.

Health-Care Legislation

Internet Research

America's Health Insurance Programs

For current information on legislative and regulatory health-care issues affecting American consumers, visit this Website at: http://thomsonedu.com/management/mathis.

The importance of health-care benefits to employers and employees has led to a variety of federal and state laws being created. Some laws have been enacted to provide protection for employees who leave their employers, either voluntarily or involuntarily. To date, the two most important ones are COBRA and HIPAA.

COBRA Provisions The Consolidated Omnibus Budget Reconciliation Act (COBRA) requires that most employers (except

FIGURE 14-10   Overview of COBRA Provisions

Qualifying Event	Qualified Beneficiaries	Coverage Period
Employee termination / reduction in hours (except for misconduct)	Employee, spouse, and dependent children	18–29 months
Divorce or death of employee	Spouse and dependent children	36 months

churches and the federal government) with 20 or more employees offer extended health-care coverage to certain groups, as follows:

- Employees who voluntarily quit
- Widowed or divorced spouses and dependent children of former or current employees
- Retirees and their spouses whose health-care coverage ends

Employers must notify eligible employees and/or their spouses and qualified dependents within 60 days after the employees quit, die, get divorced, or otherwise change their status. The chart in Figure 14-10 shows the coverage that must be offered depending on the qualifying circumstances. The individual no longer employed by the organization must pay the premiums, but the employer may charge this individual no more than 102% of the premium costs to insure a similarly covered employee. The 2% premium addition generally does not cover all relevant costs, because those costs often run several percentage points more.

Compliance with COBRA regulations can be very complex. For most employers, the COBRA requirements mean additional paperwork and related costs.[32] For example, firms must not only track the former employees but also notify their qualified dependents.

HIPAA Provisions The Health Insurance Portability and Accountability Act (HIPAA) of 1996 allows employees to switch their health insurance plans when they change employers, and to get new health coverage with the new company regardless of pre-existing health conditions. The legislation also prohibits group insurance plans from dropping coverage for a sick employee, and requires them to make individual coverage available to people who leave group plans.

One of the greatest impacts of HIPAA comes from its provisions regarding the privacy of employee medical records. These provisions require employers to provide privacy notices to employees. They also regulate the disclosure of protected health information without authorization.[33]

Flexible Spending Accounts Under current tax law (specifically, Section 125 of the Internal Revenue Code), employees can divert some pre-tax income into flexible spending accounts to fund certain additional benefits. Under tax law at the time of this writing, the funds in the account can be used to purchase only the following: (1) additional health care (including offsetting deductibles), (2) life insurance, (3) disability insurance, and (4) dependent-care benefits. An example illustrates the advantage of these accounts to employees. Assume an employee earns $3,000 a month and has $100 a month deducted to put into a flexible spending account. That $100 does not count as gross income for tax purposes, so the employee's taxable

Flexible spending accounts Benefits plans that allow employees to contribute pre-tax dollars to fund certain additional benefits.

income is reduced. The employee uses the money in the account to purchase additional benefits.

Flexible spending accounts have grown in popularity as more varied health-care plans have been adopted by more employers. Of course, such plans and their tax advantages can be changed as Congress passes future health-care and new tax-related legislation.[34]

RETIREMENT BENEFITS

The aging of the workforce in many countries is affecting retirement planning for individuals and retirement plan costs for employers and governments. In the United States, the number of citizens at least 55 years or older will increase 46% between 2004 and 2010, and older citizens will constitute 38% of the population in 2010. Simultaneously, the age of retirement will decline, as it has been doing for decades (see Figure 14-11). With more people retiring earlier and living longer, retirement benefits are becoming a greater concern for employers, employees, and retired employees.

Unfortunately, most U.S. citizens have inadequate savings and retirement benefits for funding their retirements. According to a study by the Employee Benefit Research Institute, almost 70% of individuals over age 55 have less than $250,000 in savings and investments.[35] Therefore, they are heavily dependent on employer-provided retirement benefits. But many employers with fewer than 100 workers do not offer retirement benefits. Therefore, individuals must rely on Social Security payments, which were not designed to provide full retirement income.

Social Security

The Social Security Act of 1935, with its later amendments, established a system providing *old-age, survivor's, disability,* and *retirement* benefits. Administered by the federal government through the Social Security Administration, this program provides benefits to previously employed individuals. Employees and employers share in the cost of Social Security through a tax on employees' wages or salaries.

FIGURE 14-11   **Median Age at Retirement by Gender**

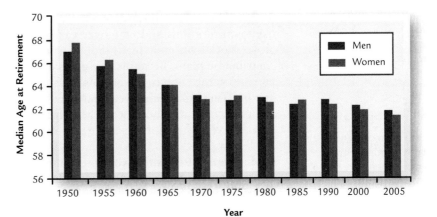

Source: U.S. Bureau of Labor Statistics, *www.bls.gov.*

Social Security Changes Since the system's inception, the Social Security payroll taxes have risen to 15.3% currently, with employees and employers each paying 7.65% up to an established maximum. In addition, Medicare taxes have more than doubled, to 2.9%.

Because the Social Security system affects a large number of individuals and is government operated, it is a politically sensitive program. The U.S. Congress has responded to public pressure by raising payments and introducing cost-of-living adjustments. Now, it is likely that legislative action will have to respond to widespread criticisms that the system is not financially sound and must consider alternatives to ensure the future viability of the Social Security system.

Pension Plans

A pension plan is a retirement program established and funded by the employer and employees. Organizations are not required to offer pension plans to employees, and fewer than half of U.S. workers are covered by them. Small firms offer pension plans less often than do large ones.

Defined-Benefit Pension Plans A "traditional" pension plan, in which the employer makes the contributions and the employee will get a defined amount each month upon retirement, is no longer the norm in the private sector. Through a defined-benefit plan, employees are promised a pension amount based on age and service. The employees' contributions are based on actuarial calculations on the *benefits* to be received by the employees after retirement and the *methods* used to determine such benefits. A defined-benefit plan gives employees greater assurance of benefits and greater predictability in the amount of benefits that will be available for retirement. Defined-benefit plans are often preferred by workers with longer service, as well as by small-business owners.

If the funding in a defined-benefit plan is insufficient, the employer may have to make up the shortfall. Therefore, many employers have dropped defined-benefit plans in favor of defined-contribution plans (discussed next) so that their contribution liabilities are known.[36] Notice in Figure 14-12 that unionized employees participate to a greater extent in defined-benefit plans than any other category.

Defined-Contribution Pension Plans In a defined-contribution plan, the employer makes an annual payment to an employee's pension account. The key to this plan is the *contribution rate;* employee retirement benefits depend on fixed contributions and employee earnings levels. Profit-sharing plans, employee stock ownership plans (ESOPs), and 401(k) plans are common defined-contribution plans. Because these plans hinge on the investment returns on the previous contributions, the returns can vary according to profitability or other factors. Therefore, employees' retirement benefits are somewhat less secure and predictable. But because of their structure, these plans are sometimes preferred by younger, shorter-service employees.

Cash Balance Pension Plans Some employers have changed traditional pension plans to hybrids based on ideas from both defined-benefit and defined-contribution plans. One such plan is a cash balance plan, in which retirement benefits are based on an accumulation of annual company contributions, expressed as a percentage of pay, plus interest credited each year. With these

Pension plan Retirement program established and funded by the employer and employees.

Defined-benefit plan Retirement program in which an employee is promised a pension amount based on age and service.

Defined-contribution plan Retirement program in which the employer makes an annual payment to an employee's pension account.

Cash balance plan Retirement program in which benefits are based on an accumulation of annual company contributions plus interest credited each year.

FIGURE 14-12	Worker Participation in Pension Plans

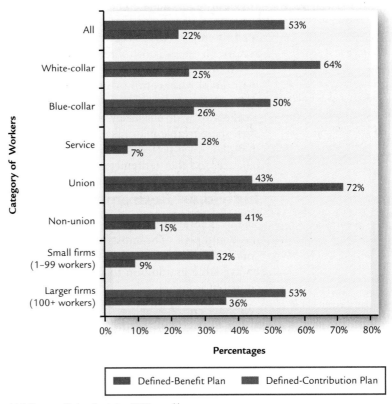

Figure 14-12 Worker Participation in Pension Plans

Source: U.S. Bureau of Labor Statistics, 2006, *www.bls.gov.*

plans, retirement benefits accumulate at the same annual rate until an employee retires. Because cash balance plans spread funding across a worker's entire career, these plans work better for mobile younger workers.

However, conversions to cash balance plans have caused discontent and even lawsuits among older employees at AT&T, EDS, and most notably IBM. At IBM, workers in the age 40 group would lose a significant amount of retirement under the new plan. Court decisions in *Cooper v. IBM Personal Pension Plan* ruled in favor of IBM. Consequently, in 2006, IBM and other firms proceeded with freezing their old plans and making the conversion to cash balance plans.[37]

Many smaller employers do not offer pension plans for a number of reasons. The primary reason, in addition to their cost, is the administrative burdens imposed by government legislation, discussed later in the chapter.

Pension Plan Concepts

Contributory plan Pension plan in which the money for pension benefits is paid in by both employees and employers.

Non-contributory plan Pension plan in which all the funds for pension benefits are provided by the employer.

Pension plans can be either contributory or non-contributory. In a contributory plan, money for pension benefits is paid in by both employees and the employer. In a non-contributory plan, the employer provides all the funds for pension benefits. As expected, the non-contributory plans are generally preferred by employees and labor unions.

Certain rights are attached to employee pension plans. Various laws and provisions have been passed to address the right of employees to receive benefits

Vesting Right of employees to receive certain benefits from their pension plans.

from their pension plans. Called vesting, this right assures employees of a certain pension, provided they work a minimum number of years. If employees resign or are terminated before they have been employed for the required vesting time, no pension rights accrue to them except the funds they have contributed. If employees stay the allotted time, they retain their pension rights and receive the funds contributed by both the employer and themselves.

Portability A pension plan feature that allows employees to move their pension benefits from one employer to another.

Another feature of some employee pensions is portability. In a portable plan, employees can move their pension benefits from one employer to another. A number of firms offer portable pension plans. Instead of requiring workers to wait until they retire to move their traditional pension plan benefits, the portable plan takes a different approach. Once workers have vested in a plan for a period of time, such as five years, they can transfer their fund balances to other retirement plans if they change jobs.

Individual Retirement Options

The availability of several retirement benefit options makes the pension area more complex. The most prominent options are individual retirement accounts (IRAs) and 401(k), 403(b), 457, and Keogh plans. These plans may be available in addition to company-provided pension plans and usually are contributory plans.

401(k) plan Agreement in which a percentage of an employee's pay is withheld and invested in a tax-deferred account.

The 401(k) plan gets its name from Section 401(k) of the federal tax code. This plan is an agreement in which a percentage of an employee's pay is withheld and invested in a tax-deferred account. Many employers match employee 401(k) contributions, up to a percentage of the employee's pay. As a result, a significant number of employees contribute to 401(k) plans. The use of 401(k) plans and of the assets in them has grown significantly in the past few years. Employers frequently have programs to encourage employees to contribute to 401(k) plans. Some employers are making employee participation in 401(k) plans automatic, unless the employees specifically opt out of them. The advantage to most employees is that they can save pre-tax income toward their retirement.

Internet Research

401K-Site.com
This Website provides investors with information on 401(k) plans. Link to the Website at: http://thomsonedu.com/management/mathis.

A special type of 401(k), the *Roth IRA*, was established effective 2006. This type is a modification of the traditional 401(k) but allows participants to be taxed in the current year for contributions. That means that under the Roth type of IRA the taxed gains in the value of the 401(k) over years is not as much with the regular 401(k). Employers may offer both types of plans.[38]

LEGAL REQUIREMENTS FOR RETIREMENT BENEFITS

A number of laws and regulations affect retirement plans. Some of the key ones are highlighted next.

Employee Retirement Income Security Act

The widespread criticism of many pension plans led to passage of the Employee Retirement Income Security Act (ERISA) in 1974. The purpose of this law is to regulate private pension plans so that employees who put money into them or depend on a pension for retirement funds actually receive the money when they retire.

ERISA essentially requires many companies to offer retirement plans to all employees if they offer retirement plans to any employees. Accrued benefits must be given to employees when they retire or leave. The act also sets minimum funding requirements, and plans not meeting those requirements are subject to financial penalties imposed by the IRS. Additional regulations require that employers pay plan termination insurance to ensure payment of employee pensions should the employers go out of business. To spread out the costs of administration and overhead, some employers use plans funded by multiple employers.

Retirement Equity in Pension Plans In the *Arizona Governing Committee v. Norris* ruling, a U.S. Supreme Court decision forced pension plan administrators to use "unisex" mortality tables, which do not reflect the gender differential in mortality.[39] To bring legislation in line with this decision, in 1984, Congress passed the Retirement Equity Act as an amendment to ERISA and the Internal Revenue Code. It liberalized pension regulations that affect women, guaranteed access to benefits, prohibited pension-related penalties due to the absences from work such as maternity leave, and lowered the vesting age.

Qualified Domestic Relations Order Created by provisions of ERISA, a *qualified domestic relations order (QDRO)* is an agreement between a divorcing couple that identifies who gets assets in a retirement plan. Use of a QDRO provides protection for both individuals and their children in a divorce. Also, use of a QDRO provides some beneficial tax provisions.[40]

Retiree Benefits and Legal Requirements

Some employers choose to offer retiree health benefits that may be paid for by the retirees, the company, or both. The costs of such coverage have risen dramatically. To ensure that firms adequately reflect the liabilities for retiree health benefits, the Financial Accounting Standards Board issued Rule 106, which requires employers to establish accounting reserves for funding retiree health-care benefits. For instance, one problem with retiree pension benefits is that a number of firms are facing unfunded pension liabilities.

Pension Protection Act of 2006 The Pension Protection Act of 2006 has numerous reporting requirements that must be met by employers. These requirements make employers disclose the assets and liabilities of pension plans. It also requires that employers increase funding to cover unfunded liabilities they face. Many of the provisions focus specifically on the deficit created by defined-benefits plans that employers must cover.[41]

Retirement Benefits and Age Discrimination

According to a 1986 amendment to the Age Discrimination in Employment Act (ADEA), most employees cannot be forced to retire at a specific age. As a result, employers have had to develop policies to comply with these regulations. In many employer pension plans, "normal retirement" is the age at which employees can retire and collect full pension benefits. Employers must decide whether individuals who continue to work past normal retirement age (perhaps 65) should receive the full benefits package, especially pension credits. Some changes in Social Security regulations have increased the age for full benefits past age 65, so modifications in policies may occur. Despite the removal of mandatory retirement provisions, the age at which individuals retire has continued to decline in the United States.

Early Retirement Many pension plans include provisions for early retirement to give workers voluntary opportunities to leave their jobs. After spending 25 to 30 years working for the same employer, individuals may wish to use their talents in other areas. Phased-in and part-time retirements offer alternatives that individuals and firms are using.

Some employers use early retirement buyout programs to cut back their workforces and reduce costs. Employers must take care to make these early retirement programs truly voluntary. Forcing workers to take advantage of an early retirement buyout program led to the passage of the federal law discussed next.

Older Workers Benefit Protection Act Passed in 1990, the Older Workers Benefit Protection Act (OWBPA) amended the ADEA and overturned a decision by the U.S. Supreme Court in *Public Employees Retirement System of Ohio v. Betts*.[42] This act requires equal treatment for older workers in early retirement or severance situations. It also sets forth some specific criteria that must be met when older workers sign waivers promising not to sue for age discrimination.

FINANCIAL BENEFITS

Employers may offer workers a wide range of special benefits that provide financial support to employees. Figure 14-13 illustrates some common financial benefits. Employers find that such benefits can be useful in attracting and retaining employees. Workers like receiving these benefits, which often are not taxed as income.

Insurance Benefits

In addition to health-related insurance, some employers provide other types of insurance. These benefits offer major advantages for employees because many employers pay some or all of the costs. Even when employers do not pay

FIGURE 14-13   Common Types of Financial Benefits

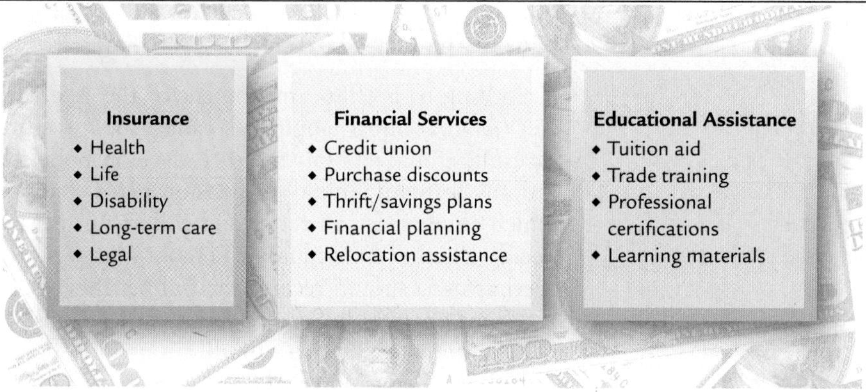

Insurance	Financial Services	Educational Assistance
• Health	• Credit union	• Tuition aid
• Life	• Purchase discounts	• Trade training
• Disability	• Thrift/savings plans	• Professional
• Long-term care	• Financial planning	certifications
• Legal	• Relocation assistance	• Learning materials

any of the costs, employees still benefit because of the lower rates available through group programs. The most common types of insurance benefits are the following:

- *Life insurance:* Bought as a group policy, the employer pays all or some of the premiums. A typical level of coverage is one-and-a-half or two times an employee's annual salary.
- *Disability insurance:* Both *short-term* and *long-term disability insurance* provide continuing income protection for employees who become disabled and unable to work. Long-term disability insurance is much more common because many employers cover short-term disability situations through sick leave programs.
- *Long-term care insurance:* Usually voluntary, these plans allow employees to purchase insurance to cover costs for long-term health care in a nursing home, an assisted-living facility, or at home. Though employees pay for the premiums, they may get cheaper rates through employer-sponsored group plans.
- *Legal insurance:* In these plans employees (or employers) pay a flat fee for a set amount of legal assistance time each month. In return, they have the right to use the service of a network of lawyers to handle their legal problems.[43]

Financial Services

Financial benefits include a wide variety of items. A *credit union* sponsored by the employer provides saving and lending services for employees. *Purchase discounts* allow employees to buy goods or services from their employers at reduced rates. For example, a furniture manufacturer may allow employees to buy furniture at wholesale cost plus 10%, or a bank may offer employees use of a safe deposit box and free checking.

Stock purchase plan Plan in which the corporation provides matching funds equal to the amount invested by the employee for the purchase of stock in the company.

Employee *thrift plans, savings plans,* or *stock investment plans* of different types may be available. To illustrate, in a stock purchase plan, the employer provides matching funds equal to the amount invested by the employee for the purchase of stock in the company. Often, employees may buy the stock at a discount. This type of plan allows employees to benefit from the future growth of the corporation. Also, the intent of such a plan is to develop greater employee loyalty and interest in the organization and its success.

Financial planning and counseling are especially valuable services for executives, many of whom may need information on investments and tax shelters, as well as comprehensive financial counseling, because of their higher levels of compensation. The importance of these financial planning benefits likely will grow as a greater percentage of workers approach retirement age and need to plan financially for retirement.

Relocation Assistance Relocation benefits of various types are offered by many firms. Some employers offer temporary relocation benefits, while others provide assistance in finding a job for the spouse of a transferred employee. Numerous other financial-related benefits may be offered as well, including the use of a company car, company expense accounts, and assistance in buying or selling a house.

Educational Assistance

Another benefit that saves financial resources of employees comes in the form of *educational assistance* and tuition aid, which pays some or all of the costs associated with formal education courses and degree programs. Some employers pay for schooling on a proportional schedule, depending on the grades received; others simply require a passing grade of C or above. Often the costs of books and laboratory materials are covered. Unless the education paid for by the employer meets certain conditions, the cost of educational aid must be counted as taxable income by employees.

ROI of Tuition Aid Providing educational benefits through tuition aid programs is a very popular benefit with employers. Over 90% of employers offer some form of education assistance to their employees, according to one survey. Interestingly, three-fourths of those employers indicated that fewer than 15% of their workers use the educational benefits.[44] Some employers are using incentives such as free tuition or bonuses upon completion of degrees to encourage greater participation by employees.[45] One concern is that it has been estimated that in one year, U.S. employers spend over $10 billion for tuition aid, but only 2% of those firms conduct HR analyses to determine the return on their investment in tuition aid for those involved in these programs.[46] To make educational benefits programs more effective, the following factors could be measured: employee retention, internal promotions, increased employee satisfaction, and others.

FAMILY-ORIENTED BENEFITS

The composition of families in the United States has changed significantly in the past few decades. The number of traditional families, in which the man went to work and the woman stayed home to raise children, has declined significantly, while the percentage of two-worker families has more than doubled. The growth in dual-career couples, single-parent households, and work demands on many workers has increased the emphasis some employers are placing on family-oriented benefits. As mentioned in earlier chapters, balancing family and work demands presents a major challenge to many workers at all levels of organizations. Therefore, employers have established a variety of family-oriented benefits. Since 1993, employers have also been required to provide certain benefits to comply with the Family and Medical Leave Act.

Family and Medical Leave Act

The Family and Medical Leave Act (FMLA) covers all federal, state, and private employers with 50 or more employees who live within 75 miles of the workplace. Only employees who have worked at least 12 months and 1,250 hours in the previous year are eligible for leave under the FMLA.

FMLA Leave Provisions The law requires that employers allow eligible employees to take a total of 12 weeks' leave during any 12-month period for one or more of three situations:

- Birth, adoption, or foster care placement of a child
- Caring for a spouse, a child, or a parent with a serious health condition
- Serious health condition of the employee

Serious health condition
Health condition requiring in-patient, hospital, hospice, or residential medical care or continuing physician care.

A serious health condition is one requiring in-patient, hospital, hospice, or residential medical care or continuing physician care. An employer may require an employee to provide a certificate from a doctor verifying such an illness. The FMLA provides a number of guidelines regarding employee leaves:

- Employees taking family and medical leave must be able to return to the same job or a job of equivalent status or pay.
- Health benefits must be continued during the leave at the same level and conditions. If, for a reason other than serious health problems, the employee does not return to work, the employer may collect the employer-paid portion of the premiums from the non-returning employee.
- The leave may be taken intermittently rather than in one block, subject to employee and employer agreements, when birth, adoption, or foster child care is the cause. For serious health conditions, employer approval is not necessary.
- Employees can be required to use all paid-up vacation and personal leave before taking unpaid leave.
- Employees are required to give 30-day notice, where practical.

Results of the FMLA Since the passage of the act, several factors have become apparent. First, a significant percentage of employees have been taking family and medical leave. As Figure 14-14 indicates, numerous women and employees in the 25- to 34-year-old age group take more family and medical leave, primarily due to childbirth reasons.

Second, many employers have not paid enough attention to the law. Some employers are denying leaves or failing to reinstate workers after leaves are completed. Consequently, numerous lawsuits have resulted, many of which are lost by employers. Many employers' problems with the FMLA occur because of the variety of circumstances in which employees may request and use family leave. Often, employers have difficulty interpreting when and how the provisions are to be applied.[47] It took a U.S. Supreme Court decision in *Ragsdale v. Wolverine Worldwide* to clarify the notice obligations that employers have regarding FMLA leave granted to employees.[48]

FIGURE 14-14   Percentages of Employees Taking Family or Medical Leave

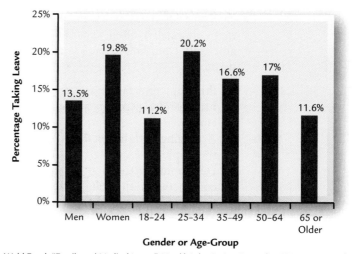

Source: Jane Wald Fogel, "Family and Medical Leave," *Monthly Labor Review*, September 2001, 17–23; and U.S. Bureau of Labor Statistics, *www.bls.gov*.

Third, employers are not required to pay employees for leave taken under the FMLA, other than for sick leave or accumulated unused vacation time. However, some states have passed or are considering laws requiring employers to provide *paid family leave*. California law provides workers as much as 55% of their pay up to a weekly maximum, for leaves as long as six weeks. This controversial and complex law covers about 13 million workers in California.[49]

Finally, one challenge for employers has been covering the workload for employees on family leave. This difficulty is compounded because the law requires that workers on these leaves be offered similar jobs at similar levels of pay when they return to work. Balancing work demands for many different employees and their family and medical situations has placed significant demands on HR professionals to ensure compliance with FMLA provisions.

Family-Care Benefits

Family issues are growing in importance for many organizations and for many workers. One repercussion of this emphasis is that employees without families may feel some resentment against those who seem to get special privileges because they have families. Many employees do not have children under the age of 18 and are offered fewer opportunities to use personal days off, flexible scheduling, telecommuting, etc. Further, they are more frequently asked to travel or put in overtime because they "don't have a family." Nevertheless, a variety of family benefits are available in many organizations.

Adoption Benefits Many employers provide maternity and paternity benefits to employees who give birth to children. A comparatively small number of employees adopt children, and in the interest of fairness, some organizations provide benefits for them. For example, Microsoft gives a cash benefit and four weeks of paid leave to employees who adopt children. Wendy's provides cash payments to help defray adoption expenses and up to six weeks of paid leave for employee adoptions. Estimates are that 35% to 42% of firms provide some type of adoption benefits.[50]

Child-Care Assistance Balancing work and family responsibilities is a major challenge for many workers. Whether single parents or dual-career couples, these employees often experience difficulty obtaining high-quality, affordable child care. Employers are addressing the child-care issue in the following ways:

- Providing referral services to help parents locate child-care providers
- Establishing discounts at day-care centers, which may be subsidized by the employer
- Arranging with hospitals to offer sick-child programs partially paid for by the employer
- Developing after-school programs for older school-age children, often in conjunction with local public and private school systems
- Offering on-site child-care centers

Elder-Care Assistance Another family issue of importance is caring for elderly relatives. Various organizations have surveyed their employees and found that as many as 25% to 30% of them have had to miss work to care for aging relatives. The responsibilities associated with caring for elderly family members have resulted in reduced work performance, increased absenteeism, and more personal stress for the affected employees. Lost productivity and absenteeism caused by workers caring for elders cost employers billions of dollars a year. Some responses by employers have included conducting needs surveys, providing resources, and giving referrals to elder-care providers.

Measuring the Effectiveness of Family Benefits

Employers that have provided child-care and other family-friendly assistance have found the programs beneficial for several reasons. The greatest advantage is in aiding employee retention.[51] Employees are more likely to stay with employers who aid them with work/life balancing. Child-care benefits can produce significant savings, primarily due to decreased employee absenteeism and turnover. Analyses of elder-care costs-benefits show similar results. To determine such metrics, costs for recruiting, training, turnover, and lost productivity often are included.

Benefits for Domestic Partners

As lifestyles change in the United States, employers are being confronted with requests for benefits from employees who are not married but have close personal relationships with others. The terms often used to refer to individuals with such arrangements are *domestic partners* or spousal equivalents. The employees who are submitting these requests are: (1) unmarried employees who are living with individuals of the opposite sex and (2) gay and lesbian employees who have partners.

The argument made by these employees is that if an employer provides benefits for the spouses of married employees, then benefits should be provided for employees without spouses but with alternative lifestyles and relationships.[52] This view is reinforced by data showing that a significant percentage of heterosexual couples live together before or instead of formally marrying. Also, gay employees are being increasingly more open about their lifestyles.

The debate about *same-sex marriages* has amplified the issue for HR professionals and their employers. In a number of states and cities, laws have been enacted to require employers to grant domestic partners the same benefits rights that they give to traditional married couples. Employers providing domestic partner benefits usually have policies that define what the qualifying relationship is and what documentation is required to verify eligibility. At some firms, both the employee and the "eligible partner" must sign an Affidavit of Spousal Equivalence. With this affidavit, the employee and the partner are asked to affirm the following:

- Each is the other's only spousal equivalent.
- They are not blood relatives.
- They are living together and jointly share responsibility for their common welfare and financial obligations.

Decisions to extend benefits to domestic partners have come under attacks from certain religious leaders opposed to homosexual lifestyles. However, it must be noted that most employees using the domestic partner benefits are of the opposite sex and are in heterosexual relationships.

TIME-OFF AND OTHER BENEFITS

Time-off benefits represent a significant portion of total benefits costs. Employers give employees paid time off for a variety of circumstances. Paid lunch breaks and rest periods, holidays, and vacations are common. But time off is given for a number of other purposes as well. As Figure 14-15 indicates, these time-off benefits also include various leaves of absence.

Holiday Pay

Most employers provide pay for a variety of holidays. U.S. employers commonly offer 10 to 12 holidays annually. Employers in many other countries are required to provide a significantly higher number of holidays, approaching 20 to 30 days in some cases. In both the United States and other countries, the number of holidays offered can vary depending on state/provincial laws and union contracts.

As an abuse-control measure, employers commonly require employees to work the last scheduled day before a holiday and the first scheduled workday after a holiday to be eligible for holiday pay. Some employers pay time-and-a-half to hourly employees who must work holidays. Also, some employers provide company holiday parties and holiday bonus programs such as food gifts (e.g., turkeys at Thanksgiving) or holiday gift cards.

Vacation Pay

Paid vacations are a common benefit. Employers often use graduated vacation-time scales based on employees' lengths of service. Some organizations have a "use it or lose it" policy whereby accrued vacation time cannot be carried

FIGURE 14-15   Percentage of Companies with Various Paid-Time-Off Plans

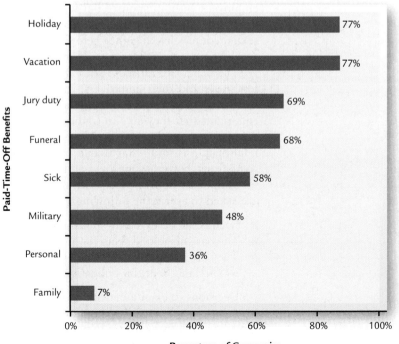

Source: U.S. Bureau of Labor Statistics, 2005, *www.bls.gov.*

over from year to year. One survey found that workers on average forfeit three vacation days per year.[53]

Some employers have policies to "buy back" unused vacation time. Other employers, such as banks, may have policies requiring employees to take a minimum number of vacation days off in a row. Regardless of the vacation policies used, employees are often required to work the day before and the day after vacation time off.

Leaves of Absence

Employers grant *leaves of absence,* taken as time off with or without pay, for a variety of reasons. All the leaves discussed here add to employer costs even if unpaid. That is because the missing employee's work must be covered, either by other employees working additionally or by temporary employees working under contract.

Other types of leaves are given for a variety of purposes. Some, such as *military leave, election leave,* and *jury leave,* are required by various state and federal laws. Employers commonly pay the difference between the employee's regular pay and the military, election, or jury pay. Some firms grant the employees military time off and provide regular pay while the employees also receive military pay. Federal law prohibits taking discriminatory action against military reservists by requiring them to take vacation time when deployed or in training. However, the leave request must be reasonable and truly required by the military.

Funeral leave or *bereavement leave* is another common method of leave offered. An absence of up to three days for the death of immediate family members is usually granted. Some policies also give unpaid time off for the death of more distant relatives or of friends.

Family Leave As mentioned earlier in the chapter, the passage of the Family and Medical Leave Act clarified the rights of employees and the responsibilities of most employers. Even though *paternity leave* for male workers is available under the FMLA, a relatively low percentage of men take it. The primary reason for the low usage is a perception that it is not as socially acceptable for men to stay home for child-related reasons. That view has begun changing as the number of dual-career couples in the workforce has risen.[54]

Sick Leave Medical and sick leave are closely related. Many employers allow employees to miss a limited number of days because of illness without losing pay. Over 50% of all U.S. workers receive paid sick leave. But U.S. employers do not provide paid sick leave to as many workers percentagewise as do the employers in other developed countries.

Some employers allow employees to accumulate unused sick leave, which may be used in case of catastrophic illnesses. Others pay their employees for unused sick leave. A problem employers face is that only about 35% of unscheduled employee absences are due to illnesses.[55] Some organizations have shifted emphasis to reward people who do not use sick leave by giving them well-pay— extra pay for not taking sick leave. Another approach is to use paid time off.

Well-pay Extra pay for not taking sick leave.

Paid-time-off (PTO) plans Plans that combine all sick leave, vacation time, and holidays into a total number of hours or days that employees can take off with pay.

Paid-Time-Off Plans

A growing number of employers have made use of a paid-time-off (PTO) plan, which combines all sick leave, vacation time, and holidays into a total number of hours or days that employees can take off with pay. Studies have found that about 37% of all employers have PTO plans.[56] More importantly, many of those employers have found PTO plans to be more effective than other means of reducing absenteeism and in having time off scheduled more efficiently. Other advantages cited by employers with PTO plans are ease of administration and as an aid for recruiting and retention and for increasing employee understanding and use of leave policies.[57]

Miscellaneous Benefits

Employers offer a wide variety of miscellaneous benefits. Some of the benefits are voluntary, meaning that employees can participate in them and pay for the costs themselves, often at group discount rates. Various types of voluntary insurance programs are the most common offered.[58] Others are unique to employers and are provided at little or no cost to employees.

Some benefits and services are social and recreational in nature, such as tennis courts, bowling leagues, picnics, parties, employer-sponsored athletic teams, organizationally owned recreational lodges, and other sponsored activities and interest groups. As interest in employee wellness has increased, more firms are providing recreational facilities and activities. The idea behind social and recreational programs is to promote employee happiness and team spirit. Employees may appreciate this type of benefit, but managers should not necessarily expect increased job productivity or job satisfaction as a result. Further, employers should retain control of all events associated with their organizations because of possible legal responsibility.

SUMMARY

- Benefits provide additional compensation to some employees as a reward for organizational membership. Because benefits generally are not taxed, they are highly desired by employees.
- Strategic considerations for benefits include their value in creating a competitive advantage and aiding in attracting and retaining employees.
- Benefits design and cost-control actions are crucial to strategic benefits efforts.
- Flexible benefits plans, which can be tailored to individual needs and situations, are increasing in popularity.
- Because of the variety of benefit options available and the costs involved, employers must develop effective systems to communicate benefits information to their employees.
- Benefits can be viewed as mandatory or voluntary. The general types of benefits include security, health care, retirement, financial, family oriented, and time off.
- Three prominent security benefits are workers' compensation, unemployment compensation, and severance pay.
- Because health-care benefits costs have increased significantly, employers are managing their health benefits costs more aggressively.

- Efforts to control the costs of health benefits have included changing employee co-payments and employee contributions, using managed care, and switching to consumer-driven health (CDH) plans.
- Organizations provide retirement benefits through defined-benefit, defined-contribution, or cash balance plans.
- The pension area is a complex one that is governed by the Employee Retirement Income Security Act (ERISA) and other laws.
- Use of defined-contribution plans and individual retirement accounts is growing.
- Various types of financial services, insurance benefits, relocation assistance, educational assistance, and other benefits enhance the appeal of an organization to employees.
- Family-oriented benefits include complying with the Family and Medical Leave Act (FMLA) of 1993 and offering adoption benefits, child-care assistance, and elder-care assistance.
- Holiday pay, vacation pay, various leaves of absence, and paid-time-off plans are another means of providing benefits to employees.

REVIEW AND APPLICATION QUESTIONS

1. Why are benefits strategically important to employers, and what are some key strategic considerations?
2. Discuss the following statement: "Health-care costs are out of control in the United States, and increasing conflicts between employers and employees are likely as employers try to reduce their health benefits costs."
3. Assume that as an HR staff member, you have been asked to research consumer-driven health plans because your employer is considering implementing one. Go to a leading benefits information resource, *Employee Benefit News*, at *www.benefitnews.com,* and identify the elements of a successful CDH and some examples of firms that use them.

CASE

Delivering Benefits

Employers of all sizes and in a variety of industries have made changes in their benefits programs to deal with rising costs. How FedEx Corporation, a worldwide transportation and shipping firm, responded to the cost pressures resulted in the firm receiving the Optimas award from *Workforce Management* magazine. The decisions made by FedEx provide some insights on approaches that other employers may wish to consider.

For years FedEx offered health-care benefits only through managed care programs such as HMOs and PPOs. But beginning in 2004, FedEx established a program that allows employees to use health-care providers inside or outside of the designated network of providers. Employees who want "freedom of choice" have the higher co-payment and payroll deduction. Also, FedEx expanded its health benefits plan to have four different levels of coverage, so that employees can choose a benefits package that fits their needs and their personal budgets.

But FedEx does not just provide health-care benefits; it also has established services to help employees improve their overall health. Many FedEx locations have wellness centers. Because many FedEx employees lift boxes and packages, the firm established a lower-back pain program to help reduce back injuries. For employees with chronic health problems such as arthritis, asthma, and diabetes, there is a disease management program to give them guidance, which also reduces their use of health-care services. A telephone hotline staffed by nurses is available around the clock for employees to call with health-related questions.

FedEx uses a variety of means to communicate benefits information, including an internal TV network that features a variety of health-related programs. Employees can also access information electronically or contact a benefits call center.

Overall, FedEx employees have responded positively to these health-related efforts, despite increases in their payroll deductions for health benefits. It is likely that FedEx will have to keep making changes in its benefits because of increasing health-care costs. But through planning, continuing communication, and education, FedEx will likely continue delivering its health-care benefits to meet both the company's and the employees' needs.[59]

Questions

1. Why is having multiple health-care plans important for FedEx in slowing down increases in the cost of benefits?
2. Discuss how the availability of disease management programs, training programs, and a nursing hotline might help with health benefits costs.

SUPPLEMENTAL CASE

Benefiting Connie

This case describes the problems that can occur when trying to coordinate time-off leaves for employees. (For the case, go to http://thomsonedu .com/management/mathis.)

NOTES

1. "Top Five Total Rewards Priorities for 2006," Deloitte Development LLC, 2006, *www.deloitte.com*; "Up, Up, and Away," *Employee Benefit News,* December 2006, 64; and "Insured Americans Accept Rising Health Care Costs—But Are Not Prepared for Them," *Newsline,* April 20, 2007, *www.worldatwork.org.*

2. Stephen Miller, "Alternative Benefit Strategies: Not Whether But Which," *SHRM Compensation & Benefit News,* June 2006, *www.shrm.org/ rewards.*

3. Linda Lisanti, "Happy Employees, Happy Customers," *Convenience Store News,* September 18, 2006, 97.

4. "An Executive Perspective on Employee Benefits," *McKinsey Quarterly Survey,* April 2006, 1, *www. mckinseyquarterly.com.*

5. "Incorporate 'Employer of Choice' Goals into Strategic, Benefits Planning," *Best Practices in HR,* September 22, 2006, 3.

6. Kevin Sweeney, "Around the Benefits World," *Employee Benefit News,* October 2003, 35–36.

7. "A Strong Benefits Mix May Be Answer to Recruiting, Retention Woes," *Workindex.com,* May 3, 2006, *www.workindex.com.*

8. For an overview and details, see Jerry S. Rosenbloom, *The Handbook of Employee Benefits: Design, Funding, and Administration,* 6th ed., (New York: McGraw-Hill, 2005).

9. U.S. Bureau of Labor Statistics, *www.bls.gov.*

10. Elayne Robertson Demby, "Nothing Partial About These Benefits," *HR Magazine,* August 2003, 72–81.

11. Karen Lee, "Study Shows Six Out of Ten Companies Outsource Benefits," *Employee Benefit News,* October 2004, 11.

12. "Online Benefits Expected to Become Predominant," *Best's Review,* April 2005, 106.

13. Examples of metrics for benefits can be found in Jim Simon, "Weighing the Cost of Employee Benefits," *Workspan,* March 2003, 56–57; and Jac Fitz-Enz and Barbara Davidson, *How to Measure Human Resources Management,* 3rd ed. (New York: McGraw-Hill, 2002), 141–156.

14. "Cost Control Is Shifting to a Long-Term View," *HR Focus,* September 2006, 1.

15. "Few Employees Understand and Appreciate Their Total Compensation Package," *WorldatWork News,* November 29, 2006. For details go to *www.Charltonconsulting.com.*

16. Dennis Ackley, "Communication: The Key to Putting the Benefit Back in Benefits," *Workspan,* February, 2006, 31–34.

17. Michal Kisilevitz, Shub Debgupta, and Daniel Metz, "Improving Employee Benefits Through Effective Communication," *WorldatWork Journal,* First Quarter 2006, 52–60.

18. "Workers Could Get Medical Records," *Omaha World-Herald,* December 6, 2006, D1.

19. Jill Elswick, "Loaded Statements: Web-Based Total Compensation Statements Keep Employees in the Know," *BenefitNews.com,* May, 2005, *www.benefitnews.com.*

20. U.S. Bureau of Labor Statistics, *www.bls.gov.*

21. Richard Breeden, "Firms Consider End to Employee Health Insurance," *The Wall Street Journal,* August 14, 2006, B8.

22. "Retiree Health-Care Costs Climb to $63.4 Billion at GM," *Omaha World-Herald,* March 12, 2004, B1.

23. "Health Benefit Costs to Keep Growing for Retirees," *Omaha World-Herald,* December 14, 2006, 7A.

24. Bryce G. Hoffman, "Ford to Freeze Health Plans," *The Denver Post,* December 14, 2005, 3C.

25. Vanesa Fuhrmans, "More Employers Try Limited Health Plans," *The Wall Street Journal,* January 17, 2006, D1; and Chris Silva, "Employers Turn to Mini-Med Plans as Stop Gaps," *Employee Benefit News,* December 2006, 39.

26. "More Firms Adopting Consumerism," *Benefits News.com,* September 14, 2006, *www .employeebenefitnews.com.*

27. Steve Neeleman, "Making Health Savings Accounts Work," *Compensation and Benefits Review,* March/ April 2005, 33.

28. Leah Carlson Shepard, "Enrollment in New CDHPs Remains Low," *Benefits News.com,* June 15, 2006, *www.employeebenefitnews.com.*

29. "Two-Thirds of Large Employers Now Offering Incentives to Improve Employees' Health," *Management Barometer,* April 10, 2006, *www .barometersurveys.com.*

30. Jeremy Smerd, "You Can Do Anything But Don't Mess with My Health Insurance," *Workforce Management,* April 12, 2007, *www.workforce.com.*

31. Based on Susan J. Wells, "Will Employees Orchestrate Their Own Health Care?" *HR Magazine,* December 2006, 62–67.

32. Darli Dunkelberger, "Avoiding COBRA's Bite: Three Keys to Compliance," *Compensation and Benefits Review,* March/April 2005, 44.

33. For details on HIPAA, see *www.hhs .gov/ocr/hipaa.*

34. Annette L. Halpin and Thomas M. Brinker Jr., "Tax Relief Through Cafeteria Plans and Flexible Spending Accounts," *Journal of Financial Services Professionals,* 57 (2003), 14.

35. *EBRI 2004 Retirement Confidence Study, www.ebri.org.*

36. Stephanie L. Costo, "Trends in Retirement Plan Coverage over the

Last Decade," *Monthly Labor Review*, February 2006, 58–64.

37. Ellen E. Schultz and Theo Francis, "What You Need to Know About Pension Changes," *The Wall Street Journal*, August 15, 2006, D1; and A. J. Bianchi, "Futurecast: Cash Balance Retirement Plans After *Cooper v. IBM*," *Employee Benefit News*, October 2006, 72.

38. Rachel D. Kugelmass and Richard Koski, "The Roth 401(k)," *Workspan*, December 2005, 36.

39. *Arizona Governing Committee v. Norris*, 103 S. Ct. 3492, 32 FEP Cases 233 (1983).

40. John Nownes, "What Every Plan Administrator Needs to Know About QDROs," *HRAM Highlights*, October 2003, 8.

41. Debbie Powell, "Reporting and Disclosure Requirements Under the Pension Protection Act of 2006," *Employee Benefit News*, December 2006, 52; and Anoinette M. Pilzner, "Pension Protection Act of 2006: Mandates and Options for Retirement Plans," *SHRM HR Legal Report*, October/November, 2006, 1+.

42. *Public Employees Retirement System of Ohio v. Betts*, 109 S. Ct. 256 (1989).

43. Angela Maas, "Legal Transformation," *Employee Benefit News*, April 15, 2005, 27.

44. "Participation Remains Low for Tuition Assistance Programs," *BenefitNews.com*, June 20, 2006, www.benefitnews.com.

45. Matt Bolch, "Bearing Fruit," *HR Magazine*, March 2006, 57–60.

46. Andy Meister, "A Matter of Degrees," *Workforce Management*, May 2004, 32–38.

47. Sara Schaefer Munoz, "A Good Idea, But . . . . ," *The Wall Street Journal*, January 24, 2005, R6.

48. *Ragsdale v. Wolverine Worldwide*, 122 S. Ct. 1155 (2002).

49. Tom Klett, "Challenges Loom from California's Paid Family Leave," *Employee Benefit News*, July 2003, 35.

50. Lynn Gresham, "Employers Honored for Adoption Benefits," *Employee Benefit News*, May 2007, 1.

51. Reagan Baughman, Daniela DiNardi, and Douglas Holtz-Eakin, "Productivity and Wage Effects of 'Family Friendly' Fringe Benefits," *International Journal of Manpower*, 24 (2003), 247.

52. M. A. Ash and M. V. Lee Badgett, "Separate and Unequal: The Effect of Unequal Access to Employment-Based Health Insurance on Same-Sex and Unmarried Different-Sex Couples," *Contemporary Economic Policy*, 24(2006), 582.

53. Leah Carlson, "Surveys Show Fewer Vacation Days Taken, Offered," *Employee Benefit News*, November 2004, 20.

54. Ron Lieber, "The Next Frontier: Paternity Leave," *The Wall Street Journal*, July 8, 2006, B1.

55. "Too Many Workers Take Advantage of Sick Days," *BenefitNews.com*, October 31, 2006, www.benefitnews.com.

56. George Faulkner, "Absent and Accounted For," *Human Resource Executive*, May 2, 2006, 56–57.

57. M. Michael Markowich, *Paid Time-Off Banks* (Scottsdale, AZ: Worldat-Work, 2007).

58. Carolyn Hirschman, "Employees' Choice," *HR Magazine*, February 2006, 95.

59. Based on "Choice Offsets Cost for FedEx Workers," *Workforce Management*, www.workforce.com.

Managing Employee Relations

CHAPTER

15

Risk Management and Worker Protection

After you have read this chapter, you should be able to:

■ Identify the components of risk management.

■ Discuss three legal areas affecting safety and health.

■ Identify the basic provisions of the Occupational Safety and Health Act of 1970 and recordkeeping and inspection requirements.

■ Discuss the activities that constitute effective safety management.

■ List three workplace health issues and how employers are responding to them.

■ Explain workplace violence as a security issue and describe some components of an effective security program.

■ Describe the nature and importance of disaster preparation and recovery planning for HR.

HR Headline

The Future Is Now for Risk Management

The focus of HR managers on risk management and worker protection has grown significantly in the past several years. Previously, most HR efforts emphasized providing work environments that are safe, healthy, and secure. Risk management has a number of different facets beyond complying with safety and health regulations. Some include:

■ Preparing the organization for and responding to natural disasters, such as massive hurricanes like Katrina, earthquakes, tsunamis in the Pacific, and forest fires in Arizona, California, and other states

■ Planning responses to terrorism and other violent attacks that disrupt company operations and the safety of employees

■ Anticipating global diseases such as an Avian flu infection spread by international business travelers and how to respond to quarantine requests

■ Protecting employees and others from workplace violence and personal attacks at work sites, such as the one that occurred at Virginia Tech University in 2007

■ Ensuring that HR data are secure and that data backup and prevention of employee identify theft are addressed

These examples illustrate how the role of HR has expanded. Planning for and handling risk management and worker protection are increasing priorities for HR and all managers today and in the future.

FIGURE 15-1   Risk Management Components

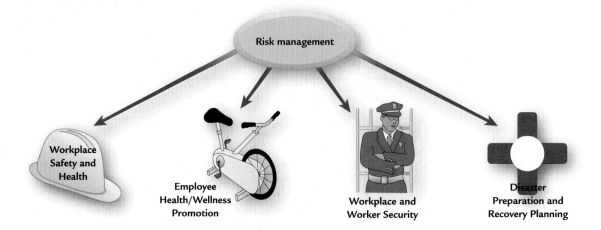

The HR Headline highlights how HR has had to expand its traditional view of worker safety and health. The importance of this expansion is seen in the addition of risk management, disaster recovery, and other revised topics to the Human Resource Certification Institute test specifications for HR professionals. In the United States and most developed nations, the concept of using prevention and control to minimize or eliminate a wide range of risks in workplaces has been expanding. Effective risk management also is becoming a key component of strategic HR management.[1]

Risk management
Involves responsibilities to consider physical, human, and financial factors to protect organizational and individual interests.

Risk management involves responsibilities to consider physical, human, and financial factors to protect organizational and individual interests. For HR management, risk management includes a number of areas, as Figure 15-1 depicts. Its scope ranges from workplace safety and health to disaster preparation. The nature and extent of risk management efforts are affected by a number of factors, including:

- Size and location of organizations
- Industry characteristics and demands
- Geographic and global location factors
- Government-mandated programs and requirements
- Strategic priorities of each organization
- Involvement and capabilities of HR professionals in the different risk management areas.

NATURE OF HEALTH, SAFETY, AND SECURITY

Health General state of physical, mental, and emotional well-being.

The first emphasis in risk management in most organizations is health, safety and security, which is discussed next. The terms *health, safety,* and *security* are closely related. The broader and somewhat more nebulous term is health, which refers to a general state of physical, mental, and emotional well-being. A healthy person is free from illness, injury, or mental and emotional problems that impair normal human activity. Health management practices in organizations strive to maintain the overall well-being of individuals.

Safety Condition in which the physical well-being of people is protected.

Typically, safety refers to a condition in which the physical well-being of people is protected. The main purpose of effective safety programs in organizations is to prevent work-related injuries and accidents.

Security Protection of employees and organizational facilities.

The purpose of security is protecting employees and organizational facilities. With the growth of workplace violence and other risk management concerns, security has become an even greater concern for both employers and employees alike.

Health, Safety, and Security Responsibilities

The general goal of providing a safe, secure, and healthy workplace is reached by operating managers and HR working together. As Figure 15-2 indicates, the greatest areas of HR responsibilities are worker compensation and health and wellness programs. The figure also indicates that HR works with other departments or perhaps outsources some activities, including safety.

A position that is utilized in many companies is that of risk management officer. This person focuses on safety, health, and environmental issues. This combination may make sense where danger results from chemical or other sources of pollution that may be hazardous to both employees and the public or the environment. The person in this role also can coordinate disaster and recovery planning efforts by working with federal, state, and local agencies.

Security also affects everyone in an organization and is often an HR responsibility. Since the terrorist attacks of September 11, 2001, the security issues that an employer might worry about have grown in number and scope. Certainly, workplace violence, computer security, and theft at work have been and continue to be concerns. But for some employers now, security issues include protecting employees from terrorist attacks, loss of electric service, bomb threats, and hostage situations. Perhaps more correctly labeled *crisis management planning* at its most extreme, dealing with such issues provides an opportunity for HR to mitigate some risks to the company.[2]

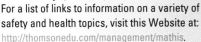

Internet Research

National Institute for Occupational Health and Safety (NIOSH)

For a list of links to information on a variety of safety and health topics, visit this Website at:

http://thomsonedu.com/management/mathis.

FIGURE 15-2   **Health and Safety—Who Handles These Responsibilities?**

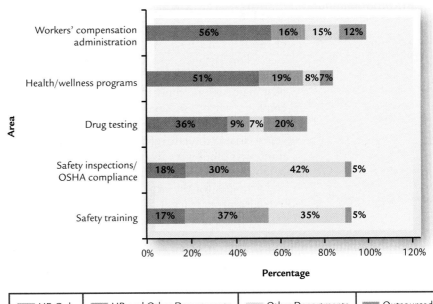

Source: *HR Department Benchmarks and Analysis Survey 2007* (Washington, D.C.: BNA, Inc., 2006), 146.

Current State of Health, Safety, and Security

In the United States, about 4.2 million non-fatal injuries and illnesses occur at work annually. Specific rates vary depending on the industry, job type, etc. The number of workplace injuries varies by employer size also, with smaller employers having more injuries per employee. The three major causes of injury (overextending, falling, and bodily reaction) were responsible for over 40% of the direct costs of injuries. Accident costs have gone up faster than inflation because of the rapid increase in medical costs, even though the total number of accidents has been decreasing for some time.[3]

Self-Employed and Safety An interesting phenomenon is that self-employed workers have higher accident rates than do those who work for others. While self-employed individuals make up only 7.4% of the U.S. civilian workforce, self-employed workers have 20% of the workplace fatalities. When comparing self-employed workers with those working for someone else, the self-employed individuals were almost three times as likely to be killed.

The self-employed were more likely to work in industries and occupations with higher fatality rates, especially farming. For instance, over 25% of the self-employed who died on the job were farmers.[4] The conclusion that can be drawn is that the self-employed are willing to work in more dangerous circumstances; therefore, they are more vulnerable to illnesses, injuries, and death. Those who are self-employed should be aware of the additional safety risks that they face.

Global Health, Safety, and Security

Safety and health laws and regulations vary from country to country, ranging from virtually non-existent to more stringent than those in the United States. The importance placed on health, safety, and security relates somewhat to the level of regulation and other factors in each country.

International Emergency Health Services With more and more expatriates working internationally, especially in some less-developed countries, significant health and safety issues require attention. Addressing these issues is part of the HR role. One consideration is provision of emergency evacuation services. For instance, evacuating and caring for an expatriate employee who sustains internal injuries in a car accident in the Ukraine or Sierra Leone may be a major issue. Many global firms purchase coverage for their international employees from an organization that provides emergency services, such as International SOS, Global Assistance & Healthcare, or U.S. Assist. If an emergency arises, the emergency services company dispatches physicians or even transports employees by chartered aircraft. If adequate medical assistance can be obtained locally, the emergency services company maintains a referral list and arranges for the expatriate to receive treatment. Emergency services firms may also provide legal counsel in foreign countries, emergency cash for medical expenses, and assistance in reissuing lost documents.

International Security and Terrorism As more U.S. firms operate internationally, the threat of terrorist actions against those firms and their employees increases. The extent to which employees are likely to experience security problems and violence depends on the country. It is crucial that the HR staff regularly check the security conditions in countries where expatriates are traveling and working.

Global firms take a variety of actions to address security concerns.[5] For example, one U.S. firm removed signs identifying its offices and facilities in a Latin American country in order to reduce the visibility of the firm and thus reduce its potential as a target for terrorist acts. Many international firms screen entry by all employees, and many use metal detectors to scan all packages, briefcases, and other items. Firms commonly use physical barriers such as iron security fences, concrete barricades, bulletproof glass, and electronic surveillance devices in offices as part of their security efforts.

Kidnapping Not all violence occurs at work. Kidnapping, murder, home invasion, robberies, and carjackings happen relatively frequently in some cities, such as Mexico City. In a number of countries throughout the world, U.S. citizens are especially vulnerable to extortion, kidnapping, bombing, physical harassment, and other terrorist activities.

To counter such threats, many global firms have *kidnap and ransom insurance*. This insurance covers the costs of paying ransoms to obtain releases of kidnapped employees and family members, pay for the bodily injuries suffered by kidnap victims, and deal with negotiations and other expenses.[6]

Individual employees and their family members working and living abroad must constantly be aware of security concerns. Both pre-departure and ongoing security training should be given to all expatriates, their dependents, and employees of global firms working internationally, especially if located in high-risk areas.

LEGAL REQUIREMENTS FOR SAFETY AND HEALTH

Employers must comply with a variety of federal and state laws when developing and maintaining healthy, safe, and secure workforces and working environments. Three major legal areas are workers' compensation legislation, the Americans with Disabilities Act, and child labor laws.

Workers' Compensation

First passed in the early 1900s, workers' compensation laws in some form are on the books in all states today. Under these laws, employers contribute to an insurance fund to compensate employees for injuries received while on the job. Premiums paid reflect the accident rates of the employers, with employers that have higher incident rates being assessed higher premiums. These laws usually provide payments to replace wages for injured workers, depending on the amount of lost time and the wage level. They also provide payments to cover medical bills and for re-training if a worker cannot go back to the current job. Most state laws also set a maximum weekly amount for determining workers' comp benefits.[7]

Workers' compensation coverage has been expanded in many states to include emotional impairment that may have resulted from physical injury, as well as job-related strain, stress, anxiety, and pressure. Some cases of suicide have also been ruled to be job related, with payments due under workers' compensation.

Another aspect of workers' compensation coverage relates to the increasing use of telecommuting by employees. In most situations while working at home for employers, individuals are covered under workers' compensation laws. Therefore, if an employee is injured while doing employer-related work at home, the employer likely is liable for the injury. This aspect of workers' compensation liability is not widely known.

Controlling Workers' Compensation Costs Workers' compensation costs have become a major issue for many employers. These costs usually represent from 2% to 10% of payroll for most employers. The major contributors to increases have been higher medical costs and litigation expenses. However, the frequency of workers' compensation claims for lost time has decreased some in all industry groups.

Key to these reductions have been *return-to-work plans*.[8] These plans monitor employees who are off work due to injuries and illness. Also, the plans focus on returning the individuals to do *light-duty work* that is less physically demanding until they are fully able to perform their full range of job duties.

Workers' compensation fraud is a fast-growing and expensive problem. It is estimated that 25% of the workers' compensation claims filed are fraudulent. False and exaggerated claims make up the bulk of the fraud—costing employers $5 billion annually.[9] Employers must continually monitor their workers' compensation expenditures. Efforts to reduce workplace injuries, illnesses, and fraud can reduce workers' compensation premiums and claims costs. Many of the safety and health management suggestions discussed later in this chapter can contribute to reducing workers' compensation costs.

FMLA and Workers' Compensation The Family and Medical Leave Act (FMLA) affects workers' compensation as well. Because the FMLA allows eligible employees to take up to 12 weeks of leave for their serious health conditions, injured employees may ask to use that leave time in addition to the leave time allowed under workers' comp, even if it is unpaid. Some employers have policies that state that FMLA runs concurrently with any workers' comp leave.

Americans with Disabilities Act and Safety Issues

Employers sometimes try to return injured workers to "light-duty" work in order to reduce workers' compensation costs. However, under the Americans with Disabilities Act (ADA), when making accommodations for injured employees through light-duty work, employers may undercut what are really essential job functions. Also, making such accommodations for injured employees for a period of time may require employers to make similar accommodations for job applicants with disabilities.

Additionally, health and safety recordkeeping practices have been affected by an ADA provision that requires all medical-related information to be maintained separately from all other confidential files. Specific access restrictions and security procedures must be adopted for medical records of all types, including employee medical benefits claims and treatment records.

Child Labor Laws

Safety concerns are reflected in restrictions affecting younger workers, especially those under the age of 18. Child labor laws, found in Section XII of the Fair Labor Standards Act (FLSA), set the minimum age for most employment at 16 years. For "hazardous" occupations, 18 years is the minimum. Figure 15-3 lists 17 occupations that the federal government considers hazardous for children who work while attending school.

| FIGURE 15-3 | Selected Child Labor Hazardous Occupations (minimum age: 18 years) |

Hazardous Work

- Manufacturing or storing explosives
- Driving a motor vehicle and being an outside helper
- Coal mining
- Logging and saw milling
- Using power-driven woodworking machines*
- Exposure to radioactive substances and to ionizing radiations
- Operating power-driven hoisting apparatus
- Operating power-driven, metal forming, punching, and shearing machines*
- Mining, other than coal mining

- Slaughtering or meatpacking, or rendering
- Using power-driven bakery machines
- Operating power-driven paper products machines*
- Manufacturing brick, tile, and related products
- Using power-driven circular saws, and guillotine shears*
- Wrecking, demolition, and shipbreaking operations
- Roofing operations*
- Excavation operations*

* In certain cases, the law provides exemptions for apprentices and student learners in these occupations.

Two examples illustrate violations of these provisions. At a fast-food restaurant specializing in roast beef sandwiches, a teenage worker operated a meat slicer, which is a hazard covered by the FLSA. At a national discount retailer, teenage workers were found to have operated the mechanical box crushers. Both situations resulted in enforcement actions and fines for violating the FLSA.

Work-related injuries of younger workers is a significant issue for employers with many youth employees. Industries such as retail and fast food consistently face safety and health issues with these workers. One characteristic of many youth workers is to be more risk taking at work, much like when they drive cars. The degree to which co-workers engage in work-related risks is a significant factor that affects the injuries and safety practices of younger workers.[10]

In addition to complying with workers' compensation, ADA, and child labor laws, most employers must comply with the Occupational Safety and Health Act of 1970. This act has had a tremendous impact on the workplace. Therefore, any person interested in HR management must develop knowledge of the provisions and implications of the act, which is administered by the Occupational Safety and Health Administration.

OCCUPATIONAL SAFETY AND HEALTH ACT

The Occupational Safety and Health Act of 1970 was passed "to assure so far as possible every working man or woman in the Nation safe and healthful working conditions and to preserve our human resources." Every employer that is engaged in commerce and has one or more employees is covered by the act. Farmers having fewer than 10 employees are exempt. Employers in

FIGURE 15-4   Percent of Non-Fatal Workplace Injuries by Private Industry Group

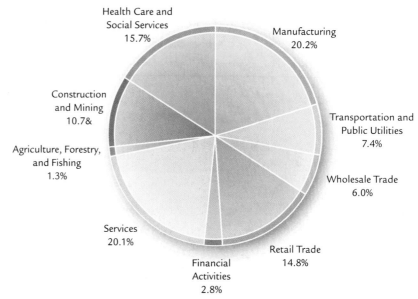

Source: U.S. Department of Labor, Bureau of Labor Statistics, "Workplace Injuries and Illnesses," *News*, October 19, 2006, 4, *www.bls.gov*.

specific industries, such as coal mining, are covered under other health and safety acts. Federal, state, and local governments are covered by separate statutes and provisions.

The Occupational Safety and Health Act of 1970 established the Occupational Safety and Health Administration, known as OSHA, to administer its provisions. The act also established the National Institute for Occupational Safety and Health (NIOSH) as a supporting body to do research and develop standards. In addition, the Occupational Safety and Health Review Commission (OSHRC) has been established to review OSHA enforcement actions and to address disputes between OSHA and employers who have been cited by OSHA inspectors.

By making employers and employees more aware of safety and health considerations, OSHA has significantly affected organizations. OSHA regulations do appear to have contributed to reductions in the number of accidents and injuries in some cases. But in other industries, OSHA has had little or no effect. Figure 15-4 indicates the percentage of workplace illnesses and injuries by industry. In the figure the legal, hospitality, education, and other services are grouped in the services category.

OSHA Enforcement Standards

To implement OSHA regulations, specific standards were established to regulate equipment and working environments. National standards developed by engineering and quality control groups are often used. OSHA rules and standards are frequently complicated and technical. Small-business owners and managers who do not have specialists on their staffs may find the standards difficult to read and understand. In addition, the presence of many minor standards has hurt the credibility of OSHA.

A number of provisions have been recognized as key to employers' efforts to comply with OSHA. Two basic ones are as follows:

■ *General duty:* The act requires that the employer has a "general duty" to provide safe and healthy working conditions, even in areas where OSHA standards have not been set. Employers who know or reasonably should know of unsafe or unhealthy conditions can be cited for violating the general duty clause.

■ *Notification and posters:* Employers are required to inform their employees of safety and health standards established by OSHA. Also, OSHA posters must be displayed in prominent locations in workplaces.

Hazard Communication OSHA established process safety management (PSM) standards that focus on hazardous chemicals. As part of PSM through a risk management program, hazard communication standards require manufacturers, importers, distributors, and users of hazardous chemicals to evaluate, classify, and label these substances. Employers also must make available information about hazardous substances to employees, their representatives, and health professionals. This information is contained in material safety data sheets (MSDSs), which must be kept readily accessible to those who work with chemicals and other substances. The MSDSs also indicate antidotes or actions to be taken should someone come in contact with the substances. The HR On-Line describes one means for providing accessible details.

If the organization employs a number of workers for whom English is not the primary language, then the MSDSs should be available in the necessary languages. Also, workers should be trained in how to access and use the MSDS information.

As part of hazard communications, OSHA has established lockout/tag-out regulations. To comply with these regulations, firms must provide mechanics

Lockout/tag-out regulations Requirement that locks and tags be used to make equipment inoperative for repair or adjustment.

HR ONLINE

Hazard Communication

The availability of the Internet has made it much quicker and easier for employers to meet OSHA's hazard communication requirements. There are two parts to the use of on-line resources.

First, employers can access safety information produced by vendors and suppliers on hazardous materials and chemicals. Many of the firms that sell the supplies have Websites that contain safety, treatment, and antidote specifications. An employer can immediately access and download updated information and details on new or revised chemicals.

Additionally, information technology allows employers to use the Internet to maintain MSDSs on chemicals and workplace substances. Using MSDS software, firms can update electronic MSDSs regularly rather than having to reissue printed manuals regularly. An employer can place all MSDSs on an intranet, through an Internet link, or access manufacturers' information sheets.

Many MSDSs also can be found on Websites. For example, at a warehouse for a company, an employee was injured when a chemical spilled on him. The company used an on-line link to retrieve MSDSs. Co-workers took the employee to the hospital. By the time they got there, the current version of the MSDS for the solvent had been faxed to the hospital, and a company safety person was on the phone with the hospital staff to provide information about the chemical and the injured employee's treatment.

and tradespeople with locks and tags for use when they make equipment inoperative for repair or adjustment to prevent accidental start-up of defective machinery. Only the person whose name is printed on the tag or engraved on the lock may remove the device.

Bloodborne Pathogens OSHA has issued a standard regarding exposure to hepatitis B virus (HBV), human immunodeficiency virus (HIV), and other bloodborne pathogens. This regulation was developed to protect employees who regularly are exposed to blood and other such substances from contracting AIDS and other serious diseases. Obviously, health-care laboratory workers, nurses, and medical technicians are at greatest risk. However, all employers covered by OSHA regulations must comply in workplaces where cuts and abrasions are common. Regulations require employers with the most pronounced risks to have written control and response plans and to train workers in following the proper procedures.

Personal Protective Equipment One goal of OSHA has been to develop standards for personal protective equipment (PPE). These standards require that employers analyze job hazards, provide adequate PPE to employees in hazardous jobs, and train employees in the use of PPE items. Common PPE items include safety glasses, hard hats, and safety shoes.[11] If the work environment presents hazards or if employees might have contact with hazardous chemicals and substances on the job, then employers are required to provide PPE to all those employees.

Ergonomics and OSHA

Ergonomics Study and design of the work environment to address physiological and physical demands placed on individuals.

Ergonomics is the study and design of the work environment to address physiological and physical demands placed on individuals. In a work setting, ergonomic studies look at such factors as fatigue, lighting, tools, equipment layout, and placement of controls. Ergonomics has been identified as providing economic value to employers.[12]

For a number of years, OSHA focused on the large number of work-related injuries due to repetitive stress, repetitive motion, cumulative trauma disorders, carpal tunnel syndrome, and other causes. Cumulative trauma disorders (CTDs) are muscle and skeletal injuries that occur when workers repetitively use the same muscles to perform tasks. *Carpal tunnel syndrome*, a cumulative trauma disorder, is an injury common to people who put their hands through repetitive motions such as typing, playing certain musical instruments, cutting, and sewing.

Cumulative trauma disorders (CTDs) Muscle and skeletal injuries that occur when workers repetitively use the same muscles to perform tasks.

Problems caused by repetitive and cumulative injuries occur in a variety of work settings. The meatpacking industry has a very high level of CTDs. Grocery cashiers experience CTDs from repetitively twisting their wrists when they scan bar codes on canned goods. Office workers experience CTDs too, primarily from doing extensive typing and data entry on computers and computer-related equipment. Most recently, attention has focused on the application of ergonomic principles to the design of work stations where workers extensively use personal computers, portable message devices, cell phones, and video display terminals for extended periods of time.

Internet Research

Office of Ergonomics Research Committee
For ergonomic research findings and links to ergonomic information, visit this Website at: http://thomsonedu.com/management/mathis.

OSHA and Ergonomics OSHA has approached ergonomics concerns by adopting voluntary guidelines for specific problem industries and jobs, gone after industries with serious ergonomic problems, and given employers tools for identifying and controlling ergonomics hazards. Among the industries receiving guidelines are nursing homes, poultry processors, and retail grocery stores.

Successful Ergonomics Programs A successful ergonomics program has several components. First, management must commit to reducing injuries caused by repetition and cumulative trauma, including providing financial and other resources to support the efforts. Involvement of employees is key to getting employee support.[13] Other actions should include reviewing jobs where CTD problems could exist and ensuring that proper equipment, seating, lighting, and other engineering solutions are utilized. Also, supervisors and managers should be trained to observe signs of CTD and on how to respond to employee complaints about musculoskeletal and repetitive motion problems.

Work Assignments and OSHA

The rights of employees regarding certain work assignments have been addressed as part of OSHA regulations. Two prominent areas where work assignments and concerns about safety and health meet are reproductive health and unsafe work.

Work Assignments and Reproductive Health Related to unsafe work is the issue of assigning employees to work in areas where their ability to have children may be affected by exposure to chemical hazards. Women who are able to bear children or who are pregnant have presented the primary concerns, but in some situations the possibility that men might become sterile has also been a concern.

In a court case involving reproductive health, the Supreme Court held that Johnson Controls violated the Civil Rights Act and the Pregnancy Discrimination Act through a policy of keeping women of childbearing capacity out of jobs that might expose them to lead.[14] Although employers have no *absolute* protection from liability, the following actions can help:

- Maintain a safe workplace for all by seeking the safest working methods.
- Comply with all state and federal safety laws.
- Inform employees of any known risks.
- Document employee acceptance of any risks.

Refusing Unsafe Work Both union and non-union workers have refused to work when they considered the work unsafe. In many court cases, that refusal has been found to be justified. The conditions for refusing work because of safety concerns include the following:

- The employee's fear is objectively reasonable.
- The employee has tried to have the dangerous condition corrected.
- Using normal procedures to solve the problem has not worked.

OSHA Recordkeeping Requirements

Employers are generally required to maintain a detailed annual record of the various types of injuries, accidents, and fatalities for inspection by OSHA representatives and for submission to the agency. OSHA guidelines state that facilities whose accident records are below the national average rarely need inspecting. Many organizations must complete OSHA Form 300 to report workshop accidents and injuries. These organizations include firms having frequent hospitalizations, injuries, illnesses, or work-related deaths, and firms in a labor statistics survey conducted by OSHA each year. However, no one knows how many industrial accidents go unreported. It may be many more than anyone suspects, despite increased surveillance of accident-reporting records by OSHA.

Reporting Injuries and Illnesses Four types of injuries or illnesses are defined by the Occupational Safety and Health Act. They are as follows:

- *Injury- or illness-related deaths:* fatalities at workplaces or caused by work-related actions
- *Lost-time or disability injuries:* job-related injuries or disabling occurrences that cause an employee to miss regularly scheduled work on the day following the accident
- *Medical care injuries:* injuries that require treatment by a physician but do not cause an employee to miss a regularly scheduled work turn
- *Minor injuries:* injuries that require first aid treatment and do not cause an employee to miss the next regularly scheduled work turn

The recordkeeping requirements for these injuries and illnesses are summarized in Figure 15-5. Notice that only very minor injuries do not have to be recorded for OSHA. For example: As Brian was repairing a conveyor belt, his hand slipped and hit the sharp edge of a steel bar. His hand was cut, and he was rushed to the hospital. He received five stitches and was told by the doctor not to use his hand for three days. This injury is recorded in the OSHA Form 300 log because the stitches and restricted duty require that it be recorded.

OSHA Inspections

The Occupational Safety and Health Act provides for on-the-spot inspections by OSHA representatives, called compliance officers or inspectors. In *Marshall v. Barlow's, Inc.,* the U.S. Supreme Court held that safety inspectors must produce a search warrant if an employer refuses to allow an inspector into the plant voluntarily. The Court also ruled that an inspector does not have to show probable cause to obtain a search warrant. A warrant can easily be obtained if a search is part of a general enforcement plan.[15]

Dealing with an Inspection When an OSHA compliance officer arrives, managers should ask to see the inspector's credentials. Next, the HR representative for the employer should insist on an opening conference with the compliance officer. The compliance officer may request that a union representative, an employee, and a company representative be present while the inspection is conducted. During the inspection, the officer checks organizational records to see if they are being maintained and to determine the number of accidents that have occurred. Following this review of the safety records, the officer conducts an on-the-spot inspection and may use a wide variety of equipment to test compliance with standards. After the inspection, the compliance officer can issue citations for any violations of standards and provisions of the act.

Citations and Violations Although OSHA inspectors can issue citations for violations of the provisions of the act, whether or not a citation is issued depends on the severity and extent of the problems, and on the employer's

FIGURE 15-5	Guide to Recordability of Cases Under the Occupational Safety and Health Act

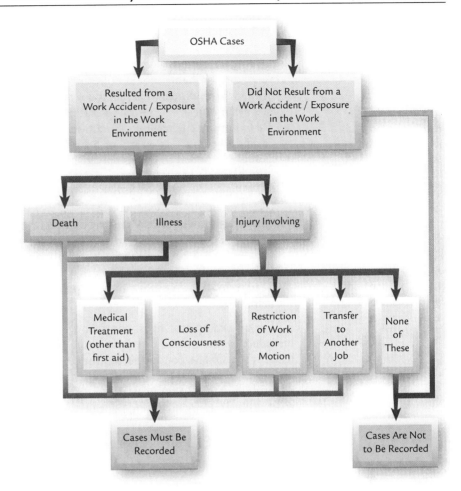

Source: U.S. Department of Labor Statistics, *What Every Employer Needs to Know About OSHA Record Keeping,* www.bls.gov.

knowledge of them. In addition, depending on the nature and number of violations, penalties can be assessed against employers. The nature and extent of the penalties depend on the type and severity of the violations as determined by OSHA officials.

A number of different types of violations are cited by OSHA. Ranging from the most severe to minimal, including a special category for repeated violations, the most common are as follows:

- *Imminent danger:* When there is reasonable certainty that the condition will cause death or serious physical harm if it is not corrected immediately, an imminent-danger citation is issued and a notice posted by an inspector. Imminent-danger situations are handled on the highest-priority basis. They are reviewed by a regional OSHA director and must be corrected immediately. If the condition is serious enough and the employer does not cooperate, a representative of OSHA may obtain a federal injunction to close the company until the condition is corrected. The absence of guardrails to prevent employees from falling into heavy machinery is one example of an imminent danger.

- *Serious:* When a condition could probably cause death or serious physical harm, and the employer should know of the condition, OSHA issues a serious-violation citation. Examples of serious violations are the absence of a protective screen on a lathe and the lack of a blade guard on an electric saw.
- *Other than serious:* Violations that could impact employees' health or safety but probably would not cause death or serious harm are called "other than serious." Having loose ropes in a work area might be classified as an other-than-serious violation.
- *De minimis:* A *de minimis* condition is one not directly and immediately related to employees' safety or health. No citation is issued, but the condition is mentioned to the employer. Lack of doors on toilet stalls is a common example of a *de minimis* violation.
- *Willful and repeated:* Citations for willful and repeated violations are issued to employers who have been previously cited for violations. If an employer knows about a safety violation or has been warned of a violation and does not correct the problem, a second citation is issued. The penalty for a willful and repeated violation can be high. For example, if death results from an accident that involves such a safety violation, a jail term of six months can be imposed on responsible executives or managers.

For an example of fines, consider a case in which a West Virginia metal manufacturer instructed its employees to operate the machines differently than usual when OSHA conducted an inspection. It also hid pieces of equipment, and management lied about its usual practices. These actions led to a "willful" violation and $288,000 in fines for 23 violations, primarily because the firm tried to cover up its non-compliance.[16]

Critique of OSHA Inspection Efforts

OSHA has been criticized on several fronts. Because the agency has so many work sites to inspect, many employers have only a relatively small chance of being inspected. Some suggest that many employers pay little attention to OSHA enforcement efforts for this reason. Labor unions and others have criticized OSHA and Congress for not providing enough inspectors. For instance, it is common to find that many of the work sites at which workers suffered severe injuries or deaths had not been inspected in the previous five years.

Employers, especially smaller ones, continue to complain about the complexity of complying with OSHA standards and the costs associated with penalties and with making changes required to remedy problem areas. Larger firms can afford to hire safety and health specialists and establish more proactive programs. However, smaller firms that cannot afford to do so still have to comply with the regulations, which leads to managers having to be more involved in safety compliance.

SAFETY MANAGEMENT

Well-designed and well-managed safety programs can pay dividends in reduced accidents and associated costs, such as workers' compensation and possible fines. Further, accidents and other safety concerns usually decline as a result of management efforts that emphasize safety. Often, the difference between high-performing firms with good occupational safety records and other firms

FIGURE 15-6	Typical Division of HR Responsibilities: Health, Safety, and Security

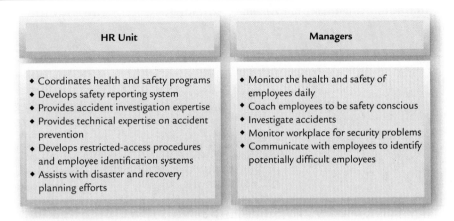

HR Unit	Managers
• Coordinates health and safety programs • Develops safety reporting system • Provides accident investigation expertise • Provides technical expertise on accident prevention • Develops restricted-access procedures and employee identification systems • Assists with disaster and recovery planning efforts	• Monitor the health and safety of employees daily • Coach employees to be safety conscious • Investigate accidents • Monitor workplace for security problems • Communicate with employees to identify potentially difficult employees

is that the former have effective safety management programs. As Figure 15-6 indicates, both HR and operating managers must coordinate health, safety, and security efforts.

Successful safety management has been researched extensively.[17] A summary of what is known about managing safety effectively includes the following components:

■ Organizational commitment
■ Policies, discipline, and recordkeeping
■ Training and communication
■ Participation (safety committees)
■ Inspection, investigation, and evaluation

Organizational Commitment and a Safety Culture

At the heart of safety management is an organizational commitment to a comprehensive safety effort that should be coordinated at the top level of management and include all members of the organization. It also should be reflected in managerial actions. If the president of a small electrical manufacturing firm does not wear a hard hat in the manufacturing shop, he can hardly expect to enforce a requirement that all employees wear hard hats in the shop.

Support by management and continuing management/employee relations are two key aspects affecting the extent of occupational accidents.[18] One result of a strong commitment to safety is that a "safety culture" pervades the organization. Firms such as Johnson & Johnson, DuPont Chemical and Energy Operations, and Frito-Lay are well known for emphasizing safety as part of their organizational cultures.

Three approaches are used by employers in managing safety. Figure 15-7 shows the organizational, engineering, and individual approaches and their components. Successful programs may use all three in dealing with safety issues.

Safety and Engineering Employers can prevent some accidents by designing machines, equipment, and work areas so that workers who perform potentially dangerous jobs cannot injure themselves and others. Providing safety equipment and guards on machinery, installing emergency switches, installing

FIGURE 15-7   Approaches to Effective Safety Management

safety rails, keeping aisles clear, and installing adequate ventilation, lighting, heating, and air conditioning can all help make work environments safer.

Designing a job properly requires consideration of the physical setting of the job. The way the work space surrounding a job is utilized can influence the worker's performance of the job itself. Several factors that affect safety have been identified, including size of work area, kinds of materials used, sensory conditions, distance between work areas, and interference from noise and traffic flow.

Individual Considerations and Safety Engineers approach safety from the perspective of redesigning the machinery or the work area. Industrial psychologists and "human factors" experts see safety differently. They address the proper match of individuals to jobs and emphasize employee training in safety methods, fatigue reduction, and health awareness.

Numerous field studies with thousands of employees, conducted by experts, have looked at the human factors in accidents. The results have shown a definite relationship between cognitive factors and occupational safety.[19] Similarly, behavior-based safety (BBS) approaches are efforts to reduce *risky behavior* and increase safe behavior by defining unsafe behavior and attempting to change it.[20] While BBS is beneficial, it does not constitute a complete approach to dealing with safety.

Work schedules can be another cause for accidents. The relationship between work schedules and accidents can be explained as follows: Fatigue based on physical exertion sometimes exists in the industrial workplace of today. Boredom, which occurs when a person is required to do the same tasks for a long period of time, is rather common. As fatigue increases, motivation decreases; when motivation decreases, workers' attention wanders, and the likelihood of accidents increases.[21] A particular area of concern is *overtime* in work scheduling. Overtime work has been consistently related to accident

UPS Delivers Safety

The brown trucks and facilities of United Parcel Service are seen worldwide. But what is not seen by most customers is the significant improvement in safety that UPS has achieved in the past several years. Many of UPS's more than 300,000 employees are constantly handling packages, lifting boxes, driving vehicles, and otherwise are at risk of injuries.

UPS received an Optimas award from *Workforce Management* for efforts that led to a decrease in worker injury rates from 27.2 injuries per 200,000 hours worked in 1996 to 10.2 injuries per 200,000 hours worked in 2004. Over the next three years the firm saw a continuing decrease in injuries.

Key to the dramatic decrease was creating 2,400 safety committees of drivers and parcel handlers to create a company program, Comprehensive Health and Safety Process. The program focused first on reducing worker sprains and strains, the most common injuries. The committees conduct injury investigations, train employees on workplace safety, and evaluate every accident. Checklists for safety issues have been developed for use in training committee members and employees on ways to avoid sprains and strains. Committee members even counsel employees who are seen lifting or bending improperly. These examples illustrate how UPS is delivering safety to its employees, which is paying off in reduced costs for the company as well.[23]

incidence because the more overtime worked, the higher the incidence of severe accidents.

Another area of concern is the relationship of accident rates to *different shifts,* particularly late-night shifts. Because there tend to be fewer supervisors and managers working the "graveyard" shifts, workers tend to receive less training and supervision. Both of these factors lead to higher accident rates.

Safety Policies, Discipline, and Recordkeeping

Designing safety policies and rules and disciplining violators are important components of safety efforts. Frequently reinforcing the need for safe behavior and frequently supplying feedback on positive safety practices are also effective ways of improving worker safety. Such safety-conscious efforts must involve employees, supervisors, managers, safety specialists, and HR staff members.[22]

For policies about safety to be effective, good recordkeeping about accidents, causes, and other details is necessary. Without records, an employer cannot track its safety performance, compare benchmarks against other employers, and may not realize the extent of its safety problems.

Safety Training and Communication

Good safety training reduces accidents. Supervisors should receive the training first, and then employees should receive it as well, because untrained workers are more likely to have accidents. The HR Best Practices describes how UPS improved its safety performance.

Safety training can be done in various ways. Regular sessions with supervisors, managers, and employees are often coordinated by HR staff members. Communication of safety procedures, reasons why accidents occurred, and what to do in an emergency is critical. Without effective communication about safety, training is insufficient. To reinforce safety training, continuous communication to develop safety consciousness is necessary. Merely sending safety memos is not enough. Producing newsletters, changing safety posters, continually updating bulletin boards, and posting safety information in visible areas are also recommended. A study in the food processing industry found that after supervisory safety training, a significant reduction in worker compensation claims was seen in the areas where the trained supervisors worked.[24]

Employers may need to communicate in a variety of media and languages. Such efforts are important to address the special needs of workers who have vision, speech, or hearing impairments; who are not proficient in English; or who are challenged in other ways.

Safety Committees

Employees frequently participate in safety planning through safety committees, often composed of workers from a variety of levels and departments. A safety committee generally meets at regularly scheduled times, has specific responsibilities for conducting safety reviews, and makes recommendations for changes necessary to avoid future accidents. Usually, at least one member of the committee comes from the HR department. The UPS example from the HR Best Practices feature illustrates the impact that safety committees can have.

Companies must take care to ensure that managers do not compose a majority on their safety committees. Otherwise, they may be in violation of provisions of the National Labor Relations Act, commonly known as the Wagner Act. That act, as explained in detail in Chapter 17, prohibits employers from "dominating a labor organization." Some safety committees have been ruled to be labor organizations because they deal with working conditions.

In approximately 32 states, all but the smallest employers may be required to establish safety committees. From time to time, legislation has been introduced at the federal level to require joint management/employee safety committees. But as yet, no federal provisions have been enacted.

Inspection, Investigation, and Evaluation

It is not necessary to wait for an OSHA inspector to check the work area for safety hazards. Inspections may be done by a safety committee or by a safety coordinator regularly. Problem areas should be addressed immediately in order to keep work productivity at the highest possible levels. Also, OSHA inspects organizations with above-average rates of lost workdays more frequently.

When accidents occur, they should be investigated by the employer's safety committee or safety coordinator. The phases of accident investigation are depicted in Figure 15-8. Identifying why an accident occurred is useful; taking steps to prevent similar accidents from occurring is even more important.

Closely related to accident investigation is research to determine ways of preventing accidents. Employing safety engineers or having outside experts evaluate the safety of working conditions is useful. If many similar accidents seem to occur in an organizational unit, a safety training program may be necessary to emphasize safe working practices. As an example, an Oregon medical center reported a greater-than-average number of back injuries among employees who lifted heavy patients. Installation of patient lifting devices and safety training on the proper way to use them was initiated . As a result, the number of worker injuries was reduced over two years.[25]

FIGURE 15-8   Phases of Accident Investigation

ACCIDENT → 1. Review the Scene → 2. Interview Employees/Others → 3. Prepare Report → 4. Identify Recommendations

Measuring Safety Efforts Organizations should monitor and evaluate their safety efforts. Just as organizational accounting records are audited, a firm's safety efforts should be audited periodically as well. Accident and injury statistics should be compared with previous accident patterns to identify any significant changes. This analysis should be designed to measure progress in safety management.

Various activities should be measured. Some common ones are workers' compensation costs per injury/illness, percentage of injuries/illnesses by department, work shifts, and job categories, and incident rate comparisons with industry and benchmark targets. Regardless of the specific measures used, it is critical to be able to track and evaluate safety management efforts using relevant HR metrics.

Employers in a variety of industries have found that emphasizing health and safety pays off in a number of ways. Lower employee benefits costs for health care, fewer work-related accidents, lower workers' compensation costs, and more productive employees are all results of employers' stressing health and safety.

EMPLOYEE HEALTH

Employee health problems are varied—and somewhat inevitable. They can range from minor illnesses such as colds to serious illnesses related to the jobs performed. Some employees have emotional health problems; others have alcohol or drug problems. Some problems are chronic; others are transitory. All may affect organizational operations and individual employee productivity.

Employers face a variety of workplace health issues. Previously in this chapter, cumulative trauma injuries and exposure to hazardous chemicals were discussed because OSHA has addressed these concerns through regulations or standards. Other concerns associated with employee health include substance abuse, emotional/mental health, workplace air quality, smoking, and obesity.

Substance Abuse

Substance abuse Use of illicit substances or misuse of controlled substances, alcohol, or other drugs.

Use of illicit substances or misuse of controlled substances, alcohol, or other drugs is called substance abuse. The millions of substance abusers in the workforce cost global employers billions of dollars annually, although recently there has been a decline in illegal drug use by employees from 13% in 1988 to 4% currently.[26]

In the United States, the incidence of substance abuse is greatest among young single men. Also, blue-collar workers are more likely than white-collar

FIGURE 15-9   Common Signs of Substance Abuse

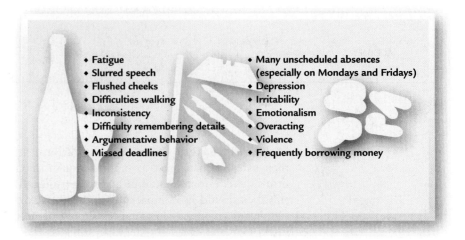

- ◆ Fatigue
- ◆ Slurred speech
- ◆ Flushed cheeks
- ◆ Difficulties walking
- ◆ Inconsistency
- ◆ Difficulty remembering details
- ◆ Argumentative behavior
- ◆ Missed deadlines
- ◆ Many unscheduled absences (especially on Mondays and Fridays)
- ◆ Depression
- ◆ Irritability
- ◆ Emotionalism
- ◆ Overacting
- ◆ Violence
- ◆ Frequently borrowing money

workers to abuse substances. Figure 15-9 shows common signs of substance abuse. However, not all signs are present in any one case. A pattern that includes some of these behaviors should be a reason to pay closer attention.

Employers' concerns about substance abuse stem from the ways it alters work behaviors, causing increased tardiness, increased absenteeism, a slower work pace, a higher rate of mistakes, and less time spent at the work station. It can also cause an increase in withdrawal (physical and psychological) and antagonistic behaviors, which may lead to workplace violence.

Alcohol testing and drug testing are used by many employers, especially following an accident or some other reasonable cause. Some employers also use random testing programs. The U.S. Department of Transportation requires drug testing for aviation workers, commercial freight carrier employees, railroad workers, mass transit employees, pipeline employees, and commercial vessel operators.

Types of Drug Tests There are several different types of tests for drug use: urinalysis, radioimmunoassay of hair, surface swiping, and fitness-for-duty testing.[27] The innovative *fitness-for-duty tests* can be used alone or in conjunction with drug testing. These tests can distinguish individuals under the influence of alcohol or prescription drugs to the extent that their abilities to perform their jobs are impaired. Some firms use fitness-for-duty tests to detect work performance safety problems before putting a person behind dangerous equipment. As an example, in one firm when a crew of delivery truck drivers comes to work, they are asked to "play" a video game—one that can have serious consequences. Unless the video game machine presents a receipt saying they passed the test, they are not allowed to drive their trucks that day. It works like this: the computer has already established a baseline for each employee. Subsequent testing measures the employees against their baselines. Interestingly, most test failures are not drug or alcohol related. Rather, fatigue, illness, and personal problems more frequently render a person unfit to perform a sensitive job.

Handling Substance Abuse Cases The Americans with Disabilities Act (ADA) affects how management can handle substance abuse cases. Current users of *illegal* drugs are specifically excluded from the definition of *disabled* under the act. However, those addicted to *legal* substances (alcohol, for example) and prescription drugs are considered disabled under the ADA. Also, recovering substance abusers are considered disabled under the ADA.

To encourage employees to seek help for their substance abuse problems, a *firm-choice option* is usually recommended and has been endorsed legally. In this procedure, a supervisor or a manager confronts the employee privately about unsatisfactory work-related behaviors. Then, in keeping with the disciplinary system, the employee is offered a choice between help and discipline. Treatment options and consequences of further unsatisfactory performance are clearly discussed, including what the employer will do. Confidentiality and follow-up are critical when employers use the firm-choice option.

Emotional/Mental Health

Many individuals today are facing work, family, and personal life pressures. Although most people manage these pressures successfully, some individuals have difficulty handling the demands. Also, specific events, such as death of a spouse, divorce, or medical problems, can affect individuals who otherwise have been coping successfully with life pressures. A variety of emotional/mental health issues arise at work that must be addressed by employers. It is important to note that emotional/mental illnesses such as schizophrenia and depression are considered disabilities under the ADA. Employers should be cautious when using disciplinary policies if employees diagnosed with such illnesses have work-related problems.

Stress that keeps individuals from successfully handling the multiple demands they face is one concern. All people encounter stress; when "stress overload" hits, work-related consequences can result. HR professionals, managers, and supervisors all must be prepared to handle employee stress; otherwise, employees may "burn out" or exhibit unhealthy behaviors, such as drinking too much alcohol, misusing prescription drugs, and bursting out in anger. Beyond trying to communicate with the employees and relieving some workload pressures, it is generally recommended that supervisors and managers contact the HR staff, who may intervene and then refer affected employees to outside resources through employee assistance programs.

Depression is another common emotional/mental health concern. The effects of depression are seen at all organizational levels, from warehouses and accounting offices to executive suites. Often, employees who appear to be depressed are guided to employee assistance programs and helped with obtaining medical treatment.

Workplace Air Quality

A number of employees work in settings where air quality is a health issue. Poor air quality may occur in "sealed" buildings (where windows cannot be opened) and when airflow is reduced to save energy and cut operating costs. Also, inadequate ventilation, as well as airborne contamination from carpets, molds, copy machines, adhesives, and fungi, can cause poor air quality and employee illnesses. In industrial settings, the presence of various chemicals and substances also can lead to poor air quality.

Air quality concerns prompted the U.S. Environmental Protection Agency (EPA) to define *sick building syndrome* as a situation in which occupants experience acute health problems and discomfort that appear to be linked to time spent in a building. Also, OSHA has investigated workplace illnesses caused by poor air quality. One major contributor to air quality problems is smoking in workplaces.

Smoking at Work

Arguments and rebuttals characterize the smoking-at-work controversy, and statistics abound. A multitude of state and local laws deal with smoking in the workplace and in public places. In response to health studies, complaints by non-smokers, and resulting state laws, many employers have instituted no-smoking policies throughout their workplaces. Although employees who smoke tend to complain initially when a smoking ban is instituted, they seem to have little difficulty adjusting within a few weeks. Many quit smoking or reduce the number of cigarettes they inhale and exhale each workday. Some employers also offer smoking cessation workshops as part of health promotion efforts.

Health Promotion

Health promotion
Supportive approach of facilitating and encouraging healthy actions and lifestyles among employees.

Employers concerned about maintaining a healthy workforce must move beyond simply providing healthy working conditions and begin promoting employee health and wellness in other ways. Health promotion is a supportive approach of facilitating and encouraging healthy actions and lifestyles among employees. Health promotion efforts can range from providing information and increasing employee awareness of health issues to creating an organizational culture supportive of employee health enhancements, as Figure 15-10 indicates. Going beyond simple compliance with workplace safety and health regulations, organizations engage in health promotion by encouraging employees to make physiological, mental, and social choices that improve their health.

The first level of health promotion (see Figure 15-10) leaves much to individual initiatives for following through and making changes in actions and behaviors. Employers provide information on such topics as weight control, stress management, nutrition, exercise, and smoking cessation. Even though such efforts may be beneficial for some employees, employers who wish to impact employees' health must offer second-level efforts, such as more comprehensive programs and actions that focus on the lifestyle "wellness" of employees. The third level requires a commitment to wellness that is seldom seen in employers.

Obesity Nearly one-third of U.S. adults are obese and another one-third are overweight. Obesity is a fact of modern life and a concern to employers, and a movement to involve employers in employee weight management is apparently gaining momentum. The reason employers are concerned is cost. The

FIGURE 15-10   Health Promotion Levels

LEVEL 1
Information and Awareness
- Brochures and materials
- Health risk screenings
- Health tests and measurements
- Special events and classes

LEVEL 2
Lifestyle Wellness
- Wellness education program
- Regular health classes
- Employee assistance programs
- Support groups
- Health incentives

LEVEL 3
Health Emphasis
- Benefits integrated with programs
- Dedicated resources and facilities
- Continous health promotion
- Health education curriculum

economic costs of obesity include doctor visits, diabetes, high blood pressure, higher health-care premiums, and lost workdays.[28] To address the increasing problem of obese employees, employers are taking a number of actions. Some firms are offering incentives to workers who are involved in physical fitness programs and lose weight. One firm with an active program is Microsoft. Over 2,000 employees have lost over 61,000 pounds as part of a program focusing on obese employees. Both employees and Microsoft have benefited from this program.[29]

Wellness Programs Employers' desires to improve productivity, decrease absenteeism, and control health-care costs have come together in the "wellness" movement. Wellness programs are designed to maintain or improve employee health before problems arise by encouraging self-directed lifestyle changes. Early wellness programs were aimed primarily at reducing the cost and risk of disease. Newer programs emphasize healthy lifestyles and environment, including reduced cholesterol and heart disease risks and individualized exercise programs and follow-up. Employer-sponsored support groups have been established for individuals dealing with health issues such as weight loss, nutrition, and smoking cessation. The top-rated topics for wellness programs are stress management, exercise/fitness, screenings/checkups, health insurance education, disease management (heart disease, diabetes, etc.), nutrition and diet, and smoking cessation.

On-line and Web-based wellness programs have grown in popularity. Ford, Microsoft, Chevron, and Watson Wyatt are just a few of the companies that offer on-line wellness programs. These programs use information and subtle psychology to motivate people to live healthier lifestyles. They typically focus on exercise, nutrition, sleep, stress, and life balance.[30]

Employee Assistance Programs One method organizations use as a broad-based response to health issues is an employee assistance program (EAP), which provides counseling and other help to employees having emotional, physical, or other personal problems. In such a program, an employer contracts with a counseling agency. Employees who have problems may then contact the agency, either voluntarily or by employer referral, for assistance with a broad range of problems. Counseling costs are paid for by the employer, either in total or up to a pre-established limit.

EAPs commonly provide help with troubled employees, problem identification, short-term intervention, and referral services. The most common employee issues dealt with in EAPs are: (1) depression and anxiety, (2) marital and relationship problems, (3) legal difficulties, and (4) family and children concerns. Other areas commonly addressed as part of an EAP include substance abuse, financial counseling, and career advice. EAP participation rates by employees are only 5% to 7%, which is low, and indicates that many individuals are not using this health benefit as often as would be expected.[31]

Critical to employee usage of an EAP is preserving confidentiality. For that reason, employers outsource EAPs to trained professionals, who usually report only the numbers of employees and services provided, rather than details on individuals using an EAP. The effectiveness of EAPs depends on how well employers integrate and support them in the workplace. Done well, EAPs can help reduce health-care and other costs.[32]

Wellness programs
Programs designed to maintain or improve employee health before problems arise by encouraging self-directed lifestyle changes.

Internet Research

Wellness Councils of America
This Website provides free resources for corporate and hospital wellness programs. Visit the site at: http://thomsonedu.com/management/mathis.

Employee assistance program (EAP)
Program that provides counseling and other help to employees having emotional, physical, or other personal problems.

Internet Research

Employee Assistance Program Directory
This Website contains a nationwide directory of employee assistance program providers and consultants in the United States. Link to their Website at: http://thomsonedu.com/management/mathis.

Measuring Health Promotion Effects Organizations can assess the effectiveness of their health promotion programs in a number of ways. Looking at participation rates by employees is one means. Although participation rates are not as high as desired, the programs have resulted in healthier lifestyles for more employees. Cost-benefit analyses by organizations also tend to support the continuation of such programs. The return on investment (ROI) for one firm has been estimated to be $50 million total savings over a five-year period. This ROI represents a payoff of $3 for every $1 spent on employee wellness efforts.[33]

SECURITY CONCERNS AT WORK

Traditionally, when employers have addressed worker health, safety, and security, they have been concerned about reducing workplace accidents, improving workers' safety practices, and reducing health hazards at work. However, in the past decade, providing security for employees has become important. Notice that virtually all of these areas have significant HR implications. Heading the list of security concerns is workplace violence.

Workplace Violence

Worldwide violence in workplaces is increasing. In the United States, in a typical week in workplaces 25 employees are seriously injured and 1 is killed. A significant number of workplace fatalities involve attacks against workers such as police officers, taxi drivers, and convenience store clerks. Often, these deaths occur during armed robbery attempts. However, in most of the remaining cases, the killer has some relationship with the workplace, such as a co-worker, former employee, customer, etc. What has shocked many employers in a variety of industries has been the number of disgruntled employees or former employees who have resorted to violence, including homicide in the workplace, to deal with their anger and grievances. Certainly the tragedy at Virginia Tech University illustrated the consequences of workplace violence.

Workplace Violence Warning Signs There are a number of warning signs and characteristics of a potentially violent person at work. Individuals who have committed the most violent acts have had the relatively common profile depicted in Figure 15-11. A person with some of these signs and characteristics may cope for years until a trauma pushes the individual over the edge. A profound humiliation or rejection, the end of a marriage, the loss of a lawsuit, or termination from a job may make a difficult employee turn violent.

Domestic Causes of Workplace Violence Too often, violence that begins at home with family or "friends" can spill over to the workplace. One in five homicides of women at work are perpetrated by current or former husbands or boyfriends. Also, many abused women report being harassed frequently at work, by telephone, or in person by abusing partners.

An inappropriate reaction by employers is to ignore obvious signs of domestic violence. In fact, some employers have been sued and found liable for ignoring pleas for help from employees who later are victims of domestic violence in company parking lots or on employer premises.[34]

FIGURE 15-11	Profile of a Potentially Violent Employee

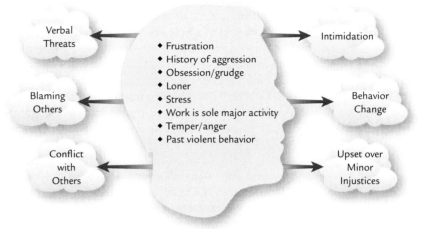

Management of Workplace Violence The increase in workplace violence has led many employers to develop policies and practices for preventing and responding to workplace violence. One aspect of HR policies is to identify how workplace violence is to be dealt with in conjunction with disciplinary actions and referrals to EAPs. Training of managers and others is crucial, as the HR On the Job indicates.

One application of these policies is a *violence response team*. Composed of security personnel, key managers, HR staff members, and selected employees, this team functions much like a safety committee but with a different focus.

HR ON-THE-JOB

Workplace Violence Training

Managers, HR staff members, supervisors, and employees should be trained on how to recognize the signs of a potentially violent employee and what to do when violence occurs. During training at many firms, participants learn the typical profile of potentially violent employees and are trained to notify the HR department and to refer employees to outside counseling professionals.

Specific suggestions addressed in training for dealing with potentially violent employees typically include the following:

■ Notice verbal and non-verbal reactions by individuals that may indicate anger or hostility.
■ Listen to individuals exhibiting such reactions, and pay attention to the words, actions, and unspoken "messages."

■ Ask questions requiring explanations and longer answers that allow individuals to "vent."
■ Respond calmly and non-threateningly to individuals' emotions, and acknowledge concerns and understanding about how the individuals feel.
■ Get assistance from others, particularly HR staff members or a manager not directly affected by the situation being discussed.
■ Indicate the need for time to respond to the concerns voiced, and then set up another time for follow-up.
■ Notify security personnel and HR staff members whenever employees' behaviors change dramatically or when job disciplinary action may provoke significant reactions by employees.

Such teams conduct analyses, respond to and investigate employee threats, and may even help calm angry, volatile employees.

Employers must be careful because they may face legal action for discrimination if they discharge employees for behaviors that often precede violent acts. For example, in several cases, employees who were terminated or suspended for making threats or even engaging in physical actions against their co-workers then sued their employers by claiming they had mental disabilities covered under the Americans with Disabilities Act.

Post-violence response is another part of managing workplace violence. Whether the violence results in physical injuries or deaths or just intense interpersonal conflicts, it is important that employers have plans to respond afterward. Their response must reassure employees who may be fearful of returning to work or who experience anxiety and sleeplessness, among other reactions. Providing referrals to EAP resources, allowing employees time to meet with HR staff, and arranging for trained counselors on-site are all part of post-violence response efforts.

Security Management

An overall approach to security management is needed to address a wide range of issues, including workplace violence. Often, HR managers have responsibility for security programs or work closely with security managers or consultants.

Security audit
Comprehensive review of organizational security.

Security Audit In a security audit, HR staff conduct a comprehensive review of organizational security. Sometimes called a *vulnerability analysis,* such an audit uses managers inside the organization (such as the HR manager and the facilities manager) and outsiders (such as security consultants, police officers, fire officials, and computer security experts) to assess security issues.

Typically, a security audit begins with a survey of the area around the facility. Such factors as lighting in parking lots, traffic flow, location of emergency response services, crime in the surrounding neighborhood, and the layout of the buildings and grounds are evaluated. The audit also may include a review of the security available within the firm, including the capabilities of guards. Another part of the security audit reviews disaster plans, which address how to deal with events such as earthquakes, floods, tornadoes, hurricanes, and fires. Efforts to prepare for catastrophes like these have become even more prominent since 9/11, the Katrina hurricane in 2005, and other recent events.

Controlled Access A key part of security involves controlling access to the physical facilities of the organization. As mentioned earlier, many workplace homicides occur during robberies. Therefore, employees who are most vulnerable, such as taxi drivers and convenience store clerks, often are provided bulletproof partitions and restricted access areas.

Many organizations limit access to facilities and work areas by using electronic access or keycard systems. Although not foolproof, these systems can make it more difficult for an unauthorized person, such as an estranged spouse or a disgruntled ex-employee, to enter the premises. Access controls can also be used in elevators and stairwells to prevent unauthorized persons from entering designated areas within a facility.

Computer Security Yet another part of security centers on controlling access to computer systems. With so many transactions and records being handled by computers, adequate security provisions are crucial to prevent unauthorized access to computer information systems. Growth of the Internet and of e-mail systems has made computer security issues an even greater concern. This concern is magnified when individuals are terminated or leave an organization. HR staff must coordinate with information technology staff to change passwords, delete access codes, and otherwise protect company information systems.[35]

Employee Screening and Selection

A key facet of providing security is screening job applicants. HR management is somewhat limited on what can be done, particularly regarding the use of psychological tests and checking of references. However, firms that do not screen employees adequately may be subject to liability if an employee commits crimes later. For instance, an individual with a criminal record for assault was hired by a firm to maintain sound equipment in clients' homes. The employee used a passkey to enter a home and assaulted the owner; consequently, the employer was ruled liable. Of course, when selecting employees, employers must be careful to use only valid, job-related screening means and to avoid violating federal EEO laws and the Americans with Disabilities Act.

Security Personnel

Providing adequately trained security personnel in sufficient numbers is a critical part of security management. Many employers contract for these personnel with firms specializing in security. If security is handled in-house, security personnel must be selected and trained to handle a variety of workplace security problems, ranging from dealing with violent behavior by an employee to taking charge in natural disasters.

DISASTER PREPARATION AND RECOVERY PLANNING

During the past several years, a number of significant disasters have occurred. Some have been natural disasters, such as Hurricane Katrina, major snow storms in Colorado, flooding in various states, tornadoes in Texas, and forest fires in Arizona and California. Additionally, there has been growing concern about terrorism after 9/11. Also, some firms have been damaged by fires and explosions. All of these situations have led to HR management having an expanded role in disaster planning.

To prepare for any instance in which organizations and their employees are impacted by such events, *crisis management* has become an important issue.[36] Yet various surveys have found that about one-third of organizations do not have disaster plans. Of those that do, about 40% have not tested or revised their plans.[37]

Disaster Planning

For disaster planning to occur properly, three components must be addressed by HR, as depicted in Figure 15-12. Imagine that a hurricane destroys the work facility were employees work, as well as many of their homes. Or an explosion or terrorist attack prohibits workers from getting to their workplaces. Those situations illustrate why each of the components in Figure 15-12 has human dimensions to be addressed.[38]

FIGURE 15-12 Disaster Planning Components

Organizational Assessment A crucial part of organizational assessment is to establish a disaster planning team, often composed of representatives from HR, security, information technology, operations, and other areas. The purpose of this team is to conduct an organizational assessment of how various disasters might affect the organization and its employees. Then a disaster recovery plan is developed to identify how the organization will respond to different situations.

Human Impact Planning A number of areas are part of human impact planning. Such items as having backup databases for numerous company details, including employee contact information, are vital.[39] Who will take responsibilities for various duties and how these efforts will be coordinated must be identified. For instance, following Hurricane Katrina many employers could not reach employees, nor could employees contact their employers. However, firms such as Home Depot and Wal-Mart had databases outside of the Gulf Coast area. Employees could contact any other company location or a national hot-line and learn about receiving paychecks, benefits questions, and even continuing employment elsewhere. Home Depot allowed evacuees to become employees at any other U.S. location, and these stores had access to employment history and payroll data, making the worker transition easier. This example illustrates why maintaining current employee contact information is crucial. Yet estimates are that about a third of employee contact information in employer files is not current.[40]

Disaster Training All of the planning efforts may be wasted if managers and employees are not trained on what to do when disasters occur. This training covers a wide range of topics, including the following:

- First aid/CPR
- Hazardous materials containment
- Disaster escape means
- Employer contact methods
- Organizational restoration efforts

But this training is not sufficient without conducting exercises for managers and employees to use the training. Much like public schools have tornado evacuation exercises, employers may have site evacuation drills. Regular tests to ensure that information technology and databases are security accessible outside of the main location should occur. Testing responses if a workplace violence attack occurs may identify additional activities needed in an organization. Therefore, training must be a continuing consideration, and must reflect updated disaster planning efforts.

Disaster Planning for Avian Flu

A significant worldwide concern is the occurrence of environmental risks. One such concern during the past few years has been the spread of Avian flu, a virus that has occurred throughout the world, especially in Asia. The global nature of business travel has increased the likelihood of the spread of this or another deadly virus. Two key issues are whether to evacuate expatriate employees from locations where Avian flu occurs and how to protect local employees if the flu symptom occurs within an area.[41]

The concerns about Avian flu and other pandemic diseases have led OSHA to establish guidelines for employers to use. The guidelines have special sections for firms in the poultry production industry due to their higher vulnerability.[42] Of great concern is that relatively few U.S. employers and other worldwide organizations are prepared for the spread of Avian flu or any other critical environmental disease. Many of the recommendations for preparations are generally similar to other types of disaster planning, but specialized policies, programs, and training may be needed. Experts project that there could be a major epic disease spread, whether a natural one or one instigated by terrorism. Thus, risk management preparation for this specialized area is part of broader disaster preparation and recovery planning efforts.[43]

SUMMARY

- The four components of risk management are workplace safety and health, employee health/wellness promotion, workplace and worker security, and disaster preparation and recover planning.
- Health is a general state of physical, mental, and emotional well-being. Safety is a condition in which the physical well-being of people is protected. Security is the protection of employees and organizational facilities.
- Global security is a growing importance, and emerging health services, terrorism, and kidnapping are key concerns.
- Workers' compensation coverage is provided by employers to protect employees who suffer job-related injuries and illnesses.
- Both the Family and Medical Leave Act (FMLA) and the Americans with Disabilities Act (ADA) affect employer health and safety policies and practices.
- The Fair Labor Standards Act (FLSA) limits the types of work that younger employees, especially those under the age of 18, can perform.

- The Occupational Safety and Health Act states that employers have a general duty to provide safe and healthy working conditions.
- The Occupational Safety and Health Administration (OSHA) has established enforcement standards to aid in a number of areas, including hazard communication.
- Ergonomics looks at the physiological and physical demands of work.
- OSHA addresses employee work assignments, requires employers to keep records on occupational illnesses and injuries, inspects workplaces, and can issue citations for several levels of violations.
- Effective safety management requires integrating three approaches: organizational, engineering, and individual.
- Developing safety policies, disciplining violators, keeping safety records, conducting safety training, communicating on safety issues, establishing safety committees, inspecting work areas for safety concerns, investigating accidents, and evaluating safety efforts are all part of comprehensive safety management.

- Substance abuse, emotional/mental health, workplace air quality, and smoking at work, as common health issues, are growing concerns for organizations and employees.
- Employee health is promoted by employers at several levels to improve organizational operations and individual employee productivity.
- Employers have responded to health problems by establishing and supporting wellness programs and employee assistance programs (EAPs).
- Establishing and maintaining an organizational culture of health continues to pay off for a number of employers.

- Security of workplaces is important, particularly as the frequency of workplace violence increases.
- Employers can enhance security by conducting a security audit, controlling access to workplaces and computer systems, screening employees adequately during the selection process, and providing security personnel.
- Disaster preparation and recovery planning have grown as important HR concerns.

REVIEW AND APPLICATION QUESTIONS

1. How does one go about controlling workers' compensation costs, and why is that important?
2. What should an employer do when facing an OSHA inspection?
3. As the HR manager of a distribution and warehouse firm with 600 employees, you plan to discuss a company wellness program at an executive staff meeting next week. The topics to cover include what a wellness program is, how it can benefit the company and employees, and the process for establishing it. To aid in developing your presentation to the executives, consult the Website *www.welcoa.org* and other applicable Websites you can locate.

CASE

Communicating Safety and Wellness Success

Many different organizations in various industries have focused on safety and health for employees. Two examples in the communications industry illustrate how such efforts have been successful.

NorthStar Communications, based in Birmingham, Alabama, provides engineering, network, and infrastructure services to numerous communications industry firms. With 500 employees, NorthStar has emphasized safety to all managers and employees. The success of its safety efforts resulted in NorthStar's efforts being designated "Safety Program of the Year" by an international safety forum.

To emphasize the importance of safety, every NorthStar individual signs a safety pledge upon being employed. After hire, all employees are expected to identify any potential safety problems and assist co-workers as needed. A safety guidebook is posted on the firm's Website, with a special section being set for safety training and information. A safety newsletter is posted every month also.

The success of NorthStar's safety efforts is evident. Compared with an industry incident rate of 9.6%, NorthStar's rate is less than 1%. In a recent year the firm had zero lost workdays, which is extremely unusual. The safety focus of NorthStar is paying off for the employees in terms of their personal safety, as well as maintaining low safety costs for the firm.

A much larger and well-known communications firm is Cox Communications, with thousands of employees throughout the United States. At its Orange County, California, operations with 750 employees, emphasizing safety and health has produced significant results. The firm has had a 93% decline in workers' compensation incidents, and a 94% reduction in the average worker compensation claim costs over 4 years.

Safety and wellness are linked at Cox Communications. The firm offers a variety of activities to support its efforts. Health fairs, on-site physical fitness programs, stretching classes for employees, and other efforts have gotten extensive individual employee involvements. Workstations are ergonomically reviewed and changed as needed. A safety incentive program has been successful in rewarding employees for improved safety and health.

The efforts of these two different communications industry firms illustrate how safety and health are crucial parts of effective HR management. The firms, their staff members, and even customers are benefiting from these efforts.[44]

Questions

1. Identify how these two firms have incorporated elements of safety management and health promotion described in the chapter into their programs.

2. Discuss how the reductions in injuries can be used to justify the expenditures on the various programs at NorthStar and Cox.

SUPPLEMENTAL CASE

"What's Happened to Bob?"

This case concerns some of the warning signs of possible alcohol abuse and the consequences at work. (For the case, go to http://thomsonedu.com/management/mathis.)

NOTES

1. The authors acknowledge the input and contribution of ideas and research aspects on risk management by Tasha Barton, John Fleharty, and Shantell Nelson.

2. Philip S. Deming, "Crisis Management Planning: A Human Resource Challenge," *SHRM White Paper,* April 2002, 1–5.

3. Occupational Safety and Health Administration, *www.osha.gov.*

4. Stephen M. Pegula, "Occupational Fatalities: Self-Employed Workers and Wages and Salary Workers," *Monthly Labor Review,* March 2004, 30–40.

5. Mark Sawyer, "Personal Safety for Expatriates," *Workspan,* August 2006, 37–38.

6. "A King's Ransom," *The Economist,* August 26, 2006, 58–59.

7. "Benefits for Temporary Total Disability Provided by Workers' Compensation Statutes in the U.S.," U.S. Department of Labor, Office of Workers' Compensation Programs, 2006, *www.dol.gov.esa.*

8. D. Mealy, "2006 State of the Line: Analysis of Workers' Compensation Results," National Council on Compensation Insurance, 2006.

9. Jerry Landsma, "Red Flags to Spot Possible Comp Fraud," *Business Insurance,* November 24, 2003, 11–14.

10. James D. Westaby and J. Krister Lowe, "Risk-Taking Orientation and Injury Among Youth Workers," *Journal of Applied Psychology,* 90 (2005), 1027–1035.

11. Janice Comer Bradley, "How to Select the Right Protective and High-Visibility Foot and Full Protection," *Occupational Hazards,* April 2006, 20.

12. Laura Baron, James Vander Spek, and Wendy Young, "The Economics of Ergonomics," *Journal of Accountancy,* December 2006, 34–40.

13. "Report: Employee Buy-In Crucial to Ergonomic Improvement," *Human Resource Executive,* June 16, 2005, 16.

14. *United Autoworkers v. Johnson Controls, Inc.,* 111 S. Ct. 1196 (1991).

15. *Marshall v. Barlow's, Inc.,* 98 S. Ct. 1816 (1978).

16. "Labor Department Official Warns Companies Against Trying to Thwart OSHA Inspections," *Safety Director's Report No. 2-10,* October 2002, 1.

17. J. Craig Wallace, "Can Accidents and Industrial Mishaps Be Predicted?" *Journal of Business and Psychology,* 17 (2003), 503–514; and Lovisa Olafsdottir, "Prevention Health and Safety Programs in Companies Provide a More Successful

and Healthier Workplace," *Work,* 22 (2004), 27–30.

18. J. C. Wallace, Eric Popp, and Scott Mondore, "Safety Climate as a Mediator Between Foundation Climates and Occupational Accidents: A Group-Level Investigation," *Journal of Applied Psychology,* 91 (2006), 681–688.

19. J. C. Wallace and Gillad Chen, "Development and Validation of a Work-Specific Measure of Cognitive Failure: Implications for Occupational Safety," *Journal of Occupational and Organizational Psychology,* 78 (2005), 615–633.

20. Don J. Eckenfelder, "Why We Need an Antidote for Behavior-Based Safety," *Occupational Hazards,* September 2003, 98–105; and Steve Roberts, "How to Play It Safe," *Safety Management,* July 2003, 57–62.

21. Denny Holland and Joe Luetzinger, "Fatigue Management: A Literature Review," *Journal of Employee Assistance,* 33 (2003), 24–35.

22. Pamela Babcock, "Safety Consciousness," *HR Magazine,* July 2005, 67–70.

23. Based on Douglas P. Shuit, "A Left Turn for Safety," *Workforce Management,* March 2005, 49–50.

24. W. S. Shaw et al., "A Controlled Case Study of Supervisor Training to Optimize Response to Injury on the Food Processing Industry," *Work,* 26 (2006), 107.

25. Al Karr, "Lifts Help Workers Handle Patients Safely, Cut Injury Rate," *The Wall Street Journal,* February 28, 2006, B1.

26. Stephanie Armour and Del Jones, "Workers' Positive Drug Tests Decrease," *USA Today,* June 20, 2006, 3B.

27. Anne Freedman, "Drug Tests of Choice," *Human Resource Executive,* June 17, 2005, *www.workindex.com.*

28. Kelly M. Kawczynski, "Obesity and the Rise of Health-Care Costs," *WorldatWork Journal,* Fourth Quarter 2006, 68–76.

29. Michelle Conlin, "More Micro, Less Soft," *Business Week,* November 27, 2006, 42.

30. Traci Purdim, "Healthy, Wealthy, Wise and Web Based," *Industry Week,* May 2004, 52–53.

31. Gina Ruiz, "Expanded EAPs Lend a Hand to Employers' Bottom Lines," *Workforce Management,* January 16, 2006, 46–47.

32. David A. Sharar and Edward Hertenstein, "Perspectives on Commodity Pricing in Employee Assistance Programs (EAPs): A Survey of the EAP Field," *WorldatWork Journal,* First Quarter 2006, 32–41.

33. "Wellness Programs: Do They Pay a Return on Investment?" *Best Practices in HR,* Business and Legal Reports, 2006, *www.blr.com.*

34. Robert J. Nesbit, "Workplace Intervention: Domestic Violence . . . ," *Employee Benefit News,* August 2006, *www.benefitnews .com.*

35. Will Strother, "A Security Primer," *SHRM White Paper, www.shrm .org/hrtx.*

36. For an overview of HR and crisis management, see Nancy R. Lockwood, "Crisis Management in Today's Business Environment: HR's Strategic Role," *SHRM Research Quarterly,* Fourth Quarter, 2005, *www.shrm.org.*

37. Kevin Lindsey, "Crisis Alert!" *HR Magazine,* August 2006, 121–125.

38. G. Sapirsteir, "Preparing Employees for Disasters," *Business Insurance,* June 5, 2006, *www.businessinsurance .com.*

39. B. M. Testa, "One Year After Katrina. . . ." *Workforce Management,* August 28, 2006, 46.

40. R. Zeidner, "Technology Becomes HR," *SHRM Technology News,* June 2006, *www.shrm.org.*

41. J. J. Smith, "HR Needed in Firms' Avian Flu Policies to Cut Panic, Help Recovery," *SHRM Global News,* June 2006, *www.shrm.org.*

42. "OSHA Unveils New Guidance for Protecting Employees Against Avian Flu," *OSHA National News Release,* November 14, 2006, *www.osha .org.*

43. Nancy H. Woodward, "Pandemic," *HR Magazine,* May 2006, 46–52; and Connie Harden, "Preparing for a Pandemic," *Workspan,* July 2006, 22–27.

44. Based on "Safety Is a Way of Life for These Employees," *Best Practices in HR,* Business & Legal Reports, Inc., October 13, 2006, 3; and Patricia Vowinkel, "Hog Wild for Health," *Human Resource Executive,* February 2006, 61–63.

CHAPTER

16

Employee Rights and Responsibilities

After you have read this chapter, you should be able to:

- Explain the difference between statutory rights and contractual rights.

- Define employment-at-will and discuss how wrongful discharge, just cause, and due process are interrelated.

- Identify employee rights associated with free speech and access to employee records.

- Discuss issues associated with workplace monitoring, employer investigations, and drug testing.

- List elements to consider when developing an employee handbook.

- Differentiate between the positive approach and progressive approach to discipline.

HR Headline

RFID Chips to Identify Employees?

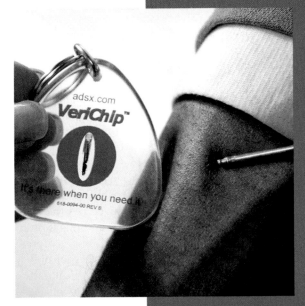

CityWatcher, a video surveillance company, recently embedded silicone chips in four of its employees. This firm was testing the technology as a way to control access to a secure room where it stores security materials for the government. The chips were embedded voluntarily in the employees' upper arms and are about the size of a dime. This technology ushered in a new means by which employees can be positively identified with electronic ID chips.

Radio-frequency identification (RFID) chips are inexpensive radio transmitters that can send a unique signal and are used to identify pets, cattle, merchandise, shipments, and apparently employees. CityWatcher's use is the first known application to employees in the United States, although the Mexican government has used RFID chips for controlling access to their Organized Crime Division.

Of course, privacy and civil liberties issues are raised by the use of RFID chips in employees. Concerns include the capacity to monitor *all* individual actions and company pressure to have the implants as a requirement for keeping one's job. The biggest selling point when compared with alternatives such as ID badges is convenience, because the devices cannot be lost. However, some people have suggested that counterfeits or swaps could be made if the payoff were sufficiently great. As with any kind of security precaution, an employer needs to compare the benefits of such precautions against its costs—and not necessarily solely in monetary terms.[1]

Three very interrelated HR issues are considered in this chapter: *employee rights, HR policies,* and *discipline.* How are they related? Employees come to work with some rights, but many more are granted or constrained by the HR policies and rules an employer sets. Further, discipline used against those who fail to follow policies and rules has employee rights dimensions as well as employer prerogative dimensions. The three concepts of rights, policies, and discipline change and evolve as laws and societal values change. Indeed, at one time the right of an employer to operate an organization as it might see fit was very strong. Today, however, that right is offset to varying extents by the increase in employee rights.

EMPLOYEE RIGHTS AND RESPONSIBILITIES

Rights Powers, privileges, or interests that belong to a person by law, nature, or tradition.

Rights generally do not exist in the abstract. Instead, they exist only when someone is successful in demanding their application. **Rights** are powers, privileges, or interests that belong to a person by law, nature, or tradition. Of course, defining a right presents considerable potential for disagreement. For example, does an employee have a right to privacy of communication in personal matters when using the employer's computer on company time? Moreover, *legal rights* may or may not correspond to certain *moral rights,* and the reverse is true as well—a situation that opens "rights" up to controversy and lawsuits.

Recently Luo Guangfu and 300 other workers sent a letter to the manager of the textile factory where they work in Guangzhou, China. They demanded that their wages be raised from less than $60 per month to the legal minimum of $69 per month. By doing so they asserted a "right" that they had as workers under Chinese law.[2]

Responsibilities Obligations to perform certain tasks and duties.

Rights are offset by **responsibilities,** which are obligations to perform certain tasks and duties. Employment is a reciprocal relationship in that both sides have rights and obligations. For example, if an employee has the right to a safe working environment, then the employer must have an obligation to provide a safe workplace. If the employer has a right to expect uninterrupted, high-quality work from the employee, then the worker has the responsibility to be on the job and to meet job performance standards. The reciprocal nature of rights and responsibilities suggests that both parties to an employment relationship should regard the other as having rights and should treat the other with respect.

Statutory Rights

Statutory rights Rights based on laws or statutes passed by federal, state, or local government.

Employees' **statutory rights** are the result of specific laws or statutes passed by federal, state, or local governments. Various federal, state, and local laws have granted employees certain rights at work, such as equal employment opportunity, collective bargaining, and workplace safety. These laws and their interpretations also have been the subjects of a considerable number of court cases.

Contractual Rights

Contractual rights Rights based on a specific contract between an employer and an employee.

An employee's **contractual rights** are based on a specific contract with an employer. For instance, a union and an employer may agree on a labor contract that specifies certain terms, conditions, and rights that employees represented by the union have with the employer.

Contracts formalize the employment relationship. For instance, when hiring an independent contractor or a consultant, an employer should use a contract to spell out the work to be performed, expected timelines, parameters, and costs and fees to be incurred. Such rights can be spelled out formally in written employment contracts or implied in employer handbooks and policies disseminated to employees.

Employment contract
Agreement that formally outlines the details of employment.

Employment Contracts An employment contract is a formal agreement that outlines the details of employment. Written employment contracts are often very detailed. Traditionally, employment contracts have been used mostly for executives and senior managers, but the use of employment contracts is filtering down the organization to include highly specialized professional and technical employees who have scarce skills.

Depending on the organization and individuals involved, employment agreements may contain a number of provisions. Figure 16-1 shows common provisions. Typically, an *identification section* lists the parties to the contract and the general nature of the employee's job duties. The level of compensation and types of benefits are often addressed, including any special compensation, benefits, incentives, or perquisites to be provided by the employer. The employment contract may also note whether the employment relationship is to be for an indeterminate time, or whether it can be renewed automatically after a specified period of time. The contract may spell out a severance agreement, continuation of benefits, and other factors related to the employee's leaving the employer.

FIGURE 16-1   Provisions in Employment Contracts

Employment Contract

- Parties to the contract
- General job duties and expectations
- Compensation and benefits
- Terms and conditions of employment
- Termination/resignation factors
- Non-compete and non-piracy agreements
- Non-solicitation of current employees
- Intellectual property and trade secrets

Date:

Employee's signature:

Company representative's signature:

Seal

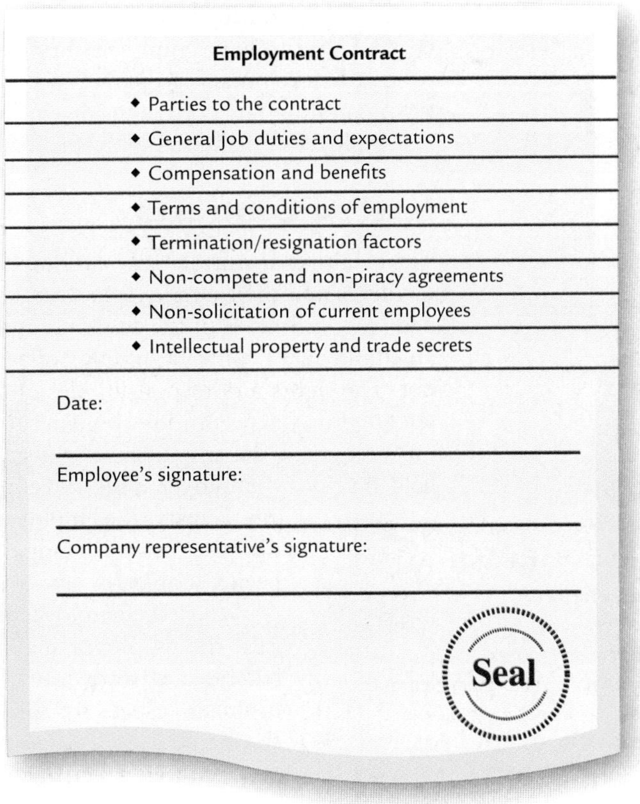

Non-compete agreements
Agreements that prohibit
individuals who leave
an organization from
competing with an
employer in the same line
of business for a specified
period of time.

Non-Compete Agreements Employment contracts may include non-compete agreements, which prohibit individuals who leave an organization from working with an employer in the same line of business for a specified period of time. A non-compete agreement may be presented as a separate contract or as a clause in an employment contract. Though primarily used with newly hired employees, some firms have required existing employees to sign non-compete agreements. Different court decisions have ruled for or against employers that have fired employees who refused to sign the agreements.[3] For example, Google hired a distinguished computer scientist who had been a Microsoft vice president. He had signed a non-compete agreement with Microsoft that he would not accept employment that competed with Microsoft for one year. Within 10 days of Google's press release, a Seattle court issued a temporary restraining order barring him from working on projects for Google similar to those he had worked on for Microsoft.[4]

Employment contracts also may contain *non-piracy agreements,* which bar former employees from soliciting business from former customers and clients for a specified period of time. For instance, a company was able to enforce a non-piracy-type agreement when two ex-employees started a competing firm and attempted to provide services to a major customer of their former company.[5] Also, clauses requiring *non-solicitation of current employees* can be incorporated into employment agreements. These clauses are written to prevent a former employee from contacting or encouraging co-workers at the former firm to join a different company, often a competitor.

Intellectual Property An additional area covered in employment contracts is protection of *intellectual property* and *trade secrets.* A 1996 federal law made the theft of trade secrets a federal crime punishable by fines up to $5 million and 15 years in jail. Employer rights in this area include the following:

- The right to keep trade secrets confidential
- The right to have employees bring business opportunities to the employer first before pursuing them elsewhere
- A common-law copyright for works and other documents prepared by employees for their employers

Implied Contracts

The idea that a contract (even an implied or unwritten one) exists between individuals and their employers affects the employment relationship. The rights and responsibilities of the employee may be spelled out in a job description, in an employment contract, in HR policies, or in a handbook, but often they are not. The rights and responsibilities of the employee may exist *only* as unwritten employer expectations about what is acceptable behavior or performance on the part of the employee. For instance, a number of court decisions have held that if an employer hires someone for an indefinite period or promises job security, the employer has created an implied contract. Such promises establish employee expectations, especially if there has been a long-term business relationship.

When the employer fails to follow up on the implied promises, the employee may pursue remedies in court. Numerous federal and state court decisions have held that such implied promises, especially when contained in an employee handbook, constitute a contract between an employer and its employees, even without a signed contract document.

Internet Research

**Human Resources
Law Index**

For legal information on workplace issues such as employment contracts and other issues, link to this Website at: http://thomsonedu.com/management/mathis.

Employment Practices Liability Insurance

Workplace litigation has reached epidemic proportion as employees who feel that their rights have been violated sue their employers. As a result, some employers have purchased insurance to try to cover their risks from numerous lawsuits. Employment practices liability insurance (EPLI) policies typically cover employer costs for legal fees, settlements, and judgments associated with employment actions. For example, at one telecommunications firm, an EPLI policy covered virtually all of a $10 million judgment against the company for racial discrimination.[6]

To determine the level of risk and premiums to be charged to employers wanting EPLI, most insurance carriers review the employers' HR policies and practices. The review may include a detailed look at an employer's HR policy manuals, employee handbooks, employment forms, and other items. It may also involve an examination of the employer's history of employment-related charges and complaints during the past three to five years. In a sense such a review can be viewed as an audit of the organization's policies and practices regarding employee rights.

RIGHTS AFFECTING THE EMPLOYMENT RELATIONSHIP

As employees increasingly regard themselves as free agents in the workplace—and as the power of unions declines in the United States—the struggle between individual employee and employer "rights" is heightening. Employers frequently do not fare well in court in employee "rights" cases. Not only the employer is liable in many cases. Individual managers and supervisors have been found liable when hiring or promotion decisions have been based on discriminatory factors, or when they have had knowledge of such conduct and have not taken steps to stop it. Several concepts from law and psychology influence the employment relationship: employment-at-will, wrongful or constructive discharge, just cause, due process, and distributive and procedural justice.

Employment-at-Will

Employment-at-will (EAW) Common-law doctrine stating that employers have the right to hire, fire, demote, or promote whomever they choose, unless there is a law or a contract to the contrary.

Employment-at-will (EAW) is a common-law doctrine stating that employers have the right to hire, fire, demote, or promote whomever they choose, unless there is a law or a contract to the contrary. Conversely, employees can quit whenever they want and go to another job under the same terms. An employment-at-will statement in an employee handbook usually contains wording such as the following:

> *This handbook is not a contract, express or implied, guaranteeing employment for any specific duration. Although we hope that your employment relationship with us will be long term, either you or the Employer may terminate this relationship at any time, for any reason, with or without cause or notice.*

In the past three decades, numerous state courts have questioned the *fairness* of an employer's decision to fire an employee without just cause and due process. Many suits have stressed that employees' job rights must be checked against the EAW doctrine to balance legal and ethical concerns.[7]

EAW and the Courts In general, the courts have recognized three rationales for hearing EAW cases:

- *Public policy exception:* This exception to EAW holds that an employee can sue if he or she was fired for a reason that violates public policy. For example, if an employee refused to commit perjury and was fired, he or she can sue the employer.
- *Implied contract exception:* This exception to EAW holds that an employee should not be fired as long as he or she does the job. Long service, promises of continued employment, and lack of criticism of job performance imply continuing employment.
- *Good-faith and fair-dealing exception:* This exception to EAW suggests that a covenant of good faith and fair dealing exists between the employer and the at-will employee. If the employer breaks this covenant by unreasonable behavior, the employee may seek legal recourse.

Nearly all states have enacted one or more statutes to limit an employer's right to discharge employees. National restrictions include prohibitions against the use of race, age, sex, national origin, religion, and disabilities as bases for termination. Restrictions on other areas vary from state to state.[8]

Wrongful Discharge

Wrongful discharge
Termination of an individual's employment for reasons that are illegal or improper.

Employers who run afoul of EAW restrictions may be guilty of wrongful discharge, which is the termination of an individual's employment for reasons that are illegal or improper. Some state courts have recognized certain nonstatutory grounds for wrongful-discharge suits. Additionally, courts generally have held that unionized workers cannot pursue EAW actions as at-will employees because they are covered by the grievance arbitration process.

A landmark court case in wrongful discharge was *Fortune v. National Cash Register Company.* The case involved the firing of a salesperson (Mr. Fortune) who had been with National Cash Register (NCR) for 25 years.[9] The employee's termination came shortly after he got a large customer order that would have earned him a big commission. Based on the evidence, the court concluded that he was wrongfully discharged because NCR dismissed him to avoid paying the commission, thus violating the covenant of good faith and fair dealing.

Employers should take several precautions to reduce wrongful-discharge liabilities. Having a well-written employee handbook, training managers, and maintaining adequate documentation are key. Figure 16-2 offers suggestions for preparing a defense against wrongful-discharge lawsuits.

Constructive discharge
Process of deliberately making conditions intolerable to get an employee to quit.

Constructive Discharge Closely related to wrongful discharge is constructive discharge, which is deliberately making conditions intolerable to get an employee to quit. Under normal circumstances, an employee who resigns rather than being dismissed cannot later collect damages for violation of legal rights. An exception to this rule occurs when the courts find that the working conditions were made so intolerable as to *force* a reasonable employee to resign. Then, the resignation is considered a discharge. For example, an employee was told he should resign but refused. He was then given lesser assignments, publicly ridiculed by his supervisor, and threatened each day with dismissal. He finally resigned, sued his employer, and won the lawsuit because he had been "constructively discharged."

| FIGURE 16-2 | Keys for Preparing a Defense Against Wrongful Discharge: The "Paper Trail" |

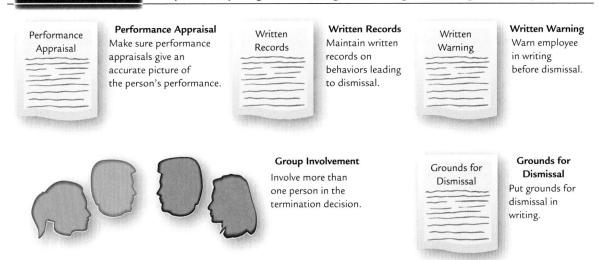

Performance Appraisal
Make sure performance appraisals give an accurate picture of the person's performance.

Written Records
Maintain written records on behaviors leading to dismissal.

Written Warning
Warn employee in writing before dismissal.

Group Involvement
Involve more than one person in the termination decision.

Grounds for Dismissal
Put grounds for dismissal in writing.

There are a number of factors to watch for that might constitute the finding of "constructive discharge."[10] Key ones include:

- Intolerable working conditions
- Dangerous duties
- Demeaning assignments
- Failure to provide work to do
- Conditions under which a "reasonable employee" would quit

Just Cause

Just cause Reasonable justification for taking employment-related action.

Just cause is reasonable justification for taking employment-related action. A "good reason" or just cause for disciplinary actions such as dismissal can usually be found in union contracts, but not in at-will situations. The United States has different just-cause rules than do some other countries. Even though definitions of *just cause* vary, the overall concern is fairness. To be viewed by others as *just*, any disciplinary action must be based on facts in the individual case.

One case involving a female employee with three years' experience illustrates how just cause can be interpreted. After taking most of her maternity leave, she was told two weeks before her return that she was being terminated due to a business slowdown. The company said she was among 23 employees fired because of poor performance. Yet the employee had received pay increases and a promotion, had never had any performance problems documented, and was replaced by a full-time employee. Pointing to these facts, the court ruled that the employee could sue the company.[11]

Due Process

Due process Requirement that the employer use a fair process to determine employee wrongdoing and that the employee have an opportunity to explain and defend his or her actions.

Due process, like just cause, is about fairness. Due process is the requirement that the employer use a fair process to determine if there has been employee wrongdoing and that the employee have an opportunity to explain and defend his or her actions. Figure 16-3 shows some factors to be considered when

FIGURE 16-3   Criteria for Evaluating Just Cause and Due Process

Just-Cause Determinants
- Was the employee warned of the consequences of the conduct?
- Was the employer's rule reasonable?
- Did management investigate before disciplining?
- Was the investigation fair and impartial?
- Was there evidence of guilt?
- Were the rules and penalties applied evenhandedly?
- Was the penalty reasonable, given the offense?

Due Process Considerations
- How have precedents been handled?
- Is a complaint process available?
- Was the complaint process used?
- Was retaliation used against the employee?
- Was the decision based on facts?
- Were the actions and processes viewed as fair by outside entities?

Distributive justice
Perceived fairness in the distribution of outcomes.

Procedural justice
Perceived fairness of the processes used to make decisions about employees.

evaluating just cause and due process. How HR managers address these factors determines whether the courts perceive employers' actions as fair.

Whether employees' perceive fairness or justice in their treatment depends on at least two other factors that are more psychological than legal in nature. First, people obviously prefer *favorable outcomes* for themselves. They decide the favorability of their outcomes by comparing them with the outcomes of others, given their relative situations. This decision involves the concept of distributive justice, which deals with the question "Were outcomes distributed fairly?" Fairness would not include disciplinary action based on favoritism when some are punished and others are not. Therefore, fairness often is dependent on employee perceptions. It is ultimately a *subjective* determination.

The second factor, procedural justice, focuses on whether the *procedures* that led to an action were appropriate, were clear, and provided an opportunity for employee input. Procedural justice deals with the question "Was the decision-making process fair?" Due process is a key part of procedural justice when making promotion, pay, discipline, and other HR decisions.[12] If organizations provide procedural justice, employees tend to respond with positive behaviors that benefit the organization in return. For instance, one study found that procedural justice was a key factor in the level of trust subordinates had in their managers.[13]

Complaint Procedures and Due Process Complaint procedures are provided by employers to resolve employee complaints or grievances. In most cases, the complaint procedures used to provide due process for unionized employees differ from those for non-union employees. For unionized employees, due process usually refers to the right to use the grievance procedure specified in the union contract. Due process may involve including specific steps in the grievance process, imposing time limits, following arbitration procedures, and providing knowledge of disciplinary penalties. More discussion of the grievance process and procedures in unions can be found in Chapter 17.

Due process procedures for at-will employees are more varied than for union workers and may address a broader range of issues. Many organizations, especially smaller ones, use an "open door" policy. This policy means that anyone with a complaint can talk with a manager, an HR representative, or an executive. Often, however, the door is not really open, especially if criticisms or conflicts are part of the complaint. Therefore, non-union organizations generally benefit from having formal complaint procedures that provide due process for their employees. Just the presence of such a formal complaint mechanism provides one indicator that an employee has been given due process. Further, if employees view a due process procedure as fair and available for use, they may be less likely to sue their employers or quit their jobs. For example, the federal government provides a complaint process for returning military reservists who are not quickly rehired by their old employer. The process uses mediation and volunteers to deal with the complaints.[14]

ALTERNATIVE DISPUTE RESOLUTION

Disputes between management and employees over different work issues are normal and inevitable, but how the parties resolve their disputes can become important. Formal grievance procedures and lawsuits provide two resolution methods. However, more and more companies look to alternative means of ensuring that due process occurs in cases involving employee rights. Employers that handle disputes effectively have lower legal costs and faster resolution times.[15] Dissatisfaction with the expenses and delays that are common in the court system when lawsuits are filed explains the growth in alternative dispute resolution (ADR) methods such as arbitration, peer review panels, and ombuds.

Arbitration

Disagreements between employers and employees often can result in lawsuits and large legal bills for settlement. Most employees who believe they have experienced unfair discrimination do not get legal counsel, but their discontent and complaints are likely to continue. Consequently, to settle disputes, a number of employers are using arbitration in non-union situations.

Arbitration Process that uses a neutral third party to make a decision.

Arbitration is a process that uses a neutral third party to make a decision, thereby eliminating the necessity of using the court system. Arbitration has been a common feature in union contracts. However, it must be set up carefully if the employers want to use it in non-union situations.[16] Because employers often select the arbitrators, and because arbitrators may not be required to issue written decisions and opinions, many see the use of arbitration in employment-related situations as unfair.

Some firms use *compulsory arbitration*, which requires employees to sign a pre-employment agreement stating that all disputes will be submitted to arbitration, and that employees waive their rights to pursue legal action until the completion of the arbitration process. Continuing pressure from state courts, federal employment regulatory commissions, and additional cases have challenged the fairness of compulsory arbitration in some situations. Requiring arbitration as a condition of employment is legal. In other situations, however, exceptions have been noted, so a legal check of where compulsory arbitration as part of ADR is allowed should be done before adopting the practice.

Peer Review Panels

Some employers allow their employees to appeal disciplinary actions to an internal committee of employees. This panel reviews the actions and makes recommendations or decisions. Panel members are specially trained volunteers who sign confidentiality agreements, after which the company empowers them to hear appeals. Eastman Kodak uses peer review panels as part of its Resolution Support Services Program. Employees from all parts of the company serve as panel members.[17]

Peer review panels use fellow employees and a few managers to resolve employment disputes. They have several advantages including fewer lawsuits, provision of due process, lower costs, and management and employee development. Basic "how-to" considerations are these:

- Recruit and train volunteers who are interested in serving on the panel—use a lottery to choose panelists for a particular case.
- Use a five- or seven-person panel with no more than one or two management members.
- When dealing with a bias issue, members of the affected protected group must be on the panel.
- The panel must be objective—either side should be able to remove individual members believed to be biased.
- Management must not attempt to alter or appeal the decision.[18]

Peer review panels can serve as the last stage of a formal complaint process for non-union employees, and their use has reduced the likelihood of unhappy employees' filing lawsuits. If an employee does file a lawsuit, the employer presents a stronger case if a group of the employee's peers previously reviewed the employer's decision and found it to be appropriate. In general, these panels reverse management decisions much less often than might be expected.

Ombuds

Some organizations ensure process fairness through ombuds, who are individuals outside the normal chain of command that act as problem solvers for both management and employees. At a number of large and medium-sized firms, ombuds have effectively addressed complaints about unfair treatment, employee/supervisor conflicts, and other workplace behavior issues. Ombuds address employees' complaints and operate with a high degree of confidentiality. Any follow-up to resolve problems is often handled informally, except when situations include unusual or significant illegal actions.

INDIVIDUAL EMPLOYEE RIGHTS ISSUES

Employees join organizations in the United States and some other countries with certain rights, including *freedom of speech, due process,* and *protection against unreasonable search and seizure.* Although the U.S. Constitution grants these and other rights to citizens, over the years, laws and court decisions have identified limits on them in the workplace. For example, an employee who voices threats against other employees may face disciplinary action by the employer without the employee's freedom of speech being violated.

HR ONLINE

Blogs and Wikis

"Blogs" or web logs provide an easy way for people to post opinions or views on any subject—including work, the boss, the company, products, and people at work. Some such representations on a blog can bring negative publicity to a company. Yet some businesses have established their own blogs—often written by the CEO to address customer and employee perceptions of products or to deal with rumors.[20]

Some companies (Google and Delta Air Lines among others) have fired or disciplined employees for what they say on their blogs.[21] As an example, consider three employees: Diane, who airs strong and extreme political views on her blog; Greg, who vents frustration with his employer and its products; and Sally, whose blogging concocts sexual fantasies that would make a statue blush. The CEO disagrees with Diane's politics and fears several major customers will too; she is also very unhappy that Greg is airing the company's dirty laundry, and she feels that Sally's blogging is a major embarrassment, especially since Sally is a recruiter—and very visible to the public. Can these employees be dismissed? Probably, except in California or New York, and Diane might be safe in a few states that exempt political views.[22]

Wikis are group-editable Web pages. They can be quite helpful for creating agendas for meetings and revising documents and schedules. In fact, some initial studies suggest they can cut the number of e-mails for a project substantially.[23] However, Wikis, like blogs, can cause difficulties in that some people may have inside knowledge not meant for publication, or others may plagiarize sources unwittingly. Procedural guidance might be appropriate here as well.

Employees' Free Speech Rights

The right of individuals to freedom of speech is protected by the U.S. Constitution. However, that freedom is *not* an unrestricted one in the workplace. Three areas in which employees' freedom of speech have collided with employers' restrictions are controversial views, blogs and wikis, and whistle-blowing.

Employee Advocacy of Controversial Views Questions of free speech arise over the right of employees to advocate controversial viewpoints at work (see HR On-Line). Numerous examples can be cited. For instance, can an employee of a tobacco company join in anti-smoking demonstrations outside of work? Can a disgruntled employee at a non-union employer wear a union badge on his cap at work? In one U.S. case, a court decision ruled against a white worker who displayed Confederate flags on his toolbox, which offended some African American employees. The court said that the worker's free speech right was not violated when the employer fired him for refusing to remove the flags.[19] In situations such as these, employers must follow due process procedures and demonstrate that disciplinary actions taken against employees can be justified by job-related reasons.

However, simply because an employer *might be able* to punish public embarrassments, should it do so? Perhaps not—this is the sort of management activity that might be viewed by employees as overreacting by the employer. It may cause other employees to leave, or at least not respect the employer. The best way to handle these concerns is to make clear what the boundaries and expectations of personal blogging might be. An employee blogging policy that spells out the boundaries and then a signed non-disclosure privacy agreement is the best approach.

Whistle-Blowing and Sarbanes-Oxley Individuals who report real or perceived wrongs committed by their employers are called whistle-blowers. The reasons why people report actions that they question vary and are often individual in nature. Many well-known whistle-blowing incidents have occurred in the past several years at companies such as Enron, Adelphia Communications, and WorldCom. For instance, a former employee of Warner-Lambert reported that the pharmaceutical firm used illegal means to market an epilepsy drug. The employee won a lawsuit that cost the firm millions of dollars.[24]

The culture of the organization often affects the degree to which employees report inappropriate or illegal actions internally or resort to using outside contacts. Employers need to address two key questions in regard to whistle-blowing: (1) When do employees have the right to speak out with protection from retribution? (2) When do employees violate the confidentiality of their jobs by speaking out? Even though the answers may be difficult to determine, retaliation against whistle-blowers clearly is not allowed, according to numerous court decisions.[25]

Whistle-blowers are less likely to lose their jobs in public employment than in private employment because most civil service systems follow rules protecting whistle-blowers. However, no comprehensive whistle-blowing law fully protects the right to free speech of both public and private employees.

The Sarbanes-Oxley Act is intended to remedy company ethical breaches. It adds protection for whistle-blowers. But by its express terms, the whistle-blower anti-retaliation provision covers *only* complaints made to certain entities[26]:

- Federal regulatory or law enforcement agencies
- Any member of Congress
- A supervisor

Privacy Rights and Employee Records

As a result of concerns about protecting individual privacy rights in the United States, the Privacy Act of 1974 was passed. It includes provisions affecting HR recordkeeping systems. This law applies *only* to federal agencies and to organizations supplying services to the federal government; however, similar state laws, somewhat broader in scope, have also been passed. For the most part, state rather than federal law regulates private employers on this issue. In most states, public-sector employees are permitted greater access to their files than are private-sector employees.

Employee Medical Records Recordkeeping and retention practices have been affected by the following provision in the Americans with Disabilities Act (ADA):

> *Information from all medical examinations and inquiries must be kept apart from general personnel files as a separate confidential medical record available only under limited conditions specified in the ADA.*

As interpreted by attorneys and HR practitioners, this provision requires that all medical-related information be maintained separately from all other confidential files. The Health Insurance Portability and Accountability Act also contains regulations designed to protect the privacy of employee medical records. As a result of all the legal restrictions, many employers have established several separate files on each employee, as illustrated in Figure 16-4.

FIGURE 16-4   Employee Record Files

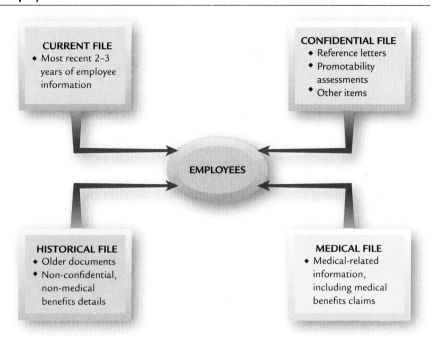

Security of Employee Records It is important that specific access restrictions and security procedures for employee records be established. These restrictions and procedures are designed to protect the privacy of employees and to protect employers from potential liability for improper disclosure of personal information. A recent regulation—the Data Protection Act—requires employers keep personnel records up to date and keep only the details that are needed.[27] The following guidelines are offered regarding employer access and storage of employee records:

- Restrict access to records to a limited number of individuals.
- Use confidential passwords for accessing employee records in various HR databases.
- Set up separate files and restricted databases for especially sensitive employee information.
- Inform employees about which types of data are retained.
- Purge employee records of outdated data.
- Release employee information only with employee consent.

Personnel files and records should usually be maintained for three years. However, different types of records should be maintained for shorter or longer periods of time based on various legal and regulatory standards.

Employee Rights and Personal Behavior

An additional employee rights issue concerns personal behavior off the job. Employers encounter special difficulty in establishing "just cause" for disciplining employees for their off-the-job behavior. Most people believe an employer should not control the lives of its employees off the job except in the case of clear job-related consequences. For example, what should an employer do if an employee is an acknowledged transvestite, a member of an activist environmental group, a leader in a racist group, or an exotic dancer on weekends? In some cases the answer should be "nothing"; in others, action must be taken. These are just a few cases in which employee rights and personal behaviors can conflict with employer expectations.

Numerous legal issues have been addressed in various lawsuits by employees. If an employer investigates deeply into an employee's personal life, an "invasion-of-privacy" claim can result. However, failure to investigate could jeopardize necessary and legal disciplinary actions that should be taken by employers.

Body Appearance Limitations Employers have put limits on appearance in some situations, which may include tattoos and body piercing. One example is Costco Wholesaler, which had an appearance policy that stated employees should be "dressed professionally at all times . . . no visible facial or tongue jewelry (earrings permitted)." A cashier refused to remove her piercings. She was fired and took the case to court. The court held that Costco had a legitimate interest in a reasonably professional appearance and upheld the dismissal. Appearance issues can be the subject of rights policies if they are job related. Boeing allows piercings provided they do not pose safety risks, Wal-Mart allows tattoos but not facial piercings, Subway allows "discreet" tattoos but limits piercings to one per ear.[28]

Off-Duty Behavior Some companies require employees to take nicotine tests even if they do not use tobacco on the job. Failing the test leads to dismissal. Companies say it is a way to curb health-care costs; employees say the companies are violating privacy rights.[29]

Employees have been disciplined for drinking on their own time, using competitors' products, gaining weight, and displaying political bumper stickers.[30] There really is no law that says you cannot discriminate against off-the-job behavior, but society has reservations about employers intruding into personal lives. However, the litmus test is whether the employee's off-the-job behavior puts the company in legal or financial jeopardy.[31]

BALANCING EMPLOYER SECURITY AND EMPLOYEE RIGHTS

Balancing employer and employee rights is becoming more difficult. On one side, employers have a legitimate need to ensure that employees are performing their jobs properly in a secure environment. On the other side, employees expect the rights that they have both at work and away from work to be protected. Technology gives employees who leave the employer the opportunity to take a great deal of valuable company secrets or data with them.[32] For this reason (and others as well), workplace monitoring has increased.[33]

Workplace Monitoring

The commonplace monitoring of e-mail and voice mail is only one way employers watch the workplace. In the United States, the right of protection from unreasonable search and seizure protects an individual against activities of the government only. Thus, employees of private-sector employers can be monitored, observed, and searched at work by representatives of the employer. However, several court decisions have reaffirmed the principle that both private-sector and government employers may search desks, files, lockers, and computer files without search warrants if they believe that work rules were violated.

Several forces have led to a growth in workplace monitoring. One major force is the expansion in available technology, ranging from the Internet to global tracking devices to enhanced video capabilities and improved information systems software. Second, the terrorist attacks of September 11, 2001, led to passage of the USA Patriot Act, which expanded legislation to allow government investigators to engage in broader monitoring of individuals, including in workplaces, in order to protect national security.

Greater use of computers, cameras, and telecommunications systems is transforming many workplaces. The use of these items by employers to monitor employee actions is amplifying concerns that the privacy rights of employees are being threatened.

The right to privacy is defined in legal terms as an individual's freedom from unauthorized and unreasonable intrusion into personal affairs. Although the right to privacy is not specifically identified in the U.S. Constitution, a number of past U.S. Supreme Court cases have established that such a right must be considered. Also, several states have enacted right-to-privacy statutes. A scope of privacy concerns exists in other countries as well.

Right to privacy An individual's freedom from unauthorized and unreasonable intrusion into personal affairs.

Internet Research

Privacy Rights Clearinghouse
Fact sheets and information on workplace monitoring rights can be found at this Website by linking to it at: http://thomsonedu.com/management/mathis.

Tracking Internet Use Many employers have developed and disseminated Internet use policies. Communicating these policies to employees, enforcing them by monitoring employee Internet use, and disciplining offenders are means used by employers to ensure that the Internet is used appropriately. These efforts are necessary because more than 90% of employees admit to visiting non-work Websites during work hours and many companies are watching them do it. The numbers vary, but as many as 76% of firms always or sometimes monitor employees' Internet use.[34]

Through such monitoring, employers attempt to guard against some employees' accessing pornographic or other Websites that could create problems for the employers. If law enforcement investigations find evidence of such access, the employer could be accused of aiding and abetting illegal behavior. In a New Jersey case, a computer log showed an employee accessing porn Websites. His supervisor told him to stop but did not inform higher-ups. Later it was clear the employee had not stopped but the supervisor was told *not* to access the employee's logs again. Later the employee was arrested on child pornography charges. The court found that the company knew of the employee's actions and was under a duty to act either by firing the employee or by reporting him to law enforcement because the employer's failure to act could lead to harm to innocent third parties.[35]

Many employers have purchased software that tracks the Websites accessed by employees. Also, some employers use software programs for blocking certain categories of Websites that are inappropriate for business use.

Monitoring Employee Performance Employee activity may be monitored to measure performance, ensure performance quality and customer service, check for theft, or enforce company rules or laws. The common concerns in a monitored workplace usually center not on whether or not monitoring should be used, but on how it should be conducted, how the information should be used, and how feedback should be communicated to employees.

At a minimum, employers should obtain a signed employee consent form that indicates that performance will be monitored regularly and phone calls will be taped regularly. Also, it is recommended that employers provide employees with feedback on monitoring results to help employees improve their performance and to commend them for good performance. For example, one major hotel reservation center allows employees to listen to their customer service calls and rate their own performance. Then, the employees meet with their supervisors to discuss both positive and negative performance issues.

Conducting Video Surveillance at Work Numerous employers have installed video surveillance systems in workplaces. Some employers use these systems to ensure employee security, such as in parking lots, garages, and dimly lit exterior areas. Other employers have installed them on retail sales floors and in production areas, parts and inventory rooms, and lobbies. When video surveillance is extended into employee restrooms, changing rooms, and other more private areas, employer rights and employee privacy collide. As with other forms of monitoring, it is important that employers develop a video surveillance policy, inform employees about the policy, perform the surveillance only for legitimate business purposes, and strictly limit those who view the surveillance results.

Monitoring of E-Mail and Voice Mail Employers have a right to monitor what is said and transmitted through their e-mail and voice-mail systems, despite employees' concerns about free speech. Advances in information and telecommunications technology have become a major issue for employers regarding employee privacy. The use of e-mail and voice mail increases every day, along with employers' liability if they improperly monitor or inspect employees' electronic communications. Many employers have specialized software that can retrieve deleted e-mail, and even record each keystroke made on their computers.

There are recommended actions for employers to take when monitoring e-mail and voice mail. Those actions include creating an *electronic communications policy* and getting employees to sign a *permission form*. With those steps in place, employers should monitor only for business purposes and strictly enforce the policy. One problem with both e-mail and voice mail is that most people express themselves more casually than they would in formal memos. This tendency can create sloppy, racist, sexist, or otherwise defamatory messages. Court cases have been brought over jokes that were forwarded that had profanity or racial undertones. Another problem is that e-mail messages can be sent rapidly to multiple (sometimes unintended) recipients. Also, both e-mail and voice mail can be stored, and often legal cases hinge on retrieval of those messages. Figure 16-5 depicts recommended employer actions regarding electronic communications.

To address the various concerns regarding monitoring of e-mail and voice mail, many employers have established policies with four elements, as follows:

- Voice mail, e-mail, and computer files are provided by the employer and are for business use only.
- Use of these media for personal reasons is restricted and subject to employer review.
- All computer passwords and codes must be available to the employer.
- The employer reserves the right to monitor or search any of the media, without notice, for business purposes.

FIGURE 16-5   Recommended Employer Actions Regarding Electronic Communications

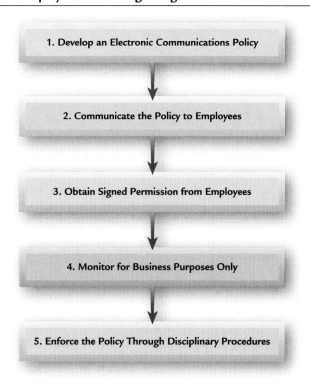

1. Develop an Electronic Communications Policy

2. Communicate the Policy to Employees

3. Obtain Signed Permission from Employees

4. Monitor for Business Purposes Only

5. Enforce the Policy Through Disciplinary Procedures

Employer Investigations

Another area of concern regarding employee rights involves workplace investigations. The U.S. Constitution protects public-sector employees in the areas of due process, search and seizure, and privacy at work, but private-sector employees are not protected. Whether on or off the job, unethical or illegal employee behavior can be a serious problem for organizations. Employee misconduct may include illegal drug use, falsification of documents, misuse of company funds, disclosure of organizational secrets, workplace violence, employment harassment, and theft.

Employee Theft A problem faced by employers is *employee theft* of property and vital company secrets. Retailers are estimated to lose more than $12 billion a year to employee theft. White-collar theft through embezzlement, accepting bribes, and stealing company property also is a concern.[36] If the organizational culture encourages or allows questionable behavior, then employees are more likely to see theft as acceptable.

Employee theft and other workplace misconduct can be addressed using a number of methods, as Figure 16-6 indicates. Besides watching current employees through various types of surveillance and monitoring, firms may screen applicants through means such as honesty testing and background checks in order to avoid hiring individuals who are likely to violate workplace standards of conduct.

Honesty and Polygraph Tests Pencil-and-paper honesty tests are alternatives to polygraph testing. These tests are widely used, particularly in the retail

FIGURE 16-6   **Means Used to Reduce Employee Theft and Misconduct**

Before Hire	After Hire
· Applicant screening	· Workplace monitoring
· Honesty testing	· Review of unusual behavior changes
· Background investigation	· Selective use of polygraph testing

industry and in other selected industries, and more than two dozen variations of them are available. However, their use has been challenged successfully in some court decisions. For current employees, polygraph testing (performed with lie detectors) is used by some organizations. The Employee Polygraph Protection Act prohibits the use of polygraphs for most pre-employment screening. The act also requires that employees must:

■ Be advised of their rights to refuse to take a polygraph exam.
■ Be allowed to stop the exam at any time.
■ Not be terminated because they refuse to take a polygraph test or solely because of the exam results.

Reviewing Unusual Behavior Another method of addressing workplace conduct is to review unusual behavior on and off the job. For instance, if an employee is suddenly wearing many new clothes and spending lavishly, inquiries as to the reasons why and the resources used might be warranted. In one case, inquiries at a county government office revealed that the county clerk had "borrowed" over $50,000 to purchase numerous items and take several trips to gambling destinations.

Conducting Work-Related Investigations Workplace investigations are frequently conducted using technology. Technological advances allow employers to review e-mails, access computer logs, conduct video surveillance, and use other investigative tactics. When using audiotaping, wiretapping, and other electronic methods, care should be taken to avoid violating privacy and legal regulations.

Workplace investigations can be conducted internally or externally. Often, HR staff and company security personnel lead internal investigations. Until recently, the use of outside investigators—the police, private investigators, attorneys, or others—was restricted by the Fair Credit Reporting Act. However, passage of the Fair and Accurate Credit Transactions (FACT) Act changed the situation. Under FACT, employers can hire outside investigators without first notifying the individuals under investigation or getting their permission.[37]

Substance Abuse and Drug Testing

Employee substance abuse and drug testing have received a great deal of attention. Concern about substance abuse at work is appropriate given that absenteeism, accident/damage rates, health-care expenses, and theft/fraud are higher for workers using illegal substances or misusing legal substances such as drugs and alcohol. Figure 16-7 identifies some of the financial effects of substance abuse. Ways to address substance abuse problems were discussed in Chapter 15; employee rights concerned with those means are discussed in the following sections.

FIGURE 16-7   How Substance Abuse Affects Employers Financially

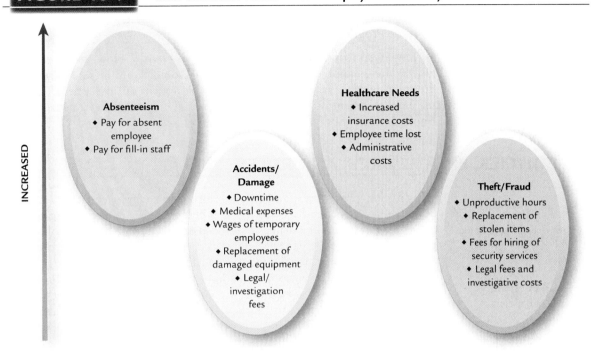

Drug-Free Workplace Act of 1988 The U.S. Supreme Court has ruled that certain drug-testing plans do not violate the Constitution. Private-employer programs are governed mainly by state laws, which can be a confusing hodgepodge. The Drug-Free Workplace Act of 1988 requires government contractors to take steps to eliminate employee drug use. Failure to do so can lead to contract termination. Tobacco and alcohol do not qualify as controlled substances under the act, and off-the-job drug use is not included. Additionally, the U.S. Department of Transportation requires regular testing of truck and bus drivers, train crews, mass-transit employees, airline pilots and mechanics, pipeline workers, and licensed sailors.

Drug Testing and Employee Rights Unless state or local law prohibits testing, employers have a right to require applicants or employees to submit to a drug test. Pre-employment drug testing is widely used: 84% of employers use it.[38] Where employers conduct drug testing of current employees, they use one of three policies: (1) random testing of everyone at periodic intervals, (2) testing only in cases of probable cause, or (3) testing after accidents.

If testing is done for probable cause, it needs to be based on performance-related consequences, such as excessive absenteeism or reduced productivity, not just the substance usage itself. From a policy standpoint, it is most appropriate to test for drugs when the following conditions exist:

■ Job-related consequences of the abuse are severe enough that they outweigh privacy concerns.

■ Accurate test procedures are available.

- Written consent of the employee is obtained.
- Results are treated confidentially, as are any medical records.
- Employer offers a complete drug program, including an employee assistance program.

Employers win most drug testing cases in court.[39] However, not all employers are enamored with drug testing and some claim the rate of testing is dropping because it shows no demonstrable return on investment. Also, as the unemployment rate is reduced, drug testing may restrict getting additional employees into jobs.[40]

HR POLICIES, PROCEDURES, AND RULES

Policies General guidelines that focus organizational actions.

Procedures Customary methods of handling activities.

Rules Specific guidelines that regulate and restrict the behavior of individuals.

HR policies, procedures, and rules greatly affect employee rights (just discussed) and discipline (discussed next). Where there is a choice among actions, **policies** act as general guidelines that focus organizational actions. Policies are general in nature, whereas procedures and rules are specific to the situation. The important role of policies requires that they be reviewed regularly.

Procedures provide customary methods of handling activities and are more specific than policies. For example, a policy may state that employees will be given vacations according to years of service, and a procedure establishes a specific method for authorizing vacation time without disrupting work.

Rules are specific guidelines that regulate and restrict the behavior of individuals. They are similar to procedures in that they guide action and typically allow no discretion in their application. Rules reflect a management decision that action be taken—or not taken—in a given situation, and they provide more specific behavioral guidelines than do policies. An example of a rule might be that a vacation day may not be scheduled the day before or after a holiday. Of course, there are always exceptions in cases, as the HR Perspective demonstrates.

HR PERSPECTIVE

I-Deals

Sometimes individual employees negotiate special terms of employment with their employers. This often occurs when the employee has special skills, talents, experience, or other unique value to the employer. These so-called "I-deals" (for idiosyncratic employment arrangements) may allow employers to retain or hire employees who otherwise would not be willing to work or continue to work for them.

I-deals can run the gamut of possibilities from the retired employee who has vast institutional knowledge and is allowed to return as a consultant, to the distinguished senior professor who is allowed to teach one course every spring semester. Another example is an exceptional salesperson who gets twice the vacation amount as anyone else in order to keep the salesperson's services. But I-deals can send divergent messages to other employees and may be resented if not clearly understood.

Although standardizing employment conditions through policies, procedures, and rules is the common method for promoting consistency in HR, I-deals will always be a possibility. They are not a substitute for good HR policy, but they can provide potentially advantageous opportunities to both parties. Often HR professionals suggest that no deals be made that would not be suitable for posting on the employee bulletin board in public view for all to see.[41]

| **FIGURE 16-8** | **Typical Division of HR Responsibilities: Policies, Procedures, and Rules** |

HR Unit	Managers
◆ Designs formal mechanisms for coordinating HR policies ◆ Assists in development of organization-wide HR policies, procedures, and rules ◆ Provides information on application of HR policies, procedures, and rules ◆ Trains managers to administer policies, procedures, and rules	◆ Help in developing HR policies and rules ◆ Review policies and rules with all employees ◆ Apply HR policies, procedures, and rules ◆ Explain rules and policies to all employees ◆ Give feedback on effectiveness of policies and rules

Perhaps more than any other part of the organization, the HR function needs policies, procedures, and rules. People react strongly to differential treatment regarding time off, pay, vacation time, discipline, etc. New and smaller employers often start without many of these HR issues well defined. But as they grow, issues become more complex, with policy decisions being made on an ad hoc basis. Before long the inconsistency and resulting employee complaints bring on the need for policies, procedures, and rules that apply to everyone.

Responsibilities for HR Policies, Procedures, and Rules

For HR policies, procedures, and rules to be effective, coordination between the HR unit and operating managers is vital. As Figure 16-8 shows, managers are the main users and enforcers of rules, procedures, and policies, and they should receive some training and explanation in how to carry them out. The HR unit supports managers, reviews policies and disciplinary rules, and trains managers to use them. Often policies, procedures, and rules are provided in employee handbooks.

Employee Handbooks

An employee handbook can be an essential tool for communicating information about workplace culture, benefits, attendance, pay practices, safety issues, and discipline.[42] They are often written in a formal paternalistic or legalistic fashion but need not be. The language used can make the handbook a more positive element. Even small organizations can prepare handbooks relatively easily using available computer software. When preparing handbooks, management should consider legal issues, readability, and use. Handbooks may contain many different areas but common are policies regarding:

- At-will prerogatives
- Harassment
- Electronic communication
- Pay and benefits
- Discipline
- Hours worked

Legal Review of Language As mentioned earlier, one current trend in the courts is to use employee handbooks against employers in lawsuits charging a broken "implied" contract. This tendency should not eliminate the use of employee handbooks as a way of communicating policies to employees. In fact, not having an employee handbook with HR policies spelled out can leave an organization open to costly litigation and out-of-court settlements. A more sensible approach is to first develop sound HR policies and employee handbooks to communicate them, and then have legal counsel review the language contained in them. Recommendations include the following:

- *Eliminate controversial phrases.* For example, the phrase "permanent employee" may be used to describe a person who has passed a probationary period. This wording can lead to disagreement over what the parties meant by "permanent." A more appropriate phrase is "regular employee."

- *Use disclaimers.* Courts generally uphold disclaimers, but only if they are prominently shown in the handbook. To ensure that disclaimers do not negate the positive image presented by the handbook, they should not be overused. A disclaimer in the handbook can read as follows:

  > *This employee handbook is not intended to be a contract or any part of a contractual agreement between the employer and the employee. The employer reserves the right to modify, delete, or add to any policies set forth herein without notice and reserves the right to terminate an employee at any time with or without a specific cause.*

- *Keep the handbook current.* Many employers simply add new material to handbooks rather than deleting old, inapplicable rules. Those old rules can become the bases for new lawsuits. Consequently, handbooks and HR policies should be reviewed periodically and revised every few years.

To communicate and discuss HR information, a growing number of firms are distributing employee handbooks electronically using an intranet, which enables employees to access policies in employee handbooks at any time. It also allows changes in policies to be made electronically rather than distributed as paper copies.

Communicating HR Information

HR communication focuses on the receipt and dissemination of HR data and information throughout the organization. *Downward communication* flows from top management to the rest of the organization, informing employees about what is and will be happening in the organization, and what the expectations and goals of top management are. *Upward communication* enables managers to learn about the ideas, concerns, and information needs of employees. Various methods are used to facilitate both types of communication.

Organizations communicate with employees through internal publications and media, including newspapers, company magazines, organizational newsletters, videotapes, Internet postings, and e-mail announcements. Whatever the formal means used, managers should make an honest attempt to communicate information employees need to know. The spread of electronic communications allows for more timely and widespread dissemination of HR information, but can present some problems. For example, a court refused to require an employee who had been fired to arbitrate his claim, because the company had e-mailed its new workplace dispute resolution policy in a mass e-mailing.

General Dynamics Government Systems Corporation sent an e-mail advising all employees that arbitration would thereafter be the exclusive means of resolving workplace disputes. One employee was later fired for persistent absenteeism and tardiness. He sued and the court refused to require him to arbitrate the claim because the e-mail notification lacked several important components of proper notice.[43]

EMPLOYEE DISCIPLINE

Discipline Form of training that enforces organizational rules.

The earlier discussion about employee rights provides an appropriate introduction to the topic of employee discipline, because employee rights often are a key issue in disciplinary cases. Discipline is a form of training that enforces organizational rules. Those most often affected by the discipline systems are problem employees. Fortunately, problem employees comprise a small number of employees. If employers fail to deal with problem employees, negative effects on other employees and work groups often result. Common disciplinary issues caused by problem employees include absenteeism, tardiness, productivity deficiencies, alcoholism, and insubordination.

Approaches to Discipline

The disciplinary system can be viewed as an application of behavior modification to a problem or unproductive employee. The best discipline is clearly self-discipline. Most people can usually be counted on to do their jobs effectively when they understand what is required at work. Yet some find that the prospect of external discipline helps their self-discipline. One approach is positive discipline.

Positive Discipline Approach The positive discipline approach builds on the philosophy that violations are actions that can usually be corrected constructively without penalty. In this approach, managers focus on using fact-finding and guidance to encourage desirable behaviors, rather than using penalties to discourage undesirable behaviors. The four steps to positive discipline are as follows:

1. *Counseling:* The goal of this phase is to heighten employee awareness of organizational policies and rules. Often, people simply need to be made aware of rules, and knowledge of possible disciplinary actions may prevent violations.
2. *Written documentation:* If the employee fails to correct her or his behavior, then a second conference becomes necessary. Whereas the first stage took place as a conversation between supervisor and employee, this stage is documented in written form, and written solutions are identified to prevent further problems from occurring.
3. *Final warning:* If the employee does not follow the written solutions noted in the second step, a final warning conference is held. In that conference, the supervisor emphasizes to the employee the importance of correcting the inappropriate actions. Some firms incorporate a decision day off, in which the employee is given a day off with pay to develop a firm, written action plan to remedy the problem behaviors. The decision day off is used to emphasize the seriousness of the problem and the manager's determination to see that the behavior is changed.

FIGURE 16-9   **Progressive Discipline Process**

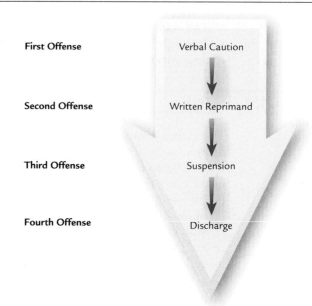

First Offense	Verbal Caution
Second Offense	Written Reprimand
Third Offense	Suspension
Fourth Offense	Discharge

4. *Discharge:* If the employee fails to follow the action plan that was developed, and further problems exist, then the supervisor can discharge the employee.

The advantage of this positive approach to discipline is that it focuses on problem solving. The greatest difficulty with the positive approach to discipline is the extensive amount of training required for supervisors and managers to become effective counselors, and the need for more supervisory time with this approach than with the progressive discipline approach, which is discussed next.

Progressive Discipline Approach Progressive discipline incorporates steps that become progressively more stringent and are designed to change the employee's inappropriate behavior. Figure 16-9 shows a typical progressive discipline process; most progressive discipline procedures use verbal and written reprimands and suspension before resorting to dismissal. At one manufacturing firm, an employee's failure to call in when he or she will be absent from work may lead to a suspension after the third offense in a year. Suspension sends the employees a strong message that undesirable job behaviors must change or termination is likely to follow.

Although appearing similar to positive discipline, progressive discipline is more administrative and process oriented. Following the progressive sequence ensures that both the nature and the seriousness of the problem are clearly communicated to the employee. Not all steps in the progressive discipline procedure are followed in every case. Certain serious offenses are exempted from the progressive procedure and may result in immediate termination. Typical offenses leading to immediate termination include intoxication at work, alcohol or drug use at work, fighting, and theft. However, if a firm has a progressive discipline policy, it should be followed. Several court decisions have ruled that failure to follow written policies for progressive discipline can invalidate an employee's dismissal.[44]

Reasons Why Discipline Might Not Be Used

For a number of reasons, managers may be reluctant to use discipline. Some of the main ones include the following:

- *Organizational culture of avoiding discipline:* If the organizational "norm" is to avoid penalizing problem employees, then managers are less likely to use discipline or to dismiss problem employees.
- *Lack of support:* Many managers do not want to use discipline because they fear that their decisions will not be supported by higher management. The degree of support is also a function of the organizational culture.
- *Guilt:* Some managers realize that before they became managers, they committed the same violations as their employees, and feel that they cannot discipline others for doing something they used to do.
- *Fear of loss of friendship:* Managers may fear losing friendships or damaging personal relationships if they discipline employees.
- *Avoidance of time loss:* When applied properly, discipline requires considerable time and effort. Sometimes, it is easier for managers to avoid taking the time required for disciplining, especially if their actions may be overturned on review by higher management.
- *Fear of lawsuits:* Managers are increasingly concerned about being sued for disciplining someone, particularly for taking the ultimate disciplinary step of termination.

Effective Discipline

Because of legal concerns, managers must understand discipline and know how to administer it properly. Effective discipline should be aimed at the problem behaviors, not at the employee personally, because the reason for discipline is to improve performance. Distributive and procedural justice suggest that if a manager tolerates unacceptable behavior, other employees may resent the unfairness of that tolerance.

Training of Supervisors Training supervisors and managers on when and how discipline should be used is crucial. Employees see disciplinary action given by trained supervisors who base their responses on procedural justice as more fair than discipline done by untrained supervisors. Regardless of the disciplinary approach used, training in counseling and in communications skills provides supervisors and managers with the tools necessary to deal with employee performance problems.

Discharge: The Final Disciplinary Step

The final stage in the disciplinary process is termination. Both the positive and the progressive approaches to discipline clearly provide employees with warnings about the seriousness of their performance problems before dismissal occurs. Terminating workers because they do not keep their own promises is more likely to appear equitable and defensible to a jury. One difficult phase of employee termination is removal of ex-employees and their personal possessions from the company facilities.

The standard advice from legal experts is to physically remove the employee as quickly as possible. This is often done by having the employee escorted by security guards out of the building. Some firms allow terminated employees to return to their desks, offices, or lockers to retrieve personal items

HR ON-THE-JOB

Termination Procedure

Dismissal of an employee can be problematic. The following practices can make it less difficult:

1. *Review evidence.* The disciplining manager, that manager's superior, and an HR representative should review the documentation and make the final determination.
2. *Select a neutral location.* Termination should occur in a neutral location, not the supervisor/manager's office.
3. *Conduct the termination meeting.* The HR representative and/or the manager informs the employee of the reason for the termination. The manager and the HR representative should remain professional and calm, not be apologetic or demeaning.

4. *Have HR discuss termination benefits.* The HR representative explains the employee's final payroll and benefits. A specific letter can serve as evidence that the employee was notified of the termination decision and details of those rights.
5. *Escort the employee from the building.* This phase is controversial. The goal is to ensure that the employee, who is likely to be upset, is removed from the premises quickly without obvious conflicts or concerns about security.
6. *Notify the department staff.* The manager notifies the department staff that the individual is no longer employed. No details or explanations should be provided.[45]

under the observation of security personnel and the department supervisor/manager. But this means the ex-employee may be seen by and may talk with co-workers while still upset or angry. The HR On-the-Job shows how a large insurance firm handles dismissal.

Separation agreement
Agreement in which a terminated employee agrees not to sue the employer in exchange for specified benefits.

Separation Agreements In some termination situations, formal contracts may be used. One type is a separation agreement, in which an employee who is being terminated agrees not to sue the employer in exchange for specified benefits, such as additional severance pay or other "considerations."

For such agreements to be legally enforceable, the considerations usually should be additional items not part of normal termination benefits. For international employees, different legal requirements may exist in various countries, including certain requirements for severance pay and benefits. When using separation agreements, care must be taken to avoid the appearance of constructive discharge of employees. Use of such agreements should be reviewed by a legal counsel.

SUMMARY

- The employment relationship is a reciprocal one in which both employers and employees have statutory and contractual rights, as well as responsibilities.
- Contractual rights can be spelled out in an employment contract or be implied as a result of employer promises.
- Employment-at-will gives employers the right to hire or terminate employees with or without notice or cause.

- Courts are changing aspects of employment-at-will relationships through exceptions for violations of public policy, an implied contract, and good faith and fair dealing.
- Wrongful discharge occurs when an employer improperly or illegally terminates an individual's employment.
- Constructive discharge is the process of making conditions intolerable to get an employee to quit.

- Just cause for employment-related actions should exist. When just cause is absent, constructive discharge may occur, in which the employee is forced to "voluntarily" quit the job.
- Although due process is not guaranteed for at-will employees, the courts expect to see evidence of due process in employment-related cases.
- Due process is important for both unionized and non-union employees. In non-union situations, alternative dispute resolution (ADR) means may be used.
- Balancing employer security concerns and employee rights becomes an issue when dealing with access to employee records, free speech, workplace monitoring, employer investigations, and substance abuse and drug testing.
- Employers increasingly are facing privacy and free speech issues in areas such as blogs and wikis and whistle-blowing.

- Employer investigations must be done to protect both employer and employee rights.
- Drug testing provides a widely used and legal method for employers to deal with increasing drug problems at work.
- To be effective, HR policies, procedures, and rules should be consistent, necessary, applicable, understandable, reasonable, and communicated.
- Courts sometimes view employee handbooks as implied contracts.
- Although employee self-discipline is the goal, positive or progressive discipline is sometimes necessary to encourage self-discipline.
- Managers may fail to discipline for a variety of reasons. However, effective discipline can have positive effects on the productivity of employees.

REVIEW AND APPLICATION QUESTIONS

1. Identify how the issues of due process and just cause are linked to employer disciplinary actions.
2. Discuss the following statement: "Even though efforts to restrict employees' free speech at work may be permissible, such efforts raise troubling questions affecting individual rights."
3. Assume that as the HR manager, you have decided to prepare some guidelines for supervisors to use when they have to discipline employees. Gather the information needed, using Internet resources such as *http://hr.blr.com*, and prepare a guide for supervisors on both positive and progressive discipline.

CASE

Employer Liable for "Appearance" Actions

A ruling by the California Supreme Court held that L'Oreal USA, a large cosmetics company, was liable for ordering a supervisor to terminate a female employee. The details of the case are described next.

Elysa Yanowitz was a regional sales manager for L'Oreal USA in California when her boss ordered her to fire a sales associate with a strong performance record because the employee was not attractive enough. The boss said she "wasn't good looking enough" and that in her place should be hired someone who was "hot." Yanowitz refused, contending that the boss's order was discrimination because male sales associates did not have to be attractive. She repeatedly refused to fire the female employee and said that the company retaliated against her. Ultimately,

Yanowitz left the company on a disability leave due to stress.

The court ruling addressed protection for those who refuse orders that they believe are discriminatory. The court also stated that an appearance standard applied to one gender but not the other is sexual discrimination. Yanowitz left the company after retaliation but won the case after the court held that her whistle-blowing was protected.[46]

Questions

1. Do you agree that the company was guilty of illegal actions? Why or why not?
2. Discuss some examples when appearance can be a legitimate work issue.

SUPPLEMENTAL CASE

George Faces Challenges

This case describes the problem facing a new department supervisor when HR policies and discipline have been handled poorly in the past. (For the case, go to http://thomsonedu.com/management/mathis.)

NOTES

1. Based on Mark McGraw, "Positive ID?" *Human Resource Executive,* June 16, 2006, 58–62.
2. Dexter Roberts, "Waking Up to Their Rights," *Business Week,* August 22, 2005, 123–128.
3. Michael J. Garrison and Charles D. Stevens, "Sign This Agreement Not to Compete or You're Fired," *Employee Responsibilities and Rights Journal,* September 2003, 103.
4. Paul Salvatore, "On Raiding and Noncompetes," *Workindex.com,* February 16, 2006.
5. "Court Affirms Duty-of-Loyalty Injunction Against Two Former Sales Representatives," *Bulletin to Management,* May 15, 2003, 155.
6. Dave Lenckus, "EPLI Policy Pays Off for Verizon," *Business Insurance,* April 7, 2003, 28.
7. Mark V. Roehling, "The Employment-at-Will Doctrine, Second Level Ethical Issues and Analysis," *Journal of Business Ethics,* 47 (2003), 115–124.
8. Robert J. Lanza and Martin Warren, "United States: Employment at Will Prevails Despite Exceptions," *Legal Report SHRM,* October/November 2005, 1–8.
9. *Fortune v. National Cash Register Co.,* 373 Mass. 96, 36 N.E.2d 1251 (1977).
10. "What Is Constructive Discharge and How Do We Avoid It?" *Ceridian Abstracts, http://www.hrcompliance.ceridian.com.*
11. *Batka v. Prime Charter, Ltd.,* S.D.N.Y., No. 2 Civ. 6265 (February 4, 2004), as described in *Workforce Management,* May 2004, 20.
12. G. S. Alder and M. L. Ambrose, "Toward Understanding Fairness Judgments Associated with Computer Performance Monitoring," *Human Resource Management Review,* 15 (2005), 43–67.

13. Julia Connell, Natalie Ferrs, and Tony Travaglione, "Engendering Trust in Manager–Subordinate Relationships: Predictors and Outcomes," *Personnel Review,* 32 (2003), 569–580.
14. Tom McGhee, "Reservists See Woes in Rehire," *The Denver Post,* October 8, 2006, 1K.
15. Richard Nimark, "Getting Dispute-Wise," *Dispute Resolution Journal,* February/April 2004, 56–57.
16. Chad Schultz, "The Jury Is Still Out—Way Out," *HR Magazine,* January 2005, 97–100.
17. Margaret M. Clark, "A Jury of Your Peers," *HR Magazine,* January 2004, 54–59.
18. "What Is Peer Review and How Does It Work?" *Ceridian Abstracts, http://www.hrcompliance.ceridian.com.*
19. *Dixon v. Coburg Dairy Inc.,* No. 02-1266 (4th Cir. May 30, 2003).
20. Jennifer Schramm, "Revising the Internet," *HR Magazine,* August 2005, 168.
21. Stephanie Armour, "Warning: Your Clever Little Blog Could Get You Fired," *USA Today,* June 15, 2005, B1–2.
22. J. A. Segal, "Beware Bashing Bloggers," *HR Magazine,* June 2005, 165–171.
23. Robert Hof, "Web 2.0: The New Guy at Work," *Business Week,* June 19, 2006, 58–59.
24. Jayne O'Donnell, "$26.6M Won't Change Me, Whistle-Blower Says," *USA Today,* May 14, 2004, 2B.
25. Philip Berkowitz, "Sarbanes-Oxley Whistleblower Claims," *Legal Report SHRM,* July/August 2005, 1–3.
26. D. Solomon, "For Financial Whistleblowers New Shield Is an Imperfect One," *The Wall Street Journal,* October 4, 2004, A1; and D. Shadowitz, "Supreme Court Delivers

Blow to Whistleblowers," *Human Resources Executive Online,* June 1, 2006, http://www.hreonline.com.
27. Anna West, "Knowing Your Rights," *Cabinet Maker,* April 7, 2006, 14.
28. Mark McGraw, "Limiting Cooks," *Human Resource Executive,* October 2, 2005, 46–49.
29. Stephanie Armour, "Trend: You Smoke? You're Fired," *USA Today,* October 12, 2006, 1; and Kris Maher, "Companies Are Closing Doors on Job Applicants Who Smoke," *The Wall Street Journal,* December 21, 2004, B6.
30. Stephanie Armour and Julie Appleby, "Off Duty Behavior Can Affect Job," *USA Today,* June 13, 2005, 4B.
31. "Regulating Off Duty Conduct: How Far Can You Go?" *The HR Specialist,* March 2005, 1.
32. Carol Hymowitz, "Balancing Security and Trust," *The Wall Street Journal,* August 16, 2005, B1.
33. "Does Workplace Surveillance Help Security or Does It Go Too Far?" *Security Director's Report,* August 2005, 1–2.
34. Richard Breeden, "Small Talk/Internet Time," *The Wall Street Journal,* May 10, 2005, B4; and "Electronic Monitoring," *Human Resource Executive,* August 2005, 15.
35. Christopher Vaz, "Employer on Notice of Illicit Internet Use Has Duty to Investigate," January 6, 2006, www.shrm.org/hrnews.
36. John M. Ivancevich et al., "Deterring White-Collar Crime," *Academy of Management Executive,* May 2003, 114–127.
37. Gregory M. Davis, "Just the FACT Act, Please," *HR Magazine,* April 2004, 131–138.
38. "Survey Finds Pre-Employment Testing Most Popular Employer Choice,"

Workplace Substance Abuse Advisor, May 9, 2006, 1.

39. David Shadvitz, "Employers Win Most Drug-Testing Cases," *Human Resources Executive*, April 11, 2006, 27.

40. Diane Cadrain, "Drug Testing Falls Out of Employees Favor, " *HR Magazine*, June 2006, 38–48.

41. Based on Denise Rousseau et al., "I-Deals: Idiosyncratic Terms in Employment Relationships," *Academy of Management Review*, October 2006, 977–994.

42. W. S. Hubbartt, "Ten Reasons to Write (or Revise) Your Employee Handbook," *SHRM White Paper*, February 2006, 1–6.

43. James Thelen, "Arbitration Policy Found Wanting," *HR Magazine*, August 2005, 118.

44. Stuart R. Buttrick, "NLRB Punishes Employer for Failing to Follow Progressive Discipline Policy," *Indiana Employment Letter*, January 2004.

45. Provided by Nicholas Dayan, SPHR, and Saralee Ryan.

46. Based on Maura Dolan, "Court: Firm Liable for 'Ugly' Actions," *The Denver Post*, August 12, 2005, A5.

CHAPTER 17

Union/Management Relations

After you have read this chapter, you should be able to:

- Describe what a union is and explain why employees join and employers resist unions.

- Identify several reasons for the decline in union membership.

- Explain the acts that compose the National Labor Code.

- Discuss the stages of the unionization process.

- Describe the typical collective bargaining process.

- Define grievance and identify the stages in a grievance procedure.

HR Headline

Unions—Continuing Decline or Changing to Win?

Membership statistics in the United States are discouraging for unions and reflect continuing decline in union participation. Currently unions represent only 12% of the civilian U.S. workforce and only 7.4% of the private-sector employees. Unions represent 15.4 million of the 130 million U.S. workers.

The continuing losses have led to disagreements among unions about how to fight the decline. Rather than remaining a part of the traditional AFL-CIO labor organization, seven unions split into a new group in 2005. Calling itself the Change to Win Federation (CTWF), this association has a goal of taking a more aggressive approach to adding union members and affecting U.S. political legislation. Some of the industries and workers targeted by the CTWF include:

- Low-skilled workers in service industries such as home health-care workers, retail clerks, hotel housekeepers, and school bus drivers
- Professional employees, especially nurses and lower-level engineers
- Immigrant workers, whether legally documented or not, who serve as day workers in construction, food processing, ware-house, and other industry firms
- Firms that outsource jobs overseas, in order to protect U.S. employees who may be affected by such global moves

Whether or not the CTWF efforts will offset the continuing decline in union membership will take several years to determine. But if not successful, union membership in the United States is likely to continue to represent a diminishing part of the U.S. workforce.[1]

The changing nature of unions and unionization efforts will be interesting to observe during the next decade. How the economic and workforce changes affect employers and unions will be major factors. Even though fewer workers have chosen to be union members than in the past, employers and HR professionals still need to have an understanding of the system of laws, regulations, court decisions, and administrative rulings related to the nature of unions. This is important because unions remain an alternative for employees in the event of poor HR management.

NATURE OF UNIONS

Union Formal association of workers that promotes the interests of its members through collective action.

A union is a formal association of workers that promotes the interests of its members through collective action. Why employees join unions and why employers resist unionization are part of understanding the current state of unionization in the United States.

Why Employees Unionize

Whether a union targets a group of employees or the employees request union assistance, the union must win support from the employees to become their legal representative. Over the years employees have joined unions for two general reasons: (1) they are dissatisfied with how they are treated by their employers and (2) they believe that unions can improve their work situations. If employees do not receive what they perceive as fair treatment from their employers, they may turn to unions for help obtaining what they believe is equitable. As Figure 17-1 shows, the major factors that can trigger unionization are issues of compensation, working environment, management style, and employee treatment.

The primary determinant of whether employees unionize is management. Reasonably competitive compensation, a good working environment, effective management and supervision, and fair and responsive treatment of workers all act as antidotes to unionization efforts. Unionization results when employees feel disrespected, unsafe, underpaid, and unappreciated, and see a union as a viable option. Once unionization occurs, the union's ability to foster commitment from members and to remain as their bargaining agent depends on how well the union succeeds in providing services that its members want.

Why Employers Resist Unions

Employers usually would rather not have to deal with unions because doing so constrains what managers can and cannot do in a number of areas. Generally, union workers receive higher wages and benefits than do non-union workers.

| **FIGURE 17-1** | Factors Leading to Employee Unionization |

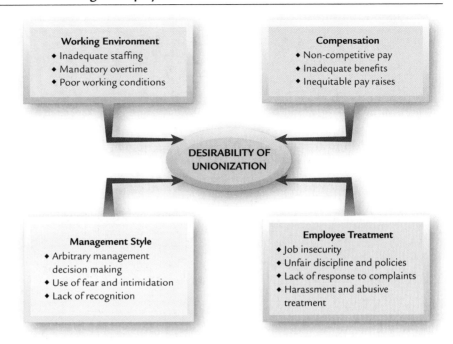

In turn, unions sometimes can be associated with higher productivity, although management must find labor-saving ways of doing work to offset the higher labor costs. Some employers pursue a strategy of good relations with unions. Others may choose an aggressive, adversarial approach.

HR Responsibilities and Unionization To prevent unionization, as well as to work effectively with unions already representing employees, both HR professionals and operating managers must be attentive and responsive to employees. The pattern of dealing with unionization varies among organizations. In some organizations, operating management handles labor relations and HR has limited involvement. In other organizations, the HR unit takes primary responsibility for resisting unionization or dealing with unionized employees.

UNIONS WORLDWIDE

As the world economy becomes more integrated, unions worldwide are facing changes. The status of global unions is being affected in several ways, as highlighted next.

Union Membership Globally

The percentage of union membership varies significantly from country to country as Figure 17-2 indicates. According to historical data, a survey of 30 countries found that since 1970, union membership percentages have increased in only four countries (Belgium, Denmark, Finland, and Sweden).[2]

Union membership is falling in many advanced countries, but collective bargaining is set in law as the way wages are determined in Europe. In many

FIGURE 17-2   **Adjusted Union Membership as a Percentage of the Workforce for Selected Countries**

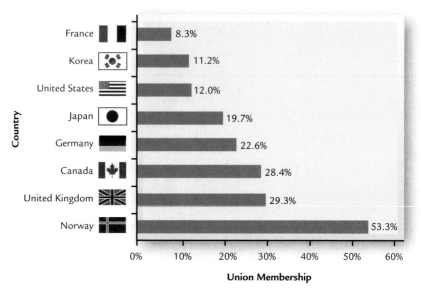

Source: U.S. Department of Labor, *Monthly Labor Review,* January 2006, 45.

European countries, artificially high wages and generous benefits have kept the unemployment rate high, however, the pressures for change are increasing. The range of labor concerns is quite wide and varies from country to country.[3] Child labor is an issue in some countries, whereas changes in participatory employment practices are issues in others.

In some countries, unions either do not exist at all or are relatively weak. In other countries, unions are closely tied to political parties. For instance, in Italy and France, national strikes occur regularly to protest proposed changes in government policy on retirement, pension programs, and regulations regarding dismissal of employees.

Co-determination Practice whereby union or worker representatives are given positions on a company's board of directors.

Co-Determination Some countries require that firms have union or worker representatives on their boards of directors. This practice, called co-determination, is common in European countries. Differences from country to country in how collective bargaining occurs also are quite noticeable. In the United States, local unions bargain with individual employers to set wages and working conditions. In Australia, unions argue their cases before arbitration tribunals. In Scandinavia, national agreements with associations of employers are the norm. In France and Germany, industry-wide or regional agreements are common. In Japan, local unions bargain but combine at some point to determine national wage patterns. Recent labor reform regulations in China are leading to increased union and worker representation in the management of Chinese-owned factories.

Global Labor Organizations

Global labor relations standards are being addressed by several organizations. The International Labour Organization, based in Switzerland, coordinates the efforts of labor unions worldwide and has issued some principles and rights at work.[4] Such coordination is increasingly occurring as unions deal with multinational firms having operations in multiple countries.

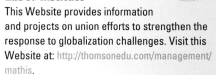

Internet Research

**Cornell Global
Labor Institute**

This Website provides information
and projects on union efforts to strengthen the
response to globalization challenges. Visit this
Website at: http://thomsonedu.com/management/
mathis.

Unions throughout the world also are linking up as part of global labor federations.[5] The Union International Network (UIN) is an entity composed of unions from numerous countries. This and other international groups are working to establish international policies on child labor, worker safety and health, training, and other aspects. Also, the UIN is providing aid and guidance to unions in developing countries, such as those in Africa and Asia.[6] U.S. unions are very active in these global entities. In some situations establishing agreements with employers based in the European Union has led to more U.S. union membership in the multi-national firms.[7]

U.S. and Global Unionization Differences

The union movement in the United States has some approaches different from those used in other countries. In the United States, the key emphases have been the following:

- *Economic issues:* In the United States, unions have typically focused on improving the "bread-and-butter" issues for their members—wages, benefits, job security, and working conditions.[8] In other countries, integration with ruling governmental and political power and activism are equal concerns along with economic issues.

- *Organization by kind of job and employer:* In the United States, carpenters often belong to the carpenters' union, truck drivers to the Teamsters, teachers to the American Federation of Teachers or the National Education Association, etc. Also, unionization can be done on a company-by-company basis. In other countries, national unions bargain with the government or with employer groups.

- *Collective agreements as "contracts":* In the United States, collective bargaining contracts usually spell out compensation, work rules, and the conditions of employment for several years. In other countries, the agreements are made with the government and employers, sometimes for only one year because of political and social issues.

- *Competitive relations:* In the United States, management and labor traditionally take the roles of competing adversaries who often "clash" to reach agreement. In many other countries, "tripartite" bargaining occurs between the national government, employers' associations, and national labor federations.

UNION MEMBERSHIP IN THE UNITED STATES

The statistics on union membership tell a disheartening story for organized labor in the United States during the past several decades. As shown in Figure 17-3, unions represented over 30% of the workforce from 1945 to 1960. But by 2006, unions in the United States represented less than 12% of all civilian workers and only 7.4% of the private-sector workforce. Even more disheartening for the unions, the actual number of members has declined in most years even though more people are employed than previously. Of the approximately 130 million U.S. workers, only about 15.4 million belong to a union.[9]

But within those averages, some unions have prospered. In the past several years, certain unions have organized thousands of janitors, health-care workers, cleaners, and other low-paid workers using publicity, pickets, boycotts, and strikes.

FIGURE 17-3   Union Membership as a Percentage of the U.S. Civilian Workforce

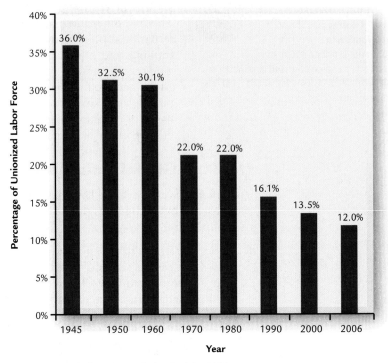

Source: U.S. Department of Labor, Bureau of Labor Statistics, 2007.

Reasons for U.S. Union Membership Decline

Several general reasons have contributed to the decline of unions: deregulation, foreign competition, a larger number of people looking for jobs, and a general perception by firms that dealing with unions is expensive compared with non-union alternatives. Also, management at many employers has taken a much more activist stance against unions than during the previous years of union growth.

To some extent, unions may be victims of their own successes. Unions historically have emphasized helping workers obtain higher wages and benefits, shorter working hours, job security, and safe working conditions from their employers. Some experts and union leaders believe that one cause for the decline of unions has been their success in getting those important issues passed into law for everyone. Therefore, unions are not seen as necessary for many workers, even though those workers enjoy the results of past union efforts to influence legislation.

Geographic Changes During the past decade, job growth in the United States has been the greatest in states located in the South, the Southwest, and the Rocky Mountains. Most of these states have little tradition of unions, "employer-friendly" laws, and relatively small percentages of unionized workers.

Another geographic issue involves the movement of many low-skill jobs outside the United States. Primarily to take advantage of cheaper labor, many manufacturers with heavily unionized U.S. workforces have moved a significant number of low-skill jobs to the Philippines, China, Thailand, and Mexico.

The passage of the North American Free Trade Agreement provided a major impetus for moving low-skill, low-wage jobs to Mexico. It removed tariffs and restrictions affecting the flow of goods and services among the United States, Canada, and Mexico. Because of significantly lower wage rates in Mexico, a number of jobs previously susceptible to unionization in the United States have been moved there.

Industrial Changes Much of the decline of union membership can be attributed to the shift in U.S. jobs from industries such as manufacturing, construction, and mining to service industries. There is a small percentage of union members in wholesale/retail industries and financial services, the sectors in which many new jobs have been added, whereas the number of industrial jobs continues to shrink.

One area that has led to union membership decline is the retirement of many union members in older manufacturing firms. But the extremely high retiree pensions and health benefits costs have led employers such as Goodyear Tire, Ford Motor Company, General Motors, and others to demand cuts in benefits for both current and retired employees These demands have led to employers cutting the number of current plants and workers as union concessions attempt to maintain benefits costs and job security for remaining workers.[10] In summary, private-sector union membership is primarily concentrated in the shrinking part of the economy, and unions are not making significant inroads into the fastest-growing segments in the U.S. economy. A look at Figure 17-4 reveals that non-governmental union members are heavily concentrated in transportation, utilities, and other "industrial" jobs.

FIGURE 17-4   **Union Membership by Industry**

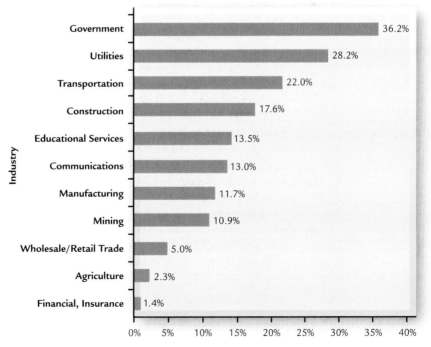

Union Members as Percentage of Total Workers in Industry

Source: U.S. Department of Labor, Bureau of Labor Statistics, 2007.

Workforce Changes Many of the workforce changes discussed in earlier chapters have contributed to the decrease in union representation of the labor force. The decline in many blue-collar jobs in manufacturing has been especially significant. For instance, the United Auto Workers' membership has dropped from 1.5 million in 1980 to about 600,000 currently.[11]

As mentioned earlier, the primary growth in jobs in the U.S. economy has been in technology, financial, and other service industries where union membership has typically been much lower. There are growing numbers of white-collar employees such as clerical workers, insurance claims representatives, data input processors, mental health aides, computer technicians, loan officers, auditors, and retail sales workers. Unions have increased efforts to organize white-collar workers as advances in technology have boosted their numbers in the workforce. However, unions face challenges in organizing these workers.

Many white-collar workers see unions as resistant to change and not in touch with the concerns of the more educated workers in technical and professional jobs. In addition, many white-collar workers exhibit attitudes and preferences quite different from those held by blue-collar union members, and they view unions as primarily blue-collar oriented.[12]

The growing percentage of women in the U.S. workforce presents another challenge to unions. In the past, unions have not been as successful in organizing female workers as they have been in organizing male workers.[13] Some unions are trying to focus more on recruiting female members, and unions have been in the forefront in the push for legislation on such family-related goals as child care, maternity and paternity leave, pay equity, and flexible work arrangements. Women in "pink-collar" low-skill service jobs have been somewhat more likely to join unions than women working in white-collar jobs.

Public-Sector Unionism

Unions have had significant success with public-sector employees. The government sector (federal, state, and local) is the most highly unionized part of the U.S. workforce, with 36% of government workers represented by unions. Local government workers at 42% have the highest unionization percentage of any group in the U.S. workforce.[14]

Unionization of state and local government employees presents some unique problems and challenges. First, some employees work in critical service areas. Allowing police officers, firefighters, and sanitation workers to strike endangers public health and safety. Consequently, more than 30 states have laws prohibiting work stoppages by public employees. These laws also identify a variety of ways to resolve negotiation impasses, including arbitration. But unions still give employees in these areas greater security and better ability to influence decisions on wages and benefits than non-union workers have.

Although unions in the federal government hold the same basic philosophy as unions in the private sector, they do differ somewhat. Previous laws and Executive Orders established methods of labor/management relations that consider the special circumstances present in the federal government.

Union Targets for Membership Growth

To attempt to counteract the overall decline in union membership, unions are focusing on a number of industries and types of workers. One reason why the Change to Win Federation split off from the AFL-CIO was to target more effectively the addition of members in the retail, hospitality, home health care, and other service industries.

Professionals Traditionally, professionals in many occupations have been skeptical of the advantages of unionization. However, professionals who have turned to unionization include engineers, physicians, nurses, and teachers. The health-care industry has been a specific focus for unionization of professionals such as physicians and physical therapists. Another area of union growth in the past few years has been nursing. The primary reason health-care employees consider union membership is the growth of managed care and health maintenance organizations (HMOs). A frequent complaint of health-care professionals is that they have lost control of patient-care decisions as a result of managed care and the spreading drive to reduce health-care costs. These complaints have led more health-care employees to join unions.

Low-Skill Workers On the other end of the labor scale, unions have targeted low-skill workers, many of whom have lower-paying, less desirable jobs. Janitors, building cleaners, nursing home aides, and meatpacking workers are examples of groups targeted by unions. For instance, in the health-care industry, workers in nursing homes dealing with the elderly are a fast-growing segment of the workforce. Many employees in this industry are relatively dissatisfied. The industry is often noted for its low pay and hard work, and many employees are women who work as nurses' aides, cooks, and launderers and in other low-wage jobs.

Another group of individuals targeted by unions is immigrant workers in low-skill jobs. Some unions have also been politically active regarding legislation to allow illegal immigrant workers to get work permits and citizenship over time. Although these efforts are not always successful, unions are likely to continue pursuing industries and employers with numerous low-skill jobs and workers. The advantages of unionization are especially strong for these employees.

Contingent and Part-Time Workers As many employers have added contingent workers instead of full-time employees, unions have tried to target part-time, temporary, and other employees. A decision by the National Labor Relations Board (NLRB) allows temporary workers to be included in firms to be represented by unions. Time will tell if the efforts to unionize part-time workers and other groups will halt the decline of union membership in the United States. When unions are present, collective bargaining agreements frequently limit the amount of contingent labor that may be used.

UNIONS IN THE UNITED STATES

For over two centuries the union movement has existed in some form or another. During that time the nature of unions has evolved because of various occurrences, legal and political changes, and other reasons.

Historical Evolution of U.S. Unions

The union movement in the United States began with early collective efforts by workers to address job concerns and counteract management power. As early as 1794, shoemakers organized a union, picketed, and conducted strikes. In those days, unions in the United States received very little support from the courts. In 1806, when the shoemakers' union struck for higher wages, a Philadelphia court found union members guilty of engaging in a "criminal conspiracy" to raise wages.

The *American Federation of Labor (AFL)* united a number of independent national unions in 1886. Its aims were to organize skilled craft workers and to emphasize economic issues and working conditions. As industrialization increased in the United States, many factories used semiskilled and unskilled workers. However, it was not until the *Congress of Industrial Organizations (CIO)* was founded in 1938 that a labor union organization focused on semiskilled and unskilled workers. Years later, the AFL and the CIO merged to become the AFL-CIO. That federation is the major organization coordinating union efforts in the United States today despite the split described in the HR Headline.

Internet Research

AFL-CIO
The AFL-CIO's home page provides union movement information. Link to their site at: http://thomsonedu.com/management/mathis.

Union Structure

U.S. labor is represented by many different unions. But regardless of size and geographic scope, two basic types of unions developed over time. In a craft union, members do one type of work, often using specialized skills and training. Examples are the International Association of Bridge, Structural, Ornamental and Reinforcing Iron Workers, and the American Federation of Television and Radio Artists. An industrial union includes many persons working in the same industry or company, regardless of jobs held. The United Food and Commercial Workers, the United Auto Workers, and the American Federation of State, County, and Municipal Employees are examples of industrial unions.

Craft union Union whose members do one type of work, often using specialized skills and training.

Industrial union Union that includes many persons working in the same industry or company, regardless of jobs held.

Federation Group of autonomous unions.

AFL-CIO Federation Labor organizations have developed complex organizational structures with multiple levels. The broadest level is the federation, which is a group of autonomous unions. A federation allows individual unions to work together and present a more unified front to the public, legislators, and members. The most prominent federation in the United States is the AFL-CIO, which is a confederation of unions currently representing about 10 million workers.[15]

Internet Research

Change to Win Federation
For information on union campaigns and issues, link to this site at: http://thomsonedu.com/management/mathis.

Change to Win Federation The establishment of the Change to Win Federation (CTWF) in 2005 meant that seven unions with about 6 million members left the AFL-CIO. The primary reason for the split was a division between different unions about how to stop the decline in union membership, as well as some internal organizational leadership and political issues. Prominent unions in the CTWF are the Teamsters, the Service Employees International Union, and the United Food and Commercial Workers.

National and International Unions National and international unions are not governed by a federation even if they are affiliated with it. They collect dues and have their own boards, specialized publications, and separate constitutions and bylaws. Such unions as the United Steelworkers of America and the American Federation of State, County, and Municipal Employees determine broad union policy and offer services to local union units. They also help maintain financial records and provide a base from which additional organizing drives may take place. Political infighting and corruption sometimes pose problems for national unions, as when the federal government stepped in and overturned the results of an officer election held by the Teamsters Union several years ago.

Like companies, unions find strength in size. In the past several years, about 40 mergers of unions have occurred, and a number of other unions have considered merging. For smaller unions, these mergers provide financial and union-organizing resources. Larger unions can add new members to cover managerial and administrative costs without spending funds to organize non-union workers to become members.[16]

Local Unions Local unions may be centered around a particular employer organization or around a particular geographic location. The membership of local unions elects officers who are subject to removal if they do not perform satisfactorily. For this reason, local union officers tend to be concerned with how they are perceived by the union members. They often react to situations as politicians do because their positions depend on obtaining votes. The local unions are the focus and the heart of labor/management relations in most U.S. companies.

Local unions typically have business agents and union stewards. A business agent is a full-time union official who operates the union office and assists union members. The agent runs the local headquarters, helps negotiate contracts with management, and becomes involved in attempts to unionize employees in other organizations. A union steward is an employee who is elected to serve as the first-line representative of unionized workers. Stewards address grievances with supervisors and generally represent employees at the work site.

Business agent Full-time union official who operates the union office and assists union members.

Union steward Employee elected to serve as the first-line representative of unionized workers.

UNION-RELATED LABOR LAWS

The right to organize workers and engage in collective bargaining offers little value if workers cannot freely exercise it. Historical evidence shows that management has consistently developed practices calculated to prevent workers from using this right. Over a period of many years, the federal government has taken action to both hamper unions and protect them.[17]

Early Labor Legislation

Beginning in the late 1800s, federal and state legislation related to unionization was passed. The two most prominent ones are discussed next.

Railway Labor Act The Railway Labor Act (RLA) of 1926 represented a shift in government regulation of unions. As a result of a joint effort between railroad management and unions to reduce transportation strikes, this act gave railroad employees "the right to organize and bargain collectively through representatives of their own choosing." In 1936, airlines and their employees were added to those covered by the RLA. Some experts believe that some of the labor relations problems in the airline industry stem from the provisions of the RLA, and that those problems would be more easily resolved if the airlines fell within the labor laws covering most other industries.

The RLA mandates a complex and cumbersome dispute resolution process. This process allows either the unions or the management to use the NLRB, a multi-stage dispute resolution process, and even the ability of the President of the United States to appoint an emergency board. The end result of having a prolonged process that is subject to political interference has been that unions often work for two or more years after the expiration of their old contracts because the process takes so long.

FIGURE 17-5   National Labor Code

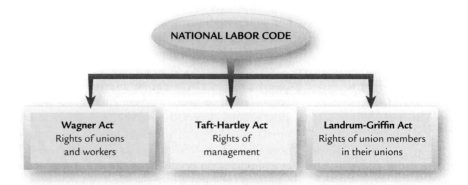

Norris-LaGuardia Act The crash of the stock market and the onset of the Great Depression in 1929 led to massive cutbacks by employers. In some industries, the resistance by employees led to strikes and violence. Under laws at that time, employers could go to court and have a federal judge issue injunctions ordering workers to return to work. In 1932, Congress passed the Norris-LaGuardia Act, which guaranteed workers some rights to organize and restricted the issuance of court injunctions in labor disputes. The economic crises of the early 1930s and the restrictions on workers' ability to organize into unions led to the passage of landmark labor legislation. Later acts reflected other pressures and issues that required legislative attention.

Following the Norris-LaGuardia Act, three acts were passed over a period of almost 25 years. These three acts constitute what has been labeled the "National Labor Code": (1) the Wagner Act, (2) the Taft-Hartley Act, and (3) the Landrum-Griffin Act. Each act was passed to focus on some facet of the relations between unions and management. Figure 17-5 indicates the primary focus of each act. Two other pieces of legislation, the Civil Service Reform Act and the Postal Reorganization Act, also affect governmental aspects of union/management relations.

Wagner Act (National Labor Relations Act)

The National Labor Relations Act, more commonly referred to as the Wagner Act, has been called the Magna Carta of labor and was, by anyone's standards, pro-union. Passed in 1935, the Wagner Act was an outgrowth of the Great Depression. With employers having to close or cut back their operations, workers were left with little job security. Unions stepped in to provide a feeling of solidarity and strength for many workers. The Wagner Act declared, in effect, that the official policy of the U.S. government was to encourage collective bargaining. Specifically, it established the right of workers to organize unhampered by management interference through unfair labor practices.

Unfair Labor Practices To protect union rights, the Wagner Act prohibited employers from utilizing unfair labor practices. Five of those practices are identified as follows:

- Interfering with, restraining, or coercing employees in the exercise of their right to organize or to bargain collectively
- Dominating or interfering with the formation or administration of any labor organization

- Encouraging or discouraging membership in any labor organization by discriminating with regard to hiring, tenure, or conditions of employment
- Discharging or otherwise discriminating against an employee because he or she filed charges or gave testimony under the act
- Refusing to bargain collectively with representatives of the employees

National Labor Relations Board The Wagner Act established the National Labor Relations Board as an independent entity to enforce the provisions of the act. The NLRB administers all provisions of the Wagner Act and of subsequent labor relations acts. The primary functions of the NLRB include conducting unionization elections, investigating complaints by employers or unions through its fact-finding process, issuing opinions on its findings, and prosecuting violations in court. The five members of the NLRB are appointed by the President of the United States and confirmed by the U.S. Senate.

Internet Research

National Labor Relations Board

For information on workplace rights and other issues, visit the NLRB's Website at: http://thomsonedu.com/management/mathis.

Taft-Hartley Act (Labor-Management Relations Act)

The passage in 1947 of the Labor-Management Relations Act, better known as the Taft-Hartley Act, was accomplished as a means to offset the pro-union Wagner Act by limiting union actions. Therefore, it was considered to be pro-management and became the second part of the National Labor Code.

The new law amended or qualified in some respect all the major provisions of the Wagner Act and established an entirely new code of conduct for unions. The Taft-Hartley Act forbade unions from engaging in a series of unfair labor practices, much like those management was prohibited from engaging in. Coercion, discrimination against non-members, refusing to bargain, excessive membership fees, and other practices were not allowed by unions. A 1974 amendment extended coverage of the Taft-Hartley Act to private, non-profit hospitals and nursing homes.

The Taft-Hartley Act also established the Federal Mediation and Conciliation Service (FMCS) as an agency to help management and labor settle labor contract disputes. The act required that the FMCS be notified of disputes over contract renewals or modifications if they were not settled within 30 days after the designated date.

National Emergency Strikes The Taft-Hartley Act allows the President of the United States to declare that a strike presents a national emergency. A national emergency strike is one that would impact an industry or a major part of it in such a way that the national economy would be significantly affected. The act allows the U.S. President to declare an *80-day "cooling off" period* during which union and management continue negotiations. Only after that period can a strike occur if settlements have not been reached.

Over the decades national emergencies have been identified in the railroad, airline, and other industries. In 2002, the national emergency provisions were involved for the first time in 25 years because of a strike of transportation and dock workers throughout the U.S. West Coast states. During the 80-day period a contract agreement was reached, so a strike was averted.[18]

National emergency strike Strike that would impact the national economy significantly.

Internet Research

Right-to-Work

This Website contains information from the National Right to Work Legal Defense Foundation. Link to their Website at: http://thomsonedu.com/management/mathis.

Right-to-Work Provision One specific provision of the Taft-Hartley Act, Section 14(b), deserves special explanation. This

Right-to-work laws State laws that prohibit requiring employees to join unions as a condition of obtaining or continuing employment.

section allows states to pass laws that restrict compulsory union membership. Accordingly, some states have passed right-to-work laws, which prohibit requiring employees to join unions as a condition of obtaining or continuing employment. The laws were so named because they allow a person the right to work without having to join a union.

The states that have enacted these laws are shown in Figure 17-6. In states with right-to-work laws, employers may have an open shop, which indicates workers cannot be required to join or pay dues to a union. Thus, even though a union may represent an entire group of employees at a company, individual workers cannot be required or coerced to join the union or pay dues. Consequently, in many of the right-to-work states, individual membership in union groups is significantly lower. For instance, at one Midwestern firm where the employee group is unionized, fewer than 25% of those represented actually belong to the union and pay dues.

Open shop Firm in which workers are not required to join or pay dues to a union.

The National Right to Work Legal Defense Foundation is an organization that has lobbied for more states to become right-to-work states. Also, that organization has become involved in lawsuits where workers have claimed to have been coerced to join unions.[19]

Closed shop Firm that requires individuals to join a union before they can be hired.

The nature of union/management relations is affected by the right-to-work provisions. The Taft-Hartley Act generally prohibits the closed shop, which is a firm that requires individuals to join a union before they can be hired. Because of concerns that a closed shop allows a union to "control" who may be considered for employment and who must be hired by an employer, Section 14(b) prohibits the closed shop except in construction-related occupations.

FIGURE 17-6   Right-to-Work States

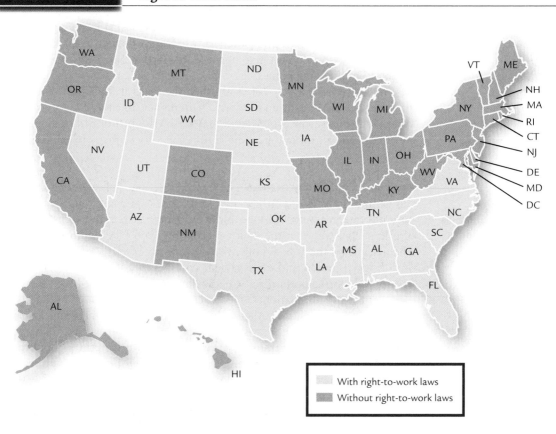

With right-to-work laws

Without right-to-work laws

In states that do not have right-to-work laws, there may be a number of different types of arrangements. Three of the different types of "shops" are as follows:

- *Union shop:* Requires that individuals join the union, usually 30 to 60 days after being hired.
- *Agency shop:* Requires employees who refuse to join the union to pay amounts equal to union dues and fees in return for the representation services of the union.
- *Maintenance-of-membership shop:* Requires workers to remain members of the union for the period of the labor contract.

The nature of those shops are negotiated between the union and the employer.[20] Often employees who fail to meet the requirements are terminated from their jobs.

Landrum-Griffin Act (Labor-Management Reporting and Disclosure Act)

The third segment of the National Labor Code, the Landrum-Griffin Act, was passed in 1959. Because a union is supposed to be a democratic institution in which union members vote on and elect officers and approve labor contracts, the Landrum-Griffin Act was passed in part to ensure that the federal government protects the democratic rights of those members. Under the Landrum-Griffin Act, unions are required to establish bylaws, make financial reports, and provide union members with a bill of rights. The law appointed the U.S. Secretary of Labor to act as a watchdog of union conduct.

In a few instances, union officers have attempted to maintain their jobs by physically harassing or attacking individuals who have tried to oust them from office. In other cases, union officials have "milked" pension fund monies for their own use. Such instances are not typical of most unions, but illustrate the need for legislative oversight to protect individual union members.

Civil Service Reform Act of 1978

Passed as part of the Civil Service Reform Act of 1978, the Federal Service Labor-Management Relations statute made major changes in how the federal government deals with unions. The act also identified areas subject to bargaining and established the Federal Labor Relations Authority (FLRA) as an independent agency similar to the NLRB. The FLRA, a three-member body, was given the authority to oversee and administer union/management relations in the federal government and to investigate unfair practices in union organizing efforts.

In a somewhat related area, the Postal Reorganization Act of 1970 established the U.S. Postal Service as an independent entity. Part of the 1970 act prohibited postal workers from striking and established a dispute resolution process for them to follow.

UNIONIZATION PROCESS

The typical union organizing process is outlined in Figure 17-7. The process of unionizing an employer may begin in one of two primary ways: (1) a union targeting an industry or a company, or (2) employees requesting union

FIGURE 17-7   **Typical Unionization Process**

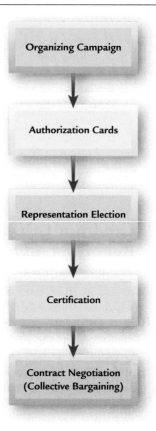

representation. In the first case, the local or national union identifies a firm or an industry in which it believes unionization can succeed. The logic for targeting is that if the union succeeds in one firm or a portion of the industry, then many other workers in the industry will be more willing to consider unionizing.

In the second case, the impetus for union organizing occurs when individual workers at an employer contact a union and express a desire to unionize. The employees themselves—or the union—may then begin to campaign to win support among the other employees.

Organizing Campaign

Like other entities seeking members, a union usually mounts an organized campaign to persuade individuals to support its efforts. As would be expected, employers respond to unionization efforts by taking various types of actions.

Employers' Union Prevention Efforts Management representatives may use various tactics to defeat a unionization effort. Such tactics often begin when union publicity appears or during the distribution of authorization cards. Some employers such as Con Agra, Coca-Cola, and Wal-Mart, hire expert consultants who specialize in combating unionization efforts. Using these "union busters," as they are called by unions, appears to enhance employers' chances of winning the representation election (discussed later). Union prevention efforts that may be conducted by consultants or done by management and outside labor attorneys include[21]:

- Holding mandatory employee meetings.
- Distributing anti-union leaflets at work and mailing anti-union letters to employees' homes.
- Providing and using anti-union videos, e-mails, and other electronic means.

Many employers have a written "no-solicitation" policy to restrict employees and outsiders from distributing literature or soliciting union membership on company premises. Employers without such a policy may be unable to prevent those acts. A policy against solicitation must be a long-term, established approach, not a single action taken to counter a specific and immediate unionization attempt. For example, the Steelworkers union sought certification by the NLRB to be the bargaining agent for the Canton, Ohio, facility of Schuler Engineering. After the union lost the election by one vote, it protested that the company had interfered with the right to organize when, just before the election, it adopted a rule prohibiting the posting of pro-union material on an employee bulletin board. The NLRB set aside the first election, and the company lost the second election.[22]

Employers may make strategic decisions and take aggressive steps to remain non-union. Such a choice is perfectly rational, but may require some specific HR policies and philosophies. For example, "preventive" employee relations may emphasize good morale and loyalty based on concern for employees, competitive wages and benefits, a fair system for dealing with employee complaints, and safe working conditions. Other issues may also play a part in employees' decisions to stay non-union, but if employers adequately address the points just listed, fewer workers are likely to feel the need for a union to represent them.

Unions' Organizing Efforts The persuasion efforts by unions can take many forms, including personally contacting employees outside work, mailing materials to employees' homes, inviting employees to attend special meetings away from the company, and publicizing the advantages of union membership. Brochures and leaflets can be given to employees as they leave work, mailed to their homes, or even attached to their vehicles, as long as they comply with the rules established by laws and the NLRB. The HR On-Line feature describes how unions use electronic communications in their organizing efforts. The purpose of all this publicity is to encourage employees to sign authorization cards.

Unions sometimes pay organizers to infiltrate a targeted employer and try to organize workers. In this practice, known as salting, the unions hire and pay people to apply for jobs at certain companies; when the people are hired, they begin organizing efforts. The U.S. Supreme Court has ruled that refusing to hire otherwise qualified applicants, even if they are also paid by a union, violates the Wagner Act. However, employers may refuse to hire "salts" for job-related and non-discriminatory reasons.[23]

Salting Practice in which unions hire and pay people to apply for jobs at certain companies to begin organizing efforts.

Authorization Cards

Union authorization card Card signed by an employee to designate a union as her or his collective bargaining agent.

A union authorization card is signed by an employee to designate a union as her or his collective bargaining agent. At least 30% of the employees in the targeted group must sign authorization cards before an election can be called.

HR ONLINE

E-Organizing Aids Unions

To encourage individuals to become involved in unionization efforts, unions have been quite willing to adopt electronic means, such as establishing Web-sites where interested workers can read about benefits of unionization. For instance, the Service Employees International Union has Websites and chat rooms where nurses at non-union hospitals can exchange information with unionized nurses. The Change to Win Federation and the AFL-CIO both have Web links and blogs available through their Websites to provide union information on-line. These sites explain workers' rights and give examples of the advantages of being union members. Successes in unionizing groups of employees are described. Also, the differences between wages, benefits, and job security are contrasted before and after unionization occurred.

E-mail has also changed union organizing efforts because unions can receive e-mails from workers wanting information on unionization and their rights to union representation. Other unions have gathered the home e-mail addresses of workers who are targets for unionization and sent those workers union solicitation information.

Employers with e-mail restrictions may enforce them when union solicitation e-mails are received, sent, or forwarded using employer-provided systems. But if they do so, they must also restrict all personal, non-business messages for everyone in the organization. This means that employees using e-mail to protest or comment on employers' actions or the desirability of unionization may be protected unless employers have clear, established, and enforced policies.

Unionization and Possible Legislative Changes Union advocates have lobbied for changing laws so that elections are not needed if over 50% of the eligible employees sign authorization cards. Some states have enacted such laws for public-sector unionization. Also, some employers have taken a "neutral" approach, and agreed to recognize unions if a majority of workers sign authorization cards.[24] Some employers' agreements allow for *card checks* to be done by a neutral outside party to verify union membership and authorization cards.

A number of politicians, such as Senator Edward Kennedy, have supported changing laws on union elections. Called the *Employee Free Choice Act*, the proposed regulations would do the following:

- Eliminate the secret ballot for electing union representation. Instead, if over 50% of employees sign authorization cards, the union is automatically the representative of all workers.
- Require mandatory contract arbitration 120 days after the election, rather than allowing employers to negotiate longer or resist certain contract provisions.

Because this act has been opposed actively by employers and some politicians, it has not been passed as of the publication of this text. However, as political forces and representation change, it is possible that this act could ultimately become law.

In reality, the fact that an employee signs an authorization card does not mean that the employee is in favor of a union; it means only that the employee would like the opportunity to vote on having a union. Employees who do not want a union might sign authorization cards because they want management to know they are disgruntled or to avoid upsetting a co-worker advocating unionization.

Employers and some politicians argue that eliminating elections violates the personal secrecy and democracy rights of employees. The extent of legislative changes will depend on the political composition of the U.S. Congress and Presidential reactions to such efforts.

Representation Election

An election to determine if a union will represent the employees is supervised by the NLRB for private-sector organizations and by other legal bodies for public-sector organizations. If two unions are attempting to represent employees, the employees will have three choices: union A, union B, and no union.

Bargaining unit Employees eligible to select a single union to represent and bargain collectively for them.

Bargaining Unit Before any election, the appropriate bargaining unit must be determined. A bargaining unit is composed of all employees eligible to select a single union to represent and bargain collectively for them. If management and the union do not agree on who is and who is not included in the unit, the regional office of the NLRB must make the determination. A major criterion in deciding the composition of a bargaining unit is what the NLRB calls a "community of interest." At a warehouse distribution firm, for example, delivery drivers, accounting clerks, computer programmers, and mechanics would probably not be included in the same bargaining unit; these employees have widely varying jobs, areas of work, physical locations, and other differences that would likely negate a community of interest. Employees who constitute a bargaining unit have mutual interests in the following areas:

- Wages, hours, and working conditions
- Traditional industry groupings for bargaining purposes
- Physical location and amount of interaction and working relationships between employee groups
- Supervision by similar levels of management

Supervisors and Union Ineligibility Provisions of the National Labor Relations Act exclude supervisors from protection when attempting to vote for or join unions. As a result, supervisors cannot be included in bargaining units for unionization purposes, except in industries covered by the Railway Labor Act.

But who qualifies as a supervisor is not always clear. The NLRB expanded its definition to identify a supervisor as any individual with authority to hire, transfer, discharge, discipline, and use independent judgment with employees.[25] Numerous NLRB and court decisions have been rendered on specific situations. A major case decided by the U.S. Supreme Court found that charge nurses with RN degrees were supervisors because they exercised independent judgment.[26] This case and others have provided employers and unions with some guidance about who should be considered supervisors and thus excluded from bargaining units.

Unfair Labor Practices Employers and unions engage in a number of activities before an election. Both the Wagner Act and the Taft-Hartley Act place restrictions on these activities. In a recent year, when unfair labor practice charges were filed with the NLRB, about one-third of them were found to be valid. About 90% of those were settled once the NLRB rulings were made, while the remaining ones went to court.[27]

HR ON-THE-JOB

Unionization Do's and Don'ts for Managers

Employers can take numerous actions to prevent unionization. All managers and supervisors must adhere to NLRB and other requirements to avoid unfair labor practices. Listed below are some common do's and don'ts.

✔ Do (Legal)	✘ Don't (Illegal)
■ Tell employees how current wages and benefits compare with those in other firms.	■ Promise employees pay increases or promotions if they vote against the union.
■ Tell employees why the employer opposes unionization.	■ Threaten to close down or move the company if a union is voted in.
■ Tell employees the disadvantages of having a union (dues, assessments, etc.).	■ Spy on or have someone spy on union meetings.
■ Show employees articles about unions and relate negative experiences elsewhere.	■ Make a speech to employees or groups at work within 24 hours of the election. (Before that, it is allowed.)
■ Explain the unionization process to employees accurately.	■ Ask employees how they plan to vote or if they have signed authorization cards.
■ Forbid distribution of union literature during work hours in work areas.	■ Encourage employees to persuade others to vote against the union.
■ Enforce disciplinary policies and rules consistently and appropriately.	■ Threaten employees with termination or discipline union-advocate employees.

Once unionizing efforts begin, all activities must conform to the requirements established by applicable labor laws. Both management and the union must adhere to those requirements, or the results of the effort can be appealed to the NLRB and overturned. The HR On-the-Job highlights some of the legal and illegal actions managers must be aware of during unionization efforts.

Election Process If an election is held, the union need receive only a *majority of the votes*. For example, if a group of 200 employees is the identified bargaining unit, and only 50 people vote, only 26 (50% of those voting plus 1) need to vote yes for the union to be named as the representative of all 200 employees. Typically, the smaller the number of employees in the bargaining unit, the higher the likelihood that the union will win. In recent years the unions have won a majority of the elections held.[28]

If either side believes that the other side used unfair labor practices, the election results can be appealed to the NLRB. If the NLRB finds evidence of unfair practices, it can order a new election. If no unfair practices were used and the union obtains a majority in the election, the union then petitions the NLRB for certification.

Certification and Decertification

Official certification of a union as the legal representative for designated private-sector employees is given by the NLRB, or for public-sector employees by an equivalent body. Once certified, the union attempts to negotiate a contract with the employer. The employer *must* bargain; refusing to bargain with a certified union constitutes an unfair labor practice.

When members no longer wish to be represented by the union, they can use the election process to sever the relationship between themselves and the union. Similar to the unionization process, decertification is a process whereby a union is removed as the representative of a group of employees. Employees attempting to oust a union must obtain decertification authorization cards signed by at least 30% of the employees in the bargaining unit before an election may be called. If a majority of those voting in the election want to remove the union, the decertification effort succeeds. Some reasons that employees decide to vote out a union are that the treatment provided by employers has improved, the union has been unable to address the changing needs of the organizational workforce, or the image of the union has declined. Current regulations prohibit employers from initiating or supporting decertification because it is a matter between employees and unions, and employers must stay out of the process.

Decertification Process whereby a union is removed as the representative of a group of employees.

Contract Negotiation (Collective Bargaining)

Collective bargaining, the last step in unionization, is the process whereby representatives of management and workers negotiate over wages, hours, and other terms and conditions of employment. This give-and-take process between representatives of the two organizations attempts to establish conditions beneficial to both. It is also a relationship based on relative power.

Management/union relations in collective bargaining can follow one of several patterns. Figure 17-8 depicts them as a continuum, ranging from conflict to collusion. On the left side of the continuum, management and the union see each other as enemies. On the right side, the two entities join together in collusion, which is relatively rare in U.S. labor history and is illegal. Most positions fall between these two extremes.

The power relationship in collective bargaining involves conflict, and the threat of conflict seems necessary to maintain the relationship. But perhaps the most significant aspect of collective bargaining is that it is a continuing relationship that does not end immediately after agreement is reached. Instead, it continues for the life of the labor agreement and beyond. Therefore, the more cooperative management is, the less hostility and conflict with unionized employees there is that carries over to the workplace.[29] However, this cooperation does not mean that the employer agrees to all union demands.

Collective bargaining Process whereby representatives of management and workers negotiate over wages, hours, and other terms and conditions of employment.

FIGURE 17-8   **Continuum of Collective Bargaining Relations**

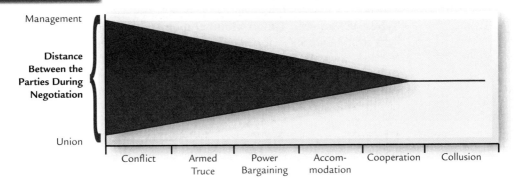

Bargaining Pattern

COLLECTIVE BARGAINING ISSUES

A number of issues can be addressed during collective bargaining. Although not often listed as such in the contract, management rights and union security are two important issues subject to collective bargaining. These and other issues may be classified in several ways, as discussed next.

Management Rights

Management rights
Rights reserved so that the employer can manage, direct, and control its business.

Virtually all labor contracts include management rights, which are rights reserved so that the employer can manage, direct, and control its business. By including such a provision, management attempts to preserve its unilateral right to make changes in areas not identified in a labor contract. A typical provision might read as follows:

> The employer retains all rights to manage, direct, and control its business in all particulars, except as such rights are expressly and specifically modified by the terms of this or any subsequent agreement.

Union Security

Union security provisions
Contract clauses to help the union obtain and retain members.

A major concern of union representatives when bargaining is the negotiation of union security provisions, which are contract clauses to help the union obtain and retain members. A growing type of union security in labor contracts is the *no-layoff policy,* or *job security guarantee.* Such a provision is especially important to many union workers because of all the mergers, downsizings, and job reductions taking place in many industrial, textile, and manufacturing firms.

Union Dues Issues One union security provision is the *dues checkoff,* which provides for the automatic deduction of union dues from the payroll checks of union members. The dues checkoff makes it much easier for the union to collect its funds; without it, the union must collect dues by billing each member separately.

However, federal court cases have been filed that restrict unions from using such checkoffs for contributions to political and congressional candidates. A recent U.S. Supreme Court case supported the constitutionality of state laws that require labor unions to get written consent before using non-member fees for political purposes. The court noted that Washington, like many other states, allows public sector unions to levy fees on non-member employees, as well as "agency shop" agreements. But it held that under such arrangements, the union must obtain express authorization from the non-members to use their agency fees for election-related purposes.[30]

Types of Required Union Membership Another form of union security results from *requiring union membership* of all employees, subject to state right-to-work laws. As mentioned earlier, a closed shop is illegal except in limited situations within the construction industry. But other types of arrangements can be developed, including union shops, agency shops, and maintenance-of-membership shops, which were discussed earlier.

Classification of Bargaining Issues

The NLRB has defined collective bargaining issues in three ways. The categories it has used are mandatory, permissive, and illegal.

Mandatory issues
Collective bargaining issues identified specifically by labor laws or court decisions as subject to bargaining.

Mandatory Issues Issues identified specifically by labor laws or court decisions as subject to bargaining are mandatory issues. If either party demands that issues in this category be subject to bargaining, then that must occur. Generally, mandatory issues relate to wages, benefits, nature of jobs, and other work-related subjects. Mandatory subjects for bargaining include the following:

- Discharge of employees
- Grievances
- Work schedules
- Union security and dues checkoff
- Retirement and pension coverage
- Vacations and time off
- Rest and lunch break rules
- Safety rules
- Profit-sharing plans
- Required physical exam

Permissive issues
Collective bargaining issues that are not mandatory and that relate to certain jobs.

Permissive Issues Issues that are not mandatory and that relate to certain jobs are permissive issues. For example, the following issues can be bargained over if both parties agree: benefits for retired employees, product prices for employees, or performance bonds.

Illegal issues Collective bargaining issues that would require either party to take illegal action.

Illegal Issues A final category, illegal issues, includes those issues that would require either party to take illegal action. Examples would be giving preference to union members when hiring employees or demanding a closed-shop provision in the contract. If one side wants to bargain over an illegal issue, the other side can refuse.

COLLECTIVE BARGAINING PROCESS

The collective bargaining process consists of a number of stages: preparation and initial demands, negotiations, settlement or impasse, and strikes and lockouts. Throughout the process, management and labor deal with the terms of their relationship.

Preparation and Initial Demands

Both labor and management representatives spend considerable time preparing for negotiations. Employer and industry data concerning wages, benefits, working conditions, management and union rights, productivity, and absenteeism are gathered. If the organization argues that it cannot afford to pay what the union is asking, the employer's financial situation and accompanying data become all the more relevant. However, the union must request such information before the employer is obligated to provide it. Typical bargaining includes initial proposals of expectations by both sides. The amount of rancor or calmness exhibited may set the tone for future negotiations between the parties.

Core Bargaining Issues The primary focus of bargaining for both union and management is on the core areas of wages, benefits, and working hours and conditions. The importance of this emphasis is seen in several ways.

Union wages and benefits generally are higher than in non-unionized firms. As shown in Figure 17-9, in a recent year median earnings for union members were $833/week compared with non-union amount of $642/week. The additional $191/week represents almost $10,000/year more for union members' wages than non-union wages. In the unionized American companies building cars (GM, Ford, and Chrysler), labor costs average over $1,600 per car more compared with the non-unionized Japanese companies building cars in the United States (Toyota, Nissan, and Honda). Thus, it is common for wages and benefits to be higher in unionized firms.[31]

FIGURE 17-9   Industry Weekly Earnings of Union and Non-Union Workers

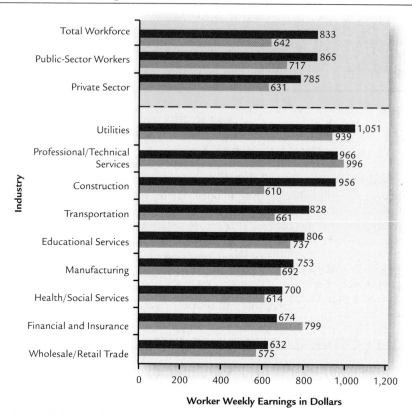

Source: Bureau of Labor Statistics, "Union Members in 2006," January 25, 2007, *www.bls.gov/cps.*

Continuing Negotiations

After taking initial positions, each side attempts to determine what the other side values highly so that the best bargain can be struck. For example, the union may be asking the employer to pay for dental benefits as part of a package that also includes wage increases and retirement benefits. However, the union may be most interested in the retirement benefits, and may be willing to trade the dental payments for better retirement benefits. Management must determine what the union has as a priority and decide exactly what to give up.

Good Faith Provisions in federal law require that both employers and union bargaining representatives negotiate in good faith. In good-faith negotiations, the parties agree to send negotiators who can bargain and make decisions, rather than people who do not have the authority to commit either group to a decision. To be more effective, meetings between the parties should be conducted professionally and address issues, rather than being confrontational. Refusing to bargain, scheduling meetings at absurdly inconvenient hours, or other conflicting tactics may lead to employers or unions filing complaints with the NLRB.

Settlement and Contract Agreement

Ratification Process by which union members vote to accept the terms of a negotiated labor agreement.

After reaching an initial agreement, the bargaining parties usually return to their respective constituencies to determine if the informal agreement is acceptable. A particularly crucial stage is ratification of the labor agreement, which occurs when union members vote to accept the terms of a negotiated labor

FIGURE 17-10   Typical Items in a Labor Agreement

Labor Agreement

1. Purpose of agreement
2. Non-discrimination clause
3. Management rights
4. Recognition of the union
5. Wages
6. Incentives
7. Hours of work
8. Vacations
9. Sick leave and leaves of absence
10. Discipline

11. Separation allowance
12. Seniority
13. Bulletin boards
14. Pension and insurance
15. Safety
16. Grievance procedure
17. No-strike or lockout clause
18. Definitions
19. Terms of contract (dates)
20. Appendices

agreement. Before ratification, the union negotiating team explains the agreement to the union members and presents it for a vote. If the members approve the agreement, it is then formalized into a contract. Figure 17-10 lists typical items in labor agreements.

Bargaining Impasse

Conciliation Process by which a third party assists union and management negotiators to reach a voluntary settlement.

Mediation Process by which a third party helps the negotiators reach a settlement.

Arbitration Process that uses a neutral third party to make a decision.

Regardless of the structure of the bargaining process, labor and management do not always reach agreement on the issues. If they reach an impasse, then the disputes can be taken to conciliation, mediation, or arbitration.

Conciliation and Mediation When an impasse occurs, an outside party such as the Federal Mediation and Conciliation Service may help the two deadlocked parties to continue negotiations and arrive at a solution. In conciliation, the third party assists union and management negotiators to reach a voluntary settlement, but makes no proposals for solutions. In mediation, the third party helps the negotiators reach a settlement.[32]

In neither conciliation nor mediation does the third party attempt to impose a solution. Sometimes, *fact-finding* helps to clarify the issues of disagreement as an intermediate step between mediation and arbitration.

Arbitration In arbitration, a neutral third party makes a decision. Arbitration can be conducted by an individual or a panel of individuals. "Interest" arbitration attempts to solve bargaining impasses, primarily in the public sector. This type of arbitration is not frequently used in the private sector because companies generally do not want an outside party making decisions about their rights, wages, benefits, and other issues. However, grievance or "rights" arbitration is used extensively in the private sector. Fortunately, in many situations, agreements are reached through negotiations without the need for arbitration.[33] When disagreements continue, strikes or lockouts may occur.

Internet Research

Federal Mediation and Conciliation Service
This Website provides information on the services and resources available through the agency of the U.S. government that handles arbitration and mediation of labor disputes and contract negotiations. Visit their site at:
http://thomsonedu.com/management/mathis.

Strikes and Lockouts

Strike Work stoppage in which union members refuse to work in order to put pressure on an employer.

Lockout Shutdown of company operations undertaken by management to prevent union members from working.

If a deadlock cannot be resolved, an employer may revert to a lockout—or a union then may revert to a strike. During a strike, union members refuse to work in order to put pressure on an employer. Often, the striking union members picket or demonstrate against the employer outside the place of business by carrying placards and signs. In a lockout, management shuts down company operations to prevent union members from working. This action may avert possible damage or sabotage to company facilities or injury to employees who continue to work. It also gives management leverage in negotiations.

Types of Strikes Five types of strikes can occur:

- *Economic strikes* happen when the parties fail to reach agreement during collective bargaining.
- *Unfair labor practices strikes* occur when union members leave their jobs over what they feel are illegal employer actions, such as refusal to bargain.
- *Wildcat strikes* occur during the life of the collective bargaining agreement without approval of union leadership and violate a no-strike clause in a labor contract. Strikers can be discharged or disciplined.
- *Jurisdictional strikes* exist when members of one union walk out to force the employer to assign work to them instead of to members of another union.
- *Sympathy strikes* take place when one union chooses to express support for another union involved in a dispute, even though the first union has no disagreement with the employer.

As a result of the decline in union power, work stoppages due to strikes and lockouts are relatively rare. In a recent year only 22 strikes and lockouts occurred. Over three-fourths of the work stoppages ended within 20 days.[34] This is occurring because many unions are reluctant to go on strike due to the financial losses their members would incur or the fear that a strike would cause the employer to go bankrupt. In addition, management has shown its willingness to hire replacements, and some strikes have ended with union workers losing their jobs.

Replacement of Workers on Strike Management retains and sometimes uses its ability to simply replace workers who strike. Workers' rights vary depending on the type of strike that occurs. For example, in an economic strike, an employer is free to replace the striking workers. But with an unfair labor practices strike, the workers who want their jobs back at the end of the strike must be reinstated.

UNION/MANAGEMENT COOPERATION

The adversarial relationship that naturally exists between unions and management may lead to strikes and lockouts. However, such conflicts are relatively rare. Even more encouraging is the recognition on the part of some union leaders and employer representatives that cooperation between management and labor unions offers a useful route if organizations are to compete effectively in a global economy, as the HR Best Practices describes.

HR BEST PRACTICES

Management/Union Cooperation Flies

Typically, management resists union efforts and has had limited cooperation with unions. But a few firms have found that working with unions as workforce partners has paid off.

One company that illustrates such a partnership effort is Southwest Airlines. Southwest is one of the few airlines that has cooperated extensively with the International Association of Machinists and Aerospace Workers (IAMAW) and several other unions to focus on job security, workplace effectiveness, and workforce productivity. While conflicts with unions at Southwest Airlines sometimes still arise, contrast this with what occurs at several other airlines. Northwest Airlines and

U.S. Airways have had strikes and ongoing contentious relations. The cooperative relationship that Southwest Airlines has had with its unions is believed to be one major reason that Southwest Airlines has been more profitable than other airlines and has consistently been viewed by customers as a better performing airline.

Cooperative partnership efforts throughout all industries are still less common than more confrontational efforts. For instance, of the 5,000 firms where IAMAW represents workers, only 12 have established similar partnership-type efforts. Employers and unions will not always agree on issues, but efforts at Southwest Airlines and others have been effective.[35]

Internet Research

National Labor Management Association

For information and articles geared toward helping management and organized labor work together effectively, visit the National Labor Management Association's Website at: http://thomsonedu.com/management/mathis.

During the past decade, numerous firms have engaged in organizational and workplace restructuring in response to competitive pressures in their industries. Restructurings have had significant effects, such as lost jobs, changed work rules, and altered job responsibilities. When restructurings occur, unions can take different approaches, ranging from resistance to cooperation. Specifically, when unions have been able to obtain information and share that information with their members in order to work constructively with the company management at various levels, then organizational restructurings have been handled more successfully. At three different automobile industry plants (GM, Ford, and Chrysler Group), the United Auto Workers and each employer increased cooperative efforts, resulting in increased production savings.[36] An example in the public sector of labor/management collaboration occurred in the city of Indianapolis, Indiana. This effort has been helpful with organizational reforms in such areas as revising disciplinary policies and changing work practices.[37]

Employee Involvement Programs

Suggesting that union/management cooperation or involving employees in making suggestions and decisions could be bad seems a little illogical. Yet, some decisions by the NLRB appear to have done just that. Some historical perspective is required to understand the issues that surrounded the decisions.

In the 1930s, when the Wagner Act was written, certain employers would form sham "company unions," coercing workers into joining them in order to keep legitimate unions from organizing the employees. As a result, the Wagner Act contained prohibitions against employer-dominated labor organizations. These prohibitions were enforced, and company unions disappeared. But the use of employee involvement programs in organizations today have raised new concerns.

Because of the Wagner Act, many employee involvement programs set up in recent years may be illegal, according to an NLRB decision dealing with Electromation, an Elkhart, Indiana, firm. Electromation used teams of employees to solicit other employees' views about such issues as wages and working conditions. The NLRB labeled these teams "labor organizations," in line with requirements of the Wagner Act. It further found that the teams were "dominated" by management, which had formed them, set their goals, and decided how they would operate. The result of this and other decisions forced many employers to re-think and re-structure their employee involvement efforts.

Federal court decisions have upheld the NLRB position in some cases and reversed it in others. One key to decisions allowing employee involvement committees and programs seems to be that these entities should not deal directly with traditional collective bargaining issues such as wages, hours, and working conditions. Other keys are that the committees should be composed primarily of workers and that they have broad authority to make operational suggestions and decisions.

Unions and Employee Ownership

Unions in some situations have encouraged workers to become partial or complete owners of the companies that employ them. These efforts were spurred by concerns that firms were preparing to shut down, merge, or be bought out. Such results were likely to cut the number of union jobs and workers.

Unions have been active in helping members put together employee stock ownership plans to purchase all or part of some firms.[38] Such programs have been successful in some situations but have caused problems in others. Some in the labor movement fear that such programs may undermine union support by creating a closer identification with the concerns and goals of employers, instead of "union solidarity."

GRIEVANCE MANAGEMENT

Complaint Indication of employee dissatisfaction.

Unions know that employee dissatisfaction is a potential source of trouble for employers, whether it is expressed or not. Hidden dissatisfaction grows and creates reactions that may be completely out of proportion to the original concerns. Therefore, it is important that dissatisfaction be given an outlet. A complaint, which is merely an indication of employee dissatisfaction, is one outlet. Complaints often are made by employees who are not represented by unions.

Grievance Complaint formally stated in writing.

If an employee is represented by a union, and the employee says, "I should have received the job transfer because I have more seniority, which is what the union contract states," and she submits it in writing, then that complaint becomes a grievance. A grievance is a complaint formally stated in writing.

Management should be concerned with both complaints and grievances, because both indicate potential problems within the workforce.[39] Without a grievance procedure, management may be unable to respond to employee concerns because managers are unaware of them. Therefore, a formal grievance procedure provides a valuable communication tool for the organizations, whether a union is present or not.[40]

| **FIGURE 17-11** | Typical Division of HR Responsibilities: Grievance Management |

HR Unit	Managers
• Assists in designing the grievance procedure • Monitors trends in grievance rates for the organization • May assist in preparing grievance cases for arbitration • May have responsibility for settling grievances	• Operate within provisions of the grievance procedure • Attempt to resolve grievances where possible • Document grievance cases for the grievance procedure • Engage in grievance prevention efforts

Grievance Responsibilities

The typical division of responsibilities between the HR unit and operating managers for handling grievances is shown in Figure 17-11. These responsibilities vary considerably from one organization to another, even between unionized firms. But the HR unit usually has more general responsibilities. Managers must accept the grievance procedure as a possible constraint on some of their decisions.

Grievance Procedures

Grievance procedures
Formal channels of communication used to resolve grievances.

Grievance procedures are formal channels of communication designed to resolve grievances as soon as possible after problems arise. First-line supervisors are usually closest to a problem. However, these supervisors are concerned with many other matters besides one employee's grievance, and may even be the subject of an employee's grievance. To receive the appropriate attention, grievances go through a specific process for resolution.

Union Representation in Grievance Procedures A unionized employee generally has a right to union representation if he or she is being questioned by management and if discipline may result. If these so-called *Weingarten rights* (named after the court case that established them) are violated and the employee is dismissed, he or she usually will be reinstated with back pay. A recent case concerns an NLRB decision to extend these rights to non-union employees involved in disciplinary grievance situations. The decision in the case involving IBM was positive for employers. That decision meant that employers are not required to allow non-union workers to have co-workers present in grievance procedure meetings. However, employers may voluntarily allow such presence.[41]

Steps in a Grievance Procedure

Grievance procedures can vary in the number of steps they include. Figure 17-12 shows a typical grievance procedure, which consists of the following steps:

1. The employee discusses the grievance with the union steward (the representative of the union on the job) and the supervisor.

FIGURE 17-12   Steps in a Typical Grievance Procedure

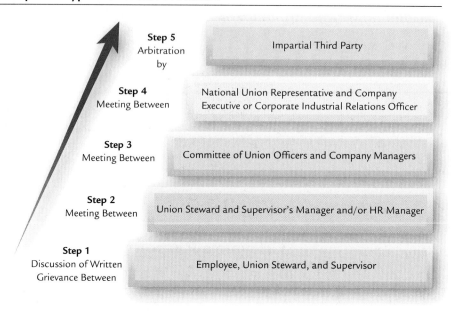

Step 5
Arbitration
by   Impartial Third Party

Step 4
Meeting Between   National Union Representative and Company
Executive or Corporate Industrial Relations Officer

Step 3
Meeting Between   Committee of Union Officers and Company Managers

Step 2
Meeting Between   Union Steward and Supervisor's Manager and/or HR Manager

Step 1
Discussion of Written   Employee, Union Steward, and Supervisor
Grievance Between

2. The union steward discusses the grievance with the supervisor's manager and/or the HR manager.
3. A committee of union officers discusses the grievance with appropriate company managers.
4. The representative of the national union discusses the grievance with designated company executives or the corporate industrial relations officer.
5. If the grievance is not solved at this stage, it goes to arbitration. An impartial third party may ultimately dispose of the grievance.

Grievance arbitration
Means by which a third party settles disputes arising from different interpretations of a labor contract.

Grievance arbitration is a means by which a third party settles disputes arising from different interpretations of a labor contract. This process should not be confused with contract or issues arbitration, discussed earlier, in which arbitration is used to determine how a contract will be written. The U.S. Supreme Court has ruled that grievance arbitration decisions issued under labor contract provisions are enforceable. Grievance arbitration includes more than 50 topic areas, with discipline and discharge, safety and health, and security issues being most prevalent.

SUMMARY

- A union is a formal association of workers that promotes the interests of its members through collective action.
- Workers join unions primarily because of management's failure to address organizational and job-related concerns.
- Unions are becoming more global as the world economy expands, and global labor federations are expanding, despite differences in approaches.
- The history of unions in the United States indicates that they primarily focus on wages, hours, and working conditions.
- In the United States, current union membership as a percentage of the workforce is down dramatically, being about 12% of the civilian workforce.
- While public-sector unions have grown, unions in general have experienced a decline in membership due to geographic, industrial, and workforce changes.
- In attempts to grow, unions are targeting professionals, low-skill workers, and contingent and part-time workers.
- The history of unions in the United States has evolved and the structural levels of U.S. unions include federations, national and international unions, and local unions.
- The National Labor Code is composed of three laws that provide the legal basis for labor relations today: the Wagner Act, the Taft-Hartley Act, and the Landrum-Griffin Act.
- The Wagner Act was designed to protect unions and workers; the Taft-Hartley Act restored some powers to management; and the Landrum-Griffin Act was passed to protect individual union members.
- Issues addressed by the different acts include unfair labor practices, national emergency strikes, and right-to-work provisions.
- The unionization process includes an organizing campaign, authorization cards, a representation election, certification and decertification, and contract negotiation through collective bargaining.
- Collective bargaining occurs when management negotiates with representatives of workers over wages, hours, and working conditions.
- The issues subject to collective bargaining fall into three categories: mandatory, permissive, and illegal.
- The collective bargaining process includes preparation and initial demands, negotiations, and settlement and contract agreement.
- Once an agreement (contract) is signed between labor and management, it becomes the document governing what each party can and cannot do.
- When an impasse occurs, work stoppages through strikes or lockouts can be used to pressure the other party.
- Union/management cooperation has been beneficial in a number of situations, although care must be taken to avoid violations of NLRB provisions.
- Grievances express workers' written dissatisfactions or differences in contract interpretations.
- A grievance procedure begins with the first-level supervisor and may end—if the grievance is not resolved along the way—with arbitration by a third party.

REVIEW AND APPLICATION QUESTIONS

1. Discuss the following statement: "If management gets a union, it deserves one."
2. Suppose a co-worker just brought you a union leaflet urging employees to sign an authorization card. What may happen from this point on?
3. As the HR manager, you have heard rumors about potential efforts to unionize your warehouse employees. Use the *www.genelevine.com* Website to develop a set of guidelines for supervisors if they are asked questions by employees about unionization as part of a "union prevention" approach.

CASE

Wal-Mart and Watching Its "Union Prevention"

Wal-Mart is one company that works hard to avoid unionization. The company says it does not have unions because it takes care of its employees. It surveys employees regularly, and many workers have been promoted from cashier and stocker jobs to management jobs. A company-wide stock ownership program has generated significant long-term returns for employees.

Unions counter that Wal-Mart uses aggressive and even unfair labor practices to prevent unionization. When a union tries to organize workers, the company often reacts with a coordinated "union prevention" program. Mandatory employee meetings are held in stores, where managers and supervisors read prepared scripts explaining the consequences of unionizing and show videos emphasizing the negatives of unionization.

As a result, at Wal-Mart in the United States, virtually no workers are unionized. In fact, when unions have won elections in some Wal-Mart locations, the firm has outsourced the jobs to independent contractors or even closed stores. Even outside the United States, Wal-Mart has been aggressive at resisting unionization of any workers in Canada, despite more union-friendly Canadian laws.

To put more pressure on Wal-Mart, unions have formed a coalition called Wal-Mart Watch. This organization has targeted Wal-Mart orga-nizational practices. For instance, extensive publicity about deficiencies in health benefits offered by Wal-Mart have led to the firm revising its plans. The Watch also has encouraged workers to file legal complaints that Wal-Mart has violated anti-discrimination laws. The watch has established its own Website (*http://walmartwatch.com*) that contains numerous articles discussing Wal-Mart actions. That Website has a blog that allows previous and current employees to post comments, as well as outsiders to provide input and opinions also.

The ultimate goal of the Watch is to be able to unionize employees at Wal-Mart because of its huge number of workers. As Wal-Mart grows and adds more stores, its growth also results in the decline or closing of other retailers, in which there are often a significant number of unionized workers. How Wal-Mart will change over the next years and the effects of the Watch on those changes will be interesting to observe.[42]

Questions

1. Describe the advantages and disadvantages of Wal-Mart's aggressive union prevention efforts.

2. Go to *http://walmartwatch*, and review some of the articles and blogs. Then identify your view of the Watch's efforts.

SUPPLEMENTAL CASE

The Wilson County Hospital

The case deals with labor disputes in a unionized hospital. (For the case, go to http://thomsonedu.com/management/mathis.)

NOTES

1. Kris Maher, "Are Unions Relevant?" *The Wall Street Journal*, January 22, 2007, B5; Jonathan Wegner, "Breakaway Unions Still Working to Get It Together," *Omaha World-Herald*, September 4, 2006, D1; and *www.changetowin.org*.

2. Based on data from Jelle Visser, "Union Membership Statistics in 24 Countries," *Monthly Labor Review*, January 2006, 38.

3. Carola M. Frege and John Kelly, *Varieties of Unionism: Strategies for Union Revitalization in a Globalizing Economy* (Oxford, U.K.: Oxford University Press, 2004).

4. For details, go to *www.ilo.org*.

5. Peter Fairbrother and Nikolaus Hammer, "Global Unions: Past Efforts and Future Prospects," *Relations Industrielles*, 60 (2005), 405.

6. John Gennard, "Global Union Federations," *Employee Relations,* 28 (2006), 100.

7. Jessica Marquez, "U.S. Unions Act Globally, Benefit Locally," *Workforce Management,* January 30, 2006, 31–33.

8. Sian Moore, "The Relationship Between Legislation and Industrial Practice," *Employee Relations,* 28 (2006), 363.

9. U.S. Bureau of Labor Statistics, "Union Members in 2006," January 25, 2007, *www.bls.gov/pub/news.release.*

10. "Demands for Labor Givebacks Grow More Aggressive," *The Wall Street Journal,* October 27, 2005, A1; and Jessica Marquez, "Good Year Fight Hints at Rough Road for Unions," *Workforce Management,* November 20, 2006, 12.

11. Jessica Marquez, "As Buyouts Continue, UAW Struggles with Membership Decline." *Workforce Management,* December 5, 2006, *www.workforce.com.*

12. Robert G. Matthews and Kris Maher, "Labor's PR Problem," *The Wall Street Journal,* August 15, 2005, B1.

13. J. R. B. Halbesleben and M. R. Buckley, "The Effect of Economic Conditions on Union Membership of Men and Women: A Quantitative and Historical Analysis," *Journal of Management History,* 12 (2006), 293.

14. U.S. Bureau of Labor Statistics, *www.bls.gov.*

15. For details on the unions and membership in the AFL-CIO, see *www.afl-cio.org.*

16. "Here, Unite Latest Duo to Tie Knot," *Nation's Restaurant News,* March 22, 2004, 30.

17. Joseph Adler, "The Past as Prologue? A Brief History of the Labor Movement in the United States," *Public Personnel Management,* 34 (2006), 311.

18. "Fallout," *Fortune,* October 28, 2002, 32.

19. For examples of right-to-work cases, go to *www.nrtw.org.*

20. Nancy R. Lockwood, "Elements of a Labor Contract," *SHRM Research,* October 5, 2006, *www.shrm.org/research.*

21. Kris Maher, "Unions' New Foe: Consultants," *The Wall Street Journal,* August 15, 2006, B1.

22. Maria Greco Danaher, "Inconsistent Bulletin Board Rule Tanks an Employer's Election Win," *www.SHRM.org/hrnews.*

23. Margaret M. Clark, "When the Union Knocks on the Recruiter's Door: Legal Rules on the Hiring of Union 'Salts,'" *SHRM Legal Report,* October 2003, 7–8.

24. Craig Becker et al., "Neutrality Agreements Take Center Stage at the National Labor Relations Board," *Labor Law Journal,* 51 (2006), 17.

25. Allen Smith, "NLRB's Expansive Definition of 'Supervisor' Could Cut Union Strength," *SHRM News,* October 14, 2006, *www.shrm.org/hrnews.*

26. *NLRB v. Kentucky River Community Care, Inc.,* 121 S.Ct. 1861 (2001).

27. National Labor Relations Board, 2006, *www.nlrb.org.*

28. "Unions' Elections Win Rate Increased in 2005," *Management Report,* August 2006, 1.

29. Leib Leventhal, "Implementing Internet-Based Negotiation," *Dispute Resolution Journal,* August/October, 2006, 50–58.

30. "High Court Upholds Limits on Political Use of Non-Members Union Fees," *SHRM Workplace Law Library,* June 15, 2007, *www.shrm.org/law/library/cms.*

31. Richard Vedder and Charlene Kalenkoski, "The Economic Status of Union Workers in the United States," *Journal of Labor Research,* 27 (2006), 593.

32. Richard A. Posthuma et al., "Mediator Tactics and Sources of Conflict," *Industrial Relations,* 41 (2002), 94–109.

33. Corinne Bendersky, "Organizational Dispute Resolution Systems: A Complementaries Model," *Academy of Management Review,* 28 (2003), 643–656.

34. "Major Work Stoppages," *Bureau of Labor Statistics News,* March 2, 2006, *www.bls.gov/cba.*

35. Based on Robert J. Grossman, "Unions Follow Suit," *HR Magazine,* May 2005, 47–51.

36. Chris Woodyard, "Working Hand-In-Hand," *USA Today,* February 6, 2007, 1B.

37. Barry Rubin and Richard Rubin, "Labor-Management Relations: Conditions for Collaboration," *Public Personnel Management,* 35 (2006), 283.

38. Jacquelyn Yates, "Unions and Employee Ownership: A Road to Economic Recovery?" *Industrial Relations,* 45 (2006), 709.

39. Barry Mordsley and Carol Aylott, "A Grievance by Any Other Name," *People Management,* July 13, 2006, 19.

40. Lawrence Nurse and Dwayne Devonish, "Grievance Management and Its Links to Workplace Justice," *Employee Relations,* 29 (2007), 89.

41. C. R. Deitsch, D. A. Ditts, and Francine Guice, "Weingarten Rights in the Non-Union Workplace," *Dispute Resolution Journal,* May/July 2006, 46.

42. Anthony Bianco, "No Union, Please, We're Wal-Mart," *Business Week,* February 13, 2006, 78.

Appendix A

HUMAN RESOURCE CERTIFICATION INSTITUTE TEST SPECIFICATIONS*

The following two levels of certification are for the **Professional in Human Resources (PHR) and the Senior Professional in Human Resources (SPHR)**. Two different exams are used for certification testing. PHR questions tend to be at an operational/technical level, whereas SPHR questions tend to be more at the strategic and/or policy level.

Examination questions for both levels cover a wide range of topics. Each multiple choice exam consists of 200 scored questions plus 25 pre-test questions for a total of 225 questions. Pre-test questions are not counted in the scoring of the examination and are used for statistical purposes only. Each question lists *four possible answers,* only one of which is correct.

Item Classification Components

The test specifications identify six *Functional Areas* plus a *Core Knowledge* section. Listed after the title of each major functional area are the weightings for that area. **The first number in the parentheses is the PHR percentage weighting and the second number is the SPHR percentage weighting.** Within each area *responsibilities* and *knowledge* topics are specified.

Readers of this book can identify specific content information for the HRCI outline topics using the extensive subject index at the end of the text. *Relevant page numbers are noted in that index.*

FUNCTIONAL AREAS:

01 STRATEGIC MANAGEMENT (12%, 29%)

Developing, contributing to, and supporting the organization's mission, vision, values, strategic goals, and objectives; formulating policies; guiding and leading the change process; and evaluating HR's contributions to organizational effectiveness.

Responsibilities

01 Interpret information related to the organization's operations from internal sources, including financial/accounting, business development, marketing, sales, operations, and information technology, in order to contribute to the development of the organization's strategic plan.

02 Interpret information from external sources related to the general business environment, industry practices and developments, technological developments, economic environment, labor pool, and legal and regulatory environment, in order to contribute to the development of the organization's strategic plan.

03 Participate as a contributing partner in the organization's strategic planning process.

*©Human Resource Certification Institute. Used with permission. For more information go to *www.hrci.org.*

04 Establish strategic relationships with key individuals in the organization to influence organizational decision-making.

05 Establish relationships/alliances with key individuals and organizations in the community to assist in achieving the organization's strategic goals and objectives.

06 Develop and utilize metrics to evaluate HR's contributions to the achievement of the organization's strategic goals and objectives.

07 Develop and execute strategies for managing organizational change that balance the expectations and needs of the organization, its employees, and all other stakeholders.

08 Develop and align the organization's human capital management plan with its strategic plan.

09 Facilitate the development and communication of the organization's core values and ethical behaviors.

10 Reinforce the organization's core values and behavioral expectations through modeling, communication, and coaching.

11 Develop and manage the HR budget in a manner consistent with the organization's strategic goals, objectives, and values.

12 Provide information for the development and monitoring of the organization's overall budget.

13 Monitor the legislative and regulatory environment for proposed changes and their potential impact to the organization, taking appropriate proactive steps to support, modify, or oppose the proposed changes.

14 Develop policies and procedures to support corporate governance initiatives (for example, board of directors training, whistleblower protection, code of conduct).

15 Participate in enterprise risk management by examining HR policies to evaluate their potential risks to the organization.

16 Identify and evaluate alternatives and recommend strategies for vendor selection and/or outsourcing (for example, HRIS, benefits, payroll).

17 Participate in strategic decision-making and due diligence activities related to organizational structure and design (for example, corporate restructuring, mergers and acquisitions [M&A], off-shoring, divestitures). **SPHR ONLY**

18 Determine strategic application of integrated technical tools and systems (for example, HRIS, performance management tools, applicant tracking, compensation tools, employee self-service technologies).

Knowledge of:
01 The organization's mission, vision, values, business goals, objectives, plans, and processes.

02 Legislative and regulatory processes.

03 Strategic planning process and implementation.

04 Management functions, including planning, organizing, directing, and controlling.

05 Techniques to promote creativity and innovation.

06 Corporate governance procedures and compliance (for example, Sarbanes-Oxley Act).

07 Transition techniques for corporate restructuring, M&A, offshoring, and divestitures. **SPHR ONLY**

02 WORKFORCE PLANNING AND EMPLOYMENT (26%, 17%)

Developing, implementing, and evaluating sourcing, recruitment, hiring, orientation, succession planning, retention, and organizational exit programs necessary to ensure the workforce's ability to achieve the organization's goals and objectives.

Responsibilities:
01 Ensure that workforce planning and employment activities are compliant with applicable federal, state, and local laws and regulations.

02 Identify workforce requirements to achieve the organization's short- and long-term goals and objectives (for example, corporate restructuring, M&A activity, workforce expansion or reduction).

03 Conduct job analyses to create job descriptions and identify job competencies.

04 Identify and document essential job functions for positions.

05 Establish hiring criteria based on job descriptions and required competencies.

06 Analyze labor market for trends that impact the ability to meet workforce requirements (for example, SWOT analysis, environmental scan, demographic scan). **SPHR ONLY**

07 Assess skill sets of internal workforce and external labor market to determine the availability

of qualified candidates, utilizing third party vendors or agencies as appropriate.

08 Identify internal and external recruitment sources (for example, employee referrals, online job boards, résumé banks) and implement selected recruitment methods.

09 Evaluate recruitment methods and sources for effectiveness (for example, return on investment [ROI], cost per hire, time to fill).

10 Develop strategies to brand/market the organization to potential qualified applicants.

11 Develop and implement selection procedures, including applicant tracking, interviewing, testing, reference and background checking, and drug screening.

12 Develop and extend employment offers and conduct negotiations as necessary.

13 Administer post-offer employment activities (for example, execute employment agreements, complete I-9 verification forms, coordinate relocations, schedule physical exams).

14 Implement and/or administer the process for non-U.S. citizens to legally work in the United States.

15 Develop, implement, and evaluate orientation processes for new hires, rehires, and transfers.

16 Develop, implement, and evaluate retention strategies and practices.

17 Develop, implement, and evaluate succession planning process.

18 Develop and implement the organizational exit process for both voluntary and involuntary terminations, including planning for reductions in force (RIF).

19 Develop, implement, and evaluate an AAP, as required.

Knowledge of:

08 Federal/state/local employment-related laws and regulations related to workforce planning and employment (for example, Title VII, ADA, ADEA, USERRA, EEOC Uniform Guidelines on Employee Selection Procedures, Immigration Reform and Control Act, Internal Revenue Code).

09 Quantitative analyses required to assess past and future staffing effectiveness (for example, cost-benefit analysis, costs per hire, selection ratios, adverse impact).

10 Recruitment sources (for example, Internet, agencies, employee referral) for targeting passive, semi-active and active candidates.

11 Recruitment strategies.

12 Staffing alternatives (for example, temporary and contract, outsourcing, job sharing, part-time).

13 Planning techniques (for example, succession planning, forecasting).

14 Reliability and validity of selection tests/tools/methods.

15 Use and interpretation of selection tests (for example, psychological/personality, cognitive, motor/physical assessments, performance, assessment center).

16 Interviewing techniques (for example, behavioral, situational, panel).

17 Relocation practices.

18 Impact of total rewards on recruitment and retention.

19 International HR and implications of global workforce for workforce planning and employment. **SPHR ONLY**

20 Voluntary and involuntary terminations, downsizing, restructuring, and outplacement strategies and practices.

21 Internal workforce assessment techniques (for example, skills testing, skills inventory, workforce demographic analysis) and employment policies, practices, and procedures (for example, orientation and retention).

22 Employer marketing and branding techniques.

23 Negotiation skills and techniques.

03 HUMAN RESOURCE DEVELOPMENT (17%, 17%)

Developing, implementing, and evaluating activities and programs that address employee training and development, performance appraisal, talent and performance management, and the unique needs of employees to ensure that the knowledge, skills, abilities, and performance of the workforce meet current and future organizational and individual needs.

Responsibilities:

01 Ensure that human resource development programs are compliant with all applicable federal, state, and local laws and regulations.

02 Conduct a needs assessment to identify and establish priorities regarding human resource development activities. **SPHR ONLY**

03 Develop/select and implement employee training programs (for example, leadership skills, harassment prevention, computer skills) to increase individual and organizational effectiveness. Note that this includes training design and methods for obtaining feedback from training (e.g., surveys, pre- and post-testing).

04 Evaluate effectiveness of employee training programs through the use of metrics (for example, participant surveys, pre- and post-testing). **SPHR ONLY**

05 Develop, implement, and evaluate talent management programs that include assessing talent, developing talent, and placing high-potential employees. **SPHR ONLY**

06 Develop/select and evaluate performance appraisal process (for example, instruments, ranking and rating scales, relationship to compensation, frequency).

07 Implement training programs for performance evaluators. **PHR ONLY**

08 Develop, implement, and evaluate performance management programs and procedures (for example, goal setting, job rotations, promotions).

09 Develop/select, implement, and evaluate programs (for example, flexible work arrangements, diversity initiatives, repatriation) to meet the unique needs of employees. **SPHR ONLY**

Knowledge of:

24 Applicable federal, state, and local laws and regulations related to human resources development activities (for example, Title VII, ADA, ADEA, USERRA, EEOC Uniform Guidelines on Employee Selection Procedures).

25 Career development and leadership development theories and applications.

26 OD theories and applications.

27 Training program development techniques to create general and specialized training programs.

28 Training methods, facilitation techniques, instructional methods, and program delivery mechanisms.

29 Task/process analysis.

30 Performance appraisal methods (for example, instruments, ranking and rating scales).

31 Performance management methods (for example, goal setting, job rotations, promotions).

32 Applicable global issues (for example, international law, culture, local management approaches/practices, societal norms). **SPHR ONLY**

33 Techniques to assess training program effectiveness, including use of applicable metrics (for example, participant surveys, pre- and post-testing).

34 E-learning.

35 Mentoring and executive coaching.

04 TOTAL REWARDS (16%, 12%)

Developing/selecting, implementing/administering, and evaluating compensation and benefits programs for all employee groups that support the organization's strategic goals, objectives, and values.

Responsibilities:

01 Ensure that compensation and benefits programs are compliant with applicable federal, state, and local laws and regulations.

02 Develop, implement, and evaluate compensation policies/programs and pay structures based on internal equity and external market conditions that support the organization's strategic goals, objectives, and values.

03 Administer payroll functions (for example, new hires, deductions, adjustments, terminations).

04 Conduct benefits programs needs assessments (for example, benchmarking, employee survey).

05 Develop/select, implement/administer, and evaluate benefits programs that support the organization's strategic goals, objectives, and values (for example, health and welfare, retirement, stock purchase, wellness, employee assistance programs [EAP], time-off).

06 Communicate and train the workforce in the compensation and benefits programs and policies (for example, self-service technologies).

07 Develop/select, implement/administer, and evaluate executive compensation programs (for example, stock purchase, stock options, incentive, bonus, supplemental retirement plans). **SPHR ONLY**

08 Develop, implement/administer, and evaluate expatriate and foreign national compensation and benefits programs. **SPHR ONLY**

Knowledge of:

36 Federal, state, and local compensation, benefits, and tax laws (for example, FLSA, ERISA, COBRA, HIPAA, FMLA, FICA).

37 Total rewards strategies (for example, compensation, benefits, wellness, rewards, recognition, employee assistance).

38 Budgeting and accounting practices related to compensation and benefits.

39 Job evaluation methods.

40 Job pricing and pay structures.

41 External labor markets and/or economic factors.

42 Pay programs (for example, incentive, variable, merit).

43 Executive compensation methods. **SPHR ONLY**

44 Non-cash compensation methods (for example, stock options, ESOPs). **SPHR ONLY**

45 Benefits programs (for example, health and welfare, retirement, wellness, EAP, time-off).

46 International compensation laws and practices (for example, expatriate compensation, entitlements, choice of law codes). **SPHR ONLY**

47 Fiduciary responsibility related to total rewards management. **SPHR ONLY**

05 EMPLOYEE AND LABOR RELATIONS (22%, 18%)

Analyzing, developing, implementing/administering, and evaluating the workplace relationship between employer and employee in order to maintain relationships and working conditions that balance employer and employee needs and rights in support of the organization's strategic goals, objectives, and values.

Responsibilities:

01 Ensure that employee and labor relations activities are compliant with applicable federal, state, and local laws and regulations.

02 Assess organizational climate by obtaining employee input (for example, focus groups, employee surveys, staff meetings).

03 Implement organizational change activities as appropriate in response to employee feedback.

04 Develop employee relations programs (for example, awards, recognition, discounts, special events) that promote a positive organizational culture.

05 Implement employee relations programs that promote a positive organizational culture.

06 Evaluate effectiveness of employee relations programs through the use of metrics (for example, exit interviews, employee surveys).

07 Establish workplace policies and procedures (for example, dress code, attendance, computer use) and monitor their application and enforcement to ensure consistency.

08 Develop, administer, and evaluate grievance/dispute resolution and performance improvement policies and procedures.

09 Resolve employee complaints filed with federal, state, and local agencies involving employment practices, utilizing professional resources as necessary (for example, legal counsel, mediation/arbitration specialists, and investigators).

10 Develop and direct proactive employee relations strategies for remaining union-free in nonorganized locations.

11 Participate in collective bargaining activities, including contract negotiation and administration. **SPHR ONLY**

Knowledge of:

48 Applicable federal, state, and local laws affecting employment in union and nonunion environments, such as antidiscrimination laws, sexual harassment, labor relations, and privacy (for example, WARN Act, Title VII, NLRA).

49 Techniques for facilitating positive employee relations (for example, employee surveys, focus groups, dispute resolution, labor/management cooperative strategies and programs).

50 Employee involvement strategies (for example, employee management committees, self-directed work teams, staff meetings).

51 Individual employment rights issues and practices (for example, employment at will, negligent hiring, defamation, employees' rights to bargain collectively).

52 Workplace behavior issues/practices (for example, absenteeism and performance improvement).

53 Unfair labor practices (for example, employee communication strategies and management training).

54 The collective bargaining process, strategies, and concepts (for example, contract negotiation and administration). **SPHR ONLY**

55 Positive employee relations strategies and non-monetary rewards.

06 RISK MANAGEMENT (7%, 7%)

Developing, implementing/administering, and evaluating programs, plans, and policies that provide a safe and secure working environment and to protect the organization from liability.

Responsibilities:

01 Ensure that workplace health, safety, security, and privacy activities are compliant with applicable federal, state, and local laws and regulations.

02 Identify the organization's safety program needs.

03 Develop/select and implement/administer occupational injury and illness prevention, safety incentives, and training programs. **PHR ONLY**

04 Develop/select, implement, and evaluate plans and policies to protect employees and other individuals and to minimize the organization's loss and liability (for example, emergency response, evacuation, workplace violence, substance abuse, return-to-work policies).

05 Communicate and train the workforce on the plans and policies to protect employees and other individuals and to minimize the organization's loss and liability.

06 Develop and monitor business continuity and disaster recovery plans.

07 Communicate and train the workforce on the business continuity and disaster recovery plans.

08 Develop internal and external privacy policies (for example, identity theft, data protection, HIPAA compliance, workplace monitoring).

09 Administer internal and external privacy policies.

Knowledge of:

56 Federal, state, and local workplace health, safety, security, and privacy laws and regulations (for example, OSHA, Drug-Free Workplace Act, ADA, HIPAA, Sarbanes-Oxley).

57 Occupational injury and illness compensation and programs.

58 Occupational injury and illness prevention programs.

59 Investigation procedures of workplace safety, health, and security enforcement agencies (for example, OSHA, National Institute for Occupational Safety and Health [NIOSH]).

60 Workplace safety risks.

61 Workplace security risks (for example, theft, corporate espionage, asset and data protection, sabotage).

62 Potential violent behavior and workplace violence conditions.

63 General health and safety practices (for example, evacuation, hazard communication, ergonomic evaluations).

64 Incident and emergency response plans.

65 Internal investigation, monitoring, and surveillance techniques.

66 Issues related to substance abuse and dependency (for example, identification of symptoms, substance abuse testing, discipline).

67 Business continuity and disaster recovery plans (for example, data storage and backup, alternative work locations and procedures).

68 Data integrity techniques and technology (for example, data sharing, firewalls).

CORE KNOWLEDGE REQUIRED BY HR PROFESSIONALS

69 Needs assessment and analysis.

70 Third-party contract negotiation and management, including development of requests for proposals (RFPs).

71 Communication skills and strategies (for example, presentation, collaboration, influencing, diplomacy, sensitivity).

72 Organizational documentation requirements to meet federal and state requirements.

73 Adult learning processes.

74 Motivation concepts and applications.

75 Training techniques (for example, computer-based, classroom, on-the-job).

76 Leadership concepts and applications.

77 Project management concepts and applications.

78 Diversity concepts and applications.

79 Human relations concepts and applications (for example, interpersonal and organizational behavior).

80 HR ethics and professional standards.

81 Technology to support HR activities (for example, HRIS, employee self-service, e-learning, ATS).

82 Qualitative and quantitative methods and tools for analysis, interpretation, and decision-making purposes (for example, metrics and measurements, cost/benefit analysis, financial statement analysis).

83 Change management methods.

84 Job analysis and job description methods.

85 Employee records management (for example, electronic/paper, retention, disposal).

86 The interrelationships among HR activities and programs across functional areas.

87 Types of organizational structures (for example, matrix, hierarchy).

88 Environmental scanning concepts and applications.

89 Methods for assessing employee attitudes, opinions, and satisfaction (for example, opinion surveys, attitude surveys, focus groups/panels).

90 Basic budgeting and accounting concepts.

91 Risk management techniques.

Appendix B

CURRENT LITERATURE IN HR MANAGEMENT

Students are expected to be familiar with the professional resources and literature in their fields of study. Five groups of resources are listed in this appendix.

A. Research-Oriented Journals

In HR management, the professional journals are the most immediate and direct communication link between researchers and the practicing managers. These journals contain articles that report on original research. Normally, these journals contain either sophisticated writing and quantitative verifications of the author's findings, or conceptual models and literature reviews of previous research.

Academy of Management Journal
Academy of Management Review
Administrative Science Quarterly
American Behavioral Scientist
American Journal of Health Promotion
American Journal of Psychology
American Journal of Sociology
American Psychological Measurement
American Psychologist
American Sociological Review
Annual Review of Psychology
Applied Psychology: An International Review
Behavioral Science
British Journal of Industrial Relations
British Journal of Management
Business Ethics
Cognitive Studies
Decision Sciences
Dispute Resolution Quarterly
Employee Responsibilities and Rights Journal
Entrepreneurship Theory and Practice
Ethics and Critical Thinking Journal
Group and Organization Studies
Human Organization
Human Relations
Human Resource Development Review
Human Resource Management Journal
Human Resource Management Review

Human Resources Abstracts
Industrial & Labor Relations Review
Industrial Relations
Industrial Relations Journal
Industrial Relations Law Journal
Interfaces
International Journal of Entrepreneurial Behavior and Research
International Journal of Human Resource Management Education
International Journal of Management Reviews
International Journal of Training and Development
International Journal of Selection and Assessment
Journal of Abnormal Psychology
Journal of Applied Behavioral Science
Journal of Applied Business Research
Journal of Applied Psychology
Journal of Business
Journal of Business Communications
Journal of Business and Industrial Marketing
Journal of Business and Psychology
Journal of Business Ethics
Journal of Business Research
Journal of Business Strategy
Journal of Collective Negotiations
Journal of Communication
Journal of Comparative International Management

Journal of Compensation & Benefits
Journal of Counseling Psychology
Journal of Experimental Social Psychology
Journal of Human Resources
Journal of Individual Employment Rights
Journal of Industrial Relations
Journal of International Business Studies
Journal of International Management
Journal of Knowledge Management
Journal of Labor Economics
Journal of Labor Research
Journal of Leadership and Organizational Studies
Journal of Management
Journal of Management Development
Journal of Management Education
Journal of Management Studies
Journal of Managerial Psychology
Journal of Occupation and Organization
    Psychology
Journal of Organizational Behavior
Journal of Organizational Change Management
Journal of Organizational Excellence
Journal of Pension Planning
Journal of Personality and Social Psychology
Journal of Quality & Participation
Journal of Quality Management
Journal of Social Issues
Journal of Social Psychology
Journal of Social Policy
Journal of Social Psychology
Journal of Vocational Behavior
Journal of Workplace Learning
Labor History
Labor Relations Yearbook
Labour
Management Science
New Technology, Work, and Employment
Occupational Psychology
Organization Behavior and Human Decision
    Processes
Personnel Monographs
Personnel Psychology
Personnel Review
Psychological Bulletin
Psychological Review
Public Personnel Management
Quarterly Review of Distance Education
Social Forces
Social Science Research
Sociology Perspective
Sociometry
Work and Occupations

B. Selected Professional/ Managerial Journals

These journals generally cover a wide range of subjects. Articles in these publications normally are aimed at HR professionals and managers. Most articles in these publications are written to interpret, summarize, or discuss the implications of research. They also provide operational and administrative ideas.

Academy of Management Executive
Across the Board
Administrative Management
Arbitration Journal
Australian Journal of Management
Benefits and Compensation Solutions
Berkeley Journal of Employment and Labor
    Law
Business
Business Horizons
Business Management
Business Monthly
Business Quarterly
Business and Social Review
Business Week
California Management Review
Canadian Manager
Columbia Journal of World Business
Compensation and Benefits Management
Compensation and Benefits Review
Corporate Governance
Directors and Boards
Economist
Employee Benefit Plan Review
Employee Benefits News
Employee Relations
Employee Relations Law Journal
Employment Practices Decisions
Employment Relations
Employment Relations Today
Forbes
Fortune
Global HR
Harvard Business Review
Hospital and Health Services Administration
HR Magazine
Human Behavior
Human Capital Management
Human Resource Development International
Human Resource Executive
Human Resource Management

Human Resource Management International
    Digest
Human Resource Planning
IHRIM Link
INC.
Incentive
Industrial Management
Industry Week
International Management
Journal of Systems Management
Labor Law Journal
Long Range Planning
Manage
Management Consulting
Management Planning
Management Research News
Management Review
Management Solutions
Management Today
Management World
Managers Magazine
Michigan State University Business
    Topics
Monthly Labor Review
Nation's Business
Occupational Health & Safety
Occupational Outlook Quarterly
Organizational Dynamics
Pension World
Personnel Management
Personnel Management Abstracts
Psychology Today
Public Administration Review
Public Manager
Public Opinion Quarterly
Recruiting Today
Research Management
SAM Advanced Management
    Journal
Security Management
Sloan Management Review
Supervision
Supervisory Management
Training
Training and Development
Workforce
Workforce Management
Working Woman
Workplace Ergonomics
Workplace Visions
Workspan
WorldatWork Journal

C. Selected HR-Related Internet Links

American Arbitration Association
    http://www.adr.org
Academy of Management
    http://www.aom.pace.edu
American Federation of Labor/Congress of
    Industrial Organizations (AFL-CIO)
    http://www.aflcio.org
American Institute for Managing Diversity
    http://www.aimd.org
American Psychological Association
    http://www.apa.org
American Society for Industrial Security
    http://www.asisonline.org
American Society for Payroll Management
    http://www.aspm.org
American Society for Training and Development
    http://www.astd.org
Australian Human Resource Institute
    http://www.ahri.com.au
CPR Institute for Dispute Resolution
    http://www.cpradr.org
Employee Benefit Research Institute
    http://www.ebri.org
Employment Management Association
    http://www.shrm.org/ema
Foundation for Enterprise Development
    http://www.fed.org
Hong Kong Institute of Human Resource
    Management
    http://www.hkihrm.org
Human Resource Certification Institute
    http://www.hrci.org
Industrial Relations Research Association
    http://www.irra.uiuc.edu
Institute for International Human Resources
    http://www.shrm.org/docs/IIHR.html
Institute of Personnel and Development (UK)
    http://www.ipd.co.uk
International Association for Human Resource
    Information Management
    http://ihrim.org
International Association of Industrial Accident
    Boards and Commissions
    http://www.iaiabc.org
International Foundation of Employee Benefit
    Plans (IFEBP)
    http://www.ifebp.org
International Personnel Management Association
    http://www.ipma-hr.org

International Personnel Management Association
Assessment Council
http://ipmaac.org
National Center for Employee Ownership
http://www.nceo.org
National Health Information Research Center
http://www.nhirc.org
Society for Human Resource Management
http://www.shrm.org
Union Resource Network
http://www.unions.org
World at Work
http://www.worldatwork.org

D. Selected Government Internet Links

Bureau of Labor Statistics
http://stats.bls.gov
Census Bureau
http://www.census.gov
Department of Labor
http://www.dol.gov
Economic Statistics Briefing Room
http://www.whitehouse.gov/fsbr/esbr.html
Employment and Training Administration
http://www.doleta.gov
Equal Employment Opportunity Commission
http://www.eeoc.gov
FedStats
http://www.fedstats.gov
National Institute of Environmental Health
Sciences
http://www.niehs.nih.gov
National Institute for Safety and Health (NIOSH)
http://www.cdc.gov/niosh/homepage.html
National Labor Relations Board
http://www.nlrb.gov
Occupational Safety and Health Administration
http://www.osha.gov
Office of Personnel Management
http://www.opm.gov
Pension and Welfare Benefits Administration
http://www.dol.gov/ebsa/welcome.html
Pension Benefit Guaranty Corporation
http://www.pbgc.gov
Small Business Administration
http://www.sba.gov

Social Security Administration
http://www.ssa.gov
Training Technology Resource Center
http://www.ttrc.doleta.gov
U.S. House of Representatives
http://www.house.gov
U.S. Senate
http://www.senate.gov

E. Abstracts, Indices, and Databases

ABI Inform Global
ACM Digital
ArticleFirst
Arts & Humanities Search
Book Review Digest
Books in Print
Business and Company ASAP
ComAbstracts
ContentsFirst
Criminal Justice Abstracts
Dissertation Abstracts
Ebsco Masterfile Premier
Ebsco Online Citations
ECO: Electronic Collections Online
EconLit
Education
ERIC
Essay and General Literature Index
Expanded Academic Index
Government Periodicals
GPO Monthly Catalog
Health Reference Center
HRAF: Human Relations Area
Human Resource Abstracts
Index to Legal Periodicals and Books
Internet and Personal Computing Abstracts
NCJRS Justice Information Center
NetFirst
Newspaper Source from Ebsco
PAIS: Public Affairs Information Service
PapersFirst
PsycInfo
Readers Guide Abstracts
Sociological Abstracts

Glossary

Acceptance rate Percent of applicants hired divided by total number of applicants offered jobs.

Active practice Performance of job-related tasks and duties by trainees during training.

Adverse selection Situation in which only higher-risk employees select and use certain benefits.

Affirmative action Employers are urged to hire groups of people based on their race, age, gender, or national origin to make up for historical discrimination.

Affirmative action plan (AAP) Formal document that an employer compiles annually for submission to enforcement agencies.

Applicant pool All persons who are actually evaluated for selection.

Applicant population A subset of the labor force population that is available for selection using a particular recruiting approach.

Arbitration Process that uses a neutral third party to make a decision.

Assessment centers Collections of instruments and exercises designed to diagnose individuals' development needs.

Attitude survey A survey that focuses on employees' feelings and beliefs about their jobs and the organization.

Autonomy Extent of individual freedom and discretion in the work and its scheduling.

Availability analysis Identifies the number of protected-class members available to work in the appropriate labor markets for given jobs.

Balance-sheet approach Compensation plan that equalizes cost differences between the international assignment and the same assignment in the home country.

Bargaining unit Employees eligible to select a single union to represent and bargain collectively for them.

Base pay Basic compensation that an employee receives, usually as a wage or a salary.

Behavior modeling Copying someone else's behavior.

Behavioral interview Interview in which applicants give specific examples of how they have performed a certain task or handled a problem in the past.

Benchmark jobs Jobs found in many organizations.

Benchmarking Comparing specific measures of performance against data on those measures in other organizations.

Benefit Indirect reward given to an employee or a group of employees for organizational membership.

Blended learning Learning approach that combines short, fast-paced, interactive computer-based lessons and teleconferencing with traditional classroom instruction and simulation.

Blind to differences Differences among people should be ignored and everyone should be treated equally.

Bona fide occupational qualification (BFOQ) Characteristic providing a legitimate reason why an employer can exclude persons on otherwise illegal bases of consideration.

Bonus One-time payment that does not become part of the employee's base pay.

Broadbanding Practice of using fewer pay grades with much broader ranges than in traditional compensation systems.

Burden of proof What individuals who file suit against employers must prove in order to establish that illegal discrimination has occurred.

Business agent Full-time union official who operates the union office and assists union members.

Business necessity Practice necessary for safe and efficient organizational operations.

Business process re-engineering (BPR) Measures for improving such activities as product development, customer service, and service delivery.

Career Series of work-related positions a person occupies throughout life.

Career paths Represent employees' movements through opportunities over time.

Cash balance plan Retirement program in which benefits are based on an accumulation of annual company contributions plus interest credited each year.

Central tendency error Occurs when a rater gives all employees a score within a narrow range in the middle of the scale.

Churn Hiring new workers while laying off others.

Coaching Training and feedback given to employees by immediate supervisors.

Closed shop Firm that requires individuals to join a union before they can be hired.

Co-determination Practice whereby union or worker representatives are given positions on a company's board of directors.

Cognitive ability tests Tests that measure an individual's thinking, memory, reasoning, verbal, and mathematical abilities.

Collective bargaining Process whereby representatives of management and workers negotiate over wages, hours, and other terms and conditions of employment.

Commission Compensation computed as a percentage of sales in units or dollars.

Compa-ratio Pay level divided by the midpoint of the pay range.

Compensation committee Subgroup of the Board of Directors, composed of directors who are not officers of the firm.

Compensable factor Job value commonly present throughout a group of jobs.

Competencies Individual capabilities that can be linked to enhanced performance by individuals or teams.

Competency-based pay Rewards individuals for the capabilities they demonstrate and acquire.

Complaint Indication of employee dissatisfaction.

Compressed workweek Schedule in which a full week's work is accomplished in fewer than five 8-hour days.

Conciliation Process by which a third party assists union and management negotiators to reach a voluntary settlement.

Concurrent validity Measured when an employer tests current employees and correlates the scores with their performance ratings.

Constructive discharge Process of deliberately making conditions intolerable to get an employee to quit.

Consumer-driven health (CDH) plan Health plan that provides employer financial contributions to employees to help cover their own health-related expenses.

Content validity Validity measured by a logical, non-statistical method to identify the KSAs and other characteristics necessary to perform a job.

Contractual rights Rights based on a specific contract between an employer and an employee.

Contrast error Tendency to rate people relative to others rather than against performance standards.

Contributory plan Pension plan in which the money for pension benefits is paid in by both employees and employers.

Co-payment Strategy requiring employees to pay a portion of the cost of insurance premiums, medical care, and prescription drugs.

Core competency A unique capability that creates high value and differentiates an organization from its competition.

Correlation coefficient Index number that gives the relationship between a predictor and a criterion variable.

Cost-benefit analysis Comparison of costs and benefits associated with training.

Craft union Union whose members do one type of work, often using specialized skills and training.

Criterion-related validity Validity measured by a procedure that uses a test as the predictor of how well an individual will perform on the job.

Cross training Training people to do more than one job.

Culture Societal forces affecting the values, beliefs, and actions of a distinct group of people.

Cumulative trauma disorders (CTDs) Muscle and skeletal injuries that occur when workers repetitively use the same muscles to perform tasks.

D

Decertification Process whereby a union is removed as the representative of a group of employees.

Defined-benefit plan Retirement program in which an employee is promised a pension amount based on age and service.

Defined-contribution plan Retirement program in which the employer makes an annual payment to an employee's pension account.

Development Efforts to improve employees' abilities to handle a variety of assignments and to cultivate employees' capabilities beyond those required by the current job.

Disabled person Someone who has a physical or mental impairment that substantially limits life activities, who has a record of such an impairment, or who is regarded as having such an impairment.

Discipline Form of training that enforces organizational rules.

Disparate impact Occurs when members of a protected class are substantially underrepresented as a result of employment decisions that work to their disadvantage.

Disparate treatment Occurs when members of a protected class are treated differently from others.

Distributive justice Perceived fairness in the distribution of outcomes.

Draw Amount advanced from and repaid to future commissions earned by the employee.

Dual-career ladder System that allows a person to advance up either a management or a technical/professional ladder.

Due process Requirement that the employer use a fair process to determine employee wrongdoing and that the employee have an opportunity to explain and defend his or her actions.

Duty Work segment composed of several tasks that are performed by an individual.

E

Economic value added (EVA) Net operating profit of a firm after the cost of capital is deducted.

Effectiveness The extent to which goals have been met.

Efficiency The degree to which operations are done in an economical manner.

E-learning Use of the Internet or an organizational intranet to conduct training on-line.

Employee assistance program (EAP) Program that provides counseling and other help to employees having emotional, physical, or other personal problems.

Employee stock ownership plan (ESOP) Plan whereby employees have significant stock ownership in their employers.

Employment-at-will (EAW) Common-law doctrine stating that employers have the right to hire, fire, demote, or promote whomever they choose, unless there is a law or a contract to the contrary.

Employment contract Agreement that formally outlines the details of employment.

Employment "test" Any employment factor used as the basis for making an employment-related decision.

Entitlement philosophy Assumes that individuals who have worked another year are entitled to pay increases, with little regard for performance differences.

Environmental scanning Process of studying the environment of the organization to pinpoint opportunities and threats.

Equal employment Employment that is not affected by illegal discrimination.

Equal employment opportunity (EEO) The concept that all individuals should have equal treatment in all employment-related actions.

Equity Perceived fairness between what a person does and what the person receives.

Ergonomics Study and design of the work environment to address physiological and physical demands placed on individuals.

Essential job functions Fundamental job duties.

Exempt employees Employees to whom employers are not required to pay overtime.

Exit interview An interview in which individuals are asked to give their reasons for leaving the organization.

F

Federation Group of autonomous unions.

Feedback Amount of information employees receive about how well or how poorly they have performed.

Flexible benefits plan Program that allows employees to select the benefits they prefer from groups of benefits established by the employer.

Flexible spending accounts Benefits plans that allow employees to contribute pre-tax dollars to fund certain additional benefits.

Flexible staffing Use of workers who are not traditional employees.

Flextime Scheduling arrangement in which employees work a set number of hours a day but vary starting and ending times.

Forced distribution Performance appraisal method in which ratings of employees' performance are distributed along a bell-shaped curve.

Forecasting Using information from the past and the present to identify expected future conditions.

4/5ths rule Discrimination exists if the selection rate for a protected group is less than 80% (4/5ths) of the selection rate for the majority group or less than 80% of the majority group's representation in the relevant labor market.

401(k) plan Agreement in which a percentage of an employee's pay is withheld and invested in a tax-deferred account.

G

Gainsharing System of sharing with employees greater-than-expected gains in profits and/or productivity.

Garnishment A court order that directs an employer to set aside a portion of an employee's wages to pay a debt owed a creditor.

Glass ceiling Discriminatory practices that have prevented women and other protected-class members from advancing to executive-level jobs.

Global market approach Compensation plan that attempts to be more comprehensive in providing base pay, incentives, benefits, and relocation expenses regardless of the country to which the employee is assigned.

Global organization Firm that has corporate units in a number of countries integrated to operate as one organization worldwide.

Graphic rating scale Scale that allows the rater to mark an employee's performance on a continuum.

Green-circled employee Incumbent who is paid below the range set for the job.

Grievance Complaint formally stated in writing.

Grievance arbitration Means by which a third party settles disputes arising from different interpretations of a labor contract.

Grievance procedures Formal channels of communication used to resolve grievances.

H

Halo effect Occurs when a rater scores an employee high on all job criteria because of performance in one area.

Health General state of physical, mental, and emotional well-being.

Health maintenance organization (HMO) Plan that provides services for a fixed period on a pre-paid basis.

Health promotion Supportive approach of facilitating and encouraging healthy actions and lifestyles among employees.

Health reimbursement arrangement (HRA) Health plan in which the employer sets aside money in a health reimbursement account to help employees pay for qualified medical expenses.

Health Savings Accounts (HSAs) High-deductible health plans with federal tax advantages.

Hostile environment Sexual harassment in which an individual's work performance or psychological well-being is unreasonably affected by intimidating or offensive working conditions.

HR audit Formal research effort that evaluates the current state of HR management in an organization.

HR generalist A person who has responsibility for performing a variety of HR activities.

HR metrics Specific measures tied to HR performance indicators.

HR specialist A person who has in-depth knowledge and expertise in a limited area of HR.

Human capital The collective value of the capabilities, knowledge, skills, life experiences, and motivation of an organizational workforce.

Human Resource (HR) management Designing management systems to ensure that human talent is used effectively and efficiently to accomplish organizational goals.

Human resource management system (HRMS) An integrated system providing information used by HR management in decision making.

Human resource planning Process of analyzing and identifying the need for and availability of human resources so that the organization can meet its objectives.

I

Illegal issues Collective bargaining issues that would require either party to take illegal action.

Immediate confirmation Based on the idea that people learn best if reinforcement and feedback are given as soon as possible after training.

Importing and exporting Buying and selling goods and services with organizations in other countries.

Independent contractors Workers who perform specific services on a contract basis.

Individual-centered career planning Career planning that focuses on an individual's responsibility for a career rather than on organizational needs.

Industrial union Union that includes many persons working in the same industry or company, regardless of jobs held.

Informal training Training that occurs through interactions and feedback among employees.

In-shoring Foreign businesses shifting activities to the United States.

J

Job Grouping of tasks, duties, and responsibilities that constitutes the total work assignment for an employee.

Job analysis Systematic way of gathering and analyzing information about the content, context, and human requirements of jobs.

Job description Identification of the tasks, duties, and responsibilities of a job.

Job design Organizing tasks, duties, responsibilities, and other elements into a productive unit of work.

Job duties Important elements in a given job.

Job enlargement Broadening the scope of a job by expanding the number of different tasks to be performed.

Job enrichment Increasing the depth of a job by adding responsibility for planning, organizing, controlling, or evaluating the job.

Job evaluation Formal, systematic means to identify the relative worth of jobs within an organization.

Job family Group of jobs having common organizational characteristics.

Job posting System in which the employer provides notices of job openings and employees respond by applying.

Job rotation Process of shifting a person from job to job.

Job satisfaction A positive emotional state resulting from evaluating one's job experiences.

Job sharing Scheduling arrangement in which two employees perform the work of one full-time job.

Job specifications The knowledge, skills, and abilities (KSAs) an individual needs to perform a job satisfactorily.

Just cause Reasonable justification for taking employment-related action.

K

Knowledge management The way an organization identifies and leverages knowledge in order to be competitive.

L

Labor force population All individuals who are available for selection if all possible recruitment strategies are used.

Labor markets External supply pool from which organizations attract employees.

Leniency error Occurs when ratings of all employees fall at the high end of the scale.

Living wage One that is supposed to meet the basic needs of a worker's family.

Lockout Shutdown of company operations undertaken by management to prevent union members from working.

Lockout/tag-out regulations Requirement that locks and tags be used to make equipment inoperative for repair or adjustment.

Lump-sum increase (LSI) One-time payment of all or part of a yearly pay increase.

M

Managed care Approaches that monitor and reduce medical costs through restrictions and market system alternatives.

Management by objectives (MBO) Performance appraisal method that specifies the performance goals that an individual and manager mutually identify.

Management mentoring Relationship in which experienced managers aid individuals in the earlier stages of their careers.

Management rights Rights reserved so that the employer can manage, direct, and control its business.

Mandatory issues Collective bargaining issues identified specifically by labor laws or court decisions as subject to bargaining.

Marginal job functions Duties that are part of a job but are incidental or ancillary to the purpose and nature of the job.

Market banding Grouping jobs into pay grades based on similar market survey amounts.

Market line Graph line that shows the relationship between job value as determined by job evaluation points and job value as determined by pay survey rates.

Market pricing Use of market pay data to identify the relative value of jobs based on what other employers pay for similar jobs.

Massed practice Practice performed all at once.

Mediation Dispute resolution process in which a third party helps negotiators reach a settlement.

Motivation The desire within a person causing that person to act.

Multi-national enterprise (MNE) Organization that has operating units located in foreign countries.

N

National emergency strike Strike that would impact the national economy significantly.

Negligent hiring Occurs when an employer fails to check an employee's background and the employee injures someone on the job.

Negligent retention Occurs when an employer becomes aware that an employee may be unfit for work, but continues to employ the person, and the person injures someone.

Nepotism Practice of allowing relatives to work for the same employer.

Non-compete agreements Agreements that prohibit individuals who leave an organization from competing with an employer in the same line of business for a specified period of time.

Non-contributory plan Pension plan in which all the funds for pension benefits are provided by the employer.

Non-directive interview Interview that uses questions developed from the answers to previous questions.

Non-exempt employees Employees who must be paid overtime.

O

Off-shoring U.S. businesses contracting out activities to unaffiliated companies or their affiliates in another country.

Open shop Firm in which workers are not required to join or pay dues to a union.

Organizational commitment The degree to which employees believe in and accept organizational goals and desire to remain with the organization.

Organizational culture The shared values and beliefs in an organization and its workforce.

Organization-centered career planning Career planning that focuses on identifying career paths that provide for the logical progression of people between jobs in an organization.

Orientation Planned introduction of new employees to their jobs, co-workers, and the organization.

Outsourcing Businesses contracting out activities to unaffiliated companies either at home or abroad.

P

Paid-time-off (PTO) plans Plans that combine all sick leave, vacation time, and holidays into a total number of hours or days that employees can take off with pay.

Panel interview Interview in which several interviewers meet with candidate at the same time.

Pay compression Occurs when the pay differences among individuals with different levels of experience and performance become small.

Pay equity Similarity in pay for all jobs requiring comparable knowledge, skills, and abilities, even if actual job duties and market rates differ significantly.

Pay grades Groupings of individual jobs having approximately the same job worth.

Pay survey Collection of data on compensation rates for workers performing similar jobs in other organizations.

Pay-for-performance philosophy Requires that compensation changes reflect performance differences.

Pension plan Retirement program established and funded by the employer and employees.

Performance appraisal Process of determining how well employees do their job relative to a standard and communicating that information to the employee.

Performance consulting Process in which a trainer and the organizational client work together to determine what needs to be done to improve organizational and individual results.

Performance management Series of activities designed to ensure that the organization gets the performance it needs from its employees.

Performance standards Define the expected levels of performance in key areas of the job description.

Permissive issues Collective bargaining issues that are not mandatory and that relate to certain jobs.

Perquisites (perks) Special benefits—usually non-cash items—for executives.

Person/job fit Matching characteristics of people with characteristics of jobs.

Person/organization fit The congruence between individuals and organizational factors.

Phased retirement Approach in which employees gradually reduce their workloads and pay levels.

Physical ability tests Test that measure an individual's abilities such as strength, endurance, and muscular movement.

Placement Fitting a person to the right job.

Policies General guidelines that focus organizational actions.

Portability A pension plan feature that allows employees to move their pension benefits from one employer to another.

Predictive validity Measured when test results of applicants are compared with subsequent job performance.

Predictors Measurable or visible indicators of a selection criterion.

Preferred provider organization (PPO) A health-care provider that contracts with an employer or an employer group to supply health-care services to employees at a competitive rate.

Primacy effect Occurs when a rater gives greater weight to information received first when appraising an individual's performance.

Procedural justice Perceived fairness of the process and procedures used to make decisions about employees.

Procedures Customary methods of handling activities.

Productivity Measure of the quantity and quality of work done, considering the cost of the resources used.

Profit sharing System to distribute a portion of the profits of an organization to employees.

Protected class Individuals within a group identified for protection under equal employment laws and regulations.

Psychological contract The unwritten expectations employees and employers have about the nature of their work relationships.

Psychomotor tests Tests that measure dexterity, hand–eye coordination, arm–hand steadiness, and other factors.

Q

Quid pro quo Sexual harassment in which employment outcomes are linked to the individual granting sexual favors.

R

Ranking Performance appraisal method in which all employees are listed from highest to lowest in performance.

Rater bias Occurs when a rater's values or prejudices distort the rating.

Ratification Process by which union members vote to accept the terms of a negotiated labor agreement.

Realistic job preview Process through which a job applicant receives an accurate picture of a job.

Reasonable accommodation A modification to a job or work environment that gives a qualified individual an equal employment opportunity to perform.

Recency effect Occurs when a rater gives greater weight to recent events when appraising an individual's performance.

Recruiting Process of generating a pool of qualified applicants for organizational jobs.

Red-circled employee Incumbent who is paid above the range set for the job.

Reinforcement Based on the idea that people tend to repeat responses that give them some type of positive reward and avoid actions associated with negative consequences.

Reliability Consistency with which a test measures an item.

Repatriation Planning, training, and reassignment of global employees to their home countries.

Responsibilities Obligations to perform certain tasks and duties.

Retaliation Punitive actions taken by employers against individuals who exercise their legal rights.

Return on investment (ROI) Calculation showing the value of expenditures for HR activities.

Reverse discrimination When a person is denied an opportunity because of preferences given to protected-class individuals who may be less qualified.

Right to privacy An individual's freedom from unauthorized and unreasonable intrusion into personal affairs.

Rights Powers, privileges, or interests that belong to a person by law, nature, or tradition.

Right-to-work laws State laws that prohibit requiring employees to join unions as a condition of obtaining or continuing employment.

Risk management Involves responsibilities to consider physical, human, and financial factors to protect organizational and individual interests.

Rules Specific guidelines that regulate and restrict the behavior of individuals.

S

Sabbatical Time off the job to develop and rejuvenate oneself.

Safety Condition in which the physical well-being of people is protected.

Salaries Consistent payments made each period regardless of the number of hours worked.

Salting Practice in which unions hire and pay people to apply for jobs at certain companies.

Security Protection of employees and organizational facilities.

Security audit Comprehensive review of organizational security.

Selection Process of choosing individuals with qualifications needed to fill jobs in an organization.

Selection criterion Characteristic that a person must possess to successfully perform work.

Selection rate Percentage hired from a given group of candidates.

Self-directed team Organizational team composed of individuals who are assigned a cluster of tasks, duties, and responsibilities to be accomplished.

Self-efficacy Person's belief that he or she can learn the training program content.

Seniority Time spent in the organization or on a particular job.

Separation agreement Agreement in which a terminated employee agrees not to sue the employer in exchange for specified benefits.

Serious health condition Health condition requiring in-patient, hospital, hospice, or residential medical care or continuing physician care.

Severance pay Security benefit voluntarily offered by employers to individuals whose jobs are eliminated or who leave by mutual agreement with their employers.

Sexual harassment Actions that are sexually directed, are unwanted, and subject the worker to adverse employment conditions or create a hostile work environment.

Situational interview Structured interview that contains questions about how applicants might handle specific job situations.

Situational judgment tests Tests that measure a person's judgment in work settings.

Skill variety Extent to which the work requires several different activities for successful completion.

Spaced practice Practice performed in several sessions spaced over a period of hours or days.

Special-purpose team Organizational team formed to address specific problems, improve work processes, and enhance the overall quality of products and services.

Statutory rights Rights based on laws or statutes passed by federal, state, or local government.

Stock option plan Plan that gives employees the right to purchase a fixed number of shares of company stock at a specified exercise price for a limited period of time.

Stock purchase plan Plan in which the corporation provides matching funds equal to the amount invested by the employee for the purchase of stock in the company.

Straight piece-rate system Pay system in which wages are determined by multiplying the number of units produced by the piece rate for one unit.

Strategic HR management Use of employees to gain or keep a competitive advantage.

Strategy A general framework that provides guidance for actions.

Stress interview Interview designed to create anxiety and put pressure on applicants to see how they respond.

Strictness error Occurs when ratings of all employees fall at the low end of the scale.

Strike Work stoppage in which union members refuse to work in order to put pressure on an employer.

Structured interview Interview that uses a set of standardized questions asked of all job applicants.

Substance abuse Use of illicit substances or misuse of controlled substances, alcohol, or other drugs.

Succession planning Process of identifying a long-term plan for the orderly replacement of key employees.

T

Talent management Concerned with enhancing the attraction, development, and retention of key human resources.

Task Distinct, identifiable work activity composed of motion.

Task identity Extent to which the job includes a "whole" identifiable unit of work that is carried out from start to finish and that results in a visible outcome.

Task significance Impact the job has on other people.

Tax equalization plan Compensation plan used to protect expatriates from negative tax consequences.

Team interview Interview in which applicants are interviewed by the team members with whom they will work.

Total rewards Monetary and non-monetary rewards provided to employees in order to attract, motivate, and retain them.

Training Process whereby people acquire capabilities to perform jobs.

Turnover The process in which employees leave an organization and have to be replaced.

U

Undue hardship Significant difficulty or expense imposed on an employer in making an accommodation for individuals with disabilities.

Union Formal association of workers that promotes the interests of its members through collective action.

Union authorization card Card signed by an employee to designate a union as her or his collective bargaining agent.

Union security provisions Contract clauses to help the union obtain and retain members.

Union steward Employee elected to serve as the first-line representative of unionized workers.

Unit labor cost Computed by dividing the average cost of workers by their average levels of output.

Utilization analysis Identifies the number of protected-class members employed in the organization and the types of jobs they hold.

Utilization review Audit of the services and costs billed by health-care providers.

V

Validity Extent to which a test actually measures what it says it measures.

Variable pay Compensation linked directly to individual, team, or organizational performance.

Vesting Right of employees to receive certain benefits from their pension plans.

Virtual team Organizational team composed of individuals who are separated geographically but linked by communications technology.

W

Wages Payments directly calculated on the amount of time worked.

Well-pay Extra pay for not taking sick leave.

Wellness programs Programs designed to maintain or improve employee health before problems arise by encouraging self-directed lifestyle changes.

Whistle-blowers Individuals who report real or perceived wrongs committed by their employers.

Work Effort directed toward accomplishing results.

Work sample tests Tests that require an applicant to perform a simulated task that is a specified part of the target job.

Workers' compensation Security benefits provided to persons injured on the job.

Workflow analysis Study of the way work (outputs, activities, and inputs) moves through an organization.

Wrongful discharge Termination of an individual's employment for reasons that are illegal or improper.

Y

Yield ratios Comparisons of the number of applicants at one stage of the recruiting process with the number at the next stage.

Author Index

Subject Index

School-to-work transitions, 276
Schuler Engineering, 535
Screenings, pre-employment, 232
Secrecy, compensation, 365
Security
 benefits, 427–428
 computer, 480–481
 current state of, 458
 defined, 457
 employee screenings, 481
 global issues, 458–459
 management, 480–481
 personnel, 481
 responsibilities, 457
 workplace monitoring, 502–505
 workplace violence, 478–480
Security audits, 480
Selection interviews
 characterization, 240
 face validity, 241
 individual's conducting, 243
 inter-rater reliability, 241
 problems in, 243–245
 types of, 241–243
Selection process
 application forms, 233–237
 background investigations,
  246–249
 case study, 253
 criteria, 227–230
 defined, 226
 flow chart, 232
 legal concerns, 251–252
 pre-employment screenings, 232
 process, 231
 rates, 219
 responsibilities, 230–236
 validity, 228–229
Selection testing
 ability, 237–238
 honesty/integrity, 239–240
 personality, 238–239
Self-assessment, 297
Self-control, 330
Self-directed teams, 168
Self-efficacy, 270
Self-image, 297
Self-ratings, 339–340
Seminars, 308–309
Seniority, 116, 384–385
Sensitivity training, 153
Sequencing, 301
Service awards, 399
Service Employees International
 Union, 528, 536
Severance pay, 428
Sex-change issues, 138

Sexual harassment
 cyber, 140
 employer responses to, 141
 nature of, 139
 statistics, 109
 types of, 140
Sexual orientation, 115, 138
Shift work, 171
SHRM. See Society for Human
 Resource Management (SHRM)
Sick building syndrome, 475
Sick leave, 447
Similar-to-me errors, 351
Situational interviews, 242
Situational judgment tests, 238
Skills
 audit, 49
 databases, 51
 demand changes, 16–17
 hard/soft, 260
 succession planning and, 317–318
Small Business Administration
 (SBA), 8
Small businesses, 8–9, 46
Smart Jobs, 276
Smith v. Jackson, 112
Snap judgments, 245
Snowfly System, 394
Social networks, 216
Social Security, 425, 435–436
Social Security Act, 428, 4358
Society for Human Resource
 Management (SHRM)
 case studies, 30–31
 certifications, 27–28
 characterization, 22
 ethics program, 23
 recruitment and, 212, 213
Socioeconomic status, 298
Southwest Airlines
 labor relations, 545
 organizational values, 76, 162
 recruiting, 201
SOX. See Sarbanes-Oxley Act (SOX)
Spaced practice, 271–272
Special-purpose teams, 168
Sports Authority, 238
Spot bonuses, 398
Staffing. See also Selection
 defined, 6
 global issues, 249–251
 job offers, 249
Standards, performance
 behavior and, 344
 defined, 186
 establishing, 331–332
Stanford University, 193

Starbucks, 422
Starwood hotels, 286
Statutory rights, 490
Steelworkers union, 535
Stereotyping, 245–246
Stillwater School District, 99
Stock plans, 404
Stock purchase plans, 441
Straight commission system,
 405–406
Strategic business partner, 13
Strategic HR management and
 planning. See also Human
 resources planning
 case study, 63
 core competency, 38
 customer service and, 41–42
 effectiveness, 58–62
 effectiveness and, 42
 financial performance and, 42
 function, 6
 global competitiveness and, 42–45
 human resources planning, 45–47
 mistakes, 35
 nature of, 36–39
 operationalizing, 38
 orientation, 12–13
 productivity and, 40–41
 seat-at-table concept, 13–14
 success with, 37
 talent management and, 292
 training and, 261–266
Stress interviews, 243
Strictness error, 349
Strikes, 531, 544
Structured interviews, 241–242
Studer Group, 242
SUBs. See Supplemental
 unemployment benefits (SUBs)
Substance abuse
 defined, 473
 employer concerns, 474
 handling cases, 474–475
 incidence of, 473–474
 testing for, 474, 506–508
Subway, 502
Success base rates, 220
Succession planning
 case study, 321
 common flaw in, 53
 common mistakes, 319–320
 considerations, 317–318
 defined, 52, 315
 metrics, 319
 process, 315–317
 values of, 319–320
Supervisors, 311–312, 338